A PEOPLE & A NATION

BRIEF EDITION

A PEOPLE & A NATION

A HISTORY OF THE UNITED STATES

BRIEF EDITION

MARY BETH NORTON   *Cornell University*

DAVID M. KATZMAN   *University of Kansas*

PAUL D. ESCOTT   *University of North Carolina, Charlotte*

HOWARD P. CHUDACOFF   *Brown University*

THOMAS G. PATERSON   *University of Connecticut*

WILLIAM M. TUTTLE, Jr.   *University of Kansas*

and

WILLIAM J. BROPHY   *Stephen F. Austin State University*

HOUGHTON MIFFLIN COMPANY   Boston

Dallas   Geneva, Illinois   Hopewell, New Jersey   Palo Alto

Cover photo: *One Sunday, July 18, Forbestown,* ca. 1852, oil on canvas, anonymous. The Oakland Museum History Department.

Map, page 212: The War in the West, 1861–July 1863, from *The Essentials of American History,* Second Edition, by Richard N. Current. T. Harry Williams and Frank Freidel. Copyright © 1976 by Alfred A. Knopf, Inc. Copyright © 1959, 1961, 1964, 1966, 1971, 1972 by Richard N. Current, T. Harry Williams and Frank Freidel. Reprinted by permission of Alfred A. Knopf, Inc.

Printed in the U.S.A.
Library of Congress Catalog Card Number: 83-80893
ISBN: 0-395-34369-0
    EFGHIJ—RM—89876

✍ Contents

1 THE MEETING OF OLD WORLD AND NEW, 1492–1650

2 AMERICAN SOCIETY TAKES SHAPE, 1650–1750

3 COLONIAL SOCIETY AT MIDCENTURY

4 SEVERING THE BONDS OF EMPIRE, 1754–1774

5 A REVOLUTION, INDEED, 1775–1783

6 FORGING A NATIONAL REPUBLIC, 1776–1789

7 POLITICS AND SOCIETY IN THE EARLY REPUBLIC, 1790–1800

8 THE REPUBLIC ENDURES, 1801–1824

9 THE ECONOMIC EVOLUTION OF THE NORTH AND WEST, 1800–1860

10 SLAVERY AND THE GROWTH OF THE SOUTH, 1800–1860

11 THE AMERICAN SCENE, 1800–1860

12 REFORM, POLITICS, AND EXPANSION, 1824–1848

13 THE UNION IN CRISIS: THE 1850s

14 TRANSFORMING FIRE: THE CIVIL WAR, 1860–1865

15 RECONSTRUCTION BY TRIAL AND ERROR, 1865–1877

16 TRANSFORMATION OF THE WEST AND SOUTH, 1877–1892

17 THE MACHINE AGE, 1877–1920

18 THE CITY AND EVERYDAY LIFE, 1877–1920

19 GILDED AGE POLITICS, 1877–1900

20 THE PROGRESSIVE ERA, 1895–1920

21 THE QUEST FOR EMPIRE, 1865–1914

22 AMERICA AT WAR, 1914–1920

23 THE NEW ERA OF THE 1920S

24 THE GREAT DEPRESSION AND THE NEW DEAL, 1929–1941

25 DIPLOMACY IN A BROKEN WORLD, 1920–1941

26 THE SECOND WORLD WAR AT HOME AND ABROAD, 1941–1945

27 COLD WAR POLITICS AND FOREIGN POLICY, 1945–1961

28   LIFE IN THE MIDDLE CLASS, 1945–1960

29   AMERICA IN A REVOLUTIONARY WORLD: FOREIGN POLICY SINCE 1961

30 REFORM, RADICALISM, AND DISAPPOINTED EXPECTATIONS, 1961–1973

31 A DISILLUSIONED PEOPLE: AMERICA SINCE 1973

APPENDIX

ꙮ Maps and Charts

ℒ PREFACE TO THE BRIEF EDITION

A few years ago six historians set out to provide students and instructors with a comprehensive survey that tells the whole story of American history, both the public and the private sides of American life. The positive response to their book, *A People and a Nation,* indicates that they succeeded admirably in their task. *A People and a Nation* incorporates Americans of all backgrounds into the nation's story and gives full coverage to minorities and women. The authors also integrate recent research in social history with the more traditional scholarship of political, diplomatic, and economic history.

Many instructors have urged the authors and the publisher to prepare a shorter version of *A People and a Nation* for use in either short courses or courses in which additional readings are assigned. This brief edition is intended to meet their needs. It is available in both a one-volume and a two-volume format. In the two-volume format, Volume A begins with the exploration of America and continues through the Reconstruction period (Chapters 1–15); Volume B begins with Reconstruction and extends to the present (Chapters 15–31). Chapter 15 on Reconstruction appears in both volumes in order to provide greater flexibility in matching the appropriate volume with the beginning and closing dates of a course.

In the preparation of this brief edition the authors collaborated with William J. Brophy, who prepared the condensation. Our goal was to make the brief version approximately half as long as the full-length edition, while still maintaining the integration of social history with political, diplomatic, and economic history. The danger in undertaking such a revision is that the results could be a patchwork condensation wherein whole sections have been deleted and the rest simply pieced together. To avoid this

danger, we have made a careful line-by-line examination of the full-length edition, deleting only details throughout. Where two examples were given, we have deleted one; where many statistics were presented, we have used a few. We have deleted some of the longer quotations from diaries and letters and some of the longer stories of individuals, but have retained many short quotations and individual experiences of everyday life. Thus we have succeeded in maintaining a thorough narrative of major events and personalities.

In the process of shortening the book, we have combined some chapters in the brief edition. Separate chapters on the city from 1877 to 1920 and on everyday life during the same period have been combined, and two chapters on the Depression have been combined. All material on the Second World War is now in one chapter, and all material on politics and foreign policy from 1945 to 1961 is in one chapter. Though each of the authors feels answerable for the whole, primary responsibility for particular chapters is as follows: Mary Beth Norton, Chapters 1–7; David M. Katzman, Chapters 8–9, 11–12; Paul D. Escott, Chapters 10, 13–15; Howard P. Chudacoff, Chapters 16–20, 23; Thomas G. Paterson, Chapters 21–22, 25, 29; William M. Tuttle, Jr., Chapters 28, 30–31; Thomas G. Paterson and William M. Tuttle, Jr., Chapters 24, 26, 27.

The brief edition covers events to the present time. In addition, we have updated the suggestions for further reading at the end of each chapter. The Appendix includes an updated list of reference works and demographic data; important documents; tables of election results, presidents and vice presidents, justices of the Supreme Court, and territorial acquisitions.

As was the case for the full-length edition, we

have prepared a *Study Guide* to accompany the brief edition of *A People and a Nation.* The *Study Guide* (in a one-volume format) begins with some suggestions on how to study, including general study habits, outlining, underlining, preparing for essay examinations, and using tables, maps, graphs, and other illustrations, with examples taken from *A People and a Nation.* For each chapter in the text, the *Study Guide* provides learning objectives and identification, multiple-choice, fill-in-the-blank, true-false, map or date-identification, and essay questions. Answers are provided for all objective questions.

Many people have contributed their thoughts and labors to this work. Special thanks go to the staff at Houghton Mifflin Company and to the following people who served as reviewers, providing detailed comments on various drafts of the brief edition:

Robin G. Buchan, *Highline Community College*
Don H. Doyle, *Vanderbilt University*
Dale T. Knobel, *Texas A & M University*
Kerby A. Miller, *University of Missouri-Columbia*
Grant Morrison, *C. W. Post College*
F. Ross Peterson, *Utah State University*
Judith Stein, *City University of New York, City College*
Howard L. Taslitz, *Cerritos College*
Carl Ubbelohde, *Case Western Reserve University*

Finally, we welcome responses and comments on the brief edition of *A People and a Nation.*

W.J.B.

ᔑ PREFACE TO THE FULL-LENGTH EDITION

We are always recreating our past, rediscovering the personalities and events that have shaped us, inspired us, or bedeviled us. When we are buffeted by the erratic winds of current affairs, we look back for reassuring precedents. But we do not always find that history is comforting. The past holds much that is disturbing, for the story of a people or a nation—like any story—is never one of unbroken progress. As with our own personal experience, it is both triumphant and tragic, filled with injury as well as healing.

This volume is our recreation of the American past: our rediscovery of its people and of the nation they founded and sustained. Drawing on recent research as well as on seasoned, authoritative works, we have sought to offer a comprehensive book that tells the whole story of American history. Presidential and party politics, congressional legislation, Supreme Court decisions, diplomacy and treaties, wars and foreign interventions, economic patterns, and state and local politics have been the stuff of American history for generations. Into this traditional fabric we have woven social history, broadly defined. We have investigated the history of the majority of Americans—women—and of minorities. And we have sought to illuminate the private side of the American story: work and play; dress and diet; entertainment; family and home life; relationships between men and women; and race, ethnicity, and religion. From the ordinary to the exceptional—the steelworker, the office secretary, the plantation owner, the slave, the ward politician, the president's wife, the actress, the canal builder—Americans have had personal stories that have intersected with the public policies of their government. Whether victors or victims, dominant or dominated, all have been actors in their own right, with feelings, ideas,

and aspirations that have fortified them in good times and bad. All are part of the American story.

Several questions guided our telling of this intricate narrative. On the official, or public, side

| Major themes |

of American history, we have sought to identify Americans' expectations of their government, to show who governs and how power is exercised, to explain the origins of reform movements, and to compare the everyday practice of government and politics with the egalitarian principles to which Americans theoretically subscribe. We have looked at the domestic sources of foreign policy and at the reasons why the United States has chosen to intervene abroad or to wage war. We have sought as well to capture the mood or mentality of an era, in which Americans reveal what they think about themselves and their public officials through their letters, music, and literature, their rallies and riots.

In the social and economic spheres, we have emphasized technological development and its effects on the worker and the workplace. We have traced major economic trends. And because geographic mobility is such a striking part of American history, we have given considerable attention to the questions of why people migrate and how they adapt to new environments. The interactions of racially and ethnically diverse people, the social divisions that have resulted and the efforts that have been made to heal them, are also, it seems to us, central to the study of the American past.

In the private domain of the family and the home, we have examined sex roles, childbearing and childrearing, diet and dress. We have attempted to show how public policy and technological development—war and mass production, for example—have forced change on these most basic institutions. Finally, we have asked how Americans have chosen to entertain themselves, as participants or spectators, with sports, music, the graphic arts, reading, theater, film, and television.

Our experience as teachers of American history has shown us that students not only need to address these questions, but can and want to address them. Unfortunately, dull, abstract writing often kills their natural curiosity. Thus we have taken pains to write in clear, concrete language and to include wherever possible the stories of real people, as told in their letters and diaries and in oral histories. We have tried to stimulate readers to think about the meaning of American history—not just to memorize it.

In planning the book, we decided to open each chapter with the true story of an American,

| Structure of the book |

ordinary or exceptional, whose experience was representative of the times. Following the story we devote a few paragraphs to placing it in historical perspective and introducing the major themes and events of the chapter. Students should find these introductory sections, which in effect provide an overview of the chapters, useful study guides.

We have used boxed glosses to highlight key persons, events, concepts, and trends. Our illustrations, maps, tables, and graphs are closely related to important points in the text. Similarly, the four full-color photographic studies of changing patterns in work and leisure are specifically related to the chapters in which they appear.

Most chapters close with a chronological list of important events, and all chapters end with a bibliography for follow-up reading. In the Appendix we have provided a bibliography of general reference books by subject; important documents; tables of election results, administrations (including Cabinet members), party strength in Congress, justices of the Supreme Court, and territorial acquisitions; and a statistical profile of the American people.

During the long and painstaking course of writing and revision the six of us read and reread one another's work and debated one another across note-strewn tables. In our effort to produce a unified and spirited book, we became friends and better scholars. Though each of us feels answerable for the whole, we take primary responsibility for particular chapters as follows: Mary Beth Norton, Chapters 1–7; David M. Katzman, Chapters 8–9, 11–12; Paul D. Escott, Chapters 10, 13–15; Howard P. Chudacoff, Chapters 16–21, 24; Thomas G. Paterson, Chapters 22–23, 25, 27–28, 32; and William M. Tuttle, Jr., Chapters 26, 29–31, and 33–34.

| Acknowledg-ments |

We have been alert to the constructive suggestions of the many teachers and scholars who have read and criticized our manuscript in successive drafts. Their advice has been invaluable, and we are grateful for it:

Robert Abzug, *University of Texas, Austin*
Lois Banner, *George Washington University*
William Barney, *University of North Carolina, Chapel Hill*
Michael C. Batinski, *Southern Illinois University, Carbondale*
Susan Becker, *University of Tennessee, Knoxville*
Barton Bernstein, *Stanford University*
Stephen Botein, *Michigan State University*
Jonathan Chu, *University of Massachusetts, Boston*
Allen Davis, *Temple University*
Peter Filene, *University of North Carolina, Chapel Hill*
Lewis Gould, *University of Texas, Austin*
J. William Harris, *Committee on Degrees in History & Literature, Harvard University*
George Herring, *University of Kentucky, Lexington*
William Holmes, *University of Georgia, Athens*
Michael F. Holt, *University of Virginia, Charlottesville*
Nancy Jaffe, *Riverside City College, California*
Charles Johnson, *University of Tennessee, Knoxville*
Alice Kessler-Harris, *Hofstra University*
Richard Lowitt, *Iowa State University*
George Lubick, *Northern Arizona University*

John G. MacNaughton, *Monroe Community College, Rochester, New York*

Pauline Maier, *Massachusetts Institute of Technology*

Robert Martin, *St. Louis Community College at Florissant Valley*

Arthur F. McClure, *Central Missouri State University*

Russell Menard, *University of Minnesota, Minneapolis*

Eric Monkkonen, *University of California, Los Angeles*

Philip D. Morgan, *Institute of Early American History and Culture, Williamsburg, Virginia*

Jerome Mushkat, *University of Akron*

William O'Neill, *Rutgers The State University of New Jersey, New Brunswick*

George Pilcher, *University of Colorado, Boulder*

Jackson Putnam, *California State University, Fullerton*

Harvard Sitkoff, *University of New Hampshire, Durham*

James Smallwood, *Oklahoma State University*

Sue Taishoff, *University of South Florida, Tampa*

David Thelen, *University of Missouri, Columbia*

John Trickel, *Richland College, Dallas, Texas*

James Turner, *University of Massachusetts, Boston*

Ronald Walters, *Johns Hopkins University*

Darold Wax, *Oregon State University*

William Bruce Wheeler, *University of Tennessee, Knoxville*

We acknowledge with thanks the special contributions of Warren I. Cohen, Jeffrey Crow, Gregory DeLapp, Paul Dest, John Emond, Shirley Harman, Pam Harrison, Chico Herbison, Sharyn A. Katzman, Roberta Ludgate, Jean Manter, Sally McMillen, Paula Oliver, Holly Izard Paterson, and Mary Erickson Tuttle. We also appreciate the guidance and generous assistance of the many members of the staff of Houghton Mifflin Company who worked on the book.

T.G.P.

I ～

THE MEETING OF
OLD WORLD AND NEW,
1492–1650

"It spread over the people as great destruction," the old man told the priest. "Covered, mantled with pustules, very many people died of them. And very many starved; there was death from hunger. . . ."

By European reckoning, it was September 1520. Spanish troops led by Hernando Cortés abandoned the Aztec capital of Tenochtitlan after failing in their first attempt to gain control of the city. But they unknowingly left behind the smallpox germs that would ensure their eventual triumph. Three months later they returned to besiege the Aztec capital; the disease-weakened defenders finally surrendered in the Aztec year Three House, on the day One Serpent (August 1521). The Spaniards had conquered Mexico, and on the site of Tenochtitlan they constructed what is now Mexico City.

By the time Spanish troops occupied Tenochtitlan, the age of European expansion and colonization was already well under way. Over the next three hundred and fifty years, Europeans would spread their civilization across the globe. The history of the thirteen tiny English colonies in North America that eventually became the United States must be seen in the broader context of worldwide exploration and exploitation.

Two themes pervade the early history of English settlement in America: the clash of divergent cultures—European and Indian—and the English settlers' adaptation to an alien environment. Unlike the Spaniards, the Englishmen found very little gold and silver in the area they settled. Therefore, they began to establish agricultural settlements. The colonists' attempts to transplant English ways of life to the New World led to repeated conflicts with the native peoples. For some years the Indians' determination to resist seizure of their lands, coupled with the Europeans' difficulties adjusting to the unfamiliar surroundings, called into question the ultimate survival of the settlements. But by the middle of the seventeenth century English colonies had taken firm root in American soil.

European exploration of America

October 12, 1492, is one of those historical rarities: a well-known date that deserves the significance attributed to it. On that day Christopher Columbus, a forty-one-year-old Genoese

| Christopher Columbus | sea captain sailing under the flag of the Spanish monarchs Ferdinand and Isabella, |

landed on a Caribbean island he named San Salvador (one of the Bahamas). He had sailed west from Palos, Spain, on August 3, in hopes of reaching China and the East Indies. Columbus did not accomplish his goal, but he changed the dimensions of the known world.

Like other well-informed men of his time, Columbus believed the world to be round. He also thought that the distance from Portugal to Japan was less than 3,000 miles and that no land mass lay in his path. These two notions were scoffed at by the experts and convinced several monarchs not to support his planned expedition to China. But Columbus was obsessed with his idea and persisted in his quest for financial backing for more than a decade. Finally, Queen Isabella of Spain agreed to fund the voyage.

Columbus found support because in the fifteenth century four developments combined to propel Europeans out into the unknown oceans. The first development was purely technical: the invention and refinement of navigational instruments, which allowed mariners to spend weeks and months out of sight of land and still have some rough idea of their location. The other three factors—political changes in Europe, the quest for scarce trade goods, and a desire to convert heathen peoples to Christianity—were more complex.

Throughout Europe, the fifteenth century witnessed the consolidation of power and authority in the hands of kings. These political changes were important preconditions for exploration. In England, Henry VII founded the Tudor dynasty and began uniting a land divided for generations. In France, Francis I similarly established a claim to unchallenged authority. In Spain, Ferdinand and Isabella, rulers of the independent states of Aragon and Castile, married and combined their kingdoms. Only such powerful monarchies could muster the resources necessary to support large-scale colonial enterprises.

The third factor impelling the westward thrust was greed—the desire to find an easy trade route to the East. For centuries, Europeans had

| Search for a trade route to the East |

traded with the Orient via the ports of the eastern Mediterranean and the long land route across Asia known as the Silk Road. In 1477 the publication of Marco Polo's *Travels* stimulated Europeans' interest in China and helped to convince many, including Christopher Columbus, that that land of fabulous wealth could be reached by ship.

Columbus was not the first to cherish thoughts of tapping the riches of the Indies directly. During the first half of the fifteenth century, Prince Henry the Navigator, son of King John I of Portugal, had dispatched ship after ship southward along the coast of Africa in an attempt to discover a passage to the East. In 1488, long after Prince Henry's death, Bartholomew Dias first rounded the Cape of Good Hope, and a decade later Vasco da Gama reached India by sailing south around Africa. The Portuguese, then, found what Columbus did not: a usable oceanic trade route to the East.

But Columbus did not realize he had failed, especially on his first voyage. He insisted that the islands lay close to the Asian mainland and that he could have found vast stores of gold and spices had he had more time to explore. Columbus also expressed his belief that the Indians (as he called the natives, thinking them residents of the Indies) could easily be converted to Christianity. As a fifteenth-century European, Columbus was convinced that Christianity was the only true religion. Such a man considered it his duty to spread Jesus Christ's message. Thus, the fourth motive for exploration, the conversion of "heathens," was a factor from the beginning.

Columbus made four voyages to the Western Hemisphere, sailing along the coasts of Central and South America and further exploring the Caribbean. John Cabot, a Genoese backed by England, and then Giovanni da Verrazano, a Florentine dispatched by France, explored the North American coast. In 1534, Jacques Cartier, also sailing for France, found the mouth of the

St. Lawrence River and ventured inland as far as the first rapids. By then, everyone realized that a new world had been discovered.

Most Europeans saw the Americas as a barrier on the route to the Indies. But Spain, with its reinvigorated monarchy and belief in Columbus's prediction of vast wealth in the interior of the continent, immediately moved to take advantage of the discoveries. On his first voyage, Columbus had established a base on the island

Conquistadores

of Hispaniola. From there, Spanish explorers fanned out around the Caribbean basin. The Spaniards' dreams of wealth were realized when Cortés conquered the Aztec empire, killing its ruler, Moctezuma, and seizing a fabulous treasure of gold and silver. Moreover, Francisco Pizarro, who explored south along the western coast of South America, conquered and enslaved the Incas in 1535, thus acquiring the richest silver mines in the world. Just half a century after Columbus's first voyage, the Spanish monarchs controlled the richest, most extensive empire Europe had known since ancient Rome.

The costs to the New World were extraordinarily high. The conquistadores destroyed sophisticated Indian civilizations that had built huge urban centers, developed a calendar more accurate than the Europeans' own, invented systems of writing and mathematics, and constructed roads, bridges, and irrigation canals. As they razed Aztec, Incan, and Mayan structures, the Spaniards deliberately attempted to erase all vestiges of Indian culture.

But the greatest destruction wrought by the Europeans was unintended. Diseases carried from the Old World to the New killed millions

Effects of disease

of native Americans who had no immunity to germs that had infested Europe, Asia, and Africa for centuries. The greatest killer was smallpox, which was spread by direct human contact. Indeed, the reason Pizarro conquered the Incas so easily was that their society had been devastated by the epidemic shortly before

his arrival. Smallpox was not the only villain; influenza, measles, and other diseases added to the destruction.

The statistics are staggering. When Columbus landed on Hispaniola in 1492, about one million Indians resided there. Fifty years later, only five hundred were still alive. According to the best current estimates, five to ten million Indians inhabited central Mexico before Cortés's invasion. By the end of the century, fewer than one million remained. Even in the north, where smaller Indian populations encountered only a few European explorers, traders, and fishermen, disease ravaged the countryside.

The Americans, though, took a revenge of sorts. They gave the Europeans a disease previously unknown in the Old World: syphilis. The first recorded case of syphilis in Europe occurred in Barcelona, Spain, in 1493, shortly after Columbus's return from the Caribbean. Although less deadly than smallpox, syphilis was more virulent in sixteenth-century Europe than it is today, and doctors did not know how to treat it.

The exchange of diseases was only part of a broader mutual transfer of plants and animals that resulted directly from Columbus's voyages.

Exchange of plants and animals

Europeans introduced large domesticated mammals to the Americas, and they obtained from the New World a variety of vegetables (corn, beans, squash, and potatoes) that were more nutritious than the Old World's wheat and rye. Thus, the diets of both peoples were enriched.

The exchange of two other commodities significantly influenced the two civilizations. In America the Europeans discovered tobacco, and smoking and chewing the "Indian weed" quickly became a fad in the Old World. But more important than tobacco's influence on Europe was the impact of horses on certain native American cultures. The conquistadores brought with them the first horses Americans had ever seen. Inevitably, some escaped or were stolen by the natives; such horses were traded north through Mexico into the Great Plains, where they eventually changed the lifestyles of tribes like the Apache, Comanche, Sioux, and Blackfeet, who made the horse the focal point of their existence.

The first English outposts in America

During the sixteenth century, northern European nations had only sporadic contacts with the New World. Fishermen from a number of countries discovered that the Newfoundland Banks offered an abundant supply of cod and other fish. These fishermen set up summer camps on the shore, but returned to Europe each autumn.

Other Europeans who sailed along the coast soon found that the American natives, who still used stone implements, were eager to trade for steel knives, brass kettles, and other metal goods, along with beads and cloth. In exchange, the Indians offered the Europeans furs. As the trade developed, some nations began to establish permanent trading posts on North American soil. In 1608 the French, led by the explorer Samuel de Champlain, founded Quebec. Seventeen years later the Dutch built a trading post on Manhattan Island, at the mouth of the river Henry Hudson had discovered in 1609 and named for himself. And in 1638, Sweden sent a small number of traders to the Delaware River valley.

| Early trading posts |

The French, Dutch, and Swedish settlements differed considerably from those of New Spain. The northern European colonists made no attempt to subject the Indians to European rule, although—particularly in New France—they did try to convert them to Christianity. Unlike the Spaniards, they viewed the Indians as trading partners rather than laborers to be enslaved.

Moreover, their trading posts were not intended as beachheads for a large-scale European migration.

The English were slow to establish settlements in North America, and their first colonization efforts were stimulated by their hostility to Spain. In 1533, Henry VIII had divorced his Spanish queen, Catherine of Aragon. After the pope refused to approve his divorce, Henry left the Catholic Church, founded the Protestant Church of England, and proclaimed himself its head. These actions seriously damaged the once friendly relations between England and Spain. Attempts were made at reconciliation, but the ascension to the throne in 1558 of a Protestant, Elizabeth I, left the nations bitter enemies.

Two Englishmen, Sir Humphrey Gilbert and Sir Walter Raleigh, persuaded the queen that New World colonies could serve as bases for attacks on New Spain. But Gilbert's attempt to colonize in Newfoundland and Raleigh's attempt at Roanoke Island (now North Carolina) failed. Nearly two decades later, however, a new monarch, James I, authorized the chartering of a joint-stock company to colonize Virginia, the name Raleigh had given to the English New World.

Joint-stock companies had been developed in England during the sixteenth century as a mechanism for pooling the resources of a large number of small investors. Since they were funded through the sale of stock, investors would receive returns only in proportion to their share of the whole enterprise. Such companies did not hold forth the promise of immense wealth, but they allowed the gentry to invest moderate sums of money and to avoid the risk of bankruptcy. Joint-stock companies had drawbacks. Most investors wanted quick profits, which in the English colonies were rarely forthcoming. Many of the early colonization efforts thus suffered from a chronic lack of capital, causing dissent within the companies and conflicts with the settlers in America, who often accused the parent companies of failing to support them adequately.

| Joint-stock companies |

The charter James I granted the Virginia Company in 1606 gave it the right "to digg, mine, and searche for all manner of mines of goulde, silver, and copper." The company's West Country investors (the Virginia Company of Plymouth) tried and failed to plant a colony at Sagadahoc, in what is now Maine. Meanwhile the merchant group (the Virginia Company of London) turned its attention southward. Although the settlers it sent to America at first searched for the precious metals named in the charter, they soon realized that Virginia was not another Mexico. Within twenty years the Virginia settlement had taken an entirely new form.

English and Indians encounter each other

In the fifteenth century, when Europeans first came to the New World in large numbers, the Indian tribes living in what is now the United States varied dramatically in culture and lifestyle. The tribes along the Pacific coast lived largely by fishing, combined with some agriculture. While settled agriculture was the norm in the Southwest, tribes of nomadic hunters and gatherers roamed the Great Basin and the Great Plains. East of the Mississippi, most tribes lived a settled or seminomadic existence, combining hunting, fishing, and agriculture. A majority of the eastern coastal tribes encountered by the English spoke variants of the Algonkian languages.

To an outside observer, had one existed, the cultures of seventeenth-century English and Algonkian peoples might have appeared similar at first glance. Both lived mainly in small villages, depending for subsistence chiefly on the cultivation of crops. Both supplemented a largely vegetable diet with meat and fish. Both peoples were deeply religious, orienting their lives around festivals and rituals. Both societies featured clearcut social and political hierarchies. And finally,

both cultures were characterized by sharply defined sex roles, with men and women occupying distinctly different spheres.

Such similarities were, however, outweighed by significant differences. For example, Algonkian women bore the prime responsibility for cultivating crops, whereas in English society that was men's work. Thus English people thought Indian women were overworked and Indian men lazy, while Indian people thought English men were effeminate, because they did women's work in the fields.

Cultural differences between the Indians and the English

Although both societies were hierarchical, the nature of the hierarchies differed considerably. Among the east-coast Algonkian tribes, people were not born to automatic positions of leadership, nor were political power and social status necessarily inherited through the male line. In English society, the gentry normally inherited their position from their fathers. English leaders tended to rule autocratically; the authority of Indian leaders rested largely on a consensus they shared with their fellow tribesmen. Accustomed to the European concept of powerful kings, the English sought such figures within the tribes. If they found none, they created them. Often (for example, when negotiating treaties) they willfully overestimated the ability of chiefs to make independent decisions for their people.

Furthermore, the Indians and the English had very different notions of property ownership. In most eastern tribes, land was held communally by the entire group. The concept of absolute sale of property was utterly alien. The English, on the other hand, were accustomed to individual landholding. Perhaps more important, the English believed that nomadic peoples could not own land. To the English only those groups who intensively cultivated land could own it. They therefore paid little attention to tribal claims to traditional hunting territories and sites occupied only occasionally.

An aspect of the cultural clash that needs particular emphasis is the English settlers' unwaver-

Secota, an unfortified Indian village on the Carolina coast, as drawn by John White, an artist with Raleigh's 1585 expedition. Letters A, B, C, D, and K identify ritual sites and show the dancing and feasting that were an important part of the Indians' religion. The picture also shows the Indians' chief crops—tobacco (E), corn in two stages of growth (G and H), and pumpkins (I). The hut labeled F housed a watchman assigned to keep animals and birds away from the fields. The river (L) was the village's source of water. Note the hunters shooting deer at top left. Rare Book Division, The New York Public Library, Astor, Lenox and Tilden Foundations.

ing belief in the superiority of their civilization. They expected the Indians to adopt English customs and to convert to Christianity. When most tribes resisted, the English concluded that the Indians were irredeemable. Most colonists reached that conclusion quite early in the history of their settlements.

The Englishmen dispatched by the Virginia Company settled in a region dominated by the

Powhatan Confederacy

Powhatan Confederacy (see map, page 8). Powhatan, the chief of six allied tribes on the coast of what is now Virginia, was consolidating his control over about twenty-five other tribes in the area when the English colonists arrived. Fortunately for the Englishmen, Powhatan seems not to have viewed them as enemies but as potential allies in his struggle to establish uncontested authority over his Indian neighbors.

Initially at least, Powhatan had good cause for self-assurance. The 104 men and boys who in May 1607 established the settlement called

Founding of Jamestown

Jamestown were indeed ill-equipped for survival. Many of the first immigrants were gentlemen unaccustomed to working with their hands and artisans with irrelevant skills like glassmaking. They resisted living "like savages," retaining English dress and casual work habits. Such attitudes, combined with the effects of chronic malnutrition and epidemic disease, took a terrible toll. During the notorious "starving time," the winter of 1609–1610, some colonists even resorted to cannibalism. As late as 1624, fewer than 1,300 of the more than 8,000 immigrants to Virginia had survived.

The one Englishman who fully understood the necessity of adapting to the realities of life in Virginia was Captain John Smith. An adventurer, Smith took charge of the colony in 1608 and imposed military discipline on the settlers, requiring all to work. Smith's previous experience with alien peoples (he had lived in Turkey) gave him an understanding of Powhatan lacking in his fellow colonists. Powhatan and Smith respected and sparred with each other as

Pocahontas (1595/96?–1617), here called Matoaka alias Rebecka, portrayed in Elizabethan dress. During her visit to England with her husband John Rolfe in 1616, the Indian princess became the toast of London society. She died the following year, just as she was leaving England to return to her homeland, and was buried in the parish church at Gravesend. National Portrait Gallery, Smithsonian Institution, Washington, D.C.

equals. Though their relationship was never cordial, it was founded upon a reluctant mutual admiration.

The early Virginia settlers had frequent contacts with the Indians. Powhatan's people traded life-saving corn to the English and obtained steel knives, hatchets, and guns. A regular visitor to Jamestown was Powhatan's favorite daughter, Pocahontas, who greatly admired Smith and on several occasions warned him of her father's plots against the colony.

Smith left Virginia forever in 1609. But Pocahontas continued to visit Jamestown, and in 1613 the Englishmen seized her as a hostage. In captivity she fell in love with a widowed planter,

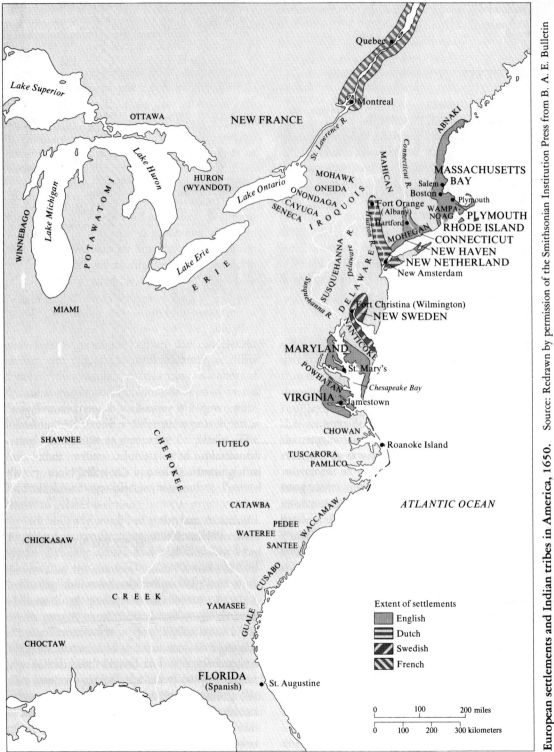

European settlements and Indian tribes in America, 1650. Source: Redrawn by permission of the Smithsonian Institution Press from B. A. E. Bulletin 145, *Indian Tribes of North America*, John Swanton, Smithsonian Institution, Washington, D.C. 1952.

Lake Superior

OTTAWA

NEW FRANCE

Quebec

Montreal

WINNEBAGO

Lake Michigan

Lake Huron

POTAWATOMI

HURON
(WYANDOT)

Lake Ontario

St. Lawrence R.

MOHAWK
ONEIDA
ONONDAGA
CAYUGA
SENECA
IROQUOIS

Lake Erie

ERIE

MIAMI

ABNAKI

MAHICAN

Connecticut R.

MASSACHUSETTS
BAY

Salem
Boston
Plymouth

Fort Orange
(Albany)

Hartford

WAMPA-
NOAG

PLYMOUTH

RHODE ISLAND
CONNECTICUT
NEW HAVEN
NEW NETHERLAND

MOHEGAN

Hudson R.

New Amsterdam

SUSQUEHANNA

Susquehanna R.

Delaware R.

DELAWARE

Fort Christina (Wilmington)
NEW SWEDEN

NANTICOKE

MARYLAND

St. Mary's

POWHATAN

Chesapeake Bay

VIRGINIA

Jamestown

SHAWNEE

CHEROKEE

TUTELO

CHOWAN

Roanoke Island

TUSCARORA
PAMLICO

CATAWBA

ATLANTIC OCEAN

CHICKASAW

PEDEE
WATEREE
SANTEE

WACCAMAW

CREEK

CUSABO

YAMASEE

GUALE

CHOCTAW

FLORIDA
(Spanish)

St. Augustine

Extent of settlements

English
Dutch
Swedish
French

0   100   200 miles

0   100   200   300 kilometers

John Rolfe, and married him the following year. Her father approved the match, agreeing as well to a formal treaty with the colonists. Pocahontas's marriage linked Powhatan with the whites; the treaty cemented the alliance, strengthening his position with respect to the thirty tribes he had subjected to his rule.

The peace established in 1614 lasted eight years, persisting beyond Pocahontas's death in 1617 and Powhatan's the next year. But even before 1614 the force that would eventually destroy the peace had been set in motion. That force was the spread of tobacco cultivation.

In tobacco the settlers and the Virginia Company found the saleable commodity for which they had been searching. The tobacco native to North America was harsh and unpleasant, but John Rolfe imported the seeds of preferable varieties from South America, planting his first crop in 1611. Within twenty years, 1.5 million pounds were being exported annually—tobacco had become the foundation of Virginia's prosperity.

Successful tobacco cultivation required abundant land, since the crop quickly drained soil of nutrients. Planters soon learned that a field could produce only about three satisfactory crops before it had to lie fallow for several years to regain its fertility. Thus the once small English settlements began to expand rapidly: eager planters applied to the Virginia Company for large land grants on both sides of the James and its tributary streams.

Opechancanough, Powhatan's brother and successor, watched the English colonists steadily encroaching on Indian lands and attempting to convert members of the tribes to Christianity. He recognized the danger his brother had overlooked. On March 22 (Good Friday), 1622, under his leadership, the confederacy launched coordinated attacks all along the river. By the end of the day, 347 colonists (about one-third of the total) lay dead. The colony survived both this war and the one waged by Opechancanough in 1644. His defeat in the latter war cost him his life and ended the Powhatan Confederacy's efforts to resist the spread of white settlement.

| Opechanca-nough's attack |

Life in the Chesapeake

After the 1622 massacre, James I revoked the company's charter and made Virginia a royal colony. But he allowed the company's headright system and a representative assembly to survive. The headright granted each colonist fifty acres of land, with a proportional number of headrights allotted to those financing the passage of others. The assembly, called the House of Burgesses, had been created in 1619. It gave the settlers a representative system of government with considerable local autonomy.

In 1634, Virginia acquired a neighbor; the proprietorship of Maryland was founded in the area north of the Potomac River. The Calvert family, who founded Maryland, intended the colony to serve as a haven for their fellow Roman Catholics, who were being persecuted in England. Cecilius Calvert, second Lord Baltimore, became the first colonizer to offer prospective settlers freedom of religion, as long as they were practicing Christians. In that respect Maryland differed from Virginia, where the Church of England was the only officially recognized religion. In other ways, however, the two Chesapeake colonies resembled each other. In Maryland as in Virginia, tobacco planters spread out along the river banks, establishing isolated farms instead of towns.

| Founding of Maryland |

The planting, cultivation, and harvesting of tobacco had to be done by hand; these tasks did not take much skill, but they were repetitious and time-consuming. When the headright system was adopted in Maryland in 1640, a prospective tobacco planter anywhere in the Chesapeake could simultaneously obtain both land and the labor to work it. Through good management a planter could use his profits to pay for the passage of more workers, gain title to more land, and accumulate substantial wealth rapidly.

There were two possible sources of laborers for the growing tobacco farms of the Chesapeake: Africa and England. In 1619, a Dutch privateer brought more than twenty blacks from the Spanish Caribbean islands to Virginia; they were the first known black inhabitants of the English colonies in North America. Over the next few decades, small numbers of blacks were carried to the Chesapeake, but even as late as 1670 the black population of Virginia was at most 2,000. Chesapeake planters looked to England, not Africa or the West Indies, to supply their labor needs. Workers migrated from England as indentured servants: that is, in return for their passage they contracted to work for planters for periods ranging from four to seven years.

Who were the thousands of English people who chose to emigrate to the Chesapeake as servants in the seventeenth century? Most of them were men between the ages of fifteen and twenty-four who had been farmers and laborers. Many had been skilled tradesmen and even clerks, teachers, and accountants. They were what their contemporaries called the "common" or "middling" sort. Judging by their youth, though, most had probably not yet established a firm foothold for themselves in England.

Immigrants to the Chesapeake

What motivated the servants to leave their homeland? Many of the servants came from areas of England that were experiencing severe economic disruption. For such people the Chesapeake appeared to offer good prospects. Once they had fulfilled the terms of their indentures, servants were promised "freedom dues," consisting of clothes, tools, livestock, casks of corn and tobacco, and sometimes even land.

What did indentured servants actually find in Virginia and Maryland? Their lives were not easy. Servants typically worked six days a week, ten to fourteen hours a day, in a climate much

Conditions of servitude

warmer than they were accustomed to. Their masters could discipline or sell them, and they faced severe penalties for running away. Even so, they did have some rights enforceable in the courts. Their masters had to supply them with sufficient food, clothing, and shelter; they had to be allowed to rest on Sundays; and they could not be physically abused. Yet few seem to have been happy with their lot.

Servants also had to contend with epidemic disease and a death rate higher than England's. After surviving a process called "seasoning"—a bout with disease (probably malaria)—immigrants were confronted with dysentery, influenza, typhoid, and recurrences of malaria. As a result, approximately 40 percent of the male servants did not survive long enough to become freedmen.

For those who survived the term of their indentures, however, the opportunities for advancement were real. Until the last decades of the century, former servants were usually able to become independent planters ("freeholders") and to live a modest but comfortable existence. Some even became prominent. But after 1670 tobacco prices fell, land became expensive, and Maryland dropped its requirement that freed servants receive land as part of their freedom dues. By 1700 the Chesapeake was no longer the land of opportunity it had once been.

Life in the seventeenth-century Chesapeake was hard for everyone. Most people subsisted on pork and corn, not a particularly nutritious diet. Thus the health problems caused by epidemic disease were magnified by diet deficiencies and the near-impossibility of preserving food for safe winter consumption. Few farm households had many material possessions. Among the settlers' most valuable property was their clothing, since cloth usually had to be imported from England. Spinning and weaving were traditionally done by women, and the few women in the Chesapeake could not supply the needs of the population.

Chapter 1: The meeting of Old World and New, 1492–1650

The predominance of males and the high mortality rates combined to produce unusual patterns of family life. Because there were so few women, many men were never able to marry.

| Family life in the Chesapeake |

Meanwhile, nearly every adult free woman in the Chesapeake married, and widows remarried quickly. Servant women, though, usually remained single during their term of indenture, since most masters denied them permission to marry, fearing pregnancy would make them unable to work. The high death rates also produced many widows, widowers, and orphans. In one Virginia county, for example, three-fourths of the children had lost at least one parent by the time they married or reached age twenty-one.

Marriage and family patterns in the Chesapeake thus differed from those in England. Families in England were patriarchal (dominated by the husband-father figure). But Chesapeake immigrants, separated from their families, could determine their futures for themselves. So too could the first native-born generation, since the high mortality rates usually deprived them of at least one parent while they were still children. Servant women, who could not marry until their late twenties, normally bore only one or two children who lived to maturity. Their daughters, by contrast, married shortly after puberty and bore many more offspring. Thus the Chesapeake population began to grow slowly through natural increase, although not until the 1720s did native-born residents outnumber immigrants.

The fact that the Chesapeake population was primarily immigrant for nearly a century had important implications for politics in Maryland and Virginia. Both Virginia's House of Burgesses and Maryland's House of Delegates (established in 1635) were composed almost entirely of immigrants until late in the seventeenth century. The same was true

| Political instability |

of the governors' councils, which acted as the upper house of the legislature and as executive advisor to the governor. Such immigrants came from different parts of England and had few ties to each other or to their new colonial homes. They tended to look to England for solutions to their problems. Moreover, most of the elected representatives felt little need to be responsive to their constituents, about whom they knew very little. Their bitter and prolonged struggles for power and personal economic advantage often thwarted the colonial governments' ability to function effectively. As a result, the existence of representative institutions failed to lead to political stability. Thus, the people of the Chesapeake paid a high price for the area's unusual population patterns.

The Chesapeake was not, however, representative of all the English settlements in North America. In New England, immigrants seeking freedom of religion established a very different society.

The founding of New England

England's Protestant Reformation began the chain of events that eventually brought thousands of English men and women to the northern portion of Virginia, otherwise known as New England. The establishment of the Church of England set into motion forces that neither Henry VIII nor his successors could entirely control. To be sure, Henry and Elizabeth reformed the theology and structure of the new church, but many people were not satisfied. Critics of England's mild reformation wanted to abolish the church hierarchy, free the church from political interference, and make church membership more restrictive. These people were called Puritans, because of their desire to purify the church.

The Puritans were followers of John Calvin, a Swiss cleric who stressed the omnipotence of

| Puritanism |

God and people's powerlessness to affect their ultimate fate. He rejected the Catholic doctrine that one could attain salvation through good works, and declared that God predestines souls to heaven or hell before their births. Only the elect—those selected by God for reasons humans could not understand—would go to heaven when they died. Only they should be allowed to be church members. But this doctrine posed a problem for Puritans, because they believed it was difficult, if not impossible, to know with certainty if one was of the elect.

Some Puritans, the Congregationalists, wanted to reform the Anglican Church rather than abandon it. Another group, known as Separatists, believed the Church of England to be so corrupt it could not be salvaged. They wanted to establish their own religious bodies, with membership restricted to the elect (as nearly as they could be identified). Both groups were subjected to religious persecution in England.

In 1620, the Separatists, many of whom had earlier migrated to Holland in quest of the right to practice their religion freely, obtained permission to settle in part of the territory controlled by the Virginia Company of Plymouth. A total of 101 men and women, some of them "strangers" (non-Separatists), set sail in Septem-

| Founding of Plymouth |

ber on the aged, crowded *Mayflower.* Two months later they sighted land—the tip of Cape Cod, which was outside the northern boundary of the company's territory. But by then it was too late in the fall to go elsewhere. The Pilgrims located their settlement on a fine harbor. While everyone was still on board the ship, the Pilgrims drafted the Mayflower Compact through which they established a "Civil Body Politic" and a rudimentary legal authority for the colony.

Though the weather that year was quite mild, the Pilgrims were ill prepared to survive the rigors of a New England winter. They were racked by disease and suffered seriously from malnutrition. When spring arrived, only half the *Mayflower's* passengers were still alive. But spring also brought what one of them termed "a special instrument sent of God" in the person of Squanto, a friendly Indian. Squanto, an escaped kidnap victim of an English sea captain, spoke good English and served as the Pilgrims' interpreter. He also showed them how to plant corn Indian-style and where to fish.

Further contributing to their good fortune was a climate healthier than that of the Chesapeake and an epidemic that had weakened the tribes near Cape Cod before the Pilgrims arrived. Moreover, Massasoit, chief of the powerful Wampanoags, agreed to a peace with the Pilgrims in 1621. The treaty lasted for more than half a century.

Before the 1620s had ended, a group of Congregationalists launched the colonial enterprise that would come to dominate New England. Under the auspices of the New England Company, which held a land grant from the Council for New England (the successor to the Virginia Company of Plymouth), a group of Congrega-

| Founding of Massachusetts Bay |

tionalist merchants sent out a body of settlers to Cape Ann, north of Cape Cod, in 1628. The following year the merchants obtained a royal charter, constituting themselves as the Massachusetts Bay Company. In a dramatic move, the Congregationalist merchants boldly decided to transfer the headquarters of the Massachusetts Bay Company to New England. The settlers would then be answerable to no one in the mother country and would be able to handle their affairs, secular and religious, as they pleased.

The most important recruit to the new venture was John Winthrop, a pious but practical landed gentleman from Suffolk and a justice of the peace. In October 1629, the members of the Massachusetts Bay Company elected the forty-

| Governor John Winthrop |

one-year-old Winthrop as their governor. It thus fell to Winthrop to organize the initial segment of the great Puritan migration to America. In 1630 more than 1,000 English men and women were transported to Massachusetts—most of them to Boston, which soon became the largest town in North America. By 1643 nearly 20,000 compatriots had followed them.

Winthrop had a transcendent vision. The society he foresaw in America was a true commonwealth, a community in which each person put the good of the whole ahead of private concerns. In America, he asserted, "we shall build a city upon a hill, the eyes of all people are upon us." People in this "city upon a hill" were to live according to the precepts of Christian charity, loving friends and enemies alike. The creation of an ideal society was a special mission to Puritans.

The Puritans' communal ideal was expressed chiefly in the doctrine of the covenant. As Winthrop's words indicated, they believed God had

| *Ideal of the covenant* | made a covenant—that is, an agreement or contract—with them when He chose them |

for the mission to America. In turn they covenanted with each other, promising to work together toward their goals. The founders of churches and towns in the new land often drafted formal documents setting forth the principles on which such institutions would be based. The leaders of Massachusetts Bay interpreted their original joint-stock company charter in ways that enabled them to establish a covenanted community based on mutual consent. They gradually transformed the General Court, officially merely the company's governing body, into a colonial legislature, and opened the status of "freeman," or voting member of the company, to all adult male church members resident in Massachusetts. Less than two decades after the first large group of Puritans had arrived in Massachusetts Bay, the colony had a functioning system of self-government composed of a governor and a two-house legislature.

The colony's method of distributing land helped to further the communal ideal. Unlike Virginia and Maryland, where individual applicants sought headrights for themselves and their servants, in Massachusetts groups of families—often from the same region of England—applied together to the General Court for grants of land

| *Town land grants* | on which to establish towns. The men who received the original grant had the sole |

authority to determine how the land would be distributed. Understandably, they copied the villages from which they came. First they laid out town lots for houses and a church. Then they gave each family parcels of land scattered around the town center: pasture here, a woodlot there, an arable field elsewhere. They also reserved the best and largest plots for the most distinguished among them (usually including the minister); people who had been low on the social scale in England received far smaller allotments. Even when immigrants began to move beyond the territorial limits of the Bay Colony into Connecticut (1636), New Haven (1638), and New Hampshire (1638), the same pattern of town land grants was maintained. In their towns the settlers quickly established diversified farms instead of raising one primary crop, as was done in the Chesapeake.

The migration to Connecticut ended the Puritans' relative freedom from clashes with neighboring Indian tribes. The first English settlers in the Connecticut River valley moved there from Newtown (Cambridge), under the direction of their minister, Thomas Hooker. Connecticut was fertile, and the wide river promised easy access to the ocean for purposes of trade. The site had just one problem: it fell within the territory controlled by the Pequot tribe.

The strong Pequots, themselves recent migrants from the upper Hudson valley, dominated the weaker tribes native to the region. After two incidents in which Indians (probably

| *Pequot War* | not Pequots) brutally killed white men, a Massachusetts |

force in 1636 burned some Pequot villages and crops. That raid set off a brief but bloody war that ended when a force of Englishmen accom-

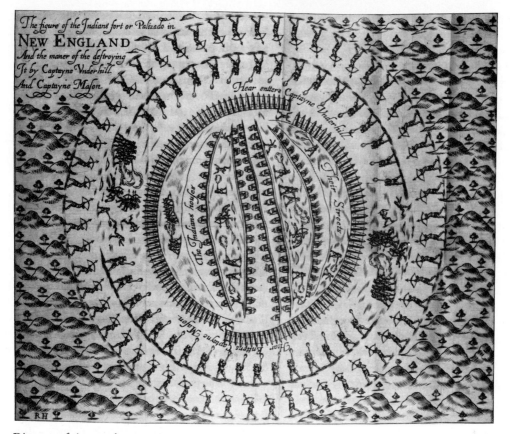

Diagram of the attack on the Pequot fort at Mystic. The Puritans and their Narragansett allies surround the fort, shooting everyone who tries to escape the flames. Drawn by Captain John Underhill, who participated in the attack. The Library Company of Philadelphia.

panied by some Narragansett Indians attacked one of the main Pequot villages on May 26, 1637. The Puritans and their allies set the town on fire. At least four hundred Pequots, including many women and children, were slaughtered. Of the English, only two were killed and twenty wounded. The power of the Pequots was broken. The few surviving members of the tribe, dispirited and despairing, were captured and enslaved by the colonists and their Indian allies. Since the Pequots had been the only tribe strong enough to oppose the migration into the New England interior, the way was cleared for English expansion.

Life in New England

Colonists in New England led lives dramatically different from those of their contemporaries in the Chesapeake. The chief differences lay in their patterns of settlement, in the relative importance of religion in the settlers' daily lives, and in their family organization and behavior.

Although religion seems to have played a minor role in the lives of seventeenth-century Chesapeake settlers, it was ever-present in the lives of New Englanders, even those who were not Puritans. The governments of Massachusetts Bay, Plymouth, Connecticut, and the other northern colonies were all controlled by Puritans. Congregationalism was the only officially recognized religion; members of other sects had no freedom of worship except in Rhode Island. Only male church members could legally vote in colony elections, although some non-Puritans appear to have voted in town meetings. All households were taxed to build meetinghouses and pay ministers' salaries. Moreover, penalties were prescribed for failing to attend church regularly.

In the New England colonies, church and state were intertwined. Puritans objected to secular interference in religious affairs, but at the same time expected the church to influence the conduct of politics. They also believed that the state had an obligation to support and protect the one true church—theirs. As a result, though they came to America seeking freedom of worship, they saw no contradiction in their refusal to grant that freedom to others. Indeed, the two most significant divisions in early Massachusetts were caused by religious disputes, and by Massachusetts Bay's unwillingness to tolerate dissent.

Roger Williams, a Separatist, immigrated to Massachusetts Bay in 1631 and became assistant pastor at Salem. Williams soon began to express the eccentric ideas that the king had no right to give away land belonging to the Indians, that church and state should be separated, and that Puritans had no right to force their beliefs upon others. Banished from Massachusetts in 1635, Williams founded the town of Providence on Narragansett Bay. Because of his beliefs, Providence and other towns in what became the colony of Rhode Island adopted a policy of tolerating all religions, including Judaism.

The other dissenter, and an even greater challenge to Massachusetts Bay orthodoxy, was Anne Marbury Hutchinson. She was a follower of John Cotton, a minister who stressed God's free gift of salvation to unworthy humans (the covenant of grace). In 1636 Hutchinson began holding meetings in her home. At first, her gatherings included only women, but later men attended as well. She talked about the covenant of grace, going beyond the views of John Cotton. Indeed, Hutchinson embraced the Antinomian heresy—the belief that the elect can communicate directly with God and be assured of salvation. She thus offered Puritans relief from the tension associated with the uncertainty of salvation.

Anne Hutchinson posed a dual threat, one theological and one social, to the Puritan world. She was charged by the General Court with having libeled the colony's clerics by claiming that they preached salvation through works. Her banishment to Rhode Island was assured when she stated that God had spoken directly to her. Equally significant was her challenge to traditional gender roles. Her judges were almost as outraged by her "masculine" behavior as by her heretical beliefs. As one of them told her, "You have stept out of your place, you have rather bine a Husband than a Wife and a preacher than a Hearer; and a Magistrate than a Subject."

The vehemence with which the General Court reacted to Anne Hutchinson's disregard of customary feminine behavior indicates the extent to which traditional English family patterns had been duplicated in New England, in contrast to the Chesapeake. First, Puritans commonly migrated as families—sometimes even three-generation families—rather than as individuals. That meant that the age range of the immigrants was wider and the sexes more balanced numerically, so that the population could immediately begin to reproduce itself. Second, New England's climate was much healthier than that of the Chesapeake. Indeed, New England proved to be even healthier than the mother country.

Important events

1477	Marco Polo's *Travels* published
1488	Bartholomew Dias rounds Cape of Good Hope
1492	Christopher Columbus discovers Bahama Islands
1493	Syphilis first recorded in Europe
1497	John Cabot charts coast of Newfoundland
1498	Vasco da Gama reaches India
1518–30	Smallpox pandemic decimates Indian population of New World
1521	Tenochtitlan surrenders to Cortés; Aztec empire falls to Spaniards
1524	Giovanni da Verrazano explores North American coast
1533	Henry VIII divorces Catherine of Aragon
1535	Francisco Pizarro conquers Inca empire
1558	Elizabeth I becomes queen
1587–90	Sir Walter Raleigh's Roanoke colony fails
1603	James I becomes king
1606	Virginia Company chartered
1607	Jamestown founded
1609	Henry Hudson explores Hudson River
1611	First Virginia tobacco crop
1619	First blacks arrive in Virginia
1620	Plymouth Colony founded
1622	Powhatan Confederacy attacks Virginia colony
1624	Virginia Company charter revoked; Virginia becomes royal colony
1625	Charles I becomes king
1629	Massachusetts Bay Company chartered
1630	Massachusetts Bay Colony founded
1634	Maryland founded
1635	Roger Williams expelled from Massachusetts Bay; founds Providence, Rhode Island
1636	Connecticut founded
1637	Pequot War / Anne Hutchinson expelled from Massachusetts Bay
1638	New Haven Colony founded / New Hampshire founded
1640	Great Migration to New England ends

While Chesapeake families were few in number, small in size, and transitory, New England ones were numerous, large, and long-lived. In

Family life in New England

New England more men were able to marry, since there were more female migrants; immigrant women married earlier (at twenty, on the average); and marriages lasted longer and produced more children, who were more likely to live to maturity. If seventeenth-century Chesapeake women could expect to rear three healthy children, New England women could anticipate raising six to eight.

The nature of the population had other major implications for family life. New England in effect created grandparents, since in England people rarely lived long enough to know their children's children. To be sure, conflict between the generations existed in New England. Parents attempted to exercise control even over their adult children. Because of the land-grant system, young men were dependent upon their fathers to supply them with acreage to cultivate. Yet parents needed their children's labor on their farms. On the whole, though, children seem to have obeyed their parents' wishes. They had few alternatives.

In 1630 John Winthrop wrote to his wife Margaret, who was still in England, "my deare wife, we are heer in a paradise." Yet even though America was not a paradise, it was a place where English men and women could worship as they wished or attempt to better their economic circumstances. Many died, but those who lived laid the foundation for subsequent colonial prosperity. That they did so by dispossessing the Indians bothered few besides Roger Williams. By the middle of the seventeenth century, one fact was indisputable: English people had come to the New World to stay.

Suggestions for further reading

GENERAL Charles M. Andrews, *The Colonial Period of American History: The Settlements*, 3 vols. (1934–1937); John E. Pomfret, *Founding the American Colonies, 1583–1660* (1970); Robert V. Wells, *Revolutions*

in Americans' Lives: A Demographic Perspective on the History of Americans, Their Families, and Their Society (1982)

INDIANS Harold E. Driver, *Indians of North America,* 2nd ed. (1969); Alvin Josephy, Jr., *The Indian Heritage of America* (1968); Neal Salisbury, *Manitou and Providence: Indians, Europeans, and the Making of New England, 1500–1643* (1982); Robert F. Spencer, Jesse D. Jennings, et al., *The Native Americans: Ethnology and Backgrounds of the North American Indians,* 2nd ed. (1977).

ENGLAND Peter Laslett, *The World We Have Lost* (1965); Wallace Notestein, *The English People on the Eve of Colonization 1603–1630* (1954); Michael Walzer, *The Revolution of the Saints* (1965).

EXPLORATION AND DISCOVERY Alfred W. Crosby, Jr., *The Columbian Exchange: Biological and Cultural Consequences of 1492* (1972); J.H. Elliott, *The Old World and the New, 1492–1650* (1970); Charles Gibson, *Spain in America* (1966); Samuel Eliot Morison, *The European Discovery of America: The Northern Voyages, A.D. 1500–1600* (1971), *The Southern Voyages, A.D. 1492–1616* (1974); J.H. Parry, *The Age of Reconnaissance* (1963); David B. Quinn, *North America from Earliest Discovery to First Settlements* (1977).

EARLY CONTACT BETWEEN WHITES AND INDIANS Francis Jennings, *The Invasion of America: Indians, Colonialism, and the Cant of Conquest* (1975); Frances Mossiker, *Pocahontas: The Life and the Legend* (1976); Alden T. Vaughan, *American Genesis: Captain John Smith and the Founding of Virginia* (1975); Alden T. Vaughan, *The New England Frontier: Puritans and Indians 1620–1675,* rev. ed. (1979).

NEW ENGLAND John Demos, *A Little Commonwealth: Family Life in Plymouth Colony* (1970); Philip J. Greven, Jr., *Four Generations: Population, Land, and Family in Colonial Andover, Massachusetts* (1970); Sydney V. James, *Colonial Rhode Island* (1975); Lyle Koehler, *A Search for Power: The "Weaker Sex" in Seventeenth-Century New England* (1980); Kenneth A. Lockridge, *A New England*

Town: The First Hundred Years (Dedham, Massachusetts, 1636–1736) (1970); Edmund S. Morgan, The Puritan Dilemma: The Story of John Winthrop (1958); Edmund S. Morgan, The Puritan Family: Religion and Domestic Relations in Seventeenth-Century New England, rev. ed. (1966); Edmund S. Morgan, Visible Saints: The History of a Puritan Idea (1963); Sumner Chilton Powell, Puritan Village: The Formation of a New England Town (1963); Darrett Rutman, American Puritanism: Faith and Practice (1970); Darrett Rutman, Winthrop's Boston: A Portrait of a Puritan Town, 1630–1649 (1965); Alan Simpson, Puritanism in Old and New England (1955).

CHESAPEAKE   Lois Green Carr and Lorena Walsh, "The Planter's Wife: The Experience of White Women in Seventeenth-Century Maryland," William and Mary Quarterly, 3rd ser., 34 (1977), 542–571; Wesley Frank Craven, The Southern Colonies in the Seventeenth Century, 1607–1689 (1949); Wesley Frank Craven, White, Red, and Black: The Seventeenth Century Virginian (1971); David Galenson, White Servitude in Colonial America: An Economic Analysis (1981); Edmund S. Morgan, American Slavery, American Freedom: The Ordeal of Colonial Virginia (1975); Abbot E. Smith, Colonists in Bondage: White Servitude and Convict Labor in America, 1607–1776 (1947); Thad W. Tate and David L. Ammerman, eds., The Chesapeake in the Seventeenth Century: Essays on Anglo-American Society & Politics (1979); William and Mary Quarterly, 3rd ser., 30, No. 1 (Jan. 1973): Chesapeake Society.

2

AMERICAN SOCIETY TAKES SHAPE, 1650–1750

Olaudah Equiano was eleven years old in 1756 when black raiders in search of slaves kidnapped him from his village in what is now Nigeria. Until then, he had lived peacefully with his family. As a captive, Equiano passed from master to master, finally arriving at the coast, where an English slave ship lay at anchor. Terrified by the light complexions, long hair, and strange language of the sailors, he was afraid that "I had gotten into a world of bad spirits and that they were going to kill me." Equiano was placed below decks, where "with the loathsomeness of the stench and crying together, I became so sick and low that I was not able to eat, nor had I the least desire to taste anything."

The youthful Equiano was carried to Virginia where he was separated from the other Africans and put to work weeding and clearing rocks from the fields. "I was now exceedingly miserable and thought myself worse off than any of the rest of my companions," Equiano recalled in a narrative of his life, "for they could talk to each other, but I had no person to speak to that I could understand. In this state I was constantly grieving and pining and wishing for death rather than anything else."

If the most important aspect of the first fifty years of English colonization was the meeting of European and Indian, the key occurrence of the next century was the importation of more than two hundred thousand Africans into North America. That massive influx of black slaves, and the geographic patterns it took, has dramatically influenced the shaping of American society ever since.

Many other major events also marked the years between 1650 and 1750. New colonies were founded, populating the gap between the widely separated New England and Chesapeake settlements. England also took over the coastal outposts established by other European nations. As English settlements spread to the north, west, and south, they moved onto territory controlled by the powerful Indian tribes of the interior. After many years of peace, colonists and native Americans once again went to war. Furthermore, internal disputes within the colonies often resulted in open rebellions against established governments. Yet by the middle of the eighteenth century, stable political and social structures had evolved in all the colonies. After a century and a half of English colonization, the American provinces assumed a mature form.

The forced migration of Africans

Few Africans were imported into the English mainland colonies before the last quarter of the seventeenth century. This pattern was in sharp contrast to that of Britain's Caribbean colonies, where blacks outnumbered whites by the 1680s. What accounted for the difference between the island and mainland colonies with respect to black slavery? More important, since England itself had no tradition of slavery, why did English settlers in the New World begin to enslave Africans at all? The answers to both questions lie in the combined effects of economics and racial attitudes.

The English were an ethnocentric people. They believed firmly in the superiority of their values and civilization. Furthermore, they believed that fair-skinned peoples like themselves were superior to the darker-skinned races. Those beliefs alone did not cause them to enslave Indians and Africans, but the idea that other races were inferior to whites helped to justify slavery.

Although the English had not previously practiced slavery, the Spanish and Portuguese had; moreover, Christian doctrine allowed the enslavement of heathen peoples as a means of converting them. Yet the Indians' familiarity with the American environment made them difficult to enslave, and Indian captives were often able to escape from their white masters. But Africans were a different story. Transported far from home and set down in alien surroundings, they were frequently unable to communicate with their fellow workers. They were also the darkest (and thus, to European eyes, the most inferior) of all peoples. Black Africans therefore seemed to be ideal candidates for perpetual servitude.

Nevertheless, a fully developed system of lifelong slavery did not emerge immediately in the English colonies. Lack of historical evidence makes it difficult to determine the legal status of blacks during the first two or three decades of English settlement, but at least a few of them seem to have been free. After 1640, on the other

| Emergence of slavery |

hand, some blacks were being permanently enslaved in each of the English colonies. Soon Barbados (1661) and then the main-

land colonies adopted comprehensive slave codes.

The question still remains: why did Chesapeake and Caribbean colonists differ at first in their choice of laborers, and why did the Chesapeake tobacco planters turn increasingly to blacks after 1675? Both supply and demand factors were influential.

In the West Indies, the environment was decisive. English people did not adapt easily to life in the tropics; they died in droves from epidemic diseases their doctors did not know how to treat. Potential servant migrants to the Caribbean may well have learned of the area's dangers and decided to go elsewhere. In any event, sugar planters soon came to prefer African laborers, who were accustomed to the tropical climate and resistant to the most serious of the diseases that killed whites. Thus the black population of the Caribbean islands grew rapidly due to continuing importation.

The Chesapeake environment, though dangerous, was measurably less deadly to whites than the Caribbean, and tobacco planters relied almost exclusively on white indentured servants for fully half a century. But after about 1675,

| Decline in white immigration |

England's declining birth rate and improved economy made indentured servants more difficult to secure. When the shortage of servants became acute, the importation of Africans increased dramatically. By 1690 the Chesapeake colonies contained more black slaves than white indentured servants.

Yet not all white planters could afford to devote so much money to purchasing workers. Accordingly, the transition from indentured to enslaved labor increased the social and economic distance between richer and poorer planters. Whites with enough money could acquire slaves and accumulate greater wealth, while less affluent whites could not. As time passed, white Chesapeake society thus became more and more stratified; that is, the gap between rich and poor steadily widened.

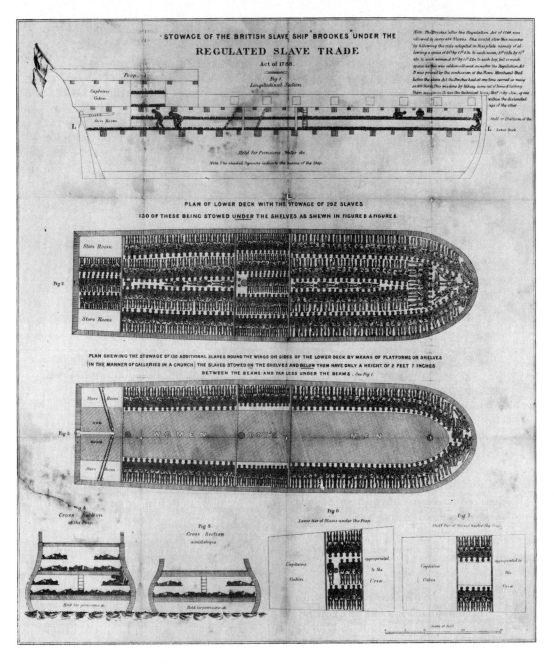

Eighteenth-century diagram of a slave ship, with its human cargo stowed according to British regulations. Many captains did not give slaves even this much room. On the assumption that a large number of Africans would die en route, shipmasters packed as many slaves as possible into the hold to increase their profit.   Library of Congress.

The forced migration of Africans

Slavery also affected Carolina, the other southern colony chartered in the seventeenth century (1669). Carolina's proprietors planned

Founding of the Carolinas

to establish a colony governed by an elaborate hierarchy of landholding aristocrats. But Carolina failed to follow the course outlined for it. Instead it quickly developed two distinct population centers, which in 1730 split into separate colonies.

The Albemarle region that became North Carolina was first settled by Virginians. They established a society much like their own, with an economy based on tobacco cultivation and the export of such forest products as pitch, tar, and timber. South Carolina developed quite differently. Its first settlers—who founded Charleston in 1670—came from Barbados with their slaves. Perhaps one-quarter to one-third of the first residents of South Carolina were black, and of those three-fourths were male. The high proportion of Africans and Caribbean-born blacks in South Carolina's population from the very beginning inexorably shaped the colony's early history.

Their central position in the colony's economy was not established, however, until almost the end of the century. In the 1670s and 1680s, white Carolinians, like other English people in the New World, employed white indentured servants and Indian slaves as well as blacks. But in the last decade of the century South Carolin-

Introduction of rice and indigo

ians developed a new staple crop: rice. Europeans knew little about techniques of cultivating and processing rice, but slaves from Africa's so-called Rice Coast (present-day Ghana and Sierra Leone) had spent their lives working in the rice fields. It may well have been their expertise that enabled their English masters to grow rice successfully. As the colony's commitment to rice cultivation grew, so did the demand for African workers. As a result, by 1710 a majority of South Carolina's residents were black.

South Carolina later developed another staple crop, and it too made use of blacks' special skills. The crop was indigo, much prized in Europe as a blue dye for clothing. In the 1740s, Eliza Lucas, a young Antigua woman who was managing her father's South Carolina plantations, began to experiment with indigo cultivation. Drawing on the knowledge of West Indians familiar with the crop, she developed the planting and processing techniques later adopted throughout the colony. Indigo was grown on high ground, and rice was planted in low-lying swampy areas; rice and indigo also had opposite growing seasons. Thus the two crops complemented each other perfectly.

After 1700 white southerners were irrevocably committed to black slavery as their chief source of labor. The same was not true of white northerners, for small-scale northern agriculture did not require slave labor. Still, wealthy northerners wanted domestic servants, and slaves could fill that need. By the 1740s, blacks constituted more than 10 percent of the population of New York City, Newport, Rhode Island, and other cities.

Between 1492 and 1770 more Africans than Europeans came to the New World. But only about 275,000 of the millions of enslaved Afri-

Slave importation, 1492–1770

cans were taken to the English mainland colonies in the eighteenth century. Most slaves were destined for lives in the Caribbean or South America. Of the English colonies, the West Indies had the harshest environment and the most rigorous work schedules, and thus had the highest black mortality rate.

On the mainland, South Carolina most closely resembled the West Indies. Rice cultivation was difficult and unhealthful, partly because the rice swamps were ideal breeding-grounds for malaria-carrying mosquitoes. Furthermore, Carolina planters, like those of the islands, maintained a slave population with a high proportion of males to females (about two-to-one). During the mid-eighteenth century, therefore, South Carolina slaves barely managed to reproduce themselves, and the black population increased in size only because of massive imports of slaves from Africa.

In the Chesapeake, by contrast, imports accounted for black population growth only until about 1720. From 1740 on, the black population of Maryland and Virginia grew chiefly through natural increase. Precisely how and why such a transition occurred is not yet clear. The more moderate climate and less demanding work routines in the Chesapeake probably contributed to greater survival rates among the immigrants. Moreover, by the middle of the eighteenth century some whites had begun to recognize the advantages of encouraging their slaves to marry and have children.

Natural increase of the slave population

The increase of the black population through natural means had important consequences. A planter with a few slave families could watch the size of his work force grow without additional investment. Natural increase brought a balance between the sexes, and that brought marriage and childbearing. There was a direct relationship between the emergence of the Chesapeake's first large plantations in the 1740s and the slave population's natural increase. Finally, marital unions and children were essential elements in the creation of a distinctive Afro-American society.

The secularization and commercialization of New England

In 1642 civil war broke out in England between Puritans led by Oliver Cromwell and Anglicans supporting Charles I, who not only persecuted Puritans but also ruled autocratically. The Puritans, who dominated Parliament, successfully overthrew the king after several years of war and executed him in 1649. Cromwell then controlled the government until his own death in 1658. Two years later the Stuart family was peacefully restored to the throne in the person of Charles II, son of Charles I.

These events had profound consequences for the American colonies, especially New England. The Puritans' triumph at home eliminated their major incentive for immigration to America. The Puritan migration largely ceased. New England's population growth in the seventeenth century, therefore, resulted almost entirely from natural increase.

Population growth and land use

Families were larger, and children tended to live longer, on the average, than their Chesapeake contemporaries. By 1700 New England's population had quadrupled to approximately 100,000 and equaled that of the Chesapeake.

In New England, the area of settlement and the number of towns constantly expanded as members of each subsequent generation sought land on which to establish and support their families. This process was not always smooth, nor was there an infinite amount of land available for farming. Since sons (and occasionally daughters) usually shared equally in their father's property, the size of landholdings tended to decrease with each generation. The earliest settlers of some of the first Massachusetts towns, for example, eventually received land grants averaging about 150 acres during their lifetimes. By the third quarter of the eighteenth century, the average landholding in the same towns was only 30 to 50 acres.

Although these smaller farms were still adequate to support a family, pressure was being placed on the supply of arable land. Members of the first American-born generation could usually farm in their home towns. But their children and grandchildren often had to migrate. Others learned skills and became artisans in their home towns or in the region's seaports.

As the population increased, New England towns changed in shape and character. The settlement pattern of each family living on a village lot and cultivating scattered pieces of land gave way to consolidated farms located some distance from the town center. When the population in an outlying area had reached a sufficient number, the farmers there commonly asked the town for permission to construct their own church, so they would not have to travel so far on Sundays. Often the next step was a formal division of the town.

Just as inevitable as changes in the land-population ratio and alterations in town boundaries was the major religious crisis caused by a conflict between two basic tenets of New England Puritanism. The first was a belief in infant baptism for the children of all church members. The second was the requirement that potential church members prove to the congregation that they had experienced the gift of God's grace, or "saving faith," before they could be admitted to full membership.

By the 1650s, baptized American-born children of immigrant church members were themselves marrying and having children. But many of them had not applied for full church membership, since they had not experienced saving faith. What was to be done when such families presented their infants for baptism? A synod of Massachusetts ministers, convened in 1662 to consider the problem, responded by establishing a category of "halfway" membership in the church. In a statement that has become known as the Halfway Covenant, the clergymen declared that adults who had been baptized as children but were not full church members could have their children baptized. In return, such parents would have to acknowledge the authority of the church and live according to moral precepts. They would not be allowed to vote in church affairs or take communion.

By the 1660s another change in church membership was evident: the proportion of females in the typical congregation was increasing. Indeed, at the end of the century women constituted a majority in many churches. In response, clerics such as Cotton Mather began to preach sermons outlining woman's proper role in church and society. Mather's sermons were the first formal examination of that theme in

American history. In "Ornaments for the Daughters of Zion," Mather instructed women to be submissive to their husbands, watchful of their children, and attentive to religious duty. The evidence from church membership rolls suggests a growing division between pious women and their more worldly husbands. It also reflects the significant economic changes occurring in New England.

Before 1640 furs obtained by trading with the Indians were the only dependable export from the northern colonies. But the proceeds from furs alone were insufficient to purchase all the manufactured goods the settlers needed. Furthermore, when the outbreak of the English Civil War virtually ended the flow of immigrants, it became apparent that the colonies' economy had depended heavily on a continuing influx of new settlers. New England farmers had been producing surplus crops—such as seed grains and cattle—which they sold to the newcomers, who in return supplied them with clothing, plows, and other such items. When there were no longer many newcomers, New England's first economic system collapsed.

The Puritans then began a search for new saleable crops and markets. They found such crops in the waters off the coast—fish—and on their own land—grain and wood products. By 1643 they had also found the necessary markets: first the Wine Islands (the Azores and Canaries)

Rise of a mercantile economy | in the Atlantic, and then the new English colonies in the Caribbean, which were beginning to cultivate sugar intensively and to invest heavily in slaves. The islands lacked precisely the goods New England could produce in abundance: cheap food (corn and salted fish) to feed the slaves and wood for barrels to transport wine and molasses.

Thus developed the series of transactions that has become known, inaccurately, as the triangular trade. Since New England's products duplicated England's, the northern colonists sold their goods in the West Indies and elsewhere to earn the money with which to purchase English products. There soon grew up in New Eng-

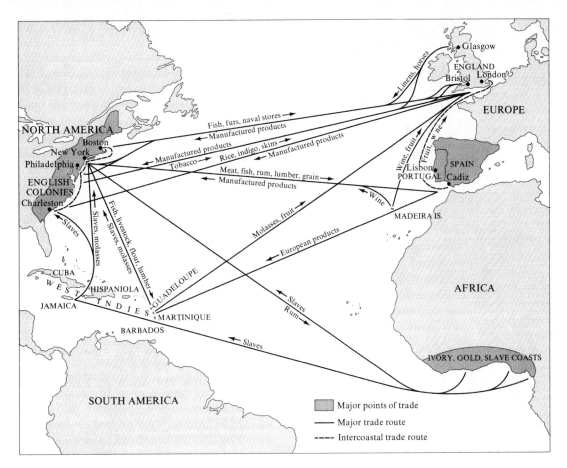

Atlantic trade routes

land's ports a cadre of merchants who acquired—usually through barter—cargoes of timber and foodstuffs, which they then dispatched to the West Indies for sale. In the Caribbean the ships sailed from island to island, exchanging fish, barrel staves, and grains for molasses, fruit, spices, and slaves. Then they would return to Boston, Newport, or New Haven to dispose of their cargoes. Thus the trading pattern was not a neat triangle but a shifting set of irregular polygons (see map). Its sole constant was uncertainty, due to the weather, rapid changes of supply and demand in the small island markets, and the delicate system of credit on which the entire structure depended.

The Puritan New Englanders who ventured into commerce were soon differentiated from their rural counterparts by their ties to a wider transatlantic world and by their preoccupation with material endeavors. The gulf between commercial and farming interests widened after 1660, when Anglican merchants began to migrate to New England. Such men had little stake in the survival of Massachusetts Bay and Connecticut in their original form, and some were openly antagonistic to Puritan traditions. As non-Congregationalists they were denied the vote, and they resented their exclusion from the governing elite.

A clash between the commercial community and Puritan political leaders was inevitable. In 1684, encouraged by the merchants and their al-

Sea Captains Carousing in Surinam, a scene that could have occurred in any tavern in any Caribbean port. Several recognizable Rhode Island merchants are included among the merrymakers. Painted by John Greenwood (1758), a Bostonian who lived in Surinam (Dutch Guiana), on the northern coast of South America.   The St. Louis Art Museum.

lies, England revoked the Massachusetts Bay Colony's charter. After several years of experimentation with a combined government for all of the New England provinces, a new charter making Massachusetts a royal colony was issued in 1691. Henceforth, its governors were to be appointed by the king, and church membership could no longer be a condition for voting. An Anglican parish was even established in the heart of Boston. John Winthrop's dream of a "city upon a hill" seemed to be no more.

The extreme stress New England was undergoing as a result of upheavals in its religious life, social organization, and economic system gave rise in 1692 to accusations of witchcraft in Salem

| Witchcraft in Salem Village | Village (now Danvers), Massachusetts. Like their contemporaries elsewhere, seventeenth-century New Englanders believed in and greatly feared witches. If they could not find rational explanations for their troubles, they tended to suspect they were being bewitched.

The crisis began when a group of adolescent girls accused a number of older women—mostly outsiders—of having bewitched them. Before the hysteria spent itself ten months later, nineteen people (including several men, most of them related to accused female witches) had been hanged, another pressed to death by heavy stones, and more than one hundred others jailed. Historians have puzzled ever since about the origins of the witchcraft episode.

The most plausible explanation may lie in the uncertainty of life in late seventeenth-century New England. Salem Village, a farming town on the edge of a commercial center, was torn between old and new styles of life. Most people were uncertain about their destiny, but none more so than adolescent girls, whose destiny depended on whether their future husbands would be farmers or artisans or merchants. By lashing out and in effect seizing command of the entire town, the girls gave their lives a certainty previously lacking. At the same time, they afforded

Chapter 2: American society takes shape, 1650–1750

their fellow townspeople an opportunity to vent their frustrations at the unsettling changes in their lives. The accused witches were scapegoats for the shattered dreams of an isolated Bible Commonwealth.

The founding of the middle colonies

New Netherland was founded in 1624 as a trading outpost of the Dutch West India Company. Because the Dutch faced few economic and religious pressures, immigration remained sparse. In the 1660s New Netherland had only about 5,000 white and black inhabitants. It had two chief settlements: Fort Orange (Albany) in the north and New Amsterdam (on Manhattan Island) in the south. At Fort Orange the Dutch traded with the Mohawk Indians for the furs that were the colony's chief export.

The powerful Mohawk tribe was the easternmost component of the Iroquois Confederacy, which also included the Seneca, Cayuga, Onon-

| *Iroquois Confederacy* |

daga, and Oneida tribes. Under the terms of a defensive alliance forged in the sixteenth century, the key decisions of war and peace for the entire confederacy were made by a council composed of tribal representatives. The Five Nations vigorously protected their territory against encroachments by whites and other Indians alike, and sought to destroy or subjugate potential rivals.

Because the Dutch traders and the Iroquois needed each other, their relationship was—if sometimes uneasy—generally cordial. But this was a matter of circumstance rather than principle. When Dutch colonists wanted land, not pelts, as they did near Manhattan in the 1640s, conflict developed. In 1655 the Indians attacked New Amsterdam itself, but failed to dislodge the Dutch.

The English were more successful in achiev-

ing that goal. In March 1664, in total disregard of Dutch claims to the area, Charles II gave the entire region between the Connecticut and Delaware rivers, including the Hudson valley, to his brother James, Duke of York. James immediately organized an invasion fleet. In late Au-

| *English conquest of New Netherland* |

gust the vessels anchored off the coast of New Netherland and demanded the colony's surrender. The Dutch complied without firing a shot. Although the Netherlands regained control of the colony in 1672, it permanently ceded the province two years later.

Thus James (and—after he became king in 1685—the English nation) acquired a tiny but heterogeneous possession. Together, the Dutch and the English accounted for the majority of the population. But New York, as it was now called, also included sizable numbers of Germans, French-speaking Walloons, Scandinavians, and Africans, as well as a smattering of other European peoples.

Recognizing the diversity of the population, the Duke of York's representatives moved slowly and cautiously in their efforts to establish English authority. Dutch forms of local government were maintained and Dutch land titles confirmed. Religious toleration was guaranteed through a sort of multiple establishment: each town was permitted to decide which church to support with its tax revenues. Much to the chagrin of English residents of the colony, the duke did not agree to the colonists' requests for an elected legislature until 1683.

The English takeover thus had little immediate effect on the colony. A major reason for the lack of change in New York was that the Duke of York quickly regranted the land between the Hudson and Delaware rivers—New Jersey—to his friends Sir George Carteret and John Lord

| *Founding of New Jersey* |

Berkeley. That left his own colony confined between Connecticut to the east and New Jersey to the west, depriving it of much fertile land and hindering its economic growth. He also failed to promote immigration. Mean-

Penn's Treaty with the Indians, by Benjamin West (1771), one of the first great American-born artists. A Pennsylvanian, West had been raised on stories of Penn's benevolent Indian policies. His painting of Penn's negotiations with the Delawares captured the spirit of the colony's founder.   Joseph and Sarah Harrison Collection, Pennsylvania Academy of the Fine Arts.

while the New Jersey proprietors acted rapidly to attract settlers, promising generous land grants, freedom of religion, and a representative assembly. In response, large numbers of Puritan New Englanders migrated southward to New Jersey, along with some Dutch New Yorkers and a contingent of families from Barbados. New Jersey grew quickly; at the time of its first census in 1726, it had 32,500 inhabitants, only 8,000 fewer than New York.

Within twenty years, Berkeley and Carteret sold large portions of New Jersey to Quakers who were seeking refuge from persecution in England. The Quakers, formally known as the Society of Friends, denied the need for an intermediary between the individual and God. Anyone, they believed, could receive the "inner light" and be saved, and all were equal in God's sight. They had no formally trained clergy; any Quaker, male or female, who felt the call could become a "public Friend" and travel from meeting to meeting to discuss God's word. More-

Chapter 2: American society takes shape, 1650–1750

over, any member of the Society could speak in meetings if he or she desired. In short, the Quakers were true religious radicals, Antinomians in the mold of Anne Hutchinson.

The Quakers obtained a colony of their own in 1681, when Charles II granted the region between Maryland and New York to William Penn, one of the sect's most prominent mem-

| Pennsylvania, a Quaker haven |

bers. Penn held the colony as a personal proprietorship, and the vast property holdings earned profits for his descendants until the American Revolution. Even so, Penn saw the province not merely as a source of revenue, but also as a haven for his persecuted co-religionists. Penn offered land to all comers on liberal terms, promised toleration for all religions, guaranteed such English liberties as the right to bail and trial by jury, and pledged to establish a representative assembly. He also publicized the ready availability of land in Pennsylvania through promotional tracts published in German, French, and Dutch.

Penn's activities and the natural attraction of his lands for Quakers gave rise to a migration whose magnitude was equalled only by the Puritan exodus to New England in the 1630s. By mid-1683, over 3,000 people—among them Welsh, Irish, Dutch, and Germans—had already moved to Pennsylvania. Philadelphia, carefully planned to be the major city in the province, almost immediately attracted 2,000 residents and began to challenge Boston's commercial preeminence.

A pacifist with egalitarian principles, Penn was determined to treat the Indians of Pennsylvania fairly. He purchased tracts of land from the Delawares (or Lenni Lenape), the dominant tribe in the region, before selling them to settlers. Penn also established strict regulations for the Indian trade. News of the Quakers' exemplary Indian policies spread to other tribes, some of whom decided to move to Pennsylvania. By a supreme irony, however, the same toleration that attracted Indians to Penn's domains also brought non-Quaker Europeans who showed little respect for Indian claims to the soil.

Relations between whites and Indians

As the area of English settlement expanded after 1650, white colonists came into contact with increasing numbers of Indian tribes. Two circumstances helped to bring the races together. First, there was no clearly defined frontier: white settlements and Indian villages were often located near each other, and in many cases tribal lands were surrounded, rather than overrun, by whites. As a result, Indians were a common sight in many English towns, and white merchants frequently visited Indian villages. Second, as has been seen, the Indian trade contributed significantly to the colonial economies, especially in the earliest years of settlements.

But some of that trade was involuntary from the Indians' standpoint. Tribes frequently warred

| Indian slave trade |

with each other, a fact that white Carolinians, for example, exploited by urging victorious tribes to sell their captives into slavery and even by fomenting wars. Initially the whites kept many enslaved Indians within the colony. But the Indians' ability to escape, coupled with fears of a general Indian uprising, soon caused the Carolina whites to export most enslaved Indians to the West Indies and New England.

By contrast, whites captured by Indians were often adopted into the tribes as full members of Indian families. A number of such people (especially women captured when young) refused to return to white society when offered the chance to do so. One such captive was Mary Jemison, taken by the Senecas when she was only twelve. She married, bore children, and became a respected matron among the Iroquois. In her memoirs, written late in life, Jemison explained that she had stayed with the Indians not only because of her ties to her husband and children, but also because she preferred the work life of an Iroquois. Women labored in the fields together, keeping their children with them, and, as Jemison remarked, "[we] had no master to oversee or drive us, so that we could work as leisurely as we pleased." Though the lives led by white captives of the Indians should not be romanticized, it is clear that some of them found a "savage" existence preferable to a "civilized" one. The mere existence of such captives indicated, of course, that relations between Indians and whites were not always cordial. And after 1670, a new cycle of hostilities began as English colonists gradually moved beyond the territory of the coastal tribes they had already defeated.

In the mid-1670s, Metacomet–known to the English as King Philip–set out to expel the whites from New England. Metacomet, whose father, Massasoit, had signed a treaty with the Pilgrims in 1621, was concerned because his lands on Narragansett Bay were being surrounded by white settlements. He was further

King Philip's War

concerned over the impact of European culture on his people. When a Plymouth colony court presumed to apply English law to three Wampanoags accused of killing another Wampanoag (they were hanged), Metacomet and his warriors took the act as a grievous insult. In late June 1675, they began to attack nearby white communities.

Soon two other local tribes, the Nipmucs and the Narragansetts, joined Metacomet's forces. In the fall, the three tribes jointly attacked settlements in the northern Connecticut River valley; in the winter and spring of 1676, they totally destroyed twelve of the ninety Puritan towns and attacked forty others. New England's very survival seemed at stake, but after Metacomet was killed the alliance crumbled. Surviving members of the tribes were captured and enslaved.

At the same time Indian-white relations in

Virginia became violent. There settlers, coveting Indian lands, started the war. After whites attacked their villages, the Susquehannock tribe began to raid plantations in the winter of 1676. The land-hungry whites rallied behind the leadership of Nathaniel Bacon, a planter who had arrived in the colony only two years before. Governor William Berkeley, however, hoped to avoid setting off a major war like that raging in New England.

Berkeley and Bacon soon clashed. After Bacon forced the House of Burgesses to authorize him to attack the Indians, Berkeley declared Bacon and his men to be in rebellion. As the

Bacon's Rebellion

chaotic summer of 1676 wore on, Bacon alternately pursued Indians and battled with the governor's supporters. In September he marched on Jamestown itself and burned the capital to the ground. But after Bacon died of dysentery the following month, the rebellion collapsed. Still, a new treaty signed in 1677 opened most of the disputed territory to whites.

Warfare also broke out in the Carolinas. In 1709, a group of Swiss and German settlers expropriated without payment lands belonging to the Tuscarora tribe, an Iroquoian people who had migrated southward many years earlier. In 1711, the Tuscaroras and their allies struck back, initially killing more than one hundred whites.

Tuscarora and Yamasee wars

Since thinly populated North Carolina was incapable of raising a force large enough to oppose the Indians, South Carolina came to its aid in 1712 and again in 1713. The Tuscaroras, badly defeated in the second campaign, gradually began drifting northward to New York, where they became the sixth nation in the Iroquois Confederacy.

Two years later the Yamasees, who had helped the South Carolina whites subdue the Tuscaroras, themselves rose against the English colonists. Their chief grievance was exploitation at the hands of Carolina traders, who regularly engaged in corrupt and deceptive practices. One contemporary observer noted that the traders bragged openly about raping Yamasee women.

Furthermore, the traders overcharged the Yamasees, and then seized women and children to sell as slaves in payment of the Indians' "debts."

With the aid of the Creeks, the Yamasees began coordinated attacks on outlying white settlements on April 15, 1715. That summer the Creek-Yamasee offensive came close to driving the whites from the mainland altogether. But the key to victory lay in the hands of the Cherokees. Wooed by both sides, they finally decided to align themselves with the whites against their ancient enemies, the Creeks. Their cause lost, the Yamasees moved south into Florida to seek the protection of the Spanish, and the Creeks retreated to their villages in the western highlands.

By the end of the first quarter of the eighteenth century, therefore, the colonists had effectively destroyed the power of all the Indian tribes east of the Appalachian Mountains. The one dangerous gap was plugged in 1732 with the chartering of Georgia, the last of the colonies that would become part of the original United States. Intended as a haven for debtors by its founder James Oglethorpe, Georgia was specifically designed as a garrison province. Since all its landholders were expected to serve as militiamen to defend English settlements against the Spanish, the charter prohibited women from inheriting or purchasing land in the colony. That clause was soon altered, but it, and a similarly short-lived injunction against the introduction of slavery, revealed the founders' intention that Georgia should be peopled by sturdy yeoman farmers who could take up their weapons at a moment's notice.

Colonial political development and imperial reorganization

From the mid-1630s to the restoration of the Stuarts in 1660, England was too concerned with its own internal disputes to pay much attention to its New World possessions. The American provinces were thus left to develop political structures and practices largely on their own. In the absence of direct intervention from England, the colonists gradually evolved governments composed of a governor and a two-house legislature. In New England, the governors were elected by the people or the legislature; in the Chesapeake, they were appointed by the king or the proprietor. A council, elected in some colonies and appointed in others, advised the governor on matters of policy and sometimes served as the province's highest court. The council also developed into the upper house of the colonial legislature, with the lower house being composed of representatives elected by white male voters in specific districts.

Colonial political structures

The English colonies established later in the century adopted similar political structures. Charles II, who authorized the new settlements, included in each charter (except that of New York) a provision requiring the inhabitants' consent to governmental measures. None of the charters specified the form such consent should take or defined the voting population; such questions were left in the hands of the proprietors. In the Carolinas, Pennsylvania, and New Jersey, representative assemblies were established as the means of obtaining consent. Pennsylvania's legislature had only one house, but the other colonies followed the two-house pattern. And an assembly was formed in New York in 1683 at the urging of the people.

By late in the seventeenth century, therefore, the American colonists were accustomed to exercising a considerable degree of local political autonomy. The tradition of consent was especially firmly established in New England. Massachusetts, Connecticut, and Rhode Island were, in effect, independent entities, subject neither to the direct authority of the king nor to a proprietor. In the colonies to the south, political structures were somewhat less stable and assemblies less powerful because the largely immigrant population prevented the development of coherent colonial interests and consistent leadership. The desire for local control was basically identical in North and South, but greater continuity of officeholding in New England made for more political coherence and less instability throughout most of the seventeenth century.

After the restoration of the monarchy in 1660, England's Stuart rulers took a new interest in the American colonies. Even though James II was overthrown in a bloodless rebellion known as the Glorious Revolution in 1688–1689, his successors, William and Mary, continued his colonial policies. The monarchs realized that the American colonies could make important contributions to England's well-being. They wanted to ensure that colonial commerce would benefit England rather than competing with the mother country or aiding other nations. They also wanted to tighten England's administrative controls over the colonies.

English administrators in the late seventeenth century based their commercial policy on a theory usually called *mercantilism,* though the term was not coined until a century later. The economic world was seen as a collection of national states, each competing for shares of a finite amount of wealth. What one nation gained was automatically another nation's loss. Each nation's goal was to become as economically self-sufficient as possible. Colonies had an important role to play in such a scheme. They could supply the mother country with valuable raw materials to be consumed at home or sent abroad, and they could serve as a market for the mother country's manufactured goods.

Parliament applied that mercantilist theory to the American colonies in a series of laws known as the Navigation Acts. The major acts—passed in 1660, 1663, and 1673—established three main principles. First, only English or colonial merchants and ships could engage in trade in the colonies. Second, certain valuable American products could be sold only in the mother country. At first these "enumerated" goods were wool, sugar, tobacco, indigo, ginger,

Navigation Acts

and dyes; later acts added rice, naval stores (masts, spars, pitch, tar, and turpentine), copper, and furs to the list. Third, all foreign goods destined for sale in the colonies had to be shipped via England and English import duties had to be paid. Some years later, a new series of laws declared a fourth principle: the colonies could not make or export items that competed with English products (such as wool clothing, hats, and iron).

The intention of the Navigation Acts was clear: American trade was to center on England. The mother country was to benefit from colonial imports and exports both. But the American provinces, especially those in the north, produced many goods that were not enumerated—such as fish, flour, and barrel staves. These products could be traded directly to foreign purchasers as long as they were carried in English or American ships.

The English authorities soon learned that it was easier to write mercantilist legislation than to enforce it. The many harbors of the American coast provided ready havens for smugglers, and colonial officials often looked the other way when illegally imported goods were offered for sale. Consequently, Parliament in 1696 enacted another Navigation Act designed to strengthen enforcement of the first three. This law established in America a number of vice-admiralty courts, which operated without juries, since colonial juries had demonstrated a tendency to favor local smugglers over customs officers.

England took another major step in colonial administration in 1696 by creating the Board of Trade and Plantations to replace the loosely structured standing committee of the Privy Council that had handled colonial affairs since 1675. The fifteen-member Board of Trade thereafter served as the chief organ of government concerned with the American colonies. Still, the Board of Trade did not have any direct powers of enforcement; its chief functions were to gather information and to give advice to policymakers. Furthermore, it shared jurisdiction over American affairs with other agencies. In short, although the Stuart monarchs' reforms consid-

Important events

1642	English Civil War begins
1649	Charles I executed
1658	Oliver Cromwell dies
1660	Stuarts restored to throne; Charles II becomes king First Navigation Act passed
1662	Halfway Covenant drafted Connecticut granted charter
1663	Rhode Island granted charter
1664	English conquer New Netherland; New York founded New Jersey established
1669	Carolina chartered
1670	Charleston founded
1674	Netherlands permanently cede New York to England
1675–76	King Philip's (Metacomet's) War (New England)
1676	Bacon's Rebellion (Virginia)
1677	Culpeper's Rebellion (North Carolina)
1679	New Hampshire becomes royal colony
1670s	Imports of African slaves to southern colonies increase dramatically
1681	Pennsylvania chartered
1684	Massachusetts Bay charter revoked
1685	James II becomes king
1686–89	Dominion of New England
1688–89	James II deposed in Glorious Revolution; William and Mary ascend throne
1689	Protestant Association Rebellion (Maryland) Leisler's Rebellion (New York)
1691	Massachusetts Bay and Plymouth colonies combined under one royal charter
1692	Witchcraft outbreak in Salem Village
1696	Board of Trade and Plantations established
1690s	Rice cultivation begins in South Carolina
1702	New Jersey becomes royal colony
1710	Blacks become a majority in South Carolina
1711–13	Tuscarora War (North Carolina)
1715	Yamasee War (South Carolina)
1720s	Native-born Americans become a majority in Chesapeake
1729	North and South Carolina become separate royal colonies
1732	Georgia chartered
1740s	Indigo cultivation begins in South Carolina Black population of Chesapeake begins to grow chiefly through natural increase

erably improved the quality of colonial administration, supervision of the American provinces remained decentralized and haphazard.

As part of the same campaign to bring more order into the administration of the colonies, colonial charters were changed. Thus New Hampshire (1679), Massachusetts (1691), New Jersey (1702), and the Carolinas (1729) became royal colonies. The most drastic change was reserved for that hotbed of Puritanism and smuggling—

| **Dominion of New England** | New England. There, in 1686, all charters were revoked and the crown created |

the Dominion of New England. Sir Edmund Andros, the governor, was given immense power: all the assemblies were dissolved, and he needed only the consent of an appointed council to make laws and levy taxes. New Englanders endured Andros's autocratic rule for more than two years. Then, after hearing that William and Mary had assumed the throne in England, they overthrew Andros and resumed their customary form of government.

In other American colonies too, the Glorious Revolution proved to be a signal for revolt. In Maryland the Protestant Association overturned the government of the Catholic proprietor, and in New York Jacob Leisler, a militia officer of German origin, assumed control of the province. When these three uprisings are seen in conjunction with those of the previous decade—Bacon's Rebellion in Virginia (1676) and Culpeper's Rebellion in North Carolina (1677)—it is clear that the late seventeenth century was a time of turmoil for the American colonies.

In the wake of that turmoil, the representative assembly became the chief vehicle through which politically talented Americans expressed

| **Rise of the representative assembly** | their opinions on colonial policy. Denied access to top appointive posts, which usually went to Englishmen, |

such men sought to increase their power by expanding the role of the assembly. Colonial assemblies began to claim privileges associated with the House of Commons, such as the right to initiate all tax legislation and to control the

militia. The assemblies also developed effective ways of influencing governors, judges, customs officers, and other appointed officials (including threats to withhold their salaries). Colonial assemblies were often wracked by internal disputes, but Americans agreed on one point: members of the assembly represented the people in a way that appointed English officials did not.

By the middle of the eighteenth century, the colonists had developed a standard way of thinking about their political system. They believed that their governments mimicked the balance between king, lords, and commons found in Great Britain—a combination that was thought to produce a stable polity. Although the analogy was not exact, the colonists equated their governors with the monarch, their councils with the aristocracy, and their assemblies with the House of Commons. All three were thought essential to good government, but the colonists did not regard them with the same degrees of approval. They saw the governors and appointed councils as aliens who posed a potential threat to colonial freedoms and customary ways of life. As representatives of England rather than America, the governors and councils were to be feared and guarded against rather than trusted. The colonists saw the assemblies, on the other hand, as the people's protectors. Elected in most colonies by men who met minimal property-holding requirements, the assemblies regarded themselves as representatives of the people. Their constituents shared the same view.

That vision of politics, which emerged slowly over the first half of the eighteenth century, was to be of immense importance in the revolutionary crisis that developed in the years following 1763. The colonists had become accustomed to a political structure in which the executive was feared and the legislature trusted, in which authority was widely dispersed and decentralized, and in which the supreme power (England, in this case) had little direct effect on most people. What they were familiar with, in other words, was a *limited* government—though limited more by circumstances than by design. When Americans had to create governmental structures for themselves after 1775, they incorporated all those elements of their past experience into a formal political theory.

Suggestions for further reading

GENERAL Charles M. Andrews, *The Colonial Period of American History,* vol. 4 (1938); Stuart Bruchey, *Roots of American Economic Growth, 1607–1861* (1965); Wesley Frank Craven, *The Colonies in Transition, 1660–1713* (1968.)

AFRICA AND THE SLAVE TRADE Philip D. Curtin, *The Atlantic Slave Trade: A Census* (1969); Basil Davidson, *Black Mother* (1969); David B. Davis, *The Problem of Slavery in Western Culture* (1966).

BLACKS IN ANGLO-AMERICA Edgar J. McManus, *Black Bondage in the North* (1973); Edmund S. Morgan, *American Slavery, American Freedom: The Ordeal of Colonial Virginia* (1975); Peter H. Wood, *Black Majority: Negroes in Colonial South Carolina from 1670 through the Stono Rebellion* (1974).

INDIAN-WHITE RELATIONS James Axtell, "The White Indians of Colonial America," *William and Mary Quarterly,* 3rd ser., 32 (1975), 55–88; Verner W. Crane, *The Southern Frontier, 1670–1732* (1929); Douglas Leach, *Flintlock and Tomahawk: New England in King Philip's War* (1958).

NEW ENGLAND Bernard Bailyn, *The New England Merchants in the Seventeenth Century* (1955); Paul Boyer and Stephen Nissenbaum, *Salem Possessed: The Social Origins of Witchcraft* (1974); Richard Bushman, *From Puritan to Yankee: Character and the Social Order in Connecticut, 1690–1765* (1967); John Putnam Demos, *Entertaining Satan: Witchcraft and the Culture of Early New England* (1982); Perry Miller, *The New England Mind: From Colony to Province* (1953); Robert G. Pope, *The Half-Way Covenant: Church Membership in Puritan New England* (1969).

NEW NETHERLAND AND THE RESTORATION COLONIES Edwin B. Bronner, *William Penn's "Holy Experiment": The Founding of Pennsylvania 1681–1701* (1962); Wesley Frank Craven, *New Jersey and the English Colonization of North America* (1964); Michael Kammen, *Colonial New York: A History* (1975); Robert C. Ritchie, *The Duke's Province: A Study of Politics and Society in Colonial New York, 1660–1691* (1977); M. Eugene Sirmans, *Colonial South Carolina: A Political History, 1663–1763* (1966).

COLONIAL POLITICS Bernard Bailyn, *The Origins of American Politics* (1968); Jack P. Greene, *The Quest for Power: The Lower Houses of Assembly in the Southern Royal Colonies, 1689–1776* (1963); David S. Lovejoy, *The Glorious Revolution in America* (1972); Charles S. Sydnor, "Gentlemen Freeholders": Political Practices in Washington's Virginia* (1952).

IMPERIAL ADMINISTRATION Thomas C. Barrow, *Trade and Empire: The British Customs Service in Colonial America 1660–1775* (1967); Michael Kammen, *Empire and Interest: The American Colonies and the Politics of Mercantilism* (1970); I.K. Steele, *Politics of Colonial Policy: The Board of Trade in Colonial Administration* (1968); Stephen Saunders Webb, *The Governors-General: The English Army and the Definition of the Empire, 1569–1681* (1979).

3

COLONIAL SOCIETY

AT MIDCENTURY

Around the middle of the eighteenth century, the immigrant Alexander McAllister received a letter from a cousin in Scotland asking whether he too should consider moving to the American colonies. McAllister, who had settled in North Carolina along with many fellow Scotsmen, responded encouragingly. He told his cousin, "you would do well to advise all poor people whom you wish well to take curradge and com to this Country it will be of Benefite to ther riseing generation." A few years later Martha McClouting, a Scotch-Irish woman living in Charleston, expressed the same attitude to her mother in Derry: "I have got Sex Negros wich keps me Easey From hard Lebar and I wish that meney moor of you had the good fortun to Cum to this Contry with me. . . ."

McAllister and McClouting were two among the hundreds of thousands of European immigrants who flooded into England's mainland colonies during the years from 1715 to 1775. Their attitude was representative. Migrants from overpopulated and distressed areas of Europe, especially Scotland, northern Ireland (Ulster), and Germany, found opportunities in America undreamed of in their homelands. The arrival of these immigrants was one of the most important occurrences in eighteenth-century America.

The life they found in the colonies was less primitive and precarious than it had been during the first century of settlement. A majority of colonists, black and white, were now native-born, and the colonies were beginning to de-

velop a distinctive identity of their own. Colleges had been founded, newspapers established, social clubs and literary societies formed, a regular postal service begun, roads built, laws codified, and histories of the colonies written. The provinces could no longer be seen as extensions of England. Individually and collectively, they had become quite different.

Population growth

One of the most striking characteristics of the mainland colonies in the eighteenth century was their rapid population growth. Only about 250,000 people (excluding Indians) resided in the colonies in 1700; by 1775 it had become 2.5 million. Although immigration accounted for a considerable share of the growth, most of it resulted from natural increase. By 1750 the sex ratio among both whites and blacks was approximately equal throughout the mainland colonies. Most white women married in their early twenties, most black women in the late teens. Women usually bore between five and eight children, becoming pregnant every two or three years throughout their fertile years, and a large proportion of their children survived to maturity. In 1755 about half the American population, white and black, was under sixteen years of age.

This portrait of an eighteenth-century family shows the typical colonial childbearing pattern in the large number of "stairstep" children, born at approx-imately two-year intervals.   Museum of Fine Arts, Boston, Julia Knight Knox Fund.

Such a dramatic phenomenon did not escape the attention of contemporaries. As early as the 1720s, Americans began to point with pride to their fertility, citing population growth as evidence of the advantages of living in the colonies. In 1755 Benjamin Franklin published his *Observations Concerning the Increase of Mankind,* which predicted that America's amazing growth rate would within a century make it more populous than Britain.

Interestingly enough, Franklin's purpose in writing his *Observations* was to argue that Britain should stop allowing Germans to emigrate to Pennsylvania. Since the English population in America was increasing so rapidly, he asked, "Why should Pennsylvania, founded by the English, become a Colony of *Aliens,* who will shortly be so numerous as to Germanize us instead of Anglifying them, and will never adopt our Language or Customs?" Franklin's fears, while exaggerated, were not wholly misplaced. By the late eighteenth century, emigrants from the Rhineland—known as "Pennsylvania Dutch," a corruption of *Deutsch*—comprised one-third of the colony's residents.

Not all the approximately 100,000 Germans

who emigrated to Pennsylvania, mainly between 1730 and 1755, stayed in that colony. Some who landed at Philadelphia moved west and then south along the eastern slope of the Appala-

German immigration chian Mountains, eventually finding homes in western Maryland and Virginia. Others sailed first to Charleston or Savannah and settled in the interior of South Carolina or Georgia. The German immigrants belonged to a wide variety of Protestant sects—primarily Lutheran, German Reformed, and Moravian.

Many Germans arrived in America as redemptioners. Under that variant form of indentured servitude, immigrants paid as much as possible of the cost of their passage before sailing from Europe. After they landed in the colonies, the rest of the fare had to be "redeemed." If poor immigrants had no friends or relatives in America willing to take on the burden of payment, they were indentured for a term of service proportional to the amount they still owed. That term could be as brief as a year or two, but was more likely to be four.

The largest group of white non-English emigrants to America was the Scotch-Irish, chiefly descended from Presbyterian Scots who had set-

Scotch-Irish and Scottish immigration tled in Protestant portions of Ireland during the seventeenth century. Perhaps as many as 250,000 Scotch-Irish people moved to the colonies. Fleeing economic distress and religious discrimination, they were lured as well by hopes of obtaining land in America. Like the Germans, the Scotch-Irish often landed in Philadelphia. They also moved west and south from that city, settling chiefly in the western portions of Pennsylvania, Maryland, Virginia, and the Carolinas. Frequently unable to afford any acreage, they squatted on land belonging to Indian tribes, land speculators, and colonial governments.

In addition to the Scotch-Irish, more than 25,000 settlers came directly to America from Scotland. Many Scottish immigrants were Jacobites—supporters of the Stuart claimants to the throne of England. After the death of Queen Anne in 1714, the British throne had passed to the German house of Hanover, in the person of King George I. In 1715 and again in 1745, Jacobite rebels attempted unsuccessfully to capture the crown for the Stuart pretender, and many were exiled to America as punishment for their treason. Most of the Jacobites settled in North Carolina. Ironically, they tended to become loyalists during the Revolutionary War because of their strong commitment to monarchy. Another wave of Scottish immigration began in the 1760s and flowed mainly into northern New York.

Due to these migration patterns and the concentration of slaveholding in the South, half the colonial population south of New England was of non-English origin by 1775. Yet, with the exception of certain religious sects like the Mennonites, Amish, and Dunkards, most immigrants assimilated fairly readily into Anglo-American culture. In Germantown, Pennsylvania, for example, German continued to be spoken in churches and within families. But English soon became the language of public communication. English was also the language of instruction in the town's first school.

Social stratification

The vast majority of eighteenth-century immigrants entered white society at the bottom of the social scale and on the geographic fringes of settlement. By the time they arrived, American society was dominated by wealthy, native-born

Distribution of wealth elite families. Furthermore, the social and economic structure was more rigid than it had been before 1700. Unlike their seventeenth-century predecessors, the new non-English immigrants had little opportunity to improve their circumstances dramatically. The most they could realistically hope for was to accumulate a modest amount of property over a lifetime of hard work.

Increasing social stratification—a widening gap between rich and poor—was most noticeable in the cities, which contained less than 10 percent of the population but displayed greater extremes of wealth and poverty than did rural areas outside the plantation South. There were few large cities in mid-eighteenth-century America. The biggest—as it had been since 1630—was Boston, with about 17,000 residents. Next came Philadelphia (approximately 13,000), closely followed by New York (about 11,000). Charleston, South Carolina, the only city of appreciable size in the South, had approximately 7,000 inhabitants, about half of whom were black. Smaller but still important were Newport, New Haven, Salem, and Hartford in the North and Norfolk, Annapolis, and Savannah in the South.

In late seventeenth- and early eighteenth-century America, there was little dire poverty and little ostentatious wealth. Surviving city tax records show that at the turn of the century the bottom half of the population possessed about one-tenth of the property, and the richest 10 percent owned perhaps 40 percent. Sixty to seventy years later, conditions had changed significantly. In Philadelphia, for example, by 1774 the upper tenth possessed 55 percent of the wealth and the poorest third owned less than 2 percent.

What had happened? In the cities, obviously, the rich had gotten significantly richer and the poor had gotten poorer. But who were the rich? And who were the poor? The first question is easier to answer than the second. The rich were those American families who had begun the century with sufficient capital to take advantage of changes in the colonial economy—especially changes associated with the Atlantic trade. Controlling much of this expanded commerce, and earning sizable profits from it, were the merchants of urban America. In contrast to the late seventeenth century, when most voyages were joint ventures by a large number of small investors, mid-eighteenth-century voyages

Merchants and professionals

were funded by fewer merchants with larger amounts of capital. That meant greater individual risk (making marine insurance a thriving field) but also potentially greater individual profits.

In addition to the merchants, the cities contained a growing well-to-do professional class composed of doctors, lawyers, and government officials. Judges, members of governors' councils, customs officers, and the like were amply rewarded for their labors on behalf of the crown. Prominent families thus often sought political alliances with colonial governors or English administrators, for it was through such connections that coveted positions could be won. As the economy became more complex, the legal system also grew more elaborate, and the need for lawyers increased. By the 1750s, lawyers who had studied in London were practicing in all the major cities. They handled the legal transactions necessitated by the more sophisticated economy. Successful lawyers could earn sizable incomes, as could the doctors educated in England or Scotland who had begun to practice medicine in Boston, Philadelphia, and smaller colonial cities.

The urban poor are more difficult to identify. Recent immigrants must have been among the poor; whether indentured or not, they often hired themselves out as live-in servants so as at least to have food and lodging. Elderly, disabled, and female colonists (especially widows) were also components of the urban poor. In the eighteenth century, like today, women were paid less than men for comparable work. (Female servants, for example, earned about half the salary of male servants.) And, though opportunities for employment were better in the city than in the countryside, a woman's chances of finding well-paid work were considerably more limited than a man's. Sewing and nursing commanded far lower fees than did blacksmithing, shipbuilding, and other male occupations.

The effects of increasing poverty can be seen in city records. Philadelphia is a case in point. From the 1730s on, city taxpayers were assessed a three-penny annual fee to supply the needy

| Poor relief |

with food and firewood (distributed to applicants by city officials). A private Hospital for the Sick Poor was founded in 1751 under the leadership of Benjamin Franklin. But in the 1760s, such arrangements proved inadequate. The poor tax was raised to five pennies, then to six; a Bettering House—a combined almshouse and workhouse—was founded to shelter the growing number of poor people and to give employment to the able-bodied among them. The problem, however, was insoluble.

Stratification was increasing in the countryside as well. In the Chesapeake, the natural increase of the slave population had spurred the development of a planter aristocracy. Such planters increased their wealth still further by serving as middlemen in the tobacco trade. They loaned less well-to-do planters money, marketed their crops, sold them imported goods, and enriched themselves in the process. In New England, meanwhile, the continuing population growth and the relatively static amount of land under cultivation forced more and more men either to migrate or accept landless status. The same trend appeared even in such fertile areas as Chester County, Pennsylvania.

It is impossible to tell from the available evidence whether a class of permanently impoverished people was forming in eighteenth-century America, or whether poverty was a phase many people passed through (usually during youth or old age). But this much can be said: the gap between rich and poor was widening, and it had become more difficult for a person starting out at the bottom of the economic ladder to reach its upper rungs.

The transition to a more rigid social and economic structure did not occur without conflict. People who had trouble earning a living wage occasionally exploded into violence when

| Social conflict |

goaded by particularly blatant examples of profiteering. Urban crowds tended to direct their hostility toward merchants suspected of monopolizing or hoarding necessary commodities in

hopes of driving up prices. In Boston in both 1710 and 1713, for example, rioters prevented a wealthy merchant from exporting large quantities of grain at a time of severe bread shortages. (On the second occasion they cleaned out his warehouse.) Attempts by the British navy to press colonists into the service also brought collective protests from the poor.

Rural riots frequently erupted over land titles—a matter of much concern to farmers. In the 1740s, for example, New Jersey farmers holding land under grants from the governor of New York (dating from the brief period when both provinces were owned by the Duke of York) clashed repeatedly with agents of the Jersey proprietors. The proprietors claimed the land as theirs and demanded annual payments, called quitrents, for the use of the property. Similar violence occurred in the 1760s in the region that later became Vermont. In both cases the rioters saw themselves as virtuous yeomen defending their way of life against monied interlopers.

The same theme can be detected in the most serious land riots of the period, which took place along the Hudson River in 1765 and 1766. Late in the seventeenth century, Governor Benjamin Fletcher of New York had granted several huge tracts in the lower Hudson valley to prominent colonial families. The proprietors in turn divided these estates into small farms, which they rented chiefly to poor Dutch and German immigrants.

After 1740, though, New Englanders in search of land squatted on vacant portions of the manors and resisted all attempts to evict them. In the 1760s, New York courts ordered some of the squatters to make way for tenants with valid leases. They rebelled, terrorizing proprietors and loyal tenants. Finally, troops from New York City put down the rebellion.

The land riots in New York, New Jersey, and Vermont revealed the tenacity with which eighteenth-century Americans would defend their cherished positions as independent yeomen farmers. That status played a major part in colonial Americans' perceptions of themselves and their culture.

Colonial culture

During the 1750s, the future reluctant revolutionary John Dickinson of Pennsylvania studied law in London. In letters written to his parents, Dickinson expressed the prevailing colonial belief that life in America was simpler, purer, and less corrupt than life in England. If America could not boast of a literary culture equal to London's, it could at least point to publications displaying good common sense. If the colonists lacked polish, they nevertheless had unaffected manners. If residence in the colonies meant remoteness from centers of power and influence, it also conveyed immunity to the vice that automatically accompanied the exercise of power. Dickinson and his fellow Americans were, in other words, making a virtue out of a necessity.

But while they were still part of the British Empire, Americans could not reject categorically the standards by which English people were commonly judged. In mid-eighteenth-century America, two opposing tendencies prevailed in the thinking of the colonial cultural, political, and economic elite. One—reflected in John Dickinson's letters—celebrated the simple virtues of life in the colonies and openly criticized England's failings. The other stressed the links between European and American culture. Colonial intellectuals prided themselves on reading the latest English books and corresponding with leading thinkers in the mother country and on the Continent. Wealthy colonists imitated as best they could the manners, dress, and behavior of English aristocrats.

The most important aspect of the transatlantic cultural connection was Americans' participation in the European intellectual movement known as the Enlightenment. Since the six-

| American Enlightenment |

teenth century, some continental thinkers had been analyzing nature in an effort to determine the laws that govern the universe. Enlightenment philosophers emphasized acquiring knowledge through reason, rather than intuition and revelation. Many European Enlightenment thinkers, like John Locke—whose *Essay on Human Understanding* disputed the Calvinist notion that human beings were innately depraved—wrote abstract analytical philosophy. Colonial participants in the Enlightenment, meanwhile, oriented their studies toward the concrete and particular.

For example, Americans were intensely interested in their natural surroundings. The Western Hemisphere housed many plants and animals unknown in the Old World. Naturalists like John Bartram of Pennsylvania and Cadwallader Colden of New York eagerly assisted a transatlantic attempt to identify and classify plant species. American naturalists also sought evidence to disprove the claim that the American environment was unhealthy.

The American Philosophical Society epitomized the colonists' participation in the Enlightenment. The society was founded in Philadelphia in 1769. Among its first members were political leaders, educators, physicians, and skilled artisans (notably the clockmaker David Rittenhouse, who was constructing an orrery, a mechanical model of the solar system). Benjamin Franklin, the best-known American scientist, was selected as the organization's president even though he was living in London.

It was in the realm of medicine that Enlightenment activity had the greatest impact on the lives of ordinary colonists. The key figure in the drama was the Reverend Cotton Mather, the Puritan divine, who was a member of England's Royal Society. In a Royal Society publication Mather read about the benefits of inoculation as

| Smallpox inoculations |

a protection against the dreaded smallpox. In 1720 and 1721, when Boston suffered a major smallpox epidemic, Mather and a doctor urged people to be inoculated; there was fervent opposition, including that of Boston's leading physician. When the epidemic had ended, the statistics bore out Mather's opinion: of those inoculated, fewer than 3 percent died; of those who became ill without inoculation, nearly 15 percent perished.

On the whole, though, few Americans were

affected by the transatlantic intellectual currents of the day. Indeed, of all the arts, music alone had a significant effect on the general public. And the roots of American music were less European than local. America was filled with people who could neither read nor write. Colonial hymns (the music of the common people was chiefly religious) were written in short, rhyming, metrical lines that were easy to learn and remember. Many churches also aided singing by "lining-out"—that is, having a leader read each line aloud before the congregation sang it.

The shortcomings of colonial education ensured that there would be many illiterate Americans who needed such assistance. In New England, which probably had the highest literacy rates in the colonies, 80 to 90 percent of adult men but only about 50 percent of adult women could sign their names at the time of the Revolution. Indeed, of all the colonies, only Massachusetts Bay had a law (enacted in 1647) requiring the towns to maintain public schools, and this law was widely ignored.

Whether colonial children learned to read and write thus depended largely on their parents. Most youngsters learned their ABCs at home, often using the Bible or an almanac—the

| *Primary education* |

most commonly owned books—as a text. Their first teachers were their parents or older siblings. Later, if their parents were willing and able to pay for further education, they might attend a private "dame school" run by a local widow, where they would learn more of the basics. A few fortunate boys might then go on to a grammar school, to study with a minister and prepare to enter college at age fourteen or fifteen.

Girls were usually not educated beyond the rudiments. Only a very few daughters of elite families received any advanced intellectual training. One such girl was Eliza Lucas, whose father, a West Indian planter, sent her to school in England because he did not want her mind to be "vacant and uninformed." Just before she married Charles Pinckney in 1745, Eliza thanked her father "[for] the pains and mony you laid

out in my Education which I esteem a more valuable fortune than any you could now have given me."

Ironically, the colonial system of higher education, for those males fortunate enough to attend college, was more fully

| *Higher education* |

developed than was basic instruction for either sex. Virtually all colonial colleges, however, were established primarily to train ministers. Harvard, which was authorized in 1636 and began instruction in 1638, was the first of the colleges. Like Yale (1701), it trained clerics for the Congregational Church. In the eighteenth century, the Anglican, Presbyterian, Baptist, and Dutch Reformed churches also chartered colleges for the purpose of educating future ministers. Dartmouth (1769) had a different religious mission: Christianizing the Indians. Only the College of Philadelphia (later the University of Pennsylvania, 1755) had nonsectarian origins.

The College of Philadelphia was largely the creation of two men: Benjamin Franklin, who first outlined its purposes and curriculum, and William Smith, a Scots emigrant who became its first provost. Franklin, born in Boston in 1706, was the perfect example of a self-made, self-educated man. His *Experiments and Observations on Electricity* (1751) was the most important scientific work by a colonial American.

In 1749 and 1751 Franklin published pamphlets proposing the establishment of a new educational institution in Pennsylvania. The purpose of Franklin's "English School" was not to produce clerics or scholars but to prepare young

| *Benjamin Franklin on education* |

men "for learning any business, calling or profession, except such wherein languages are required." The students he envisioned were to be perfect representatives of colonial culture. Free of the Old World's traditions and corruptions, the ideal American would achieve distinction through hard work and the application of common-sense principles. He would be unlettered but not unlearned, simple but not ignorant, virtuous but not priggish. The American would be a true child of the Enlightenment, knowledgeable about European culture yet not bound by its fetters, advancing through reason and talent alone.

The contrast with the original communal ideals of the early New England settlements could not have been sharper. Franklin's American was an individual, free to make choices about his future, able to contemplate a variety of possible careers. John Winthrop's American had been a component of a greater whole that required his unhesitating, unquestioning submission. But the two visions had one point in common: both described only white males. Neither blacks—nearly one-fifth of the total population—nor females—about half of the population—played any part in them.

Life on farms and in towns

The basic unit of colonial society was the household. Headed by a white male (or perhaps his widow), the household was the chief mechanism of production and consumption in the colonial economy. Its members—bound by ties of blood or servitude—worked together to produce goods for consumption or sale. The white male head of the household represented it to the outside world, serving in the militia or political posts, casting the household's sole vote in elections. He managed the finances and held legal authority over the rest of the family—his wife, his children, and his servants or slaves. (Eighteenth-century Americans used the word *family* for people who lived together in one house, whether or not they were blood kin.) Such households were considerably larger than American families today; in 1790, the average home contained seven people, one of whom was black.

The vast majority of eighteenth-century American families—more than 90 percent of them—lived in rural areas. Northern and southern households, other than plantations, had many common characteristics. Nearly all adult

men were farmers and all adult women farm wives. The tasks each member of the household performed were clearly differentiated by sex. Servants, slaves, and children aided either the master or the mistress of the household, laboring under his or her supervision.

Men and women had their own separate but complementary spheres. Women had the do-

| *Sex roles* |

mestic or "indoor" sphere and men had the "outdoor" one. Men performed the heavy outdoor tasks—clearing and planting fields, butchering livestock, chopping wood, and building fences. The phrase "indoor sphere" is somewhat deceptive. The preparation of food, an "indoor" function, involved planting and cultivating a garden, harvesting and preserving vegetables, salting and smoking meat, drying apples and pressing cider, milking cows and making butter and cheese, not to mention cooking and baking. Women's single most time-consuming task was making clothing, which required spinning and weaving as well as sewing.

Farm households were governed by the seasons and by the hours of daylight. Men and boys had the most leisure in the winter, when

| *Rhythms of rural life* |

there were no crops that needed care. Women and girls were freest in the summer, before embarking on autumn food preservation and winter spinning and weaving. Other activities, including education, had to be subordinated to seasonal work. The seasons also affected travel plans. Because the roads were muddy in spring and fall, most visiting took place in summer and especially winter, when sleighs could be used.

Because most farm families were relatively isolated from their neighbors, and because of heavy seasonal work obligations, rural folk took advantage of every possible opportunity for socializing. Men taking grain to be milled would stop at a crossroads tavern for a drink and conversation with friends. Women gathering to assist at childbirth would drink tea and exchange news. And work itself provided opportunities for visiting. Harvest frolics, corn-husking bees,

At the Loom. One of the earliest known pictures of an American woman at work, this painting shows the mistress of a household making an elaborate coverlet. Note the spinning wheel beside the fireplace. Downtown Gallery Papers, American Folk Art Gallery. Microfilm roll ND/47, Archives of American Art, Smithsonian Institution.

barn raisings, quilting parties, spinning bees, and other communal endeavors brought together neighbors from miles around, often for several days of work followed by feasting, dancing, and singing in the evenings.

Although seasonality also touched the lives of city dwellers, they were not tied so inextricably to nature's rhythms. Women could purchase meat, vegetables, butter, and cheese at well-stocked city markets. They could buy cloth at dry goods stores and—if they had the money—even hire seamstresses and milliners to make their family's clothing. Men could purchase wood already chopped, and they had no fields to tend. Nor were visits to friends seasonally determined. The well-to-do in particular had more hours of leisure to read, attend dances, plays, and concerts, take walks around town or rides in the countryside, play cards, or simply relax.

Rhythms of urban life

City people had much more contact with the world beyond their own homes than did their rural compatriots. By the middle of the century, every major city had at least one weekly newspaper, and most had two or three. Newspapers printed the latest "advices from London" and news of events in other English colonies, as well as reports on matters of local interest. However, contact with the outside world also had drawbacks. Contagious diseases were sometimes brought into port cities by sailors, causing epidemics that the countryside largely escaped.

The merchants and professionals at the top of

Chapter 3: Colonial society at midcentury

the social and economic scale typically earned

Urban social structure

more than £200 annually. Of similar social but lesser economic standing were teachers and clergymen, whose salaries rarely exceeded £100. The yearly incomes of the urban "middling sort," mostly artisans and shopkeepers, ranged from under £50 to over £100. Below them were the unskilled laborers, who earned perhaps £20 a year (bare subsistence for an average family), and then the free servants and apprentices, who were compensated mainly with room and board and no more than £10 a year. At the very bottom of the social ladder were indentured servants and, finally, slaves, who could earn money only with the permission of their masters.

Most of the very few colonial women (less than 10 percent of the female population) who ran businesses lived in the cities where they could find customers for their services as teachers, nurses, seamstresses, or innkeepers. Only single women could run independent businesses, because of the provisions of English and colonial law regarding women's

Status of women

status. Under the common law doctrine of coverture, a married woman became one person with her husband. She could not sue or be sued; make contracts; buy, sell, or own property; or draft a will. A married woman, in other words, was completely subordinate to her husband by law, and she had little chance to escape a bad marriage. Divorces were practically impossible to obtain.

A wife's subordination to her husband was more than just legal. Colonial men expected their wives to defer to their judgment, and most wives seem to have accepted secondary status without murmuring. A Virginia woman remarked, for example, that it was the wives' responsibility "to give up to their husbands" whenever differences of opinion arose between them. Not until very late in the eighteenth century would some women question these traditional notions.

The man's authority extended to his children

as well. Eighteenth-century Americans regarded child rearing as primarily the father's responsibility. That responsibility did not, however, encompass the day-to-day care of children, which was the mother's task. Instead, the father disciplined the children and determined the general

Child rearing

standards by which they were raised. The sexual division of tasks within the home brought mothers and daughters especially close together. Colonial mothers and daughters accordingly often referred to each other as "friend" and "companion." Fathers and sons rarely developed the same sort of egalitarian relationship.

In seventeenth-century New England, parents had exercised considerable control over their children's marriages. By the middle of the eighteenth century, children were marrying out of birth order and choosing spouses from other towns and of lesser economic standing. Most important of all, the premarital pregnancy rate soared. In one Massachusetts town in the latter decades of the century, nearly 40 percent of brides were pregnant at the time of their marriage. Parents had apparently lost either the ability or the desire to control their children's lives.

Life on plantations

A plantation was a rural household writ large. The planter and his wife perceived everyone in the household, white and black alike, as belonging to their family, and, indeed, the plantation was organized along familial lines. The master and mistress of the household were responsible for the same tasks as their counterparts on small farms, but on plantations they supervised black workers instead of doing the jobs themselves. Children of planter families, like northern youngsters, learned from the parent of the same sex.

The lives of wealthy white planter families differed markedly from those of their poorer compatriots in both North and South. Since mothers did not have to perform the household

White family and social life chores themselves, they could devote much more time to their offspring. Accordingly, wealthy southern youngsters received more attention than did most of their contemporaries. They were also probably the first American children whose parents were not centrally concerned with matters of discipline and control. Their more relaxed upbringing foreshadowed nineteenth-century Americans' greater indulgence of children.

Though life on the larger plantations was comfortable, whites still led an isolated existence. Thus like other colonists they took advantage of all opportunities for socializing. In tidewater Virginia and Maryland, attending church was just as much a social occasion as it was in backcountry South Carolina. The Sunday entries in the diary of one Virginia teen-ager, for instance, barely mentioned the sermon topic but devoted many lines to listing the people she had seen and talked to. Barbecues and week-long house parties were popular, as were horse racing, cock fighting, and gambling. In South Carolina, planters from the swampy lowcountry traditionally lived in Charleston from May until December to escape the worst heat—and seasonal illnesses like malaria. Consequently Charleston developed as wide a variety of diversions as northern cities.

Yet southern whites made up only slightly more than half the region's population. In South Carolina, a majority of the population was black; in Georgia, about half; and in the Chesapeake, 40 percent. The trend toward consolidation of landholding and slave ownership after 1740 had a profound effect on the lives of Afro-Americans. In the tidewater Chesapeake in the 1780s, nearly three-quarters of all blacks lived on plantations with more than ten slaves, and 43 percent were owned by planters with at least twenty slaves. In the lowcountry, where most of South Carolina's slaves lived in the 1760s, 88 percent were on plantations with ten or more slaves, and 40 percent lived in units of fifty or more. It must always be remembered,

however, that a sizable minority of southern blacks lived on farms with only one or two other slaves.

The large size of many plantation households allowed for the specialization of labor. Encouraged by planters whose goal was to create as self-sufficient a household as possible, Afro-American men and women became highly skilled at various tasks. Each plantation had its own blacksmiths, carpenters, dairy maids, seamstresses, cooks, valets, shoemakers, gardeners, and at least one midwife, who attended pregnant white and black women alike. Their presence meant that the colonial South required the services of fewer white artisans than did the North.

The typical Chesapeake tobacco plantation or Georgia or Carolina rice-indigo plantation was divided into small "quarters" located at some distance from one another. In the Chesapeake, white overseers supervised work on the distant **Operation of the plantation** quarters, while the planter personally took charge of the "home" quarter. In the Carolina lowcountry, black drivers often supervised their fellow slaves. The work force on the outlying quarters was typically composed of both Africans and Afro-Americans, whereas Afro-Americans alone lived at the home quarter. Planters usually sent "outlandish" (African-born) slaves to do field labor on outlying quarters in order to accustom them to plantation work routines and to enable them to learn some English. Those chosen to be artisans were usually Afro-Americans.

Eighteenth-century planters were considerably less worried that their slaves might run away than were their counterparts fifty years later. Slavery legally existed in all the colonies. Thus slaves had no place to seek refuge. With whites in control of the guns and ammunition, violent resistance was even less of an option than running away. Under these conditions owners allowed their slaves to move freely from one quarter to another. This is not to say that slaves never ran away. They did, in large numbers. But they did so to visit friends or relatives,

An Overseer Doing His Duty, by Benjamin H. Latrobe. Most slave women were field hands like these, sketched in 1798 near Fredericksburg, Virginia.

White women were believed to be unsuited for heavy outdoor labor.   Maryland Historical Society.

or simply to escape their normal work routines for a few days or months.

Afro-Americans did try to improve the conditions of their bondage and gain some measure of control over their lives. Their chief vehicle for doing so was the family. Members of extended kin groups provided support, assistance, and comfort to each other. On the quarters of the Virginia plantation, Nomini Hall, for example, Nanny's complaint about the excessive punishment an overseer had inflicted on her sons caused her master, Robert Carter, to admonish the overseer; and George won his daughter's transfer from one quarter to another so that she could live with her stepmother. Moreover, if the nuclear family was broken up by sale, the extended family was there to help with child rearing and other tasks.

| Black family life |

Despite white intrusions into their lives, most black families managed to carve out a small measure of autonomy. On many plantations, slaves were allowed to plant their own gardens, hunt, or fish in order to supplement the standard diet of corn and salt pork. Some Chesapeake mistresses permitted their female slaves to raise chickens, which they could then sell or exchange for such items as extra clothing or blankets.

In South Carolina, slaves were often able to accumulate property, because most rice and indigo plantations operated on a task system. Once slaves had completed their assigned tasks for the day, they were free to work for themselves. In Maryland and Virginia, where by the end of the century some whites had begun to hire out their slaves to others, blacks were sometimes allowed to keep a small part of the wages they earned. Such advances were slight, but against the bleak backdrop of slavery they deserve to be highlighted.

Relations between blacks and whites varied considerably from household to household. In some, masters and mistresses enforced their will chiefly through physical coercion. On other plantations, like Robert Carter's, masters were

Life on plantations

more lenient and respectful of slaves' property and their desire to live with other members of their families. Yet even in households where whites and blacks displayed genuine affection for one another, there were inescapable tensions. Such tensions were caused not only by the whites' uneasiness about the slave system in general but also by the dynamics of day-to-day relationships when a small number of whites wielded absolute legal power over the lives of many blacks.

A few thoughtful white Americans were deeply concerned about the implications of the system in which they were enmeshed. But what troubled them was not so much the plight of enslaved blacks as the impact of slavery on whites. Thomas Jefferson summed up the common viewpoint when he observed: "The whole commerce between master and slave is a perpetual exercise of the most boisterous passions, the most unremitting despotism on the one part, and degrading submission on the other. Our children see this, and learn to imitate it. . . ." Before the Revolution, only a tiny number of Quakers (most notably John Woolman in his *Some Considerations on the Keeping of Negroes,* published in 1754) took a different approach, criticizing slavery out of sympathy for blacks. The few other white colonists who questioned slavery took Jefferson's approach, stressing the institution's adverse effect on whites.

Underlying anxieties

During the entire colonial period, there were only two (or perhaps three) occasions when blacks sought to win their freedom through rebellion. The first was in New York City in 1712, when about twenty-five slaves set fire to a building, killed nine whites, and wounded others who came to put out the fire. The conspirators were caught and executed, some barbarously (by burning or starvation). In 1741 white residents of New York, fearing another similar plot, executed thirty-one blacks and four whites. In that

case, though, the so-called conspirators appear to have been a biracial gang of thieves who were also arsonists. The other colonial rebellion, however, posed a real danger to whites.

Early one morning in September 1739, about twenty South Carolina slaves, most of them An-

| Stono Rebellion |

golans, gathered near the Stono River south of Charleston. After seizing guns and ammunition from a store, they killed the storekeeper and some nearby planter families. Then, joined by other slaves from the area, they headed south toward Spanish Florida. Later that day the militia caught up with the fugitives (about one hundred) and killed a number of them. Within a week most of the remaining conspirators were captured. Those not killed on the spot were later executed.

And there were other signs of conflict within the colonies at midcentury. In the late 1760s, the so-called Regulator movement erupted in the South Carolina backcountry. Angry frontier dwellers, most of them Scotch-Irish, protested that they had little voice in the government of the colony, which was dominated by low-country planters. For some months they policed the countryside in vigilante bands, contending that regular law enforcement was too lax. The early 1770s saw the rise of another Regulator movement in North Carolina; there, the western farmers and eastern grandees were unable to resolve their difficulties without bloodshed in a battle at Alamance in 1771. But the most significant evidence of unrest in the colonies was the Great Awakening.

The first decades of the eighteenth century had witnessed two unmistakable trends in American religion: a decline in the influence of the clergy and a movement toward rationalism in theology. Protestant clerics never entirely abandoned the Calvinist emphasis on people's powerlessness to affect their own fates. But they were affected by the Enlightenment view that God was a rational rather than an irrational and unforgiving creator.

By the late 1720s a reaction to this "enlightened" notion had emerged. Clerics such as Theodore Frelinghuysen (Dutch Reformed), Gilbert Tennent (Presbyterian), and Jonathan Edwards (Congregationalist) returned to basic Calvinistic principles. People were evil and had to surrender to God's will. Such surrender, when it came, brought release from worry and sin. Above all else the process was emotional and ran counter to the rationalist trend. In Edwards's congregation, for example, a single identifiable moment of conversion signified the surrender to God.

The effects of such conversions remained isolated until 1739, when George Whitefield, an English adherent of the Methodist branch of Anglicanism, arrived in America. For fifteen months Whitefield toured the colonies, preaching to large audiences, and he became the chief generating force behind the Great Awakening. Regular clerics at first welcomed Whitefield, as well as other evangelist preachers. But many churchmen soon realized that the revived religion ran counter to their own more rationalistic faith.

| First Great Awakening |

Opposition to the Awakening heightened rapidly, and large numbers of churches splintered in its wake. "Old Lights"—traditional clerics and their followers—engaged in bitter disputes with the "New Light" evangelicals. American religion, already characterized by numerous sects, became further divided as the major denominations split into Old Light and New Light factions, and as new evangelical sects—Methodists and Baptists—quickly gained adherents. This rapid rise in the number of distinct denominations contributed to Americans' growing willingness to tolerate religious diversity.

The most important effect of the Awakening, though, was its impact on American modes of thought. Colonial society was deferential; that is, common folk were expected to accept unhesitatingly the authority of their "betters," whether wealthy gentry, government officials, or educated clergyman. The message of the Great Awakening directly challenged that tradition of deference. The revivalists, many of whom were not ordained clergymen (some were even illiter-

Important events

ate), claimed they understood the word of God far better than orthodox clerics. The Awakening's emphasis on emotion rather than learning as the road to salvation further undermined the validity of received wisdom.

By midcentury the Great Awakening had injected an egalitarian strain into American life. Although primarily a religious movement, the Awakening also had important social and political consequences, calling into question habitual modes of behavior in the secular as well as the religious realm. By the 1750s, some Americans were challenging previously unassailed colonial authorities; during the next decade, Americans began to challenge English rule as well.

Suggestions for further reading

GENERAL Alice Hanson Jones, *Wealth of a Nation To Be: The American Colonies on the Eve of the Revolution* (1980); James A. Henretta, *The Evolution of American Society, 1700-1815* (1973); Richard Hofstadter, *America at 1750: A Social Portrait* (1971).

RURAL SOCIETY Carl Bridenbaugh, *Myths and Realities: Societies of the Colonial South* (1963); Sung Bok Kim, *Landlord and Tenant in Colonial New York: Manorial Society, 1664-1775* (1978); James T. Lemon, *The Best Poor Man's Country: A Geographical Study of Early Southeastern Pennsylvania* (1972); Gloria Main, *Tobacco Colony: Life in Early Maryland, 1650-1720* (1982); Michael Zuckerman, *Peaceable Kingdoms: New England Towns in the Eighteenth Century* (1970).

URBAN SOCIETY Carl Bridenbaugh, *Cities In Revolt: Urban Life In America, 1743-1776* (1955); Gary B. Nash, *The Urban Crucible: Social Change, Political Consciousness, and the Origins of the American Revolution* (1979); Frederick B. Tolles, *Meeting House and Counting House: The Quaker Merchants of Colonial Philadelphia 1682-1763* (1948).

IMMIGRATION Marcus L. Hanson, *The Atlantic Migration, 1607-1860: A History of the Continuing Settlement of America* (1940).

BLACKS Ira Berlin, "Time, Space, and the Evolution of Afro-American Society in British Mainland America," *American Historical Review,* 85 (1980), 44-78; Allan Kulikoff, "The Origins of Afro-American Society in Tidewater Maryland and Virginia, 1700 to 1790," *William and Mary Quarterly,* 3rd ser., 35 (1978), 228-259; Gerald W. Mullin, *Flight and Rebellion: Slave Resistance in Eighteenth-Century Virginia* (1972).

WOMEN AND FAMILY J. William Frost, *The Quaker Family in Colonial America* (1972); Philip J. Greven, *The Protestant Temperament: Patterns of Child-Rearing, Religious Experience, and the Self in Early*

America (1977); Mary Beth Norton, *Liberty's Daughters: The Revolutionary Experience of American Women 1750-1800* (1980); Daniel Blake Smith, *Inside the Great House: Planter Family Life in Eighteenth-Century Chesapeake Society* (1980); Laurel Ulrich, *Good Wives: Image and Reality in the Lives of Women in Northern New England, 1650-1750* (1982).

COLONIAL CULTURE AND THE ENLIGHTENMENT Daniel J. Boorstin, *The Americans: The Colonial Experience* (1958); Richard Beale Davis, *Intellectual Life in the Colonial South, 1585-1763,* 2 vols. (1978); Howard Mumford Jones, *O Strange New World, American Culture: The Formative Years* (1964); Henry F. May, *The Enlightenment in America* (1976); Louis B. Wright, *The Cultural Life of the American Colonies, 1607-1763* (1957).

EDUCATION James Axtell, *The School upon a Hill: Education and Society in Colonial New England* (1974); Bernard Bailyn, *Education in the Forming of American Society* (1960); Patricia Cohen, *A Calculating People: The Spread of Numeracy in Early America* (1982); Lawrence A. Cremin, *American Education: The Colonial Experience 1607-1783* (1970); Kenneth A. Lockridge, *Literacy in Colonial New England: An Inquiry into the Social Context of Literacy in the Early Modern West* (1974).

SCIENCE AND MEDICINE Jane Donegan, *Women and Men Midwives: Medicine, Morality, and Misogyny in Early America* (1978); Brooke Hindle, *The Pursuit of Science in Revolutionary America* (1956); Raymond P. Stearns, *Science in the British Colonies of America* (1970).

RELIGION AND THE GREAT AWAKENING Carl Bridenbaugh, *Mitre and Sceptre: Transatlantic Faiths, Ideas, Personalities, and Politics, 1689-1775* (1962); J.M. Bumsted and John E. Van de Wetering, *What Must I Do To Be Saved? The Great Awakening in Colonial America* (1976); Edwin S. Gaustad, *The Great Awakening in New England* (1957); Alan E. Heimert, *Religion and the American Mind: From the Great Awakening to the Revolution* (1966); Sidney E. Mead, *The Lively Experiment: The Shaping of Christianity in America* (1963).

4

SEVERING THE BONDS

OF EMPIRE,

1754-1774

Forty years after the battles at Lexington and Concord, John Adams in a letter to Thomas Jefferson asked, "What do We Mean by the Revolution?" Answering his own question, Adams said that to him "the Revolution was in the Minds of the people, and this was effected, from 1760 to 1775 . . . before a drop of blood was drawn at Lexington." At first glance Adams's statement seems peculiar. His view of what constituted the Revolution certainly differs from that held by most Americans today. To us, the Revolution was the war for independence fought from 1775 to 1783—a military, political, and constitutional struggle. To Adams, the Revolution was quite a different thing: it was the American colonists' change of heart about their traditional loyalty to the mother country. Adams's opinion has much to recommend it. In 1750 white colonists gloried in their identity as Britons. Just twenty-five years later, they were engaged in open revolt. What had caused the dramatic shift, a change so startling that it can be termed revolutionary?

The answer lies largely in the events of the two decades preceding the outbreak of war. To be sure, some friction had always marred the relationship between colonies and mother country. But no one on either side of the Atlantic was prepared for the explosive protests against

parliamentary acts that began in the mid-1760s. Ironically, the event that may be said to have started the movement toward revolution was England's overwhelming victory in the worldwide war that ended in 1763. That victory altered the balance of power in America and fundamentally changed the nature of the British Empire. As a result, Parliament and successive ministries adopted a new approach to Britain's colonial possessions. It was in response to those measures that the North American colonists eventually turned to revolution.

1763: a turning point

Pontiac, the war chief of an Ottawa village near Detroit, was one of the first Americans to understand the changes wrought by the British triumph. A man of vision and commanding bearing, Pontiac quickly reacted to the British victory. Using all his powers of persuasion, he forged an unprecedented alliance among the Ottawas and their neighbors. Then, in May and June 1763, the Indians launched devastating attacks on settlements and forts on the frontier.

Franklin's Join, or Die cartoon, produced at the beginning of the French and Indian War, was used during the Revolution as a symbol of America's need to unite.   The Library Company of Philadelphia.

But why did the British triumph motivate Pontiac and his allies to take such a drastic step?

For hundreds of years Britain and France had fought each other in Europe. After they established outposts in North America, the continuing warfare enveloped their colonial posses-

Anglo-French warfare in the colonies

sions as well. Inhabitants of the colonies—white, black, and red—found themselves involved in struggles that had begun in Europe over issues of little importance to Americans. Because the colonists cared which nation controlled the chief portion of their continent, though, they fought willingly on England's side. In the colonies, the War of the League of Augsburg (1689–1697) was called King William's War, the War of the Spanish Succession (1702–1713) was Queen Anne's War, and the War of the Austrian Succession (1740–1748) was King George's War. All three conflicts were inconclusive; neither side was ever able to achieve an unqualified success in America or Europe.

If the European disputes that started the three wars seemed irrelevant to white colonists, they were even less meaningful to American Indians. But the tribes reaped many advantages from the whites' quarrels. Above all, the Indians

of the interior wanted to protect their territory from white settlement and to avoid the fate already suffered by their seacoast counterparts. Most of the tribes concluded that their goals could best be achieved by maintaining outward neutrality and playing off the European powers against one another. Their strategy proved resoundingly successful—as long as the Europeans were evenly matched.

The conditions that allowed the tribes to preserve the balance of power in the American interior ended forever with the close of the conflict known in Europe as the Seven Years' War (1756–1763) and in America as the French and Indian War. What distinguished this war from its three predecessors was not only its decisive outcome, but also the fact that it began on the North American continent. For the first time a war spread to Europe from America rather than vice versa. Specifically, the war arose from the clash between England and France over which nation would dominate the land west of the Appalachian Mountains. Because that land was the home of the interior tribes, they necessarily became involved in the struggle.

In 1753 the French began to push southward from Lake Erie into the Ohio country. That threat stimulated an intercolonial conference in June 1754. Encouraged by authorities in Lon-

Albany Congress

don, delegates from seven northern and middle colonies met with representatives of the Iroquois at Albany, New York, in an attempt to persuade the confederated Indian nations to ally themselves with the British. But the Albany Congress failed to convince the Iroquois tribes to abandon their neutrality.

The delegates at Albany also adopted a Plan of Union designed to coordinate the defenses of the colonies. They proposed the establishment of an elected intercolonial legislature with the power to tax, headed by a president-general appointed by the king. But their home governments, fearing the resulting loss of autonomy, uniformly rejected the idea. The Congress thus failed to achieve its major objectives, but it did produce an enduring symbol of union—Ben-

Chapter 4: Severing the bonds of empire, 1754–1774

jamin Franklin's famous cartoon of a segmented snake captioned "Join, or Die."

The delegates to the Congress did not know that, while they deliberated, the war they sought to prepare for was already beginning. The governor of Virginia, which claimed the region that is now western Pennsylvania, had sent a small militia force westward to counter the French moves. But the Virginia militiamen arrived too late. The French had already taken possession of the strategic point—now Pittsburgh—where the Allegheny and Monongahela rivers meet to form the Ohio, and they were constructing Fort Duquesne there. The foolhardy and inexperienced young colonel who commanded the Virginians allowed himself to be trapped by the French in his crudely built Fort Necessity at Great Meadows, Pennsylvania. After the twenty-two-year-old George Washington surrendered, he and his men were allowed to return to Virginia.

Beginning of the Seven Years' War

Washington had blundered grievously. He had sparked a war that would eventually encompass nearly the entire world. In 1755, General Edward Braddock, two regiments of regulars, and some colonial troops suffered a disastrous defeat a few miles south of Fort Duquesne. For the next three years, the French were consistently victorious.

Finally, under the leadership of William Pitt, who was named secretary of state in 1757, the British mounted the effort that won them the war in North America. They captured the fortress at Louisbourg in 1758, Quebec in 1759, and Montreal—the last French stronghold—in 1760. The war in America was over, but it continued elsewhere for three more years. When the Treaty of Paris was finally signed in 1763, France ceded its major North American holdings to Britain. Spain, an ally of France toward the end of the war, gave Florida to the victorious English. And since Britain feared the presence of France in Louisiana, it forced the cession of that region to Spain, a weaker power. No longer would the English seacoast colonies have to worry about the threat to their existence posed by France's extensive North American territories.

In order to achieve this stunning victory, Pitt had had to alter many of the policies his predecessors had pursued in their dealings with the colonies. When the war began, the British intended to rely heavily on American enlistments. But after the British defeats, enlistments lagged, and British officers adopted coercive techniques to fill the ranks. In 1757, American crowds resisted forced recruitment in New York City and elsewhere. Other clashes developed over the army's heavy-handed attempts to commandeer wagons and supplies from American farmers and merchants and to house troops in private homes wherever public accommodations were inadequate.

Anglo-American tensions

In 1758, Pitt acted to ease the strains that were threatening to disrupt the Anglo-American war effort. He agreed to reimburse the colonies for their military expenditures, and placed the recruitment of American troops in their hands. The result was an immediate increase in the number and enthusiasm of colonial volunteers. The colonial governments, assured of financial aid from the mother country, began to devote more of their resources to the task of winning the war. At the same time, Pitt dispatched a large number of British regulars to the colonies. The well-trained redcoats did most of the actual fighting, with colonial militia relegated to support roles.

Pitt's measures won the war, but they also caused discord within the Anglo-American ranks. British commanders could not understand why the colonies seemed so reluctant to contribute to the war effort; they were especially angry at the merchants who continued to trade with the French West Indies. Redcoat officers and enlisted men alike looked down on their American counterparts as undisciplined and ignorant of military procedures. For their part, the Americans resented the Britons' condescension, and soldiers and civilians both chafed at the restrictions imposed on their behavior by military regulations. In the years after 1760, memories of wartime friction were to contribute to the growing tensions between colonies and mother country.

It was several years before white colonists felt the full impact of the British victory in the French and Indian War. The Indians, however, felt it almost immediately. The Ottawas and their neighbors, the Chippewas and the Potawatomis, became angry when Britain, lacking competition, raised the price of trade goods and ended the French custom of giving them ammunition for hunting. Even more significantly, the British refused to pay the customary rent for forts established within tribal territory. They also permitted white settlers to move into the Monongahela and Susquehanna valleys, which belonged to the Iroquois and Delawares. Thus the British signalled their disregard for Indian claims to sovereignty over the interior.

Pontiac, the Ottawa chief who realized the meaning of the British victory, had been a loyal ally of the French since the 1740s. In early May, he laid seige to Fort Detroit while his war parties attacked the other British outposts in the Great Lakes region. Detroit withstood the siege, but by the end of June all the other forts west of Niagara and north of Fort Pitt (old Fort Duquesne) had fallen to the Indian alliance.

That was the high point of the uprising. The tribes raided the Virginia and Pennsylvania frontiers at will throughout the summer, killing at least two thousand whites. But they could not take the strongholds of Niagara, Fort Pitt, or Detroit. In early August, a combined Indian force was soundly defeated at Bushy Run, Pennsylvania, by troops sent from the coast. Conflict ceased when Pontiac broke off the siege of Detroit in late October. A formal treaty ending the war was finally negotiated in 1766.

In the aftermath of the bloody summer of 1763, white frontiersmen from Paxton Township, Pennsylvania, sought revenge on the only Indians within reach, a peaceful band of Christian converts living at Conestoga. In December the whites raided the Indian village twice, killing twenty people. Two months later hundreds

of frontier dwellers known to history as the Paxton Boys marched on Philadelphia to demand military protection against future Indian attacks. City officials feared violence and mustered the militia to repel the westerners, but the protesters presented their request in an orderly fashion and returned home.

Pontiac's uprising and the march of the Paxton Boys showed that Great Britain would not find it easy to govern the huge territory it had just acquired from France. In October, in a futile attempt to assert control over the interior, the ministry issued the Proclamation of 1763, which declared the headwaters of rivers flowing into the Atlantic from the Appalachian Mountains to be the temporary western boundary for colonial settlement (see map). The proclamation was intended to prevent future clashes between Indians and colonists by forbidding whites to move onto Indian lands until the tribes had given up their land by treaty. But many whites had already established farms west of the proclamation line, and the policy was doomed to failure from its outset.

The beginnings of colonial protest

At the close of the war George Grenville, who had been named prime minister, and George III, who became king in 1760, faced an immediate problem: Britain's immense war debt. The figures were staggering. England's burden of indebtedness had nearly doubled since 1754, from £73 million to £137 million. Clearly Grenville's ministry had to find new sources of funds, and the English people themselves were already heavily taxed. Since the colonists had been major beneficiaries of the wartime expenditures, Grenville concluded that the Americans should be asked to pay a greater share of the cost of running the empire.

When Grenville decided to tax the colonies,

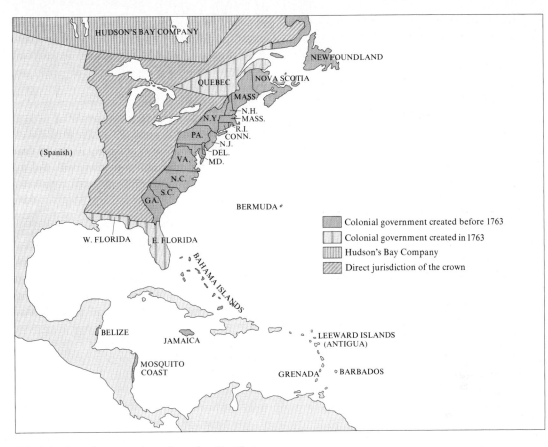

Britain's American empire after the Proclamation of 1763

he did not stop to consider whether Parliament had the authority to do so. Like all his countrymen, he believed that the government's legitimacy derived ultimately from the consent of the people, but he defined consent far more loosely than did the colonists. Americans had come to believe that they could be represented only by men for whom they or their property-holding neighbors had actually voted. To Grenville and his English contemporaries, however, Parliament by definition represented all English subjects, wherever they lived. According to this theory of government, called *virtual representation,* the colonists were said to be virtually, if not actually, represented in Parliament. Thus their consent to acts of Parliament could be presumed. Before Grenville proposed to tax the colonists, the two notions existed side by side without apparent contradiction.

> **Theories of representation**

In the years before 1763, the colonists had become accustomed to a government that wielded only limited authority over them and affected their daily lives very little. In consequence, they believed that a good government was one that largely left them alone, a view in keeping with the theories of a group of British writers known as the Real Whigs. These writers stressed the dangers inherent in a powerful government, particularly one headed by a monarch. They warned

The beginnings of colonial protest

55

that rulers would try to corrupt and oppress the people, that government was always to be feared, and that only the perpetual vigilance of the people and their elected representatives could preserve freedom.

Britain's attempts to tighten the reins of colonial government in the 1760s and early 1770s convinced many Americans that the Real Whigs' reasoning applied to their circumstances. They began to see evil designs behind the actions of Grenville and his successors. In the mid-1760s, the colonists did not, however, immediately accuse Grenville of an intent to oppress them. They at first simply questioned the utility of the new laws.

The first such measures, the Sugar and Currency Acts, were passed by Parliament in 1764. The Sugar Act revised the existing system of

| **Sugar and Currency Acts** |

customs regulations; laid new duties on certain foreign imports into the colonies; established a vice-admiralty court at Halifax, Nova Scotia; and included special provisions aimed at stopping the widespread smuggling of molasses, one of the chief commodities in American trade. The Currency Act in effect outlawed colonial issues of paper money. Americans could accumulate little hard cash, since they imported more than they exported; thus the act seemed to the colonists to deprive them of the means of doing business.

Since the American economy was suffering a severe postwar depression, it is not surprising that both individual colonists and colonial governments decided to protest the new policies. But, lacking any precedent for a united campaign against acts of Parliament, Americans in 1764 took only hesitant and uncoordinated steps. Eight colonial legislatures sent separate petitions to Parliament requesting repeal of the Sugar Act. They argued that the act placed severe restrictions on their commerce and that they had not consented to its passage. They also instructed their agents in London to lobby against another proposed levy, the stamp tax.

That tax was modeled on a law that had been in effect in England for nearly a century. It would touch nearly every colonist by requiring tax stamps on most printed materials. Anyone

| **Stamp Act** |

who purchased a newspaper or pamphlet, made a will, transferred land, bought dice or playing cards, needed a liquor license, accepted a government appointment, or borrowed money would have to pay the tax. Never before had a revenue measure of such scope been proposed for the colonies. The act would also require that tax stamps be paid for with hard money and that violators be tried in vice-admiralty courts, without juries. Finally, such a law would break decisively with the colonial tradition of self-imposed taxation.

The most important colonial pamphlet protesting the Sugar Act and the proposed stamp act was *The Rights of the British Colonies Asserted and Proved,* by James Otis, Jr., a brilliant young Massachusetts attorney. Otis starkly exposed the ideological dilemma that was to confound the colonists for the next decade. How could they justify their opposition to certain acts of Parliament without questioning Parliament's authority over them? On the one hand, Otis asserted that Americans were "entitled to all the natural, essential, inherent, and inseparable rights" of Britons, including the right not to be taxed without their consent. On the other hand, Otis was forced to admit that, under the British system, "the power of parliament is uncontroulable, but by themselves, and we must obey. . . ."

Otis thus implied on one hand that Parliament could not tax the colonies because Americans were not represented in its ranks. On the other hand, however, he accepted the prevailing British theory of parliamentary supremacy. In an effort to find a middle ground, Otis proposed colonial representation in Parliament; the idea was never seriously considered on either side of the Atlantic. The British believed that the colonists were already virtually represented in Parliament, and the Americans quickly realized that a handful of colonial delegates to London would simply be outvoted.

The Stamp Act crisis

When Americans learned of the passage of the Stamp Act in the spring of 1765, they did not at first know how to proceed. Colonial opposition to it was nearly universal, even among government officials. But the colonists had already failed to prevent its adoption, and further lobbying appeared futile. Perhaps Otis was right, and the only course open to them was to pay the stamp tax, reluctantly but loyally. Acting on that assumption, colonial agents in London sought the appointment of their American friends as stamp distributors, so that the law would at least be enforced equitably.

Not all the colonists were resigned, however, to paying the new tax without a fight. One who was not was a twenty-nine-year-old lawyer serving his first term as a member of the Virginia House of Burgesses. Patrick

| Patrick Henry |

Henry later recalled that he was appalled by his fellow legislators' unwillingness to oppose the Stamp Act openly. Henry decided to act. "Alone, unadvised, and unassisted, on a blank leaf of an old law book," he wrote the Virginia Stamp Act Resolves.

Patrick Henry introduced his proposals in late May, near the end of the legislative session. Henry's fiery speech in support of his resolutions led the Speaker of the House to accuse him of treason, but Henry quickly denied the charge. The small number of burgesses remaining in Williamsburg formally adopted five of Henry's seven resolutions by a bare majority. Though they repealed the most radical resolution the next day, their action had far-reaching effects.

The four propositions adopted by the burgesses resembled the arguments James Otis had advanced the previous year. The colonists had never forfeited the rights of British subjects, they declared, and consent to taxation was one of the most important of those rights. The other three resolutions went much further. The one that was repealed claimed for the burgesses "the only exclusive right" to tax Virginians. The fi-nal two asserted that residents of the colony did not have to obey tax laws passed by other legislative bodies (namely Parliament) and termed any opponent of that opinion "an Enemy to this his Majesty's Colony."

Approval of the resolutions did not reflect a desire for independence on the part of the colonists. They did, however, wish to retain some measure of self-rule. Daniel Dulany, whose *Considerations on the Propriety of Imposing Taxes on the British Colonies* was the most widely read pamphlet of 1765, accepted both America's dependence on England and the supreme authority of the British government. But, warned Dulany, a superior did not have the right "to seize the property of his inferior when he pleases"; there was a crucial distinction between a condition of "dependence and *inferiority*" and one of "absolute *vassalage* and *slavery*."

Over the course of the next ten years, Americans searched for a political formula that would enable them to control their internal affairs, especially taxation, but remain within the British Empire. The chief difficulty lay in British officials' inability to compromise on the issue of parliamentary power. The notion that Parliament could exercise absolute authority over all colonial possessions was basic to the orthodox British theory of government.

The ultimate effectiveness of Americans' opposition to the Stamp Act did not rest on ideological arguments over parliamentary power. What gave the resistance its primary force were the decisive and inventive actions of the colonists during the late summer and fall of 1765.

In August the Loyal Nine, a Boston social club of printers, distillers, and other artisans, organized a demonstration against the Stamp Act.

| Loyal Nine |

Hoping to show that people of all social and economic ranks opposed the act, they approached the leaders of the city's rival laborers' associations, the North End and South End mobs. The Loyal Nine convinced them to lay aside their differences and participate in the demonstration.

Early in the morning of August 14, the dem-

This woodcut, produced half a century after the event, shows a crowd parading the effigy of the New Hampshire stamp distributor through the steets of Portsmouth in 1765. The procession is led, as it was in many cities, by men carrying a coffin to symbolize the death and burial of the Stamp Act. The Metropolitan Museum of Art, Bequest of Charles Allen Munn.

onstrators hung an effigy of Andrew Oliver, the province's stamp distributor, from a tree on Boston Common. That night, after a peaceful parade, the crowd destroyed a building they assumed was going to be a tax office. The wood from the structure was used to build a bonfire near Oliver's house. In an unplanned act, members of the crowd broke most of Oliver's windows, and then Oliver publicly promised not to fulfill the duties of his office. Twelve nights later another mob, reportedly led by the South End leader, Ebenezer MacIntosh, attacked the homes of several customs officials. This time the violence was almost universally condemned, for the mob completely destroyed Lieutenant Governor Thomas Hutchinson's elaborately furnished townhouse.

Thoughtful residents of other colonies drew two important conclusions from the Boston mob actions. First, they realized that they could prevent implementation of the Stamp Act by forcing stamp distributors to resign. Second, they recognized the danger of inciting mob action to achieve their goals. Although mobs could be useful, they would have to be carefully controlled to avoid the kind of excessive violence that had destroyed Hutchinson's house.

The Stamp Act controversy drew disfranchised Americans into the vortex of imperial politics for the first time. Lower-class whites, blacks, and even women began to participate in public discussions and demonstrations. Such people had long expressed their opinions on local issues, often through crowd action, but never before had they been aroused by broad questions of imperial policy. In 1765, though, as Sally Franklin wrote to her father Benjamin, then serving as a colonial agent in London,

Chapter 4: Severing the bonds of empire, 1754–1774

"nothing else is talked of, the Dutch [Germans] talk of the stompt act the Negroes of the tamp, in short every body has something to say."

The aims of such newly politicized Americans were often quite different from those of resistance leaders. The Loyal Nine had accomplished their end when Oliver agreed not to distribute stamps, but the Boston crowd had its own goals. Chief among them seems to have been a desire to punish the haughty Hutchinson for his ostentatious display of wealth in a city whose average citizen's share of the economic pie had steadily decreased since about 1750. Although Hutchinson was erroneously believed to be a supporter of the Stamp Act, his self-advertised wealth probably contributed significantly to motivating the crowd's "hellish Fury."

The Loyal Nine's tactics were immediately imitated elsewhere in the colonies. The organized crowd actions were so successful that by November 1, when the law was scheduled to go into effect, not a single stamp distributor was willing to carry out the duties of his office. To coordinate their efforts at directing opposition into acceptable channels, re-

| Sons of Liberty |

sistance leaders throughout the colonies formed an association known as the Sons of Liberty. The first such group was created in New York City in early November, and branches spread rapidly through the colonies. Largely composed of merchants, lawyers, prosperous tradesmen, and the like, the Sons of Liberty linked resistance leaders in cities from Charleston, South Carolina, to Portsmouth, New Hampshire, by early 1766.

During the fall and winter of 1765 and 1766, opposition to the Stamp Act proceeded on three separate fronts. The colonial legislatures petitioned Parliament to repeal the hated law and sent delegates to an intercolonial congress, the first since 1754. In October the Stamp Act Congress met in New York to draft a unified but relatively conservative statement of protest. At the same time, the Sons of Liberty held mass meetings in an effort to win public support for the resistance movement. Finally, American merchants organized nonimportation associ-

ations to put economic pressure on British exporters. Recognizing that the colonial market contributed greatly to the exporters' profits, they reasoned that London merchants whose sales suffered would lobby for repeal. (Nonimportation also enabled colonial merchants to reduce bloated inventories.)

In March 1766, Parliament repealed the Stamp Act. The nonimportation agreements had

| Repeal of the Stamp Act |

had the anticipated effect, creating allies within the powerful circle of wealthy London merchants. Success, however, was largely a result of Grenville's replacement by Lord Rockingham. The new prime minister, an opponent of the tax, pushed for repeal. But he linked repeal to the passage of the Declaratory Act, which asserted Parliament's ability to tax and legislate for Britain's American possessions "in all cases whatsoever." As they celebrated the Stamp Act's repeal, few Americans recognized the Declaratory Act's ominous implications.

Resistance to the Townshend Acts

In 1767, Charles Townshend, the chancellor of the exchequer, decided to rely on the Declaratory Act to revive the attempts to tax the colonies. The new taxes Townshend proposed were

| Townshend Acts |

levied on trade goods like paper, glass, and tea, and thus seemed on the surface to be nothing more than extensions of the existing Navigation Acts. But the Townshend duties differed from previous customs taxes in two ways. First, they were levied on items imported into the colonies from Britain, not from foreign countries. Thus they were at odds with mercantilist theory. Second, they were designed to raise money, not to regulate the availability and use of certain commodities in America. The receipts, moreover, would pay the salaries of royal officials in the colonies. That posed a direct challenge to the colonial assemblies, which derived considerable power from threatening to withhold officials' salaries. Townshend's scheme also provided for the establishment of an American Board of Customs Commissioners, the creation of vice-admiralty courts at Boston, Philadelphia, and Charleston, and the appointment of a secretary of state for American affairs. Finally, he suspended the New York legislature for not providing certain items (like firewood and candles) to British troops stationed permanently in America.

The Townshend Acts drew a quick response. One series of essays in particular, *Letters from a Farmer in Pennsylvania* by the prominent lawyer John Dickinson, expressed the consensus prevailing among his fellow colonists. Dickinson contended that Parliament could regulate colonial trade, but could not exercise that power for the purpose of raising revenues. He thus avoided the complicated question of colonial consent to parliamentary legislation. But his argument had another flaw: it was clearly unworkable for Americans to assess Parliament's motives for passing a trade law before deciding whether to obey it.

The Massachusetts assembly responded to the acts by drafting a circular letter to the other colonial legislatures, calling for unity and suggesting a joint petition of protest to the king. It was less the letter itself than the ministry's reaction to it that united the colonies. When Lord Hillsborough, the first secretary of state for America,

| Massachusetts assembly dissolved |

learned of the circular letter, he ordered Governor Francis Bernard of Massachusetts to insist that the assembly recall it. He also directed other governors to prevent their assemblies from discussing the letter. Hillsborough's order gave the colonial assemblies the incentive they needed to forget their differences and join forces to meet the new threat to their prerogatives. In late 1768 the Massachusetts legislature met, debated, and resoundingly rejected recall by a vote of 92 to 17. Bernard immedi-

ately dissolved the assembly, and other governors followed suit when their legislatures debated the circular letter.

The figure 45 had become a symbol of resistance to Great Britain when John Wilkes, a radical Englishman sympathetic to the American cause, had been jailed for libel because of his publication of the essay *The North Briton No. 45*. Now 92, the number of votes cast against recalling the circular letter, assumed ritual significance as well. In Newport, for example, 45 members of the revived Sons of Liberty dined on 45 dishes and drank 92 toasts. Americans in other towns engaged in similar activities.

During the two-year campaign against the Townshend duties, the Sons of Liberty and other American leaders made a deliberate effort to broaden the base of the resistance movement. In addition to asking merchants not to import British products, they urged ordinary citizens not to buy them. As a result, an increasing number of Americans found themselves aligned in a united cause.

Even women, who had previously regarded politics as outside their proper sphere, joined in the formal resistance movement. In towns throughout America, young women calling themselves Daughters of Liberty met to spin in

| Daughters of Liberty |

public, in an effort to spur other women to make homespun and end the colonies' dependence on English cloth. These symbolic displays of patriotism, often held in the minister's house, served the same purpose as the male rituals involving the numbers 45 and 92. When young ladies from well-to-do families sat publicly at spinning wheels all day, eating only American food and drinking herbal tea, and afterwards listening to patriotic sermons, they were serving as political instructors.

Women also took the lead in promoting nonconsumption of tea. In Boston more than three hundred matrons publicly promised not to drink tea, "Sickness excepted." Housewives throughout the colonies exchanged recipes for tea substitutes or drank coffee instead. The best known of the protests (because it was satirized by a British cartoonist), the so-called Edenton Ladies Tea Party, actually had little to do with tea; it was a meeting of prominent North Carolina women who pledged formally to work for the public good and to support resistance to British measures.

Not all Americans acquiesced in nonimportation. Many merchants continued to import British goods, some as a matter of principle and others for economic reasons. The earlier boycotts of 1765 and 1766 had helped to revive a depressed economy; but in 1768 and 1769 merchants were enjoying boom times and had no financial incentive to support a boycott. However, artisans, who recognized that the absence of British goods would create a market for their own manufactures, used coercion to enforce nonimportation.

Such tactics were effective: colonial imports from England dropped dramatically in 1769, especially in New York, New England, and Pennsylvania. But they also aroused significant opposition. Some Americans who supported resistance to British measures began to question the use of violence to force others to join the boycott. The wealthier and more conservative colonists were frightened by the threat to private property inherent in the campaign. Moreover, political activism on the part of colonists who had once deferred to the judgment of their superiors posed a threat to the local ruling classes.

All Americans were relieved when the news arrived in April 1770 that a new prime minister, Lord North, had persuaded Parliament to repeal the Townshend duties, except the tea tax, on

| *Repeal of the Townshend duties* | the grounds that duties on trade within the empire were bad policy. Although the more radical Americans ar- |

gued that nonimportation should be maintained until even the tea tax was repealed, merchants quickly resumed importing. The rest of the

Townshend Acts remained in force, but repeal of the taxes made the other laws appear less objectionable to the colonists.

Growing rifts

At first the new ministry did nothing to antagonize the colonists. Yet on the very day Lord North proposed repeal of the Townshend duties, a clash between civilians and soldiers in Boston led to the death of five Americans. The origins of the event patriots called the Boston Massacre lay in repeated clashes between customs officers and the people of Massachusetts. One clash, a riot in 1768, led the British to station two regiments in Boston.

Bostonians, accustomed to leading their lives with a minimum of interference from government, now found themselves hemmed in at every turn. Guards on Boston Neck, the entrance to the city, checked all travelers and their goods. Redcoat patrols roamed the city day and night, questioning and sometimes harassing passers-by. Young women who ventured out on the streets were subjected to sexual insults by soldiers. But the greatest potential for violence lay in the uneasy relationship between the soldiers and Boston laborers. Many redcoats sought employment in their off-duty hours, competing for unskilled jobs with the city's ordinary workingmen, and members of the two groups brawled repeatedly.

On March 2, 1770, workers at a ropewalk (a ship-rigging factory) attacked some redcoats seeking jobs. Three days later, on the evening of March 5, a crowd began throwing hard-packed

| *Boston Massacre* | snowballs at sentries guarding the Customs House. Goaded beyond endurance, |

the sentries fired on the crowd against express orders to the contrary, killing four and wound-

Paul Revere's engraving of the Boston Massacre, a masterful piece of propaganda. At right the British officer seems to be ordering the soldiers to fire on a peaceful, unresisting crowd. The Customs House has been labeled Butcher's Hall, and smoke drifts up from a gun barrel sticking out the window. American Antiquarian Society.

ing eight, one of whom died a few days later. Resistance leaders idealized the dead rioters as martyrs for the cause of liberty, holding a solemn funeral three days later and commemorating March 5 annually with patriotic orations. The best-known engraving of the massacre, by Paul Revere, was itself a part of the propaganda campaign, for it depicted a peaceful, rather than a riotous, crowd.

The leading patriots wanted to make certain the soldiers did not become martyrs as well. Thus when the soldiers were tried for the killings in November, they were defended by John Adams and Josiah Quincy, Jr., both unwavering patriots. All but two of the accused men were acquitted, and those convicted were released after having been branded on the thumb. Undoubtedly the favorable outcome of the trials

Chapter 4: Severing the bonds of empire, 1754-1774

prevented London officials from taking further steps against the city.

For more than two years after the Boston Massacre and the repeal of the Townshend duties, a superficial calm descended on the colonies. Local incidents, like the burning of the customs vessel *Gaspée* in 1772 by Rhode Islanders, marred the relationship of individual colonies and the mother country, but nothing caused Americans to join in a unified protest. Even so, the resistance movement continued to gather momentum. The most radical colonial newspapers, for example, published essays drawing on Real Whig ideology and accusing Great Britain of a deliberate plan to oppress America.

Still, no one yet advocated complete independence from the mother country. Though the patriots were becoming increasingly convinced that they should seek freedom from parliamentary authority, they continued to acknowledge their British identity and to pledge their allegiance to George III. Indeed, they hoped to ally themselves with English radicals in working for imperial reform. They began, therefore, to try to envision a system that would enable them to be ruled largely by their own elected legislatures while remaining loyal to the king. But any such scheme was totally alien to Britons' conception of the nature of their government. Conservative colonists recognized the dangers inherent in the new mode of patriot thought.

Their fears proved correct when, in the fall of 1772, the North ministry began to implement the portion of the Townshend Acts that provided for governors and judges to be paid from customs revenues. In early November, voters at a Boston town meeting established a Committee

| Committees of Correspondence |

of Correspondence to publicize the decision by exchanging letters with other Massachusetts towns. Heading the committee was the man who had proposed its formation, Samuel Adams.

Samuel Adams was fifty-one years old in 1772, thirteen years the senior of his distant cousin John and a decade older than most other leaders of American resistance. His primary forum was the Boston town meeting. An experienced political organizer, Adams continually stressed the necessity of prudent collective action. His Committee of Correspondence thus undertook to create an informed consensus among all the citizens of Massachusetts, including residents of rural areas. The formal resistance movement had until then been largely confined to cities and towns.

The Boston town meeting directed the Committee of Correspondence "to state the Rights of the Colonists and of this Province in particular," to list "the Infringements and Violations thereof that have been, or from time to time may be made," and to send copies to the other towns in the province. Samuel Adams, James Otis, Jr., and Josiah Quincy, Jr., prepared the statement of the colonists' rights. Declaring that Americans had absolute rights to life, liberty, and property, the committee asserted that the idea that "a British house of commons, should have a right, at pleasure, to give and grant the property of the colonists" was "irreconcileable" with "the first principles of natural law and Justice . . . and of the British Constitution in particular." The list of grievances, drafted by another group of prominent patriots, was similarly sweeping. It complained of taxation without representation, the presence of unnecessary troops and customs officers on American soil, the use of imperial revenues to pay colonial officials, the expanded jurisdiction of vice-admiralty courts, and even the nature of the instructions given to American governors by their superiors in London. Significantly, the document did not attempt to define the limits of parliamentary authority.

The response of the Massachusetts towns to the committee's pamphlet must have caused Samuel Adams to rejoice. Some towns disagreed with Boston's assessment of the state of affairs, but most aligned themselves with the city. From Braintree came the assertion that "all civil officers are or ought to be Servants to the people." The citizens of Petersham commented that resistance to tyranny was "the first and highest social Duty of this people." It was beliefs like these that made the next crisis in Anglo-American affairs the final one.

The Boston Tea Party

The only one of the Townshend duties still in effect by 1773 was the tax on tea. Although a continuing tea boycott was less than fully effective, tea retained its explosive symbolic character. When in May 1773 Parliament passed an act designed to save the East India Company from bankruptcy, resistance leaders were immediately

| Tea Act | suspicious. Under the Tea Act, certain duties paid on tea were to be returned to the company. Furthermore, tea was to be sold only by designated agents, which would enable the East India Company to control the price and undersell any competitors, even smugglers. The net result would be cheaper tea for American consumers. But many colonists interpreted the new measure as a pernicious device to make them admit Parliament's right to tax them, since the less expensive tea would still be taxed under the Townshend law. Others saw the Tea Act as the first step in the establishment of an East India Company monopoly of all colonial trade.

New York, Boston, Charleston, and Philadelphia were singled out to receive the first shipments of tea. Only Boston was the site of a dramatic confrontation. There both sides—the town meeting, joined by participants from nearby towns, and Governor Thomas Hutchinson—rejected compromise.

The first of three tea ships, the *Dartmouth,* entered Boston Harbor on November 28. Under the customs law, duty had to be paid within twenty days of a ship's arrival or its cargo would be seized by customs officers. After a series of mass meetings, Bostonians voted to prevent the tea from being unloaded and to post guards on the wharf. Hutchinson, for his part, refused to permit the vessels to leave the harbor, since that too would violate the law.

On December 16, 1773, one day before the cargo would have to be confiscated, more than five thousand people (nearly a third of the city's population) crowded into Old South Church. The meeting, chaired by Samuel Adams, made a final attempt to persuade Hutchinson to send the tea back to England. But Hutchinson remained adamant. At about 6 P.M., Adams reportedly announced "that he could think of nothing further to be done—that they had now done all they could for the Salvation of their Country." As if his statement were a signal, cries rang out from the back of the crowd: "Boston harbor a tea-pot night! The Mohawks are come!" Small groups pushed their way out of the meeting. Within a few minutes, about sixty men, many of them artisans, crudely disguised as Indians, assembled at the wharf, boarded the three ships, and dumped the cargo into the harbor. By 9 P.M. their work was done: 342 chests of tea worth approximately £10,000 floated in splinters on the ebbing tide.

The North administration, after failing in an attempt to charge the resistance leaders with high treason, proposed a bill closing the port of Boston until the tea was paid for and prohibiting all but coastal trade in food and firewood. Colonial sympathizers in Parliament were easily outvoted. Later in the spring, Parliament passed three further punitive measures. The Massachusetts Government Act altered the province's charter, substituting an appointed council for an elected one, increasing the powers of the governor, and forbidding special town meetings. The Justice Act provided that a person accused of committing murder in the course of suppressing a riot or enforcing the laws could be tried outside the colony where the incident had occurred. Finally, the Quartering Act gave broad authority to military commanders seeking to house their troops in private dwellings.

After passing the last of what became known as the Coercive Acts in early June, Parliament turned its attention to much-needed reforms in the government of Quebec. The Quebec Act, though unrelated to the Coercive Acts, thus became linked with them in the minds of the patriots. The law granted religious freedom to Catholics, reinstated French civil law, and established an appointed council (rather than an elected legislature) as the colony's governing body. To protect Indians from white settlement, the act annexed to Quebec the area east of the Mississippi River and north of the Ohio River. Thus that region, parts of which were claimed by individual seacoast colonies, was removed from the colonists' jurisdiction.

The members of Parliament who had voted for the punitive legislation believed that the acts would be obeyed. But the patriots showed little inclination to bow to the wishes of Parliament. In their eyes, the Coercive Acts and the Quebec Act proved what they had feared since 1768: that Great Britain had embarked on a deliberate plan to oppress them. If the port of Boston could be closed, why not those of Philadelphia or New York? If the royal charter of Massachusetts could be changed, why not that of South Carolina? If certain people could be removed from their home colonies for trial, why not all violators of all laws? If the Roman Catholic Church could receive favored status in Quebec, why not everywhere?

The Boston Committee of Correspondence urged all the colonies to join in an immediate boycott of British goods. But the other provinces were not yet ready to take such a drastic step. Instead, they suggested that another intercolonial congress be convened to consider an appropriate response to the Coercive Acts. Few people wanted to take hasty action; even the most ardent patriots still hoped for reconciliation with Great Britain. And so the colonies agreed to send delegates to Philadelphia in September.

Suggestions for further reading

GENERAL Ian R. Christie and Benjamin W. Labaree, *Empire or Independence, 1760–1776: A British-American Dialogue on the Coming of the American Revolution* (1976); Lawrence Henry Gipson, *The Coming of the Revolution 1763–1775* (1954); Merrill Jensen, *The Founding of a Nation: A History of the American Revolution, 1763–1776* (1968); Edmund S. Morgan, *The Birth of the Republic, 1763–1789* (1956)

COLONIAL WARFARE AND THE BRITISH EMPIRE Lawrence Henry Gipson, *The British Empire Before the American Revolution,* 15 vols. (1936–1970); Howard H. Peckham, *The Colonial Wars, 1689–1762* (1963); Alan Rogers, *Empire and Liberty: American Resistance to British Authority, 1755–1763* (1974); John Shy, *Toward Lexington: The Role of the British Army in the Coming of the American Revolution* (1965).

BRITISH POLITICS AND POLICY John Brewer, *Party Ideology and Popular Politics at the Accession of George III* (1976); John Brooke, *King George III* (1972); Bernard Donoughue, *British Politics and the American Revolution: The Path to War, 1773–1775* (1965); Michael Kammen, *A Rope of Sand: The Colonial Agents, British Politics, and the American Revolution* (1968);

Lewis B. Namier, *England in the Age of the American Revolution,* 2nd ed. (1961); Lewis B. Namier, *The Structure of Politics at the Accession of George III,* 2nd ed. (1957); P.D.G. Thomas, *British Politics and the Stamp Act Crisis* (1975).

INDIANS AND THE WEST Thomas P. Abernethy, *Western Lands and the American Revolution* (1959); James T. Flexner, *Mohawk Baronet: Sir William Johnson of New York* (1959); Howard H. Peckham, *Pontiac and the Indian Uprising* (1947); Jack M. Sosin, *Whitehall and the Wilderness: The Middle West in British Colonial Policy, 1760–1775* (1961).

REVOLUTIONARY IDEOLOGY Bernard Bailyn, *The Ideological Origins of the American Revolution* (1967); H. Trevor Colbourn, *The Lamp of Experience: Whig History and the Intellectual Origins of the American Revolution* (1965); Jay Fliegelman, *Prodigals & Pilgrims: The American Revolution Against Patriarchal Authority 1750–1800* (1982); Caroline Robbins, *The Eighteenth-Century Commonwealthman: Studies in the Transmission, Development, and Circumstance of English Liberal Thought from the Restoration of Charles II until the War with the Thirteen Colonies* (1959); Clinton Rossiter, *Seedtime of the Republic: The Origin of the American Tradition of Political Liberty* (1953).

AMERICAN RESISTANCE David Ammerman, *In the Common Cause: American Response to the Coercive Acts of 1774* (1974); Joseph Albert Ernst, *Money and Politics in America, 1755–1775: A Study in the Currency Act of 1764 and the Political Economy of Revolution* (1973); Rhys Isaac, *The Transformation of Virginia, 1740–1790* (1982); Pauline R. Maier, *From Resistance to Revolution: Colonial Radicals and the Development of American Opposition to Britain, 1765–1776* (1972); Pauline R. Maier, *The Old Revolutionaries: Political Lives in the Age of Samuel Adams* (1980); Edmund S. Morgan and Helen M. Morgan, *The Stamp Act Crisis: Prologue to Revolution* (1953); Gary B. Nash, *The Urban Crucible: Social Change, Political Consciousness, and the Origins of the American Revolution* (1979); Arthur M. Schlesinger, *The Colonial Merchants and the American Revolution 1763–1776* (1918); Alfred H. Young, ed., *The American Revolution: Explorations in the History of American Radicalism* (1976).

5

A REVOLUTION,

INDEED,

1775–1783

One April morning in 1775, Hannah Winthrop awoke with a start to drumbeats, bells, and the continuous clang of the Cambridge fire alarm. She and her husband, a professor at Harvard, soon learned that redcoat troops had left Boston late the evening before, bound for Concord. A few hours later they watched British soldiers march through Cambridge to reinforce the first group. The Winthrops quickly decided to leave home and seek shelter elsewhere. They made their way to an isolated farmhouse, but it was no secure haven. They were, Mrs. Winthrop later wrote, "for some time in sight of the Battle, the glistening instruments of death proclaiming by an incessant fire that much blood must be shed, that many widowd and orphand ones be left as monuments of that persecuting Barbarity of British Tyranny."

Hannah Winthrop was convinced that nothing would be the same again. In that expectation she was wrong. The Winthrops returned to their Cambridge home and resumed their normal lives. But the Revolution did bring major changes. It uprooted thousands of civilian families, disrupted the economy, reshaped society by forcing many colonists into permanent exile, and led Americans to develop new conceptions of politics. Indeed, even before the shooting began the patriots had established functioning revolutionary governments throughout the colonies.

Government by congress and committee

When the fifty-five delegates to the First Continental Congress convened in Philadelphia in September 1774, they knew that any measures they adopted were likely to enjoy strong support among their fellow countrymen and women. During the summer of 1774, open meetings held throughout the colonies had endorsed the idea of another non-importation pact. The committees of correspondence that had been established in many communities publicized these popular meetings so effectively that Americans everywhere knew about them. Most of the congressional delegates were selected by extralegal provincial conventions because the royal governors had forbidden the regular assemblies to conduct formal elections. Thus the very act of designating delegates

First Continental Congress

to attend the congress involved Americans in open defiance of British authority.

The congressmen faced three tasks when they convened at Carpenters Hall on September 5, 1774. The first two were explicit: defining American grievances and developing a plan for resistance. The third was implicit—outlining a theory of their constitutional relationship with England—and proved troublesome. The delegates readily agreed on a list of the laws they wanted repealed (notably the Coercive Acts) and chose as their method of resistance an economic boycott coupled with petitions for relief. But they could not reach a consensus on the constitutional issue, a subject on which the delegates held widely differing views.

The most radical congressmen, like Richard Henry Lee of Virginia and Roger Sherman of Connecticut, agreed with the position published a few weeks earlier by Thomas Jefferson—who was not a delegate—in his *Summary View of the Rights of British America.* Jefferson argued that the colonists owed allegiance only to George III, and that Parliament was nothing more than "the legislature of one part of the empire" with no legitimate authority over the provinces.

Meanwhile the conservative Joseph Galloway of Pennsylvania insisted that the congress should acknowledge Parliament's supremacy over the empire and its right to regulate American trade. Galloway embodied these ideas in a formal plan of union. His plan proposed the establishment of an American legislature, its members chosen by individual colonial assemblies, which would have to consent to laws pertaining to America. The delegates rejected Galloway's proposal, though, eventually accepting instead a position outlined by John Adams.

The clause Adams drafted in the congress's Declaration of Rights and Grievances read in part: "From the necessity of the case, and a re-

| Declaration of Rights and Grievances |

gard to the mutual interest of both countries, we cheerfully consent to the operation of such acts of the British parliament, as are bona fide, restrained to the regulation of our external commerce." Note the

key phrases. "From the necessity of the case" indicated Americans' abandonment, once and for all, of their unquestioning loyalty to the mother country. "Bona fide, restrained to the regulation of our external commerce" resonated with overtones of the Stamp Act controversy and Dickinson's arguments in his *Farmer's Letters.* The delegates intended to make clear to Lord North that they would continue to resist taxes in disguise, like the Townshend duties. Most striking of all was that such language, which only a few years before would have been regarded as irredeemably radical, could be presented and accepted as a compromise in the fall of 1774.

Once the delegates had resolved the constitutional issue, they discussed the tactics by which to force another British retreat. They quickly agreed on nonimportation of all goods from Great Britain and Ireland, as well as tea and molasses from other British possessions and slaves from any source, effective December 1. An end to the consumption of British products was also readily accepted as part of the agreement that became known as the Continental Association; it would become effective on March 1, 1775. Nonexportation, on the other hand, generated considerable debate. The Virginia delegation adamantly refused to accept a ban on exports to England until after its planters had had a chance to market their 1774 tobacco crop. As a result, the congress provided that nonexportation would not begin until September 10, 1775.

More influential than the details of the Continental Association was the method the congress recommended for its enforcement: the election of committees of observation and inspection in every county, city, and town in America. Such

| Committees of Observation |

committees were officially charged only with overseeing enforcement of the association, but over the next six months they became de facto governments. Since the congress specified that committee members be chosen by all persons qualified to vote for members of the lower house of the colonial legislatures, the committees were guaranteed a broad popular base. Furthermore, their large size ensured that

Chapter 5: A revolution, indeed, 1775–1783

many new men would be incorporated into the resistance movement.

At first the committees confined themselves to enforcing the nonimportation clause. But the Continental Association also promoted home manufactures and encouraged Americans to adopt simple modes of dress and behavior. Wearing homespun garments became a sign of patriotism. Since expensive leisure-time activities were symbols of vice and corruption (characteristic of England, not of the virtuous colonies), the congress urged Americans to forgo dancing, gambling, horse racing, cock fighting, and other forms of "extravagance and dissipation." In enforcing these injunctions, the committees gradually extended their authority over nearly all aspects of American life.

The committees also attempted to identify opponents of American resistance. In their quest to protect American rights, the patriots denied freedom of speech and thought to those who disagreed with them. They developed elaborate spy networks, circulated copies of the association for signatures, and investigated reports of dissident remarks and activities. Suspected dissenters were first urged to convert to the colonial cause; if that failed, the committees had them watched or restricted their movements. Sometimes people engaging in casual political exchanges with friends one day found themselves charged with "treasonable conversation" the next.

The committees were extralegal bodies, drawing on no source of authority other than popular election. They had no connection—except in some cases overlapping membership—with the ordinary organs of government Americans were accustomed to obeying. That most colonists apparently submitted to their rule without overt complaint certainly suggests broad public support for resistance to Great Britain. As the patriots were to discover, however, many people who were willing to work for reform within the empire by means of boycotts and petitions were unwilling to seek independence by force of arms.

While the committees were expanding their power during the winter and early spring of 1775, the established governments of the colonies were collapsing. Only in Connecticut, Rhode Island, Delaware, and Pennsylvania did regular assemblies continue to meet without encountering patriot challenges to their authority.

| *Provincial conventions* |

In every other colony, popularly elected provincial conventions took over the task of running the government. In late 1774 and early 1775, these conventions approved the Continental Association, elected delegates to the Second Continental Congress (scheduled for May), organized militia units, and gathered arms and ammunition. The British-appointed governors and councils watched helplessly as their authority crumbled. Courts were prevented from holding sessions; taxes were paid to agents of the conventions rather than provincial tax collectors; sheriffs' powers were questioned; and militiamen refused to muster except by order of the local committees. In short, during the six months preceding the battles at Lexington and Concord, independence was being won at the local level, but without formal acknowledgment and for the most part without shooting or bloodshed. Not many Americans fully realized what was happening. The vast majority of colonists still proclaimed their loyalty to Great Britain and denied that they sought to leave the empire. Among the few Americans who did recognize the trend toward independence were those who opposed it.

Internal enemies

The first protests against British measures, in the mid-1760s, had won the support of most colonists. Only in the late 1760s and early 1770s did a significant number of Americans begin to question both the aims and the tactics of the resistance movement. In 1774 and 1775 such people found themselves in a difficult position.

Like their more radical counterparts, most of them objected to parliamentary policies and wanted some kind of constitutional reform. Nevertheless, if forced to a choice, these colonists sympathized with Great Britain rather than with an independent America.

In 1774 and 1775 some conservatives began to publish essays and pamphlets critical of the congress and its allied committees. In Pennsylvania, Joseph Galloway published *A Candid Examination of the Mutual Claims of Great Britain and the Colonies,* attacking the Continental Congress for rejecting his plan of union. In Massachusetts, the young attorney Daniel Leonard, writing under the pseudonym Massachusettensis, engaged in a prolonged newspaper debate with Novanglus (John Adams). All the conservative authors stressed the point that Leonard put so well in his sixth essay in January 1775: "There is no possible medium between absolute independence and subjection to the authority of parliament." Leonard and his fellows realized that what had begun as a dispute over the extent of American subordination within the empire had now raised the question of whether the colonies would remain linked to Great Britain at all.

Some colonists heeded the conservative pamphleteers' warnings. About one-fifth of the white American population remained loyal to

| *Loyalists, patriots, and neutrals* |

Great Britain, actively opposing independence. With notable exceptions, most people of the following types became loyalists: British-appointed government officials; merchants whose trade depended on imperial connections; Anglican clergy everywhere and lay Anglicans in the North; former British soldiers; non-English ethnic minorities, especially Scots; tenant farmers; members of persecuted religious sects; and many of the backcountry southerners who had rebelled against eastern rule in the 1760s and early 1770s. All these people had one thing in common: the patriot leaders were their long-standing enemies, though for different reasons. Local and provincial disputes thus helped to determine which side a person chose in the imperial conflict.

The active patriots, who accounted for about two-fifths of the population, came chiefly from the groups that had dominated colonial society, either numerically or politically. Among them were yeoman farmers, members of dominant Protestant sects (both Old and New Lights), Chesapeake gentry, merchants dealing mainly in American commodities, city artisans, elected officeholders, and people of English descent. Wives usually but not always adopted their husbands' political beliefs.

There remained the two-fifths of the population that tried to avoid taking sides. Among them were pacifist Quakers and those colonists who simply wanted to be left alone. In the southern backcountry, many Scotch-Irish took a neutral position, for they had grievances against both the British and the patriot gentry.

To American patriots there could be no neutrals or conscientious objectors. Those not with them were against them. In the winter of 1775–1776, the Continental Congress recommended to the states that all "disaffected" or "inimical" persons be disarmed and arrested. As a result of actions by the states, oaths of allegiance became common, banishment or extra taxes penalized those refusing to take loyalty oaths, and after 1778 the property of banished loyalists was confiscated. Perhaps 100,000 white loyalists were forced into exile, but they were not the only Americans to concern the patriots.

In late 1774 and early 1775 news of slave conspiracies surfaced in different parts of the colonies. All shared a common element: a plan to as-

| *Slave conspiracies* |

sist the British in return for freedom. A group of black Bostonians petitioned General Thomas Gage, commander of the troops there, promising to fight for the redcoats if he would liberate them. The governor of Maryland authorized the issuance of extra guns to militiamen in four counties where slave uprisings were expected. The most serious incident occurred during the summer of 1775 in Charleston, where Thomas Jeremiah, a free black harbor pilot, was brutally executed after being convicted of attempting to foment a slave revolt.

Connecticut imprisoned many of its loyalists in notorious Newgate prison, a converted copper mine. The offenders were housed in caverns below the large structure left of center. Some prominent loyalists (like Benjamin Franklin's son William, the last royal governor of New Jersey) were held in private homes.   The Connecticut Historical Society.

Concern over the slave population affected the level of revolutionary sentiment in the colonies. In the North, where whites greatly outnumbered blacks, revolutionary fervor was at its height. But in South Carolina, which was over 60 percent black, and Georgia, where the racial balance was nearly even, whites were noticeably less enthusiastic about resistance. Georgia, in fact, sent no delegates to the First Continental Congress, and reminded its representatives at the Second Continental Congress to consider its circumstances, "with our blacks and tories within us," when voting on the question of independence.

The whites' worst fears were realized in November 1775, when Lord Dunmore, the governor of Virginia, offered to free any slaves and indentured servants who would leave their patriot masters to join the British forces. Dunmore hoped to use black manpower in his fight against the revolutionaries, and to disrupt the economy by depriving white Americans of their labor force. But fewer blacks than expected rallied to the British standard in 1775 and 1776 (there were at most two thousand).

The patriots even turned rumors of slave uprisings to their own advantage. South Carolinians were told that whites needed the Continental Association to protect them from blacks. This appeal to white unity apparently brought wavering Carolinians into the patriot camp.

A similar factor—the threat of Indian attacks—helped to persuade some reluctant westerners to support the struggle against Great Britain. In the years since the Proclamation of 1763, British officials had won the trust and respect of the interior tribes by attempting to protect them from land-hungry whites. In 1768, the British-appointed superintendents of Indian affairs, John Stuart in the South and Sir William Johnson in the North, negotiated two treaties—signed at Hard Labor Creek, South Carolina, and Fort Stanwix, New York—with the tribes. The treaties supposedly established permanent borders for the colonies. But just a few years later, in the treaties of Lochaber (1770) and Augusta (1773), the British pushed the southern boundary even farther west to accommodate the demands of whites in western Georgia and the "overmountain" region known as Kentucky.

Indian neutrality

By the time of the Revolution, the Indians were impatient with the Americans' aggressive pressure on their lands. They also resented the whites' unwillingness to prosecute frontiersmen who wantonly killed innocent natives. In combination with the tribes' confidence in Stuart and Johnson, these grievances predisposed most Indians toward an alliance with the British. Even so, the British hesitated to make full and immediate use of their potential Indian allies. The superintendents were well aware that the tribes might prove a liability, since their aims and style of fighting were not necessarily compatible with those of the British. Accordingly, the superintendents sought only the neutrality of the tribes.

The patriots also sought the Indians' neutrality. In 1775 the Second Continental Congress sent a general message to the tribes describing the war as "a family quarrel between us and Old England" and requesting that they "not join on either side." The Overhill Cherokees, led by Chief Dragging Canoe, nevertheless decided that the whites' "family quarrel" would allow them to settle some old scores. They attacked white settlements along the western borders of the Carolinas and Virginia in the summer of 1776. But partly because the Creeks, the other major southern tribe, failed to aid them, the Cherokees were unable to drive the whites from their land. Instead, after a defeat at the hands of the colonial militia, they withdrew to the west and ceded more of their territories to the whites.

Thus, although the patriots could never completely ignore the threats posed by loyalists, blacks, neutrals, and Indians, only rarely did fear of these groups seriously hamper the revolutionary movement. Indeed, the practical impossibility of a large-scale slave revolt, coupled with tribal feuds and the patriots' successful campaign to disarm and neutralize loyalists, ensured that the revolutionaries would remain firmly in control as they fought for independence.

War begins

On January 27, 1775, the secretary of state for America, Lord Dartmouth, addressed a fateful letter to General Thomas Gage. Expressing his belief that American resistance was nothing more than the response of a "rude rabble without plan," Dartmouth ordered Gage to arrest "the principal actors and abettors in the provincial congress." If such a step were taken swiftly and silently, Dartmouth observed, no bloodshed need occur.

By the time Dartmouth's letter reached Gage on April 14, though, the major patriot leaders had already left Boston. Gage, spurred to action by the letter, decided to send a force to confiscate the provincial military supplies stockpiled at Concord. Bostonians dispatched two messengers, William Dawes and Paul Revere (later joined by a third, Dr. Samuel Prescott), to rouse the countryside. Thus when the British vanguard approached Lexington at dawn on April 19, they found a straggling group of 70 militiamen—approximately half the adult male population of the town—drawn up before them on the town common. The Americans' commander, Captain John Parker, ordered his men to withdraw, realizing that they were too few to halt the redcoat advance. But as they began to disperse, a shot rang out; the British soldiers then fired several volleys. When they stopped, 8 Americans lay dead and another 10 had been wounded. The British moved on to Concord, five miles away.

Battles of Lexington and Concord

At Concord, British troops suffered their first casualties of the war in an attack on the colonials guarding the North Bridge. Before the day ended, thousands of colonial militiamen harassed the British on their march back to Boston. The redcoats suffered 272 casualties (70 dead) and inflicted but 93 casualties on the colonists.

By the evening of April 20, perhaps as many as twenty thousand American militiamen had gathered around Boston. Many of them returned home after a week or two for spring planting, but others remained and dug siege lines around the city. For nearly a year the two armies stared at each other. The only battle occurred on June 17 when the British attacked Breed's Hill. There, in the misnamed Battle of Bunker Hill, the British incurred over 1,000 casualties (228 dead). Elsewhere, in the first eleven months of the war the colonists captured Fort Ticonderoga, with its much needed cannon, and failed in a Canadian campaign. Most significantly, the lull of the first year gave both sides time to regroup, organize, and make plans.

Lord North and his new American secretary, Lord George Germain, made three major assumptions about the war they faced. First, they concluded that patriot forces could not withstand the assaults of trained British regulars. Accordingly,

British strategy

they dispatched to America the largest single force Great Britain had ever assembled anywhere: 370 transport ships carrying 32,000 troops (including thousands of German mercenaries) and tons of supplies, accompanied by 73 naval vessels and 13,000 sailors. Such an extraordinary effort would, they thought, ensure a quick victory. Second, British officials and army officers persisted in comparing this war to wars they had fought successfully in Europe. Thus they adopted a conventional strategy of capturing major American cities. Third, they assumed that a clear-cut military victory would automatically bring about their goal of retaining the colonies' allegiance.

All these assumptions proved false. The British vastly underestimated the Americans' commitment to armed resistance. Defeats on the battlefield did not lead the patriots to abandon their political aims and sue for peace. At one time or another the British captured all major American ports, but with 1,500 miles of coastline their actions did not halt essential commerce. And since less than 5 percent of the population lived in the cities, their loss meant little to the colonists.

Most of all, the British did not at first understand that a military victory would not necessarily bring about a political victory. Securing the colonies permanently would require hundreds of thousands of Americans to return to their original allegiance. The conquest of America was thus a far more complicated task than the defeat of France twelve years earlier. The British needed not only to overpower the patriots, but also to convert them. The British never fully realized that they were not fighting a conventional European war at all, but rather an entirely new kind of conflict: the first modern war of national liberation.

Yet the British at least had a bureaucracy ready to supervise the war effort. The Americans had only the Second Continental Congress, originally intended merely as a brief gathering of colonial representatives to consider the British response to the

Second Continental Congress

Continental Association. Instead, the delegates who convened in Philadelphia on May 10, 1775, found that they had to assume the mantle of intercolonial government. That summer the congress authorized the printing of money with which to purchase necessary goods, modified the Continental Association to allow trade in needed military supplies with friendly European nations, and took steps to strengthen the militia. Most important of all, the congress created the Continental Army and appointed its generals.

Until the congress met, the Massachusetts provincial congress had taken responsibility for organizing the massive army of militia encamped at Boston. Because the cost of maintaining the army was too great, Massachusetts asked the Continental Congress to assume control of the army. Also, as the war was thus far largely a northern affair, congress, to ensure unity, selected a non–New Englander, George Washington of Virginia, to be the commander-in-chief.

Washington was no fiery radical, nor was he a reflective political thinker. He had not played a prominent role in the prerevolutionary agitation, but his devotion to the American cause was unquestioned. He was dignified, conservative, respectable, and a man of unimpeachable integrity. Though unmistakably an aristocrat, Washington was unswervingly committed to representative government. Moreover, he both looked and acted like a leader. Other patriots praised his judgment, steadiness, and discretion, and even a loyalist admitted that Washington could "atone for many demerits by the extraordinary coolness and caution which distinguish his character."

George Washington: his traits

Washington needed all the coolness and caution he could muster when he took command of the army outside Boston in July 1775. It took him months to impose hierarchy and discipline on the unruly troops and to bring order to the supply system. But by March 1776, when the arrival of cannon from Ticonderoga enabled him at last to put direct pressure on the redcoats in the city, the army was prepared to act. As it happened, an assault on Boston proved unnecessary.

Sir William Howe, who had replaced Gage as the British commander-in-chief, wanted to move his troops to a more central location, New York City. The patriots' bombardment of Boston early in the month decided the matter. On March 17, the British and more than a thousand of their loyalist allies abandoned Boston forever.

That spring of 1776, as the British fleet left Boston for the temporary haven of Halifax, Nova Scotia, the colonies were moving inexorably toward the unthinkable—a declaration of independence. One man, however, in January 1776 not only thought the unthinkable but advocated it.

Thomas Paine's *Common Sense* exploded on the American scene like a bombshell. Within three months of publication, it sold 120,000 copies. The author, a radical English printer who had lived in America only since 1774, called stridently and stirringly for independence. More than that: Paine rejected the notion that a balance of monarchy, aristocracy, and democracy was necessary to preserve freedom and advocated the establishment of a republic. Instead of acknowledging the benefits of a connection with the mother country, Paine insisted that Britain had exploited the colonies unmercifully. In place of the frequent assertion that an independent America would be weak and divided, he substituted an unlimited confidence in America's strength when freed from European control.

Thomas Paine's Common Sense

There is no way of knowing how many people were converted to the cause of independence by reading *Common Sense*. But by late spring 1776 independence had clearly become inevitable. On May 10, the Second Continental Congress formally recommended that individual colonies "adopt such governments as shall, in the opinion of the representatives of the people, best conduce to the happiness and safety of their constituents in particular, and America in general." From that source flowed the first state constitutions.

Then on June 7 came the confirmation of the

George Washington (1732–1799), painted in his uniform as commander-in-chief. His stalwart bearing, so vividly conveyed in this portrait, was one of his prime assets as a leader. Washington and Lee University, Washington-Curtis-Lee Collection.

movement toward independence. Richard Henry Lee of Virginia, seconded by John Adams of Massachusetts, introduced the crucial resolution: "that these United Colonies are, and of right ought to be, free and independent States, that they are absolved of all allegiance to the British Crown, and that all political connection between them and the State of Great Britain is, and ought to be, totally dissolved." The congress debated the resolution and named a committee composed of Thomas Jefferson,

Declaration of Independence

John Adams, Benjamin Franklin, Robert R. Livingston of New York, and Roger Sherman of Connecticut to draft a declaration of independence. The committee in turn assigned primary responsibility for writing the declaration to Jefferson, a Virginia lawyer widely read in history and political theory and with an acknowledged talent for felicitous expression.

The draft of the declaration was laid before congress on June 28. The delegates officially voted for independence four days later, then debated the wording of the declaration for two more days, adopting it with some changes on July 4. Since Americans had long since ceased to see themselves as legitimate subjects of Parliament, the Declaration of Independence concentrated on George III. But the declaration's chief importance did not lie in its lengthy catalogue of grievances against the king. It lay instead in the ringing statements of principle that have served ever since as the ideal to which Americans adhere, nominally at least.

> We hold these truths to be self evident, that all men are created equal; that they are endowed by their creator with certain inalienable rights; that among these are life, liberty and the pursuit of happiness; that, to secure these rights, governments are instituted among men, deriving their just powers from the consent of the governed, that whenever any form of government becomes destructive of these ends, it is the right of the people to alter or abolish it, and to institute new government.

These phrases have echoed down through American history like no others.

The delegates in Philadelphia who voted to accept the Declaration of Independence did not have the advantage of our two hundred years of hindsight. When they adopted the declaration, they risked their necks; they were unequivocally committing treason against the crown. Thus when they concluded the declaration with the assertion that they "mutually pledge[d] to each other our lives, our fortunes, and our sacred honor," they spoke no less than the truth. The real struggle still lay before them.

The long struggle in the North

On July 2, 1776, the first of Sir William Howe's troops from Halifax landed on Staten Island. But Howe delayed his attack on New York City until mid-August, when additional troops arrived from England. This delay allowed Washington and his force of 17,000 men to move south and defend the city.

Washington's problem was as simple as the geography of the region was complex. To protect the city adequately, he would have to divide his forces among Long Island, Manhattan Island, and the mainland. But the British fleet under Admiral Lord Richard Howe, Sir William's brother, controlled the harbors and rivers that separated the American forces. The patriots thus constantly courted catastrophe, for swift action by the British navy could cut off the possibility of retreat and perhaps even communications. Washington could not afford to surrender New York without a fight, however. Both the strategic location of the city and the number of loyalist sympathizers in the area required him to make a show of force. Only a willingness to fight would persuade waverers to join the patriot cause.

Washington's defense of the city would be characterized by the mistakes of an inexperienced commander and an untested army. After losing the first battle on Brooklyn Heights, he fell back to Manhattan and retreated north up the island into Westchester. But 3,000 men he left behind on the west shore of Manhattan at Fort Washington had to surrender to Howe. In the end, though, the Howe brothers' failure to move quickly prevented a decisive defeat of the Americans. Although Washington's army had been seriously reduced, its core remained. Through November and December, Washington led his men in a retreat across New Jersey. Howe followed at a leisurely pace, setting up a string of outposts manned mostly by Hessian mercenaries. After Washington crossed the Delaware River into Pennsylvania, the British commander turned back and settled into comfortable winter quarters in New York City.

The British now controlled most of New Jersey. Hundreds of Americans accepted the pardons offered by the Howes. The occupying troops met with little opposition, and the revolutionary cause appeared to be in disarray.

Battle for New York City

Thomas Paine's new pamphlet, *The Crisis,* declared, "These are the times that try men's souls."

In the aftermath of battle, as at its height, the British generals let their advantage slip away. The redcoats stationed in New Jersey went on a rampage of rape and plunder. Because loyalists and patriots were indistinguishable to the British and Hessian troops, families on both sides suffered equally. Nothing rallied the doubtful to the patriot cause more than the wanton murder of innocent civilians and the epidemic of rapes in New Jersey. Sixteen girls from Hopewell were held captive for days in the British camp and repeatedly molested; a thirteen-year-old was raped by six soldiers; another thirteen-year-old, two of her friends, and her aunt were similarly attacked.

The soldiers' marauding alienated potentially loyal New Jerseyites and Pennsylvanians whose allegiance the British could ill afford to lose. It also spurred Washington's determination to strike back. With enlistments of many troops scheduled to expire on December 31, Washington decided to strike quickly. He first struck the Hessian encampment at Trenton on December 26. A few days later he attacked Princeton. With these two victories the 1776 campaign ended.

Campaign of 1776

The campaign of 1776 established patterns that were to persist throughout much of the war. British forces, although numerically superior to the Americans, engaged in ponderous maneuvering, lacked familiarity with the terrain, and antagonized the populace. The British thus offset their manpower advantage. Washington always seemed to lack regular troops, but during critical moments he could usually depend on the militia. These men would not fight far from home and would leave the army to plant and harvest crops, but they were invaluable to Washington.

As the war dragged on, the Continental Army and the militia took on decidedly different characters. State militias attracted farmers with families, who preferred short-term duty, while members of the Continental Army tended to be young and single. Only they were willing to serve extended periods of time. In the North recruiters augmented white recruits with blacks, and many of the nearly 5,000 blacks who served in the army secured their freedom as a result. Female camp followers also rendered service to the army. These women (usually the wives and widows of poor soldiers) worked as cooks, nurses, and launderers for partial rations and low pay. The American army was shapeless and difficult to manage, yet this shapelessness provided an almost unlimited supply of man and woman power.

In 1777, the chief British effort was planned by the flashy "Gentleman Johnny" Burgoyne, a playboy general who had gained the ear of Lord George Germain. Burgoyne convinced Germain that he could lead an invading force of redcoats and Indians down the Hudson River from Canada, cutting off New England from the rest of the states. He proposed to rendezvous near Albany with a similar force that would move east from Niagara along the Mohawk River valley. The combined force would then presumably link up with that of Sir William Howe in New York City.

That Burgoyne's scheme would give "Gentleman Johnny" all the glory and relegate Howe to a supporting role did not escape Howe's notice. In fact, while Burgoyne was plotting in London, Howe was laying his own plans to take Philadelphia. Howe achieved his objective in an inexplicable fashion. Instead of marching his forces from New York, he waited for months and then transported them by sea. The six-week voyage brought him only forty miles closer to Philadelphia, debilitated his men, depleted his supplies, and gave Washington time to prepare a defense of the city. Washington encountered the enemy at Brandywine Creek and at Germantown. He lost both battles but the Americans handled themselves well. By the time Howe took Philadelphia in late September, the 1777 campaign was virtually over (see map, page 78).

Howe takes Philadelphia

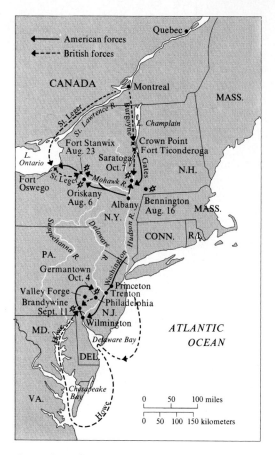

Campaign of 1777

To the north Burgoyne and his men had set out from Montreal in mid-June. After easily tak-

Burgoyne's campaign in New York

ing Fort Ticonderoga, he began having trouble on an overland march. Because of his clumsy artillery carriages and baggage wagons, Burgoyne took twenty-four days to travel twenty-three miles. Moreover, the 800 German mercenaries he sent into Vermont on a foraging expedition were soundly defeated at Bennington. Burgoyne's failure to recognize the seriousness of his situation cost the British dearly. He continued toward Albany and was surrounded by the Americans. On October 17, 1777, he surrendered 6,000 men to General Horatio Gates.

Long before, the 1,400 redcoats and Indians marching along the Mohawk River toward Albany had also been turned back. The troops, under the command of Colonel Barry St. Leger, fought the patriots at Oriskany on August 6. The British claimed victory in the battle, but they and their Indian allies lost their taste for further fighting.

The battle of Oriskany marked the division of the Iroquois Confederacy. In 1776 the Six Na-

Crumbling of the Iroquois Confederacy

tions had formally pledged to remain neutral in the Anglo-American struggle. But two influential Mohawk leaders, Joseph and Mary Brant, worked tirelessly to persuade their fellow Iroquois to join the British. Mary Brant, a powerful tribal matron in her own right, was also the widow (in fact if not in law) of the respected Indian superintendent Sir William Johnson. Her younger brother Joseph, a renowned warrior, was convinced that the Six Nations should ally themselves with the British to prevent further encroachment on their lands. The Brants won over to the British the Senecas, Cayugas, and Mohawks. But the Oneidas and Tuscaroras chose the Americans. At Oriskany, the three-hundred-year league of friendship among the Iroquois was torn apart, as confederation warriors fought on both sides.

For the Indians, Oriskany was the most significant battle of the northern campaign; for the whites, it was Saratoga. Burgoyne's surrender prompted Lord North to authorize a peace commission to offer the Americans everything they had requested in 1774—in effect, a return to the imperial system of 1763. It was, of course, far too late for that: The patriots rejected the overture and the peace commission sailed back to England empty-handed in mid-1778.

Most important of all, the American victory at Saratoga drew France into the war. Ever since 1763, the French had been seeking ways to

French entry into the war

avenge their defeat in the Seven Years' War, and the American Revolution was the perfect opportunity to do so. King Louis XVI and his ministers had covertly aided the

The Mohawk chief Joseph Brant (1742–1807), painted in London in 1786 by Gilbert Stuart. New York State Historical Association, Cooperstown.

revolutionaries with money and supplies since 1776, and American emissaries in France (notably the clever Benjamin Franklin) had worked ceaselessly to strengthen those ties. Not until Saratoga, though, did France agree to a formal alliance with the patriots. After 1778, the British could no longer focus their attention on the American mainland alone, for they had to fight the French in the West Indies and elsewhere. Spain's entry into the war in 1779 as an ally of France (but not the United States) further mag-

nified Britain's problems. In the last years of the war, French assistance was to prove vital to the Americans.

The long struggle in the South

In the aftermath of the Saratoga disaster, Lord George Germain and the military officials in London reassessed their strategy. Maneuvering in the North had done them little good; perhaps shifting the field of battle southward would bring success. The new British commander-in-chief, Sir Henry Clinton, became convinced that a southern strategy would work when Savannah and Augusta fell easily into British hands. Consequently, in late 1779, he sailed toward Charleston with an invasion force of 8,500 men.

The Americans worked hard to bolster Charleston's defenses, but on May 12, 1780,

| Fall of Charleston | General Benjamin Lincoln surrendered the city and the entire southern army of |

5,500 troops. Clinton's forces then spread throughout South Carolina. As South Carolinians professed their loyalty to the crown, Clinton organized loyalist regiments in hopes of securing the countryside.

Yet the British triumph was less complete and secure than it appeared. The widely dispersed British armies involved in the southern campaign depended on the navy to communicate with one another. But French naval power could possibly disrupt British communications and threaten the entire southern enterprise. The continuing presence of patriot guerrilla bands in the state also created problems for the crown. Finally, the loss of Charleston failed to dishearten the patriots; instead it spurred them to greater exertions.

Still the war went badly for the Americans. In August, 1780 the reorganized southern army under Horatio Gates was defeated by Lord Cornwallis at Camden, South Carolina. Moreover, the southern economy was disrupted when thousands of blacks joined the British. Many blacks served the British as scouts, guides, and laborers.

After the defeat at Camden, Washington placed General Nathanael Greene in charge of the southern campaign. Greene adopted a plan calling for conciliation and stability. Loyalists were given the chance to secure pardons, and

troops were ordered not to loot their property.

Greene also took a conciliatory approach to the southern Indians, a strategy dictated by his need for troops. When he took command, the southern army had but 1,600 regulars. Greene needed volunteers, and he could not secure them if the people's homes had to be defended against Indian attacks. Thus Greene negotiated treaties with the tribes. By the war's end only the Creeks remained allied with the redcoats.

Even before Greene took command of the southern army in December 1780, the tide had begun to turn. At King's Mountain in October, a force of "overmountain men" from the settlements west of the Appalachians had defeated a large party of redcoats and loyalists. Then in January 1781 Greene's trusted aide, Brigadier General Daniel Morgan, brilliantly defeated the crack British regiment Tarleton's Legion at Cowpens, near the border between North and South Carolina. And in March Greene engaged the main body of British troops at Guilford Court House, North Carolina. Though the Americans lost, Lord Cornwallis's force was largely destroyed.

Then Cornwallis, in violation of his orders not to leave South Carolina unless it was safely in British hands, moved north into Virginia. With a new army of 7,200 men, Cornwallis withdrew to the tip of the peninsula between the York and James rivers. There he fortified Yorktown and in effect waited for the end. Seiz-

| Surrender at Yorktown | ing the opportunity, Washington quickly moved over 7,000 troops south from |

New York City. When a French fleet under the Comte de Grasse arrived from the West Indies to cut the Britons' vital sea supply line, Cornwallis was trapped. On October 19, 1781, Cornwallis surrendered to the combined American and French forces while his military band played "The World Turned Upside Down."

When news of the surrender reached England, Lord North's ministry fell. Parliament voted to cease offensive operations in America and authorized peace negotiations. But guerrilla warfare between patriots and loyalists continued to ravage the Carolinas and Georgia for more than a year, and in the North vicious retaliatory raids by Indians and whites kept the frontier aflame.

The fighting finally ended when Americans and Britons learned of the signing of a preliminary peace treaty at Paris in November 1782. | Treaty of Paris | The American negotiators— Benjamin Franklin, John Jay, and John Adams—ignored their instructions to be guided by France and instead struck a separate agreement with Great Britain. Their instincts were sound: the French government was more an enemy to Britain than a friend to the United States. The new British ministry, headed by Lord Shelburne, was weary of war and made numerous concessions.

Under the treaty, finalized on September 3, 1783, the Americans were granted unconditional independence and unlimited fishing rights off Newfoundland. The boundaries of the new nation were generous: to the north, approximately the current boundary with Canada; to the south, the thirty-first parallel; to the west, the Mississippi River. The British conveniently overlooked the fact that their Indian allies, particularly the Iroquois and the Creeks, had joined them precisely because of their promise to protect Indian lands from white encroachment. Thus the tribes found themselves and their interests sacrificed to European power politics. Loyalists were also poorly served by the British negotiators. In effect the treaty legalized the wartime confiscation of loyalist property, forcing them into permanent exile.

The long war finally over, the victorious Americans could look back on their achievement with satisfaction and awe. In 1775, with an inexperienced ragtag army, they had taken on the greatest military power in the world—and eight years later they had won. They had accomplished their goal more through persistence and commitment than through brilliance on the bat-

Important events

1768	Treaty of Hard Labor
	Treaty of Fort Stanwix
1770	Treaty of Lochaber
1773	Treaty of Augusta
1774	First Continental Congress
	Continental Association; committees of observation formed
1775	Battles of Lexington and Concord
	Battle of Bunker Hill
	Lord Dunmore's Proclamation
	Second Continental Congress
1776	Thomas Paine, *Common Sense*
	British evacuate Boston
	Declaration of Independence
	New York campaign
	Battle of Trenton
	Cherokee War
1777	Battle of Princeton
	British take Philadelphia
	Battle of Oriskany
	Burgoyne surrenders at Saratoga
1778	British Peace Commission
	French alliance
	British take Savannah
1780	British take Charleston
	Battle of Camden
	Battle of King's Mountain
1781	Battle of Guilford Court House
	Cornwallis surrenders at Yorktown
1782	North's ministry falls
	Preliminary peace treaty
1783	Treaty of Paris

tlefield. Actual victories had been few, but their army had always survived defeat and stand-offs to fight again. Ultimately, the Americans had simply worn their enemy down.

Suggestions for further reading

ESSAY COLLECTIONS Stephen G. Kurtz and James H. Hutson, eds., *Essays on the American Revolution* (1973); Library of Congress, *Symposia on the American Revolution,* 5 vols. (1972–1976); Edmund S. Morgan, *The Challenge of the American Revolution* (1976); *William and Mary Quarterly,* 3rd ser., 33, No. 3 (July 1976), *The American Revolution;* Alfred Young, ed., *The American Revolution: Explorations in the History of American Radicalism* (1976).

MILITARY John Richard Alden, *The American Revolution 1775–1783* (1964); Don Higginbotham, *The War of American Independence: Military Attitudes, Policies, and Practice, 1763–1789* (1971); Piers Mackesy, *The War for America, 1775–1783* (1964); Charles Royster, *A Revolutionary People at War: The Continental Army and American Character, 1775–1783* (1980); John Shy, *A People Numerous & Armed: Reflections on the Military Struggle for American Independence* (1976); Marshall Smelser, *The Winning of Independence* (1972).

LOCAL AND REGIONAL Jeffrey Crow and Larry Tise, eds., *The Southern Experience in the American Revolution* (1978); Robert A. Gross, *The Minutemen and Their World* (1976).

INDIANS AND BLACKS Barbara Graymont, *The Iroquois in the American Revolution* (1972); Duncan J. MacLeod, *Slavery, Race, and the American Revolution* (1974); James H. O'Donnell, III, *Southern Indians in the American Revolution* (1973); Benjamin Quarles, *The Negro in the American Revolution* (1961); Anthony F.C. Wallace, *The Death and Rebirth of the Seneca* (1969).

LOYALISTS Bernard Bailyn, *The Ordeal of Thomas Hutchinson* (1974); Robert McCluer Calhoon, *The Loyalists in Revolutionary America 1760–1781* (1973); William H. Nelson, *The American Tory* (1961); Mary Beth Norton, *The British-Americans: The Loyalist Exiles in England, 1774–1789* (1972); Paul H. Smith, *Loyalists and Redcoats: A Study in British Revolutionary Policy* (1964).

WOMEN Linda Grant DePauw and Conover Hunt, *"Remember the Ladies": Women in America 1750–1815* (1976); Linda K. Kerber, *Women of the Republic: Intellect & Ideology in Revolutionary America* (1980); Mary Beth Norton, *Liberty's Daughters: The Revolutionary Experience of American Women, 1750–1800* (1980).

DIPLOMACY Richard B. Morris, *The Peacemakers: The Great Powers and American Independence* (1965); Richard W. Van Alstyne, *Empire and Independence: The International History of the American Revolution* (1965).

PATRIOT LEADERS Fawn M. Brodie, *Thomas Jefferson: An Intimate History* (1974); Verner W. Crane, *Benjamin Franklin and a Rising People* (1954); Marcus Cunliffe, *George Washington: Man and Monument* (1958); Eric Foner, *Tom Paine and Revolutionary America* (1976); Peter Shaw, *The Character of John Adams* (1976).

6

FORGING A
NATIONAL REPUBLIC,
1776–1789

"In the new Code of Laws which I suppose it will be necessary for you to make I desire you would Remember the Ladies," Abigail Adams wrote her congressman husband John on March 31, 1776. "Remember all Men would be tyrants if they could," she continued. "If perticuliar care and attention is not paid to the Laidies we are determined to foment a Rebelion, and will not hold ourselves bound by any Laws in which we have no voice, or Representation."

These famous words were, as John Adams recognized, a sign of the impact the Revolution and its ideology had had on American society. The colonists had ventured into revolution to protect their rights as English people, but gradually they had developed broader definitions of these rights.

During and after the war, propertyless men began to claim that they too should be allowed to vote. Others questioned the institution of slavery. Still others asked why one American should be expected to defer to the judgment of another, no matter how wealthy or well educated. Members of the dissenting religious sects, who had been legally discriminated against in the seven colonies with established (or state-supported) churches, successfully pressed their case for the liberty of conscience. And once provincial veterans returned home with a sense of national pride.

In redefining their politics and society be-

tween 1775, when the war began, and 1787, when the new Constitution was drafted, Americans drew their ideas from the ideology of resistance and from their own experiences. They designed state and national governments incorporating the features they had decided would best protect their rights: weak executives and powerful legislatures, separation of powers among branches of government, and division of sovereignty between national and state governments. Over time they modified their ideas somewhat, but these basic elements remained intact. The Articles of Confederation and the Constitution, which historians have often seen as reflecting opposing political philosophies (the "democratic" Articles versus the "aristocratic" Constitution), should instead be viewed as separate and successive attempts to solve the same problems. Both represented Americans' efforts to apply the lessons of the Revolution to their form of government.

Learning the lessons of the Revolution

Abigail Adams seems an unlikely revolutionary. In 1776 she was thirty-one years old, daughter of a minister, wife of a lawyer, and mother of four growing children. Throughout her life she emphasized the "Relative Duties" of her roles as wife, mother, and mistress of a household. She believed that each sex had its distinct role to fulfill, and that ladies like herself should avoid the rough-and-tumble world of politics and public affairs. But she had the intelligence to perceive the incongruities in her society and the initiative to point them out.

Yet not until the American Revolution began did Abigail Adams think to question the assumptions that had previously defined her world. Her husband, like many other leaders of the Revolution, was away from home for long periods of time. In their absence their wives, who had previously handled only the "indoor affairs" of the household, had to shoulder the responsibility for "outdoor affairs" as well.

Both Adamses took great pride in Abigail's developing skills as a "farmeress." Abigail Adams, like her female contemporaries, stopped calling the farm "yours" in letters to her husband, and began referring to it as "ours." (This simple change of pronoun spoke volumes.) Both men and women realized that female patriots had made a vital contribution to winning the war through their work at home. Thus, in the years after the Revolution, Americans began to develop new ideas about the role women should play in a republican society.

Although most Americans, including Abigail Adams, did not believe that women should vote, a few women thought differently. In New Jersey the state constitution of 1776 had defined voters as "all free inhabitants" who met certain property qualifications. The vote was thus given to property-holding white spinsters and widows, as well as free black men. In the 1780s and 1790s women successfully claimed the right to vote in New Jersey's local and congressional elections. They continued to exercise that right until 1807, when women and blacks were disfranchised by the state legislature on the grounds that their votes could be easily manipulated.

Such dramatic episodes were unusual. On the whole the re-evaluation of women's position had its greatest impact on private life. For instance, the traditional colonial view of marriage had stressed the subordination of wife to husband. But in 1790 a female "Matrimonial Republican" asserted that "marriage ought never to be considered as a contract between a superior and an inferior. . . . The obedience between man and wife is, or ought to be mutual." This new understanding of the marital relationship seems to have contributed to a rising divorce rate after the war. Dissatisfied wives proved less willing to remain in unhappy marriages than they had been previously.

Furthermore, though the father had previously been seen as the most influential parent, the republican decades witnessed an ever-increasing emphasis on the importance of mothers. A list of "Maxims for Republics" first published in 1779 and reprinted in 1788 declared that "it is of the utmost importance, that the women should be well instructed in the principles of liberty in a republic. Some of the first patriots of ancient times, were formed by their mothers." In 1790 one woman even argued publicly for female superiority, resting her claim on woman's maternal role.

Other Americans did not go that far. They still viewed woman's role in traditional terms. Like Abigail Adams, they accepted the notion of equality, but within the context of men's and women's separate spheres. Whereas their forebears had seen women as inferior and subordinate to men, members of the revolutionary generation regarded the sexes and their roles as more nearly equal in importance. However, equality did not mean sameness.

To white men, too, the Revolution brought change. It is estimated that 40 percent of adult white male patriots served six months or more in the Revolutionary armies. In the ranks, American men learned four new political lessons. The first was nationalism. The experience

Chapter 6: Forging a national republic, 1776–1789

In the mid-1780s Abigail Adams (1744–1818) and her husband John (1735–1826) sat for these portraits in London, where they had been reunited after a five-year wartime separation. John Adams was then American ambassador to Great Britain. Left, Boston Athenaeum. Right, New York State Historical Association, Cooperstown.

| Beginnings of nationalism | of fighting, sacrificing, and working together for a common goal had given men from different regions a new notion of where their loyalties lay. Soldiers' letters reveal their emerging nationalism. In March 1776 a Massachusetts shoemaker in the Continental Army told his wife that "I am willing to serve my contery in the Best way & manner that I am Capeble of." A surgeon assigned to Valley Forge during the difficult winter of 1777 and 1778 observed that "nothing tends to the establishment of the firmest Friendship like Mutual Sufferings." When such men returned to their homes after the war, they retained their patriotism and pride in their accomplishments. They had also acquired a knowledge of other parts of the country that few earlier Americans had possessed.

The second and third lessons concerned the theory and practice of republicanism. As John Dickinson later recalled, "there was no question concerning forms of Government. . . . We knew that the people of this country must unite themselves under some form of Government and that this could be no other than the Republican form." To Dickinson and other Americans, a republican government had to rest directly and solely on the consent of the people. Members of the revolutionary generation therefore devoted much time and attention to molding state governments into proper republican shapes. They also attempted to order their lives in accordance with republican principles.

Nowhere was this more true than in the ranks of the Revolutionary army and navy, where enlisted men repeatedly revealed their commitment to the concept of government by

| **Republican soldiers** | mutual consent. When a thousand Pennsylvania soldiers mutinied at the Ameri- |

can army's main winter encampment at Morristown, New Jersey, on January 2, 1781, their chief complaint was not poor food and clothing but that their rights had been violated. They had enlisted for three years, they argued, and their term of service was up; Pennsylvania contended that they had signed on for the duration of the war. The disgruntled soldiers chose a proper republican solution to their problem, leaving camp peacefully en masse to lay their case before Pennsylvania's civilian leaders. The military authorities agreed to a compromise that discharged most of the men.

Another republican lesson soldiers learned had to do with status and its prerequisites. Before the war, only men of distinguished social and economic standing had held political or military office in the colonies. But the unwieldy Revolutionary army required numerous officers (perhaps 15,000 to 20,000 in all). Consequently, men with no pretenses to gentlemanly status achieved posts of prestige and responsibility. At the same time, close contact with genteel officers gave many common soldiers a more realistic view of their betters. Privates who saw inexperienced officers make mistakes that cost both battles and men became less inclined to defer automatically to the gentry's judgment.

The fourth lesson of the Revolution was less heartening. In the heady days of 1775 and early 1776, the patriots had been convinced of their invincibility and of the willingness of the people to make necessary wartime sacrifices. But as the war dragged on and patriotic fervor subsided, the men serving their country grew bitter. Soldiers were often underfed and underclothed, short of guns and ammunition, and unpaid—all because state legislatures failed to support the war with adequate appropriations and because war profiteers sold the army shoddy merchandise and spoiled food. Thus once-optimistic patriots learned that many Americans were unwilling to sacrifice personal gain for public good, and that

it would be unwise to put too much confidence in their new governments.

Ironies of the Revolution

For white Americans, male and female, the war did more than change the way they thought about themselves. It also exposed them to one of the primary contradictions in their society. Just as Abigail Adams pointed out to her husband his failure to apply revolutionary doctrines to the status of women, both blacks and whites recognized the irony of slaveholding Americans claiming they wanted to prevent Britain from enslaving them.

As early as 1764, James Otis, Jr., had identified the basic problem in his pamphlet *The Rights of the British Colonies Asserted and Proved.* If according to natural law all people were born free and equal, that meant *all* humankind, black and white. "Does it follow that 'tis right to enslave a man because he is black?" Otis asked. And in 1773 Benjamin Rush, a Philadelphia doctor, warned that "the plant of liberty is of so tender a nature that it cannot thrive long in the neighborhood of slavery."

Blacks themselves were quick to recognize the implications of revolutionary ideology. In 1779 a group of slaves from Portsmouth, New Hampshire, asked the state legislature "from what authority [our masters] assume to dispose of our lives, freedom and property" and pleaded "that the name of slave may not more be heard in a land gloriously contending for the sweets of freedom." That same year several black residents of Fairfield, Connecticut, petitioned the legislature for their freedom.

Both legislatures responded negatively. But the postwar years did witness the gradual abolition of slavery in the North. Massachusetts

| **Gradual emancipation** | courts decided in the 1780s that the clause in the state constitution declaring that |

"all men are born free and equal, and have certain natural, essential, and unalienable rights" had abolished slavery in the state. Pennsylvania passed an abolition law in 1780; four years later Rhode Island and Connecticut provided for gradual emancipation, followed by New York (1799) and New Jersey (1804).

In the South the pattern differed. Antislavery impulses prompted the state legislatures of Virginia (1782), Delaware (1787), and Maryland (1790 and 1796) to pass laws allowing masters to free their slaves without legal restrictions. But South Carolina and Georgia never considered adopting such acts, and North Carolina decided to insist that all manumissions—emancipations of individual slaves—be approved by county courts. None of the southern states came close to adopting general emancipation laws.

Thus revolutionary ideology had limited impact on the well-entrenched economic interests of large slaveholders. Only in the North, where there were few slaves and where little money was invested in human capital, could state legislatures vote to abolish slavery with relative ease. Even there, legislators' concern for property rights led them to favor gradual emancipation over immediate abolition.

Despite the slow progress of abolition, the free black population of the United States grew dramatically in the first years after the Revolu-

Growth of the free black population

tion. Before the war there had been few free blacks in America. But wartime disruptions radically changed the size and composition of the free black population. Slaves who had escaped from plantations during the war, others who had served in the American army, and still others who had been emancipated by their owners or by state laws were now free. By 1790 there were nearly 60,000 free people of color in the United States; ten years later they numbered more than 108,000 and represented nearly 11 percent of the total black population. Most of them were concentrated in the states of the upper South.

But the trend toward abolition of slavery was

The Reverend Richard Allen (1760–1831) of Philadelphia, founder of the African Methodist Episcopal Church. Allen was attracted to Methodism because "the Methodists were the first people that brought glad tidings to the colored people." Later elected bishop of the AME Church, he was the first black bishop in the United States. Historical Society of Pennsylvania.

not a trend toward racial equality. Even whites who recognized blacks' right to freedom were unwilling to accept them as equals. Laws discriminated against emancipated blacks as they had against slaves; South Carolina, for example, did not permit free blacks to testify against whites in court. Public schools often refused to educate the children of free black parents. Freedmen found it difficult to purchase property and find good jobs. And white Christians rarely allowed blacks an equal voice in church affairs.

Gradually free blacks developed their own separate institutions, sometimes by choice, sometimes because whites imposed segregation on

Development of black institutions them. In Charleston, mulattoes formed the Brown Fellowship Society, which provided insurance coverage for its members, financed a school for free children, and helped to support black orphans. In 1787 blacks in Philadelphia and Baltimore founded churches that eventually became the African Methodist Episcopal (AME) denomination. AME churches later sponsored schools in a number of cities, and often became cultural centers of the free black community.

For freed blacks, then, the lesson of the Revolution was that freedom from bondage did not necessarily mean freedom from discrimination. If they were to survive and prosper, they would have to rely on their own efforts rather than the good will of their white compatriots.

To American Indians the Revolution meant the end of an independent tribal existence for most of those who lived east of the Mississippi River. The United States assumed that the Treaty of Paris (1783) cleared its title to all land east of the Mississippi except the areas still held by Spain. But recognizing that some sort of land *Encroachment on Indian lands* cession should be obtained from the major tribes, Congress initiated negotiations with both northern and southern Indians. At Fort Stanwix, New York, in 1784, and at Hopewell, South Carolina, in late 1785 and early 1786, American representatives signed treaties of questionable legality with the Iroquois and with Choctaw, Chickasaw, and Cherokee chiefs respectively. The United States took the treaties as final confirmation of its sovereignty over the Indian territories, and authorized white settlers to move onto the land. Whites soon poured over the southern Appalachians, provoking the Creeks—who had not agreed to the Hopewell treaties—to defend their territory by declaring war. Only in 1790, when the Creek chief Alexander McGillivray traveled to New York to negotiate a treaty, did the Creeks finally come to terms with the United States.

In the North, meanwhile, the Iroquois Confederacy was in disarray. The raids Americans launched against their villages in 1779 had forced many tribesmen to flee to Canada. Those who remained soon found that they had little bargaining power. In 1786 they formally repudiated the Fort Stanwix treaty and warned of new attacks on frontier settlements, but both whites and Indians knew the threat was an empty one. By 1790 the once-proud Iroquois Confederacy was confined to a few scattered reservations.

It is one of the crueler ironies of American history that a revolution fought in the name of personal liberty and property rights failed to deliver those benefits to large segments of the population. The loyalists were exiled from their homes and deprived of their property for exercising what could have been seen as their right to dissent. Eastern Indian tribes lost much of their traditional homeland, and most blacks remained slaves. However, the war had caused white men and women to look at their political and social roles in a new light. That development was to influence Americans' efforts to establish new state and national governments during and after the war.

Designing republican governments

About two months after his wife urged him to "Remember the Ladies," John Adams received a letter from a friend requesting advice on drafting the suffrage provisions of a new Massachusetts constitution and proposing that propertyless men be given the vote. It is clear from Adams's reply that he had begun to think seriously about the issues raised by his wife and by the changing circumstances in America. Government must be founded on the consent of the people, Adams observed, but what precisely did that mean? "How then does the right arise in the majority to govern the minority against their will? Whence arises the right of the men to govern the women without their consent?

whence the right of the old to bind the young without theirs?"

In response to his own questions, Adams drew a parallel between disfranchised groups. "Very few men who have no property, have any judgment of their own," he asserted. Therefore, if the franchise was to be broadened to include men without property, "the same reasoning . . . will prove that you ought to admit women and children: for, generally speaking, women and children have as good judgment, and as independent minds, as those who are wholly destitute of property." Thus Adams used the specter of women and children at the polls to argue for maintaining traditional property requirements for voting. Adams and other patriot leaders believed that government had to be based on the consent of the people and that republics were preferable to monarchies and aristocracies. But they still wanted to define the electorate as white male property-holders.

Politically aware Americans believed that republics were especially fragile forms of government that risked chronic instability. They believed that republics could succeed only if a nation were small in size, had a homogeneous population, and had a citizenry willing to sacrifice their own private interests for the good of the whole. In return for sacrifices, though, a republic offered its citizens equality of opportunity. Under such a government, rank would be based on merit rather than inherited wealth and status. Society would be ruled by members of a "natural aristocracy," men of talent who had risen from what might have been humble beginnings to positions of power and privilege. Rank would not be abolished but instead placed on a different footing.

Designing governments that put such precepts into effect proved difficult. On May 10, 1776, the Continental Congress directed the states to devise new republican governments to replace the provincial congresses and committees that had met since 1774. Thus Americans initially concentrated on drafting state constitutions. They immedi-

Drafting of state constitutions

ately faced the problem of defining just what the constitution was. The British constitution could not serve as a model because it was an unwritten mixture of law and custom; Americans wanted tangible documents specifying the fundamental structures of government. They also wanted to make their documents special. Thus they began to call conventions for the sole purpose of drafting constitutions. The states sought direct authorization from the people–the theoretical sovereigns in a republic–before establishing new governments. After the new constitutions had been drawn up, delegates submitted them to the people for ratification.

Those who wrote the state constitutions concerned themselves primarily with outlining the distribution of and limitations on governmental power. As colonists, Americans had learned to fear the power of the governor–in most cases the appointed agent of the king or the proprietor–and to trust the legislature. Accordingly, the first state constitutions typically provided for the governor to be elected annually (usually by the legislature), limited the number of terms any one governor could serve, and gave him little independent authority. At the same time the constitutions expanded the powers of the legislature. They redrew the lines of electoral districts to reflect population patterns more accurately and increased the number of members in both the upper and lower houses. Finally, most states lowered property qualifications for voting. As a result the legislatures came to include some men who before the war would not even have been eligible to vote. Thus the revolutionary era witnessed the first deliberate attempt to broaden the base of American government.

But the authors of the state constitutions knew that governments designed to be responsive to the people would not necessarily provide sufficient protection should tyrants be elected to office. Consequently, they included limitations on governmental authority in the documents they composed. Seven of the constitutions contained formal bills of rights, and the others had similar clauses. Most of them guaranteed citizens freedom of the press and of religion, the right to a fair trial, the right of consent to taxation, and protection against general search warrants. An independent judiciary was charged with upholding such rights.

In sum, the constitution makers put far greater emphasis on preventing state governments from becoming tyrannical than on making them effective wielders of political authority. But establishing such weak political units, especially in wartime, practically ensured that the constitutions would soon need revision. Invariably, the revised versions increased the powers of the governor and reduced the scope of the legislature's authority. Only then, a decade after the Declaration, did Americans start to develop a formal theory of checks and balances as the primary means of controlling governmental power. They would embody that theory in the Constitution of 1787.

The constitutional theories that Americans applied at the state level did not at first influence their conception of the nature of a national government. The powers and structure of the Continental Congress evolved by default early in the war, since Americans had little time to devote to legitimizing their de facto government while organizing the military struggle against Britain. Not until late 1777, after Burgoyne's defeat at Saratoga, did Congress send the Articles of Confederation to the states for ratification.

The chief organ of the Confederation government was a unicameral legislature in which each state had one vote. Its powers included the conduct of foreign relations, the settlement of disputes between states, control over maritime affairs, the regulation of Indian trade, and the valuation of state and national money. The articles did not give the national government the ability to tax effectively or to enforce a uniform commercial policy. The United States of America was described as "a firm league of friendship" in which each state "retains its sovereignty, freedom and independence."

The articles required the unanimous consent of the state legislatures for ratification or amendment, and a clause concerning western lands turned out to be troublesome. Because Maryland did not want to be overpowered by states with large land claims deriving from their colonial charters, the state absolutely refused to accept the articles until 1781. Only when Virginia and other states promised to surrender their holdings to national jurisdiction did Maryland accept the articles.

The fact that a single state could delay ratification for three years was a portent of the fate of American government under the Articles of Confederation. The authors of the articles had not given adequate thought to the distribution of power within the national government or to the relationship between the Confederation and the states. The congress they created was simultaneously a legislative body and a collective executive, but it had no independent income and no authority to compel the states to accept its rulings. What is surprising, in other words, is not how poorly the Confederation functioned in the following years, but rather how much the government was able to accomplish.

Trials of the Confederation

During and after the war the most persistent problem faced by the American governments, state and national, was finance. Because of a general reluctance to levy taxes, both Congress and the states tried to finance the war by simply printing currency. Even though the money was backed by nothing but good faith, it circulated freely and without excessive depreciation during 1775 and most of 1776. Indeed, the amount of money issued in those years was probably no more than what a healthy economy required as a medium of exchange.

But in late 1776, as the American army suffered major battlefield reverses in New York and New Jersey, prices began to rise and in-

Monetary problems

flation set in. The value of the currency rested on Americans' faith in their government, a faith that was sorely tested in the years that followed. Both Congress and the states attempted to control inflation, but by 1780 it took forty paper dollars to purchase one in silver. A year later Continental currency was worthless.

Although many suffered from inflation, especially those on fixed incomes, some benefited from such economic conditions. Military contractors, large-scale farmers, and investors could make sizable profits. More risky, but potentially even more profitable, was privateering against enemy shipping—an enterprise that attracted venturesome sailors and wealthy merchants alike. Indeed, as a Nantucket, Massachusetts, mother wrote her son in early 1778, "it was Never better times here for Seamen then it is Now."

But accumulations of private wealth did not help Congress with its financial problems. In 1781, faced with the total collapse of the monetary system, the delegates undertook major reforms. After establishing a department of finance under the wealthy Philadelphia merchant Robert Morris, they asked the states to amend the Articles of Confederation to allow Congress to levy a duty on imported goods. Morris put national finances on a solid footing, but the customs duty was never adopted.

Congress also faced major diplomatic problems at the close of the war. Chief among them were issues involving the peace treaty itself. Article 4, which promised the repayment of prewar debts (most of them owed by Americans to British merchants), and Article 5, which suggested that loyalists might recover their con-

Failure to enforce the Treaty of Paris

fiscated property, aroused considerable opposition. States passed laws denying British subjects the right to sue for recovery of debts or property in American courts, and town meetings decried the loyalists' return. As residents of Norwalk, Connecticut, put it, few Americans wanted to permit the "Tory Villains" to return "while filial Tears are fresh upon our Cheeks and our Murdered Brethren scarcely cold in their Graves." Because prominent patriots had purchased most of the confiscated loyalist property, state governments also did not want to enforce Article 5.

The failure of state and local governments to comply with Articles 4 and 5 gave Britain an excuse to maintain posts on the Great Lakes long after its troops were supposed to be withdrawn. Furthermore, Congress's inability to convince the states to implement the treaty pointed up its lack of power. Concerned nationalists argued publicly that enforcement of the treaty, however unpopular, was a crucial test for the republic. "Will foreign nations be willing to undertake anything with us or for us," asked Alexander Hamilton, "when they find that the nature of our governments will allow no dependence to be placed on our engagements?"

Congress's weakness was especially evident in the realm of trade, because the Articles of Confederation specifically denied it the power to establish a national commercial policy. Immediately following the war, both Britain and France restricted American trade with their colonies and flooded the United States with their products. Americans were outraged but Congress lacked the power to do anything. Though Americans opened a profitable trade with China in 1784, it was no substitute for access to closer and larger markets.

Congress also had difficulty dealing with the threat posed by Spain's presence on the southern and western borders of the United States. Determined to prevent the new nation's expansion, Spain in 1784 closed the Mississippi River to American navigation. It thus deprived the growing settlements west of the Appalachians of their major access route to the rest of the nation and the world. If Spain's policy were not reversed, westerners might have to accept Spanish sovereignty as the necessary price for survival. Congress opened negotiations with Spain in 1785, but even John Jay, one of the nation's most experienced diplomats, could not win the desired concessions on navigation.

Diplomatic problems of another sort confronted the congressmen when they considered the status of the territory north of the Ohio River. The United States had nominally acquired that land from Great Britain by the Treaty of Paris, and state land cessions had then placed the domain directly under congressional jurisdiction. But in actuality the land was still occupied by Indians—and by tribes, moreover, that had not participated in the negotiations at Fort Stanwix in 1784. An alliance of Shawnee, Chippewa, Ottawa, Potawatomi, and other western tribes demanded direct unified negotiations with the United States before further land could be ceded.

At first the national government ignored the western Indian confederacy. Shortly after the state land cessions were completed, Congress began to organize the Northwest Territory, bounded by the Mississippi River, the Great Lakes, and the Ohio River. Ordinances passed in

| Northwest Ordinances |

1784, 1785, and 1787 outlined the process through which the land could be sold to settlers and formal governments organized. To ensure orderly development, Congress directed that the land be surveyed into townships six miles square, each divided into thirty-six sections of 640 acres (one square mile). Revenue from the sale of the sixteenth section of each township was to be reserved for the support of public schools—the first instance of federal aid to education in American history. The minimum price per acre was set at one dollar, and the minimum sale was to be 640 acres ($640 was beyond the reach of most Americans). The proceeds from the land sales were the first independent revenues available to the national government.

The most important ordinance was the third, passed in 1787. The Northwest Ordinance contained a bill of rights guaranteeing settlers in the territory freedom of religion and the right to a jury trial, prohibiting cruel and unusual punishments, and abolishing slavery. It also specified the process by which residents of the territory could eventually organize state governments

and seek admission to the union "on an equal footing with the original States."

In a sense, though, the ordinance was purely theoretical at the time it was passed. The Indians in the region refused to acknowledge American sovereignty and insisted on their right to the land. They opposed white settlement violently, attacking unwary pioneers who ventured too far north of the Ohio River. It was soon apparent that the United States would have to negotiate with the western confederacy.

In January 1789 General Arthur St. Clair, the first governor of the Northwest Territory, asked the tribes to come to a council at Fort Harmar, on the Muskingum. Only a few Indians attended, none of them major chiefs. The treaty signed by St. Clair and the Indians was utterly meaningless.

After that fiasco, war was inevitable. General Josiah Harmar (1790) and then St. Clair himself (1791) were defeated in major battles near the

| War in the Northwest |

present border between Indiana and Ohio. More than six hundred of St. Clair's men were killed and scores more wounded; it was the whites' worst defeat in the entire history of the American frontier. In 1793 the tribal confederacy declared that peace could be achieved only if the United States recognized the Ohio River as the boundary between white and Indian lands. But the national government refused to relinquish its claim to the Northwest Territory. A new army under the command of General Anthony Wayne, a Revolutionary War hero, attacked and defeated the tribesmen in August 1794, at the Battle of Fallen Timbers (near Toledo, Ohio). This victory made it possible for serious negotiations to begin.

The Treaty of Greenville (1795) gave each side a portion of what it wanted. The United States gained the right to settle much of what was to become the state of Ohio, the tribes retaining only the northwest corner of the region. The Indians received the acknowledgment they had long sought: American recognition of their rights to the soil. At Greenville, the United States formally accepted the principle of Indian sovereignty, by virtue of residence, over all lands the tribes had not yet ceded. Never again would the United States government claim that it had acquired Indian territory solely through negotiation with a European or American country.

The problems the United States encountered in ensuring safe settlement of the Northwest Territory pointed up, once again, the basic weakness of the Confederation government. Not until after the Articles of Confederation were replaced with a new Constitution could the United States muster sufficient force to implement all the provisions of the Northwest Ordinance. Thus, although the ordinance is often viewed as one of the few major accomplishments of the Confederation Congress, it must be seen within a context of political impotence.

From crisis to a constitution

The most obvious deficiencies of the Articles of Confederation were in the areas of trade and foreign relations. Congress could not impose its will on the states to establish a uniform commercial policy or to ensure the enforcement of treaties. The problems involving trade were particularly serious. Trade restrictions imposed by European powers adversely affected the American economy, which slid into a depression less than a year after the war's end. Although recovery had begun by 1786, the war's effects proved impossible to erase entirely.

Indeed, the economy was significantly changed by the Revolution. Whereas the thirteen colonies had sold their goods primarily to foreign markets, the domestic market, stimulated by population growth and the spread of settlement, began to assume greater overall importance in the independent United States. In addition, freed from the mercantilist restrictions of the British Empire and drawing on European technological innovations, Americans began to establish manufacturing enterprises. The first

American textile mill, for example, opened in Pawtucket, Rhode Island in 1793.

Recognizing the Confederation Congress's inability to deal with the nation's trade problems, Virginia invited the other states to a conference at Annapolis, Maryland, to discuss commercial policy. Although eight states named representatives to the meeting in September 1786, only five delegations attended. Those present realized that they were too few in number to have any real impact on the political system. They issued a call for another convention, to be held in Philadelphia in nine months, "to devise such further provisions as shall . . . appear necessary to render the constitution of the federal government adequate to the exigencies of the Union."

That fall an incident occurred in western Massachusetts that helped to convince other Americans that broad changes were necessary in their national government. Crowds of farmers,

> **Shays' Rebellion**

angered by high taxes and the low supply of money, halted court proceedings in which the state was trying to seize property for nonpayment of taxes. The insurgents were led by Daniel Shays, a farmer who had risen to the rank of captain in the American army; many of them were respected war veterans, described as gentlemen in contemporary accounts of the riots. Clearly the incident could not be dismissed as the work of an unruly rabble.

To residents of eastern Massachusetts and other citizens of the United States, the most frightening aspect of the uprising was the rebels' attempt to forge direct links between themselves and the earlier struggle for independence. Massachusetts officials in response asserted that the formation of the republic had narrowed the range of acceptable political alternatives. The crowd actions that had once been a justifiable response to British tyranny were no longer legitimate. In a republic, reform had to come about through the ballot box rather than by force. If the nation's citizens refused to submit to legitimate authority, the result would be chaos and collapse of the government.

It was this issue that made Shays' Rebellion

A woodcut of Daniel Shays and one of his chief officers, Job Shattuck, in 1787.   National Portrait Gallery, Smithsonian Institution. Washington. D.C.

seem to challenge the existence of the entire United States, even though the rebels were easily dispersed by militia in 1787. The reality of the threat the insurgents posed was never at issue: the importance of the uprising lay in its symbolic meaning. Of the major American political thinkers, only Thomas Jefferson could view the Massachusetts incidents without alarm. "What country can preserve its liberties, if its rulers are not warned from time to time that their people preserve the spirit of resistance?" Jefferson wrote from Paris, where he was serving as American ambassador.

But Jefferson was clearly exceptional. Shays' Rebellion unquestionably accelerated the movement toward comprehensive revision of the Articles of Confederation. In February 1787, after most of the states had already appointed delegates, the Confederation Congress belatedly endorsed the convention. In mid-May, fifty-five men, repre-

Calling of the Constitutional Convention

senting all the states but Rhode Island, assembled in Philadelphia to begin their deliberations.

The vast majority of the delegates were men of property and substance. Among their number were merchants, planters, physicians, generals, governors, and especially lawyers—twenty-three had studied the law. Most had been born in America, and many came from families that had immigrated in the seventeenth century. In an era when only a tiny proportion of the population had any advanced education, more than half had attended college. A few had been educated in Britain, but most were graduates of American institutions. The youngest delegate was twenty-six, the oldest—Benjamin Franklin—eighty-one. Like George Washington, whom they elected chairman, most were in their vigorous middle years. A dozen men did the bulk of the convention's work. Of the dozen, James Madison of Virginia was the most important; he truly deserves the title Father of the Constitution.

Madison was unique among the delegates in

Chapter 6: Forging a national republic, 1776–1789

his systematic preparation for the Philadelphia meeting. Through Jefferson in Paris he bought more than two hundred books on history and government, and carefully analyzed their accounts of past confederacies and republics. In April 1787, a month before the convention began, he summed up the results of his research in a lengthy paper entitled "Vices of the Political System of the United States." After listing the eleven major flaws he perceived in the current structure of the government, Madison set forth the principle of checks and balances.

The government, he believed, had to be constructed in such a way that it could not become tyrannical or fall wholly under the influence of a particular interest group. He regarded the large size of a potential national republic as an advantage in that respect. Rejecting the common assertion that republics had to be small to survive, Madison argued that a large, diverse republic was in fact to be preferred. Because the nation would include many different interest groups, no one of them would be able to control the government. Political stability, he declared, would result from compromises among the contending parties.

Madison's conception of national government was embodied in the so-called Virginia plan, introduced on May 29 by his colleague Ed-

| *Virginia and New Jersey plans* |

mund Randolph. The plan provided for a two-house legislature with proportional representation in both houses, an executive and a judiciary (both of which the Confederation government lacked), and congressional veto over state laws. It gave Congress the broad power to legislate "in all cases to which the separate states are incompetent." Had the Virginia plan been adopted intact, it would have created a government in which national authority reigned unchallenged and state power was greatly diminished.

But the convention included many delegates who, while recognizing the need for change, believed that the Virginians had gone too far in the direction of national consolidation. The dis-

affected delegates united under the leadership of New Jersey's William Paterson. On June 15 Paterson presented an alternative scheme, the New Jersey plan, calling for modifications in the Articles of Confederation rather than a complete overhaul of the government. Although the delegates rejected Paterson's narrow interpretation of their task, he and his allies won a number of major victories.

Debate quickly focused on three key questions involving representation. Should there be proportional representation in both houses of the national legislature? (Paterson's group readily agreed to replace Congress with a bicameral body.) What should the representation in either or both houses be proportional *to*—people, property, or a combination of the two? And, finally, how should the representatives to the two houses be elected?

The easiest question to resolve was the mode of electing representatives. The Virginia plan suggested that the lower house be elected at large by the people, and that the upper house be elected by the lower. The latter proposal was quickly discarded, and a compromise was reached as early as June 21. The delegates agreed that the people should have a direct say in the choice of some national legislators (thus the House of Representatives). They also knew that the state governments, which had named delegates to the Confederation Congress, would insist on a similar privilege in the new government. In providing for senators to be selected by state legislatures, they thus adhered to republican principles but recognized political reality.

The most difficult problem was the issue of proportional representation in the Senate. On June 11 the convention accepted the principle of

| *Debate over representation* |

proportional representation in the lower house. The Senate was another matter. Delegates from the large states favored proportional representation; those from the small states wanted equal representation. After weeks of debate and deadlock, a committee was appointed to work out a compromise. The committee recommended equal representation for states in the

Senate, coupled with a proviso that all appropriation bills must originate in the lower house. The dispute continued and was finally resolved when the delegates agreed that the two senators from each state could vote as individuals rather than as a bloc.

One potentially divisive question remained unresolved: how was representation in the lower house to be apportioned among the states? Most delegates fell into one of the three groups: those who wanted representation proportional to total population; those who wanted to count only the free population; and those who proposed counting three-fifths of the slaves as well. On this issue New Englanders, who only wanted to count free people, found themselves at odds with Georgians and South Carolinians, who wanted to count everyone, including slaves. At the insistence of delegates from the upper South and the middle states, the three-fifths formula was accepted. The formula was linked to a clause allowing Congress to stop the slave trade after twenty years, thus preventing the slave population from increasing indefinitely.

Other issues proved to be less difficult to resolve. The delegates agreed to enumerate the powers of Congress but to allow it to pass all laws "necessary and proper" for carrying out its functions. Foreign policy was placed in the hands of the executive, who was also made the commander-in-chief of the armed forces. The idea of a legislative veto over state action was rejected, but an implied judicial veto was included. Moreover, the Constitution, national laws, and treaties were made the supreme law of the land. Finally, the delegates established the electoral college and a short term for the chief executive, who could seek re-election.

The key to the Constitution was the distribution of political authority—separation of powers among the executive, legislative, and judicial branches of the national government, and division of powers between states and nation. The system of checks and balances would make it difficult for the government to become tyrannical, as Madison had intended. At the same time, though, the elaborate system would sometimes prevent the government from acting quickly and decisively. Finally, the line between state and national powers was ambiguously and vaguely drawn.

The convention held its last session on September 17, 1787. Of the forty-two delegates present, only three refused to sign the Constitution. (Two of the three, George Mason and Elbridge Gerry, declined because of the lack of a bill of rights.) Though the delegates had accepted the Constitution, the question remained as to whether or not the states would ratify it.

Opposition and ratification

The ratification clause of the Constitution provided for the new system to take effect once it was approved by special conventions in at least nine states. The delegates to each state convention were to be elected by the people. Thus the national constitution, unlike the Articles of Confederation, would rest directly on popular authority.

As the states began to elect delegates to the special conventions, pro- and anti-Constitution forces emerged. Critics of the Constitution, who became known as Antifederalists, emphasized the threat to the states embodied in the new national government and stressed the dangers to individuals posed by the lack of a bill of rights. The Antifederalists saw the states as the chief protectors of individual rights. They also regarded Madison's argument that a large republic was preferable to a small one as heretical nonsense.

As the months passed and public debate continued, the Antifederalists focused more sharply on the Constitution's lack of a bill of rights. Even if the states were weakened by the new system, they believed, the people could still be protected from tyranny if their rights were specifi-

Chapter 6: Forging a national republic, 1776–1789

cally guaranteed. *Letters of a Federal Farmer,* perhaps the most widely read Antifederalist pamphlet, listed the rights that should be protected: freedom of the press and of religion, the right to trial by jury, and guarantees against unreasonable search warrants.

As the state conventions met to consider ratification, the lack of a bill of rights loomed larger and larger as a flaw in the new form of government. Four of the first five states to ratify did so

| Ratification of the Constitution |

unanimously, but serious disagreements then began to surface. Massachusetts ratified by a majority of only 19 votes out of 355 cast; in New Hampshire the Federalists won by a majority of 57 to 47. When New Hampshire ratified, in June 1788, the requirement of nine states had been satisfied. But New York and Virginia had not yet voted, and everyone realized the new constitution could not succeed unless those key states accepted it. In Virginia, despite a valiant effort by the Antifederalist Patrick Henry, the pro-Constitution forces won 89 to 79. In New York James Madison, John Jay, and Alexander Hamilton campaigned for ratification by publishing *The Federalist,* one of the most important political tracts in American history. Their reasoned arguments, coupled with the promise that a bill of rights would be added to the Constitution, helped carry the day. On July 26, 1788, New York ratified the Constitution by the slim margin of 3 votes. The new government was a reality, even though the last state (Rhode Island, which had not participated in the convention) did not formally join the union until 1790. Still the question remained: could they successfully implement the new system?

Important events

1776	Second Continental Congress directs states to draft constitutions
1777	Articles of Confederation sent to states for ratification
1780	Pennsylvania becomes first state to abolish slavery
1781	Articles of Confederation ratified
1782	Virginia becomes first southern state to allow individual manumissions without legal restrictions
1784	Treaty of Fort Stanwix Spain closes Mississippi River to American navigation
1785–86	Treaty of Hopewell
1786	Iroquois repudiate Treaty of Fort Stanwix Annapolis Convention
1786–87	Shays' Rebellion (Mass.)
1787	Northwest Ordinance Constitutional Convention
1788	Hamilton, Jay, and Madison, *The Federalist* Constitution ratified
1789	Treaty of Fort Harmar
1791	St. Clair's defeat
1794	Battle of Fallen Timbers
1795	Treaty of Greenville

Suggestions for further reading

GENERAL   Stuart Bruchey, *The Roots of American Economic Growth, 1607–1861* (1965); Staughton Lynd, *Class Conflict, Slavery, & the United States Constitution: Ten Essays* (1967); Forrest McDonald, *E Pluribus Unum: The Formation of the American Republic 1776–1790* (1965); Curtis P. Nettels, *The Emergence* of a National Economy, 1775–1815 (1962); Robert R. Palmer, *The Age of the Democratic Revolution: A Political History of Europe and America 1760–1800,* 2 vols. (1959, 1964); Garry Wills, *Inventing America: Jefferson's Declaration of Independence* (1978); Gordon S. Wood, *The Creation of the American Republic, 1776–1787* (1969).

CONTINENTAL CONGRESS AND ARTICLES OF CON-FEDERATION E. James Ferguson, *The Power of the Purse: A History of American Public Finance, 1776–1790* (1961); H. James Henderson, *Party Politics in the Continental Congress* (1974); Merrill Jensen, *The Articles of Confederation: An Interpretation of the Social-Constitutional History of the American Revolution, 1774–1781,* 2nd ed. (1959); Merrill Jensen, *The New Nation: A History of the United States during the Confederation, 1781–1789* (1950); Jack N. Rakove, *The Beginnings of National Politics: An Interpretive History of the Continental Congress* (1979).

STATE POLITICS Willi Paul Adams, *The First American Constitutions: Republican Ideology and the Making of the State Constitutions in the Revolutionary Era* (1980); Jackson Turner Main, *The Sovereign States, 1775–1783* (1973); Jackson Turner Main, *The Upper House in Revolutionary America, 1763–1788* (1967); J.R. Pole, *Political Representation in England and the Origins of the American Republic* (1966).

THE CONSTITUTION Douglass Adair, *Fame and the Founding Fathers* (1974); Charles A. Beard, *An Economic Interpretation of the Constitution of the United States* (1913); Jackson Turner Main, *The Anti-Federalists: Critics of the Constitution, 1781–1788* (1961); Frederick W. Marks, III, *Independence on Trial: Foreign Affairs and the Making of the Constitution* (1973); Clinton Rossiter, *1787: The Grand Convention* (1973); Robert A. Rutland, *The Ordeal of the Constitution* (1966); Garry Wills, *Explaining America: The Federalist* (1981).

WOMEN Charles Akers, *Abigail Adams: An American Woman* (1980); Linda K. Kerber, *Women of the Republic: Intellect & Ideology in Revolutionary America* (1980); Mary Beth Norton, *Liberty's Daughters: The Revolutionary Experience of American Women, 1750–1800* (1980).

BLACKS AND INDIANS Ira Berlin, *Slaves without Masters: The Free Negro in the Antebellum South* (1974); David Brion Davis, *The Problem of Slavery in the Age of Revolution, 1770–1823* (1975); Winthrop D. Jordan, *White Over Black: American Attitudes Toward the Negro, 1550–1812* (1968); Bernard Sheehan, *Seeds of Extinction: Jeffersonian Philanthropy and the American Indian* (1973); Anthony F.C. Wallace, *The Death and Rebirth of the Seneca* (1969).

7

POLITICS AND SOCIETY
IN THE EARLY REPUBLIC,
1790–1800

Charles Thomson, secretary to Congress, arrived at Mount Vernon, Virginia, around noon on April 14, 1789. He brought momentous news: the first electoral college convened under the new Constitution had unanimously elected George Washington president of the United States, and Congress had confirmed the choice.

The United States formally honored its first president with an outpouring of affection and respect that has rarely been equalled since. Washington's inauguration allowed the people to express their pride in the Revolution, the new Constitution, and most of all in the nation itself. The struggle against Britain had nurtured in Americans an intense nationalism that quickly manifested itself in attempts to create a distinctive cultural style. They reformed their educational system in accordance with republican principles, and pursued artistic and literary independence along with political autonomy. Their goal was to establish a nation of virtuous, self-sacrificing yeomen dedicated to the public good rather than private gain.

Yet Americans were ultimately unsuccessful in their quest for unity and unqualified independence. Nowhere was their failure more evident than in the realm of national politics. They found it difficult to understand and deal with partisan tensions that developed out of disputes over such fundamental questions as the extent to which authority, especially fiscal authority, should be centralized in the national government; the formulation of foreign policy in an era of continual warfare in Europe; and the limits of dissent within the republic. By the close of the decade they still had not come to terms with the implications of partisan politics.

Creating a virtuous republic

"Virtue, Virtue alone . . . is the basis of a republic," declared Dr. Benjamin Rush, a leading Philadelphia physician and ardent patriot, in 1778. His fellow Americans fully concurred. Every aspect of their culture should, they believed, reflect and foster the virtue so necessary to a republic. Accordingly, in the 1780s and 1790s those who sought to define American identity looked to painting, literature, and architecture, as well as politics and society, to express republican virtue.

| Republicanism in the arts |

The Americans took their artistic standards from ancient Greece and Rome–the source of their political heroes as well. The style they used is called *neoclassical,* for it was an explicit adaptation of classical forms to contemporary circumstances. Paradoxically, educated Americans wanted to create a culture embodying the highest artistic and literary ideals outlined by European Enlightenment thinkers, but free of the corrupting influence of vice-ridden Europe.

The first American literary productions were highly moralistic. William Hill Brown's *The Power of Sympathy* (1789), the first novel written in the United States, was a lurid tale of seduction intended as a warning to young women, who made up a large proportion of America's fiction readers. The most popular book of the era, Mason Locke Weems's *Life of Washington,* published in 1800 shortly after its subject's death, was, the author declared, designed to "hold up his great Virtues . . . to the imitation of Our Youth." Weems could hardly have been accused of being subtle. The famous tale he invented—six-year-old George bravely admitting cutting down his father's favorite cherry tree—ended with George's father exclaiming, "Run to my arms, you dearest boy. . . . Such an act of heroism in my son, is worth more than a thousand trees, though blossomed with silver, and their fruits of purest gold."

Painting, too, was expected to embody high moral standards. The major artists of the republican period were Gilbert Stuart, John Trumbull, and Ralph Earl. Stuart and Earl painted innumerable portraits of upstanding republican citizens. Trumbull's vast canvases depicted such milestones of American history as the Battle of Bunker Hill, Burgoyne's surrender at Saratoga, and Cornwallis's capitulation at Yorktown. Both portraits and historical scenes were intended to arouse patriotic virtues in their viewers.

Architects likewise hoped to convey in their buildings a sense of the young republic's ideals, and most of them consciously rejected British models. When the Virginia government asked Thomas Jefferson, then ambassador to France, for advice on the design of a state capitol in Richmond, Jefferson unhesitatingly recommended copying a Roman building, the Maison

Carrée at Nîmes. "It is very simple," he explained, "but it is noble beyond expression." Jefferson set forth ideals that would guide American neoclassical architecture for a generation to come: simplicity of line, harmonious proportions, a feeling of grandeur.

But republican theorists did not always have their way. By the mid-1780s, some Americans were beginning to detect signs of luxury and corruption all around them. The end of the war and resumption of European trade brought a return to fashionable clothing styles for both men and women and abandonment of the simpler homespun garments patriots had once worn with such pride. Balls and concerts resumed in the cities and were attended by well-dressed elite families. Parties no longer seemed complete without gambling and card-playing. Social clubs for young people multiplied. Especially alarming to fervent republicans was the establishment of the Society of the Cincinnati, a hereditary organization of Revolutionary War officers and their descendants. Many feared that the group would become the nucleus of a native-born aristocracy. All these developments directly challenged the United States's image as a virtuous, self-sacrificing republic.

Their deep-seated concern for the future of the infant republic focused Americans' attention on their children, the "rising generation." Education acquired new significance in the context

| *Educational reform* |

of the republic. Formerly, education had been seen chiefly as a family matter. Now, though, it would serve a public purpose. If young people were to resist the temptation of vice, they would have to learn the lessons of virtue at home and at school. In fact, the very survival of the nation depended on it. The early republican period was thus a time of major educational reform.

The 1780s and 1790s brought three significant changes in American educational practice. First, the states began to be willing to use tax money to support public elementary schools. Second, the college curriculum was reformed. Colleges like Harvard, Yale, and William and

Mary continued to instruct their students in classical languages and theology, but they added classes in history, geography, modern languages, and "natural philosophy" (science). American education thus broadened its scope and focused on producing well-informed republican citizens rather than future clergymen. Third, schooling for girls was vastly improved. The new recognition of the importance of the rising generation led to the realization that mothers would have to be properly educated if their children were to be educated. Still, colleges were not open to women, and only a few girls were able to attend academies where they could study history, geography, rhetoric, and mathematics.

The chief theorist of women's education in the early republic was Judith Sargent Murray, of Gloucester, Massachusetts. Born in 1751, Murray married a sea captain at age eighteen. Widowed in 1786, she took as her second husband John Murray, the founder of the Universalist sect. Though she began to think and write about woman's status during the American Revolution, her first published essay did not appear until 1784. Murray argued that women and men had equal intellectual capacities. Therefore, concluded Murray, boys and girls should be offered equivalent scholastic training. She further contended that girls should be taught to support themselves by their own efforts: "Independence should be placed within their grasp." Because she rejected the prevailing notion that a young woman's chief goal in life should be finding a husband, Judith Sargent Murray deserves the title of the first American feminist. (That distinction is usually accorded to better-known nineteenth-century women like Margaret Fuller or Sarah Grimké.)

By 1800, therefore, the struggle for political independence had prompted Americans to think about their society and culture in new ways. The process of breaking away from their colonial origins had already had a profound influence on the arts. Americans were also attempting to ensure their nation's future by instructing their

Judith Sargent Murray on education

Judith Sargent Murray (1751–1820), painted by John Singleton Copley about the time of her marriage to the sea captain John Stevens. Although her steady gaze suggests clear-headed intelligence, there is little in the stylized portrait–typical of Copley's work at the time–to suggest her later emergence as the first notable American feminist theorist. Frick Art Reference Library.

children–and themselves–in the principles of virtue and morality. All their efforts would prove useless, though, if the new federal government was not placed on a sound footing.

Building a workable government

In 1788 Americans celebrated the ratification of the Constitution with a series of parades, held in many cities on the Fourth of July. The processions were carefully planned to symbolize the unity of the new nation and to recall its history to the minds of the watching throngs.

The nationalistic spirit expressed in the ratification processions carried over into the first session of Congress. In the congressional elections,

| First Congress | held late in 1788, only a few Antifederalists had run or

been elected to office. Thus the First Congress was composed chiefly of men who were considerably more inclined toward a strong national government than had been the delegates to the Constitutional Convention. Since the Constitution had deliberately left many key issues undecided, the nationalists' domination of Congress meant that their views on those points quickly prevailed.

Congress faced four immediate problems when it convened in April 1789: raising revenue to support the new government, responding to the state ratification conventions' calls for amendments to the Constitution, establishing executive departments, and organizing the federal judiciary. The latter task was especially important. The Constitution declared only that there should be a Supreme Court and other lower federal courts, leaving it to Congress to work out not just the details of the national judiciary but also its basic structure.

The Virginian James Madison, who had been elected to the House of Representatives, soon became as influential in Congress as he had been at the Philadelphia convention. Only a few months into the session, he persuaded Congress to impose a tariff on certain imported goods. The new government was to have its problems, but a lack of sufficient revenue was not one of them.

Madison also took the lead on the issue of constitutional amendments. He thought it unnecessary to guarantee the people's rights when the government was one of limited powers, but public sentiment clearly favored some explicit constitutional protection for basic rights. Accordingly, Madison drafted and introduced nineteen proposed amendments,

| Bill of Rights | of which Congress accepted

twelve and the states ten. These ten amendments officially became part of the Constitution on December 15, 1791. Not for many years, though, did they become known collectively as the Bill of Rights.

The first amendment specifically prohibited Congress from passing any law restricting the people's right to freedom of religion, speech, press, peaceable assembly, or petition. The next two arose directly from the former colonists' fear of standing armies as a threat to freedom. The second guaranteed the people's right "to keep and bear arms" because of the need for a "well regulated Militia"; the third defined the circumstances in which troops could be quartered in private homes. The next five amendments pertained to judicial procedures. The fourth amendment prohibited "unreasonable searches and seizures"; the fifth and sixth established the rights of accused persons; the seventh specified the conditions for jury trials in civil, as opposed to criminal, cases; and the eighth forbade "cruel and unusual punishments." Finally, the ninth and tenth amendments reserved to the people and the states other unspecified rights and powers. In short, the authors of the amendments made clear that in listing some rights explicitly they did not mean to preclude the exercise of others.

While debating the proposed amendments, Congress also concerned itself with the organization of the executive branch. It was readily agreed to continue the three administrative departments established under the Articles of Confederation: War, Foreign Affairs (renamed State), and Treasury. Congress also instituted two lesser posts: the attorney general—the nation's official lawyer—and the postmaster general, who would oversee the Post Office. The only serious controversy was whether the president alone could dismiss officials whom he had originally appointed with the consent of the Senate. After some debate, the House and Senate agreed that he had such authority. Thus was established the important principle that the heads of the executive departments are responsible solely to the president.

Aside from the constitutional amendments,

the most far-reaching piece of legislation enacted by the First Congress was the Judiciary Act of 1789. The Judiciary Act provided for the Supreme Court to have six members: a chief justice and five associate justices. It also defined the jurisdiction of the federal judiciary and established thirteen district courts and three circuit courts of appeal.

> **Judiciary Act of 1789**

The act's most important provision may have been its section 25, which allowed appeals from state courts to the federal court system when certain types of constitutional issues were raised. This section was intended to implement Article VI of the Constitution, which stated that federal laws and treaties were to be considered "the supreme Law of the Land." If Article VI was to be enforced uniformly, the national judiciary clearly had to be able to overturn state court decisions in cases involving the Constitution, federal laws, or treaties.

During the first decade of its existence, the Supreme Court handled few cases of any importance. But in a significant 1796 decision, *Ware* v. *Hylton,* the Court for the first time declared a state law unconstitutional. That same year it also reviewed the constitutionality of an act of Congress, upholding its validity in the case of *Hylton* v. *U.S.* The most important case of the decade, *Chisholm* v. *Georgia* (1793), established that states could be freely sued in federal courts by citizens of other states; this decision, unpopular with the states, was overruled five years later by the Eleventh Amendment to the Constitution.

Domestic policy under Washington

During his first months in office Washington acted cautiously, knowing that whatever he did would set precedents for the future. His first major task was to choose the men who would head the executive departments. For the War Department he selected an old comrade-in-arms, Henry Knox, who had been his reliable general of artillery during much of the Revolution. His choice for the State Department was his fellow Virginian Thomas Jefferson, who had just returned to the United States from his post as ambassador to France. Finally, for the crucial position of secretary of the treasury, the president chose the brilliant, intensely ambitious Alexander Hamilton, who had been born in poverty in the West Indies.

Two traits distinguished Hamilton from most of his contemporaries. First, he displayed an undivided, unquestioning loyalty to the nation as a whole. As a West Indian who had lived on the mainland only briefly before the war, Hamilton had no ties to an individual state. He showed little sympathy for, or understanding of, demands for local autonomy. Thus his fiscal policies aimed always at consolidation of power at the national level. Furthermore, he never feared the exercise of centralized executive authority, as did his older counterparts who had clashed repeatedly with colonial governors.

Second, he regarded his fellow human beings with unvarnished cynicism. Perhaps because of his difficult early life and his own overriding ambition, Hamilton believed people to be motivated primarily, if not entirely, by self-interest—particularly economic self-interest. He placed absolutely no reliance on people's capacity for virtuous and self-sacrificing behavior. That outlook immediately set him apart from other republicans who foresaw a rosy future in which public-spirited citizens would pursue the common good rather than their own private advantage. More important, his beliefs significantly influenced the way in which he tackled the monumental task before him: straightening out the new nation's tangled finances.

In 1789 Congress ordered the new secretary of the treasury to study the state of the public debt and to submit recommendations for supporting the government's credit. Hamilton discovered that the country's remaining war debts fell into three categories: those owed by the United States to foreign governments and investors, mostly to France (about $11 million);

Alexander Hamilton (1757–1804), painted by John Trumbull in 1792. Hamilton was then at the height of his influence as secretary of the treasury, and his haughty, serene expression reveals his supreme self-confidence. Trumbull, an American student of the English artist Benjamin West, painted the portrait at the request of John Jay.   National Gallery of Art, Gift of the Avalon Foundation.

solidation of the debt in the hands of the national government would unquestionably help to concentrate both economic and political power at the national level.

Hamilton's "Report on Public Credit," sent to Congress in January 1790, reflected both his national loyalty and his cynicism. It proposed

> **Hamilton's "Report on Public Credit"**

that Congress assume outstanding state debts, combine them with national obligations, and issue new securities covering both principal and accumulated unpaid interest. Current holders of state or national debt certificates would have the option of taking a portion of their payment in western lands. Hamilton's aims were clear: he wanted to expand the financial reach of the United States government and reduce the economic power of the states. He also wanted to ensure that the holders of public securities–many of them wealthy merchants and speculators–would have a significant financial stake in the survival of the national government.

Hamilton's plan stimulated lively debate in Congress. The opposition coalesced around his former ally James Madison. Believing with some reason that speculators had purchased large quantities of debt certificates at a small fraction of their face value, Madison proposed that the original holders of the debt also be compensated by the government. But Madison's plan was exceedingly complex and perhaps impossible to administer. The House of Representatives accordingly rejected it.

At first, however, the House also rejected the assumption of state debts. Since the Senate, by contrast, adopted Hamilton's plan largely intact, a series of compromises followed. The traditional story that Hamilton and Madison agreed over Jefferson's dinner table to locate the nation's capital city in the South in exchange for assumption of state debts is distorted and simplistic, but in the end the Potomac River was designated as the site for the capital. Simultaneously, the four congressmen from Maryland and Virginia whose districts contained the most likely locations for the new city switched from

those owed by the national government to merchants, former soldiers, holders of revolutionary bonds, and the like (about $27 million); and finally, similar debts owed by state governments (roughly estimated at $25 million). With respect to the national debt, there was little disagreement: Americans uniformly recognized that if their new government was to succeed it would have to pay the obligations the nation incurred while winning independence.

The state debts were quite another matter. Some states had already paid off most of their war debts. They would oppose the national government's assumption of responsibility for other states' debts. Conversely, states with large debts favored assumption. The possible assumption of state debts also had political implications. Con-

opposition to support for assumption. As a result, the first part of Hamilton's financial program became law in August 1790.

Four months later Hamilton submitted to Congress a second report on public credit, recommending the chartering of a national bank. Debate on the bank focused on constitutional issues and arose primarily after Congress had already passed the law.

Hamilton modeled his proposed bank on the Bank of England. The Bank of the United States was to be capitalized at $10 million, with only $2 million coming from public funds. The rest would be supplied by private investors. Its charter was to run for twenty years, and one-fifth of its directors were to be named by the government. Its bank notes would circulate as the nation's currency; it would also act as the collecting and disbursing agent for the treasury and lend money to the government. Most people recognized that such an institution would benefit the country. But did the Constitution give Congress the power to establish such a bank?

First Bank of the United States

James Madison pointed out that the delegates to the Philadelphia convention had specifically rejected a clause authorizing Congress to issue corporate charters. Washington, disturbed by Madison's contention, decided to seek other opinions. Thomas Jefferson, the secretary of state, agreed with Madison that the bank was unconstitutional. Jefferson referred to Article I, section 8 of the Constitution, which gave Congress the power "to make all Laws which shall be necessary and proper for carrying into Execution the foregoing Powers." *Necessary* was the key word, Jefferson argued: Congress could do what was needed but it could not do what was merely desirable without specific constitutional authorization.

Washington asked Hamilton to reply to these negative assessments of his proposal. Hamilton's "Defense of the Constitutionality of the Bank," presented to Washington in February 1791, was a brilliant exposition of what has become known as the broad-constructionist view

of the Constitution. Hamilton argued forcefully that Congress could choose any means not specifically prohibited by the Constitution to achieve a constitutional end. In short, he said, if the end was constitutional and the means was not *un*constitutional, then the means was also constitutional. Washington accepted Hamilton's logic and signed the bill.

In December, Hamilton presented to Congress his "Report on Manufactures," the third and last of his prescriptions for the American economy. In it he outlined an ambitious plan for encouraging and protecting the United States's infant industries, like shoemaking and textile manufacturing. He urged Congress to promote the immigration of technicians and laborers, enact protective tariffs, and support industrial development. But because most congressmen were convinced that America's future was agrarian, they rejected Hamilton's report.

That same year Congress did accept the other part of Hamilton's financial program, an excise tax on whiskey, because of the need for additional government revenues. The tax fell most heavily on New England, where most of the nation's large distilleries were located, and on western farmers. Because transportation over the mountains was difficult and expensive, the frontier-dwellers' most salable "crop" was whiskey made from the corn they raised.

News of the excise law set off immediate protests in frontier areas of Pennsylvania and the Carolinas. But matters did not come to a head until the summer of 1794, when western Pennsylvania farmers tried to stop a federal **Whiskey Rebellion** marshal from arresting some men charged with violating the law. Washington, being determined to prevent a recurrence of Shays' Rebellion, ordered the insurgents to disperse by September 1 and summoned more than 12,000 militiamen. But the troops arrived after the riots were over. Only two of those arrested were convicted of treason, and Washington pardoned them.

The chief importance of the Whiskey Rebellion lay in the message it forcefully conveyed to the American public. The national government, Washington had demonstrated, would not allow violent organized resistance to its laws. In the new republic, change would be effected peacefully, by legal means.

By 1794, a group of Americans had already begun to seek change systematically within the confines of electoral politics, even though traditional political theory regarded organized opposition—especially in a republic—as illegitimate. The leaders of the opposition, Jefferson and Madison, saw themselves as the true heirs of the revolution. To emphasize their support of republican principles, they and their followers called themselves Republicans. Hamilton and his supporters claimed to be the rightful interpreters of the Constitution and took the name Federalists. Each side contended the other was a faction bent upon subversion. (By traditional definition, a faction was opposed to the public good.)

The beginnings of partisan politics

The first years under the Constitution were blessed by international peace. Eventually, however, the French Revolution, which began in 1789, brought about the resumption of hostilities between France, America's wartime ally, and Great Britain, America's most important trading partner.

At first, Americans welcomed the news that France was turning toward republicanism. But by the early 1790s the reports from France were disquieting. Outbreaks of violence continued, ministries succeeded each other with bewildering rapidity, and executions were commonplace. The king himself was beheaded in early 1793. Although many Americans, including Jefferson and Madison, retained their sympathy for the French revolutionaries, others, including Hamilton, began to view France as a prime example of the perversion of republicanism.

At that juncture, France declared war on Brit-

ain, Spain, and Holland. The Americans thus faced a dilemma. The 1778 treaty with France bound them to that nation "forever," and a mutual commitment to republicanism created ideological bonds. Yet the United States was connected to Great Britain as well. Aside from sharing a common history and language, America and England were economic partners.

The political and diplomatic climate was further complicated in April 1793, when Citizen Edmond Genêt, a representative of the French

| *Citizen Genêt* |

government, landed in Charleston. As Genêt made his leisurely way northward toward New York City, he was wildly cheered and lavishly entertained at every stop. En route, he recruited Americans for expeditions against British and Spanish possessions in the Western Hemisphere and distributed privateering commissions with a generous hand. Genêt's arrival raised a series of key questions for President Washington. Should he receive Genêt, thus officially recognizing the French revolutionary government? Should he acknowledge the United States's obligation to aid France under the terms of the 1778 treaty? Or should he proclaim American neutrality in the conflict?

For once, Hamilton and Jefferson saw eye to eye. Both told Washington that the United States could not afford to ally itself firmly with either side. Washington agreed; thus he received Genêt officially, but also issued a proclamation informing the world that the United States would adopt "a conduct friendly and impartial toward the belligerent powers." However, the domestic divisions Genêt had helped to widen were perpetuated by clubs called Democratic-Republican societies.

Americans sympathetic to the French Revolution and worried about trends in the Washing-

| *Democratic-Republican societies* |

ton administration formed forty of these Democratic-Republican societies between 1793 and 1800. Their members saw themselves as the heirs of the Sons of Liberty, seeking the same goal as their predecessors: protection of the people's liberties against

Chapter 7: Politics and society in the early republic, 1790–1800

encroachment by corrupt and evil rulers. Like the Sons of Liberty, the Democratic-Republican societies were composed chiefly of artisans and craftsmen of various kinds, although professionals, farmers, and merchants also joined.

The rapid growth of such groups, outspoken in their criticism of the Washington administration for its failure to come to the aid of France and for its domestic economic policies, deeply disturbed Hamilton and eventually Washington himself. Newspapers sympathetic to the Federalists charged that the societies were subversive agents of a foreign power.

In retrospect, Washington's and Hamilton's reaction to the Democratic-Republican societies seems hysterical and overwrought. But it must be kept in mind that the Democratic-Republican societies were the first formally organized political dissenters in the United States. As such, they aroused the fear and suspicion of elected officials who had not yet accepted the idea that one component of a free government was an organized loyal opposition.

In 1794 George Washington decided to send Chief Justice John Jay to England to try to reach agreement on four major unresolved questions affecting Anglo-American affairs. The first point at issue was recent British seizures of American merchant ships trading in the French West Indies. The United States wanted to establish the principle of freedom of the seas and to assert its right, as a neutral nation, to trade freely with both sides. Second, Great Britain had not yet carried out its promise in the Treaty of Paris (1783) to evacuate its posts in the American Northwest. Third and fourth, the Americans hoped for a commercial treaty and sought compensation for the slaves who had left with the British army at the end of the war.

The negotiations in London proved difficult, since Jay had little to offer Britain in exchange for the concessions he wanted. In the end, Britain did agree to evacuate the

Jay Treaty

western forts and ease the restrictions on American trade to England and the West Indies. No compensation for lost slaves was agreed to, but Jay accepted a provision establishing an arbitration commission to deal with the matter of prewar debts owed to British creditors. A similar commission was to handle the question of compensation for the seizures of American merchant ships. Under the circumstances, Jay had done remarkably well: the treaty averted war with England. Nevertheless, most Americans, including the president, were dissatisfied with at least some parts of the treaty.

At first, however, potential opposition was blunted, because the Senate debated and ratified the treaty in secret. Not until after it was formally approved on June 24, 1795, was the public informed of its provisions. The Democratic-Republican societies led protests against the treaty. After Washington reluctantly signed the treaty, though, the only hope left to its critics lay in Congress.

In March 1796, treaty opponents in the House tried to prevent approval of the appropriations needed to implement various treaty provisions. To that end, they called on Washington to submit to the House all documents pertinent to the negotiations. In successfully resisting the House's request, Washington developed the doctrine of executive privilege—that is, the power of the president to withhold information from Congress if he believes circumstances warrant doing so. At first the treaty's opponents seemed to be in the majority. But the desires of frontier residents to have the British posts evacuated and of merchants to trade with the British Empire weakened their position. Finally, Federalist senators threatened to reject a treaty Thomas Pinckney had negotiated with Spain unless the funds for Jay's Treaty were approved. Since Pinckney's Treaty had secured American navigation rights on the Mississippi, it was popular with southerners and westerners. For these reasons the House by a 51 to 48 margin voted the necessary funds.

Analysis of the vote reveals both the regional nature of the division and the growing cohesion of the Republican and Federalist factions in

Republicans and Federalists

Congress. Voting in favor of the appropriations were 44 Federalists and 7 Republicans: voting against were 45 Republicans and 3 Federalists. The final tally was also split by region. The vast majority of votes against the bill were cast by southerners. The bill's supporters were largely from New England and the middle states.

The growing division cannot be accurately explained in the terms used by Jefferson and Madison (aristocrats versus the people) or by Hamilton and Washington (true patriots versus subversive rabble). Simple economic differences between agrarian and commercial interests do not provide the answer either, since more than 90 percent of Americans in the 1790s lived in rural areas. Yet certain distinctions can be made. Republicans tended to be self-assured, confident optimists who were not fearful of instability and who sought to widen the people's participation in government. Federalists, on the other hand, were insecure, uncertain of the future. They stressed the need for order, authority, and regularity in the political world. Unlike Republicans, they had no grass-roots political organization and put little emphasis on involving ordinary people in government. The nation was, in their eyes, perpetually threatened by potential enemies, both internal and external, and best protected by a continuing alliance with Great Britain.

If the factions' respective attitudes are translated into economic and regional affiliations, the pattern is clear. Northern merchants and commercially oriented farmers, well aware of the uncertainties of international trade, tended to be Federalists. Since New England's soil was poor and agricultural production could not be expanded, northern subsistence farmers also gravitated toward the more conservative party, which wanted to preserve the present (and past) rather than look to the future.

Republican southern planters, on the other hand, firmly in control of their region and of a class of enslaved laborers, could anticipate unlimited westward expansion. Many Tidewater planters successfully shifted from cultivating soil-draining tobacco to grains and other foodstuffs. The invention of the cotton gin in 1793 allowed them to plant many more acres of cotton. For their part, small farmers in the South found the Republicans' democratic rhetoric (despite aristocratic leadership) more congenial than the approach of the Federalists, who said and did little to attract the allegiance of such folk.

Finally, the two sides drew supporters from different ethnic groups. Americans of English stock tended to be Federalists, while those of Celtic origin (Welsh, Irish, Scots) were more likely to be Republicans. The third largest group, the Germans, were split fairly evenly at first but eventually moved into the Republican camp. To what degree traditional antagonisms between English and Celts in particular contributed to the growing political split is impossible to say. But it is conceivable that ethnicity was as important as other factors in determining eventual political alignments.

In September 1796, at the end of his second term, Washington published his "Farewell Address," most of which was written by Hamilton. In it Washington outlined two principles that guided American foreign policy until the late 1940s: maintain commercial but not political ties to other nations and enter no permanent alliances. He also attacked the legitimacy of the Republican opposition to his presidency.

The presence of the two organized groups, not yet parties in the modern sense but nonetheless active contenders for office, made the presidential election of 1796 the first that was seriously contested. To succeed Washington, the Federalists put forward the candidacy of Vice President John Adams, with the diplomat

Election of 1796

Thomas Pinckney of South Carolina as his vice-presidential running mate. The Republicans in Congress chose Thomas Jefferson as their candidate; the lawyer, revolutionary war veteran, and active Republican politician Aaron Burr of New York agreed to run for vice president.

That the election was contested did not mean that its outcome was decided by the people. Under the Constitution, electors, not the people, voted. Though in most cases the people chose their electors, over 40 percent of the electors were selected by state legislatures. The system provided that each elector would cast two votes. The man receiving the highest vote total became the president; the second highest became vice president. Thus Adams, the Federalist with 71 votes, became the new president and Jefferson, the Republican with 68 votes, became vice president.

John Adams and political dissent

John Adams took over the presidency peculiarly blind to the partisan developments of the past four years. He kept Washington's cabinet intact, despite its key members' allegiance to his chief rival, Alexander Hamilton. He often adopted a passive posture, letting others (usually Hamilton) take the lead, when he should have acted decisively. When Adams's term ended, the Federalists were severely divided and the Republicans had won the presidency. But at the same time Adams's detachment from Hamilton's maneuverings enabled him to weather the greatest international crisis the republic had yet faced: the so-called Quasi-War with France.

The Jay Treaty improved America's relationship with England, but it provoked retaliation from England's rival, France. When French vessels began seizing American ships carrying British goods, Adams sent three special commissioners to France to reach a settlement: Elbridge Gerry of Massachusetts, John Marshall of Virginia, and Charles Cotesworth Pinckney of South Carolina. At the same time Congress increased military spending. The negotiations never materialized, however, because of a French precondition that a $250,000 bribe had to be paid before talks could begin. Upon receiving word of the French demand, Adams informed Congress of the impasse and recommended further appropriations for the military.

| XYZ Affair |

THE PROVIDENTIAL DETECTION

This Federalist political cartoon was probably drawn shortly after the presidential election of 1796. Jefferson kneels in front of the altar of French despotism, kindling a fire from the controversial writings of radicals. He is stopped from adding the Constitution to the flames by an American eagle—meant to symbolize John Adams, whose election has saved the nation from disorder.   The Library Company of Philadelphia.

Convinced that Adams had deliberately sabotaged the negotiations, congressional Republicans insisted that the dispatches be turned over to Congress. Aware that releasing the reports would work to his advantage, Adams complied. He withheld only the names of the French agents, referring to them as X, Y, and Z. The revelation that the Americans had been treated with utter contempt stimulated a wave of anti-French sentiment in the United States. Cries for war filled the air. Congress formally abrogated the 1778 treaty with France and authorized American ships to seize French vessels.

The Federalists saw this climate of opinion as an opportunity to deal a death blow to their Republican opponents. Now that the country seemed to see the truth of what they had been saying ever since the Whiskey Rebellion in 1794–that the Republicans were subversive foreign agents–the Federalists sought to codify that belief into law. In the spring and summer of 1798, the Federalist-controlled Congress adopted a set of four laws known as the Alien and Sedition Acts, intended to suppress dissent and prevent further growth of the Republican party.

Three of the acts were aimed at immigrants, whom the Federalists quite correctly suspected of being Republican in their sympathies. The Naturalization Act lengthened the residency period required for citizenship from five to fourteen years and ordered all resident aliens to register with the federal government. The Alien

| Alien and Sedition Acts | Enemies Act provided for the detention of enemy aliens in time of war. The Alien

Friends Act, which was to be in effect for only two years, gave the president almost unlimited authority to deport any alien he deemed dangerous to the nation's security. (Adams never used that authority. The Alien Enemies Act was not implemented either, since war was never formally declared.)

The fourth law, the Sedition Act, sought to control both citizens and aliens. It outlawed conspiracies to prevent the enforcement of federal laws and set the maximum punishment for such offenses at five years in prison and a $5,000 fine. The act also tried to control speech. Writing, printing, or uttering "false, scandalous and malicious" statements "against the government of the United States, or the President of the United States," became a crime punishable by as much as two years imprisonment and a $2,000 fine.

In all, there were fifteen indictments and ten convictions under the Sedition Act. Most of the accused were outspoken Republican newspaper editors who failed to mute their criticism of the administration in response to the law. But the first victim–whose story may serve as an example of the rest–was a Republican congress-man from Vermont, Matthew Lyon. The congressman received a $1,000 fine and a four-month prison sentence for declaring in print that John Adams had "an unbounded thirst for ridiculous pomp, foolish adulation, and selfish avarice."

Faced with the prosecutions of their major supporters, Jefferson and Madison sought an effective means of combating the Alien and Sedition Acts. They turned to constitutional theory and the state legislatures. Carefully concealing their own role, Jefferson and Madison each drafted a set of resolutions. Introduced into the Kentucky and Virginia legislatures, respectively, in the fall of 1798, the resolutions differed somewhat but their import was the same. Since the Constitution was created by a compact among the states, they contended, the people speaking through their states had a legitimate right to judge the constitutionality of actions by the federal government. Both sets of resolutions pronounced the Alien and Sedition Acts unconstitutional and asked other states to join in the protest.

Although no other state replied positively to the Virginia and Kentucky resolutions, they nevertheless had major significance. First, they were superb political propaganda, rallying Republican opinion throughout the country. They placed the opposition party squarely in the revolutionary tradition of resistance to tyrannical authority. Second, the theory of union they proposed was expanded on by southern states'-rights advocates in the 1830s and thereafter.

Adams's decision not to seek a declaration of war against France had, in the meantime, split the Federalists, for Hamilton wanted a declared war. When the French government privately indicated that it regretted the earlier treatment of the three commissioners, Adams sent an envoy who successfully negotiated a settlement. But the results of the negotiations were not known until after the election of 1800, and by then the split in the Federalist ranks had already cost Adams his re-election.

The Republicans entered the 1800 presidential race firmly united behind the Jefferson-Burr ticket. Though they won the

Election of 1800

election, their lack of foresight almost cost them dearly. The problem was caused by the system of voting in the electoral college. All Republican electors voted for both Jefferson and Burr, giving each of them 73 votes (Adams had 65). Because neither Republican had a plurality, the Constitution required that the contest be decided in the House of Representatives, with each state's congressmen voting as a unit. In the House, Federalist congressmen decided the election by selecting Jefferson on the thirty-fifth ballot. As a result of the tangle, the Twelfth Amendment to the Constitution (1804) changed the method of voting in the electoral college to allow for a party ticket.

Religious dissent and racial ferment

Ever since the fervor of the Great Awakening had burned itself out in the 1760s, America's churches had been largely quiescent. But in the

Second Great Awakening

late 1790s a few revivals began to occur in New England, and in 1800 a full-fledged Second Awakening broke out in Kentucky and Tennessee. Itinerant Presbyterian and Methodist ministers spread over the countryside, carrying the word of salvation to all who would listen.

Frontier folk, for the most part poor, uneducated, and rootless, were particularly receptive to the enthusiastic preachers. At camp meetings, sometimes attended by thousands of people and usually lasting from three days to a week, clergymen exhorted their audiences to repent their sins and become genuine Christians. They stressed that salvation was open to all, downplaying the doctrine of predestination. The emotional nature of the conversion experience was emphasized far more than the need for careful study and preparation. Such preachers were in effect "democratizing" American religion, making it available to all rather than to a preselected and educated elite. The religious ferment left an indelible legacy of evangelism to American Protestantism.

The revivals also led to increasingly female church congregations. Unlike the First Great Awakening, when converts were evenly divided by sex, more women than men—particularly young women—answered the call of Christianity during the Second Awakening. The increase in female converts seems to have been directly related to major changes in women's circumstances at the end of the eighteenth century. In some areas of the country, especially New England, women outnumbered men after 1790. Thus girls could no longer count on finding marital partners. The uncertainty of their social and familial position may well have led them to seek spiritual certainty in the church. And in these churches they formed innumerable female associations to dispense charity to widows and orphans or to support foreign missions.

The religious ferment among both blacks and whites in frontier regions of the upper South contributed to racial ferment as well. People of both races attended the camp meetings, and sometimes black preachers exhorted whites in addition to members of their own race. When revivals spread eastward into more heavily slave-holding areas, white planters became fearful of the egalitarianism implied in the evangelical message of universal salvation and harmony. At the same time, revivals created a group of respected black leaders—preachers—and provided them with a ready audience for a potentially revolutionary doctrine.

In Virginia a revolt was planned by Gabriel Prosser, a blacksmith who argued that blacks should fight to obtain the same rights as whites.

Prosser's Rebellion

Prosser placed himself in the tradition not only of the French Revolution but also in that of the successful slave rebellion on Haiti, which had been led by Toussaint l'Ouverture.

Important events

1789	George Washington inaugurated Judiciary Act of 1789 French Revolution		1796	First contested presidential election: John Adams elected president, Thomas Jefferson vice president *Ware* v. *Hylton*
1790	Alexander Hamilton's first "Report on Public Credit"		1798	XYZ Affair Alien and Sedition Acts Virginia and Kentucky resolutions Eleventh Amendment
1791	First National Bank chartered Hamilton's "Report on Manufactures" First ten amendments (Bill of Rights) ratified			
1793	France declares war on Britain, Spain, and Holland Neutrality Proclamation Democratic-Republican societies founded Invention of cotton gin *Chisholm* v. *Georgia*		1798–99	"Quasi-War" with France
			1800	United States and France reach peace agreement Jefferson elected president, Aaron Burr vice president Second Great Awakening begins Prosser's Rebellion (Virginia) Mason Locke Weems, *Life of* *Washington*
1794	Whiskey Rebellion (Pennsylvania)			
1795	Jay Treaty		1804	Twelfth Amendment

At revival meetings held by his brother, Prosser recruited other blacks like himself—artisans who moved easily in both black and white circles and who lived in semifreedom under minimal white supervision. The artisan leaders then enlisted rural blacks in the cause. The conspirators planned to attack Richmond on the night of August 30, 1800, setting fire to the city, seizing the state capital, and capturing the governor. Their plan showed considerable political sophistication, but heavy rain made it impossible to execute the plot as scheduled. Several whites then learned of the plan from their slaves and spread the alarm. Prosser avoided capture for some weeks, but most of the other leaders of the rebellion were quickly arrested and interrogated. The major conspirators, including Prosser himself, were

hanged, but in the months that followed other insurrectionary scares continued to frighten Virginia slaveowners.

As the eighteenth century ended, then, white and black inhabitants of the United States were moving toward an accommodation to their new circumstances. The United States was starting to take shape as an independent nation no longer dependent on England. In domestic politics, the Jeffersonian interpretation of republicanism had prevailed over the Hamiltonian approach. The country would be characterized by a decentralized economy, minimal government (especially at the national level), and maximum freedom of action and mobility for individual white males.

But that freedom would be purchased at the expense of white females and black men, women, and children. In the decades to come, both groups would be subject to further control. Within a few years after the establishment of the republic, women and blacks had little realistic hope that the egalitarian ideals of the Declaration of Independence would apply to them. And a pattern was set that would deny Indians not only their rights but also their land.

Suggestions for further reading

NATIONAL GOVERNMENT AND ADMINISTRATION John R. Howe, *The Changing Political Thought of John Adams* (1966); Stephen G. Kurtz, *The Presidency of John Adams: The Collapse of Federalism, 1795–1800* (1957); Forrest McDonald, *Alexander Hamilton: A Biography* (1979); Forrest McDonald, *The Presidency of George Washington* (1974); John C. Miller, *The Federalist Era, 1789–1801* (1960); Merrill D. Peterson, *Thomas Jefferson & The New Nation: A Biography* (1970).

PARTISAN POLITICS Lance Banning, *The Jeffersonian Persuasion: Evolution of a Party Ideology* (1978); Richard W. Buel, Jr., *Securing the Revolution: Ideology in American Politics, 1789–1815* (1972); William Nisbet Chambers, *Political Parties in a New Nation: The American Experience, 1776–1809* (1963); Joseph Charles, *The Origins of the American Party System* (1956); Noble E. Cunningham, *The Jeffersonian Republicans: The Formation of Party Organization, 1789–1801* (1957); Manning J. Dauer, *The Adams Federalists* (1953); Richard Hofstadter, *The Idea of a Party System: The Rise of Legitimate Opposition in the United States, 1780–1840* (1970); Adrienne Koch, *Jefferson and Madison: The Great Collaboration* (1950); John Zvesper, *Political Philosophy and Rhetoric: A Study of the Origins of American Party Politics* (1977).

DIPLOMACY Harry Ammon, *The Genet Mission* (1973); Samuel F. Bemis, *Jay's Treaty,* 2nd ed. (1962); Samuel F. Bemis, *Pinckney's Treaty,* 2nd ed. (1960); Alexander DeConde, *Entangling Alliance: Politics and Diplomacy under George Washington* (1958); Alexander DeConde, *The Quasi-War: Politics and Diplomacy of the Undeclared War with France, 1797–1801* (1966); Felix Gilbert, *To the Farewell Address: Ideas of Early American Foreign Policy* (1961); Charles Ritcheson, *Aftermath of Revolution: British Policy Toward the United States, 1783–1795* (1969).

CIVIL LIBERTIES Leonard W. Levy, *Legacy of Suppression: Freedom of Speech and Press in Early American History* (1960); Robert A. Rutland, *The Birth of the Bill of Rights, 1776–1791* (1955); James Morton Smith, *Freedom's Fetters: The Alien and Sedition Laws and American Civil Liberties* (1956).

EDUCATION AND CULTURE Lawrence A. Cremin, *American Education: The National Experience, 1783–1876* (1981); Joseph J. Ellis, *After the Revolution: Profiles of Early American Culture* (1979); Russel B. Nye, *The Cultural Life of the New Nation: 1776–1803* (1960); Kenneth Silverman, *A Cultural History of the American Revolution* (1976).

WOMEN AND BLACKS Nancy F. Cott, *The Bonds of Womanhood: "Woman's Sphere" in New England, 1780–1835* (1977); Gerald W. Mullin, *Flight and Rebellion: Slave Resistance in Eighteenth-Century Virginia* (1972).

8 ᴖ

THE REPUBLIC ENDURES,

1801–1824

In November 1800, Abigail Adams took up residence in the "wilderness," the new federal capital of Washington. The president's "great castle," she wrote her sister, was still uncompleted. Because the yard was unfenced, the First Lady was forced to dry the family's wash in the "great unfinished audience-room" (the East Room). She shopped for provisions in nearby Georgetown, but found it "the very dirtyest Hole," its streets "a quagmire after every rain."

Even so, the creation of this new capital, a planned city, was among the boldest steps of the new nation. Located near the nation's center of population in eastern Maryland, Washington was beholden neither to the colonial past nor to any single state. Its design, too, reflected the political philosophy of the new nation. Just as the Constitution divided the government into three branches, so the city had three distinct areas—one centered around Congress, another around the president, and the third around the Supreme Court. At the highest elevation stood the Capitol, a single building that emphasized Congress's role as a collective body. A mile and a half away lay the president's mansion, connected to the Capitol by a broad boulevard. The Court, however, stood apart from both Congress and the mansion, without direct access to either.

The government, with only 2,875 civilian employees, was small, but that suited the republic. Americans tended to distrust the federal government. The adoption of the Constitution and the

power of the Federalists in the 1790s had been more a result of their dissatisfaction with the Articles of Confederation than a sign of their confidence in central government. In 1800 they elected the Republican Thomas Jefferson to the presidency; thus began the Virginia dynasty and a swing back to state authority.

During the early nineteenth century, much of the young republic's future success was assured. Jefferson's inauguration established the tradition of peaceful transition of power from one political party to another. The Louisiana Purchase (1803) not only secured land for westward expansion but guaranteed continued American access to the Mississippi River. And the decisions of the Supreme Court under Chief Justice John Marshall made that body an equal branch of government. The Court also gave voice to the nationalist point of view. Indeed, nationalism would be the dominant political force immediately after the War of 1812.

All, however, was not well. The United States became embroiled in Europe's struggles and went to war against Great Britain in 1812. Economic hard times were felt under Jefferson and again in 1819. On the latter occasion a depressed economy gave rise to sectionalism. Of great significance, Missouri's petition for statehood with a slave constitution demonstrated to Americans—North and South—the explosive nature of the slavery issue. Yet through both war and political division, the nation endured.

Jefferson assumes power

Nearly overnight the formality of the Washington and Adams presidencies disappeared as Thomas Jefferson set the tone for Republican Washington. Gone were the aristocratic wigs, ruffles, and breeches (short trousers) the first two presidents had favored; Jefferson wore plain garb. On March 4, 1801, the president-elect left his New Jersey Street boarding house alone and walked to the Capitol to be sworn in. Ordinary folk who had come to celebrate his inaugural overran Washington and Georgetown, causing Federalists to cluck their tongues at the seeming collapse of authority and order.

Yet for all their suspicion, the Federalists gave up the reins of government peaceably. "I have this morning witnessed one of the most interesting scenes a free people can ever witness," Margaret B. Smith, a Philadelphian, wrote on March 4, 1801, to her sister-in-law. "The changes of administration, which in every government and in every age have most generally been epochs of confusion, villainy and bloodshed, in this our happy country take place without any species of distraction, or disorder." The precedent of an orderly and peaceful change of government had been established.

Jefferson delivered his inaugural address in the Senate chamber, the only part of the Capitol that had been completed. "We are all Republicans, we are all Federalists," he told the assembly in an appeal for national unity. Confidently addressing those with little faith in the people's ability to govern themselves, he called America's republican government "the world's best hope."

Jefferson's inaugural address

The new president went on to outline his own and his party's goals:

a wise and frugal government, which shall restrain men from injuring one another, which shall leave them otherwise free to regulate their own pursuits. . . .

equal and exact justice to all men, of whatever state or persuasion, religious or political. . . .

the support of the state governments in all their rights, as the most competent administrators for our domestic concerns and the surest bulwarks against antirepublican tendencies.

At the same time, he assured Federalists that he shared some of their concerns as well:

the preservation of the general government in its whole constitutional vigor. . . .

the honest payment of our debts and sacred preservation of the public faith. . . .

encouragement of agriculture and of commerce as its handmaid.

But more than lofty principles was at stake in the rivalry between the two groups. On assuming the presidency, Jefferson found that virtually all appointed officials were loyal Federalists. To counteract this Federalist power, Jefferson first refused to recognize Adams's last-minute "midnight appointments" to local offices in the District of Columbia. Next he dismissed Federalist customs collectors from New England ports. Vacant treasury and judicial offices were awarded to Republicans, until by July 1803 only 130 of 316 presidentially controlled offices were held by Federalists. Jefferson saw these actions not as distributing the spoils of victory, but as equalizing the power of the parties. Nonetheless, he had used patronage both to reward his friends and to build a party organization.

Meanwhile, the Republican Congress proceeded to affirm its Republicanism. Guided by Secretary of the Treasury Albert Gallatin and John Randolph of Virginia, Jefferson's ally in the House, the federal government went on a diet. Congress repealed all internal taxes, even the whiskey tax. Gallatin cut the army budget in half, to just under $2 million, and reduced the navy budget from $3.5 to $1 million in 1802. Moreover, Gallatin laid plans to reduce the national debt—Hamilton's engine of economic growth—from $83 to $57 million, as part of a plan to retire it altogether by 1817.

More than frugality, however, separated Republicans from Federalists. Opposition to the Alien and Sedition laws of 1798 had helped to

An 1801 Republican victory flag. Above a cameo portrait of Jefferson the eagle holds a banner reading "Jefferson President of the United States of America." He tramples disdainfully on a second banner, "John Adams no more." Smithsonian Institution.

unite Republicans. Now Congress let them expire in 1801 and 1802 and repealed the Naturalization Act of 1798. The act that replaced it required only five years of residency, acceptance of the Constitution, and the forsaking of foreign allegiance and titles (1802).

The Republicans turned next to the judiciary, the last stronghold of unchecked Federalist power. During the 1790s not a single Republican had been appointed to the federal bench. Moreover, the Judiciary Act of 1801, passed in the last days of the Adams administration, had created fifteen new judgeships (which Adams filled in his midnight appointments) and reduced by attrition the number of justices on the Supreme Court from

Attacks on the judiciary

six to five. Since that reduction would have deprived Jefferson of the chance to appoint a new justice when the next vacancy occurred, one of the first acts of the new Republican-dominated Congress was to repeal the Judiciary Act of 1801.

But the Republicans were not yet finished. At Jefferson's suggestion, the House impeached (indicted) and in 1804 the Senate removed from office Federal District Judge John Pickering of New Hampshire. Although he was an alcoholic and emotionally disturbed, Pickering had not committed any crime.

The same day Pickering was convicted, the House impeached Supreme Court Justice Samuel Chase for judicial misconduct. Chase had repeatedly denounced Jefferson's administration from the bench. The Republicans, however, failed to muster the two-thirds majority necessary to convict him; they had gone too far. Their failure to remove Chase preserved the Court's independence and established a precedent for narrow interpretation of the grounds for impeachment (criminal rather than political grounds).

Far more momentous than frugality in government or the politics of federal appointments was the Louisiana Purchase (1803). The territory

| Louisiana Purchase | of Louisiana was vital to the American West. By 1800 nearly a million Americans

living west of the Appalachians were dependent on the Ohio and Mississippi rivers. Farmers shipped their produce down the two rivers to New Orleans for shipment both to American ports and overseas. In 1802, Napoleon acquired the vast territory from Spain. At about the same time, the Spanish intendant of Louisiana withdrew from Americans the privilege of duty-free shipping through the port of New Orleans. Most Americans suspected a Napoleonic plot behind the change of policy. Eastern merchants and western farmers, both hurt by the decline in trade, clamored for war.

To relieve the pressure for war and to prevent westerners from joining Federalists in opposition to his administration, Jefferson simultaneously prepared for war and explored the possibility of purchasing Louisiana. In January 1803 he sent James Monroe to France to help the American minister Robert Livingston in negotiating to buy New Orleans and Florida for $10 million. Meanwhile, Congress authorized a call-up of 80,000 militia if it proved necessary. Arriving in Paris on April 12, Monroe was astonished to learn that on the previous day France had offered to sell all of Louisiana—more than 825,000 square miles—to the United States for $15 million. On April 30 Monroe and Livingston signed a treaty to purchase the territory, whose borders were left undefined.

The Louisiana Purchase doubled the size of the nation, opened the way for westward expansion across the continent, and prevented the United States from being drawn into European politics. The acquisition was the boldest of federal actions and the single most popular achievement of Jefferson's presidency. But its legality was questionable. The Constitution gave him no clear authority to acquire new territory and incorporate it into the nation. Jefferson considered requesting a constitutional amendment to allow the purchase, but in the end he justified it on the grounds that it was part of the president's implied powers to protect the nation. The people, he knew, would accept or reject the purchase on election day.

In 1804 the voters expressed their overwhelming approval of Jefferson's action; he and his running mate, George Clinton, rode the wave of popularity to a second term. Charles C. Pinckney and Rufus King, their Federalist opponents, carried only Connecticut and Delaware.

Republicans versus Federalists

Until the Republican successes in 1800 and 1804, Federalists had disdained widespread electioneering. They believed in government by the "best" people—those whose education, wealth, and experience marked them as leaders. For candidates to debate their qualifications before their inferiors—the voters—was unnecessary and undignified. The direct appeals of the Republicans therefore struck them as a subversion of the natural political order.

But after their resounding defeat in 1800, a younger generation of Federalists began to imitate the Republicans. They organized statewide,

| Younger Federalists | and led by men like Josiah Quincy, a young congressman from Massachusetts,

they began to campaign for popular support. Quincy cleverly identified the Federalists as the people's party, attacking Republicans as autocratic slaveholding planters. The self-styled Younger Federalists also exploited westerners' concern about Indians, New Englanders' con-

Citizens gather at the State House in Philadelphia to whip up support for their candidates and parties. This picture, drawn on Election Day in 1816, suggests the overwhelmingly white, exclusively male composition of the electorate. Historical Society of Pennsylvania.

cern about commerce, and everyone's concern about national strength.

In response to the new competition, the Republicans introduced the political barbecue, which became the symbol of grassroots campaigning. Soon both parties were using barbecues to appeal directly to voters. Holidays became occasions for partying and electioneering, a practice that helped to make the Fourth of July a day of national celebration and local oratory.

Older Federalists still opposed such blatant campaigns. And although they were strong in a few states like Connecticut and Delaware, the Federalists never offered the Republicans sustained competition. Divisions between Older and Younger Federalists often hindered them, and the extremism of some Older Federalists tended to discredit the party. A case in point was Timothy Pickering, a Massachusetts congressman who urged the secession of New England in 1803 and 1804. Pickering won some support among the few Federalists in Congress, but others opposed his plan for a northern confederacy. When Vice President Burr lost his bid to become governor of New York in 1804, the plan collapsed. (Burr, more an opportunist than a loyal Republican, was to have led New York into secession, with the other states to follow.)

Both political parties suffered from factionalism. In 1804, for instance, the Federalist Alex-

Chapter 8: The republic endures, 1801–1824

ander Hamilton backed a rival Republican faction against Burr in his race for the governorship of New York; Hamilton had caught wind of the Pickering-Burr conspiracy. Burr, his political career in ruins, turned his resentment on Hamilton and challenged him to a duel. Hamilton accepted the challenge and was killed.

The Burr-Hamilton duel reflected the intensity of party factionalism, which combined with the personal nature of political conflict to keep both Republicans and Federalists from becoming full-blown parties in the modern sense. Where Federalists were too weak to be a threat, Republicans succumbed to the temptation to fight among themselves. Even Jefferson's congressional leader, John Randolph, abandoned the president in 1806 to start a third party.

Thus, although this period is commonly called the era of the first party system, parties as such never fully developed. Competition encouraged party organization, but personal ambition, personality clashes, and local, state, and regional loyalties worked against it. And as the election of 1804 revealed, the Federalists could offer only weak competition at the national level. Indeed, after the death of Alexander Hamilton, only one Federalist played a strong and sustained role in national politics: Chief Justice John Marshall.

Under Marshall's domination from 1801 until 1835, the Supreme Court remained a Federalist stronghold even after Republican justices achieved a majority in 1811. *John Marshall* Throughout his tenure the Court upheld federal supremacy over the states and protected the interests of commerce and capital. More important, Marshall made the Court the equal of the other branches of government in practice as well as theory. First, he made a place on the Court a coveted honor. Second, he built a unified Court, influencing the justices to issue a single majority opinion rather than individual concurring judgments. Marshall himself became the voice of the majority. From 1801 through 1805 he wrote 24 of the Court's 26 decisions.

Finally, Marshall increased the Court's power. Ironically *Marbury* v. *Madison* (1803), the landmark case that enabled Marshall to strengthen the Court, involved another of Adams's midnight appointees. William Marbury, whom **Marbury v. Madison** Adams had designated a justice of the peace in the District of Columbia, sued the new secretary of state, James Madison, for canceling Marbury's appointment so Jefferson could appoint a Republican. In his suit Marbury requested a writ of mandamus, or a court order compelling Madison to appoint him.

At first glance, the case presented a political dilemma. It was highly possible that even if the Supreme Court ruled in favor of Marbury and issued a writ of mandamus, the president would not comply. On the other hand, if the Court refused to issue the writ, it would be handing the Republicans a victory. Marshall avoided both alternatives and turned what seemed like a no-win situation into a Federalist triumph. Speaking for the Court, he ruled that Marbury had a right to his commission but that the Court could not compel Madison to honor it, because the Constitution did not grant the Court power to issue a writ of mandamus. Thus Marshall declared unconstitutional section 13 of the Judiciary Act of 1789, which authorized the Court to issue such writs. Marbury lost his job and the justices denied themselves the power to issue writs of mandamus, but the Supreme Court claimed its great power of judicial review.

In succeeding years Marshall fashioned the theory of judicial review. Since the Constitution was the supreme law, he reasoned, any act of Congress contrary to the Constitution must be null and void. And since the Supreme Court was responsible for upholding the law, it had a duty to decide whether a conflict existed between a legislative act and the Constitution. If such a conflict did indeed exist, the Court would declare the congressional act unconstitutional.

Under Marshall, the Supreme Court also be-

Hamilton-Burr duel

came the bulwark of a nationalist point of view. In *McCulloch* v. *Maryland* (1819), the Court

McCulloch *v.* Maryland

struck down a Maryland law taxing the federally chartered Second Bank of the United States. Maryland had adopted the tax in an effort to destroy the bank's Baltimore branch. The issue was thus one of state versus federal power. Speaking for a unanimous Court, Marshall asserted the supremacy of the federal government over the states.

Having established federal supremacy, the Court went on to consider whether Congress could issue a bank charter. No such power was specified in the Constitution. But Marshall noted that Congress had the authority to pass "all laws which shall be necessary and proper for carrying into execution" the enumerated powers of the government (Article I, Section 8). Therefore Congress could legally exercise "those great powers on which the welfare of the nation essentially depends." If the ends were legitimate and the means were not prohibited, Marshall ruled, a law was constitutional. The bank charter was declared legal.

In *McCulloch* v. *Maryland* Marshall combined Federalist nationalism with Federalist economic views. By asserting federal supremacy he was protecting the commercial and industrial interests that favored a national bank. This was Federalism in the tradition of Alexander Hamilton. The decision was only one in a series. In *Fletcher* v. *Peck* (1810) the Court voided a Georgia law that violated individuals' right of contract. Similarly, in the famous *Dartmouth College* v. *Woodward* (1819), the Court nullified a New Hampshire act altering the charter of Dartmouth College, which Marshall ruled constituted a contract. In protecting such contracts, Marshall thwarted state interference in commerce and business.

The struggle for power between Marshall's Federalist court and Republican legislatures, though fierce, proved benign. A certain amount of sparring was to be expected in the process of hammering out governmental relationships in a new republic. If the nation were to be threatened in these times, it would be not from within but from without.

Preserving American neutrality

"Peace, commerce, and honest friendship with all nations, entangling alliance with none," President Jefferson had sensibly proclaimed in his first inaugural address. And Jefferson's efforts to stand clear of European conflict worked until 1805. Thereafter he found peace and undisturbed commerce an elusive goal.

The renewal of the Napoleonic wars in May 1803 again trapped the United States between France and Great Britain. For two years American commerce actually benefited from the conflict. As the world's largest neutral carrier, the United States became the chief supplier of food to Europe. American merchants also gained control of most of the West Indian trade, which was often transshipped through American ports to Europe.

Meanwhile, the United States victory over Tripolitan pirates on the north coast of Africa provided Jefferson with his one clear success in protecting American trading rights. In 1801 Jefferson had refused the demands of the Sultan of Tripoli for payment of tribute. Instead he sent a naval squadron to the Mediterranean to protect American merchant ships from Barbary Coast pirates. The United States signed a peace treaty with Tripoli in 1805, but continued to pay tribute to other Barbary states.

But in 1805 American merchants became victims of Anglo-French enmity. First Britain tightened its control over the high seas with its victory over the French and Spanish fleets at the Battle of Trafalgar in October 1805. Two months later Napoleon defeated the Russian and Austrian armies at Austerlitz. Stalemated, the two powers waged commercial war, blockading and counterblockading each other's trade.

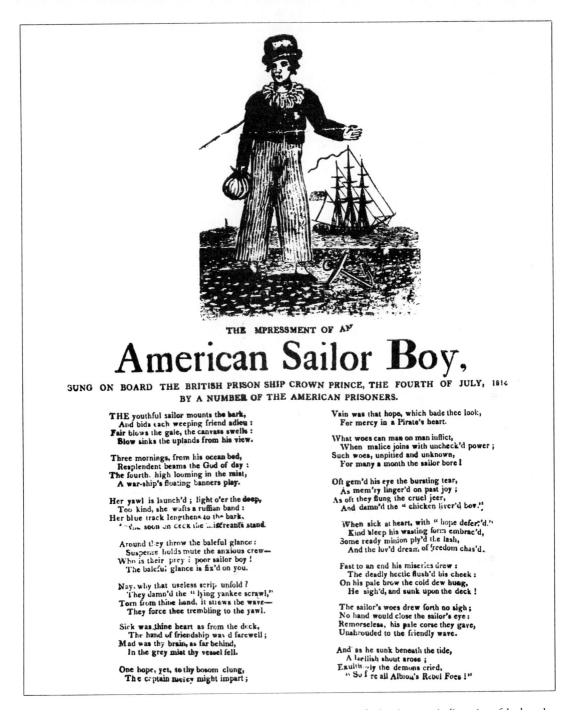

THE IMPRESSMENT OF AN

American Sailor Boy,

SUNG ON BOARD THE BRITISH PRISON SHIP CROWN PRINCE, THE FOURTH OF JULY, 1814
BY A NUMBER OF THE AMERICAN PRISONERS.

THE youthful sailor mounts the bark,
  And bids each weeping friend adieu :
Fair blows the gale, the canvass swells :
  Slow sinks the uplands from his view.

Three mornings, from his ocean bed,
  Resplendent beams the God of day :
The fourth. high looming in the mist,
  A war-ship's floating banners play.

Her yawl is launch'd ; light o'er the deep,
  Too kind, she wafts a ruffian band :
Her blue track lengthens to the bark,
  And soon on deck the miscreants stand.

Around they throw the baleful glance :
  Suspense holds mute the anxious crew—
Who is their prey ? poor sailor boy !
  The baleful glance is fix'd on you.

Nay, why that useless scrip unfold ?
  They damn'd the " lying yankee scrawl,"
Torn from thine hand, it strews the wave—
  They force thee trembling to the yawl.

Sick was thine heart as from the deck,
  The hand of friendship wav'd farewell ;
Mad was thy brain, as far behind,
  In the grey mist thy vessel fell.

One hope, yet, to thy bosom clung,
  The captain mercy might impart ;

Vain was that hope, which bade thee look,
  For mercy in a Pirate's heart.

What woes can man on man inflict,
  When malice joins with uncheck'd power ;
Such woes, unpitied and unknown,
  For many a month the sailor bore !

Oft gem'd his eye the bursting tear,
  As mem'ry linger'd on past joy ;
As oft they flung the cruel jeer,
  And damn'd the " chicken liver'd boy."

When sick at heart, with " hope defer'd."
  Kind sleep his wasting form embrac'd,
Some ready minion ply'd the lash,
  And the lov'd dream of freedom chas'd.

Fast to an end his miseries drew :
  The deadly hectic flush'd his cheek :
On his pale brow the cold dew hung,
  He sigh'd, and sunk upon the deck !

The sailor's woes drew forth no sigh ;
No hand would close the sailor's eye :
Remorseless, his pale corse they gave,
Unshrouded to the friendly wave.

And as he sunk beneath the tide,
  A hellish shout arose ;
Exultingly the demons cried,
  " So fare all Albion's Rebel Foes !"

Ballad of an American sailor impressed by the British during the War of 1812. References to the British captain as a "Pirate" and the British crew as "de- mons" reveal the intense indignation felt by the American public.   The New-York Historical Society.

Preserving American neutrality

As a trading partner of both countries, the United States paid a high price.

At the same time the British navy stepped up impressments of American sailors. Britain, whose navy was the world's largest, was suffering a severe shortage of sailors. Few enlisted, and those already in service frequently deserted. The Royal Navy resorted to stopping American ships and forcibly removing British deserters, British-born naturalized American seamen, and other unlucky sailors mistakenly suspected of being British. About six to eight thousand Americans were drafted in this manner between 1803 and 1812.

In February 1806 the Senate denounced British impressment as aggression and a violation of neutral rights. To protest the insult Congress passed the Non-Importation Act, prohibiting importation from Great Britain of a long list of cloth and metal articles. In November Jefferson suspended the act temporarily while William Pinckney joined James Monroe in London in an attempt to negotiate a settlement. But the treaty Monroe and Pinckney carried home violated their instructions—it did not mention impressment—and Jefferson never submitted it to the Senate for ratification.

Less than a year later the *Chesapeake* Affair exposed American military weakness. In June 1807 the forty-gun frigate U.S.S. *Chesapeake* left Norfolk, Virginia. About ten miles out, still inside American territorial waters, it met the fifty-gun British frigate *Leopard*. When the *Chesapeake* refused to be searched for deserters, the *Leopard* repeatedly emptied its guns broadside into the American ship. Three Americans were killed and eighteen wounded. Four sailors were impressed—three of them American citizens, all of them deserters from the Royal Navy. Wounded and humiliated, the *Chesapeake* crept back into port.

President Jefferson responded by strengthening the military and putting economic pressure on Great Britain: In July Jefferson closed American waters to British warships to prevent

similar incidents and soon thereafter he increased military and naval expenditures. On December 14, 1807, Jefferson again invoked the Non-Importation Act, followed eight days later by a new measure, the Embargo Act.

Intended as a short-term measure, the Embargo Act forbade virtually all exports from the United States to any country. Imports came to a halt as well, since foreign ships delivering goods would have to leave American ports with empty holds. Smuggling blossomed overnight.

Few American policies have been as unsuccessful as Jefferson's embargo. The lucrative American merchant trade collapsed; exports fell 80 percent from 1807 to 1808. Federalist New England felt the brunt of the depression. Ships rotted in harbors and grass grew on wharves; unemployment soared. In the winter of 1808 and 1809, talk of secession spread through New England port cities. Great Britain, in contrast, was only mildly affected by the embargo. Finally, the policy gave the French an excuse to privateer against American ships that had managed to escape the embargo by avoiding American ports. The French argued that such ships must be British ships in disguise, since the embargo barred American ships from the seas.

In the election of 1808, the Republicans faced the Federalists, the embargo, and factional dissent in their own party. Jefferson followed Washington's example, renouncing a third term and supporting James Madison, his secretary of state, as the Republican standard-bearer. Madison and his running mate, George Clinton, defeated the Federalist ticket of Charles C. Pinckney and Rufus King.

As for the embargo, it eventually collapsed under the weight of domestic opposition. Jefferson withdrew it in his last days in office, replacing it with the Non-Intercourse Act of 1809. The act reopened trade with all nations except Britain and France, and authorized the president to resume trade with either country if it ceased to violate neutral rights. But the new act solved only the problems that had been created by the embargo; it did not convince Britain and France to change their policies.

When the Non-Intercourse Act expired in spring 1810, the United States tried to sell old wine in a new bottle, relabeled Macon's Bill Number 2. A congressional invention, the bill reopened trade with both Great Britain and France, but provided that if either nation ceased to violate American rights, the president could shut down American commerce with the other. This effort, like the first, failed.

Because the British navy controlled the Atlantic, Britain was the main target of American hostility, not France. Angry American leaders tended to blame even Indian resistance in the West on British agitation, ignoring the Indians' legitimate protests against white encroachment and treaty violations. Frustrated and having exhausted all efforts to alter British policy, the United States in 1811 and 1812 drifted into war with Great Britain.

Meanwhile, unknown to the president and Congress, Great Britain was changing its policy. The Anglo-French conflict had ended much of British commerce with the European continent, and exports to the United States had fallen 80 percent. Depression had hit the British Isles. On June 16, 1812, Britain opened the seas to American shipping. But two days later, before word had crossed the Atlantic, Congress declared war.

The War of 1812 was the logical outcome of United States policy since the renewal of war in Europe in 1803. The grievances enumerated in President Madison's message to Congress on June 1, 1812, were old ones: impressment, interference with neutral commerce, and the stirring-up of western Indians. Unmentioned was the resolve to defend American independence and honor—and the thirst of expansionists for British Canada. Yet Congress and the country were divided. Much of the sentiment for war came from the War Hawks, land-hungry southerners and westerners led by Henry Clay of Kentucky and John C. Calhoun of South Carolina. Most representatives from the coastal states opposed war, since armed conflict with the great naval power threatened to close down all American shipping. The vote for war—79 to 49 in the House, 19 to 13 in the Senate—was close and reflected these sharp regional differences. The split would also be reflected in the way Americans fought the war.

The War of 1812

Militarily, war was a foolish adventure for the United States in 1812; despite six months of preparation, American forces were still ill equipped. Because the army had neither an able staff nor an adequate force of enlisted men, the burden of fighting fell on the state militia—and not all the states cooperated. The navy did have a corps of well-trained, experienced officers, but next to the Royal Navy, the ruler of the seas, the U.S. Navy was minuscule.

For the United States, the only readily available battlefront on which to confront Great Britain was Canada. The mighty Royal Navy was | *Invasion of Canada* | useless on the waters separating the United States and Canada, since no river afforded it access from the sea. Invasion of Canada, thousands of miles from British supply sources, therefore would give the United States an edge.

Begun with high hopes, the invasion of Canada proved disastrous. The American strategy was to concentrate on the West, splitting Canadian forces and isolating the Indians who supported the British. General William Hull marched his troops into Upper Canada, near Detroit. But the British anticipated the invasion, moved troops into the area, and demanded Hull's surrender. When pro-British Indians captured Fort Dearborn, near Detroit, Hull capitulated. Farther to the west, other American forts surrendered. By the winter of 1812 and 1813, the British controlled about half the Old Northwest (Ohio, Indiana, Illinois, Michigan, and Wisconsin).

The United States had no greater success on the Niagara front, where New York borders

Canada. At the Battle of Queenstown, north of Niagara, the United States regular army met defeat because the New York state militia refused to leave the state. This scene was repeated near Lake Champlain, where American plans to attack Montreal were foiled when the militia declined to cross the border.

In 1813 the two sides also vied over control of the Great Lakes, the key to the war in the Northwest. The contest was largely a ship-building

| Great Lakes campaign |

ing race. Under Master Commandant Oliver Hazard Perry and shipbuilder Noah Brown, the United States outbuilt the British on Lake Erie and defeated them at the bloody Battle of Put-in-Bay on September 10. Through their victory, the Americans gained control of Lake Erie.

General William Henry Harrison then began the campaign that would prove to be the United States' brightest moment in the war. Harrison's 4,500-man force, mostly Kentucky volunteers, crossed Lake Erie and pursued the British and their Indian allies into Canada, defeating them at the Battle of the Thames on October 5. The great Shawnee Chief Tecumseh died in that battle, and with him, the Indian confederacy he had formed to resist American expansion. Once again the United States controlled the Old Northwest.

Outside the Old Northwest the British dominated the war. In December 1812 the Royal Navy blockaded the Chesapeake and Delaware

| British naval blockade |

bays. By 1814 the blockade extended southward from New England down the Atlantic coast and then westward along the Gulf of Mexico. The blockade was so effective that between 1811 and 1814 American trade declined by nearly 90 percent.

Following their overthrow of Napoleon in April 1814, the British stepped up the land campaign against the United States, concentrating their efforts in the Chesapeake. In retaliation for the American burning of the Canadian capital, York (now Toronto)—and to divert American

troops from Lake Champlain, where the British planned a new offensive—royal troops occupied Washington and set it to the torch. The attack on the capital was, however, only a raid. The major battle occurred at Baltimore, where the Americans held firm. Although the British inflicted heavy damages both materially and psychologically, they achieved no more than a stalemate.

The last campaign of the war was waged in the South, along the Gulf of Mexico. It began when Tennessee militia general Andrew Jackson defeated the Creeks and Cherokees at the Battle of Horseshoe Bend in March 1814. The battle ended the year-long Creek War. As a result, the Creeks ceded two-thirds of their land and withdrew to southern and western Alabama. Jackson became a major general in the regular army and continued south toward the Gulf. To forestall a British invasion at Pensacola Bay, which provided an overland route to New Orleans, Jackson seized Pensacola—in Spanish Florida—on November 7, 1814. After securing Mobile, he marched on to New Orleans.

The Battle of New Orleans was the final engagement of the war. Early in December the British fleet had landed east of New Orleans,

| Battle of New Orleans |

7,500 strong, hoping to gain control of the Mississippi River. They faced an American force of regular army troops, plus a larger contingent of Tennessee and Kentucky frontiersmen and two companies of free black volunteers from New Orleans. Finally, on January 8, 1815, the two forces met head on. Jackson and his mostly untrained army held their ground against two frontal assaults. It was a massacre. More than 2,000 British soldiers lay dead or wounded at the day's end; the Americans suffered only 21 casualties. Andrew Jackson was a national hero. Ironically, the Battle of New Orleans was fought two weeks after the end of the war; unknown to Jackson, a treaty had been signed in Ghent, Belgium, on December 24, 1814.

The Ghent treaty made no mention of the issues that had led to war. The United States received no satisfaction on impressment, block-ades, or other maritime rights. Likewise, British demands for a neutral Indian buffer state in the Northwest and territorial cessions from Maine to Minnesota went unmet. Essentially, the Treaty of Ghent restored the prewar status quo. It provided for an end to hostilities, release of prisoners, restoration of conquered territory, and arbitration of boundary disputes. Other questions—notably compensation for losses and fishing rights—would be negotiated by joint commissions.

Why did the negotiators settle for so little? Events in Europe had made peace and the status quo acceptable at the end of 1814, as they had not been in 1812. Napoleon's fall from power allowed the United States to abandon its demands, since peace in Europe made impressment and interference with American commerce moot questions. Similarly, war-weary Britain, its treasury nearly depleted, gave up pressing for a military victory.

The war did reinforce the independence of the young American republic. Although conflict with Great Britain continued, it never again led to war. The experience strengthened America's resolve to steer clear of European politics. It also convinced the government to maintain a standing army of 10,000 men—three times its size under Jefferson.

The war also sealed the fate of the Federalist party. Their presidential nominee in 1812, De Witt Clinton, lost by a wide margin to James Madison. But it was their extremism that was the Federalists' undoing. During the war Older Federalists had revived talk of secession, and from December 15, 1814, to January 5, 1815, Federalist delegates from New England met in Hartford, Connecticut, to take action. With the war in a stalemate and trade in ruins, they planned to revise the national compact or pull out of the republic. Moderates prevented a resolution of secession, but convention members continued to call for radical changes in the Constitution. The changes sought would have limited presidents to one term and weakened the Republicans.

If nothing else, the timing of the Hartford Convention proved fatal. The victory at New Orleans and news of the peace treaty made the Hartford Convention, with its talk of secession and proposed constitutional amendments, look ridiculous. Rather than harassing a beleaguered wartime administration, the Federalists now retreated before a rising tide of nationalism. Though it remained strong in a handful of states until the 1820s, the Federalist party began to dissolve.

Possibly most important of all, the war stimulated economic change. The embargo, the Non-Importation and Non-Intercourse acts, and the war itself had spurred the production of manufactured goods—cloth and metal—to replace banned imports. And in the absence of commercial opportunities abroad, New England capitalists had begun to invest in manufactures. The effects of these changes were to be far reaching.

Postwar nationalism

With peace came a new sense of American nationalism. Five new states joined the union: Indiana (1816), Mississippi (1817), Illinois (1818), and Alabama (1819). (Louisiana had been admitted in 1812.) Self-confidently, the nation asserted itself at home and abroad as Republicans aped Federalists in encouraging economic development and commerce. In his last message to Congress in December 1815, President Madison embraced Federalist doctrine by recommending military expansion and a program to stimulate development and growth. Wartime experiences had, he said, demonstrated the need for a national bank (the first bank had expired) and for better transportation. To raise government revenues and perpetuate the wartime growth in manufacturing, Madison called for a protective tariff—a tax on imported goods. Yet in straying from Jeffersonian Republicanism, Madison did so within limits. Only a constitutional amendment, he argued, could give the federal government authority to build roads and canals that were less than national in scope.

The congressional leadership pushed Madison's nationalist program energetically. Representative John C. Calhoun and Speaker of the House Henry Clay, who named the program the American System, believed it would unify the

American System

country. They looked to the tariff on imported goods to stimulate industry. New mills would purchase raw materials; new mill workers would buy food from the agricultural South and West. New roads would make possible the flow of produce and goods, and tariff revenues would provide the money to build them. Finally, the national bank would facilitate all these transactions.

In 1816 Congress enacted into law much of the nationalistic program. The Second Bank of the United States was chartered. Like its predecessor, the bank had a twenty-year charter, was a blend of public and private ownership, and had one-fifth of its directors appointed by the government. The nation's first protective tariff was also passed. Duties were placed on imported cottons and woolens and on iron, leather, hats, paper, and sugar.

Congress did not share Madison's reservations about the constitutionality of using federal funds to build local roads. "Let us, then, bind the republic together," Calhoun declared, "with a perfect system of roads and canals." But Madison vetoed Calhoun's internal improvements bill, which provided for the construction of roads of mostly local benefit, adamantly insisting that it was unconstitutional. Internal improvements were the province of the states and of private enterprise. (Madison did, however, approve funds for the continuation of the National Road, on the grounds that it was a military necessity.)

The 1816 presidential election pitted Rufus King, the last Federalist to seek that office, against James Monroe, a Republican. Monroe, who won decisively, declared that the American people were "one great family with a common interest." For his first term that was true. He retained Madison's domestic program, supporting the bank and tariffs and vetoing internal improvements.

Monroe's secretary of state, John Quincy Adams, managed the nation's foreign policy brilliantly from 1817 to 1825. An experienced

John Quincy Adams as secretary of state

diplomat, Adams stubbornly pushed for expansion, political distance from the Old World, and peace. Party politics, he firmly believed, had no place in foreign relations; the national interest, not loyalty or good intentions, should guide American policy. A small, austere man who described himself as a bulldog, Adams was a giant as a diplomat.

Adams's first step was to strengthen the peace with Great Britain. In April 1817 the two nations agreed to the Rush-Bagot Treaty. Through the treaty Great Britain and the United States agreed to limit their Great Lakes naval forces to one ship each on Lake Ontario and Lake Champlain and two vessels each on the other lakes. This first disarmament treaty of modern times began the process that led to demilitarization of the United States–Canadian border. Adams then pushed for the Convention of 1818, which fixed the United States–Canadian border from Lake of the Woods west to the Rockies. When agreement could not be reached on the territory west of the mountains, the two nations settled on joint occupation of Oregon for ten years.

Adams moved next to settle long-term disputes with Spain. During the War of 1812, the United States had seized Mobile and West Florida. Afterward it took advantage of Spain's preoccupation with domestic and colonial troubles to negotiate for the purchase of Florida. Talks took place in 1818, while General Andrew Jackson's troops occupied much of Florida on the pretext of suppressing Seminole raids against American settlements across the border. The following year, under dictated terms, Spain agreed to cede Florida to the United States without payment. In this Transcontinental, or Adams-Onís Treaty, the United States also defined the southern boundary of the Louisiana Purchase from the Gulf of Mexico to the Pacific Ocean. In return, the United States government assumed $5 million worth of claims by American citizens against Spain and gave up its dubious claim to Texas. Expansion had thus been achieved at little cost and without bloodshed, and American claims now stretched from the Atlantic to the Pacific.

The Panic of 1819 and renewed sectionalism

Monroe's domestic achievements could not match his diplomatic successes. The period of harmony that began his presidency—dubbed the Era of Good Feelings by a Boston newspaper—was short-lived. By 1819 postwar nationalism and confidence had eroded, and financial panic darkened the land. (Neither panic nor the resurgence of sectionalism hurt Monroe politically; without a rival political party to rally opposition, he won a second term unopposed.)

But hard times spread. The postwar expansion had been built on loose money and widespread speculation. When it slowed, the manufacturing depression that had begun in 1818 deepened. Distressed urban workers lobbied for relief and began to take a more active role in politics. Manufacturers demanded greater tariff protection—and eventually got it in the Tariff of 1824. Farmers, on the other hand, wanted lower tariffs. Southern planters, for example, railed at the protective Tariff of 1816, which had raised prices at the same time cotton prices were falling sharply.

Western farmers suffered too. Those who had purchased public land on credit could not repay their loans. To avoid mass bankruptcy, Congress delayed payment of the money, and western state legislatures passed "stay laws" restricting mortgage foreclosures. Many westerners blamed the panic on the Second Bank of the United States, which in self-protection had cut off loans it had issued in the previous three years.

Even more divisive was the question of slavery. Ever since the drafting of the Constitution, political leaders had avoided the issue. In February 1819, however, slavery finally crept into the political agenda when Missouri residents petitioned Congress for admission to the Union as a slave state. For the next two-and-one-half years the issue dominated all congressional action.

The debate transcended slavery in Missouri. At stake was the undoing of the compromises that had kept the issue quarantined since the Constitutional Convention. Missouri was on the same latitude as free Illinois, Indiana, and Ohio, and its admission as a slave state would thus thrust slavery further northward. It would also tilt the political balance toward the states committed to slavery. In 1819 the Union consisted of an uneasy balance of eleven slave and eleven free states. If Missouri entered as a slave state, the slave states would have a two-vote edge in the Senate.

But what made the issue so divisive was not the politics of admission to statehood, but people's emotional attitudes toward slavery. Many northerners had come to the conclusion that it was evil. Thus when Representative James Tallmadge, Jr., of New York introduced an amendment providing for gradual emancipation in Missouri, it led to passionate and sometimes violent debate on moral grounds. The

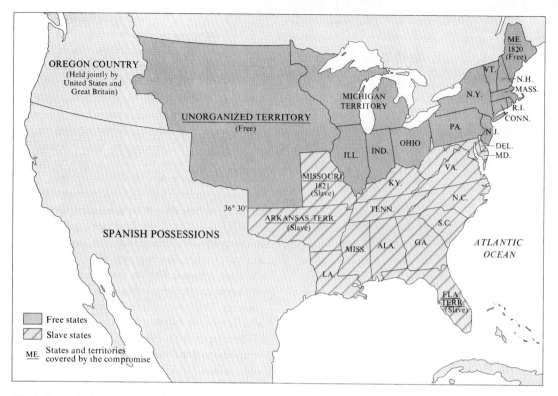

The Missouri Compromise of 1820

House, which had a northern majority, passed the Tallmadge amendment, but the Senate rejected it. The two sides were deadlocked.

A compromise emerged in 1820 under pressure from House Speaker Henry Clay: the admission of free Maine, carved out of Massachusetts, was linked with that of slave Missouri. In the rest of the Louisiana Territory north of 36°30′ (Missouri's southern boundary), slavery was prohibited forever (see map). Though the compromise carried, the issue ultimately destroyed Republican unity and ended the reign of the Virginia dynasty.

Missouri Compromise

In foreign policy, one thorny issue remained to be resolved: recognition of revolutionary forces in Latin America. The United Provinces of the Rio de la Plata (Argentina), Chile, Peru, Colombia, and Mexico had broken free of Spain between 1808 and 1822, and Americans clam-ored to recognize them officially. But Monroe and Adams moved slowly in acknowledging Latin American independence. They sought to avoid conflict with European powers and to assure themselves of the stability of the revolutionary regimes. Shortly after the Adams-Onís Treaty with Spain was safely signed and ratified, in 1823, however, the United States became the first nation outside Latin America to recognize the new states.

Later the same year, events in Europe again threatened the stability of the New World. Spain experienced a domestic revolt, and France occupied Spain in an attempt to bolster the weak monarchy against the rebels. The United States feared that France and its allies might also seek to overturn the new Latin American states and restore them to Spanish rule. Great Britain, which shared this concern, proposed joint United States–British protection of South America. But Adams rejected the British overture, fearing any European intervention in the New World. He insisted that the United States act independently and on its own initiative; action in concert with Britain would violate the principle of avoiding foreign entanglements.

The result was the Monroe Doctrine, a unilateral declaration against European interference in the New World. The president enunciated the famous doctrine in his last message to Congress on December 2, 1823.

| Monroe Doctrine |

Monroe called for, first, *noncolonization* of the Western Hemisphere by European nations, a principle that expressed American anxiety not only about Latin America but also about Russian expansion in Alaska. Second, he demanded *nonintervention* by Europe in the affairs of independent New World nations. Finally, Monroe pledged *noninterference* by the United States in European affairs, including those of Europe's existing New World colonies.

The Monroe Doctrine, however, had no force behind it. Indeed, the policy could not have succeeded without the support of the British, who were already committed to keeping other European nations out of the New World. Europeans ignored the doctrine; it was the Royal Navy they respected, not American policy.

The foreign-policy problems confronting the infant republic from the turn of the century through the mid-1820s strikingly resembled those faced today by the newly established nations of the Third World. The mother country often treated its former colony as if it had not won its independence. And like Third World nations today, the young United States steered clear of alliances with superpowers, preferring neutrality and unilateralism.

At home the United States worked to establish an enduring central government. As a union of states whose boundaries were an inheritance from the colonial past, the republic was no more than a shaky federation. And although Federalist talk of secession never led to action, sectional differences ran deep. Some issues, like slavery, seemed beyond resolution, though com-

Important events

1801	John Marshall becomes Chief Justice Jefferson inaugurated
1801–05	Tripoli War
1803	*Marbury* v. *Madison* Louisiana Purchase
1803–12	British impressment of American seamen
1804	Jefferson re-elected
1806	Non-Importation Act
1807	*Chesapeake* Affair Embargo Act
1808	James Madison elected president
1809–10	Non-Intercourse Acts
1810	Macon's Bill No. 2
1812–15	War of 1812
1814	Treaty of Ghent
1814–15	Hartford Convention
1815	Battle of New Orleans
1816	James Monroe elected; last Federalist presidential candidate
1817	Second Bank of the United States Rush-Bagot Treaty
1819	*McCulloch* v. *Maryland* Adams-Onís Treaty
1819–23	Financial panic; depression
1820	Missouri Compromise
1821	Missouri admitted as state
1823	Monroe Doctrine

promise did succeed in delaying the judgment day. Political division in itself proved benign, and the young country established a tradition of peaceful transition of power through presidential elections. It was the Supreme Court that made the first advances toward national unity, establishing federal power over the states and encouraging commerce. After the war all branches of the government, responding to the popular mood, pursued a more vigorous national policy. Their efforts would help to transform the nation and its economy.

Suggestions for further reading

GENERAL   Marcus Cunliffe, *The Nation Takes Shape, 1789–1837* (1959); Marshall Smelser, *The Democratic Republic, 1801–1815* (1968); Charles M. Wiltse, *The New Nation, 1800–1845* (1961).

PARTY POLITICS   Noble E. Cunningham, Jr., *The Jeffersonian Republicans in Power: Party Operations, 1801–1809* (1963); David Hackett Fischer, *The Revolution of American Conservatism: The Federalist Party in the Era of Jeffersonian Democracy* (1965); Richard Hofstadter, *The Idea of a Party System* (1969); Linda K. Kerber, *Federalists in Dissent* (1970); James S. Young, *The Washington Community, 1800–1828* (1966).

THE VIRGINIA PRESIDENTS   Harry Ammon, *James Monroe: The Quest for National Identity* (1971); Irving Brant, *The Fourth President: A Life of James Madison* (1970); Noble E. Cunningham, Jr., *The Process of Government Under Jefferson* (1978); Alexander De Conde, *The Affair of Louisiana* (1976); James Ketcham, *James Madison* (1970); Forrest McDonald, *The Presidency of Thomas Jefferson* (1976); Merrill D. Peterson, *The Jefferson Image in the American Mind* (1960); Merrill D. Peterson, *Thomas Jefferson and the New Nation* (1970).

THE SUPREME COURT AND THE LAW   Leonard Baker, *John Marshall: A Life in Law* (1974); Richard E. Ellis, *The Jeffersonian Crisis: Courts and Politics in the Young Republic* (1971); Charles G. Haines, *The Role of the Supreme Court in American Government and Politics, 1789–1835* (1944); Morton J. Horowitz, *The Transformation of American Law, 1780–1860* (1977); R. Kent Newmyer, *The Supreme Court under Marshall and Taney* (1968).

THE WAR OF 1812   Roger H. Brown, *The Republic in Peril: 1812* (1964); Harry L. Coles, *The War of 1812* (1965); Reginald Horsman, *The Causes of the War of 1812* (1962); Reginald Horsman, *The War of 1812* (1969).

NATIONALISM AND SECTIONALISM   George Dangerfield, *The Awakening of American Nationalism, 1815–1828* (1965); George Dangerfield, *The Era of Good Feelings* (1952); Glover Moore, *The Missouri Compromise 1819–1821* (1953); Murray N. Rothbard, *The Panic of 1819* (1962).

THE MONROE DOCTRINE   Samuel F. Bemis, *John Quincy Adams and the Foundations of American Foreign Policy* (1949); Walter LaFeber, ed., *John Quincy Adams and American Continental Empire* (1965); Ernest R. May, *The Making of the Monroe Doctrine* (1976); Dexter Perkins, *Hands Off: A History of the Monroe Doctrine* (1941).

9

THE ECONOMIC EVOLUTION OF THE NORTH AND WEST, 1800–1860

John Jervis's life bridged the old and the new. His roots lay in the rural area of upstate New York. He had learned to read and write during occasional attendance at common school, and to farm and handle an axe from his father. But in 1817 he left behind much of that tradition and became involved in undertakings that would lead to a new, far different nation. Hired to clear a cedar swamp for the Erie Canal, Jervis had to acquire skills not used on the farm: the ability to follow construction plans and to work precisely in tandem with others. As he learned new skills, he advanced from axeman to surveyor to engineer to superintendent of a division.

When the Erie Canal was completed in 1825, Jervis moved on to become second-in-command of the Delaware and Hudson Canal project. Later, as a supervisor of an early rail experiment, he redesigned the locomotive's wheel assembly. Jervis spent two decades building the 98-mile Chenango Canal and the fresh-water supply system for New York City. In 1864, at age sixty-nine, he returned home to Rome, New York, and organized an iron mill.

The canals and railroads John Jervis helped build were the most visible signs of the evolution of the American economy from 1800 through 1860. The canal boat, the steamboat, the locomotive, and the telegraph were all agents of change and economic growth. They helped to open up the frontier and brought mostly self-sufficient farmers into the market economy. They made it profitable to manufacture cloth in New England and ship the finished goods to retail outlets in New Orleans or St. Louis or even, by the 1850s, San Francisco. They forged the beginnings of a national, capitalist economy.

But for Americans living in this era of rapid economic growth, the rewards of economic improvement were accompanied by problems and tensions. Not everyone profited, as John Jervis did, in wealth and opportunity. As traditional ways began to give way to the demands of a market economy, survival required that most free Americans sell their labor for wages. By the second half of the nineteenth century, the engine of economic change and growth roared ahead full-steam; economic growth would not be derailed.

The transition to a market economy

The base of the old economy had been staple exports—grain, tobacco, and other crops grown by free farmers and slaves for overseas markets. By the Civil War, however, the United States had an industrializing economy in which an increasing number of men and women worked in factories or offices for a wage, and in which most citizens—farmers and workers—had become dependent on store-bought necessities.

In the new economy crops were grown and goods were produced for sale in the marketplace, at home or abroad. The money received in market transactions, whether from the sale of goods or of a person's labor, was used to purchase items produced by other people. Such a system encouraged specialization. Formerly self-sufficient farmers, for example, began to grow just one or two crops. Farm women gave up spinning and weaving at home and purchased fabric produced by wage-earning farm girls in Massachusetts textile mills.

Sustained growth was the result of this economic evolution. Improvements in transportation and technology, the division of labor, and new methods of financing all fueled expansion of the economy—that is, the multiplication of goods and services. In turn, this growth prompted new improvements. The effect was cumulative; by the 1840s the economy was growing more rapidly than in the previous four decades. Per-capita income doubled between 1800 and 1860.

Though such economic growth was sustained, it was not even. Prosperity reigned during two long periods, from 1823 to 1835 and from 1843 to 1857. But there were long stretches of economic contraction as well. During the time from Jefferson's 1807 embargo through 1815, the growth rate was ac-

tually negative—that is, fewer goods and services were produced. Contraction and deflation occurred again during the depressions of 1819 through 1823, 1839 through 1843, and 1857. These periods were characterized by the collapse of banks, business bankruptcies, and a decline in wages and prices. For workers, the down side of the cycle meant lower wages and higher rates of unemployment.

Working people, a Baltimore physician noted during the depression of 1819, felt hard times "a thousand fold more than the merchants." Yet even during good times wage earners could not build up sufficient financial reserves to get them through the next depression; often they could not make it through the winter without drawing on charity for food, clothing, and firewood. In the 1820s and 1830s, free laborers in Baltimore found steady work from March through October and unemployment and hunger from November through February.

What caused the cycles of boom and bust? In general, they were a direct result of the new market economy. Prosperity inevitably stimulated greater demand for staples and finished goods. Increased demand led in turn to higher prices and still higher production, to speculation in land, and to the flow of foreign currency into the country. Eventually production surpassed demand, leading to lower prices and wages; and speculation outstripped the true value of land and stocks. The inflow of foreign money led first to easy credit and then to collapse when unhappy investors withdrew their funds.

Some economists considered this process healthy—a self-adjusting cycle in which unprofitable economic ventures were eliminated. In theory, people concentrated on the activities they did best, and the economy as a whole became more efficient. Advocates of the system argued also that it furthered individual freedom, since ideally each seller, whether of goods or labor, was free to determine the conditions of the sale. But in fact the system put workers on a perpetual rollercoaster; they had become dependent on wages—and the availability of jobs—for their very existence.

Government promotion of the economy

To stimulate economic growth, the federal and state governments intervened actively during these years in the economy. Beginning with the purchase of Louisiana in 1803, the nation embarked on a deliberate program of westward expansion, western settlement, and promotion of agriculture. In 1803 President Jefferson dispatched Meriwether Lewis and William Clark to explore the new territory and report on its flora, fauna, minerals, and metals. The Lewis and Clark expedition was the beginning of a continuing federal interest in geographic and geologic surveying, which were the first steps in opening western land to exploitation and settlement.

| *Survey and sale of land* |

To encourage western agriculture, the federal government offered public lands for sale at reasonable prices and evicted Indian tribes from their traditional lands. And because transportation was crucial to development of the frontier, the government financed roads and subsidized railroad construction through land grants. Even the State Department aided agriculture: Its consular offices overseas collected horticultural information, seeds, and cuttings and published technical reports in an effort to improve American farming.

The federal government also played a key role in technological and industrial growth. Federal arsenals pioneered new manufacturing techniques and helped to develop the machine-tool industry. The United States Military Academy at West Point, founded in 1802, emphasized technical and scientific subjects in its curriculum.

And the U.S. Post Office stimulated interregional trade and played a brief but crucial role in the development of the telegraph. Finally, to create an atmosphere conducive to economic growth, the government protected inventions and domestic industries. Patent laws gave inventors a seventeen-year monopoly on their inventions, and tariffs protected American industry from foreign competition.

The federal judiciary, too, promoted business enterprise. In *Gibbons* v. *Ogden* (1824), the Supreme Court overturned a New York state law that had given Robert Fulton and Robert Livingston a monopoly on the New York–New Jersey steamboat trade. Ogden, their successor, lost his monopoly when Chief Justice Marshall ruled that the trade fell under the sway of the commerce clause of the Constitution. Thus Congress, not New York, had the controlling power. Since the federal government issued such licenses on a nonexclusive basis, the decision ended monopolies on waterways throughout the nation. In defining interstate commerce broadly, the Marshall Court expanded federal powers over the economy while limiting the ability of states to control economic activity within their borders.

| *Legal foundations of commerce* |

Federal and state courts, through their interpretation of state laws, also encouraged the proliferation of corporations. In 1800 the United States had about 300 incorporated firms; in 1830 the New England states alone had issued 1,900 charters. At first each firm needed a special legislative act to incorporate, but after the 1830s applications became so numerous that incorporation was authorized by general state laws.

State governments far surpassed the federal government in promoting economic growth. From 1815 through 1860, for example, 73 percent of the $135 million invested in canals was government money, mostly from the states. In the 1830s the states shifted their investments to rail construction. Even though the federal government

| *State promotion of the economy* |

played a larger role in building railroads than canals, state and local governments provided more than half of southern rail capital. Overall, railroads received 131 million acres in land subsidies, 48 million of which were provided by the states. States actually equalled or surpassed private enterprise in their investments.

From the end of the War of 1812 until 1860 the United States experienced uneven but sustained economic growth largely as a result of these government efforts. Though political controversy raged over questions of state versus federal activity—especially with regard to internal improvements and banking—all parties agreed on the general goal of economic expansion. Indeed, the major restraint on government action during these years was not philosophical but financial: both the government and the public purse were small.

Transportation and regionalization

From 1800 through 1860 the North, South, and West followed distinctly different paths economically. Everywhere agriculture remained the foundation of the American economy. Nevertheless, factories and merchant houses came to characterize the North, plantations the South, and frontier farms the West. Paradoxically, this tendency toward regional specialization made the sections at once more different and more dependent on each other.

The revolution in transportation and communications was probably the single most important cause of these changes. It was the North's heavy investment in canals and railroads that made it the center of American commerce. The South, with most of its capital invested in slave labor, remained largely rural and undeveloped.

Before the canal and railroad fevers, it was by no means self-evident that New England and the Middle Atlantic states would dominate American economic life. In fact, the southward-flowing Ohio and Mississippi rivers oriented the

Change in trade routes frontier of 1800—Tennessee, Kentucky, and Ohio—to the South. But the pattern changed in the 1820s and 1830s. New roads and turnpikes opened up east-west travel. The National Road, a stone-based gravel-topped highway beginning in Cumberland, Maryland, reached Columbus, Ohio, in 1833. More important, the Erie Canal, completed in 1825, forged an east-west axis from the Hudson River to Lake Erie, linking the Great Lakes with New York City and the Atlantic Ocean. Railroads and later the telegraph would solidify these east-west links. By contrast, only at one place—Bowling Green, Kentucky—did a northern railroad actually connect with a southern one. In 1850 the bulk of western trade flowed eastward. Thus, by the eve of the Civil War, the northern and Middle Atlantic states were closely tied to the former frontier of the Old Northwest.

Construction of the 363-mile-long Erie Canal was a visionary enterprise. Vigorously promoted **Canals** by Governor De Witt Clinton, the Erie cost $7 million. It shortened the journey between Buffalo and New York City from twenty to six days and reduced freight charges from $100 to $5 a ton.

The Erie triggered an explosion of canal building. Other states and cities, fearing the advantage New York had gained, rushed to follow suit. By 1840 canals crisscrossed the Northeast and Midwest, and canal mileage in the United States had reached 3,300—an increase of more than 2,000 miles in a single decade. Unfortunately for investors, none of these canals enjoyed the financial success achieved by the Erie. Investment in canals began to slump in the 1830s. By 1850 more miles were being abandoned than built, and the canal era had ended.

Meanwhile, railroad construction was on the upswing. The railroad era began in 1830 when **Railroads** Peter Cooper's locomotive *Tom Thumb* first steamed along 13 miles of track constructed by the Baltimore and Ohio Railroad. By 1850 the United States had nearly 9,000 miles of railroad; by 1860, roughly 31,000. Canal fever stimulated

A mid-nineteenth-century poster boasts of the superior services of the New York Central Railroad. American Antiquarian Society.

this early railroad construction. Promoters of the Baltimore and Ohio had turned to the railroad in an effort to compete with the Canal. Similarly, the line between Boston and Worcester, Massachusetts, was intended as the first link in a line to Albany, at the eastern end of the Erie Canal.

The earliest railroads connected two cities or one city and its surrounding area. But in the 1850s technological improvements, competition, and economic recovery prompted the development of regional and later national rail networks. The West experienced a railroad boom. By 1853 rail lines linked New York to Chicago,

and a year later track had reached the Mississippi River. By 1860 rails stretched as far west as St. Joseph, Missouri—the edge of the frontier. In that year the railroad network east of the Mississippi approximated its physical pattern for the next century, but the process of corporate integration had only begun. Most lines were still independently run, separated by gauge, scheduling, differences in car design, and a commitment to serve their home towns first and foremost.

Railroads did not completely replace water transportation. Steamboats, first introduced in 1807 when Robert Fulton's *Clermont* paddled up

| Steamboats | the Hudson from New York City, still plied the rivers. Until the 1850s, when western rail development blossomed, steamboats outdid railroads in carrying freight. Great Lakes steamers managed to hold their own even into the fifties, for the sealike lakes permitted the construction of giant ships and the widespread adoption of propellers in place of paddle wheels.

Gradually steamboats began to replace sailing vessels on the high seas. In 1818 square-rigged packets began making four round trips a year between New York and Liverpool, sailing on schedule rather than waiting for a full cargo as had ships before then. The breakthrough came in 1848, though, when steamship owner Samuel Cunard began the Atlantic Shuttle, which reduced travel time between Liverpool and New York from 25 days eastbound and 49 days westbound to 10–14 days each way. Sailing ships quickly lost their first-class passengers and light cargo to these swift new ocean steamships.

By far the fastest spreading technological advance of the era was the magnetic telegraph.

| Telegraph | Samuel F.B. Morse's invention freed messages from the restraint of traveling no faster than the messenger; instantaneous communication became possible even over long distances. By 1853, only nine years after construction of the first experimental line, 23,000 miles of telegraph wire spread across the United States. The first transatlantic cable was laid in 1858, and by 1861 the telegraph bridged the continent, connecting the east and west coasts. The new invention revolutionized news gathering, provided advance information for railroads and steamships, and altered patterns of business and finance. Rarely has innovation had so great an impact so quickly.

The changes in transportation and communications from 1800 to 1860 were revolutionary. Railroads reduced the number of loadings and unloadings, were cheap to build over difficult terrain, and remained in use all year. But time was the key. In 1800, for example, it took four weeks to travel from New York City to Detroit; by 1857 it was an overnight trip. In a week one could reach Texas, Kansas, or Nebraska. This reduced travel time saved money and facilitated commerce. During the first two decades of the century, wagon transportation cost 30 to 70 cents per ton per mile. By 1860, railroads in New York state carried freight at an average charge of 2.2 cents per ton per mile; wheat moved from Chicago to New York for 1.2 cents a ton-mile. In sum, the transportation revolution had transformed the economy–and with it the relationships of the North, West, and South.

The North: merchants and farmers

The development of the North as the nation's clearing-house was hastened by its rapid population growth. Between 1800 and 1860, the number of Americans increased sixfold to 31.4 million. As the population grew, the frontier receded, and rural settlements became towns and cities. In 1800 the nation had only 33 towns

| Growth of cities | with 2,500 or more people and only 3 with more than 25,000. By 1860, 392 towns exceeded 2,500 in population and 35 had more than 25,000. In the Northeast, the percentage of people living in urban areas grew from 9.3 to 35.7 from 1800 to 1860. Significantly, most of this growth occurred in northern and western communities located along the new transportation routes, where increased commerce created new jobs and opportunities.

The hundreds of small new cities were surpassed by the great metropolitan cities. In 1860 21 cities exceeded 40,000 in population and 9 exceeded 100,000. By 1810 New York City had overtaken Philadelphia as the nation's most populous city; its population soared thereafter, reaching 1,174,779 in 1860. Baltimore and New Orleans dominated the South, and San Francisco became the leading West Coast city. In the Midwest the new lake cities (Chicago, Detroit, Milwaukee, and Cleveland) began to surpass the frontier river cities (Cincinnati, Louisville, and Pittsburgh) founded a generation earlier. These cities formed a nationwide urban network whose center was the great metropolises of the North.

Rapid urban growth in turn brought about a radical change in American commerce and trade. In 1800 most merchants performed the functions of retailer, wholesaler, importer and exporter, shipper, banker, and insurer. But in New York and Philadelphia in the 1790s, and increasingly in all large cities after the War of 1812, the general merchant gave way to the specialist. As a result, the distribution of goods became more systematic. By the 1830s and 1840s, urban centers had been transformed into a pattern we would recognize today: retail shops featured such specialized lines as shoes, wines and spirits, dry goods, groceries, and hardware. Within the downtown area importers and exporters, wholesalers, jobbers, bankers, and insurance brokers clustered on particular streets, near transportation and the merchant exchanges that made it convenient to carry on their businesses more efficiently.

| *Specialization of commerce* |

In small towns the general merchant persisted for a longer time. Such merchants continued to sell some goods through barter—exchanging, for example, flour or pots and pans for eggs or other local produce. They left the sale of finished goods, such as shoes and clothing, to local craftsmen. In rural areas and on the frontier, peddlers acted as general merchants. But as transportation improved and towns grew, even small-town merchants began to specialize.

Commercial specialization made some traders in the big cities, especially New York, virtual merchant princes. These newly rich traders invested their profits in processing and then manufacturing, further stimulating the growth of northern cities. Boston merchants even founded a new city, Lowell, to house the first textile mills in Massachusetts.

Because the entire trading system was built on credit, it was extremely susceptible to the boom-and-bust cycles that characterized the era. In boom times credit was easy to come by and merchants flourished. During slumps and depressions, bank credit and investment loans contracted sharply and many merchant houses collapsed.

Beyond the town and city limits, agriculture remained the backbone of the New England economy. For although urban areas were growing quickly, America was still overwhelmingly rural. Indeed, it was rural population growth that transformed so many farm villages into bustling small cities. And it was the ability of northeastern farmers to feed the growing town and village populations that made possible the concentration of population and the resulting development of commerce and industry.

In the early part of the century New England and Middle Atlantic farmers supplied their own needs and produced a surplus of crops for sale to the growing towns. But then canals and railroads began transporting grains, especially wheat, eastward from the fertile Old Northwest. And at the same time, northeastern agriculture developed some serious problems. Northeastern farmers had already cultivated all the land they could; expansion was impossible. Moreover, these small farms with their uneven terrain did not lend themselves to the new labor-saving farm implements introduced in the 1830s—mechanical sowers, reapers, threshers, and balers. Many northeastern farms also suffered from soil exhaustion.

| *Northeastern agriculture* |

In response to all these problems, and to competition from the West, many northern farmers either went west or gave up farming for jobs in the merchant houses and factories. Those farmers who remained proved to be quite adaptable. By the 1850s New England and Middle Atlantic farmers were successfully adjusting to western competition. They abandoned commercial production of wheat and corn and stopped tilling poor land. Instead they improved their livestock, especially cattle, and specialized in vegetable and fruit production and dairy farming. They financed these changes through land sales or borrowing. In fact, their greatest profit was made from increasing land values, not from farming itself.

Even so, the Old Northwest gradually and inevitably replaced the northeastern states as the center of American agriculture. Farms in the Old Northwest were much larger than northeastern ones, and better suited to the new mech-

| Mechanization of agriculture |

anized farming implements. The farmers of the region bought machines such as the McCormick reaper on credit and paid for them with the profits from their high yields. By 1847 Cyrus McCormick was selling a thousand reapers a year. Using interchangeable parts, he expanded production to five thousand a year, but still demand outstripped supply. Similarly, John Deere's steel plow, invented in 1837, replaced the inadequate iron plow; steel blades kept the soil from sticking and were tough enough to break the roots of prairie grass. By 1856, Deere's sixty-five employees were making 13,500 plows a year.

These machines eased the problem of scarce farm labor and permitted a 70-percent surge in wheat production in the 1850s alone. By that time the western wilderness of 1800 had become one of the world's leading agricultural regions. Midwestern farmers fed an entire nation and had food left over to export.

The western frontier

Between 1800 and 1860 the frontier moved westward at an incredible pace (see map). In 1800 the edge of settlement formed an arc from western New York through the new states of

| Movement of the frontier |

Kentucky and Tennessee, south to Georgia. Twenty years later it had shifted to Ohio, Indiana, and Illinois in the North and Louisiana, Alabama, and Mississippi in the South. By 1860 settlement had reached the West Coast. Unsettled land remained—mostly between the Mississippi River and the Sierra Nevadas—but essentially the frontier and its native inhabitants, the Indians, had given way to white settlement. All that remained for whites was to people the plains and mountain territories.

The lore of the vanishing frontier forms part of the mythology of America: fur trappers, explorers, and pioneers braving an unknown environment and hostile Indians; settlers crossing the arid plains and snow-covered Rockies by Conestoga wagon to bring civilization to the wilderness; Mormons finding Zion in the Great American Desert; forty-niners sailing on clipper ships to California in search of gold.

Americans have only recently come to recognize that there are other sides to these familiar stories. Women as well as men were pioneers. The fur trappers, explorers, and pioneers did not discover North America by themselves, nor did the wagon trains fight their way across the plains—Indians guided them along traditional paths and led them to food and water. And rather than civilizing the frontier, settlers at first brought a rather primitive economy and society, which did not compare favorably with the well-ordered Indian civilizations. Moreover, all those who sought furs, gold, and lumber spoiled the virgin landscape in the name of progress and development.

No figure has come to symbolize the frontier more aptly than the footloose, rugged fur trap-

| Fur trade |

per. Indeed, the history of trapping was in essence the history of the opening up of the frontier. Early fur traders exploited friendly Indian tribes; then pioneers—mountain trappers—monopolized the trade through the systematic organization and financial backing of trading companies. Soon settlements and towns sprang up along the trappers' routes. By the 1840s, with demand at a low ebb and the beaver nearing extinction, fur trad-

The moving frontier: the edge of settlement, 1800–1860. Source: From Ross M. Robertson, *History of the American Economy,* 2nd edition. N.Y.: Harcourt Brace & World, 1964.

ing declined. The mining and cattle frontiers were to continue for another half-century, following the development of the fur-trading frontier.

But not all regions followed this pattern. By contrast, California and the Pacific Slope were settled almost overnight. In January 1848 James Marshall, a carpenter, spotted a few gold-like

California gold rush

particles in the millrace at Sutter's Mill (now Coloma, California). Word of the discovery spread, and other Californians rushed in search of instant fortunes. By 1849 the news had spread eastward; hundreds of thousands of fortune-seekers flooded in. Most forty-niners never found enough gold to pay their expenses.

"The stories you hear frequently in the States," one gold-seeker wrote home, "are the most extravagant lies imaginable—the mines are a humbug. . . .The almost universal feeling is to get home." But many stayed, unable to afford the passage back home, or tempted by the growing labor shortage in California's cities and agricultural districts. San Francisco, the gateway from the coast to the interior, became an instant city, ballooning from 1,000 people in 1848 to 35,000 just two years later.

Gold altered the pattern of settlement along the entire Pacific Coast. Before 1848 most overland traffic flowed north over the Oregon Trail; few pioneers turned south to California. But by 1849 traffic was instead flowing south, and California was becoming the new population center of the Pacific Slope. One measure of the shift was the overland mail routes. In the 1840s the Oregon Trail had been the major communications link between the Pacific and the Midwest. But the Post Office officials who organized mail routes in the 1850s terminated them in California; there was no route farther north than Sacramento.

By 1860 California, like the Great Plains and prairies farther east, had become a farmers' and merchants' frontier. What made farm settlement possible was the availability of land and credit. Some public lands were granted as a reward for

| Land grants and sales |

military service: veterans of the War of 1812 received 160 acres; veterans of the Mexican War could purchase land at reduced prices. And until 1820, civilians could buy government land at $2 an acre (a relatively high price) on a liberal four-year payment plan. More important, from 1804 to 1817 the government successively reduced the minimum purchase from 320 to 80 acres. However, when the availability of land prompted a flurry of land speculation that ended in the Panic of 1819, the government discontinued credit sales. Instead it reduced the price further, to $1.25 an acre.

Some eager pioneers settled land before it had been surveyed and put up for sale. Such illegal settlers, or squatters, then had to buy the land they lived on at auction, and faced the risk of being unable to purchase it. In 1841, to facilitate settlement, simplify land sales, and end property disputes, Congress passed the Preemption Act, which legalized settlement prior to surveying.

The rise of manufacturing

The McCormick reaper, ridiculed the London *Times,* looked like "a cross between a flying-machine, a wheelbarrow, and an Astley chariot." Put to a competitive test through rain-soaked wheat, however, the Chicago-made reaper alone passed. The reaper and hundreds of other American products made their international debut at the 1851 London Crystal Palace Exhibition, the first modern world's fair. There the design and quality of American machines and wares astonished observers. Most impressive to the Europeans were three simple machines: Alfred C. Hobb's unpickable padlocks, Samuel Colt's revolvers, and Robbins and Lawrence's six rifles with completely interchangeable parts. All were machine-made rather than hand-tooled, products of what the British called the American system of manufacturing.

The American system of manufacturing used precision machinery to produce interchangeable parts that needed no filing or fitting. In 1798 Eli

| American system of manufacturing |

Whitney had used a primitive system of interchangeable parts when he contracted with the federal government to make ten thousand rifles in twenty-eight months. By the 1820s the Connecticut manufacturer Simeon North, the Springfield (Massachusetts) Arsenal, and the Harpers Ferry (Virginia) Armory were all producing machine-made interchangeable parts for firearms. From the arsenals the American system spread, giving birth to the machine-tool industry—the mass manufacture of specialized machines for other industries. One by-product was an explosion in the production of inexpensive consumer goods whose quality was uniformly high.

Interchangeable parts and the machine-tool industry were uniquely American contributions to the industrial revolution. Both paved the way for America's swift industrialization following the Civil War. The process of industrialization began, however, in a simple and traditional way, not unlike that of other nations. In 1800 manufacturing was relatively unimportant to the American economy. What manufacturing there was took place mostly in small workshops and homes, where journeymen and apprentices worked with and under master craftsmen and made articles by hand for a specific customer.

It was the rise of merchant-investors, wholesalers, and retailers, in combination with the transportation revolution, that transformed this system. First the "putting-out" system of home

| *Putting-out system* |

manufacture established the merchant as a middleman between the worker and the customer. In the shoe industry, for instance, shoemakers worked in their homes from 1800 until about 1840, receiving the materials—leather, thread, and so on—from a merchant or master cordwainer and delivering the finished product to him. Then in the 1820s, entrepreneurs set up central shops where leather was cut into soles and uppers before being put out. This system introduced a division of labor, in which workers performed specialized tasks. By the 1850s steam-powered factory production had become widespread. In the process the master craftsman had disappeared, the journeyman had become a factory worker, and shoes were produced impersonally for distant markets.

Even more dramatic and influential was the development of the New England textile industry. The first American textile mill, built in Pawtucket, Rhode Island, in 1790, used water-powered spinning machines constructed by the English immigrant Samuel Slater. By 1800 the mill employed one hundred people.

Textile manufacturing was radically transformed in 1813 by the construction of the first American power loom and the chartering of the Boston Manufacturing Company. The corporation was capitalized at $400,000—ten times the amount behind the Rhode Island mills—by Francis Cabot Lowell and other Boston mer-

| *Waltham (Lowell) system* |

chants. Its goal was to eliminate problems of timing, shipping, coordination, and quality control inherent in the putting-out system. The owners erected their factories in Waltham, Massachusetts, combining all the manufacturing processes at a single location. They also employed a resident manager to run the mill, thus separating ownership from management. The company produced cheap, coarse cloth suitable for the mass market.

In the rural setting of Waltham not enough hands could be found to staff the mill, so the managers recruited New England farm daughters, accepting responsibility for their living conditions and their virtue. To persuade young women to come, they offered high wages, company-run boarding houses, and such cultural events as evening lectures—none of which were available on the farm. This paternalistic approach, called the Waltham or Lowell system, was adopted in other mills erected alongside New England rivers. By the 1850s, though, another work force had entered the mills—Irish immigrants. With a surplus of cheap labor available, Lowell and other mill towns abandoned their model systems. By 1860 a cotton mill had become a modern factory, and work relationships in American society had been radically altered.

Though shoe factories and textile mills were in the vanguard of industrialization, the United States experienced broad-based growth in many kinds of manufacturing. "White coal"—water power—was widely used to run the machines, and an increasing number of Americans derived their livelihood from manufacturing jobs.

Several factors, including the need for home manufactures created by the War of 1812, popu-

A Merrimack Manufacturing Company label shows the mill girls who came from rural areas to work at the looms in Lowell, Massachusetts.   Merrimack Valley Textile Museum.

lation growth, and government policy, stimulated industrialization. Especially important, however, was the development of financial institutions (banks, insurance companies, and corporations) linking savers—those who put money in the bank—with producers or speculators—those who wished to borrow money for equipment. The expiration of the Bank of the United States in 1811 after Congress refused to renew its charter, acted as a stimulus to state-chartered banks, and in the next five years the number of banks more than doubled. Nonethe-

Banking and credit systems

less, state banks proved inadequate to spur national growth, and in 1816 Congress chartered the Second Bank of the United States. From then until 1832, however, many farmers, local bankers, and politicians denounced the bank as a monster, and finally succeeded in killing it.

The closing of the Second Bank in 1836 caused a nationwide credit shortage that, along with the Panic of 1837, stimulated some major reforms in banking. Michigan and New York introduced charter laws promoting what was called *free banking*. Previously every new bank had required a special legislative charter. Under the new laws, any proposed bank that met certain minimum conditions—amount of money, notes issued, and types of loans to be made—would automatically receive a state charter.

Free banking proved a significant stimulus to the economy in the late 1840s and 1850s. New banks sprang up everywhere, providing merchants and manufacturers the credit they needed. The free banking laws also served as a precedent for general incorporation statutes, which allowed manufacturing firms to receive state charters without special acts. Investors in corporations, called shareholders, were granted *limited liability,* or freedom from responsibility for the company's debts. An attractive feature to potential investors, limited liability thus encouraged people to back new business ventures.

In the 1850s, with credit and capital both more easily obtainable, the pace of industrialization increased. In the North, industry began to rival agriculture and commerce in dollar volume. By 1860 six northern states—Massachusetts, New York, Pennsylvania, Connecticut, Rhode Island, and Ohio—were highly industrialized. The clothing, textile, and shoe industries employed more than 100,000 workers each, lumber 75,000, iron 65,000, and woolens and leather 50,000.

Mill girls and mechanics

Oh, sing me the song of the Factory Girl!
So merry and glad and free!
The bloom in her cheeks, of health how it speaks,
Oh! a happy creature is she!
She tends the loom, she watches the spindle,
And cheerfully toileth away,
Amid the din of wheels, how her bright eyes kindle,
And her bosom is ever gay.

This idyllic portrait of factory work was an anachronism when it appeared in 1850. But it was a fitting song for the first women who entered the New England textile mills: young women, most single and between fifteen and thirty years old, who left the villages and farms of New England to work in the mills. They went on their own, lured by the chance to be independent and self-supporting, to get away from home, to save for a trousseau, and to enjoy city life. The mill owners, believing that the degradations of English factory workers arose from their living conditions and not from the work itself, designed a model community offering airy courtyards and river views, secure dormitories, prepared meals, and cultural activities.

By the 1840s, however, the paternalism of the Lowell system had been replaced by exploitation. In their race for profits, owners lengthened hours, cut wages, and tightened discipline. They also introduced the speed-up and the stretch-out to expand production. The speed-up increased the speed of the machines, and the stretch-out increased the number of machines a worker had to operate.

What happened in the New England mills occurred in less dramatic fashion throughout the nation. Workers experienced undesirable changes in their tasks and in their relationships

| Changes in the workplace |

with the employers. In the old journeyman-apprentice system that skilled workers had known for centuries, the master had worked alongside his employees, often living in the same household. Work relationships were intensely personal, and there was little social distance between master and journeyman. All had an interest in the standards of their craft, and they made their finished goods to order and with pride.

But textile mills, shoe factories, insurance companies, wholesale stores, canals, and railroads were the antithesis of the old master-journeyman tradition. Supervisors separated the workers from the owners. The division of labor and the use of machines reduced the skills required of workers. And the coming and going of the large work forces was governed by the bell, the steam whistle, or the clock.

New England mill workers responded to their deteriorating working conditions by organ-

Women shoe workers strike for higher wages at
Lynn, Massachusetts, in 1860.   Culver.

| Mill girl protests | izing and striking. In 1834, in reaction to a 25-percent wage cut, they unsuccessfully |

"turned out" (struck) against the Lowell mills.
Two years later, when boarding-house rates were
raised, they turned out again. As conditions
worsened, workers changed their methods of resistance. By the 1850s strikes had given way to a
concerted effort to shorten the workday. Massachusetts mill women joined forces with other
workers to press for legislation mandating a ten-
hour day and aired their complaints in worker-
run newspapers.

Economic upheaval and divisions among the
workers (native-born versus immigrant) tended
to keep organized labor weak during this period.
Labor unions tended to be local in nature; the
strongest resembled medieval guilds. The first
unions arose among urban journeymen in printing, woodworking, shoemaking, and tailoring.
These craftsmen sought to protect themselves
against the competition of inferior workmen by
regulating apprenticeship and establishing minimum wages. In the 1820s and 1830s craft
unions—unions organized by occupation—forged
larger umbrella organizations in the cities, including the National Trades Union (1834). But
in the depression of 1839 through 1843, the
movement fell apart amidst wage reductions and
unemployment. In the 1850s the deterioration
of working conditions strengthened the labor
movement again. Workers won a reduction in
hours, and the ten-hour day became standard.
Though the Panic of 1857 wiped out the um-

brella organizations, some of the new national unions for specific trade groups survived.

Organized labor's greatest achievement during this period was in gaining recognition of its right to exist. When journeymen shoemakers organized in the first decade of the century, employers turned to the courts, charging criminal conspiracy. The cordwainers' conspiracy cases, which involved six trials from 1806 through 1815, left labor organizations in a tenuous position. Although the journeymen's right to organize was recognized, the courts ruled unlawful any coercive action that harmed other businesses or the public. In effect, therefore, strikes were unlawful. Eventually a Massachusetts case, *Commonwealth* v. *Hunt* (1842), effectively reversed the decision when Chief Justice Lemuel Shaw ruled that Boston journeymen bootmakers had a right to combine and strike "in such manner as best to subserve their own interests."

> **Right to strike**

The impact of economic and technological change, however, fell more heavily on individual workers than on their organizations. As a group, the workers' share of the national wealth declined after the 1830s. Individual producers—craftsmen, factory workers, and farmers—had less economic power than they had had a generation or two before. And workers were increasingly losing control over their own work.

For the nation as a whole, the period from 1800 through 1860 was one of sustained growth. The population grew from 5.3 to 31.5 million. Settlement, once restricted to the Atlantic seaboard and the eastern rivers, had extended more than a thousand miles inland by 1860 and was spreading east from the Pacific Ocean as well. Whereas agriculture had completely dominated the nation at the turn of the century—in 1800 nearly every American not engaged in farming either processed food or provided services for farmers—by mid-century farming was being challenged by a booming manufacturing sector. And agriculture itself was becoming mechanized.

Still, traditional work persisted. Every town had its blacksmith and tailor, stablehands and

Important events

1803–06	Lewis and Clark expedition
1807	Fulton's steamboat, *Clermont*
1810	New York becomes the most populous city
1813	Boston Manufacturing Company founded
1817–30	Canal era
1819	*Dartmouth College* v. *Woodward*
1819–23	Depression
1820s	New England textile mills expand
1824	*Gibbons* v. *Ogden*
1825	Erie Canal completed
1830	Baltimore and Ohio Railroad begins operation *Tom Thumb*
1830–86	Railroad era
1831	McCormick invents the reaper
1834	Mill women strike at Lowell
1837	Financial panic
1839–43	Depression
1842	*Commonwealth* v. *Hunt*
1848	Cunard's Atlantic shuttle
1849	Gold rush
1853	British study of American system of manufacturing
1854	Railroad reaches the Mississippi
1857	Depression
1858	Transatlantic cable

day laborers, seamstresses and domestic servants. And in the South, although some black slaves worked in the new factories and mills, the overwhelming majority of slaves still performed traditional agricultural work.

Suggestions for further reading

GENERAL Stuart Bruchey, *The Roots of American Economic Growth, 1607–1861: An Essay in Social Causation* (1965); David Klingaman and Richard Vedder, eds., *Essays in 19th Century History* (1975); Douglass North, *Economic Growth of the United States, 1790–1860* (1961); Nathan Rosenberg, *Technology and American Economic Growth* (1972).

TRANSPORTATION Robert G. Albion, *The Rise of New York Port, 1815–1860* (1939); Carter Goodrich, *Government Promotion of American Canals and Railroads, 1800–1890* (1960); Samuel E. Morison, *Maritime History of Massachusetts, 1789–1860* (1921); Harry N. Scheiber, *Ohio Canal Era: A Case Study of Government and the Economy, 1820–1861* (1969); Ronald E. Shaw, *Erie Water West: Erie Canal, 1797–1854* (1966); George R. Taylor, *The Transportation Revolution, 1815–1860* (1951).

COMMERCE AND MANUFACTURING Alfred D. Chandler, Jr., *The Visible Hand: Managerial Revolution in American Business* (1977); H.J. Habakkuk, *American and British Technology in the Nineteenth Century* (1962); Diane Lindstrom, *Economic Development in the Philadelphia Region, 1810–1850* (1978); Louis Hartz, *Economic Policy and Democratic Thought: Pennsylvania, 1776–1860* (1954); Merritt Roe Smith, *Harpers Ferry Armory and the New Technology* (1977); Peter Temin, *Iron and Steel in Nineteenth-Century America* (1964);

Joseph E. Walker, *Hopewell Village: A Social and Economic History of an Ironmaking Community* (1966); Caroline F. Ware, *Early New England Cotton Manufacturing* (1931).

AGRICULTURE Percy Bidwell and John Falconer, *History of Agriculture in the Northern United States 1620–1860* (1925); Allan G. Bogue, *From Prairie to Corn Belt: Farming on the Illinois and Iowa Prairies in the Nineteenth Century* (1963); Clarence Danhof, *Change in Agriculture: The Northern United States, 1820–1870* (1969); Paul W. Gates, *The Farmer's Age: Agriculture, 1815–1860* (1962); Benjamin H. Hibbard, *A History of Public Land Policies* (1939); Julie Roy Jeffrey, *Frontier Women: The Trans-Mississippi West 1840–1880* (1979); Edward C. Kendall, *John Deere's Steel Plow* (1959).

THE WESTERN FRONTIER Ray A. Billington, *The Far Western Frontier, 1830–1860* (1956); Gloria G. Cline, *Exploring the Great Basin* (1963); John Mack Faragher, *Women and Men on the Overland Trail* (1979); William H. Goetzmann, *Exploration and Empire: The Explorer and the Scientist in the Winning of the American West* (1966); Rodman W. Paul, *California Gold: The Beginning of Mining in the Far West* (1974); John D. Unruh, Jr., *The Overland Emigrants and the Trans-Mississippi West, 1840–1860* (1979); David J. Wishart, *The Fur Trade of the American West, 1807–1840* (1979).

WORKERS Alan Dawley, *Class and Community: The Industrial Revolution in Lynn* (1977); Thomas Dublin, *Women at Work: The Transformation of Work and Community in Lowell, Massachusetts, 1826–1860* (1979); Susan E. Hirsch, *Roots of the American Working Class: The Industrialization of Crafts in Newark, 1800–1860* (1978); Hannah Josephson, *The Gold Threads: New England's Mill Girls and Magnates* (1949); Bruce Laurie, *Working People of Philadelphia, 1800–1850* (1980); Norman Ware, *The Industrial Worker, 1840–1860* (1924).

10

SLAVERY AND THE GROWTH OF THE SOUTH, 1800–1860

He was weeping, sobbing. In a humble voice he had begged his master not to give him to Mr. King, who was going away to Alabama, but it had done no good. Now his voice rose and he uttered "an absolute cry of despair." Raving and "almost in a state of frenzy," he declared that he would never leave the Georgia plantation that was home to his father, mother, wife, and children.

To Fanny Kemble, watching from the doorway, it was a horrifying and disorienting scene. One of the most famous British actresses ever to tour America, Fanny had grown up breathing England's antislavery tradition as naturally as the air. In New England she had become friends with enlightened antislavery thinkers. Then the man she married took her away from New England to a Georgia rice plantation.

Pierce Butler, Fanny's husband, was all that a cultured Philadelphia gentleman should be. He had lived all his life in the North, though part of his family's fortune had always sprung from southern slavery. When Fanny chose him from dozens of suitors, he had seemed an attractive exemplar of American culture. Yet now he shattered his slave's hopes without hesitation. Only Fanny's tears and pleas convinced Butler not to separate the slave family.

This incident, which occurred in 1839, illustrates both the similarities between South and North and the differences that were beginning to emerge. Though racism existed in the North, its influence was far more visible on southern society. And though some northerners, like Pierce Butler, were undisturbed by the idea of human bondage, a growing number considered it shocking and backward, inappropriate to their thriving economy and contrary to natural rights.

In the South too, the years from 1800 to 1860 were a time of growth and prosperity; new lands were settled and new states peopled. But as the North grew and changed, economically the South merely grew. Steadily the South emerged as the world's most extensive and vigorous slave economy. Its people were slaves, slaveholders, and nonslaveholders rather than farmers, merchants, mechanics, and manufacturers. Its well-being depended on agriculture alone, rather than agriculture plus commerce and manufacturing. Its population was almost wholly rural rather than rural and urban.

The South remains rural

The South in the early 1800s was the product of precisely the kind of resource-exploiting

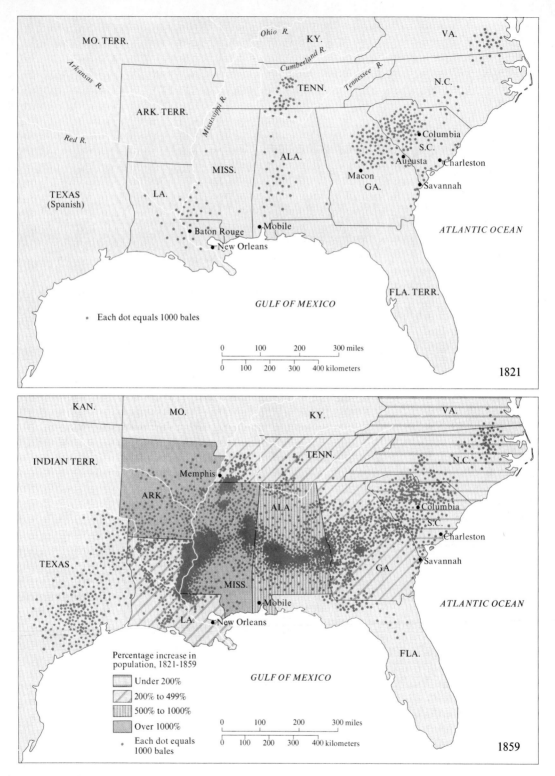

Cotton production in the South

commercial agriculture that most of the early colonies had aspired to develop. Only there, nonmechanized agriculture remained highly profitable, as it did not in the Northeast. Southern planters were not sentimentalists who held onto their slaves for noneconomic reasons. Like other Americans, they were profit-oriented. Circumstances dictated that the most profitable investment lay in the continuation of a plantation economy.

At the time of the Revolution, slave-based agriculture was not exceedingly lucrative. After the war, however, England's burgeoning textile industry required more and more cotton. Only one thing held back a major cotton explosion in the South: a device was needed to remove the sticky seeds from the fibers of the cotton. Eli Whitney solved the problem with the invention of the cotton gin (1793). By 1800 cotton and slavery were spreading rapidly westward from the seaboard states.

So the antebellum South, or Old South, became primarily a cotton South. Tobacco continued to be grown in Virginia and North Caro-

Rise of the cotton South

lina, and rice and sugar were still very important in certain coastal areas, especially in South Carolina, Georgia, and Louisiana. But cotton was the largest crop, the most widespread, and the force behind the South's hunger for new territory. Ambitious cotton growers poured into the West. The boom in the cotton economy came in the 1830s in Alabama and Mississippi. But not until the 1850s did the wave of cotton expansion cross Louisiana and pour into Texas (see maps). Migration into Texas was still strong in 1860.

An unfortunate consequence of the cotton boom was the relative indifference of farmers to the long-term fertility of the soil. In an expanding economy, with cheap and superior land available farther west, most people preferred to exhaust the land and move on rather than invest heavily in preserving it. Only in the older states of the upper South, where the major landholders stayed behind, and where the cotton

boom had less impact, did serious interest in diversified farming develop.

An even more important consequence of the boom was thin population distribution. Producers spread out over as large an area as possible in

Population distribution

order to maximize production and income. Because farms were far apart, southern society remained predominantly rural. Population density, low even in the older plantation states, was especially so in the frontier areas being brought under cultivation. In 1860 there were only 2.3 people per square mile in Texas, 15.6 in Louisiana, and 18.0 in Georgia. By contrast, the Northeast had an average of 65.4 persons per square mile, and in some places the density was much higher.

Society in such rural areas was characterized by relatively weak institutions, for it takes people to create and support organized activity. Where the concentration of people was low, it was difficult to finance and operate schools, churches, libraries, or even hotels, restaurants, and other urban amenities. Southerners were strongly committed to their churches, and some believed in the importance of universities, but all such institutions were far less developed than those in the North.

The few southern cities were likewise smaller and less developed than those in the North. As exporters, southerners did not need large cities; a small group of merchants working in connection with northern brokers sufficed to ship their cotton overseas and to import necessary

Economic development

supplies and luxuries. As planters, southerners invested most of their capital in slaves; they had little money left to build factories—another source of urban growth. A few southerners did invest in iron or textiles on a small scale. But the largest southern industrial plants were cigar factories, where slaves finished tobacco products.

Moreover, the society that developed in this largely agrarian economy was one of extremes. The social distance between a wealthy planter

Many southern yeomen led an almost frontier style of life, farming and raising livestock in sparsely populated areas.   Culver.

and a small slaveholder was as great as the distance between a slaveholder and a nonslaveholder (to say nothing of the distance between whites and slaves). And, contrary to popular belief, planters were neither the most numerous nor the most typical group. The typical white southerner was a yeoman farmer.

Yeoman farmers

More than two-thirds of white southern families owned no slaves. Some of them lived in towns and ran stores or businesses, but most were farmers who owned their own land and grew their own food. Independent and self-respecting, with a hearty share of frontier individualism, they settled the southern wilderness, first by herding livestock and then by planting crops.

Successive waves of these herdsmen and farmers moved down the southern Appalachians into the new regions of the Southwest following the War of 1812. The herdsmen grazed their cattle and pigs on the abundant natural vegetation in the woods. Before long, however, the next wave of settlers arrived and broke ground for crops. These yeomen farmers forced the herdsmen far-

Chapter 10: Slavery and the growth of the South, 1800–1860

ther and farther west, and eventually across the Mississippi. Some yeomen acquired large tracts of level land and became wealthy planters. Others clung to the beautiful mountainous areas they loved. Yeomen could not afford the richest bottomlands, which were swampy and required expensive draining, but they owned land almost everywhere else.

Observers sometimes concluded that these people were poor and idle, especially the herdsmen who sat on their cabin porches while their stock foraged in the woods. It would be more accurate to say that they were frontiersmen and farmers who did not manage to become rich. They worked hard, as farmers do everywhere,

| *Folk culture of the yeoman* |

and enjoyed a folk culture based on family, church, and community. They spoke with a drawl and their inflections were reminiscent of their Scottish and Irish backgrounds. Once a year they flocked to religious revivals called protracted meetings or camp meetings, and in between they enjoyed house raisings, log rollings, corn shuckings, and the ancient Scottish habit of burning the woods (to remove underbrush or clear land). The men did most of the farming; though the women occasionally helped in the fields, they commonly spent their time preserving and preparing food, making clothes, blankets, and candles, and tending to household matters.

Conditions were worse for another group of southerners: free blacks. In 1860 nearly a quarter

| *Free blacks* |

million of them led lives that were often little better than the slaves'. The free blacks of the upper South were descendants of men and women emancipated by their owners in the 1780s and 1790s, a period of post-Revolutionary idealism that coincided with declining tobacco prices. They had few material advantages; most did not own land and had to labor in someone else's field, frequently beside slaves. By law they could not own a gun or liquor, violate curfew, assemble except in church, testify in court, or (everywhere after 1835) vote. Despite these obstacles, a minority bought land, and others found jobs

as artisans, draymen, boatmen, and fishermen. A few owned slaves, who were almost always their wives and children, who had been purchased from bondage.

Farther south, in the cotton and Gulf regions, a large proportion of free blacks were mulattoes, the privileged offspring of wealthy planters. Some received good educations and financial backing from their fathers, who recognized a moral obligation to them. In a few cities such as New Orleans and Mobile, extensive interracial sex had produced a mulatto population that was recognized as a distinct class. Mulattoes formed a society of their own and sought a status above slaves and other freedmen, if not equal to planters. But outside New Orleans and Mobile such groups were rare, and most mulattoes encountered disadvantages more frequently than they enjoyed benefits from their light skin tone.

Slaveholding planters

At the opposite end of the spectrum from free blacks were the slaveholders. As a group slaveowners lived well, on incomes that enabled them to enjoy superior housing, food, clothing, and luxuries. But most did not live on the opulent scale that legend suggests. A few statistics tell the story: 88 percent of southern slaveholders had fewer than twenty slaves; 72 percent had fewer than ten; 50 percent had fewer than five. Thus the average slaveholder was not a man of great wealth but an aspiring farmer. Nor was he a polished aristocrat, but more usually a person of humble origins, with little formal education and many rough edges to his manner.

The wealth of the greatest planters gave ambitious men something to aspire to. If most planters lived in spacious, comfortable farmhouses, some did live in mansions. If most slaveowners sat down at mealtimes to an abundance of tempting country foods, the sophisticated elite consumed such delights as "gumbo, ducks

The North Carolina planter Duncan Cameron (1776–1853) built this spacious and comfortable farmhouse for his bride, Rebecca Bennehan, in 1804. The house, called Fairntosh, is more typical of the average planter's home than the elaborate Greek-revival-style mansions of popular legend. Courtesy of the North Carolina Division of Archives and History, Raleigh.

and olives, *suprême de volaille,* chickens in jelly, oysters, lettuce salad, chocolate cream, jelly cake, claret cup, etc."

Among the wealthiest and oldest families, a paternalistic ideology prevailed. Instead of stressing the acquisitive aspects of commercial agriculture, these people focused on *noblesse oblige.* They saw themselves as custodians of the

> **Southern paternalism**

welfare of society as a whole and of the black families who depended on them. The paternalistic planter saw himself not as an oppressor but as the benevolent guardian of an inferior race. He developed affectionate feelings toward his slaves (as long as they kept in their place) and was genuinely shocked at outside criticism of his behavior.

A few words from the letters of Paul Carrington Cameron, North Carolina's largest slaveholder, illustrate this mentality. After a period of sickness among his approximately one thousand North Carolina slaves (he owned hundreds more in Alabama and Mississippi), Cameron wrote, "I fear the Negroes have suffered much from the want of proper attention and kindness under this late distemper . . . no love of lucre shall ever induce me to be cruel, or even to make or permit to be made any great exposure of their persons at inclement seasons."

There is no doubt that the richest southern planters saw themselves in this way. It was comforting to do so, and slaves, accommodating themselves to the realities of power, encouraged their masters to think their benevolence was appreciated. Paternalism also provided a welcome defense against abolitionist criticism. Still, for most planters, paternalism affected the manner and not the substance of their behavior. It was a matter of style. Its softness and warmth covered harsher assumptions: blacks were inferior; planters should make money.

Relations between men and women in the planter class were similarly paternalistic. The southern woman was raised and educated to be a companion and helpmate to men. At an age when her brothers were studying science, law, or medicine, the wealthy young woman was expected to devote herself to drawing, music, literature, and social life. Her proper responsibility was home management. Within the domestic circle, furthermore, the husband reigned supreme. "He is master of the house," wrote South Carolina diarist Mary Boykin Chesnut. "To hear is to obey . . . all the comfort of my life depends upon his being in a good humor." In a darker mood Chesnut once observed that "there is no slave . . . like a wife." Unquestionably there were some, possibly many, close and satisfying relationships between men and women in the planter class. But it is clear that many women were oppressed.

Childbearing brought grief and sickness as well as joy to southern women. In 1840 the birthrate for southern women in their fertile years was almost 20 percent higher than the na-

| Woman's role |

tional average. At the beginning of the nineteenth century, the average southern woman could expect to bear eight children; by 1860 the figure had decreased only to six, and a miscarriage was likely among so many pregnancies. The high birthrate took a toll on women's health, for complications of childbirth were a major cause of death. Moreover, a mother had to endure the loss of many of the children she bore. In the South in 1860 almost five out of ten children died before age five.

Slavery was another source of trouble. "Violations of the moral law . . . made mulattoes as common as blackberries," protested a woman in Georgia, but wives had to play "the ostrich game." "A magnate who runs a hideous black harem," wrote Mrs. Chesnut, "under the same roof with his lovely white wife, and his beautiful accomplished daughters . . . poses as the model of all human virtues to these poor women whom God and the law have given him. From the height of his awful majesty, he scolds and thunders at them, as if he never did wrong in his life."

In the early 1800s, some southern women, especially Quakers, had spoken out against slavery. But in the 1840s and 1850s, as national and international criticism of slavery increased, southern men published a barrage of articles stressing that women should restrict their concerns to the home. Thus, the *Southern Quarterly Review* declared, "The proper place for a woman is at home. One of her highest privileges, to be politically merged in the existence of her husband."

But southern women were beginning to chafe at their customary exclusion from financial matters. Education was another sore spot. Some of the most privileged women were acquiring a taste for knowledge, and schools for women were multiplying. These academies emphasized domestic skills, but their students nevertheless picked up some knowledge of the world's affairs that they were not, after graduation, permitted to use.

For another large category of southern men and women, education in any form was not allowed. Male or female, slaves were expected to accept ignorance as part of their condition.

Slaves and the conditions of their servitude

For Afro-Americans, slavery was a curse that brought no blessings other than the strengths they developed to survive it. Slaves knew a life of poverty, coercion, toil, heartbreak, and resentment. They had few hopes that were not denied; often they had to bear separation from their loved ones; and they were despised as an inferior race. That they endured and found loyalty and strength among themselves is a tribute to their courage, but it could not make up for a life without freedom or opportunity.

Southern slaves enjoyed few material comforts beyond the bare necessities. Their diet was plain, their clothing coarse, and their housing rudimentary. A slave's diet consisted of cornmeal, fat pork, molasses, and sometimes coffee. Despite occasional supplements of green vegetables and fish, their diet was nutritionally deficient; many slaves suffered from beriberi and pellagra. The few clothes issued to slaves were made either of light cotton or a coarse heavy material called osnaburg. Because shoes were normally not issued until the weather became cool, slaves frequently contracted parasitic diseases such as hook worm. Slave quarters were one-room cabins with dirt floors, few furnishings, and straw mattresses. One and sometimes two families had to share the small cabins, fostering the spread of infection and contagious diseases.

Hard work was the central fact of the slaves' existence. Overseers rang the morning bell before dawn, making it possible for slaves to be in the fields and prepared to work at first light.

Slave work routines Except on some rice plantations, where slaves were assigned daily tasks to complete at their own pace, working from "sun to sun" became universal in the South. These long hours and hard work were at the heart of the advantage of slave labor.

Planters aimed to keep all their laborers busy all the time. Slave women did heavy field work, often as much as the men and even during pregnancy. Old people—of whom there were few—were kept busy caring for young children, doing light chores, or carding, ginning, or spinning cotton. Children had to gather kindling for the fire, carry water to the fields, or sweep the yard. But slaves had a variety of ways to keep from being worked to death. It was impossible for the master to supervise every slave every minute, and slaves slacked off when they were not being watched.

Of course the slave could not cheat too much, because the owner enjoyed a monopoly of force and violence. Whites throughout the *Physical and mental abuse of slaves* South believed that blacks "can't be governed except with the whip." Evidence suggests that whippings were less frequent on small farms than on large plantations, but the reports of former slaves show that a large majority even of small farmers plied the lash. These beatings symbolized authority to the master and tyranny to the slaves, who made them a benchmark for evaluating a master. In the words of former slaves, a good owner was one who did not "whip too much," whereas a bad owner "whipped till he'd bloodied you and blistered you."

As this testimony suggests, terrible abuses could and did occur. The master wielded virtually absolute authority on his plantation; courts did not recognize the word of chattel, and southern society was slow to put pressure on all but the most debased and vicious slaveowners. Some owners refined the cruelty of whipping by cutting open the blisters on a

Most slave families lived in crude and crowded quarters, but the five generations here drew strength from their close family ties. Photographed in Beaufort, South Carolina, in 1862. Library of Congress.

slave's back and dripping sealing wax into them, or throwing salt or pepper water onto the sores. Sometimes, pregnant women received terrible lashings after their master had dug a hole in the ground in which to lay their bellies. There were burnings, mutilations, tortures, and murders.

Slavery in the United States was physically cruel, but less so than elsewhere in the New World. In some parts of the Western Hemisphere in the 1800s, slaves were regarded as an expendable resource and scheduled for replacement after seven years. Treatment was so poor and families so uncommon that death rates were high and the heavily male slave population did not replace itself, and rapidly shrank in size. In the United States, by contrast, the slave population showed a steady natural increase, births exceeded deaths, and each generation grew larger.

The worst evil of American slavery was not

its physical cruelty but the fact of slavery itself: coercion, loss of freedom, belonging to another person. American slaves hated their oppression, and contrary to some whites' perceptions, they were not grateful to their oppressors. Although they had to be subservient and speak honeyed words in the presence of their masters, they talked quite differently later on among themselves. The evidence of their resistant attitudes comes from their actions and from their own life stories.

Former slaves reported some kind feelings between masters and slaves, but the overwhelming picture was one of antagonism and resistance. Slaves mistrusted kindness from whites and sus-

| Slaves' attitudes toward whites |

pected self-interest in their owners. A woman whose mistress "was good to us Niggers" said her owner was kind " 'cause she was raisin' us to work for her." Christmas presents of clothing from the master did not mean anything, observed another, " 'cause he was going to [buy] that anyhow."[1]

Slaves were sensitive to the thousand daily signs of their degraded status. One man recalled the general rule that slaves ate cornbread and owners ate biscuits. If blacks did get biscuits, "the flour we made the biscuits out of was the third-grade shorts." A woman reported that on her plantation "Ol' Master hunted a heap, but we never did get any of what he brought in." If the owner took slaves' garden produce to town and sold it for them, the slaves suspected him of pocketing part of the profits.

Suspicion and resentment often grew into hatred. According to a former slave from Virginia, "the white folks treated the nigger so mean that all the slaves prayed God to punish their cruel masters." When a yellow fever epidemic struck in 1852, many slaves saw it as God's retribution.

[1] Accounts by ex-slaves are quoted from *The American Slave: A Composite Autobiography,* edited by George P. Rawick (Westport, Conn.: Greenwood Press, First Reprint Edition 1972, Second Reprint Edition 1974), from materials assembled by the Library of Congress and originally published in 1941. The spelling in these accounts has been standardized.

A young slave girl who had suffered abuse as a house servant admitted that she took cruel advantage of her mistress when the woman had a stroke. Instead of fanning the mistress to keep flies away, the young slave struck her in the face with the fan whenever they were alone. "I done that woman bad," the slave confessed, but "she was so mean to me."

Slave culture and everyday life

The force that helped slaves to maintain such defiance was their culture. They had their own view of the world, a body of beliefs and values born of both their past and their present. With power overwhelmingly in the hands of whites, it was not possible for slaves to change their world. But drawing strength from their culture, they could refuse to accept their condition or to give up the struggle against it.

Slave culture changed significantly after the turn of the century. Between 1790 and 1808, when Congress banned further importation of slaves, there was a rush to import Africans. After that the proportion of native-born blacks rose steadily, reaching 96 percent in 1840 and almost 100 percent in 1860. With time the old African culture faded further into memory, though it did not disappear. Differences among slaves from various tribes became less noticeable. An Afro-American culture was visibly emerging.

In many ways African influences remained primary. For African practices and beliefs reminded the slaves that they were and ought to be different from their oppressors, and thus encouraged them to resist. The most visible aspects of African culture were the slaves' dress and rec-

| Remnants of African culture |

reation. Some slave men plaited their hair into rows and fancy designs; slave women often wore their hair "in string"—tied in small bunches with a string or piece of cloth. A few men and many women wrapped their heads in kerchiefs following the

Chapter 10: Slavery and the growth of the South, 1800–1860

styles and colors of West Africa. For entertainment, slaves made musical instruments with carved motifs that resembled some African stringed instruments. Their drumming and dancing clearly followed African patterns.

Many slaves continued to see and believe in spirits. Some whites believed in ghosts, but the belief was more widespread among slaves. It closely resembled the African concept of the living dead—the idea that deceased relatives visited the earth for many years until the process of dying was complete. Slaves also practiced conjuration, voodoo, and quasi-magical root medicine. By 1860 the most notable conjurers and root doctors were reputed to live in South Carolina, Georgia, Louisiana, and other isolated coastal areas of heavy slave importation.

These cultural survivals provided slaves with a sense of their separate past. Black achievement in music and dance was so exceptional that whites felt entirely cut off from it; in this one area some whites became aware that they stood completely outside the slave community. Conjuration and folklore also directly fed resistance; slaves could cast a spell or direct the power of a hand (a bag of articles belonging to the person to be conjured) against the master. Not all masters felt confident enough to dismiss such a threat.

In adopting Christianity, slaves fashioned it too into an instrument of support and resistance. Theirs was a religion of justice. Former | *Slave religion* | slaves scorned the preaching arranged by their masters. "You ought to heared that preachin'," said one man. " 'Obey your massa and missy, don't steal chickens and eggs and meat,' but nary a word about having a soul to save." They rejected the idea that in heaven whites would have "colored folks . . . there to wait on em." Instead, when God's justice came, the slaveholders would be "broilin' in hell for their sin."

For slaves Christianity was a religion of personal and group salvation. Beyond seeking personal guidance, these worshippers prayed "for deliverance of the slaves." Some waited "until the overseer got behind a hill" and then laid down their hoes and called on God to free them. Others held fervent secret prayer meetings that lasted far into the night. From such activities many slaves gained the unshakable belief that God would end their bondage. As one man asserted, "it was the plans of God to free us niggers." This faith and the joy and emotional release that accompanied their worship sustained blacks.

Slaves also developed a sense of racial identity. The whole experience of southern blacks taught them that whites despised their race. Blacks naturally drew together, helping each other in danger, need, and resistance. "We never told on each other," one woman declared. Former slaves were virtually unanimous in denouncing those who betrayed the group or sought personal advantage through allegiance to whites. And because most slaves lived in small units, there was no overriding class system within the black community.

The main source of support was the family. Slave families faced severe dangers. At any moment the master could sell a husband or wife, | *Slave family life* | give a slave child away as a wedding present, or die in debt, forcing a division of his property. Many families were broken in such ways. Others were uprooted in the trans-Appalachian expansion of the South. Between 1810 and 1820 alone, 137,000 slaves were forced to move from North Carolina and the Chesapeake states to Alabama, Mississippi, and other western regions. An estimated 2 million persons were sold between 1820 and 1860. When the Union Army registered thousands of black marriages in Mississippi and Louisiana in 1864 and 1865, 25 percent of the men over forty reported that they had been forcibly separated from a previous wife. Probably a substantial minority of slave families suffered disruption of one kind or another.

But this did not mean that slave families could not exist. American slaves clung tenaciously to the personal relationships that gave meaning to life. For although American law did not protect slave families, masters permitted them. In fact, slave owners expected slaves to form families and have children. As a result, there remained a normal ratio of men to women, young to old.

Following African kinship taboos, Afro-Americans avoided marriage among cousins (a frequent occurrence among aristocratic slaveowners). They did not condemn unwed mothers, although they did expect a young girl to form a stable marriage after one pregnancy, if not before. By naming their children after relatives of past generations, Afro-Americans emphasized their family histories. If they chose to bear the surname of a white slaveowner, it was often not their current master's but that of the owner under whom their family had begun.

Slaves abhorred interference in their family lives and sought to prevent the break-up of a family. Rape was a horror for both men and women. Some husbands faced death rather than permit their wives to be sexually abused; and women sometimes fought back. In other cases slaves seethed with anger at the injustice but could do nothing except to soothe each other with human sympathy and understanding. Significantly, blacks condemned the guilty party, not the victim.

Because of the pressures of bondage, black couples had more equal relationships than their white owners. Each member of the immediate family, as well as grandparents, uncles, and aunts, had to take on extra duties as the need arose; thus there was no opportunity to restrict women to narrow responsibilities. Women often worked in the fields with men, but they still cooked the meals and performed traditional household chores. The men cared for the livestock in the evening or fished and hunted on the weekends. Within the family the slave husband and father held a respected place in his home.

Slaves brought to their efforts at resistance the same common sense, determination, and practicality that characterized their family lives. American slavery produced some fearless and

| *Resistance to slavery* |

implacable revolutionaries. Gabriel Prosser's conspiracy (1800) apparently was known to more than a thousand slaves. A similar conspiracy in Charleston in 1822, headed by a free black named Denmark Vesey, involved many of the most trusted slaves of leading families. But the most famous rebel of all, Nat Turner, rose in violence in Southampton County, Virginia, in 1831.

The son of an African woman who passionately hated her enslavement, Turner was a precocious child who learned to read very young. Encouraged by his first owner to study the Bible, he enjoyed some special privileges but also knew changes of masters and hard work. In time young Turner became a preacher. He also developed a tendency toward mysticism, and he became increasingly withdrawn. After nurturing his plan for several years, Turner led a band of rebels from house to house in the predawn darkness of August 22, 1831. The group severed limbs and crushed skulls with axes or killed their victims with guns. Before they were stopped, Nat Turner and his followers had slaughtered sixty whites of both sexes and all ages. Turner and as many as two hundred blacks lost their lives as a result of the rebellion.

But most slave resistance was not violent, for the odds against revolution were especially high in North America. Consequently they directed their energies toward improving their lot as slaves. A desperate slave could run away for good, but as often or probably more often slaves simply ran off temporarily to hide in the woods. Every day that a slave "lay out" in this way the master lost a day's labor. Most owners chose not to mount an exhaustive search and sent word instead that the slave's grievances would be redressed. The runaway would then return to bargain with the master. Most owners would let the matter pass, for, like the owner of a valuable cook, they were "glad to get her back."

Other modes of resistance had the same object: to better the conditions of slavery. Appropriating food (stealing, in the master's eyes) was so common that even whites sang humorous songs about it. Blacks were also alert to the attitudes of individual whites, and learned to ingratiate themselves or play off one white person against another. Field hands frequently tested a new overseer to intimidate him or win more favorable working conditions.

Harmony and tension in a slave society

Not only for blacks but for whites too, slave labor stood at the heart of the South's social system. A host of consequences flowed from its existence, from the organization of society to an individual's personal values.

For blacks, the nineteenth century brought a strengthening and expansion of the legal restrictions of slavery. In all things, from their workaday movements to Sunday worship, slaves fell under the supervision of whites. Courts held that a slave "has no civil right" and could not even hold property "except at the will and pleasure of his master." When slaves revolted, legislators tightened the legal straitjacket.

The weight of this legal and social framework fell on nonblacks as well. All white male citizens bore an obligation to ride in patrols to discourage slave movements at night. White southerners who criticized the slave system out of moral conviction or class resentment were intimidated, attacked, or legally prosecuted. Urban residents who did not supervise their domestic slaves as closely as planters found themselves subject to criticism. And the South's few manufacturers felt pressure to use slave rather than free labor.

Small wonder, for slavery was the main determinant of wealth in the South. Ownership of slaves guaranteed the labor to produce cotton

Slavery as the basis of wealth and social standing

and other crops on a large scale. Slaves were therefore vital to the acquisition of a fortune. Beyond that, slaves were a commodity and an investment, much like gold; people bought them on speculation, hoping for a steady rise in their value. Surplus capital was invested in slaves—not factories and railroads.

It was therefore natural that slaveholding should be the main determinant of a person's social position. Wealth in slaves was the foundation on which the ambitious built their reputations. Ownership of slaves also brought political power: a solid majority of political officeholders were slaveholders, and the most powerful of them were generally large slaveholders. Though lawyers and newspaper editors were sometimes influential, they did not hold independent positions in the economy or society. Dependent on the planters for business and support, they served planters' interests and reflected their outlook.

As slavery became entrenched, its influence spread throughout the social system until even the values and mores of nonslaveholders bore its imprint. For one thing, the availability of slave labor tended to devalue free labor. Nonslaveholders therefore preferred to work for themselves rather than to hire out. This kind of thinking engendered an aristocratic value system ill-suited to a newly established democracy.

In modified form, the attitudes characteristic of the planter elite gained a considerable foot-

Aristocratic values and frontier individualism

hold among the masses. The ideal of the aristocrat emphasized lineage, privilege, power, pride, and refinement of person and manner. Some of those qualities were necessarily in short supply in an expanding economy, however; they mingled with and were modified by the tradition of the frontier. In particular, masculinity and defense of one's honor were highly valued by planter and frontier farmer alike. Thus, instead of gradually disappearing, as it did in the North, the code duello, which required men to defend their honor through the rituals of a duel, hung on in the South and gained an acceptance that spread throughout the society.

Other aristocratic values that marked the planters as a class were less acceptable to the average citizen. Simply put, planters believed they were better than other people. In their pride, they expected not only to wield power but to receive special treatment. By the 1850s, some planters openly rejected the democratic creed, vilifying Jefferson for his statement that all men were equal.

These ideas, which shaped the outlook of the southern elite for generations, led to conflict. Yeomen farmers and citizens resented their underrepresentation in state legislatures, corruption

| Democratic reform movements |

in government, and undemocratic control over local government. After vigorous debate, the reformers won most of their battles. Five states—Alabama, Mississippi, Tennessee, Arkansas, and Texas—adopted what was for that time a thoroughly democratic system: popular election of governors; white manhood suffrage; legislative apportionment based on the white population; and locally chosen county government. Indeed, only South Carolina and Virginia effectively defended property qualifications for office, legislative malapportionment, appointment of county officials, and selection of the governor by the lawmakers. Democracy had expanded with the cotton kingdom.

Even in Virginia, nonslaveholding westerners raised a basic challenge to the slave system. Following the Nat Turner rebellion, advocates of gradual abolition forced a two-week legislative debate on slavery, arguing that it was injurious to the state and inherently dangerous. When the House of Delegates finally voted, the motion favoring abolition lost by just 73 to 58. This was the last major debate on slavery in the antebellum South.

With such tensions in evidence, it was perhaps remarkable that slaveholders and non-

slaveholders did not experience frequent and serious conflict. Why were class confrontations among whites so infrequent? Historians who have considered this question have given many answers. In a rural society, family bonds and kinship ties are valued, and some of the poor nonslaveholding whites were related to the rich new planters. The experience of frontier living must also have created a relatively informal, egalitarian atmosphere. And there is no doubt that the South's racial ideology, which stressed whites' superiority to blacks and race, not class, as the social dividing line, tended to reduce conflict among whites. Moreover, the South was an expanding, mobile society in which yeomen and planters did not depend on each other.

There were signs, however, that the relative lack of conflict between slaveholders and nonslaveholders was coming to an end. As the region grew older, nonslaveholders saw their op-

| Hardening of class lines |

portunities beginning to narrow; meanwhile wealthy planters enjoyed an expanding horizon. In effect, the risk involved in substantial cotton production was becoming too great for most nonslaveholders. Thus from 1830 to 1860 the percentage of white southern families holding slaves declined steadily from 36 percent to 25 percent. At the same time, the monetary gap between the classes was widening. Though nonslaveholders were becoming more prosperous, slaveowners' wealth was increasing much faster. And though slaveowners made up a smaller portion of the population in 1860, their share of the South's agricultural wealth remained between 90 and 95 percent. In fact, the average slaveholder was almost 14 times as rich as the average nonslaveholder.

Pre–Civil War politics reflected these realities. Facing the prospect of a war to defend slavery, slaveowners expressed growing fear for the loyalty of nonslaveholders and discussed schemes to widen slave ownership. In North Carolina, a controversy over the low taxes on slaves erupted. A class-conscious nonslaveholder named Hinton R. Helper attacked slavery in his book *The Impending Crisis,* published in New

Chapter 10: Slavery and the growth of the South, 1800–1860

York in 1857. Discerning planters knew that such fiery controversies lay close at hand in every southern state.

But for the moment slaveowners stood secure. They held from 50 to 85 percent of the seats in state legislatures and a similarly high percentage of the South's congressional seats. In addition to their near-monopoly on political office, they had established their point of view in all the other major social institutions. Professors who criticized slavery had been dismissed from colleges and universities; schoolbooks that contained "unsound" ideas had been replaced. And almost all the Methodist and Baptist clergy, some of whom had criticized slavery in the 1790s, had given up preaching against the institution. In fact, except for a few obscure persons of conscience, southern clergy had become the most vocal defenders of the institution. Society as southerners knew it seemed stable, if not unthreatened.

Elsewhere in the nation, however, society was anything but stable. Social diversity was becoming one of the major characteristics of northern society, and social conflict an increasingly common phenomenon.

Suggestions for further reading

SOUTHERN SOCIETY W. J. Cash, *The Mind of the South* (1941); Avery O. Craven, *The Growth of Southern Nationalism, 1848–1861* (1953); Clement Eaton, *The Growth of Southern Civilization, 1790–1860* (1961); William W. Freehling, *Prelude to Civil War* (1965); Eugene D. Genovese, *The World the Slaveholders Made* (1964); William Sumner Jenkins, *Pro-Slavery Thought in the Old South* (1935); Robert McColley, *Slavery and Jeffersonian Virginia* (1964); Frederick Law Olmsted, *The Slave States,* ed. Harvey Wish (1959); Charles S. Sydnor, *The Development of Southern Sectionalism, 1819–1848* (1948); Ralph A. Wooster, *The People in Power* (1969); Ralph A. Wooster, *Politicians, Planters, and Plain Folk* (1975); Gavin Wright, *The Political Economy of the Cotton South* (1978); Bertram Wyatt-Brown, *Southern Honor* (1982).

SLAVEHOLDERS AND NONSLAVEHOLDERS Ira Berlin, *Slaves Without Masters* (1974); Mary Boykin Chesnut, *A Diary from Dixie,* ed. Ben Ames Williams (1949); Catherine Clinton, *The Plantation Mistress* (1982); Everett Dick, *The Dixie Frontier* (1948); Clement Eaton, *The Mind of the Old South* (1967); Frances Anne Kemble, *Journal of a Residence on a Georgia Plantation in 1838–1839* (1863); Donald G. Mathews, *Religion in the Old South* (1977); Robert Manson Myers, ed., *The Children of Pride* (1972); James Oates, *The Ruling Race* (1982); Frank L. Owsley, *Plain Folk of the Old South* (1949).

CONDITIONS OF SLAVERY Leslie Howard Owens, *This Species of Property* (1976); Willie Lee Rose, ed., *A Documentary History of Slavery in North America* (1976); Todd L. Savitt, *Medicine and Slavery* (1978); Kenneth M. Stampp, *The Peculiar Institution* (1956); Robert S. Starobin, *Industrial Slavery in the Old South* (1970).

SLAVE CULTURE AND RESISTANCE Herbert Aptheker, *American Negro Slave Revolts* (1943); John W. Blassingame, *The Slave Community* (1972); Dena J. Epstein, *Sinful Tunes and Spirituals* (1977); Paul D. Escott, *Slavery Remembered* (1979); Eric Foner, ed. *Nat Turner* (1971); Eugene D. Genovese, *Roll, Jordan, Roll* (1974); Herbert G. Gutman, *The Black Family in Slavery and Freedom, 1750–1925* (1976); Vincent Harding, *There is a River* (1981); Lawrence W. Levine, *Black Culture and Black Consciousness* (1977); Gerald W. Mullin, *Flight and Rebellion* (1972); Stephen B. Oates, *The Fires of Jubilee* (1975); Albert J. Raboteau, *Slave Religion* (1978); Robert S. Starobin, *Denmark Vesey* (1970); Peter H. Wood, *Black Majority* (1974).

11 ❧

THE AMERICAN SCENE,

1800–1860

The Englishwoman Frances Trollope, in her *Domestic Manners of the Americans* (1832), described the audience at a Cincinnati theater: "The spitting was incessant," accompanied by "the mixed smell of onions and whiskey. . . . The noises, too, were perpetual, and of the most unpleasant kind." Indeed, theater regularly evoked the strongest of passions among Americans. "When a patriotic fit seized them, and 'Yankee Doodle' was called for," Trollope observed, "every man seemed to think his reputation as a citizen depended on the noise he made."

That the theater could elicit such emotions, reflected its pre-eminent role in American life. Theater was an early development in the rise of mass popular culture in the United States. It was also a mirror of American social life. Like society itself, theater audiences were divided by occupation, wealth, status, sex, and race. But as the gap between the classes yawned wider, different houses began to cater to different classes. In New York, the Park Theater enjoyed the patronage of the carriage trade, the Bowery drew the middle class, and the Chatham attracted workers. The opera house generally became the upper-class playhouse.

As the United States grew, its society became at once more diverse and more turbulent. More and more people lived in cities, where poverty, overcrowding, and crime set them against each other. Opulent mansions existed within sight of notorious slums, and both wealth and poverty reached extremes unknown in traditional agrarian America.

Private life changed too during these years. With increasing industrialization, the home began to lose its function as a workplace, especially among the middle and upper classes. It became woman's domain, a refuge from the jungle of a man's world. At the same time birth control was more widely practiced and families became smaller.

To a great degree, many Americans were uncomfortable with the new direction of American life. Antipathy toward immigrants was common among native-born Americans, who feared competition for jobs. Blacks fought unceasingly for equality, and Indians tried unsuccessfully to resist forced removal. And some women began to raise their voices against the restrictions they faced. In a diverse and complex society, conflict became common.

Country life, city life

Although the isolated pioneer came to symbolize the United States in the decades before the Civil War, it was the farm community that dominated rural America. The farm village was the center of rural life. But

| *Farm communities* |

social life was not limited to trips to the village; families gathered on each other's farms to do as a community what they could not do individually. Barn-raising was among the activities that regularly brought people together. In preparation for the event, the farmer and an itinerant carpenter built a platform and cut beams, posts, and joists. When the neighbors arrived by buggy and wagon, they put together the sides and raised them into position. After the roof was up, everyone celebrated with a communal meal, and perhaps with singing and dancing. Similar gatherings took place at harvest time and on other special occasions.

Rural women met more formally than did men. Farm men had frequent opportunities to gather informally at general stores, markets, and taverns. Women, though, had to prearrange their regular work and social gatherings: weekly after-church dinners; sewing, quilting, and husking bees; and preparations for marriages and baptisms. These were times to exchange experiences and thoughts, offer each other support, and swap letters, books, and news.

City people had more formal amusements. As work and family life grew apart, there were fewer opportunities to turn work into festivals
| City life | or family gatherings. Entertainment became a separate activity for which one purchased a ticket—to the theater, the circus, or P.T. Barnum's American Museum; or in the 1840s, to the race track; or a decade later, to the baseball park. The concentration of population in cities supported this diversity of activities, a luxury unknown in the countryside.

By twentieth-century standards, early nineteenth-century cities were disorderly, unsafe, and unhealthy. Expansion occurred so suddenly and swiftly that few cities could handle the problems it brought. For example, migrants from rural areas were used to relieving themselves and throwing refuse in any vacant area. But in the city waste spread disease, polluted wells, and gave off obnoxious smells. In some districts scavengers and refuse collectors carted away garbage and human waste, but in much of the city it just rotted.

Crime was another problem. To keep order and provide for public safety, Boston supplemented (1837) and New York replaced (1845)

its colonial watchmen and constables with paid policemen. Nonetheless, middle-class men and women did not venture out alone at night, and during the day stayed clear of many city districts. And the influx of immigrants to the cities compounded social tensions by pitting people of different backgrounds against each other in the contest for jobs and housing. Ironically, in the midst of the dirt, the noise, the crime, and the conflict, rose the opulent residences of the very rich.

Extremes of wealth

Some observers, notably the young French visitor Alexis de Tocqueville, saw the United States before the Civil War as a place of equality and opportunity. To Tocqueville, American equality—the relative fluidity of the United States' social order—was the result of its citizens' geographic mobility. Migration offered people opportunities to start anew regardless of where they came from or who they were. Prior wealth or family or education mattered little; a person could be known by deeds alone. Talent and hard work, many Americans and Europeans believed, found their just reward in such an atmosphere. It was common advice that anyone could advance by working hard and saving money.

But other observers recorded the rise of a new aristocracy based on wealth and power, and a growing gap between the upper and working classes. Among those who disagreed with the
| Distribution of wealth | egalitarian view of American life was *New York Sun* publisher Moses Yale Beach, author of twelve editions of *Wealth and Biography of the Wealthy Citizens of New York City*. In 1845 Beach listed a thousand New Yorkers with assets of $100,000 or more. Tocqueville himself, ever sensitive to the conflicting trends in American life, had described the growth of an American aristocracy based on industrial wealth. The rich and well educated "come forward to exploit

industries," Tocqueville wrote, and become "more and more like the administrator of a huge empire. . . . What is this if not an aristocracy?"

Throughout the United States, wealth was becoming concentrated in the hands of a relatively small number of people. In New York City between 1828 and 1845, the wealthiest 4 percent of the city's population increased its holdings from an estimated 63 percent to 80 percent of all individual wealth. Inequality of wealth prevailed in rural areas as well, including the Old Northwest and West. By 1860 the top 5 percent of families owned more than half the nation's wealth; the top tenth owned over 70 percent.

Another manifestation of the growing inequality and insecurity in American society was the frequency of rioting and sporadic incidents of violence. In the 1830s riots became com-

| Urban riots |

monplace as skilled workers vented their rage against new migrants to the city and other symbols of the new industrial order. Nationwide between 1828 and 1833 there were twenty major riots; in the year 1834 alone there were sixteen; in 1835, thirty-seven. By 1840 more than 125 people had died in urban riots, and by 1860 more than a thousand.

A cloud of uncertainty hung over working men and women. Many were afraid that in periods of economic depression they would be unable to find steady work. They feared the competition of immigrant and slave labor. They feared the insecurities and indignities of poverty, chronic illness, disability, old age, widowhood, and desertion. And they had good reason.

Indeed, poverty and squalor stalked the urban working class. Cities were notorious for the dilapidated districts where newly arrived immi-

| Urban slums |

grants, indigent blacks, the working poor, and thieves, beggars, and prostitutes lived. Five Points in New York City's Sixth Ward was probably the worst slum in pre–Civil War America. The neighborhood was equally divided between Irish and blacks. Ill-suited to human habitation and lacking such amenities as running water and sewers, it exemplified all that was worst in American society.

A world apart from Five Points was the upper-class elite society of Philip Hone, one-time mayor of New York. Hone's diary, meticulously kept from 1826 until his death in 1851, records the activities of an American aristocrat. On February 28, 1840, for instance, Hone attended a masked ball at a Fifth Avenue mansion. The ball began at the fashionable hour of 10 P.M., and the five hundred ladies and gentlemen who filled the five rooms of the mansion's first floor wore costumes adorned with ermine, gold, and silver. Few balls attained such grandeur, but at one time or another similar parties were held in Boston, Philadelphia, Baltimore, Charleston, and New Orleans.

By and large the elite were not idle, although their fortunes were often built on inherited wealth. Nearly all received sizable inheritances, and their inbred marriage patterns enhanced their inherited possessions. Yet as a group they devoted at least some of their energies to increasing their fortunes and their power. Philip Hone, like other urban capitalists and southern planters, was actively engaged in transportation and manufacturing ventures. Wealth begat wealth.

New lives in America

Though they did not bring much wealth with them, immigrants contributed in other ways to the changing American scene. In numbers alone they drastically altered the United States. The 5 million immigrants who settled in the states between 1820 and 1860 outnumbered the entire population of the country at the first census in 1790. They came from all over the world—from North America, the Caribbean, Latin America, Asia, and Africa, though Europeans made up the vast majority. The peak period of pre–Civil War immigration was from 1847 through 1857; in that eleven-year period,

The infamous Five Points section of New York City's Sixth Ward, probably the worst slum in pre-Civil War America. Immodestly dressed prostitutes cruise the streets or gaze from windows, while pig roots for garbage in their midst.　Brown Brothers.

3.3 million immigrants entered the United States, 1.3 million from Ireland and 1.1 million from the German states. By 1860, 15 percent of the white population was foreign-born.

This massive migration had been set in motion decades earlier when the Napoleonic wars began one of the greatest population shifts in history. One part of the movement, increasingly significant as time went on, was the emigration of Europeans to the United States. War and revolution, crop failure and famine, industrialization and economic displacement, political and religious persecution dogged weary Europeans. Meanwhile, the United States beckoned, offering them economic opportunity and the chance to found new communities.

Background of immigration

So they came, enduring the hardships of travel and of settling in a strange land. The journey was difficult. The average crossing took six weeks; in bad weather it could take three months. Disease spread unchecked among people huddled together like cattle in steerage. More than 17,000 immigrants, mostly Irish, died from "ship fever" in 1847. On disembarking, immigrants became fair game for the con artists and swindlers who worked the docks. In 1855, in response to the immigrants' plight, New York state's commissioners of emigration established Castle Garden as an immigrant center. There, at the tip of Manhattan Island, the major port of entry, immigrants were sheltered from fraud.

Most immigrants gravitated toward the cities, since only a minority had both farming experience and the means to purchase land and

New lives in America

equipment. Many stayed in New York. By 1845, 35 percent of the city's 371,000 people were of foreign birth. Ten years later 52 percent of its inhabitants were immigrants. Boston, an important entry point for the Irish, took on a European tone. Throughout the 1850s the city was about 35 percent foreign-born, of whom more than two-thirds were Irish. In the South of 1860, New Orleans was 44 percent foreign-born, Savannah 33 percent, Charleston 26 percent, and the border city of St. Louis, 61 percent. On the West Coast, San Francisco had a foreign-born majority.

Some immigrants, however, did settle in rural areas. In particular, German, Dutch, and Scandinavian farmers gravitated toward the Midwest. Greater percentages of Scandinavians and Netherlanders became farmers than did migrants of other nationalities; both groups came mostly as religious dissenters and migrated in family units. The Dutch, under such leaders as Albertus C. Van Raalte, fled persecution in their native land to establish new and more pious communities—Holland, New Groningen, and Zeeland, Michigan, among them.

Success in America bred further emigration. "I wish, and do often say that we wish you were

| *Promotion of immigration* |

all in this happy land," wrote shoemaker John West of Germantown, Pennsylvania, to his kin in Corsley, England, in 1831. "A man nor woman need not stay out of employment one hour here," he advised. "No war nor insurrection here. *But all is plenty and peace.*" Others wrote of the room still left in America.

American institutions, both public and private, actively recruited European immigrants. Western states lured potential settlers in the interest of promoting their economies. In the 1850s, for instance, Wisconsin appointed a commissioner of emigration, who advertised the state's advantages in American and European newspapers. Wisconsin also opened a New York office and hired European agents to compete with other states and with firms like the Illinois Central Railroad for the attention of immigrants.

Before the potato blight hit Ireland, tens of thousands of Irish were lured to America by recruiters. They came to swing picks and shovels on American canals and railroads, to dig the foundations of mills and factories. Thousands of those who came, however, found bitter disappointment and returned to Ireland. Among

| *Immigrant disenchantment* |

them was Michael Gaugin, who had the misfortune of arriving in New York City during the financial panic of 1837. Gaugin, an assistant engineer in the construction of the Ballinasloe Canal in Dublin, had been attracted to the states by the promise that "he should soon become a wealthy man." Within two months of arriving in the United States, Gaugin had become a pauper. In August 1837 he declared he was "now without means for the support of himself and his family, and has no employment, and has already suffered great deprivation since he arrived in this country; and is now soliciting means to enable him to return with his family home to Ireland." Many of those who had come with the Gaugins had already returned home.

Such experiences did not deter Irish men and women from coming to the United States. Ireland was the most densely populated European country, and among the most impoverished. From 1815 on, small harvests prompted a steady stream of Irish to immigrate to America. Then

| *Irish immigration* |

in 1845 and 1846 potatoes— the basic Irish food—rotted in the fields. From 1845 to 1849, death in the form of starvation, malnutrition, and typhus stalked the island. In all, 1 million died and about 1.5 million fled, two-thirds of them to the United States. The immigrants clustered in poverty in the cities, where they met growing anti-immigrant, anti-Catholic sentiment. Everywhere "No Irish Need Apply" signs appeared.

Anti-Catholicism had erupted in the American revolutionary movement when Quebec spurned the Continental Congress's invitation to join the Revolution. Later, though, French support of the colonists and the staunch patriotism of American Catholics had soothed such feelings. But in the 1830s anti-Catholicism appeared

| Anti-Catholicism | wherever the Irish did. Attacks on the papacy and the church circulated widely in |

the form of libelous texts like *The Awful Disclosures of Maria Monk* (1836), which alleged sexual orgies among priests and nuns. Nowhere was anti-Catholicism more open and nasty than in Boston, though such sentiments were widespread.

The native-born who embraced anti-Catholicism were motivated largely by anxiety. They feared that a militant Roman church would subvert American society, that unskilled Irish workers would displace American craftsmen, and that the slums inhabited in part by the Irish were undermining the nation's values. Every American problem from immorality and the evils of alcohol to poverty and economic upheaval was blamed on immigrant Irish Catholics. Friction increased as Irish-Americans fought back against anti-Irish and anti-Catholic prejudice; in the 1850s they began to vote and to become active in politics.

Though potato blight also sent many Germans to the United States in the 1840s, other hardships contributed to the steady stream of German immigrants. Many came from areas

| German immigration | where small landholdings made it hard to eke out a living and to pass on land to |

their sons. Others were craftsmen displaced by the industrial revolution. These refugees were joined by middle-class Germans who had sought to unify the three dozen or so German states in a liberal republic. Frustration with abortive revolutions like the one that occurred in 1848 led them to immigrate to the United States. For some, the only other choice was jail.

Unlike the Irish, who tended to congregate in towns and cities, Germans settled everywhere. Many came on German cotton boats, disembarked at New Orleans, and traveled up the Mississippi. In the South they became peddlers, traders, and merchants; in the North they worked as farmers, urban laborers, and businessmen. Also unlike the Irish, they tended to migrate in families. A strong desire to maintain the German language and culture prompted them to colonize areas as a group.

In adhering to German traditions, German-Americans also met with antiforeign attitudes. More than half the German immigrants were Catholic, and their Sabbath practices were different from the Protestants'. On Sundays German families typically gathered at beer gardens to eat and drink beer, to dance, sing, and listen to band music, and sometimes to play cards. Protestants were outraged by such violations of the Lord's day.

In rural areas Germans were resented for their success as farmers. Familiar with scientific agriculture, German-Americans dominated farming in Ohio, Wisconsin, and Missouri. Their persistence in using the German language and their different religious beliefs also set them apart. Besides the Catholic majority, a significant number of German immigrants were Jewish. Even the Protestants—mostly Lutherans—founded their own churches and often educated their children in German-language schools. And many of the Germans who migrated to America after the failure of the Revolution of 1848 were liberals and freethinkers, some of whom were socialists, communists, and anarchists. The freethinkers embraced abolitionism and the Republican party.

The conflict between the immigrants and the society they joined was paralleled by the inner tensions most immigrants experienced. On the one hand they felt impelled to commit themselves wholeheartedly to their new country. On the other hand they were rooted in their own culture. Nearly all found themselves altered in significant ways, even as they successfully resisted other changes. In the process American customs and society changed as well.

Free people of color

No black person was safe, wrote the abolitionist and former slave Frederick Douglass following the Philadelphia riot of 1849. "His life—his property—and all that he holds dear are in the hands of a mob. . . ." For free people of color, mobs could take many forms. They could come in the shape of slave hunters, seeking fugitive slaves but as likely to kidnap a free black as a slave. Or they could take the form of civil authority, as in Cincinnati in 1829, when city officials, frightened by the growing black population, drove one thousand to two thousand blacks from the city by enforcing a law that required the posting of cash bonds for good behavior. In whatever form, free blacks faced insecurity daily.

Under federal law, blacks held an uncertain position. The Bill of Rights seemed to apply to free blacks; the Fifth Amendment specified that "no person shall . . . be deprived of life, liberty, or property, without due process of law." Nevertheless, early federal legislation discriminated against free people of color. In 1790 naturalization was limited to white aliens; in 1792 the militia was limited to white male citizens; and in 1810 blacks were barred from carrying the mails. Moreover, Congress approved the admission to the Union of states whose constitutions restricted the rights of blacks. Following the admission of Missouri in 1821, every new state admitted until the Civil War banned blacks from voting. And when the Oregon and New Mexico territories were organized, public land grants were limited to whites.

Dred Scott v. *Sanford* (1857) made the de facto position of free blacks official. Scott, a Mis-

| Dred Scott *v.* Sanford |

souri slave, had accompanied his master to the free state of Illinois and the free territory of Wisconsin. Once back in Missouri, he sued for his freedom on the grounds that his presence in areas where there was no slavery had made him free. After a ten-year battle, the Supreme Court ruled against Scott. Speaking for the majority, Chief Justice Roger Taney ruled that blacks "were not intended to be included, under the word 'citizens' in the Constitution, and can therefore claim none of the rights and privileges

which that instrument provides for and secures to citizens of the United States."

The Dred Scott decision affirmed what had already become practice: each state decided the legal condition of blacks within its borders. In the North blacks faced legal restrictions nearly everywhere. Only in Massachusetts, New Hampshire, Vermont, and Maine could blacks vote on an equal basis with whites throughout the pre–Civil War period. Blacks gained the right to vote in Rhode Island in 1842, but they had lost it earlier in Pennsylvania and Connecticut. No state but Massachusetts permitted blacks to serve on juries; four midwestern states and California did not allow blacks to testify against whites. In Oregon blacks could not own real estate, make contracts, or sue in court.

Legal status was important, but practice and custom were crucial. Although Ohio repealed its law barring black testimony against whites in 1849, the exclusion persisted as custom in southern Ohio counties. Throughout the North free people of color were either excluded from or

| *Exclusion and segregation of blacks* |

segregated in public places. Abolitionist Frederick Douglass was repeatedly met by the phrase "We don't allow niggers in here," during a speaking tour of the North in 1844. Hotels and restaurants were closed to blacks, as were most theaters and churches. But probably no practice inflicted greater injury than the general discrimination in hiring. Factory and skilled work were virtually closed to northern blacks.

Free people of color faced still severer legal and social barriers in the southern slave states. There the state legislatures, with the dual intent of restricting free blacks and encouraging them to migrate north, adopted "black codes." Blacks

| *Black codes* |

were required to have licenses for certain occupations and were barred from others. Some states forbade blacks to assemble without a license; some prohibited blacks from being taught to read and write. All the slave states except Delaware barred blacks from testifying against whites. In

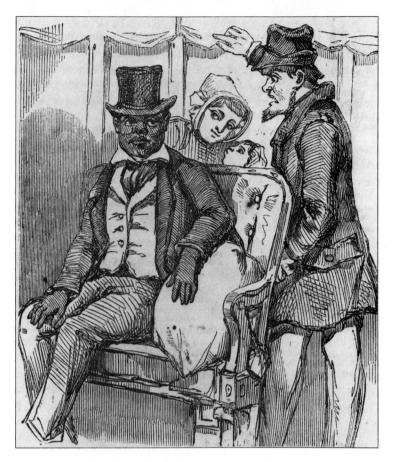

A free black man being expelled from a whites-only railway car in Philadelphia. Prior to the Civil War blacks were commonly segregated or excluded from public places in the North.   Library of Congress.

the late 1830s, when these black codes were enforced with vigor for the first time, free blacks increasingly moved northward, even though northern states discouraged the migration.

In spite of these obstacles, the free black population rose dramatically in the first part of the nineteenth century, from 108,000 in 1800 to almost 500,000 in 1860. Nearly half lived in the North, occasionally in rural settlements like Hammond County, Indiana, but more often in cities like Philadelphia, New York, or Cincinnati. Baltimore had the largest free black com-

munity; sizable free black populations also existed in New Orleans, Charleston, and Mobile.

The ranks of free blacks were constantly increased by ex-slaves. Some, like Frederick Douglass and Harriet Tubman, were fugitives. Tub-

Fugitive slaves

man, a slave on the eastern shore of Maryland, escaped to Philadelphia in 1849 when her master's death led to rumors that she would be sold out of the state. Within the next two years she returned twice to free her two children, her sister, her mother, and her brother and his family. Other slaves were voluntarily freed by their owners. Some, like a Virginia planter named Sanders who settled his slaves as freedmen in Michigan, sought to cleanse their souls by freeing their slaves in their wills. Others freed elderly slaves after a lifetime of service rather than support them in old age.

In response to their oppression, free blacks founded strong, independent self-help societies to meet their unique needs and fight their less-than-equal status. In every black community there appeared black churches, fraternal and benevolent associations, literary societies, and schools. Many black leaders believed that these mutual aid societies would encourage thrift, industry, and morality, thus equipping their members to improve their lot. But no amount of effort could counteract white prejudice. Blacks remained second-class in status.

The black convention movement, which originated in the 1830s, also promoted education and industriousness. But under the leadership of the small black middle class, which included the Philadelphia sail manufacturer James Forten and the orator Reverend Henry Highland Garnet, the convention movement quickly turned into a protest movement. Increasingly the conventions served as a forum to attack slavery and agitate for equal rights. The struggle was also joined by militant new black publications, such as *Freedom's Journal* (1827) and the *Weekly Advocate* (1837).

Although abolitionism and civil rights remained at the top of the blacks' agenda, the mood of free blacks began to shift in the late 1840s and 1850s. Some black leaders became more militant, and a few joined John Brown in his plans for rebellion. But many more were swept up in the tide of black nationalism, which stressed racial solidarity and unity, self-help, and a growing interest in Africa. Before this time, efforts to send Afro-Americans

"back to Africa" had originated with whites seeking to solve racial problems by ridding the United States of blacks. But in the 1850s blacks held emigrationist conventions of their own under the leadership of Henry Bibb and Martin Delany. With the coming of the Civil War, and emancipation, however, all but a few blacks lost interest in migrating to Africa.

The Trail of Tears

Indians faced problems similar to blacks'. They too faced massive hostility. Midwesterners and southerners sought their land, and soldiers marched them off it. Missionaries tried to Christianize them. And like blacks, their troubles involved the law, for Indians too were directly dependent on government policy—or the lack of it.

Under the Constitution, Indians had a more clearly defined status than blacks. They were not taxed, not counted in apportioning state representation, not citizens. Congress was given the power "to regulate Commerce with foreign Nations, and among the several States, and with the Indian Tribes." In exercising this mandate the federal government treated Indian tribes as separate nations.

The basis of Indian-white relations was the treaty. For its own convenience, the United States government demanded that one person or group have the power to obligate a tribe to a treaty's provisions. But like European nations in colonial times, government officials had difficulty applying this principle. Many tribes' traditions simply did not permit it. The Cherokees, for instance, were a common lingual group rather than a confederation of independent villages. No majority or unanimous leadership could sell the birthrights of all tribal members. Some frustrated United States officials simply

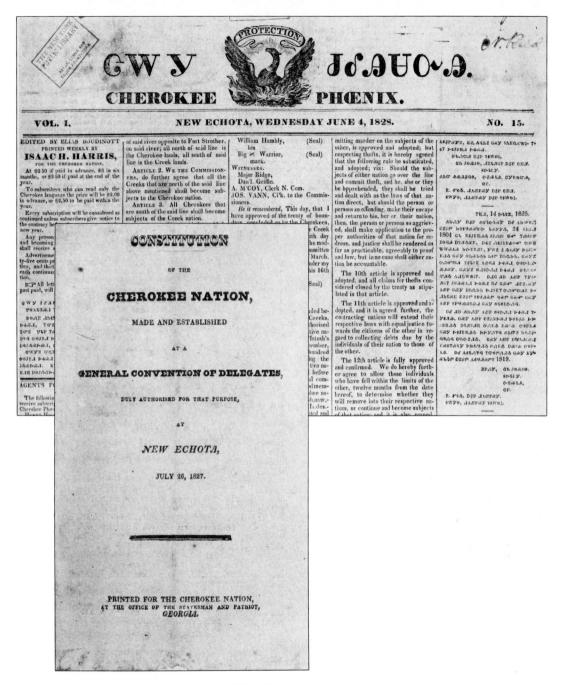

The Cherokee Phoenix, a bilingual newspaper published by the Cherokee nation (top) and the title page of the Cherokee constitution (bottom). This issue of the newspaper details the provisions of a recent treaty with the Creeks. Rate Book Division, The New York Public Library, Astor, Lenox and Tilden Foundations.

designated a tribal leader. Chiefs who worked closely with the government were well rewarded.

The Shawnee Chief Tecumseh led by far the most significant campaign of resistance to fed-

| Tecumseh |

eral pressure. Convinced that only a federation of nations and tribes could stop the advance of white society, Tecumseh sought, in the first decade of the century, to unify northern and southern Indians. His brother Laulewasika (the Prophet), like Tecumseh a powerful orator, spread the word of unity as well.

Under Tecumseh, the Indians refused to cede more land to the whites. In repudiating an Indian land sale, Tecumseh told Indiana's Governor William Henry Harrison at Vincennes in 1810 that "the only way to check and stop this evil is, for all the red men to unite in claiming a common and equal right in the land." Tecumseh then warned that the Indians would resist white occupation of the 2.5 million acres on the Wabash they had ceded to the United States in the Treaty of Fort Wayne the year before.

A year later, using a Potawatomi raid on an Illinois settlement as an excuse, Harrison attacked Prophet's Town, Tecumseh's headquarters on Tippecanoe Creek. Losses on both sides were heavy. When the War of 1812 started, Tecumseh joined the British in return for a promise of an Indian country in the Great Lakes region. But he was killed in the Battle of the Thames in October 1813, and with him died the dream of Indian unity.

By 1820 Indians in Ohio, southern Indiana and Illinois, southwestern Michigan, most of Missouri, central Alabama, and southern Mississippi had been forced to cede their lands. They had given up nearly 200 million acres for pennies an acre. But white settlers' appetites were insatiable; the demand for tribal lands east of the Great Plains continued until nearly all the Indians had been forced out.

In the 1820s the Cherokees, Creeks, Choctaws, Chickasaws, and Seminoles attempted to resist the whites' tactics and defend their ancestral lands. In 1825 President Monroe proposed

that these tribes, the last of the large Indian nations east of the Mississippi, sign new treaties and resettle between the Missouri and Red rivers. The conflict had focused on northwestern Georgia, where lay the Cherokee lands and a small portion of the Creek lands.

The Cherokees attempted to resist forced removal by adopting a written constitution and organizing themselves officially as an independent nation. But in 1828 the Georgia legislature annulled the constitution, extended state sovereignty over the Cherokees, and ordered the seizure of tribal lands. Under the new law a Cherokee named Corn Tassel was tried and convicted of murder in a state court. Though the Supreme Court issued a writ of error on appeal, Georgia refused to recognize it and executed Corn Tassel.

In 1829 the Cherokees turned to the federal courts to defend their treaty with the United States and prevent Georgia's seizure of their

| Cherokee Nation v. Georgia |

land. In *Cherokee Nation* v. *Georgia* (1831), Chief Justice John Marshall referred to the Indians as "domestic dependent nations . . . their relation to the United States resembles that of a ward to a guardian." Nevertheless, he ruled that the Indians had an unquestioned right to their lands; they could lose title only by voluntarily giving it up. A year later, in *Worcester* v. *Georgia,* Marshall defined the Cherokees' position more clearly. The Indian nation was, he declared, a distinct political community in which "the laws of Georgia can have no force," and into which Georgians could not enter without permission or treaty privilege.

"John Marshall has made his decision," President Jackson is reported to have said; "now let him enforce it." Jackson, concerned with opening up new lands for settlement, was determined to remove the Cherokees at all costs. In the Removal Act of 1830 Congress provided Jackson the funds he needed to negotiate new

| Trail of Tears |

treaties and resettle the resistant tribes west of the Mississippi. The Choctaw were the first to go (see map). Soon other tribes were forced west: the

Chapter 11: The American scene, 1800–1860

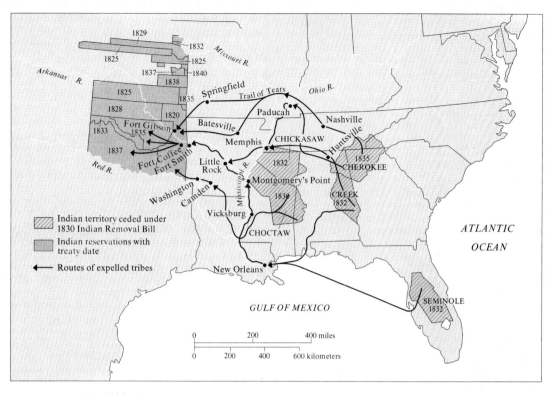

Removal of the Indians from the South, 1820–1840. Source: Redrawn by permission of Macmillan Publishing Company, Inc. From *American History Atlas* by Martin Gilbert, cartography by Peter Kingsland. Copyright © 1968 by Martin Gilbert.

Creeks in 1836 and the Chickasaws in 1837. The Cherokees, having fought to stay through the courts, found themselves divided. Some recognized the hopelessness of further resistance and accepted removal as the only chance to preserve their civilization. The leaders of this minority signed a treaty in 1835 in which they agreed to exchange their southern home for western land. But when the time for evacuation came in 1838, most Cherokees refused to move. President Martin Van Buren then sent federal troops to round up the Indians. About twenty thousand Cherokees were evicted, held in detention camps, and marched to Oklahoma under military escort. Nearly one-quarter died of disease and exhaustion on the famous Trail of Tears. When it was all over, the Indians had traded about 100 mil-

lion acres of land east of the Mississippi for 32 million acres west of the river plus $68 million.

A small band of Seminoles successfully resisted removal and remained in Florida. In the 1832 Treaty of Payne's Landing, tribal chiefs

| *Seminole War* |

agreed to relocate to the West within three years. Under Osceola, however, a minority refused to vacate their homes, and from 1835 on they waged a fierce guerrilla war against the United States. The army in turn attempted, ruthlessly but unsuccessfully, to exterminate the Seminoles. In 1842 the United States finally abandoned the Seminole War; it had cost 1,500 soldiers' lives and $20 million. Osceola's followers remained in Florida.

Among whites, the forced Indian removals

were motivated by a complex set of attitudes. Most whites merely wanted Indian lands. Others were aware of the injustice, but believed the Indians must inevitably give way to white settlement. Some, like John Quincy Adams, believed the only way to preserve Indian civilization was to remove the tribes and establish a buffer zone between Indians and whites. Others hoped to "civilize" the Indians and assimilate them slowly into American culture. But however the motivation of whites might have varied, the result was the same: the destruction of an American people and their culture.

Woman's sphere

American democracy, Alexis de Tocqueville believed, was built on the foundation of family stability. "In Europe almost all the disorders of society are born around the domestic hearth," he wrote in *Democracy in America*, "and not far from the nuptial bed." By contrast, when the American returns from the turmoil of politics to the bosom of the family, he immediately finds a perfect picture of order and peace." This regularity of family life was reflected in public affairs, Tocqueville wrote.

Whether or not the differences between the United States and Europe can be explained in terms of family stability and contentedness, Tocqueville's distinction between public and private life was an important one in the America of the first half of the nineteenth century. For the middle class and the elite, the public sphere was associated with men and the private, or domestic, sphere with women. The public sphere was the world of business and politics, of conflict and selfishness. The private sphere, the home, was a refuge from the jungle. Governed by women, it was the fount of spirituality and purity.

Changing role of women

The development of these separate spheres reflected both economic and social changes within the society. The family was no longer a unit of economic production. Once middle class and elite women were "freed" from their former economic role, they were expected to develop the home as a spiritual and cultural sanctuary. This new ideal of womanhood, however, was quite narrow. In their new role, ideal women were expected to be dominant at home but passive and submissive to men in public.

Those economically able to fulfill the new ideal were not expected to work for wages. Nursing and teaching (both extensions of the new concept of womanhood) were the only acceptable occupations for such women. Work outside the home became associated with the lower classes and quickly fell in esteem. Thus by the 1840s New England mills employed mostly immigrant Irish women; native-born farm girls shunned the work.

While woman's sphere was narrowing, family size was shrinking. A number of factors lowered the birth rate. For many people, family life became less important as migration loosened family bonds. Others came to believe that by having fewer children they could provide greater opportunities to their offspring. City life, by placing less pressure on young people to marry than did rural life, also contributed to the lower birth rate. Finally, marriage manuals stressed the harmful effects of too many births on a woman's health.

Decline in the birth rate

How did men and women limit their families in the early nineteenth century? Many married later, thus shortening the period of childbearing. More important, however, was the widespread use of birth control. The first American book on birth control, *Moral Physiology; or, A Brief and Plain Treatise on the Population Question* (1831), as well as the popular marriage guide by the physician Charles Knowlton, *Fruits of Philosophy; or, the Private Companion of Young Married People* (1832), provides us with a glimpse of contemporary birth control methods. Probably the most widespread practice was *coitus interruptus*, or withdrawal of the male before completion of the sexual act. But mechanical devices were be-

Birth control

ginning to compete with this ancient folk practice. Cheap rubber condoms were widely adopted when they became available in the 1850s. Dr. Knowlton advocated the dubious practice of douching with a chemical solution immediately after intercourse. And some couples used the rhythm method—attempting to confine intercourse to a woman's infertile periods. Knowledge of the "safe period" was so uncertain even among physicians, however, that the directions for avoiding conception were similar to today's advice to couples who want children! Another method was abstinence, or less frequent sexual intercourse. Frequently woman abstained and men visited prostitutes. For those desiring to terminate a pregnancy, surgical abortions became common after 1830. By 1860, however, twenty states had outlawed abortions.

Significantly, the birth control methods women themselves controlled—douching, the rhythm method, abstinence, and abortion—were the ones that were increasing in popularity. For the new emphasis on women's domesticity encouraged women's autonomy in the home and gave them greater control over their own bodies. According to the cult of true womanhood, the refinement and purity of women ruled the family, including the nuptial bed.

Marriage patterns changed as well. Only among elite families did the pattern of marrying kin persist. And among all but the highest classes, young people married spouses of their own choosing, not their parents'. In the new social climate marriages were made between individuals, not families, and romantic love was the yardstick by which proposals were measured.

Change in marriage patterns

Not all women accepted or could fulfill the domestic ideal. Mill girls, especially by the 1840s when they organized and resisted wage reductions, were forging new roles for women in the public sphere. So too were the women who assembled at Seneca Falls, New York, in 1848. Modeling their protest on the Declaration of Independence, they called for political, social, and economic equality for women.

The United States in 1860 was a far more diverse and divided society than it had been in 1800. Industrialization, urbanization, and immigration had altered the ways people lived and worked. Communities had become larger and more varied, and differences in wealth, ethnicity, religion, race, and sex separated individuals and groups.

As American society changed during these years, conflict became commonplace. Riots, crime, and anti-Catholicism were just a few of the many manifestations of social division in America. But conflict took other forms as well. In reform movements and religious revivals, Americans attempted to deal constructively with social change. In future years the 1820s, 1830s, and 1840s would be known as an age of reform.

Suggestions for further reading

COMMUNITIES   Stuart M. Blumin, *The Urban Threshold: Growth and Change in a Nineteenth-Century American Community* (1976); Don H. Doyle, *The Social Order of a Frontier Community: Jacksonville, Illinois, 1825–1870* (1978); Peter R. Knights, *The Plain People of Boston, 1830–1860* (1971); Raymond A. Mohl, *Poverty in New York, 1783–1825* (1971); Edward Pessen, *Riches, Class and Power Before the Civil War* (1973); Stephen Thernstrom, *Poverty and Progress: Social Mobility in a Nineteenth Century City* (1964); Alexis de Tocqueville, *Democracy in America*, 2 vols. (1835–1840); Richard C. Wade, *The Urban Frontier: 1790–1830* (1957); Anthony F.C. Wallace, *Rockdale: The Growth of an American Village in the Early Industrial Revolution* (1978).

IMMIGRANTS   Rowland Berthoff, *British Immigrants in Industrial America* (1953); Theodore C. Blegen, *Norwegian Migration to America, 1825–1860* (1931); Kathleen Neils Conzen, *Immigrant Milwaukee: 1836–1860* (1976); Charlotte Erickson, *Invisible Immigrants* (1972); Robert Ernst, *Immigrant Life in New York City, 1825–1863* (1949); Oscar Handlin, *Boston's Immigrants: A Study in Acculturation*, rev. ed. (1959);

Stuart Creighton Miller, *The Unwelcome Immigrant: The American Image of the Chinese 1785–1882* (1969); Philip Taylor, *The Distant Magnet: European Emigration to the United States of America* (1971).

FREE PEOPLE OF COLOR   Ira Berlin, *Slaves Without Masters: The Free Negro in the Antebellum South* (1974); James Horton and Lois Horton, *Black Bostonians: Family Life and Community Struggle in the Antebellum North* (1979); Luther Porter Jackson, *Free Negro Labor and Property Holding in Virginia, 1830–1860* (1942); David M. Katzman, *Before the Ghetto: Black Detroit in the Nineteenth Century* (1973); Rudolph M. Lapp, *Blacks in Gold Rush California* (1977); Leon Litwack, *North of Slavery: The Negro in the Free States, 1790–1860* (1961); Floyd J. Miller, *The Search for a Black Nationality: Black Colonization and Emigration 1787–1863* (1975); Arthur Zilversmit, *The First Emancipation: The Abolition of Slavery in the North* (1967).

NATIVE AMERICANS   Robert F. Berkhofer, Jr., *The White Man's Indian* (1978); Grant Foreman, *Indian Removal: The Emigration of the Five Civilized Tribes of Indians,* rev. ed. (1953); Charles Hudson, *The Southeastern Indians* (1976); Alvin M. Josephy, Jr., *The Patriot Chiefs: a Chronicle of American Indian Resistance* (1961); John K. Mahon, *History of the Second Seminole War, 1835–1842* (1967); Francis P. Prucha, *American Indian Policy in the Formative Years* (1962); Ronald N. Satz, *American Indian Policy in the Jacksonian Era* (1975); Glen Tucker, *Tecumseh: Vision of Glory* (1956); Wilcomb E. Washburn, *The Indian in America* (1975).

WOMEN AND THE FAMILY   Nancy F. Cott, *The Bonds of Womanhood: "Woman's Sphere" in New England, 1780–1835* (1977); Carl N. Degler, *At Odds: Women and the Family in America from the Revolution to the Present* (1980); Linda Gordon, *Woman's Body, Woman's Rights: A Social History of Birth Control in America* (1976); James C. Mohr, *Abortion in America: The Origins and Evolution of National Policy, 1800–1900* (1978); James Reed, *From Private Vice to Public Virtue: The Birth Control Movement and American Society Since 1830* (1978); Kathryn Kish Sklar, *Catherine Beecher: A Study in American Domesticity* (1973).

12

REFORM, POLITICS,
AND EXPANSION,
1824–1848

Like a biblical prophet, the gaunt, bearded New Englander Henry David Thoreau periodically withdrew from the world to meditate and listen to an inner voice. Then he would emerge, pen in hand, in defense of nature against exploitation, of simplicity against industrialism, of citizen against the state. From July 4, 1845, to September 6, 1847, Thoreau retreated to Walden Pond in Concord, Massachusetts. His sojourn there resulted in the classic *Walden, or Life in the Woods* (1854), a romantic account of his thoughts and experiences that exalted nature and individualism.

Thoreau was skeptical of the value of the artifacts of a changing economy and society: railroads, steamboats, the telegraph, factories, and cities. "There is an illusion about" such improvements, he wrote in *Walden*. "There is not always a positive advance. . . . Men think that it is essential that the *Nation* have commerce, and export ice, and talk through a telegraph, and ride thirty miles an hour . . . but whether we should live like baboons or like men, is a little uncertain."

Yet for all his idealization of the simple life, Thoreau did not withdraw from the world, much less from Concord. While at Walden he visited his mother daily, dined with townsfolk, and joined the men congregating around the grocery-store stove. In reality his everyday life

was infused with all those modern improvements he seemed to detest so much. Thoreau even raised a cash crop—beans—and sold it to support himself at Walden.

Was Thoreau a fraud? No, he was caught up in a basic ambivalence toward industrialization and urbanization. *Walden* was a romantic, idealistic response to the changes that were sweeping America—in essence, a nostalgic return to the world of his youth. Although Thoreau's answer was highly individualistic, he shared his search—and his ambivalence—with millions of other Americans. They were lured on the one hand by the simplicity and beauty of pastoral days gone by, pulled on the other by their belief in progress and the promise of machine-generated prosperity.

Indeed, the early nineteenth century was marked by the efforts of artists, writers, and reformers of all kinds to find or impose harmony on a society in which discord had reached a crescendo.

Romanticism and reform

Like Thoreau, the first distinctively American group of artists, the Hudson River school, seemed to look askance at urbanization and industrialization. Led by Thomas Cole, these artists—Asher Brown Durand, William Trost Richards, George Inness, and others—ignored cities and factories to paint romantic scenes of majestic mountains and river valleys. Their northeastern panoramas were not, however, untouched by civilization's advances. Thomas Cole's *The Oxbow* (1836), for instance, portrayed the works of both God and human beings; the focal point of the painting was cleared farm land. Similarly, William Trost Richards's *View in the Adirondacks* (about 1859) focused on an inhabited environment of toolmade houses and plowed fields. These American landscapists seemed to be saying that the land itself would restrain industrialism.

The artist's search for harmony between the vast physical changes America was experiencing and the simple landscape of the past was paralleled by various reform movements that emerged during the 1820s. Basically, reformers sought to restore order to a society made disorderly by economic and social change. Disturbed by change, convinced that the world could be improved, and confident that they could do something about it, reformers were so active from 1820 through the 1850s that the period became known as an age of reform.

Why were people upset by change? For one thing, many people felt they were no longer

Background of reform

masters of their own fate. Change was occurring so rapidly that people had difficulty keeping up with it. An apprentice shoemaker could find his trade obsolete by the time he became a journeyman; a student could find himself lacking sufficient arithmetic or geography to enter a counting house when he graduated. Other aspects of change were simply unpleasant or culturally alien. Respectable citizens found their safety threatened by urban mobs and paupers, and the Protestant majority feared the growing Catholic minority, with their strange customs and beliefs.

Reform was at its core an attempt to impose

moral direction on these social, cultural, and economic changes. The movement encompassed both individual improvement (religion, temperance, health) and institutional reform (antislavery, women's rights, and education). Not all the problems that reformers addressed were new to the nineteenth century. Slavery had existed in the United States for two centuries, and alcohol had been a colonial problem; yet neither became a national issue until the 1820s and after, when the reformist ferment prompted action.

Though reform movements played an important role in all sections of the country, they centered in the North. For one thing, slavery and the complex issues surrounding that institution tended to suppress the southern reform impulse. Fear of educating blacks, for instance, led even antislavery southerners to ignore the movement for educational reform.

Probably the prime motivating force behind reform was religion. The Second Great Awakening, which had begun in the 1790s, galvanized Protestants to try to right the wrongs of the world. Non-Protestants were also moved by the reform impulse.

Religious revival and utopianism

Evangelical Christianity was a religion of the heart, not the head. In 1821 Charles G. Finney, "the father of modern revivalism," experienced a soul-shaking conversion, which, he said, brought him "a retainer from the Lord Jesus Christ to plead his cause." In everyday language, he told his audiences that sin was a voluntary, avoidable act; Christians were not doomed by original sin. Hence anyone could achieve salvation through righteous behavior.

The Second Great Awakening raised people's hopes for the Second Coming of the Christian

Second Great Awakening

messiah and the establishment of the Kingdom of God on earth. A millennium—a thousand years—of peace, harmony, and Christian morality was supposed to precede the Day of Judgment. Thus revivalists set out to speed the Second Coming by joining the forces of good and light—reform—to combat those of evil and darkness.

In this way the Great Awakening bred reform, and evangelical Protestants became missionaries for both religious and secular salvation. Wherever they preached, voluntary societies arose. Evangelists organized an association for each issue—temperance, education, Sabbath observance, antidueling, and later antislavery; collectively these groups formed an empire of benevolent and moral reform societies.

Some people, especially middle-class businessmen and their families, were drawn to revivalism for its efforts to restore traditional communal and familial values. The new market economy tended to separate people from each other by emphasizing self above communal interest. Revivalism brought people back together and promised to restore the old order of things.

Some of these seekers of a sense of community turned away from the larger society to establish utopian towns and farms. Such settlements offered an antidote to the untamed growth of large urban communities. Whatever their particular philosophy, utopians attempted to establish order and regularity in their daily lives and to build a cooperative rather than competitive environment.

America's earliest utopian experiments were organized by the Shakers. An offshoot of the

| Shakers |

Quakers, the sect was established in America in 1774 by the English Shaker Ann Lee. Shakers believed that the end of the world was near, and that sin entered the world through sexual intercourse. They regarded existing churches as too worldly, and considered the Shaker family the instrument of salvation.

In 1787 the Shakers "gathered in" at New Lebanon, New York, to live, worship, and work communally. Other colonies soon followed. At its peak, between 1820 and 1860, the sect had about six thousand members in twenty settle-

ments in eight states. Though economically conservative, the Shakers were social radicals. They abolished individual families, practiced celibacy, and made no distinction between the sexes in their government, economy, or society. Each colony was one large family, with religious authority vested in elders and eldresses and economic leadership in deacons and deaconesses. The Shaker ministry was headed by a woman, Lucy Wright, during its period of greatest growth.

Not all utopian communities were founded by religious groups. Robert Owen's New Harmony was a short-lived attempt to found a socialist utopia in Indiana. A wealthy Scottish industrialist, Owen established the cooperative community in 1825. According to his plan, its nine hundred members were to exchange their labor for goods at a communal store. Handicrafts (hat and boot making) flourished at New Harmony. But the economic base of the community, its textile mill, failed after Owen gave it to the community to run. By 1827 the experiment had ended.

More successful were the New England transcendentalists who lived and worked at the

| Brook Farm |

Brook Farm cooperative in West Roxbury, Massachusetts. Inspired by the philosophy that the spiritual transcends the worldly, members rejected materialism and sought satisfaction in a communal life combining spirituality, work, and play. Though short-lived, Brook Farm played a significant part in the Romantic movement. There Hawthorne, Emerson, and the editor of the *Dial* (the leading transcendentalist journal), Margaret Fuller, joined Thoreau, James Fenimore Cooper, Herman Melville, and others in helping to create what is known today as the American Renaissance—the flowering of a national literature. In poetry and prose these Romanticists praised individualism and intuition, rejecting or modifying the ordered world of the Enlightenment in favor of the mysteries of nature. Rebelling against convention, both social and literary, they probed and celebrated the American character and the American experience.

Religious revival and utopianism

Far and away the most successful communitarians were the Mormons, who originated in western New York. Fleeing persecution in Illinois because of their newly adopted practice of polygamy, the Mormons trekked across the continent in 1846 and 1847 to found a New Zion in the Great Salt Lake Valley. There, under Brigham Young, head of the Twelve Apostles, they established a cohesive community of Saints—a heaven on earth. The Mormons created agricultural settlements and distributed land according to family size. In doing so, they transformed the arid valley into a rich oasis. As the colony developed, its cooperative principles gradually gave way to benevolent corporate authority, and the church elders came to control water, trade, industry, and even the territorial government of Utah.

Mormon community of Saints

Temperance, public education, and feminism

As a group, American men liked to drink alcoholic spirits. They gathered in public houses, saloons, taverns, and rural inns to socialize, gossip, discuss politics, play cards, and drink. Men drank on all occasions, social and business. And though respectable women did not drink in public, many regularly tippled alcohol-based elixirs, patent medicines promoted as cure-alls.

Why then was temperance such a vital issue? And why were women especially active in the movement? As with all reform, temperance had a strong religious base. To evangelicals, the selling of whiskey was a chronic symbol of Sabbath violation, for workers commonly labored six days a week, then spent Sunday at the public house drinking and socializing. Alcohol was seen as a destroyer of families as well, since men who drank heavily either neglected their families or could not adequately support them.

Demon rum thus became the target of the most widespread and successful of the antebellum reform movements. As the reformers gained momentum, they shifted their emphasis from temperate use of spirits to voluntary abstinence and finally to a crusade to prohibit the manufacture and sale of spirits. The American Society for the Promotion of Temperance, organized in 1826 to urge drinkers to sign a pledge of abstinence, shortly thereafter became a pressure group for state prohibition legislation. By the mid-1840s the annual per capita consumption of alcohol had fallen from more than five gallons to less than two gallons. Furthermore, many northern states, beginning with Maine in 1851, enacted laws prohibiting the manufacture and sale of alcohol.

Temperance societies

Another important part of the reform impulse was the development of new institutions to meet the social needs of citizens. Public education was one of the more lasting results of the age of institution building. In 1800 there were no public schools outside New England; by 1860 every state had some public education, although southern states lagged far behind the North and West. Massachusetts took the lead, especially under Horace Mann, secretary of the state board of education from 1837 to 1848. Under Mann, Massachusetts established a minimum school year of six months, increased the number of high schools, formalized the training of teachers, and emphasized secular subjects and applied skills rather than religion.

Horace Mann on education

Horace Mann's preaching on behalf of free state education changed schooling throughout the nation. "If we do not prepare children to become good citizens," Mann prophesied " . . . then our republic must go down to destruction." The abolition of ignorance, Mann claimed, would end misery, crime, and suffering.

In laying the basis of free public schools, Mann also broadened the scope of education. Previously, education had been religious rather than practical. Under Mann's leadership, the school curriculum became more appropriate for future clerks, farmers, and workers. Geography, American history, arithmetic, and science replaced many of the classics; teachers were trained in the new subjects at normal schools. Moral education was retained, but direct religious indoctrination was dropped.

A more controversial reform movement was the rise of American feminism in the 1840s. Ironically, it was women's traditional image as pious and spiritual that brought them into the public sphere. In the 1820s and 1830s, using their churches as a base, women began to play a prominent activist role in temperance, antislavery, and other reform movements. Organized into women's groups like the Boston Female Anti-Slavery Society, they slowly entered the public arena.

Reaction to the growing involvement of women in reform movements led many women to re-examine their position in society. In 1837 two antislavery lecturers, Angelina and Sarah Grimké, became objects of controversy when they were rebuked for speaking before mixed groups of men and women. This hostile reception turned the Grimkés' attention from slavery to women's condition. The two attacked the concept of "subordination to man."

| Angelina and Sarah Grimké |

In arguing against slavery, some women noticed the similarities between their own position and that of slaves. They saw parallels in their legal disabilities—inability to vote or control their property, except in widowhood—and their social restrictions—exclusion from advanced schooling and from most occupations. "The investigation of the rights of the slave," Angelina Grimké confessed, "has led me to a better understanding of my own." Her *Letters to Catherine E. Beecher* and Sarah Grimké's *Letters on the Condition of Women and the Equality of the Sexes*, both published in 1838, were the opening volleys in the war against the legal and social inequality of women.

Unlike other reform movements, which succeeded in building a broad base of individual and organizational support, the movement for women's rights was confined mostly to women.

Some men joined the ranks, notably abolitionist William Lloyd Garrison and ex-slave Frederick Douglass, but most opposed the movement. Though the Seneca Falls Convention, led by Elizabeth Cady Stanton and Lucretia Mott, issued a much-published indictment of women's disabilities in 1848, it had little effect. By the 1850s feminists were focusing more and more on the single issue of suffrage. But their arguments for the right to vote fell on deaf ears. Another cause eclipsed the suffrage movement, at least for a time.

The antislavery movement

Sparked by territorial expansion, the issue of slavery eventually became so overpowering that it consumed all other reforms. Passions would become so heated that they would threaten the nation itself. Above all else, those opposed to slavery saw it as a moral issue, evidence of the sinfulness of the American nation.

From colonial days to 1830 few whites, if any, advocated the immediate abolition of slavery. Some, most notably the Quakers, hoped that moral suasion would convince slaveholders to free their chattels. Others favored gradual abolition coupled with the resettling of blacks in Africa. The American Colonization Society had been founded in 1816 with this objective. Only free blacks pushed for an immediate end to slavery. By 1830 there were at least fifty black antislavery societies. These societies assisted fugitive slaves, attacked slavery at every turn, and reminded the nation that its mission as defined in the Declaration of Independence remained unfulfilled. A free black press helped to spread their word. When the climate of opinion changed and whites became more committed to antislavery, black abolitionists like Frederick Douglass, Sojourner Truth, and Harriet Tubman worked

| Black antislavery movement |

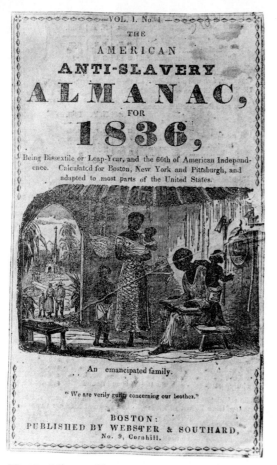

THE AMERICAN ANTI-SLAVERY ALMANAC, FOR 1836,

Being Bissextile or Leap-Year, and the 60th of American Independence. Calculated for Boston, New York and Pittsburgh, and adapted to most parts of the United States.

An emancipated family.

"We are verily guilty concerning our brother."

BOSTON: PUBLISHED BY WEBSTER & SOUTHARD, No. 9, Cornhill.

The Anti-Slavery Almanac, propaganda of the American Anti-Slavery Society. Beneath the picture of an emancipated family is the motto "We are verily guilty concerning our brother." Sophia Smith Collection, Smith College.

with white reformers in the American Anti-Slavery Society.

A full-fledged abolitionist crusade emerged in the 1830s when a small minority of white reformers made antislavery their primary commitment. The most prominent and uncompro-

William Lloyd Garrison

mising abolitionist, though clearly not the most representative, was William Lloyd Garrison, who demanded "immediate and complete emancipation." Recruited to the abolitionist cause in 1828 by Benjamin Lundy, a gradu-

alist, Garrison made his break from the moderate abolitionists in 1831. In that year he published the first issue of the *Liberator.* This paper would be his major weapon in the fight against slavery for thirty-five years.

Garrison alone could not have made antislavery a central issue. By the 1830s many northern reformers were recognizing the evils of slavery and preparing to act. Moral and religious ferment had primed evangelists to enter the fray. And the reform activities of the 1820s, including antislavery, had built a network of interrelated organizations.

Ironically, it was in defense of the constitutional rights of abolitionists, not slaves, that many whites entered the struggle. Wherever they went, abolitionists found their civil rights in danger. Southern mobs, for example, seized and destroyed much of the propaganda mailed by the American Anti-Slavery Society, and the state of South Carolina intercepted and burned abolitionist propaganda coming into the state (with the approval of the postmaster general). Elijah Lovejoy, an abolitionist editor, was killed by an Alton, Illinois, mob that had come to sack his office. Such actions gained sympathy and support for the abolitionists.

Another civil rights confrontation developed in Congress. Exercising their constitutional right to petition Congress, abolitionists had mounted a campaign to abolish slavery and the slave trade in the District of Columbia. But Congress re-

Gag rule

sponded in 1836 by adopting the so-called gag rule, which automatically tabled abolitionist petitions, effectively preventing debate on them. In a dramatic defense of the right of petition, ex-president John Quincy Adams, then a Massachusetts representative, took to the floor repeatedly to defy the gag rule and eventually succeeded in getting it repealed (1844).

The effect of the unlawful, violent, and obstructionist tactics used by proslavery advocates cannot be overestimated. Antislavery was not at the outset a unified movement. It was splintered and factionalized, and its adherents fought each other as often as they fought the defenders of slavery. They were divided over Garrison's emphasis on "moral suasion" versus the more practical political approach of James G. Birney, the Liberty party's candidate for president in 1840. And they disagreed over the place of black people in American society. Even so, abolitionists would eventually manage to unify and make antislavery a major issue in the politics of the 1850s.

Jacksonianism and the beginnings of modern party politics

Reformers were not the only Americans working to create or restore order in the 1820s and 1830s. Though their means differed, political leaders were also seeking to deal with the problems created by an expanding, urbanizing, market-oriented nation. John Quincy Adams advocated a nationalist program and an activist federal government; Andrew Jackson and his followers adhered to the Jeffersonian ideal of a limited federal government, with the primary power vested in the states.

The election of 1824, in which Adams and Jackson faced each other for the first time, signaled the beginning of a new, more open political system. From 1800 through 1820 a congressional caucus had chosen the Republican presidential nominees. In 1824, the caucus chose William H. Crawford, secretary of the treasury. But by this date most electors were selected by the voters rather than by the state legislatures. Thus, several individuals decided to ignore the caucus and seek the presidency by going directly to the voters.

End of the caucus system

John Quincy Adams drew support from New England, and westerners backed Speaker of the House Henry Clay of Kentucky. Secretary of War John C. Calhoun looked to the South for support, and hoped to win Pennsylvania as well. Andrew Jackson, a popular military hero whose political views were unknown, was nominated by resolution of the Tennessee legislature and won support everywhere. By boycotting the deliberations of the caucus and by attacking it as undemocratic, these men and their supporters ended the presidential nominating role of the congressional caucus.

Though Andrew Jackson led in both popular and electoral votes in the four-way presidential election of 1824, no one received a majority. Adams finished second, and Clay and Crawford trailed far behind. (Calhoun dropped out of the race before the election.) Under the Constitution, the selection of a president in such circumstances fell to the House of Representatives. Clay, as Speaker of the House and leader of the Ohio Valley states, was in a position to influence the House vote for either Adams or Jackson. He backed Adams, who received the votes of thirteen out of twenty-four state delegations. Clay was rewarded with the position of secretary of state in the Adams administration— the traditional stepping-stone to the presidency. Angry Jacksonians denounced the arrangement as a "corrupt bargain" that had stolen the office from them.

As president, John Quincy Adams took a strong nationalist position, emphasizing Henry Clay's American System of protective tariffs, a national bank, and internal improvements. Adams believed the federal government should take an activist role not only in the economy but in education, science, and the arts; accordingly, he proposed a national university in Washington, D.C.

Tragically, Adams was as inept a president as he was brilliant as a diplomat and secretary of state. He underestimated the lingering effects of the Panic of 1819 and the resulting bitter opposition to a national bank and protective tariffs. Distrustful of party organization, Adams failed to build a coalition to support his programs. Meanwhile, supporters of Andrew Jackson sabotaged Adam's administration at every opportunity.

The 1828 campaign between Adams and Jackson was an intensely personal conflict.

Wooden figurehead of "Old Hickory," Andrew Jackson, carved for the prow of the U.S.S. *Consitution* in 1834. Shortly after it was mounted, an enemy of Jackson sawed the head off. Museum of the City of New York.

Whatever principles the two men stood for were obscured by the mudslinging of both sides. Jackson polled 56 percent of the popular vote

and won in the electoral college, 178 to 83. For him and his supporters, the election of 1828 was the culmination of a long-fought, well-organized campaign based on party organization.

Andrew Jackson was nicknamed "Old Hickory," after the toughest American hardwood. A

> **Andrew Jackson**

rough-and-tumble, ambitious man, he rose from humble birth to become a wealthy planter and slaveholder. Jackson was the first American president not born into comfortable circumstances, a self-made man at ease among both frontiersmen and southern planters.

Jackson and his supporters offered a distinct alternative to the activist federal government Adams had advocated. They and their party, the Democratic-Republicans (shortened to Democrats), represented a wide range of beliefs but

> **Democrats**

shared some common ideals. Fundamentally, they sought to foster the Jeffersonian concept of an agrarian society, hearkening back to the belief that a strong central government was the enemy of individual liberty, a tyranny to be feared. Thus, like Jefferson, they favored limited government and emphasized state sovereignty.

Jacksonians were also fearful of concentrated economic power and hostile toward reform. They saw government intervention in the economy as benefiting special-interest groups and the rich. To counter special privilege, Jackson used the negative power of government—that is, he utilized the veto and cut federal support of banks and corporations. Democratic opposition to reform was tied to their perception of government and concern for individual rights. Reformers sought to achieve their goals through an interventionist government: Jacksonians advocated individual rights. Democrats, for example, opposed public education because it interferred with parental rights and responsibilities. Finally, neither Jackson nor many of his supporters shared the reformers' humanitarian concerns.

Like Jefferson, Jackson strengthened the executive branch of government at the same time he weakened the federal role. But his deliberate policy of combining the roles of party leader and chief of state did centralize even greater power in the White House. Invoking the principle that rotating officeholders would make government more responsive to the public will, Jackson used the spoils system to reward loyal Democrats with appointments to office. Though he removed fewer than one-quarter of federal officeholders in eight years, his use of patronage nevertheless strengthened party organization and loyalty.

In office Jackson invigorated the philosophy of limited government. In 1830 he vetoed the Maysville Road bill, which would have provided a federal subsidy to construct a sixty-mile turnpike from Maysville to Lexington, Kentucky. Jackson insisted that an internal improvement confined to one state was unconstitutional, and that such projects were properly a state responsibility. The veto undermined Henry Clay's American System and personally embarrassed Clay, since the project was in his home district.

The nullification and bank controversies

Jackson had to face more directly the question of the proper division of sovereignty between state and federal government. The slave South, especially South Carolina, was fearful of federal power. To protect their interests, South Carolinian political leaders developed the doctrine of nullification, according to which a state had the right to overrule federal legislation. The act that directly inspired this doctrine was the passage in 1828 of the Tariff of Abominations. In his unsigned *Exposition and Protest,* John C. Calhoun argued that in any disagreement between the federal government and a state, a special state convention—like those called to ratify the Constitution—would decide the conflict by either nullifying or accepting the federal law. Only the power of nullification could protect the minority against the tyranny of the majority, Calhoun asserted.

South Carolina first invoked its theory of nullification against the Tariff of 1832. Though this tariff had the effect of reducing some duties, it

| *Nullification crisis* |

retained high taxes on imported iron, cottons, and woolens. A majority of southern representatives supported the new tariff, but South Carolinians refused to go along. In their view, their constitutional right to control their own destiny had been sacrificed to the demands of northern industrialists. They feared the consequences of accepting such an act; it could set a precedent for congressional legislation on slavery. In November 1832, a South Carolina state convention nullified the tariff, making it unlawful for officials to collect duties in the state after February 1, 1833.

President Jackson responded with toughness. On December 10, 1832, Jackson issued his own proclamation nullifying nullification. He moved troops to federal forts in South Carolina and prepared United States marshals to collect the required duties. At Jackson's request, Congress passed the Force Act, which supposedly renewed Jackson's authority to call up troops; it was actually a scheme to avoid the use of force by collecting duties before ships reached South Carolina. At the same time, Jackson extended the olive branch by recommending tariff reductions. Calhoun, disturbed by South Carolina's drift toward separatism, worked with Henry Clay to draw up the compromise tariff of 1833. Quickly passed by Congress and signed by the president, the revision lengthened the list of duty-free items and reduced duties over the next nine years. Satisfied, South Carolina's convention repealed its nullification law, and in a final salvo nullified Jackson's Force Act. Jackson ignored the gesture.

The nullification controversy did represent a genuine debate on the true nature and principles of the republic. Each side believed it was upholding the Constitution. Neither side won a clear victory. Another issue, that of a central bank, would define the powers of the federal government more clearly.

At stake was the rechartering of the Second

Bank of the United States, whose twenty-year charter expired in 1836. One of the bank's func-

| Second Bank of the United States | tions was to act as a clearing-house for state banks, keeping them honest by refusing to accept their notes if they |

had insufficient gold in reserve. Many state banks resented the central bank's police role; by presenting state bank notes for redemption all at once, the Second Bank could easily ruin a state bank. Moreover, state banks found themselves unable to compete on an equal footing with the Second Bank. And many state governments regarded the national bank as unresponsive to local needs. Finally, westerners and urban workers remembered with bitterness the bank's conservative credit policies during the Panic of 1819. To many westerners the bank's conservative, anti-Jacksonian president, Nicholas Biddle, symbolized all that was wrong with the Second Bank.

Although the bank's charter would not expire until 1836, Biddle, aware of Jackson's hostility, sought to make it an issue in the presidential campaign of 1832. His strategy backfired. In July 1832 Jackson vetoed the rechartering bill, and the Senate failed to override the veto. Jackson's veto message was an emotional attack on the undemocratic nature of the bank. The bank was the major issue of the 1832 campaign, and Jackson used it to attack special privilege and economic power.

But the most dramatic institutional change that accompanied the rise of parties—the convention system of nominating presidential candidates—did not originate with the Jacksonians. It was the Anti-Masonic party that in 1831 met in a national convention, named William Wirt their standard-bearer for 1832, and adopted a party platform, the first in the nation's history. The Democrats and the major opposition party, the National Republicans, quickly followed suit. Jackson and Martin Van Buren were nominated at the Democratic convention, Clay and John Sergeant at the National Republican. Jackson was re-elected easily in a Democratic party triumph.

After his victory and second inauguration in 1833, Jackson moved not only to dismantle the Second Bank of the United States but to ensure that it would not be resurrected. He deposited federal funds in favored state-chartered ("pet") banks; without federal money, the bank shriveled. When its federal charter expired in 1836, it became just another Pennsylvania-chartered private bank. In 1841 it went bankrupt.

The Whig challenge and the second party system

Once historians described the period from 1834 through the 1840s as the Age of Jackson. Increasingly, however, historians have viewed these years as an age dominated by popularly based political parties and reformers. For it was only when the passionate concerns of evangelicals and reformers spilled into politics that party differences became important and party loyalties solidified. For the first time, grassroots political groups, organized from the bottom up, set the tone of political life.

In the 1830s the Democrats' opponents found shelter under a common umbrella, the Whig party. From 1834 through the 1840s, Whigs and Democrats built strong organizations, attracted mass popular following, and competed nearly equally. They fought at every level—city, county, and state—and achieved a sta-

| Whigs | bility previously unknown in American politics. The two |

parties took different approaches to numerous fundamental issues during these years. Though both favored economic expansion, the Whigs sought it through an activist government, the Democrats through limited government. Thus the Whigs supported corporate charters, a national bank, and paper currency; the Democrats were opposed. The Whigs also favored more humanitarian reforms than did the Democrats—public schools, abolition of capital punishment, temperance, and prison and asylum reform.

In general, Whigs were simply more optimistic than Democrats, and more enterprising. They did not hesitate to help one group if doing so would promote the general welfare. The chartering of corporations, they argued, expanded economic opportunity for everyone. Meanwhile the Democrats, distrustful of the concentration of economic power and of moral and economic coercion, held fast to their Jeffersonian principle of limited government.

Ironically, the basic economic issues of the era were not the determinants of party affiliation. Although the Whigs attracted more of the upper and middle classes, both sides drew support from manufacturers, merchants, laborers, and farmers. Religion and ethnicity, however, were more strongly correlated with party allegiance. In the North, the Whigs' concern for energetic government and humanitarian and moral reform won the favor of native-born and British-American evangelical Protestants. Democrats, on the other hand, tended to be foreign-born Catholics and nonevangelical Protestants, both groups that preferred to keep religious and secular affairs separate.

The Whig party thus became the vehicle of evangelical Christianity. Indeed, Whigs practiced a kind of political revivalism. Their rallies resembled camp meetings; their rhetoric echoed evangelical rhetoric; their programs embodied the perfectionist beliefs of reformers. In unifying evangelicals, the Whigs alienated members of other faiths. Sabbath laws, temperance legislation, and Protestant-inspired public education threatened the religious freedom of other groups, which generally opposed state interference in moral and religious questions. As a result, Catholics voted overwhelmingly Democratic.

Whigs and reformers

Jackson hand-picked Vice President Martin Van Buren to head the Democratic ticket in the presidential election of 1836. The Whigs, who had not yet coalesced into a national party, entered three sectional candidates: Daniel Webster of New England, Hugh White of the South, and William Henry Harrison of the West. By splintering the vote, they hoped to throw the election into the House, but Van Buren squeaked through with a 25,000-vote edge out of a total of 1.5 million.

Van Buren took office just weeks before the American credit system collapsed. The economic boom of the 1830s was over. Unfortunately, Van Buren followed Jackson's hard-money policies. He curtailed federal spending, thus adding to the deflation, and opposed the Whigs' advocacy of a national bank, which would have improved matters by expanding credit. Even worse, Van Buren proposed a new treasury system under which the government would keep all its funds in regional treasury offices rather than banks. The treasury branches would accept and pay out only gold and silver coin. Van Buren's independent treasury bill was passed in 1840. By creating a constant demand for hard coin, it deprived banks of gold and added to the general deflation.

Martin Van Buren and hard times

With the nation in a depression, the Whigs confidently prepared for the election of 1840. The Democrats renominated President Van Buren in a somber convention. The Whigs rallied behind the military hero General William Henry Harrison and his running mate, John Tyler of Virginia. Eighty percent of the eligible voters cast ballots, and the Whigs won.

Election of 1840

Unfortunately for the Whigs, Harrison died within a month of his inauguration. Tyler, a former Democrat who had left the party in opposition to Jackson's Nullification Proclamation, turned out to be more of a Democrat than a Whig. He consistently opposed the party's program, vetoing bills that provided for protective tariffs, internal improvements, and a revived Bank of the United States. Understandably, the Whigs virtually expelled him from the party.

Tyler thus turned his attention to territorial questions. A major dispute with Great Britain emerged over the imprecisely defined boundary between Maine and New Brunswick. In the winter of 1838–1839, Canadian lumberjacks

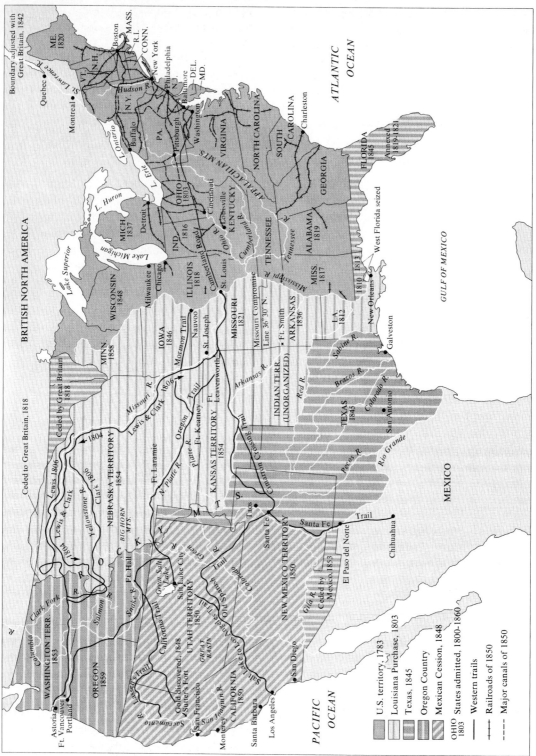

Westward expansion, 1800–1860

moved into the area. Shortly thereafter, Maine attempted to expel them. The Canadians captured the Maine land agent, both sides mobilized, and Congress authorized a call-up of fifty thousand men. Fortunately, war was avoided. Both sides compromised on their claims in the Webster-Ashburton Treaty (1842).

The border dispute with Great Britain prefigured an issue that became prominent in national politics in the mid- to late 1840s: the westward expansion of the United States. Tyler's succession to power in 1841 and a Democratic victory in the presidential election of 1844 ended activist, energetic government on the federal level for the rest of the decade. Meanwhile economic issues were eclipsed by debate over the nation's destiny to stretch from coast to coast.

Manifest destiny

Americans had always been hungry for western land. There lay virgin soil, valuable mineral resources, and the chance for a better life or a new beginning. Agrarian Democrats saw the West as an antidote to urbanization and industrialization. Enterprising Whigs looked to the new commercial opportunities the West offered. Equally important was both a fierce national pride and a desire to acquire western land to secure the nation from external enemies. Finally, Americans believed that westward expansion would extend American freedom and democracy to "less fortunate people." In the 1840s *manifest destiny*, the belief that American expansion westward was inevitable, divinely ordained, and just, served the nation's expansionists (see map).

Among the long-standing objectives of expansionists was the Republic of Texas. Originally part of Mexico, Texas attracted thousands

| Republic of Texas | of Americans in the 1820s and 1830s. The Mexican government's extremely generous land policy enticed settlers into the area. In return for the right to settle in Texas, settlers

were expected to become Mexican citizens, to obey Mexican law, and to adopt the Catholic faith.

By 1835, 35,000 Americans, including many slaveholders, lived in Texas. These new settlers ignored local laws and oppressed native Mexicans, and when the Mexican government attempted to tighten its control over the region, it stimulated a rebellion instead. The desires of Texans to avenge the defeat at the Alamo and to secure their independence were fulfilled in 1836 through Sam Houston's victory in the Battle of San Jacinto.

Americans were generally delighted with the revolution's result, but joy did not mean that the Texas request for annexation into the Union was welcomed. Texas was a slave republic and this made annexation a potentially explosive political issue. Jackson delayed recognition of Texas because of the political danger, and Van Buren ignored annexation altogether. Texans then talked about developing ties with Britain and expanding to the Pacific. President Tyler feared that a Texas alliance with the English might threaten American independence. He was also committed to expansion and hoped to build support in the South by enlarging the area of slavery. Tyler, therefore, pushed for annexation. But in a sectional vote, the Senate in April 1844 rejected a treaty of annexation.

Just as southerners sought expansion to the Southwest, northerners looked to the Northwest. In 1841 "Oregon fever" struck thousands.

| Oregon fever | Lured by the glowing reports of missionaries, emigrants organized hundreds of wagon trains and embarked on the Oregon Trail. However, the organization of a provisional government in 1843 placed the United States and Britain on a collision course.

Since the Anglo-American convention of 1818, Britain and the United States had jointly occupied the disputed Oregon territory. Beginning with the administration of President John Quincy Adams, the United States had tried to fix the boundary at the 49th parallel, but Britain had refused. Time only increased the American appetite. In 1843 a Cincinnati convention de-

Travelers on the Oregon Trail encamped at Independence Rock in Wyoming.   Denver Public Library, Western History Department.

manded that the United States obtain the entire Oregon territory, up to its northernmost border of 54°40′. Soon "Fifty-four Forty or Fight" had become the rallying cry of American expansionists.

The presidential campaign of 1844 was the first to be dominated by foreign-policy issues.

| Election of 1844 | The Democrats nominated House Speaker James K. Polk, a hard-money Jack-

sonian and avid expansionist. Their platform called for the occupation of the entire Oregon country and the annexation of Texas. Henry Clay, the Whig nominee, believed that the Democrats would provoke a war with Great Britain or Mexico. He favored expansion through negotiations.

The Democrats captured the White House by 170 electoral votes to 105 (they won the popular vote by just 38,000 out of 2.7 million). Polk carried New York's 36 electoral votes by just 6,000 votes; abolitionist James G. Birney, the Liberty party candidate, drew almost 16,000 votes away from Clay, handing the state and the election to Polk. Thus abolitionist forces had influenced the choice of a president.

Interpreting Polk's victory as a mandate for annexation, President Tyler proposed in his last days in office that Texas be admitted by joint resolution of Congress. Proslavery and antislavery congressmen debated the extension of slavery into the territory, and the resolution passed the House 120 to 98 and the Senate 27 to 25. Three days before leaving office, Tyler signed the measure. Mexico immediately broke relations with the United States.

Faced with the prospect of war in the Southwest, President Polk sought to avoid conflict with Great Britain in the Northwest. Thus he dropped the demand for a 54°40′ boundary in favor of the 49th parallel. But the United States was still demanding the lion's share of Oregon, and Britain rejected the offer. In April 1846 the United States therefore gave the required one-year notice for ending the 1818 joint-occupation agreement. Faced with what amounted to a threat of war, the British accepted the 49th parallel in the Oregon Treaty of 1846.

Meanwhile, the crisis over Texas was worsening as Polk was determined to have California and New Mexico as well as all of Texas; he intended to fulfill the nation's destiny and expand to the Pacific. After an attempt to buy the tremendous expanse of land failed, Polk resolved to ask Congress for a declaration of war, and set to work compiling a list of grievances. This task became unnecessary when word arrived that Mexican forces had engaged a body of American troops whom Polk had sent to guard the Texas border. American blood had been shed. Polk eagerly declared that "war exists by the act of Mexico itself."

Although Congress voted overwhelmingly in May 1846 to recognize a state of war between Mexico and the United States, public opinion was sharply divided. Southwesterners anticipated war with enthusiasm; New Englanders strenuously opposed it. Antislavery Whigs charged that Polk had manipulated the United States into war; abolitionists regarded the war as no less than a plot to extend slavery and proslavery influence.

As in previous wars, the United States depended on volunteers raised by the states to augment its small standing army. Nationalist and expansionist fervor generated adequate forces, however, and American troops quickly established their superiority over | **Mexican War** | the Mexicans. General Zachary Taylor attacked and occupied Monterey, securing northeastern Mexico (see map, page

192). Polk then ordered Colonel Stephen Kearney to invade the remote provinces of New Mexico and California. Once in California, Kearney joined forces with rebellious American settlers under Captain John C. Frémont and some naval units. Together they wrested control of California from Mexico with ease. General Winfield Scott's daring invasion of Mexico City brought the war to an end, and on February 2, 1848, representatives signed the Treaty of Guadalupe Hidalgo. The United States gained California and New Mexico (including present-day Nevada, Utah, and Arizona) and recognition of the Rio Grande as the southern boundary of Texas. In return, the American government agreed to settle the claims of its citizens against Mexico and to pay Mexico a mere $15 million for the new territory. The nation's manifest destiny had been achieved: the American flag waved on Atlantic and Pacific shores. The cost was thirteen thousand Americans and fifty thousand Mexicans dead, and Mexican-American enmity lasting into the twentieth century.

Ironically enough, instead of unifying the nation, the territorial expansion of the 1840s sparked sectional conflict. The debate over whether Oregon would be slave or free revived | **Sectional conflict over slavery in the territories** | old southern fears of congressional power. Northern expansionists, meanwhile, felt abandoned on the Oregon question by a South that had already won its plum–Texas. Reformers, charging that expansion was a Slave Power conspiracy, began to find a receptive audience in the North. Under the pressure of these sectional issues, the party unity of both Democrats and Whigs began to loosen.

In the presidential election of 1848, the political agenda changed radically. Prohibition of | **Election of 1848** | slavery in the territories was the one overriding issue. The Democrats tried to avoid sectional conflict by nominating General Lewis Cass of Michigan for president. Cass personally favored "squatter or popular sovereignty"–letting the inhabitants of a territory decide the

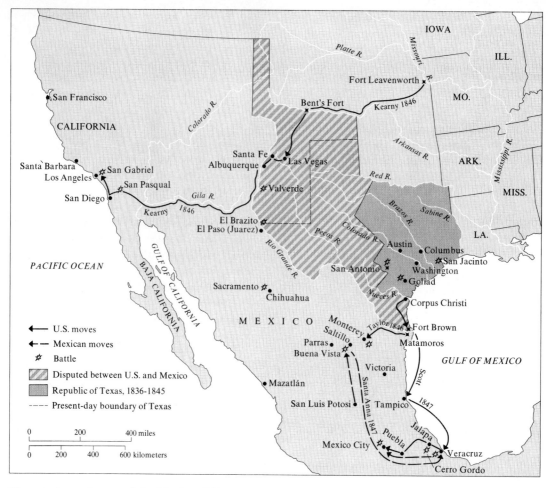

Texas independence and the Mexican War

question of slavery themselves. The party platform in turn declared that Congress did not
have the power to interfere with slavery, and
criticized those who pressed the question. Some
Democrats broke with the party and nominated
former President Van Buren. Also backed by
members of the Liberty party and abolitionist
Whigs, Van Buren became the Free-Soil candidate. The party slogan was "Free soil, free
speech, free labor, and free men."

The regular Whigs nominated General Zach-
ary Taylor, the military hero of the Mexican
War and a slaveholding southerner, along with

Millard Fillmore for vice president. Though the
Whig convention refused to assert congressional
power over slavery in the territories, its attempt
to avoid the issue proved futile. Van Buren divided the Democratic vote, allowing Taylor to
carry states he might not otherwise have won.
Again New York, Van Buren's home state, provided the crucial marginal votes—enough to put
Taylor in the White House. Antislavery crusa-
ders had again influenced the outcome of an
election.

The election of 1848 and the conflict over
slavery in the territories shaped politics in the

Important events

1790s–1840s	Second Great Awakening
1820s	Hudson River School
1824	House of Representatives elects John Quincy Adams president
1825–27	New Harmony, Indiana, experiment
1826	American Society for the Promotion of Temperance founded
1828	Tariff of Abominations Andrew Jackson elected president
1830s–40s	Second party system
1830	Maysville Road bill veto
1831	*Liberator* begins publication
1832	Veto of Second Bank of the United States recharter Jackson re-elected
1832–33	Nullification crisis
1836	Martin Van Buren elected president Republic of Texas established
1837	Financial panic
1837–39	U.S.–Canada border tensions
1837–48	Horace Mann heads Massachusetts Board of Education
1838	Sarah Grimké, *Letters on the Conditions of Women and the Equality of the Sexes*
1839–43	Depression
1840	Whigs under William Henry Harrison win presidency
1841–47	Brook Farm
1841	John Tyler assumes the presidency
1844	James K. Polk elected president
1845	Texas admitted to the Union
1846–47	Mormon trek to the Great Salt Lake Valley
1846–48	Mexican War
1846	Oregon Treaty
1848	Treaty of Guadalupe Hidalgo Seneca Falls Convention General Zachary Taylor elected president
1851	Maine Temperance law

1850s. At the national level, all issues would be seen through the prism of sectional conflict over slavery in the territories. The nation's uncertain attempts to deal with economic and social change would give way to more pressing questions about the nature of the Union itself. And the second party system developed in the 1830s and 1840s would itself succumb to crisis.

Suggestions for further reading

GENERAL Marvin Myers, *The Jacksonian Persuasion: Politics and Belief* (1960); Russel B. Nye, *Society and Culture in America, 1830–1860* (1974); Edward Pessen, *Jacksonian America: Society, Personality, and Politics*, rev. ed. (1979); John William Ward, *Andrew Jackson: Symbol for an Age* (1955).

RELIGION AND REVIVALISM   Whitney R. Cross, *The Burned-Over District* (1950); Charles A. Johnson, *The Frontier Camp Meeting* (1955); Paul E. Johnson, *A Shopkeeper's Millennium: Society and Revivals in Rochester, New York, 1815–1837* (1978); William G. McLoughlin, *Revivals, Awakenings, and Reform: An Essay on Religion and Social Change in America, 1607–1977* (1978); Timothy J. Smith, *Revivalism and Social Reform in Mid-Nineteenth Century America* (1957).

REFORM   Ray Allen Billington, *The Protestant Crusade, 1800–1860: A Study of the Origins of American Nativism* (1938); Clifford S. Griffin, *The Ferment of Reform, 1830–1860* (1967); Clifford S. Griffin, *Their Brother's Keepers: Moral Stewardship in the United States, 1800–1865* (1960); Raymond Muncy, *Sex and Marriage in Utopian Communities: 19th Century America* (1973); Wallace Stegner, *The Gathering of Zion: The Story of the Mormon Trail* (1964); Alice Felt Tyler, *Freedom's Ferment* (1944); Ronald G. Walter, *American Reformers, 1815–1860* (1978).

TEMPERANCE, EDUCATION, AND FEMINISM   Lawrence A. Cremin, *American Education: The National Experience, 1783–1876* (1980); Ellen C. Du Bois, *Feminism and Suffrage: The Emergence of an Independent Woman's Movement in America 1848–1869* (1978); Michael Katz, *The Irony of Early School Reform* (1968); Stanley K. Schultz, *The Culture Factory: Boston Public Schools, 1789–1860* (1973); Ian R. Tyrrell, *Sobering Up: From Temperance to Prohibition in Antebellum America, 1800–1860* (1979).

ANTISLAVERY AND ABOLITIONISM   Frederick Douglass, *Life and Times of Frederick Douglass* (1881); Aileen S. Kraditor, *Means and Ends in American Abolitionism: Garrison and His Critics on Strategy and Tactics* (1967); William H. Pease and Jane H. Pease, *They Would Be Free: Blacks' Search for Freedom, 1830–1861* (1974); Lewis Perry and Michael Fellman, eds., *Antislavery Reconsidered: New Perspectives on the Abolitionists* (1979); Benjamin Quarles, *Black Abolitionists* (1969); Leonard L. Richards, *"Gentlemen of Property and Standing": Anti-Abolition Mobs in Jacksonian America* (1970); Ronald G. Walter, *The Antislavery Appeal: American Abolitionism After 1830* (1976).

DEMOCRATS AND WHIGS   Lee Benson, *The Concept of Jacksonian Democracy: New York as a Test Case* (1964); James C. Curtis, *The Fox at Bay: Martin Van Buren and the Presidency, 1837–1841* (1970); Ronald P. Formisano, *The Birth of Mass Political Parties: Michigan, 1827–1861* (1971); William W. Freehling, *Prelude to Civil War: The Nullification Controversy in South Carolina* (1966); Daniel Walker Howe, *The Political Culture of the American Whigs* (1979); Richard P. McCormick, *The Second American Party System: Party Formation in the Jacksonian Era* (1966); Robert V. Remini, *Andrew Jackson* (1966); Robert V. Remini, *Andrew Jackson and the Bank War* (1967).

MANIFEST DESTINY   K. Jack Bauer, *The Mexican-American War, 1846–1848* (1974); Frederick Merk, *Manifest Destiny and Mission in American History: A Reinterpretation* (1963); David M. Pletcher, *The Diplomacy of Annexation: Texas, Oregon, and the Mexican War* (1973); John H. Schroeder, *Mr. Polk's War: American Opposition and Dissent, 1846–1848* (1973); Otis A. Singletary, *The Mexican War* (1960); Albert K. Weinberg, *Manifest Destiny* (1935).

13 &

THE UNION IN CRISIS:
THE 1850s

In the winter of 1860, President Abraham Lincoln received a letter from an old friend, Alexander Stephens of Georgia. Fearful that the growing momentum of sectional conflict would soon shatter the Union, Stephens appealed to Lincoln to make some gesture to reassure the South. But Lincoln refused to budge from his party's platform; he was unalterably opposed to the extension of slavery to the territories, though he readily acknowledged its right to exist in the southern states. Replying to Stephens, Lincoln wrote: "You think slavery is *right* and ought to be extended; while we think it is *wrong* and ought to be restricted. That I suppose is the rub." To Lincoln the conflict was fundamental.

Was compromise possible? Throughout the 1850s many Americans, North and South, worked for that end. But circumstances worked against the peacemakers. Though northerners and southerners strove to avoid conflict over slavery, westward expansion continually injected their disagreement into politics by raising the question of whether slavery would be allowed in the territories. This recurring crisis gradually convinced each side that its very way of life was jeopardized. Northerners envisioned a Slave Power intent on trampling basic liberties; southerners imagined that northerners would not stop until they had abolished slavery everywhere. Finally, changes in the political party system magnified sectional divisions. These forces jointly caused far more damage to the Union than they could have separately.

In the 1850s sectional pressures built until they eventually overwhelmed the capacity of the changing political system to deal with them. The result was a tragedy—civil war—that most American voters in 1860 clearly did not want.

The sources of conflict

The bitter debate over the morality of slavery was one cause of sectional strife. Profound questions of morality, social responsibility, and national purpose were at issue. At times the debate was explosive.

In the 1830s and 1840s, a growing body of northern abolitionists had preached against slavery, condemning it as a sin. These missionaries spoke in thousands of churches and public halls, slowly winning converts, indicting slavery as a moral wrong that brutalized all who came in contact with it.

> **Debate over the morality of slavery**

Stung by such criticism, southern slaveowners denied any wrongdoing, asserting that their slaves were well cared-for and protected. Some even argued that slavery was a social good. Senator John C. Calhoun agreed, calling slavery "a universal condition," and jurist William Harper wrote in 1837 that "It is as much the order of nature that men should enslave each other as

that animals should prey upon each other."
Even more extreme were the pronouncements
of a Virginian named George Fitzhugh, who
contended that wage labor in industry was more
inhumane than slavery and that all societies,
whatever their racial composition, should practice slavery.

These arguments generated strong emotions,
but they were not central to the conflict that
eventually divided the Union. The abolitionists
were significant because they were a growing
minority opposed in principle to the status quo.
Proslavery advocates also wanted change:
greater security and acceptance of their institution. Both constituted a threat to political stability. But their argument was only one cause of
sectional strife, and a small one at that. Most
northerners were racist, not abolitionists, and
most southerners paid scant attention to proslavery theories. The issue that ultimately led to
disunion was more obscure and complicated
than the morality of slavery. That issue was
slavery in the territories.

Throughout the 1850s Americans kept moving west, prompting Congress to create new territories. Abolitionists and
proslavery advocates were
too weak to impose their
views on each other in the
states, but the territories provided them with a
ready battleground. The prizes in these contests
were both tangible and intangible. On achieving
statehood, each territory elected two senators
who would support either slavery or freedom in
Washington. This gain directly affected sectional
power. Indirectly, there was the prestige of victory, of extending influence.

> **Debate over
> slavery in the
> territories**

Ironically, the territorial question had only
limited practical significance. Few slaves entered
any territory during the 1850s, and many areas
had few white settlers. Thus the territorial issue
in itself was probably manageable. Its explosive
power lay in its capacity to stir up other issues
and arouse other fears.

The prospect of slaves in the territories broadened the dispute over slavery to matters of basic
American liberties. It brought the conflict home
to northerners who had little interest in abolition or westward migration. And it spread fear
of an aggressive Slave Power. Abolitionists constantly warned of a threatening Slave Power; an
issue like slavery in the territories made the
threat credible.

The Slave Power idea postulated a slaveholding oligarchy in control of the South and
intent on controlling the nation. The evidence
for such domination lay in
the persecution of southern
dissenters and the suppres-
sion of their ideas. Evidence for the oligarchy's
desire to extend its control could be found in efforts to reopen the African slave trade and to acquire territory in the Caribbean, as well as in extreme proslavery arguments. A few slaveowners
were saying that if additional slaves could not be
acquired from Africa, whites would do. Eventually, warned abolitionists, these southern
oligarchs would consolidate their power, take
over the government, deprive the middle and
lower classes of their rights, and extend slavery
nationwide.

> **Fear of a Slave
> Power**

Fear of the sinister Slave Power transformed
the abolitionist impulse into a broader and more
influential antislavery movement. It turned
people who were not abolitionists—who were in
fact often racists—into opponents of slavery.
These northern whites were seeking to protect
themselves, not southern blacks, from the Slave
Power. As the prevailing issues shifted away
from the morality of slavery, they excited larger
numbers of people: more northerners cared
about the Slave Power than about the extension
of slavery, and more cared about slavery extension than about abolition.

Meanwhile, northerners and southerners were
developing ideologies—ways of viewing the
world—that hardened the lines of conflict.
Northerners attributed their own growing population, booming industries,
and increasing prosperity to
the free labor system. Free la-
bor and a free society seemed to be the key to
progress. Southerners, on the other hand,
praised the stability, order, and devotion to the

> **Conflicting
> ideologies**

Constitution of their section. They criticized the North for subverting the Constitution in the name of progress.

On top of these conflicts came the unraveling of the second party system and its replacement with a new system. This political restructuring

| Demise of the second party system |

was caused by the demise of the Whig party. Though blessed with influential congressmen, the Whigs had lacked commanding presidents in an era of strong leaders. The deaths of President Taylor (1850), Webster (1852), and Clay (1852) and discord between the party's northern and southern wings dealt a lethal blow to the Whigs. The party ran its last presidential candidate in 1852.

Although the Whig party disappeared, former Whigs accounted for approximately half the electorate, a magnificent prize for competing political organizations. Most Whigs were emotionally unable to join the Democrats. During the 1850s, three new parties (the Free Soilers, the Know Nothings, and the Republicans) appealed to the homeless Whigs by stressing such issues as temperance, immigration, tariffs, and internal improvements. For many Americans it was these issues and not slavery that were the real stuff of politics.

But this process of party building had one crucial implication: if voters joined organizations that took strong sectional stands, they added to the sectional confrontation whether the issue of slavery seemed important to them or not. Thus the interrelated problems of the 1850s reinforced each other and grew more dangerous and difficult.

Sectional problems are compromised but re-emerge

The first sectional battle of the decade involved the territory of California. More than eighty thousand Americans flooded into Califor-

nia in 1849. President Taylor urged the settlers to seek admission to the Union. The proposed state constitution submitted by California, however, prohibited slavery, and southerners objected. At a minimum southerners wanted the Missouri Compromise line extended through California.

Northern politicians were equally determined to keep slavery out of the new territories. They favored the position first taken by Representa-

| Wilmot Proviso |

tive David Wilmot in his proviso of 1846. In that year Wilmot had attached an amendment to a military appropriations bill barring slavery in any territory acquired from Mexico. It was not adopted.

Sensing that the Union was in peril, Henry Clay once more marshalled his energies. To hushed Senate galleries the "Great Pacificator" presented a series of compromise measures. Clay and Senator Stephen A. Douglas, an Illinois Democrat, moved through the Congress compromises balancing the issues of California and the nearby territories, the Texan boundary claim, runaway slaves, and the slave trade in the District of Columbia. The problems to be solved were thorny indeed, and made more so because of conflicting theories over settlers' rights in the territories. It was these theories that proved most troublesome in the continuing debate over the territories.

In 1847 Lewis Cass had introduced the idea of popular sovereignty. Though Congress had to

| Popular sovereignty |

approve statehood for a territory, it should "in the meantime," Cass said, allow the people living there "to regulate their own concerns in their own way." But, what was the meaning of "meantime"?

When could settlers bar slavery? Southerners claimed equal rights in the territories; therefore neither Congress nor a territorial legislature could bar slavery. Only when settlers framed a state constitution could they take that step. Northerners, meanwhile, argued that Americans living in a territory were entitled to local self-government, and thus could outlaw slavery at any time, if they allowed it at all. To avoid dissension within their party, northern and southern Democrats had explained Cass's statement to their constituents in these two incompatible ways. Their conflicting interpretations caused strong disagreement in the debate on Clay's proposals.

Despite bitter debate, the Compromise of 1850 finally passed. California was admitted as a free state, and the Texan | | boundary was set at its present limits. The United States paid Texas $10 million in consideration of the boundary agreement. And the territories of New Mexico and Utah were organized with power to legislate on "all rightful subjects . . . consistent with the Constitution." A stronger fugitive slave law and an act to suppress the slave trade in the District of Columbia completed the compromise.

Jubilation greeted passage of the Compromise of 1850. There was in reality, however, less cause for celebration than citizens thought. The compromise was an artful evasion of the sectional disputes. It did not solve the problems; it postponed them. Furthermore, the compromise had two basic flaws. The first pertained to popular sovereignty. What were "rightful subjects of legislation, consistent with the Constitution"? During debate, southerners had defined them one way, northerners another. In one politician's words, the legislators seemed to have enacted a lawsuit instead of a law.

The second flaw lay in the Fugitive Slave Act, which stirred up controversy instead of laying it to rest. The new law empowered slaveowners to go into court in their own states and present evidence that a slave who owed them service had escaped. The transcript of such a proceeding, including a description of the fugitive, was to be taken as conclusive proof of a person's slave status, even in free states and territories. Legal authorities had to decide only whether the black person brought before them was the person described, not whether he or she was indeed a slave. The accused was denied the right to a trial by jury and the right to present evidence or to cross-examine witnesses. Fines and penalties encouraged U.S. marshals to assist in apprehending fugitives and discouraged citizens from harboring them. (Authorities were paid $10 if the alleged fugitive was turned over to the slave-owner, $5 if he was not.)

At this point a novice writer dramatized the plight of the slave in a way that captured the sympathies of millions of northerners. Harriet Beecher Stowe wrote *Uncle Tom's Cabin* out of deep moral conviction. Her book, published in March 1852, showed how slavery brutalized the men and women who suffered under it. Stowe also portrayed slavery's evil effects on slaveholders. By mid-1853 the book had sold over a million copies. Stowe had brought the issue of slavery home to many who had never before given it much thought.

At the same time, the policies of the newly elected Pierce administration revived sectional disputes. In 1852 Franklin Pierce, a Democrat from New Hampshire, won a smashing victory over the Whig presidential nominee, General Winfield Scott. Pierce backed the Compromise of 1850, believing that the defense of each section's rights was essential to the nation's unity. Thus Pierce's victory seemed to confirm most Americans' support for the Compromise of 1850.

But Pierce did not seem able to avoid sectional conflict. His proposal for a transcontinental railroad ran into congressional dispute over where it should be built, North or South. His attempts to acquire foreign territory stirred up more trouble. An annexation treaty with Hawaii failed because southern senators would not vote for another free state, and Pierce's efforts to annex Cuba angered antislavery northerners.

But the shattering blow to sectional harmony originated in Congress, when Senator Stephen Douglas introduced a bill to organize the Kansas and Nebraska territories. Douglas, a rising Il-

An advertisement for *Uncle Tom's Cabin* indicates the tremendous effect of the book on the general public. The New-York Historical Society

linois Democrat and potential presidential candidate, hoped for a midwestern transcontinental railroad to boost Chicago's economy and encourage settlement on the Great Plains. A necessary precondition for a railroad was the organization of the territory it would cross. Thus it was probably in the interest of building such a railroad that Douglas introduced a bill that inflamed sectional passions, completed the destruction of the Whig party, damaged the northern wing of the Democratic party, gave birth to the Republican party, and injured his own national ambitions.

The Kansas-Nebraska bill exposed the first flaw of the Compromise of 1850, and conflict over popular sovereignty erupted once more. Douglas's bill clearly left "all questions pertaining to slavery in the Territories . . . to the people residing therein," but northerners and southerners still disagreed violently over what territorial settlers could constitutionally do.

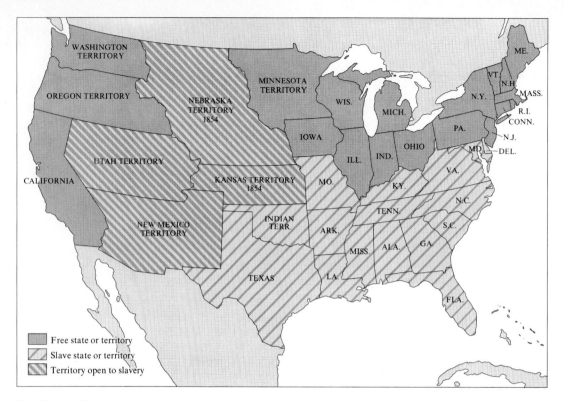

The Kansas-Nebraska Act, 1854

Political realignment

Moreover, the Kansas-Nebraska bill opened a new Pandora's box by explicitly repealing the Missouri Compromise. From a legal point of view Douglas's bill, which became law in May 1854, threw land open to slavery where it had been prohibited before (see map).

The Kansas-Nebraska Act inflamed fears and angers that had only simmered before. Abolitionists charged that the act was sinister aggression by the Slave Power. Between 1855 and 1859 seven northern states passed personal liberty laws designed to interfere with the swift action of the Fugitive Slave Act. These laws reflected northern fear of the Slave Power. Southerners saw the personal liberty laws as signs of bad faith. Finally, the Kansas-Nebraska Act had a devastating impact on the Whig and Democratic parties.

The Kansas-Nebraska Act divided the Whig party's northern and southern wings so irrevocably that it fell apart shortly thereafter. The Democrats survived, but they suffered at the polls in 1854 for their role in the legislation. Moreover, anger over the territorial issue created a new political party. In the summer and fall of 1854, antislavery Whigs and Democrats, free-soilers, and other reformers throughout the Old Northwest met to form a new Republican party, dedicated to keeping slavery out of the territories. The Republicans' influence rapidly spread to the East, and they won a stunning victory in the 1854 elections by capturing a majority of House seats in the North.

For the first time, a sectional party based on a

sectional issue had gained significant power in the political system. In the second party system, the national base of support enjoyed by both Whigs and Democrats had moderated sectional conflict. But the Whigs were gone, and politics in the 1850s would never be the same.

Nor were Republicans the only new party. An anti-immigrant organization, the American party, seemed likely for a few years to replace the Whigs. This party, also known as the Know-Nothings (because its members at first

Know-Nothings

kept their purposes secret, answering all queries with the words "I know nothing"), exploited nativist fear of foreigners. By the mid-1850s the American party was powerful and growing; in 1854 so many new congressmen won office with anti-immigrant as well as antislavery support that Know-Nothings could claim they outnumbered Republicans. But like the Whigs, the Know-Nothings could not keep their northern and southern wings together, and they melted away after 1856. That left the field to the Republicans.

The Republicans who wooed nativists and temperance advocates also appealed to groups interested in the economic development of the West. Commercial agriculture was booming in

Republicans

the Ohio-Mississippi-Great Lakes area, but residents of that region needed more canals, roads, and river and harbor improvements to reap the full benefit of their labors. There was also widespread interest in a federal land-grant program through which western land would be made available free to settlers. After vetoes of internal improvement bills by the Democratic presidents Pierce and Buchanan (elected in 1856) and of an 1859 homestead bill by Buchanan, the Republicans added internal-improvements and land-grant planks to their platform. They also backed higher tariffs as an enticement to industrialists and businessmen.

Thus the Republican party picked up support from a variety of sources. Opposition to the extension of slavery had brought the party together, but party members carefully broadened their appeal by adopting the causes of other groups. They were wise to do so. As the newspaper editor Horace Greeley wrote in 1860: "An Anti-Slavery man *per se* cannot be elected." But, he added, "a Tariff, River-and-Harbor, Pacific Railroad, Free Homestead man, *may* succeed *although* he is Anti-Slavery."

Greeley's remark was insightful. The Republican party was an amalgam of many interests, but functionally it had only one stand in the North-South controversy. Since a high proportion of the original activist Republicans were strongly opposed to slavery, the party's position on slavery and the territories was immune to change. Thus southerners perceived Republican strength as antislavery strength.

A similar process was under way in the South. The disintegration of the Whig party had left many southerners at loose ends politically. Much of the support for Whigs had come from wealthy planters and small-town businessmen and slaveholders. Some of these people gravitated to the American party, but not for long.

Southern Democrats

By advocating states' rights, Democratic leaders managed to convert most of the formerly Whig slaveholders. The party spoke to the class interests of slaveowners and the slaveowners responded.

In the South, however, yeomen rather than slaveholders were the heart of the party. Thus Democratic politicians, though often slaveowners themselves, had lauded the common man and appeared to champion his interests. The yeomen did not immediately object to the entry into the party of these ex-Whig slaveowners. Republican stands did not appeal to yeomen. Their party loyalties were strong, and as long as political issues were not posed in a class-conscious way, they did not become restive.

Slaveholding Democrats were careful to portray the sectional controversies as matters involving injustice to planter and yeoman alike.

Their ultimate weapon was the appeal to race prejudice. They argued, as Jefferson Davis put it in 1851, that slavery elevated the status of the nonslaveholder and enabled the poor man to "stand upon the broad-level of equality with the rich man." Slaveholders warned that the overriding issue was "shall negroes govern white men, or white men govern negroes?"

The result of these arguments was a one-party system in the South that emphasized sectional issues. Racial fears and traditional political loyalties kept this political alliance between yeomen and planters intact through the 1850s. In the South as in the North, political realignment obscured support for the Union and made sectional divisions seem sharper and deeper than they really were.

Free labor versus proslavery theory

While the new political parties were emerging, northerners and southerners were also developing opposing ideologies. The Republicans spoke to the image northerners had of themselves, their society, and their future when they preached "Free Soil, Free Labor, Free Men." At the time the Republicans were espousing these ideas, the northern economy was expanding. The key element in this successful economy seemed, in the eyes of many, to be free labor. Any hard-working, virtuous person, it was thought, could improve his condition and gain economic independence by applying himself.

| Free labor |

In developing their theories, Republican ideologues saw no conflict between the interests of capital and of labor. They relied on an old Whig idea, the harmony of economic interests, to justify the capitalistic system. According to this theory, farms and factories benefited each other, and the tariff safeguarded the jobs of American workers. If free labor, economic individualism, and opportunity were protected, even proper-tyless workers could save money, buy property, and command the means of production.

Thus the fate of the territories was crucial to the nation's future. The North's free-labor economic system had to be extended to the territories if coming generations were to prosper. After all, the territories were the great reservoir of opportunity for decent people without means. To allow an aristocratic system of bondage and forced labor to enter the territories would be to poison the reservoir.

Influential southerners were also developing an ideology of their own. Behind their ideology lay a deep fear that their way of life was about to collapse. Among southern politicians and slaveholders the feeling was growing that slavery was in jeopardy. The need to defend the institution became an obsession.

By the 1850s virtually all southern representatives were familiar with the latest arguments in proslavery theory. At a moment's notice they could discuss the anthropological evidence for the separate origin of the races; physicians' views on the inferiority of the black body; and sociological arguments for the superiority of the slave-labor system. But in private and in their hearts, most of these men fell back on two rationales: a belief that blacks were inferior and biblical accounts of slaveholding. Some, such as Jefferson Davis, reverted to the eighteenth-century argument that southerners were doing the best they could with a situation they had inherited.

| Proslavery theory |

The South's defenders also developed a set of arguments to prove the necessity of expanding slavery into the territories. Expansion was essential to the welfare of the Negro, they declared, for prejudice lessened where the concentration of blacks decreased. They further argued that expansion was necessary to the prosperity of the South. But few slaveholders moved into the territories. A more likely cause of southern concern over the territories was the fear that if areas like Kansas became free soil, they would be used as a base from which to spread abolitionism into the slave states.

An illustration from the *American Anti-Slavery Almanac* showing southern society as an unrelieved succession of slave torture, duels, lynchings, gambling, and cockfighting. Such blatant propaganda reinforced Republican fearmongering in the North. Library of Congress.

Southern leaders also spent a great deal of time commenting on the superior social values and practices of their region. Whereas the North was cold, materialistic, unstable, and polluted with radicalism, the South was warm, caring (thanks to its practice of paternalism), and solidly devoted to home, family, and Christianity. The turmoil and change of northern life had evidently unhinged northern minds, these critics said. Even so, their arguments were primarily rebuttals of northern criticism and attempts to suppress potential criticism from within.

But the chief tool in defending slavery was constitutional theory. Drawing on Jefferson's concept of strict construction, southern leaders emphasized that the nation arose from a compact among sovereign states; that the states were primary and the central government secondary; that the states retained all powers not expressly granted to the central government; and that the states were to be treated equally, and the rights of their citizens respected equally. Along with

these theories went the philosophy that the power of the federal government should be kept to a minimum. By keeping government close to home, southerners hoped to keep slavery safe.

But as the 1850s advanced, a growing portion of slaveholders became convinced that slavery could not be protected within the Union. Such concern was not new. As early as 1838, the Louisiana planter Bennet Barrow had written in his diary, "Northern States medling with slavery . . . must eventually cause a separation of the Union."

Political impasse: slavery in the territories

Like successive hammer blows, events reinforced these sectional differences. Controversy over Kansas did not subside; it grew. For among the settlers in the territory were partisans of both sides, each determined to make Kansas free or slave. Abolitionists and religious groups sent free-soil settlers to save the territory from slavery; southerners sent their own reinforcements. Clashes between the two groups led to violence, and soon the whole nation was talking about "Bleeding Kansas."

When elections for a territorial legislature were held in 1855, thousands of proslavery Mis-

Bleeding Kansas — sourians invaded the polls and ran up a large but unlawful majority for slavery candidates. The legislature that resulted promptly legalized slavery, and in response free-soilers called an unauthorized convention and created their own government and constitution. A proslavery posse sent to arrest the free-soil leaders sacked the town of Lawrence; in revenge, John Brown, a fanatic who saw himself as God's instrument to destroy slavery, murdered five proslavery settlers. Soon armed bands of guerrillas roamed the territory.

The passion generated by this conflict erupted in the chamber of the United States Senate in May 1856, when Charles Sumner of Massachusetts denounced "the Crime against Kansas." Idealistic and radical in his antislavery views, Sumner attacked the president, the South, and Senator Andrew P. Butler of South Carolina. Soon thereafter Butler's nephew, Congressman Preston Brooks, approached Sumner at his Senate desk and beat him brutally with a cane. Voters in Massachusetts and South Carolina seethed; the country was becoming polarized.

But the agony of personal confrontation paled beside the constitutional issues raised by the Supreme Court's decision in *Dred Scott* v.

Dred Scott *v.* Sanford — *Sanford* (1857). Scott, a Missouri slave, had sued his owner for his freedom, charging that he was free because he had resided in free territory. Chief Justice Roger B. Taney wrote that Scott was not a citizen either of the United States or Missouri; that residence in free territory did not make Scott free; and most im-

portantly, that Congress lacked the power to bar slavery from a territory, as it had done in the Missouri Compromise.

A storm of angry reaction broke in the North. Every charge against the aggressive Slave Power seemed now to be confirmed. "There is such a thing as THE SLAVE POWER," warned the *Cincinnati Daily Commercial;* the Cincinnati *Freeman* asked, "What security have the Germans and Irish that their children will not, within a hundred years, be reduced to slavery in this land of their adoption?"

Republican politicians, including Abraham Lincoln, capitalized on these fears of the Slave

Abraham Lincoln on the Slave Power — Power. At the crux of the matter was the self-interest of whites. Pointing to the southern obsession with the territories, Lincoln declared that they must be reserved "as an outlet for *free white people everywhere.*" After the Dred Scott decision, Lincoln charged that the next step in the unfolding Slave Power conspiracy would be a Supreme Court decision "declaring that the Constitution does not permit a State to exclude slavery from its limits. . . ."

Lincoln's most eloquent statement against the Slave Power was his famous House Divided speech. In it Lincoln declared: "I do not expect the Union to be dissolved—I do not expect the House to fall—but I do expect it to cease to be divided. It will become all one thing or all the other. Either the opponents of slavery will arrest the further spread of it, and place it where the public mind shall rest in the belief that it is in the course of ultimate extinction; or its advocates will push it forward, till it shall become alike lawful in all the States, old as well as new, North as well as South. Have we no tendency to the latter condition?" The concluding question was the key element of the passage, for it drove home the idea that slaveholders were trying to extend bondage over the entire nation.

The brilliance of Republican tactics offset the difficulties the Dred Scott decision posed for them. By endorsing southern constitutional arguments, the Court had invalidated the central position of the Republican party: no extension of slavery. Republicans could only repudiate the decision, appealing to a "higher law," or hope to change the personnel of the Court.

A northern Democrat like Stephen Douglas, meanwhile, faced an awful dilemma. He had to find a way to ease the fears of northerners without losing the support of southerners. Douglas chose to stand by his principle of popular sovereignty, which encountered a second test in Kansas in 1857. There, after free-soil settlers boycotted an election, proslavery forces met at Lecompton and wrote a constitution that permitted slavery. New elections to the territorial legislature, however, returned an antislavery majority, and the legislature promptly called for a popular vote on the new constitution, which was defeated by more than ten thousand votes. Despite this overwhelming evidence that Kansas did not want slavery, President Buchanan tried to force the Lecompton constitution through Congress. Douglas threw his weight against a document the people had rejected; he gauged their feelings correctly, and in 1858 Kansas voters rejected the constitution a third time. But his action infuriated southern Democrats.

In his well-publicized debates with Abraham Lincoln in 1858, Douglas further alienated the southern wing of his party. Speaking at Freeport, Illinois, he attempted to revive the notion of popular sovereignty with some tortured extensions of his old arguments. Asserting that the Court had not ruled on the powers of a *territorial* legislature, Douglas claimed that a territorial legislature could bar slavery by law or, in practice, by giving it no support. This argument, called the Freeport Doctrine, temporarily shored up Douglas's northern position but it alarmed southern Democrats. Some, like William L. Yancey of Alabama, concluded that southern rights would be safe only in a separate southern nation.

| Stephen Douglas proposes the Freeport Doctrine |

Violence inflamed passions further in October 1859, when John Brown led a small band in an attack on a federal arsenal at Harpers Ferry, Virginia, hoping to trigger a slave rebellion. Brown failed miserably, and was quickly captured, tried, and executed. It came to light, however, that Brown had had the financial backing of several prominent abolitionists, and northern intellectuals such as Emerson and Thoreau praised him as a hero and a martyr. Since slave rebellion excited the deepest fears in the white South, these disclosures multiplied southerners' fear and anger many times over. The unity of the nation was now in peril.

The election of 1860 and secession

Many observers feared that the election of 1860 would decide the fate of the Union. An ominous occurrence at the beginning of the campaign did nothing to reassure them. For several years, the Democratic party had been the only remaining organization, political or otherwise, that was truly national in scope. At the 1860 convention, however, the Democratic party broke in two.

Stephen A. Douglas wanted the party's presidential nomination, but could not afford to alienate northern opinion by accepting a strongly southern position on the territories. Southern Democrats like William L. Yancey, on the other hand, were determined to have their rights recognized, and they moved to block Douglas's nomination. When Douglas nevertheless marshalled a majority for his version of the platform, delegates from the five Gulf states plus South Carolina, Georgia, and Arkansas walked out of the convention hall in Charleston. Efforts at compromise failed, so the Democrats presented two nominees: Douglas for the northern wing, John C. Breckinridge for the southern. The Republicans nominated Abraham Lincoln; a Constitutional Union party, formed to preserve the nation but strong only in Virginia and the upper South, nominated John Bell of Tennessee.

| Splintering of the Democratic party |

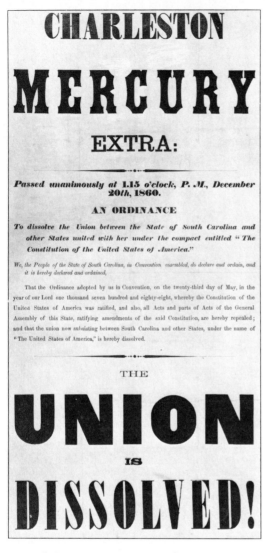

CHARLESTON

MERCURY

EXTRA:

Passed unanimously at 1.15 o'clock, P. M., December 20th, 1860.

AN ORDINANCE

To dissolve the Union between the State of South Carolina and other States united with her under the compact entitled " The Constitution of the United States of America."

We, the People of the State of South Carolina, in Convention assembled, do declare and ordain, and it is hereby declared and ordained,

That the Ordinance adopted by us in Convention, on the twenty-third day of May, in the year of our Lord one thousand seven hundred and eighty-eight, whereby the Constitution of the United States of America was ratified, and also, all Acts and parts of Acts of the General Assembly of this State, ratifying amendments of the said Constitution, are hereby repealed; and that the union now subsisting between South Carolina and other States, under the name of " The United States of America," is hereby dissolved.

THE

UNION

IS

DISSOLVED!

A handbill announcing passage of South Carolina's ordinance of secession. Rare Book Division, The New York Public Library, Astor, Lenox and Tilden Foundations.

The results of the balloting were sectional in character, but they indicated clearly that most voters were satisfied in the Union. Lincoln led in the North and Breckinridge in the South, but more votes were cast for Douglas and for Bell than for any single candidate. Moreover,

> **Election of 1860**

many supporters of Lincoln or Breckinridge did not favor secession. Even in the states that ultimately remained loyal to the Union, Lincoln gained only a plurality; his victory was won in the electoral college.

Although a majority of voters had rejected the extreme choices and the opportunity for compromise existed, Lincoln decided not to soften his party's position on the territories. In his inaugural address he spoke of the necessity of maintaining the bond of faith between voter and candidate. But Lincoln's party was *not* the majority. His refusal to compromise probably had more to do with the unity of the Republican party than with the integrity of the democratic process. Many Republicans favored compromise, but the original and strongest party members—antislavery voters and "conscience Whigs"—would not back away from the platform. To preserve the unity of his party, then, Lincoln had to take a position that endangered the Union.

Furthermore, political leaders in the North and the South tragically misjudged each other. Lincoln and other prominent Republicans believed that southerners were bluffing when they threatened secession; they expected a pro-Union majority in the South to assert itself. On their side, southern leaders had become convinced that northerners were not taking them seriously, and that a posture of strength was necessary to win respect for their position. Thus, southern leaders who hoped to avert disaster did not offer compromise for fear of inviting aggression. Nor did northern leaders who loved the Union, believing it unnecessary and unwise. The misunderstanding was complete; the communication between the two groups nil.

Meanwhile the Union was being destroyed. On December 20, 1860, South Carolina passed an ordinance of secession amid jubilation and

> **Secession of South Carolina**

cheering. This step marked the inauguration of a strategy known as separate-state secession. Despairing of persuading all the southern states to challenge the federal government simultaneously, foes of the Union had

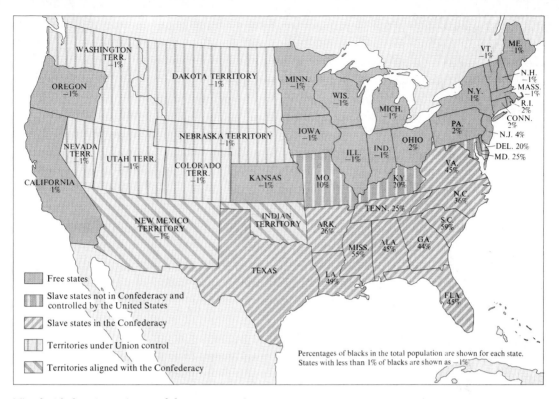

The divided nation—slave and free areas, 1861

concentrated their hopes on the most extreme proslavery state. With South Carolina out of the Union, they hoped other states would follow suit and momentum would build toward disunion.

Congress made last-minute efforts to save the Union. Both the Senate and the House established special committees to search for a satisfactory compromise. Their efforts focused on a series of proposals offered by Senator John J. Crittenden of Kentucky, who suggested that the two sections divide the territories between them at 36°30'. But his efforts came to grief when Lincoln indicated that Republicans would not make concessions on the territorial issue.

In these circumstances, southern extremists soon got their way. Overwhelming their opposition, they quickly called conventions and passed secession ordinances in six other states: Mississippi, Florida, Alabama, Georgia, Louisiana,

and Texas. By February 1861 these states had joined with South Carolina to form a new government in Montgomery, Alabama: the Confederate States of America (see map). Choosing Jefferson Davis as their president, they began to function independently of the United States.

Yet this apparent unanimity of action was deceiving. Confused and dissatisfied with the alternatives, many voters who had cast a ballot for president stayed home rather than vote for delegates who would consider secession. In some conventions the vote to secede had been close, the balance tipped by the overrepresentation of plantation districts. Furthermore, the conventions were noticeably reluctant to seek ratification of their acts by the people. Four states in the upper South—Virginia, North Carolina, Tennessee, and Arkansas—flatly rejected secession, and did not join the Confederacy until after the fighting had started. In Kentucky and

Important events

1846	Wilmot Proviso		1856	Preston Brooks attacks Charles Sumner in Senate chamber
1847	Lewis Cass proposes idea of popular sovereignty			Bleeding Kansas
				James Buchanan elected president
1848	Zachary Taylor elected president		1857	*Dred Scott* v. *Sanford*
				Lecompton constitution
1849	California applies for admission to Union as free state		1858	Voters reject Lecompton Constitution
1850	Compromise of 1850			Lincoln-Douglas debates
	Vermont enacts personal liberty law			Freeport Doctrine
			1859	Buchanan vetoes homestead bill
1852	Harriet Beecher Stowe, *Uncle Tom's Cabin*			John Brown raids Harpers Ferry
	Franklin Pierce elected president		1860	Democratic party splits in half
				Abraham Lincoln elected president
1854	Kansas-Nebraska bill			Crittenden Compromise fails
	Free-Soil party promotes settlement of Kansas			South Carolina secedes from Union
	Republican party formed			
	Pierce's effort to buy Cuba fails		1861	Six more southern states secede
	Democrats lose ground in congressional elections			Confederacy established
				Attack on Fort Sumter

Missouri popular sentiment was too divided for decisive action; these states remained under Union control, along with Maryland and Delaware.

Small wonder, since secession posed new and troubling issues for southerners, not the least of them the possibility of war and the question of who would be sacrificed. A careful look at election returns indicates that slaveholders and non-slaveholders were beginning to part company politically. Heavy slaveholding counties drew together in strong support of secession, but many counties with few slaves took an anti-secession position or were staunchly Unionist. In other words, yeomen were beginning to act on class interests. Finally, there was still considerable love for the Union in the South.

The dilemma facing President Lincoln on inauguration day in March 1861 was how to maintain the authority of the federal government without provoking war in the states that had left the Union. He decided to proceed cautiously; by holding onto federal fortifications, he reasoned, he could assert federal sovereignty while waiting for a restoration of relations. But Jefferson Davis, who could not claim to lead a sovereign nation if its ports and military facilities were under foreign control, would not cooperate. A collision was inevitable.

It came in the early morning hours of April

12, 1861, at Fort Sumter in Charleston harbor.

| Attack on Fort Sumter |

A federal garrison there was running low on food. Lincoln had decided to send a supply ship and had notified the South Carolinians of his intention. For the Montgomery government, the only alternative to an attack on the fort was submission to Lincoln's authority. Accordingly, orders were sent to obtain surrender or attack the fort. Under heavy bombardment for two days, the federal garrison finally surrendered. The Confederates permitted the soldiers to sail away on unarmed vessels while the residents of Charleston celebrated. Thus the bloodiest war in the nation's history began in a deceptively gala and gentlemanly spirit.

Suggestions for further reading

SOURCES OF CONFLICT   Eugene H. Berwanger, *The Frontier Against Slavery* (1967); Louis Filler, *The Crusade Against Slavery, 1830–1860* (1960); Eric Foner, *Free Soil, Free Labor, Free Men* (1970); George M. Fredrickson, *The Black Image in the White Mind* (1971); Eugene D. Genovese, *The World the Slaveholders Made* (1969); Michael F. Holt, *The Political Crisis of the 1850s* (1978); William Sumner Jenkins, *Pro-Slavery Thought in the Old South* (1935); Aileen S. Kraditor, *Means and Ends in American Abolitionism* (1969); Roy F. Nichols, *The Disruption of American Democracy* (1948); Russel B. Nye, *Fettered Freedom* (1949); Lewis Perry and Michael Fellman, eds., *Antislavery Reconsidered* (1979).

POLITICAL CRISES   Thomas B. Alexander, *Sectional Stress and Party Strength* (1967); William L. Barney, *The Secessionist Impulse* (1974); John Barnwell, *Love of Order* (1982); Stanley W. Campbell, *The Slave Catchers* (1968); Avery O. Craven, *The Coming of the Civil War* (1942); Don E. Fehrenbacher, *The Dred Scott Case* (1978); J. C. Furnas, *The Road to Harpers Ferry* (1959); Holman Hamilton, *Prologue to Conflict* (1964); Henry V. Jaffa, *Crisis of the House Divided* (1959); Allan Nevins, *The Emergence of Lincoln,* 2 vols. (1950); Stephen B. Oates, *To Purge the Land with Blood* (1970); David M. Potter, *The Impending Crisis, 1848–1861* (1976); Kenneth M. Stampp, *And the War Came* (1950); J. Mills Thornton, III, *Politics and Power in a Slave Society* (1978).

SECESSION AND WAR   Steven A. Channing, *Crisis of Fear* (1970); David M. Potter, *Lincoln and His Party in the Secession Crisis* (1942); Ralph A. Wooster, *The Secession Conventions of the South* (1962).

POLITICAL LEADERS   Richard N. Current, *The Lincoln Nobody Knows* (1958); David Donald, *Charles Sumner and the Coming of the Civil War* (1960); Drew Faust, *James Henry Hammond and the Old South* (1982); Don E. Fehrenbacher, *Prelude to Greatness* (1962); George B. Forgie, *Patricide in the House Divided* (1979); Robert W. Johannsen, *Stephen A. Douglas* (1973); Roy F. Nichols, *Franklin Pierce* (1958); Philip Shriver Klein, *President James Buchanan* (1962).

14 ∽

TRANSFORMING FIRE:
THE CIVIL WAR,
1860–1865

Moncure Conway, a Virginian who had converted to abolitionism and settled in New England, saw the Civil War as a momentous opportunity to bring justice to human affairs by abolishing slavery forever. In the words of one slave, it was God's "Holy War for the liberation of the poor African slave people." But Union troops took a different perspective. When a Yankee soldier ransacked a slave family's cabin and stole their best quilts, the mother exclaimed, "Why you nasty, stinkin' rascal. You say you come down here to fight for the niggers, and now you're stealin' from em." The soldier replied, "You're a G-- D--- liar, I'm fightin' for $14 a month and the Union."

White southerners too acted on limited and pragmatic motives, fighting in self-defense or out of regional loyalty. A Union officer interrogating Confederate prisoners noticed the poverty of one captive. Clearly the man was no slaveholder, so the officer asked him why he was fighting. "Because y'all are down here," replied the Confederate.

For each of these people and millions of others, the Civil War was a life-changing event. Armies numbering in the hundreds of thousands marched over the South, devastating once-peaceful countrysides. Families struggled to survive without their men; businesses tried to cope with

the loss of workers. Women, North and South, faced added responsibilities in the home and moved into new jobs in the work force. Nothing seemed untouched.

Change was most drastic in the South, where the leaders of the secession movement had launched a revolution for the purpose of keeping things unchanged. Southerners had feared that a peacetime government of Republicans would interfere with slavery and upset the routine of plantation life. Instead their own actions led to a war that turned southern life upside down and imperiled the very existence of slavery.

War altered the North as well, but not as deeply. Since the bulk of the fighting took place on southern soil, most northern farms and factories remained physically unscathed. The drafting of workers and the changing needs for products slowed the pace of industrialization somewhat, but factories and businesses remained busy. Though workers lost ground to inflation, the economy hummed. And a new probusiness atmosphere dominated Congress. To the discomfort of some, the powers of the federal government and the president increased during the emergency.

Ultimately, the Civil War forced new social and racial arrangements on the nation. Its greatest effect was to compel leaders and citizens to deal with an issue they had often tried to avoid: slavery. This issue had, in complex and indirect ways, given rise to the war; now the scope and demands of the war forced reluctant Americans to deal with it.

The South goes to war

In the first bright days of the southern nation, few foresaw the changes that were in store. Lincoln's call for troops to put down the Confederate insurrection stimulated an outpouring of regional loyalty that unified the classes. And in the South a half-million men volunteered to fight; there were so many would-be soldiers that the government could not arm them all.

This groundswell of popular support for the Confederacy generated a mood of optimism and gaiety. The first major battle of the war only increased such cockiness. On July 21, 1861, thirty thousand federal troops attacked twenty-two thousand southerners at a stream called Bull Run, near Manassas Junction, Virginia. Both armies were ill-trained, and confusion reigned on the battlefield. But nine thousand Confederate reinforcements and a timely stand by General Thomas Jackson (thereafter known as "Stonewall" Jackson) won the day for the South. Union troops fled back to Washington in disarray, and shocked northern picnickers who had expected to witness a victory suddenly feared their capital would be taken.

|Battle of Bull Run|

As 1861 faded into 1862, however, the North undertook a massive buildup of troops in northern Virginia. In the wake of Bull Run, Lincoln had given command of the army to General George B. McClellan, an officer who had always been better at organization and training than at fighting. McClellan devoted the fall and winter to readying a formidable force of a quarter-million men.

The North also moved to blockade southern ports in order to choke off the Confederacy's avenues of commerce and supply. Initially, the Union blockade of the Confederacy was woefully inadequate, but eventually it achieved near total success. Federal squadrons captured Cape Hatteras and Hilton Head, part of the Sea Islands off the South Carolina coast. Of greater significance, in April 1862, ships commanded by Admiral David Farragut smashed through log booms on the Mississippi and fought their way upstream to capture New Orleans (see map, page 212).

|Union naval campaign|

With the approach of spring 1862, the military outlook for the Confederacy darkened again, this time in northern Tennessee. There, General Ulysses S. Grant captured forts Henry and Donelson, securing two prime routes into the Confederacy's heartland. A path into Tennessee, Alabama, and Mississippi now lay open before the Union army.

|Grant's campaign in Tennessee|

But on April 6, Albert Sidney Johnston, the southern commander, caught Grant's army at Pittsburg Landing in southern Tennessee. The Confederates inflicted heavy damage, but Johnston was killed. The next day a reinforced Union army forced the enemy to withdraw to Corinth, Mississippi. Though the Battle of Shiloh was a Union victory, it was hideously destructive on both sides. Northern troops lost 13,000 of 63,000 men; southerners sacrificed 11,000 out of 40,000.

Both soldiers and civilians were beginning to recognize the enormous costs of this war. Never before in Europe or America had such massive forces pummeled each other with weapons of such destructive power. The improved range of modern rifles multiplied casualties; and, since medical knowledge was rudimentary, even minor wounds often led to death through infection. The slaughter was most vivid, of course, to the soldiers themselves, who saw the blasted bodies of their friends and comrades.

The scope and duration of the conflict had begun to have a visible effect on Confederate

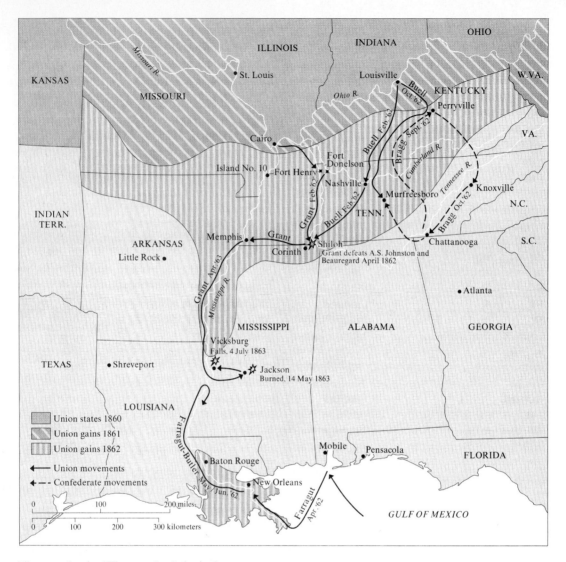

The war in the West, 1861–July 1863. Source:
Reprinted by permission of Alfred A. Knopf, Inc.

morale. As the spring of 1862 approached,
southern officials worried about the strength of

Confederacy resorts to a draft

their armies. The volunteer
spirit had died out, and three
states threatened or instituted
a draft. Finally, the Con-
federate government enacted the first national
conscription law in American history. The war

had forced an unprecedented change on states
that had seceded for fear of change.

With their ranks swelled by conscripts, southern armies moved into heavier fighting. Early in
1862 most of the combat centered in Virginia.
General McClellan sailed his troops to the York
peninsula and advanced on Richmond from the
east. But when McClellan sent his legions into

combat, generals Jackson and Lee managed to stave off his attacks. First, Jackson drew some of the federal troops away from Richmond to protect their own capital. Then, in a series of engagements culminating in the Seven Days' battles, Lee held McClellan off. On August 3 McClellan withdrew to the Potomac, and Richmond was safe for almost two more years.

Buoyed by these results, Jefferson Davis conceived an ambitious plan to turn the tide of the war and compel the United States to recognize the Confederacy. He ordered a general offensive,

 sending Lee north to Maryland and generals Kirby Smith and Braxton Bragg to Kentucky. The South would abandon the defensive and take the war north. The plan was promising, but every part of the offensive failed. In the bloodiest single day of fighting, September 17, 1862, McClellan turned Lee back in the Battle of Antietam near Sharpsburg, Maryland. Smith and Bragg had to withdraw from Kentucky just one day after Bragg had attended the inauguration of a provisional Confederate governor. The entire effort had collapsed.

But southern arms were not exhausted. On December 13, Lee decimated General Ambrose Burnside's soldiers as they charged his fortified positions at Fredericksburg, Virginia. Nevertheless, the Confederacy had marshalled all its strength for a breakthrough and had failed. Profoundly disappointed, Davis admitted to a committee of Confederate representatives that southerners had entered "the darkest and most dangerous period we have yet had."

War transforms the South

Even more than the fighting itself, changes in civilian life altered southern society beyond all expectations and with astonishing speed. Among the first traditions to fall in the states'-rights-South was limited government.

From the outset of the war, Davis pressed to bring all arms, supplies, and troops under central control. He advocated conscription when the states failed to enroll enough new soldiers.

Centralization of power in the South And he took a strong leadership role toward the Confederate congress, which raised taxes and later passed a tax-in-kind—a levy on wheat, corn, oats, rye, cotton, peas, and other farm products. Where opposition arose, the government suspended the writ of habeas corpus and imposed martial law. In the face of a political opposition that cherished states' rights, Davis proved unyielding.

Soon the Richmond administration was taking virtually complete direction of the southern economy. Because it controlled the supply of labor through conscription, the administration could regulate industry. In addition, the Confederate congress passed laws giving the central government almost full control of the railroads; and later shipping, too, came under extensive regulation. New statutes even limited corporate profits and dividends. A large bureaucracy sprang up to administer these operations: over seventy thousand civilians were needed to run the Confederate war machine. By the war's end the southern bureaucracy was proportionally larger than its northern counterpart.

The mushrooming bureaucracy expanded the cities. Clerks and subordinate officials, many of them women, crowded the towns and cities where Confederate departments had their offices.

Effects of war on southern cities and industry These sudden population booms stretched the existing housing supply and stimulated new construction. The pressure was especially great in Richmond, whose population increased two-and-a-half times.

Another prime cause of urban growth was industrialization. Because of the Union blockade, the traditionally agricultural South became interested in industry. Davis exulted that southerners were manufacturing their own goods. And indeed, though the Confederacy started from scratch, it achieved tremendous feats of industrial development.

As a result of these changes southerners adopted new values. Women, sheltered in the patriarchal antebellum society, gained substantial new responsibilities.

Change in the southern woman's role

The wives and mothers of soldiers became heads of households and undertook what had previously been considered men's work. In slaveowning families women assumed management roles. City women also found new and respectable roles and paying jobs in the workforce. "Government girls" who staffed the Confederate bureaucracy and female schoolteachers became a familiar sight. Such experiences undermined the image of the omnipotent male and gave thousands of women new confidence in their abilities.

The Confederate experience introduced and sustained many other new values. Legislative bodies yielded power to the executive branch of government, which could act more decisively in time of war. The traditional emphasis on aristocratic lineage gave way to respect for achievement and bravery under fire. Finally, sacrifice for the cause discouraged the pursuit of pleasure.

For the elite such sacrifice was symbolic, but for millions of ordinary southerners it was terrifyingly real. Mass poverty descended on the

Human suffering in the South

South. The crux of the problem was that many yeoman families had lost their breadwinners to the army. The poor sought help from relatives, neighbors, friends, anyone. Sometimes they took their cases to the Confederate government, as did an elderly Virginian who pleaded, "If you dount send [my son] home I am bound to louse my crop and cum to suffer."

Inflation became a major problem as prices rose by almost 7,000 percent. People of once-modest means looked around them and found abundant evidence that all classes were not sacrificing equally. They saw that the wealthy curtailed only their luxuries, while many poor families went without necessities. They saw that the

Inequities of the Confederate draft

government contributed to these inequities through policies that favored the upper class. Until the last year of the war, for example, prosperous southerners could avoid military service by furnishing a hired substitute. Well over fifty thousand upper-class southerners purchased substitutes.

Anger at such discrimination exploded when in October 1862 the Confederate congress exempted from military duty anyone who was supervising at least twenty slaves. The "twenty nigger law" became notorious. Immediately protests arose from every corner of the Confederacy, and North Carolina's legislators formally condemned the law. Its defenders argued, however, that the exemption preserved order and aided food production, and the statute remained on the books.

Dissension spread as growing numbers of citizens concluded that the struggle was "a rich man's war and a poor man's fight." Alert politicians and newspaper editors warned that class resentment was building to a dangerous level; letters to Confederate officials during this period contained a bitterness that suggested the depth of the people's anger. "If I and my little children suffer [and] die while there Father is in service," threatened one woman, "I invoke God Almighty that our blood rest upon the South."

The northern economy copes with war

With the onset of war, a tidal wave of change also rolled over the North. Factories and citizens' associations geared up to support the war, and the federal government and its executive branch gained power they had never had before. Civil liberties were restricted, and social values were influenced by both personal sacrifice and wartime riches. Idealism and greed flourished side by side.

HARPER'S WEEKLY.
A JOURNAL OF CIVILIZATION.

VOL. V.—No. 238.]　　　　NEW YORK, SATURDAY, JULY 20, 1861.　　　　[SINGLE COPIES SIX CENTS.
$2.50 PER YEAR IN ADVANCE.

Entered according to Act of Congress, in the Year 1861, by Harper & Brothers, in the Clerk's Office of the District Court for the Southern District of New York.

FILLING CARTRIDGES AT THE UNITED STATES ARSENAL AT WATERTOWN, MASSACHUSETTS.—[SEE NEXT PAGE.]

In both North and South women entered the factories to boost wartime production. This *Harper's Weekly* cover shows women filling cartridges in the United States arsenal at Watertown, Massachusetts.　Library of Congress.

The northern economy copes with war　　　　215

Initially, the war was a shock to business. With the sudden closing of the southern market, firms could no longer predict the demand

| Initial slump in northern business |

for their goods; many companies had to redirect their activities in order to remain open. And southern debts became uncollectible, jeopardizing not only merchants but many western banks. In farming regions, families struggled with an aggravated shortage of labor. For reasons such as these, the war initially caused an economic slump.

Overall the war slowed industrialization in the North. But the war's economic impact was not all negative. Certain entrepreneurs, such as wool producers, benefited from shortages of competing products, and soaring demand for war-related goods swept some businesses to new heights of production. To feed the voracious war machine the federal government pumped unprecedented amounts of money into the economy. As a result, industries producing weapons, munitions, uniforms, boots, camp equipment, saddles, ships, food, and other war necessities prospered.

War production also promoted the development of heavy industry in the North. The output of coal rose substantially. Iron makers

| Effects of war on northern industry and agriculture |

improved the quality of their product while boosting the production of pig iron. And although new railroad construction slowed, the manu-

facture of rails increased. Of considerable significance for the future were the railroad industry's adoption of a standard gauge for track and foundries' development of new and less expensive ways to make steel.

Another strength of the northern economy was the complementary relationship between agriculture and industry. The mechanization of agriculture had begun well before the war. Now, though, wartime recruitment and conscription gave western farmers an added incentive to purchase labor-saving machinery. This shift from human labor to machines had several beneficial effects. New markets for industry were

created and the food supply for the industrial work force was expanded. Finally, farm families whose breadwinners had gone to war did not suffer as they did in the South.

The northern workers who suffered most during the war were wage earners, particularly industrial and urban workers. Though jobs were plentiful following the initial slump, inflation took much of a worker's paycheck. Studies of the cost of living indicate that between 1860 and 1864 consumer prices rose at least 76 percent; meanwhile daily wages rose only 42 percent. To make up the difference, workers' families had to do without.

As their real wages shrank, industrial workers also lost job security. To increase production, some employers were replacing workers with labor-saving machines. Other employers urged the government to liberalize immigration procedures so they could import cheap labor. Workers responded by forming unions and

| New militancy among northern workers |

sometimes by striking. Skilled craftsmen organized to combat the loss of their jobs and status to machines; women and unskilled work-

ers, excluded by the craftsmen, formed their own unions. And in recognition of the increasingly national scope of business activity, thirteen occupational groups formed national unions during the Civil War. Because of the tight labor market, unions were able to win many of their demands without striking; but still the number of strikes rose steadily.

Troublesome as unions were, they did not prevent many employers from making a profit. The biggest fortunes were made in profiteering on government contracts. Unscrupulous businessmen sold the army clothing and blankets made of "shoddy"—wool fibers reclaimed from rags or worn cloth—that often came apart in the rain. Inferior guns were sold for double the usual price and tainted meat for the price of good. Corruption was so widespread that it led to a year-long investigation by the House of Representatives.

Legitimate enterprises also turned a neat

profit. The output of woolen mills increased so dramatically that dividends in the industry nearly tripled. Some cotton mills, though they reduced their output, made record profits on what they sold. And railroads carried immense quantities of freight and passengers, increasing their business to the point that railroad stocks doubled or even tripled.

Wartime benefits to northern business

In fact, railroads were a leading beneficiary of government largesse. Congress had failed in the 1850s to resolve the question of a northern versus a southern route for the first transcontinental railroad. But with the South out of Congress, the northern route quickly prevailed. In 1862 and 1864 Congress chartered two corporations, the Union Pacific Railroad and the Central Pacific Railroad, and assisted them handsomely in connecting Omaha, Nebraska, with Sacramento, California. For each mile of track laid, the railroads received a loan of $16,000 to $48,000 plus twenty square miles of land along a free four-hundred-foot-wide right of way. Overall, the two corporations gained approximately 20 million acres of land and nearly $60 million in loans.

Another measure that brought joy to the business community was the tariff. Northern businesses did not uniformly favor high import duties; some manufacturers desired cheap imported raw materials more than they feared foreign competition. But northeastern congressmen traditionally supported higher tariffs, and the tariff act of 1864 raised tariffs generously. And, as one would expect, some healthy industries made artificially high profits by raising their prices to a level just below that of the foreign competition. By the end of the war, tariff rates averaged 47 percent, more than double the rates of 1857.

The frantic wartime activity, the booming economy, and the Republican alliance with business combined to create a new atmosphere in Washington. The balance of opinion shifted against consumers and wage earners and toward large corporations; the notion spread that government should aid businessmen but not interfere with them. This was the golden hour of untrammeled capitalism, and railroad builders and industrialists took advantage of it.

As long as the war lasted, the powers of the federal government and the president continued to grow. Abraham Lincoln found, as had Jefferson Davis, that war required active presidential leadership. At the beginning of the conflict, Lincoln launched a major ship-building program without waiting for Congress to assemble. The lawmakers later approved his decision, and Lincoln continued to act in advance of Congress when he deemed it necessary. In one striking exercise of executive power, Lincoln suspended the writ of habeas corpus for all people living between Washington and Philadelphia. The justification for this action was practical rather than legal; Lincoln was ensuring the loyalty of Maryland. Lincoln also used his wartime authority to bolster his political power. He and his generals proved adept at arranging furloughs for soldiers who could vote in close elections. Needless to say, the citizens in arms whom Lincoln helped to vote usually voted Republican.

Wartime powers of the U.S. executive

Among the clearest examples of the wartime expansion of federal authority were the National Banking Acts of 1863, 1864, and 1865. Prior to the Civil War the nation did not have a uniform currency. Banks operating under a variety of state charters issued no fewer than seven thousand different kinds of notes. Under the new laws, Congress established a national banking system empowered to issue a maximum number of national bank notes. At the close of the war in 1865, Congress laid a prohibitive tax on state bank notes and forced most major institutions to join the system.

The rapidly increasing scale of things may have been best sensed by soldiers, whose first experiences with large organizations were often unfortunate. Blankets, clothing, and arms were often inferior. Vermin were commonplace. Hospitals were badly managed at first. Rules of hygiene in large camps were badly written or unenforced; latrines were poorly made or carelessly used. Indeed, conditions were such that 224,000 Union troops died from disease or accidents, far more than the 140,000 who died in battle.

Such conditions would hardly have predisposed the soldier to sympathize with changing social attitudes on the home front. Amid the excitement of money-making, a gaudy culture

| Self-indulgence versus sacrifice in the North |

of vulgar display flourished in the largest cities. A writer for the *New York Herald* observed, "This war has entirely changed the American character. . . . The individual who makes the most money–no matter how–and spends the most–no matter for what–is considered the greatest man. . . . The world has seen its iron age, its silver age, its golden age, and its brazen age. This is the age of shoddy."

Yet strong elements of idealism coexisted with ostentation. Abolitionists, after initial uncertainty over whether to fight the South or allow division of the Union to separate the North from slavery, campaigned to turn the war into a war against slavery. Free black communities and churches both black and white responded to the needs of slaves who flocked to the Union lines. They sent clothing, ministers, and teachers in generous measure to aid the runaways.

Northern women, like their southern counterparts, took on new roles. Those who stayed home organized over ten thousand soldiers' aid societies, rolled innumerable bandages, and raised $3 million. Thousands served as nurses in front-line hospitals, where they pressed for better care of the wounded. The professionalization of medicine since the Revolution had created a medical system dominated by men: thus dedicated and able female nurses had to fight both military regulations and professional hostility to win the chance to make their contribution. In the hospitals they quickly proved their worth, but only the wounded welcomed them. Even Clara Barton, the most famous female nurse, was ousted from her post during the winter of 1863.

Thus northern society embraced strangely contradictory tendencies. Materialism and greed flourished alongside idealism, religious conviction, and self-sacrifice. While wealthy men purchased 118,000 substitutes and almost 87,000 commutations at $300 each to avoid service in the Union army, others risked their lives out of a desire to preserve the Union or extend freedom.

The strange advent of emancipation

At the very highest levels of government there was a similar lack of clarity about the purpose of the war. Through the first several months of the struggle, both Davis and Lincoln studiously avoided references to slavery, the crux of the matter. Davis told southerners that they were fighting for constitutional liberty. He feared that stressing slavery might alienate non-slaveholders. Lincoln, hoping that a pro-Union majority would assert itself in the South, recognized that mention of slavery would end any chance of coaxing the seceded states back into the Union. Moreover, many Republicans were not vitally interested in the slavery issue. An early presidential stand making the abolition of slavery and not the preservation of the Union the war's objective could have split the party.

Lincoln first broached the subject of slavery in a major way in March 1862, when he proposed that the states consider emancipation on their own. He asked Congress to pass a resolution promising aid to any state that decided to emancipate, and he appealed to border-state representatives to give the idea of emancipation

| Lincoln's plan for gradual emancipation |

serious consideration. What Lincoln was talking about was gradual emancipation, with compensation for slaveholders and colonization of the freed slaves out-

Black troops, many of whom had been slaves, infused vital strength into the Union armies. The men above, members of Company E, Fourth U.S. Colored Infantry, were photographed at Fort Lincoln, Virginia.   Chicago Historical Society.

side the United States. This was a conservative approach in which the states, rather than Lincoln, would make the decision and assume the responsibility.

But others wanted to go much further. A group of congressional Republicans known as the Radicals had, from the early days of the war, concerned themselves with slavery. In August 1861, at the Radicals' instigation, Congress passed its first confiscation act. Designed to punish the Confederate rebels, the law confiscated all property used for "insurrectionary purposes." That is, if the South used slaves in a hostile action, those slaves were declared seized and liberated from their owners' possession. A second confiscation act (July 1862) was much more drastic: it confiscated the property of all those who supported the rebellion, even those who merely resided in the South and paid Confederate taxes. Their slaves were "forever free of

> Confiscation Acts

their servitude, and not again [to be] held as slaves."

When Lincoln refused to enforce the second confiscation act, Horace Greeley, editor of the *New York Tribune,* criticized him. Lincoln's reply was an explicit statement of his complex and calculated approach to the question. "I would save the Union," announced Lincoln. "If I could save the Union without freeing *any* slave I would do it, and if I could save it by freeing *all* the slaves I would do it; and if I could save it by freeing some and leaving others alone I would also do that. What I do about slavery, and the colored race, I do because I believe it helps to save the Union."

When he wrote those words, Lincoln had already decided to issue the Emancipation Proclamation. He waited until the opportune time. On September 22, 1862, shortly after the Battle of Antietam, Lincoln issued the first part of his two-part proclamation. Invoking his powers as

The strange advent of emancipation

Emancipation proclamations commander-in-chief of the armed forces, he announced that in a proclamation to be issued on January 1 he would emancipate the slaves in states whose people "shall then be in rebellion against the United States."

Lincoln's designation of the areas in rebellion on January 1 is worth noting. He excepted from his list every Confederate county or city that had fallen under Union control. Those areas, he declared, "are, for the present, left precisely as if this proclamation were not issued." And in a telling omission, Lincoln neglected to liberate slaves in the border slave states that remained in the Union. "The President . . . has proclaimed emancipation only where he has notoriously no powers to execute it," complained the *New York World.*

As a moral document the Emancipation Proclamation, which in fact freed no slaves, was wanting. As a political document it was nearly flawless. Because the proclamation defined the war as a war against slavery, liberals could applaud it. Yet at the same time it protected Lincoln's position with conservatives, leaving him room to retreat if he chose and forcing no immediate changes on the border slave states. The president had not gone as far as Congress had, and he had taken no position he could not change.

Lincoln seemed to take a stronger stand in June 1864. On the eve of the Republican national convention, he called the party's chairman to the White House and issued these instructions: "Mention in your speech, when you call the convention to order . . . to put into the platform as the keystone, the amendment of the Constitution abolishing and prohibiting slavery forever." It was done and, following congressional approval, the proposed Thirteenth Amendment went to the states for ratification.

But even this was not Lincoln's last word on the matter. In 1865 the newly re-elected president considered allowing the defeated southern states to re-enter the Union and delay or defeat the amendment. In February he and Secretary of State Seward met with three Confederate com- missioners at Hampton Roads, Virginia. There, Seward talked of how re-entry into the Union would allow the southern states to block the pending amendment. Lincoln spoke of ratification with a five-year delay and of a promise to seek $400 million in compensation for slaveowners. The president was apparently motivated by a desire to create a new and broader Republican party based on an alliance with southern Whigs and moderates. The proposals were not discussed in the South because of Jefferson Davis's total commitment to independence.

Hampton Roads Conference

Before the war was over, the Confederacy too addressed the issue of emancipation. Ironically, a strong proposal in favor of liberation came from Jefferson Davis. He was dedicated to independence, and he was willing to sacrifice slavery to achieve that goal. After considering the alternatives, especially the need for manpower, Davis concluded in the fall of 1864 that it was necessary to act. Thus he advocated the purchase and arming of slave soldiers. Tied to his recommendation was a proviso stipulating that such soldiers, and later their wives and children, must be freed.

Davis's plan for emancipation

Confederate emancipation began too late to revive southern armies or win diplomatic advantages with antislavery Europeans. But Lincoln's Emancipation Proclamation stimulated a vital infusion of manpower into the Union armies. Beginning in 1863 blacks shouldered arms for the North. Before the war was over, 186,000 of them had fought for freedom and the Union. Their participation was crucial to northern victory, and it discouraged recognition of the Confederacy by foreign governments.

The disintegration of Confederate unity

During the final two years of fighting, both northern and southern governments waged the war in the face of increasing opposition at home. The unrest was connected to the military stalemate: neither side was close to victory in 1863. But protest also arose from fundamental stresses in the social structures of the North and the South.

One ominous development was the increasing opposition of planters to their own government, whose actions had had a negative effect on them. As a diplomatic weapon the South had withheld most of its cotton from world markets, hurting the planters' profits. Confederate military authorities had also impressed slaves to build fortifications. And when Union forces advanced on plantation areas, Confederate commanders had sent detachments through the countryside to burn stores of cotton that lay in the enemy's path. Such interference with plantation routines and financial interests was not what Confederate planters had expected of their government.

Planters' opposition to the Confederacy

Furthermore, the Confederate constitution, drawn up by the leading political thinkers of the South, had in fact granted substantial powers to the central government, especially in time of war. But for many planters, states' rights had become virtually synonymous with complete state sovereignty. In effect, years of opposition to the federal government within the Union had frozen southerners in a defensive posture. Now they erected the barrier of states' rights as a defense against change. Planters sought a guarantee that their plantations and their lives would remain untouched; they were deeply committed neither to building a southern nation nor to winning independence. Thus, when secession revolutionized their world, they could not or would not adjust to it.

Meanwhile, at the bottom of southern society, there were other difficulties. Food riots occurred in the spring of 1863 in several communities. On April 2, a crowd assembled in the Confederate capital of Richmond to demand relief. A passerby, noticing the ex-

Food riots in southern cities

citement, asked a young girl, "Is there some celebration?" "There is," replied the girl. "We celebrate our right to live. We are starving. As soon as enough of us get together we are going to the bakeries and each of us will take a loaf of bread." Soon they did just that, sparking a riot that Davis himself had to quell at gunpoint.

Throughout the rural South, ordinary people resisted more quietly—by refusing to cooperate with impressments of food, conscription, or tax collection. "In all the States impressments are evaded by every means which ingenuity can suggest, and in some openly resisted," wrote a high-ranking commissary officer. Farmers who did provide food refused to accept certificates of credit or government bonds in lieu of cash, as required by law. And conscription officers increasingly found no one to draft—men of draft age were hiding out in the forests.

Such civil discontent was certain to affect the Confederate armies. Spurred by concern for their loved ones and resentment of the rich man's war, large numbers of men did indeed leave the armies, supported by their friends and neighbors. The problem of desertion became so acute that by November 1863, Secretary of War James Seddon admitted that one-third of the army could not be accounted for. And the situation was to worsen.

The gallantry of those who stayed on in Lee's army and the daring of their commander made for a deceptively positive start to the 1863 campaign. On May 2 and 3 at Chancellorsville, Virginia, 130,000 members of the Union Army of the Potomac bore down on fewer than 60,000 Confederates. Lee and Stonewall Jackson boldly divided their forces, ordering 30,000 men under Jackson on a day-long march westward and to the rear for a flank attack. Jackson arrived at his position late in the afternoon to witness unprepared Union troops, "laughing, smoking," and playing cards. "Push right ahead," Jackson said, and his weary but excited corps swooped down on the Federals and drove their right wing back in confusion. The Union forces left Chancellorsville the next day de-

Battle of Chancellorsville

feated. Though Stonewall Jackson had been fatally wounded, it was a remarkable southern victory.

But two critical battles in July 1863 brought crushing defeats to the Confederacy. General Ulysses S. Grant, after finding an advantageous approach to Vicksburg, laid siege to that vital western fortification. If Vicksburg fell, U.S. forces would control the Mississippi, cutting the Confederacy in half. Meanwhile, Lee proposed an invasion of the North to divert attention from Vicksburg. Both movements drew toward conclusion early in July.

In the North, Lee's troops streamed through Maryland and into Pennsylvania, where they threatened both Washington and Baltimore. The possibility of a major victory before the Union capital became more and more likely. But along the Mississippi, Confederate prospects darkened. Davis and Secretary of War Seddon repeatedly wired General Joseph E. Johnston to concentrate his forces and attack Grant's army. Johnston, despite the prodding from his superiors, did nothing to relieve the garrison. In the meantime, Grant's men were supplying themselves by drawing on the agricultural riches of the Mississippi River valley. With such provisions, they could continue their siege indefinitely. In such circumstances the fall of Vicksburg was inevitable, and on July 4, 1863, its commander surrendered.

That same day a battle that had been raging since July 1 concluded at Gettysburg, Pennsylvania. On July 1 and 2, the Union and Confederate forces had both made gains in furious fighting. Then on July 3 Lee ordered a direct assault on Union fortifications atop Cemetery Ridge. Full of foreboding, General James Longstreet warned Lee that "no 15,000 men ever arrayed for battle can take that position." But Lee, hoping success might force the Union to accept peace with independence, stuck to his plan. His brave troops rushed the position, and a hundred momentarily breached the enemy's line. But most fell in heavy slaughter. On July 4 Lee had to withdraw, having suf-

Battle of Gettysburg

fered almost 4,000 killed and approximately 24,000 missing and wounded.

Though southern troops had displayed a courage and dedication that would never be forgotten, the results had been disastrous. Intelligent southerners knew that defeat lay ahead. Equally significant, the defeats quickened the pace of the Confederacy's internal disintegration. Southern leaders began to realize that they were losing the support of the common people. Moreover, a few newspapers and politicians began to call for peace or negotiations. These movements came to naught, but they attracted several prominent southern politicians, including Vice President Alexander Stephens.

By 1864 much of the opposition to the war had moved entirely outside politics. Southerners were simply giving up the struggle, withdrawing their cooperation from the government, and forming a sort of counter-society. Deserters joined with ordinary citizens who were sick of the war to dominate whole towns and counties. Secret societies dedicated to reunion, such as the Heroes of America, sprang up. Active dissent spread throughout the South but was particularly common in upland and mountain regions. The government was losing the support of its citizens.

Antiwar sentiment in the North

In the North opposition to the war was similar in many ways, but not as severe. There was concern over the growing centralization of government, and war-weariness was a frequent complaint. Discrimination and injustice in the draft sparked protest among poor citizens, just as they had in the South. But the Union was so much richer than the South in human resources that none of these problems ever threatened the stability of the government. Fresh recruits were always available, and food and other necessaries were not subject to severe shortages.

What was more, Lincoln possessed a talent

that Davis lacked: he knew how to stay in touch with the ordinary citizen. Through letters to newspapers and to soldiers' families, he reached the common people and demonstrated that he had not forgotten them. Their grief was his also, for the war was his personal tragedy. His words helped to contain northern discontent, though they could not remove it.

Much wartime protest sprang from politics. The Democratic party, though nudged from its dominant position, was determined to regain power. Party leaders attacked the war, the expansion of federal powers, the high tariff, inflation, and the improved status of blacks. They also supported states' rights, called for reunion on the basis of "the Constitution as it is and the Union as it was," and charged that the Republicans were going to flood the North with blacks. In 1862 Democratic criticism of the war helped the party make a substantial comeback in the congressional elections.

Led by outspoken men like Clement L. Vallandigham of Ohio, the peace Democrats were highly visible. Vallandigham criticized Lincoln as a dictator who had suspended the writ of habeas corpus without congressional authority and arrested thousands of innocent citizens. He stayed carefully within legal bounds, but his attacks were so damaging to the war effort that military authorities arrested him after Lincoln suspended habeas corpus. Fearing that Vallandigham might gain the stature of a martyr, the president decided against a jail term and exiled him to the Confederacy.

Lincoln believed that antiwar Democrats were linked to secret organizations that harbored traitorous ideas. Likening such groups to a poisonous snake striking at the government, Republicans sometimes branded them—and by extension the peace Democrats—as Copperheads. Though Democrats were connected with these secret organizations, most engaged in politics rather than treason.

Most violent opposition to the government came from ordinary citizens facing the draft—especially the poor and immigrants, who were called in disproportionate numbers. Northerners witnessed scores of disturbances and melees. Enrolling officers received rough treatment in many parts of the North, and riots occurred in Ohio, Indiana, Pennsylvania, Illinois, and Wisconsin, and in such cities as Troy, Albany, and Newark. By far the most serious outbreak of violence, however, occurred in New York City in July 1863, where three days of rioting left seventy-four people dead. The riot had heavy racist overtones, for many Irish immigrants resented competition from free black workers.

Once inducted, northern soldiers reacted to their loneliness and grievances in much the same way as their southern counterparts. Thousands of men slipped away from authorities. Indeed, the Union army had a desertion rate as high as the Confederates'. Those who did not desert were often discouraged at the lack of progress in defeating the South.

Discouragement and war-weariness neared their peak during the summer of 1864. At that point the Democratic party nominated the popular General George B. McClellan for president and put a qualified peace plank into its platform. The plank, written by Vallandigham, condemned "four years of failure to restore the Union by the experiment of war" and called for an armistice. Lincoln concluded that it was "exceedingly probable that this Administration will not be re-elected." The fortunes of war, however, soon changed the electoral situation.

The northern vise closes

The year 1864 brought to fruition the North's long-term diplomatic strategy. From the outset the Union's paramount diplomatic goal had been to prevent European recognition of the Confederacy and the military and economic aid it would bring. Southerners had depended for recognition on England's need for southern cotton, but their strategy failed because England had a surplus of cotton on hand and developed new sources during the war. Britain watched the battlefield and refused to be stampeded into acknowledging the Confederacy.

On three occasions the successful Union strategy nearly broke down. A major crisis occurred in 1861 when the overzealous commander of an American frigate stopped the British steamer *Trent* and abducted two Confederate ambassadors. The British reacted strongly, but Lincoln and Seward were able to delay until public opinion allowed them to back down and return the ambassadors. In another lengthy crisis, the United States protested but could not stop the sale of six warships to the Confederacy by British shipbuilders. And in the third crisis, the victories at Gettysburg and Vicksburg helped northern officials to block delivery to the Confederacy of British warships—the formidable Laird rams, whose pointed prows were designed to break the Union blockade.

In 1864 the Union also attained military success. General William Tecumseh Sherman, in command of 100,000 men, began an advance from Chattanooga toward Atlanta. In Sherman's path the Confederacy placed the army of General Johnston, who skillfully slowed Sherman's progress. But Jefferson Davis needed a victory and not merely a tactically sound campaign. For Davis, the successful defense of Atlanta would mean the political defeat of Lincoln and the start of peace overtures. When Johnston failed to press the fight, Davis replaced him with General John Hood, who attacked but was beaten. Sherman's army occupied Atlanta on September 2, 1864. The victory buoyed northern spirits, assured Lincoln's re-election, and cleared the way for Sherman's march from Atlanta to the sea.

In Virginia the preliminaries to victory were protracted and ghastly. Throughout the spring and summer Grant hurled his troops at Lee's army and suffered appalling losses: almost 18,000 casualties in the Battle of the Wilderness, more than 8,000 at Spotsylvania, and 12,000 at

Union breakthrough in the West

Cold Harbor. But the heavy fighting did prepare the way for eventual victory: Lee's army shrank to the point that offensive action was no longer possible, while the Union army kept replenishing its forces with new recruits.

The end finally came in 1865. Sherman marched north, wreaking great destruction on South Carolina, and into North Carolina. In Virginia Grant kept battering at Lee, who tried but failed to break through the federal line east of Petersburg on March 25. With the numerical superiority of Grant's army now upwards of two-to-one, Confederate defeat was inevitable. On April 2 Lee abandoned Richmond and Petersburg. On April 9, hemmed in by federal troops, short of rations, and with fewer than 30,000 men left, Lee surrendered to Grant. Within weeks Jefferson Davis was captured, and the remaining Confederate forces laid down their arms. The war was over.

Heavy losses force Lee's surrender

Lincoln did not live to see the last surrenders. On the evening of April 14, he went to Ford's Theatre in Washington, where an assassin named John Wilkes Booth shot him at point-blank range. Lincoln died the next day. The Union had lost its wartime leader, and to many, relief at the war's end was tempered by uncertainty about the future.

Costs and effects

The costs of the Civil War were enormous. Approximately 364,222 federal soldiers died, 140,070 of them from wounds suffered in battle. Another 275,175 Union soldiers were wounded but survived. On the Confederate side, an estimated 258,000 lost their lives, and even a conservative estimate of Confederate wounded brings the total number of casualties on both sides to more than 1 million—a frightful toll for a nation of 31 million people.

Casualties

Property damage and financial costs were also

This photograph, taken four days before Lincoln's assassination, shows the effect of the burdens of war on the president.   McLellan Lincoln Collection, Brown University Library.

enormous, though difficult to tally. Federal loans and taxes during the conflict totaled almost $3 billion, and interest on the war debt

Financial cost of the war

was $2.8 billion. The Confederacy borrowed over $2 billion but lost far more in the destruction of homes, fences, crops, livestock, and other property. Thoughtful scholars have noted that small farmers lost just as much, proportionally, as planters whose slaves were emancipated.

Estimates of the total cost of the war exceed $20 billion—five times the total expenditure of the federal government from its creation to 1865. As late as the 1880s interest on the war debt constituted 40 percent of the federal budget and soldiers' pensions another 20 percent. Moreover, the war had brought an increase in both federal power and federal help to business. In political terms, too, national power increased. Extreme forms of states' rights were dead.

Costs and effects

Important events

1861	Four more southern states secede from Union		Battle of Gettysburg and surrender of Vicksburg
	Battle of Bull Run		Draft riots in New York City
	General McClellan organizes Union army	1864	Battle of the Wilderness
	Union blockade begins		Battle of Spotsylvania
	First Confiscation Act		Battle of Cold Harbor

<table>
<tr><td>1861</td><td>Four more southern states secede from Union
Battle of Bull Run
General McClellan organizes Union army
Union blockade begins
First Confiscation Act</td></tr>
</table>

1861   Four more southern states secede from Union
Battle of Bull Run
General McClellan organizes Union army
Union blockade begins
First Confiscation Act

1862   Capture of Forts Henry and Donelson
Capture of New Orleans
Battle of Shiloh
Confederacy adopts conscription
McClellan attacks Virginia
Seven Days' battles
Second Confiscation Act
Confederacy mounts offensive
Battle of Antietam
Battle of Fredericksburg

1863   Emancipation Proclamation
National Banking Act
Union adopts conscription
Black soldiers join Union army
Food riots in southern cities
Battle of Chancellorsville

  Battle of Gettysburg and surrender of Vicksburg
Draft riots in New York City

1864   Battle of the Wilderness
Battle of Spotsylvania
Battle of Cold Harbor
Battle of Petersburg
President Lincoln requests party plank abolishing slavery
McClellan nominated for presidency by northern Democrats
General Sherman enters Atlanta
Lincoln re-elected
Jefferson Davis proposes Confederate emancipation
Sherman marches through Georgia

1865   Sherman drives north through Carolinas
Congress approves Thirteenth Amendment
Hampton Roads Conference
Lee surrenders at Appomattox
Lincoln assassinated

Yet despite all these changes, one crucial question remained unanswered: what was the place of black men and women in American life? They awaited an answer, which would have to be found during Reconstruction.

Suggestions for further reading

EFFECTS OF THE WAR ON THE SOUTH   Mary Boykin Chesnut, *A Diary from Dixie,* ed. Ben Ames Williams (1949); Robert F. Durden, *The Gray and the Black* (1972); Paul D. Escott, *After Secession* (1978); J. B. Jones, *A Rebel War Clerk's Diary,* 2 vols., ed. Howard Swiggett (1935); Charles W. Ramsdell, *Behind the Lines in the Southern Confederacy,* ed. Wendell H. Stephenson (1944); James L. Roark, *Masters Without Slaves* (1977); Georgia Lee Tatum, *Disloyalty in the Confederacy* (1934); Emory M. Thomas, *The Confederacy as a Revolutionary Experience* (1971); Emory M. Thomas, *The Confederate Nation* (1979); Bell Irvin Wiley, *The Life of Johnny Reb* (1943); Bell Irvin Wiley, *The Plain People of the Confederacy* (1943); W. Buck Yearns and John G. Barrett, *North Carolina Civil War Documentary* (1980).

EFFECTS OF THE WAR ON THE NORTH   Ralph Andreano, ed., *The Economic Impact of the American Civil War* (1962); Frank L. Klement, *The Copperheads in the Middle West* (1960); Susan Previant Lee and Peter Passell, *A New Economic View of American History* (1979); George Winston Smith and Charles Burnet Judah, *Life in the North during the Civil War* (1966); Paul Studenski, *Financial History of the United States* (1952); Bell Irvin Wiley, *The Life of Billy Yank* (1952).

MILITARY HISTORY   Bruce Catton, *This Hallowed Ground* (1956); Thomas L. Connelly and Archer Jones, *The Politics of Command* (1973); Burke Davis, *Sherman's March* (1980); Shelby Foote, *The Civil War, a Narrative,* 3 vols. (1958–1974); Douglas Southall Freeman, *R. E. Lee,* 4 vols. (1934–1935); Douglas Southall Freeman, *Lee's Lieutenants,* 3 vols. (1942–1944); Allan Nevins, *The War for the Union,* 4 vols (1959–1972); Grady McWhiney and Terry D. Jamieson, *Attack and Die* (1982); T. Harry Williams, *Lincoln and His Generals* (1952).

GOVERNMENTAL POLICIES DURING THE WAR   Thomas Thomas B. Alexander and Richard E. Beringer, *The Anatomy of the Confederate Congress* (1972); David Donald, *Charles Sumner and the Rights of Man* (1970); Peyton McCrary, *Abraham Lincoln and Reconstruction* (1978); James M. McPherson, The Negro's Civil War (1965); James M. McPherson, *The Struggle for Equality* (1964); Frank L. Owsley, *State Rights in the Confederacy* (1925); James G. Randall, *Mr. Lincoln* (1957); Hans L. Trefousse, *The Radical Republicans* (1969); Glyndon G. Van Deusen, *William Henry Seward* (1967).

15 🌀

RECONSTRUCTION BY

TRIAL AND ERROR,

1865–1877

Reconstruction of the Union held many promises. For the Republican Senator Benjamin Wade of Ohio, who had demanded emancipation early in the war, it began in a reassuring way. In a meeting with the new president, Andrew Johnson, Wade spoke of both the enormous cost of the war and the need to secure the Union victory. He suggested the exile or execution of ten or twelve leading traitors to set an example. President Johnson did not blanch at the idea. Instead he replied, "How are you going to pick out so small a number? Robbery is a crime; rape is a crime; murder is a crime; *treason* is a crime; and *crime* must be punished."

At the same time, black men and women in the South were preparing to seize the advantages of freedom. Their first opportunity came in the Sea Islands. During his last campaign, General Sherman had issued Special Field Order No. 15, which set aside for exclusive Negro settlement the Sea Islands and all abandoned coastal lands thirty miles to the interior, from Charleston to the Saint John's River in northern Florida. Black refugees quickly poured into these lands; by the middle of 1865, forty thousand freedmen were living in their new home.

But neither Sherman's promise nor Johnson's was fulfilled. Although Jefferson Davis was imprisoned for two years, no Confederate leaders were executed. In fact, within a year southern aristocrats had come to view the president not as their enemy but as their friend and protector. And in the fall of 1865, the federal government began to confiscate the freedmen's land and return it to its original owners.

The resulting protests of the freedmen did not go completely unheard. The unexpected turn of events led Congress to examine the president's policies and design new plans for Reconstruction. Out of negotiations in Congress and clashes between the president and the legislators, there emerged first one and then two new plans for Reconstruction. Before the process was over the nation had adopted the Fourteenth and Fifteenth amendments and impeached its president.

For black people themselves the benefits of freedom were most often practical and ordinary. They moved out of slave quarters and built cabins of their own; they worked together in family units and worshipped in their own churches without white supervision. Blacks also took the risk of political participation, voting in large numbers and gaining some offices. But they knew their political success depended on the determination and support of the North.

In the South, opposition to Reconstruction grew steadily. By 1869 the Ku Klux Klan had added organized violence to southern whites' repertoire of resistance. Despite federal efforts to protect them, black people were intimidated at the polls, robbed of their earnings, beaten, or murdered. By the early 1870s the failure of Reconstruction was apparent.

Equality: the unresolved issue

For America's former slaves, Reconstruction had one paramount meaning: a chance to explore freedom. The slaves on one Texas plantation jumped up and down and clapped their hands as one man shouted, "We're free—no more whippings and beatings." One grandmother who had long resented her treatment "dropped her hoe" and ran to confront the mistress. "I'm free!" she yelled at her. "Yes, I'm free! Ain't got to work for you no more!" Another man recalled that he and others left the plantation, either to search for family members or just to exercise their new-found freedom of movement.

Most freedmen reacted more cautiously and shrewdly. One sign of this shrewd caution was the way freedmen evaluated potential employers. "Most all the niggers that had good owners stayed with 'em, but the others left." If a white person had been relatively considerate to blacks in bondage, blacks reasoned that he might prove a desirable employer in freedom. Other blacks left their plantation all at once, for, as one put it, "that master am sure mean."

Even more urgently than a fair employer, the freedmen wanted land of their own. Land represented their chance to farm for themselves, to

| *Blacks' desire for land* |

have an independent life. It represented compensation for their generations of travail in bondage. A northern observer noted that freedmen made "plain, straight-forward" inquiries as they settled the land set aside for them by Sherman. They wanted to be sure the land "would be theirs after they had improved it."

But no one could say how much of a chance the whites, who were in power, would give to

blacks. During the war there had been much hesitation before black people were allowed to aid and defend the Union. As soon as the fighting began, black men volunteered as soldiers. But the government and the people of the North refused their offers, saying that the conflict was "a white man's war."

Necessity forced the United States to change its policy in the fall of 1862. Because the war was going badly, the administration authorized black enlistments. By spring 1863 black troops were proving their value. "They fight like fiends," said one observer.

As black men entering the military, they, and the leadership of the black community, hoped

| *Black service in the military* |

that such service to the nation would secure their people the rights of citizenship. The wartime experiences of black soldiers, however, seemed to indicate that equal rights would not be forthcoming. Uniformed blacks immediately encountered varying forms of discrimination, including inferior pay. The government paid white privates $13 per month plus a clothing allowance of $3.50. Black troops earned $10 per month less $3 deducted for clothing. Blacks resented this injustice so deeply that in protest two regiments in South Carolina refused to accept any pay. In June 1864 Congress finally made equal pay retroactive to the date of enlistment for those who had been free on April 19, 1861. Even this law was unfair to thousands of runaway slaves who had joined the army before 1864.

Blacks, whether soldier or civilian, found that northerners had mixed attitudes on racial questions. On the one hand, wartime idealism had promoted equality and weakened discrimination. Many abolitionists had worked vigorously to extend equal rights to black Americans, and a powerful element in the Republican party had committed itself to fighting racism. In 1864 their efforts brought about the acceptance of black testimony in federal courts and the desegregation of New York City's streetcars. And one state, Massachusetts, enacted a comprehensive public accommodations law.

Andrew Johnson, a southern Unionist and an old foe of the planters. Library of Congress.

On the other hand, there were many more signs of resistance to racial equality. The Democratic party adopted an explicit and vociferous stand against blacks, charging that Republicans favored race-mixing and were undermining the status of the white worker. Moreover, voters in three states—Connecticut, Minnesota, and Wisconsin—rejected black suffrage in 1865. The racial attitudes of northerners seemed to be in flux, the outcome uncertain.

Johnson's reconstruction plan

Throughout 1865 the formation of reconstruction policy rested solely with Andrew Johnson, for shortly before he became president Congress recessed and did not reconvene until December. Thus Johnson had almost eight months to design and execute a plan of reconstruction on his own, unhindered by legislative suggestions.

Johnson had a few precedents to follow in Lincoln's wartime plans for Reconstruction. In December 1863 Lincoln had proposed a "10-percent" plan for a government being organized in captured portions of Louisiana. According to this plan, a state government could be established as soon as 10 percent of those who had voted in 1860 took an oath of future loyalty. Only high-ranking Confederate officials would be denied a chance to take the oath, and Lincoln urged that at least a few well-qualified blacks be given the ballot. At the time of his death, Lincoln had given general approval to a plan drafted by Secretary of War Stanton that would have imposed military authority and provisional governors as steps toward new state governments.

Lincoln's reconstruction plan

Johnson began with the plan Stanton had drafted for consideration by the cabinet. At a cabinet meeting on May 9, 1865, Johnson's advisors split evenly on the question of voting rights for freedmen in the South. Johnson said that he favored black suffrage, but only if the southern states adopted it voluntarily. Such views were a long-established part of his states' rights philosophy. Just as his past opinions shaped this initial act, so Johnson's personal history influenced the rest of his program.

Johnson had built his entire career on championing the cause of ordinary whites and attacking privileged planters. Born in humble circumstances, he was unable to read until taught by his wife. As he rose in Tennessee politics, he voiced his resentment of the planter aristocracy. When Tennessee seceded, Johnson refused to leave his seat in the Senate. This action commended him to Lincoln as a vice-presidential candidate in 1864.

Andrew Johnson: his early life

Now as president, Johnson was able to define the terms on which southern states and rebellious planters would re-enter the Union. He began by issuing two proclamations in May 1865.

Chapter 15: Reconstruction by trial and error, 1865–1877

The first decreed amnesty for most southerners who would take an oath of loyalty to the United States. The second established a provisional military government and prescribed steps for the creation of new civilian governments. The key aspects of both proclamations lay in the details.

Certain classes of southerners were barred from taking the oath and gaining amnesty. Federal officials, elected or appointed, who had violated their oaths to support the United States and aided the Confederacy could not take the oath. Nor could graduates of West Point or Annapolis who had resigned their commissions to fight for the South. The same was true for Confederate officers at the rank of colonel or above and for Confederate political leaders. Also barred were southerners whose taxable property was worth more than $20,000. All such individuals had to apply personally to the president for pardon and restoration of political rights, or risk legal penalties, including confiscation of land.

| Oaths of amnesty and new state governments |

Under an appointed provisional governor, elections would be held for a state constitutional convention. The delegates chosen for the convention would draft a new constitution eliminating slavery and invalidating secession. After ratification of the constitution, new governments could be elected, and the state would be restored to the Union with full congressional representation. No southerner could participate in this process who had not taken the oath of amnesty or who had been ineligible to vote on the day the state seceded. Black southerners, being in the latter category, had no voice in the process.

But the plan did not work as Johnson had hoped. Ironically, Johnson himself had a hand in subverting his own plan. He pardoned first one and then another of the aristocrats and chief rebels. By the time the southern states had completed the process of constitution-making and elections, Confederate leaders had emerged in powerful positions. The president

Confederates regain power

decided to stand by his new governments and declare Reconstruction completed. Thus in December 1865 many Confederate congressmen traveled to Washington to claim seats in the House of Representatives. And the vice president of the Confederacy, Alexander Stephens, returned to the capital as a senator.

The election of such prominent rebels was not the only result of Johnson's program that sparked negative comment in the North. Some of the state conventions were slow to repudiate secession; others only grudgingly admitted that slavery was dead. Of great concern to northern politicians was the enactment of the so-called black codes. In these laws southern state legislatures defined the status of freedmen. Some states merely revised sections of the old slave codes by substituting the word freedman for slave. Typical codes required blacks to carry passes, observe a curfew, and live in housing provided by a landowner. In some cases restrictions were created to keep blacks out of many desirable occupations. States also denied blacks access to public institutions such as schools and orphanages. To northerners, the South seemed intent on returning black people to a position of servility.

Black codes

Thus it was not surprising that a majority of northern congressmen decided to take a close look at the results of Johnson's plan. On reconvening, they voted not to admit the newly elected southern representatives, whose credentials were subject under the Constitution to congressional scrutiny. The House and Senate established a joint committee to examine Johnson's policies and advise on new ones. Reconstruction had entered a second phase, one in which Congress would play a strong role.

The congressional reconstruction plans

Northern congressmen disagreed on what to do, but they did not doubt their right to play a role in Reconstruction. The Constitution mentioned neither secession nor reunion, but it did assign Congress the injunction to guarantee to each state a republican government. Under this provision, the legislators thought they could devise policies for Reconstruction.

They soon found that other constitutional questions had a direct bearing on the policies they followed. What, for example, had the fact of rebellion done to the relationship between southern states and the Union? Lincoln had always insisted that the Union remained unbroken. But congressmen who favored vigorous reconstruction measures tended to argue that war *had* broken the Union. The southern states had committed legal suicide and reverted to the status of territories, they argued, or the South was a conquered nation subject to the victor's will. Moderate congressmen held that the states had forfeited their rights through rebellion, and had thus come under congressional supervision.

These diverse theories mirrored the diversity of Congress itself. Northern legislators fell into four major categories, no one of which held a majority: Democrats, conservative Republicans, moderate Republicans, and Radical Republicans. Overall, the Republican party had a majority, but there was considerable distance between conservative Republicans, who desired a limited federal role in Reconstruction and were fairly happy with Johnson's actions, and the Radicals. These men, led by Thaddeus Stevens, Charles Sumner, and George Julian, believed that it was essential to democratize the South, establish public education, and ensure the rights of freedmen. They favored black suffrage, often supported land confiscation and redistribution, and were willing to exclude the South from the Union for several years if necessary to achieve their goals. Between these two factions lay the moderates, who held the balance of power.

Through their actions, Johnson and the Democrats forced these diverse Republican factions to come together. The president and the northern Democrats refused to cooperate with moderate and conservative Republicans, arguing that Reconstruction was over and calling for the

| *Congress struggles for a compromise* |

seating of the southern delegates in Congress. Moreover, Johnson refused to support an apparent compromise on Reconstruction. Under its terms Johnson would have agreed to two modifications of his program. The life of the Freedmen's Bureau, which fed the hungry, negotiated labor contracts, and started schools, would be extended; and a civil rights bill would be passed to counteract the black codes. This bill, drawn up by a conservative Republican, gave federal judges the power to remove from southern courts cases in which blacks were treated unfairly.

But in spring 1866, Johnson destroyed the compromise by vetoing both bills (they were later repassed). Denouncing any change in his program, the president condemned Congress's action. In so doing he questioned the legitimacy of congressional involvement in policy making. All hope of working with the president was now gone. Instead of a compromise program, the various Republican factions developed a new Reconstruction plan. It took the form of a proposed amendment to the Constitution—the fourteenth—and it represented a compromise between radical and conservative elements of the party.

Of four points in the amendment, there was nearly universal agreement on one: the Confederate debt was declared null and void, the

| *Fourteenth Amendment* |

war debt of the United States was guaranteed. There was also fairly general support for a section prohibiting prominent Confederates from holding any national or state political office. Only at the discretion of Congress, by a two-thirds vote of each house, could these political penalties be removed.

The section of the Fourteenth Amendment that would have the greatest legal significance in later years was the first. On its face, this section was an effort to strike down the black codes and guarantee basic rights to freedmen. It conferred citizenship on freedmen and prohibited states from abridging their constitutional "privileges and immunities." Similarly, the amendment

Chapter 15: Reconstruction by trial and error, 1865–1877

barred any state from taking a person's life, liberty, or property "without due process of law" and from denying "equal protection of the laws." These clauses were phrased broadly enough to become powerful guarantees of black Americans' civil rights.

The second section of the amendment clearly revealed the compromises and political motives that had produced the document. Though many idealistic northerners favored voting rights for blacks, large portions of the electorate were just as adamantly opposed. What was more, Republicans feared that emancipation, which made every former slave five-fifths of a person instead of three-fifths for purposes of congressional representation, might increase the South's power in Congress. If it did, and if blacks were not allowed to vote, the former secessionists would gain seats in Congress.

Republicans were determined not to hand over power to their political enemies, so they offered the South a choice. According to the second section of the Fourteenth Amendment, states did not have to give black men the right to vote. But if they did not do so, their representation would be reduced proportionally. If they did, it would be increased proportionally—but Republicans would be able to appeal to the new black voters.

The Fourteenth Amendment dealt with the voting rights of black men and ignored all female citizens. Its proposal elicited a strong reaction from women's rights advocates, who had demanded to be heard during the drafting of the Fourteenth Amendment. When legislators defined females as nonvoting citizens, prominent women's leaders such as Elizabeth Cady Stanton and Susan B. Anthony decided that it was time to end their alliance with abolitionists. Thus the independent women's rights movement grew.

In 1866, however, the major question in Reconstruction politics was how the public would respond to the amendment. Johnson did his best to see that the public would reject it. Condemning Congress's plan and its refusal to seat southern representatives, the president convinced state legislatures in the South to vote

Johnson and the Fourteenth Amendment

against ratification. Every southern legislature except Tennessee's rejected the amendment. In the North, Johnson arranged a National Union convention to publicize his program. He boarded a special train for a "swing around the circle" that carried his message into the Midwest. Increasingly audiences hooted and jeered at him, however.

The election was a resounding victory for Republicans in Congress. Men whom Johnson had denounced won re-election by large margins, and the Republican majority increased as some new candidates defeated incumbent Democrats. Everywhere Radical and moderate Republicans gained strength: Thus, Republican congressional leaders received a mandate to continue with their reconstruction plan.

Recognizing that nothing could be accomplished under the existing southern governments and with blacks excluded from the electorate, Congress decided to act. It first enacted the Military Reconstruction Act of 1867. This

Military Reconstruction Act of 1867

law contained only the bare bones of the Radical program. The act called for new governments in the South, with a return to military authority in the interim. It barred from political office those Confederate leaders listed in the Fourteenth Amendment. It guaranteed freedmen the right to vote in elections for state constitutional conventions and for subsequent state governments. In addition, each southern state was required to ratify the Fourteenth Amendment; to ratify its new constitution; and to submit the new constitution to Congress for approval. Thus black people gained an opportunity to fight for a better life through the political process. The only weapon put into their hands was the ballot, however. The law required no redistribution of land and guaranteed no basic changes in southern social structure.

Congress's role as the architect of Reconstruction was not quite over. To restrict Johnson's influence and safeguard its plan, Congress passed a number of controversial laws. First it set the date for its own reconvening—an unprecedented act, since the president had traditionally summoned the legislature to Washington. Then it limited Johnson's power over the army by requiring the president to issue military orders through the General of the Army, Ulysses S. Grant, who could not be sent from Washington without the Senate's consent. Finally, Congress passed the Tenure of Office Act, which gave the Senate power to interfere with changes in the president's cabinet. Designed to protect Secretary of War Stanton, who sympathized with the Radicals, this law violated the tradition that a president controlled his own cabinet.

Johnson took several belligerent steps of his own. He issued orders to military commanders in the South limiting their powers and increasing the powers of the civil governments he had created in 1865. Then he removed army officers who conscientiously enforced Congress's new law. Finally, in August 1867 he tried to remove Secretary of War Stanton. The confrontation had reached its climax.

The House Judiciary Committee, which had twice before considered impeaching the president, again initiated the removal process. The

| Impeachment and trial | 1868 indictment concentrated on Johnson's violation of the Tenure of Office Act. Modern scholars, however, |

regard his efforts to impede enforcement of the Military Reconstruction Act as a far more serious offense.

Johnson's trial in the Senate lasted more than three months. The Radical-led prosecution argued that Johnson was guilty of "high crimes and misdemeanors." But they also advanced the novel idea that impeachment was a political matter, not a judicial trial of guilt or innocence. The Senate ultimately rejected such reasoning, which would have transformed impeachment into a political weapon against any chief executive who disagreed with Congress. Though a majority of senators voted to convict Johnson, the prosecution fell one vote short of the necessary two-thirds majority. Johnson remained in office for the few months left in his term, and

his acquittal established the precedent that only serious misdeeds merited removal from office.

In 1869, the Radicals succeeded in presenting the Fifteenth Amendment for ratification. The measure forbade states to deny the right to vote

| Fifteenth Amendment | "on account of race, color, or previous condition of servitude." Ironically, the votes of |

four uncooperative southern states—required by Congress to approve the amendment as an added condition to rejoining the Union—proved necessary to impose this principle on parts of the North. Although several states outside the South refused to ratify, the Fifteenth Amendment became law in 1870.

Thus Congress first tried to revise Johnson's program and then had to overturn it and start anew. And for black people in the South, the opportunities offered by Reconstruction did not fully come to pass until 1868. That year most of the state conventions met, and blacks participated in the democratic process for the first time. Blacks hoped to make a new life for themselves, but their task was formidable.

The response of the freedmen

Overjoyed as they were to be free, the freedmen also knew that their new status placed them in danger, for it infuriated some whites. When a Georgia planter heard a black woman singing about emancipation, he angrily knocked her down; another master threatened to "free" his servants with a shotgun.

Violence was directed at blacks from the first days of freedom. Federal troops were theoretically in control, but they could not be everywhere at all times. And sometimes racist northern troops and officials sided with local whites. Thus federal power often remained a distant or potential force, whereas the influence of local white people was immediate and continuous.

Nevertheless, blacks took risks and reached out for freedom. As soon as Congress intro-

Freed from slavery, blacks of all ages filled the schools to seek the education that had been denied them in bondage.   Valentine Museum, Richmond, Virginia.

Black suffrage and education duced black suffrage, freedmen flocked to the polls and voted solidly Republican. Former slaves also filled the schools—young and old, day and night. On "log seats" or "a dirt floor," many freedmen studied their letters in old almanacs, discarded dictionaries, or whatever was available.

Blacks and their white allies also realized that higher education was essential—colleges and universities to train teachers and equip ministers and professionals for leadership. The American

Missionary Association founded seven colleges, including Fisk and Atlanta universities, between 1866 and 1869. The Freedmen's Bureau helped to establish Howard University in Washington, D.C., and northern religious groups supported dozens of seminaries, colleges, and teachers' colleges. By the late 1870s black churches had joined in the effort, founding numerous colleges despite their smaller financial resources. Though some of the new institutions did not survive, they brought knowledge to those who would educate others and laid a foundation for progress.

Some unlettered field hands managed to educate themselves and rise to positions of leadership. But most blacks who won public office during Reconstruction came from the educated

Black political leadership

prewar elite of free people of color. Better educated and less deprived, this group had benefited from its association with wealthy whites, who were often blood relatives. The two black senators from Mississippi, Blanche K. Bruce and Hiram Revels, for example, were both privileged in their educations. Bruce was the son of a planter who had provided tutoring on his plantation; Revels was the son of free North Carolina mulattoes who had sent him to Knox College in Illinois. These men and others brought experience as artisans, businessmen, lawyers, teachers, and preachers to political office.

Black people used their new political power to seek opportunity and equality before the law. They concentrated their efforts on political and educational reform rather than sweeping economic or social change. In every southern state blacks led efforts to establish public schools. They did not press for integrated facilities; having a school to attend was the most important thing at the time, for the Johnson governments had excluded blacks from schools and other state-supported institutions. As a result, virtually every public school organized during Reconstruction was racially segregated, and these separate schools established a precedent for the segregation of the 1870s and after.

In general, freedmen depended for support on three sets of allies—northern reformers and teachers, carpetbaggers, and scalawags. In its

Reformers, carpetbaggers, and scalawags

brief life the Freedmen's Bureau founded over four thousand schools, and idealistic men and women from the North established others and staffed them ably. Thus, with the aid of religious and charitable organizations throughout the North, blacks began the nation's first assault on the problems created by slavery. The results included the beginnings of a public school system in each southern state and the enrollment of more than 600,000 blacks in elementary school by 1877.

A far more publicized ally of the freedman was the carpetbagger. Southerners opposed to Reconstruction used this derisive name to suggest an evil and greedy northern politician, recently arrived in the South with a carpetbag, into which he planned to stuff ill-gotten gains before fleeing. There were a few northerners who deserved this unsavory description. But of the thousands of northerners who settled in the South after the war, only a small portion entered politics. And most of them wanted to democratize the South and to introduce northern ways, such as industry, public education, and the spirit of enterprise.

Scalawag was a term of contempt used to discredit any native white southerner who cooperated with the Republicans. A substantial number of southerners did so. Most scalawags were men from mountain areas and small farming districts—average white southerners who saw that they could benefit from the education and opportunities promoted by Republicans. Banding together with the freedmen, they pursued common class interests and hoped to make headway against the power of the long-dominant planters. Both carpetbaggers and scalawags, however, shied away from support for racial equality.

While elected officials wrestled with the political tasks of Reconstruction, millions of freedmen concentrated on improving life at home, on their farms, and in their neighborhoods. Given the eventual failure of Reconstruction, the small practical gains they made in their daily lives often proved the most enduring and significant changes of the period. Throughout the South they devoted themselves to reuniting their families, moving away from the slave quarters, and founding black churches.

The search for long-lost family members was awe-inspiring. With only shreds of information to guide them, thousands of black people embarked on odysseys in search

| Reunification of black families |

of a husband, wife, child, or parent. By relying on the black community for help and information, many succeeded in their quest, sometimes almost miraculously. Others walked through several states and never found their loved ones.

For the thousands of husbands and wives who had belonged to different owners, freedom meant the opportunity to establish homes together for the first time. It also meant that wives would not be ordered to work in the fields. And it meant that parents finally would have the right to raise their children.

Black people frequently wanted to minimize all contact with whites. To avoid them, blacks abandoned the slave quarters and fanned out into distant corners of the land they worked. Some moved away to build new homes in the woods. Others established small all-black settlements that still exist today along the backroads of the South.

The other side of this distance from whites was closer communion within the black community. The secret church of slavery, for instance, now came out into

| Founding of black churches |

the open. Within a few years independent black branches of the Methodist and Baptist churches had attracted the great majority of black Christians in the South.

This desire to gain as much independence as possible carried over into the freedmen's economic arrangements. Since most former slaves lacked money to buy land, they preferred the next best thing—renting the land they worked. But many whites would not consider renting land to blacks; there was strong social pressure against it. And few blacks had the means to rent a farm. Therefore other alternatives had to be tried.

Northerners and officials of the Freedmen's Bureau favored contracts between owners and laborers. For a few years the Freedmen's Bureau helped to draw up and enforce such contracts, but they proved unpopular with both blacks and whites. Owners often filled the contracts with detailed requirements that reminded blacks of their circumscribed lives under slavery. Disputes frequently arose over efficiency, lost time, and other matters. Sharecropping became common.

Reconstruction in reality

From the start, many white southerners resisted Reconstruction. Some planters attempted to postpone freedom by denying or mis-

| White resistance to emancipation |

representing events. One ex-slave recalled that his mother "said we were going to be free." But "Marse Jeff said we weren't, and he didn't tell us any different until about Christmas after the War was done over with in April." Another tactic was to claim control over children or seize on guardianship and apprentice laws to bind black families to the plantation.

Sooner and later, white resistance to Reconstruction erupted in violence. Terrorism against blacks existed throughout Reconstruction—even in 1865 and 1866, bands of armed men calling themselves Regulators attacked freedmen, and confrontations often escalated into violence. But after 1867 white violence became more organ-

| Ku Klux Klan |

ized and purposeful. The Ku Klux Klan rose in a campaign to frustrate Reconstruction and keep the freedmen in subjection. Nighttime visits, whippings, beatings, and murder became common.

The testimony of former slaves suggests that the earliest purpose of the nightriders may have been to control the source of plantation labor. A man from Virginia recalled that the Klan appeared "right after the war" and whipped "the slaves that leave the plantations." Similarly, freedmen in other states recalled that the Klansmen concentrated on driving the freedmen back to their old farms.

In time, however, the Klan's purpose became more openly political and social. Lawless nightriders made active Republicans the target of their attacks. Prominent white Republicans and black leaders were killed in several states. Klansmen also attacked Union League Clubs (Republican organizations that mobilized the Negro vote) and schoolteachers who were aiding the freedmen. No one who helped to raise blacks' status was safe.

In 1870 and 1871 the violent campaigns of the Ku Klux Klan moved Congress to pass two Force Acts and an anti-Klan law. These acts permitted martial law and suspension of the writ of habeas corpus to combat murders, beatings, and threats by the Klan. General Grant, who was elected president in 1868, suspended the writ of habeas corpus in portions of South Carolina. Other federal authorities used the laws vigorously but unsuccessfully, for a conspiracy of silence frustrated many prosecutions.

Klan terror frightened many voters and weakened local party organization, but it did not stop Reconstruction. Throughout the South conventions met and drafted new constitutions. Black voters exercised their newly acquired right of suffrage, electing some black delegates to participate for the first time in the processes of democracy. The conventions promptly completed their work, and new state governments came into being. In the first elections, Republicans won majorities everywhere except Georgia.

Southern white opponents of Reconstruction (who called themselves Conservatives and later Democrats) immediately denounced the new re-

gimes, charging that they were being subjected to "black domination" and carpetbagger corruption. Such attacks were gross distortions. Blacks

| Reconstruction governments |

were a minority in eight out of ten state conventions; northerners were a minority in nine out of ten. In the new state legislatures only once—in the lower house in South Carolina—did blacks constitute a majority of either chamber; generally their numbers were far inferior to their proportion in the population. Sixteen blacks won seats in Congress before Reconstruction was over, but none was ever elected governor. Freedmen were participating in government but not dominating it.

Nor were the constitutional conventions scenes of misrule. The new constitutions were, for example, more democratic; they eliminated property qualifications for voting and officeholding, and made state and local offices elective in cases where they had been appointive. They provided for public schools and institutions to care for the mentally ill, the blind, the deaf, the destitute, and the orphaned, and they ended imprisonment for debt and barbarous punishments such as branding. Women's rights in possession of property and divorce were broadened, although white legislators ignored the call of black leaders for women's suffrage.

The Reconstruction governments also devoted themselves to stimulating industry. This policy reflected northern ideals, of course, but also sprang from a growing southern interest in industry. Accordingly, Reconstruction legislatures designed many tempting inducements to local and northern investment. Loans, subsidies, and exemptions from taxation for periods up to ten years helped to bring new industries into the region.

Despite these achievements, however, the Reconstruction governments were doomed to be unpopular. Struggling against powerful racial prejudice, they also faced major problems of taxation and public finance. Legislators wanted to continue prewar services and support such important new ventures as public schools. Rebuilding of bridges and transportation facilities devastated by the war was another obvious priority. But the Civil War had destroyed much of the South's tax base. Thus, an increase in taxes was necessary even to maintain traditional services; new ventures required even higher taxes. As taxes went up, Democrats charged the Reconstruction governments with waste and extravagance.

Corruption was another powerful charge levied against the Republicans. Unfortunately, it was true. Many carpetbaggers and black politicians sold their votes and dipped their hands in the till. Corruption was widespread in southern governments, and Democrats convinced many voters that scandal was the inevitable result of a foolish Reconstruction program. Historians have shown, however, that corruption was not merely a southern problem; it was a national one.

Political corruption

But the most lasting failure of Reconstruction governments was neither fiscal nor venal but social. The new governments failed to alter the southern social structure or its distribution of wealth and power. Exploited as slaves, freedmen remained vulnerable to exploitation during Reconstruction. Without land of their own, they were dependent on white landowners, who could use their economic power to compromise blacks' political freedom. Armed only with the ballot, southern blacks had little chance to effect major changes.

Failure of Reconstruction

The end of Reconstruction

The North's commitment to racial equality had never been total. And by the early 1870s it was evident that even its partial commitment was weakening. New issues were capturing people's attention, and soon voters began to look for reconciliation with southern whites. In the South Democrats won control of one state after another, and they threatened to defeat Republicans in the North as well. Before long the situation had returned to "normal" in the eyes of southern whites.

The Supreme Court, after first re-establishing its power, participated in the northern retreat from Reconstruction. During the Civil War the Court had been cautious and reluctant to assert itself. Reaction to the Dred Scott decision had been so violent, and the Union's wartime emergency so great, that the Court had refrained from blocking or interfering with government actions.

But in 1866 the landmark case, *Ex parte Milligan,* reached the Court. Lambdin P. Milligan of Indiana had participated in a plot to free Confederate prisoners of war and overthrow state governments; for these acts a military court had sentenced him to death. In sweeping language the Court declared that military trials were illegal when civil courts were open and functioning, thus indicating that it intended to reassert itself as a major force in national affairs.

Supreme Court decisions on Reconstruction

In 1873 the *Slaughter-House* cases tested the scope and meaning of the Fourteenth Amendment. In 1869 the Louisiana legislature had granted one company a monopoly on the slaughtering of livestock in New Orleans. Rival butchers in the city promptly sued. Their attorney argued that the Fourteenth Amendment had revolutionized the constitutional system by bringing individual rights under federal protection. But the Court refused to accept this novel argument. Neither the "privileges and immunities" clause nor the "due process" clause of the amendment guaranteed the great basic rights of the Bill of Rights against state action, the justices said. National citizenship involved only such things as the right to travel freely from state to state and to use the navigable waters of the nation. Thus the Court limited severely the amendment's potential for securing the rights of black citizens.

In 1876 the Court regressed even further, emasculating the enforcement clause of the Fourteenth Amendment and interpreting the

Fifteenth in a narrow and negative fashion. In *United States* v. *Cruikshank* the Court dealt with Louisiana whites who were indicted for attacking a meeting of blacks and conspiring to deprive them of their rights. The justices ruled that the Fourteenth Amendment did not extend federal power to cover the misdeeds of private individuals against other citizens; only flagrant state discrimination was covered. And in *United States* v. *Reese* the Court held that the Fifteenth Amendment did not guarantee a citizen's right to vote, but merely listed certain impermissible grounds for denying suffrage. Thus a path lay open for southern states to disfranchise blacks for supposedly nonracial reasons—lack of education, lack of property, or lack of descent from a grandfather qualified to vote before the Military Reconstruction Act. (Before Reconstruction, slaves and free blacks in the South could not vote.)

The retreat from Reconstruction continued steadily in politics as well. In 1868 Ulysses S. Grant defeated Horatio Seymour in a presidential election that revived sectional divisions. In office, Grant sometimes used force to support Reconstruction, but only when he had to. He hoped to avoid confrontation with the South and to erase the image of dictatorship that his military background summoned up.

In 1872 a revolt within the Republican ranks foreshadowed the end of Reconstruction. A group calling itself the Liberal Republicans bolted the party and nominated Horace Greeley, the well-known editor of the *New York Tribune,* for president. The Liberal Republicans were a varied group, including civil-service reformers, foes of corruption, and advocates of a lower tariff; they often spoke of a more lenient policy toward the South. That year the Democrats too gave their nomination to Greeley. Though the combination was not enough to defeat Grant, it reinforced his desire to avoid confrontation with white southerners.

The Liberal Republican challenge revealed the growing dissatisfaction with Grant's admin-

Liberal Republicans revolt

istration. Corruption within his administration became widespread, and Grant foolishly defended some of the culprits. As a result, Grant's popularity, and that of his party, declined; the Democrats gained control of the House in the 1874 elections.

Congress's resolve on southern issues weakened steadily. By joint resolution it had already removed the political disabilities of the Fourteenth Amendment from many former Confederates. Then in 1872 it adopted a sweeping Amnesty Act, which pardoned most of the remaining rebels and left only five hundred excluded from political participation. A Civil Rights Act passed in 1875 purported to guarantee black people equal accommodations in public places, like inns and theaters. But it was weak and contained no effective provisions for enforcement. Moreover, by 1876 the Democrats had regained control or "redeemed" all but three of the southern states (South Carolina, Louisiana, and Florida).

Amnesty Act

By the 1870s, northerners were tiring of the same old issues, and the Panic of 1873, which threw 3 million people out of work, focused attention on economic and monetary problems. Businessmen were disturbed by the strikes and industrial violence that accompanied the panic; debtors and the unemployed sought easy-money policies to spur economic expansion. In 1876 it became obvious to most political observers that the North was no longer willing to pursue the goals of Reconstruction. The results of a disputed presidential election confirmed this fact. Samuel J. Tilden, Democratic governor of New York, ran strongly in the South and took a commanding lead in both the popular vote and the electoral college over Rutherford B. Hayes, the Republican nominee. Tilden won 184 electoral votes and needed only one more for a majority. Nineteen votes from Louisiana, South Carolina, and Florida were disputed; both Democrats and Republicans claimed to have won in those states despite fraud on the part of their opponents. One vote from Oregon was undecided due to a technicality.

Election of 1876

Chapter 15: Reconstruction by trial and error, 1865–1877

All Colored People

THAT WANT TO

GO TO KANSAS,

On September 5th, 1877,

Can do so for $5.00

IMMIGRATION.

WHEREAS, We, the colored people of Lexington, Ky,. knowing that there is an abundance of choice lands now belonging to the Government, have assembled ourselves together for the purpose of locating on said lands. Therefore,

BE IT RESOLVED, That we do now organize ourselves into a Colony, as follows:— Any person wishing to become a member of this Colony can do so by paying the sum of one dollar ($1.00), and this money is to be paid by the first of September, 1877, in instalments of twenty-five cents at a time, or otherwise as may be desired.

RESOLVED, That this Colony has agreed to consolidate itself with the Nicodemus Towns, Solomon Valley, Graham County, Kansas, and can only do so by entering the vacant lands now in their midst, which costs $5.00.

RESOLVED, That this Colony shall consist of seven officers—President, Vice-President, Secretary, Treasurer, and three Trustees. President—M. M. Bell; Vice-President —Isaac Talbott; Secretary—W. J. Niles; Treasurer—Daniel Clarke; Trustees—Jerry Lee, William Jones, and Abner Webster.

RESOLVED, That this Colony shall have from one to two hundred militia, more or less, as the case may require, to keep peace and order, and any member failing to pay in his dues, as aforesaid, or failing to comply with the above rules in any particular, will not be recognized or protected by the Colony.

Exodusters, southern blacks dismayed by the failure of Reconstruction, left the South by the thousands for Kansas in 1877. This handbill advertised the establishment of a black colony in Graham County, Kansas.   Kansas State Historical Society.

To resolve this unprecedented situation, on which the Constitution gave no guidance, Congress established a fifteen-member electoral commission. In the interest of impartiality, membership on the commission was to be balanced between Democrats and Republicans. But one independent Republican, Supreme Court Justice David Davis, refused appointment in order to accept his election as a senator. A regular Republican took his place, and the Republican party prevailed 8-to-7 on every decision, a strict party vote. Hayes would then become the win-

Important events

1865	Freedmen's Bureau established President Andrew Johnson organizes new southern governments Johnson permits election of prominent Confederates and passage of black codes Congress refuses to seat southern representatives Thirteenth Amendment ratified	1870	Force Acts Four more southern states readmitted
		1871	Ku Klux Klan Act
		1872	Amnesty Act Liberal Republicans challenge party leadership Grant re-elected
1866	Congress passes Civil Rights Act over Johnson's veto Congress approves Fourteenth Amendment Freedmen's Bureau renewed by Congress over Johnson's veto Most southern states reject Fourteenth Amendment Tennessee readmitted to Union *Ex parte Milligan*	1873	*Slaughter-House* cases Economic recession
		1874	Democrats win control of House of Representatives
		1875	Several Grant appointees indicted for corruption Civil Rights Act
1867	Military Reconstruction Act; Command of the Army Act; Tenure of Office Act Constitutional conventions called in southern states	1876	*U.S.* v. *Cruikshank* *U.S.* v. *Reese* Results of presidential election disputed; Congress establishes commission to examine returns
1868	Johnson impeached by House of Representatives, tried by Senate, and acquitted Seven more southern states readmitted Fourteenth Amendment ratified Ulysses S. Grant elected president	1877	Congressional Democrats acquiesce in election of Rutherford B. Hayes President Hayes withdraws troops from South; end of Reconstruction Black Exodusters migrate to Kansas
1869	Congress approves Fifteenth Amendment		

ner if Congress accepted the commission's findings.

Congressional acceptance, however, was not sure. Democrats controlled the House. Many Americans feared that the crisis might lead to another civil war. Democrats, however, acquiesced in the election of Hayes. Scholars have found that negotiations went on between some

Chapter 15: Reconstruction by trial and error, 1865–1877

of Hayes's supporters and southerners who were interested in federal aid to railroads, internal improvements, federal patronage, and removal of troops from southern states. But the most recent studies suggest that these negotiations did not have a deciding effect on the outcome. Northern and southern Democrats simply yielded to the pressure of events and failed to contest the election. When Hayes became president, they looked forward to the removal of federal troops from the South. Reconstruction was over.

Southern Democrats rejoiced, but black Americans grieved over the betrayal of their

hopes for equality. After 1877 the hope for many southern blacks was "to go to a territory by ourselves." In South Carolina, Louisiana, Mississippi, and other southern states, thousands gathered up their possessions and migrated to Kansas. They were known as Exodusters, disappointed people still searching for their share in the American dream.

Thus the nation ended over fifteen years of bloody civil war and controversial reconstruction without establishing full freedom for black Americans. Their status would continue to be one of the major issues facing the nation. As the nation turned away from the needs of black Americans, its people and government focused attention on the problems related to industrialism.

Suggestions for further reading

NATIONAL POLICY AND POLITICS Herman Belz, *Emancipation and Equal Rights* (1978); Herman Belz, *Reconstructing the Union* (1969); Michael Les Benedict, *A Compromise of Principle* (1974); Michael Les Benedict, *The Impeachment and Trial of Andrew Johnson* (1973); Ellen Carol Dubois, *Feminism and Suffrage* (1978); John Hope Franklin, *Reconstruction* (1965); Eric L. McKitrick, *Andrew Johnson and Reconstruction* (1966); James M. McPherson, *The Abolitionist Legacy* (1975); William S. McFeely, *Grant* (1981); Kenneth M. Stampp, *Era of Reconstruction* (1965).

FREEDMEN AND RECONSTRUCTION IN THE SOUTH Edmund L. Drago, *Black Politicians and Reconstruction in Georgia* (1982); W. McKee Evans, *Ballots and Fence Rails* (1966); Herbert G. Gutman, *The Black Family in Slavery & Freedom, 1750–1925* (1976); William C. Harris, *Day of the Carpetbagger* (1979); Thomas Holt, *Black Over White* (1977); Elizabeth Jacoway, *Yankee Missionaries in the South* (1979); Leon Litwack, *Been In The Storm So Long* (1979); Robert Manson Myers, ed., *The Children of Pride* (1972); Michael Perman, *Reunion Without Compromise* (1973); Lawrence N. Powell, *New Masters* (1980); James Roark, *Masters Without Slaves* (1977); Willie Lee Rose, *Rehearsal for Reconstruction* (1964); Emma Lou Thornbrough, ed., *Black Reconstructionists* (1972); Albion W. Tourgée, *A Fool's Errand by One of the Fools* (1879); Allen Trelease, *White Terror* (1967); Sarah Woolfolk Wiggins, *The Scalawag in Alabama Politics, 1865–1881* (1977).

THE END OF RECONSTRUCTION Robert G. Athearn, *In Search of Canaan* (1978); Joseph G. Dawson III, *Army Generals and Reconstruction* (1982); William Gillette, *Retreat from Reconstruction, 1869–1879* (1980); Jay R. Mandle, *The Roots of Black Poverty* (1978); Nell Irvin Painter, *Exodusters* (1977); Keith Ian Polakoff, *The Politics of Inertia* (1973); Howard N. Rabinowitz, *Race Relations in the Urban South, 1865–1890* (1978); Roger L. Ransom and Richard Sutch, *One Kind of Freedom* (1977); C. Vann Woodward, *Origins of the New South* (1951); C. Vann Woodward, *Reunion and Reaction* (1951).

16

TRANSFORMATION OF THE WEST AND SOUTH, 1877-1892

On October 5, 1877, Chief Joseph of the Nez Perce decided he could hold out no longer. For fourteen years he had resisted the federal government's attempt to force his tribe onto a reservation in Idaho. When the army came to subdue them, the chief and eight hundred of his people fled. For four months the Nez Perce retreated through parts of Idaho, Montana, and Wyoming, outwitting hundreds of pursuing troops. Finally the army caught up with the starved and exhausted tribe thirty miles from the Canadian border. After five days of bitter resistance, Chief Joseph surrendered.

Chief Joseph's capture marked the end of an era. Men and women who called themselves Americans had displaced and scattered the original Americans, and the West had become the scene of one of the greatest migrations in human history. By 1890 farms, ranches, mines, towns, and cities could be found in almost every region of what was to become the continental United States. That year, the superintendent of the census acknowledged that a frontier line of settlement no longer existed.

In popular American thought, the frontier—which has been defined as "the edge of the unused"—has represented the birthplace of American self-confidence and individualism. Taming the continent's vast wilderness and bringing forth foodstuffs and raw materials from it, not to mention building cities in a single generation, filled Americans with a consciousness of power and a belief that anyone eager and persistent enough could succeed. Yet that very self-confidence was easily transformed into an arrogant attitude that Americans were somehow unique and special, and it was born at the expense of racial minorities and the propertyless.

Life in the newly won West was less romantic and comfortable than settlers might have anticipated. Hopeful settlers often had to contend with barren land where water, trees, and contacts with the outside world were scarce and the weather was fickle and often cruel. Moreover, farming expanded so rapidly that the impossible abruptly became a reality: productivity outstripped the nation's and the world's capacities to consume. As crop output and foreign competition increased in the 1880s, prices fell. Farmers' goals of wealth and comfort gave way to the necessity of producing more just to make ends meet. Thus the passing of the frontier and the accompanying agricultural transformation created social and economic problems that would plague the nation for several decades.

Exploitation of natural resources

In the years just before the Civil War, eager prospectors began to comb little-known forests and mountains looking for iron, coal, timber, oil, and copper. By 1900, active exploitation of the land's riches, once confined to the Northeast and Appalachian regions, had spread across the continent (see map, page 246).

The mining frontier advanced rapidly, drawing thousands of people to California, Nevada, Idaho, Montana, and Colorado in the 1850s and

| Mining and lumbering |

1860s. Prospectors tended to be restless optimists, willing to tramp mountains and deserts, searching icy streams for a telltale glint of precious metal. They shot game for food and financed their explorations by convincing merchants to advance credit for equipment in return for a share of the lode yet to be discovered. When their credit ran out, unlucky prospectors took jobs and saved up for another search for riches.

Extracting minerals from the ground involved high expenses for excavation and transportation. Thus individual prospectors who did discover veins of metal usually sold their claims to mining syndicates. The mining companies, often financed by eastern investors, had ample capital to bring in engineers, heavy machinery, railroad lines, and work crews. Although discoveries of gold and silver first drew attention to the West and its resources, such companies usually moved into the Rocky Mountain states to exploit less romantic but equally lucrative bonanzas of lead, zinc, tin, quartz, and copper.

Lumber production, unlike mineral extraction, required vast stretches of land. To get it, lumber companies exploited a piece of legislation meant to stimulate western settlement, the

Timber and Stone Act (1878). This measure, which applied to land in California, Nevada, Oregon, and Washington, allowed private citizens to buy at the low price of $2.50 per acre 160-acre plots "unfit for cultivation" and "valuable chiefly for timber." Taking advantage of the act, lumber companies hired thousands of seamen from waterfront boarding houses to register claims to timberland and turn them over to the companies. By 1900, claimants had bought over 3.5 million acres under Timber and Stone Act provisions, and most of that land belonged to corporations.

Much of the natural-resource frontier was a man's world. In 1880, men outnumbered

| Frontier society |

women by more than two to one in Colorado, Nevada, and Arizona. Yet many western communities had substantial numbers of women. Most women who went to the mining frontier did so for the same reasons men went: to find a fortune. They usually accompanied a husband or father and seldom prospected themselves. Even so, many women realized their own opportunities in the towns, where they provided cooking, laundering, and, in some cases, sexual services for the miners. Some became the family's main breadwinner when their husbands failed to strike it rich. For the most part, women's presence had a settling influence on mining communities. While they pursued new opportunities and freedoms, women also helped to bolster family life and to combat raw materialism and vice by campaigning against drinking, gambling, and whoring.

Many of the mining and lumber communities were genuinely heterogeneous, containing Mexicans and Chinese as well as some Indians and blacks. Chinese and blacks were employed in the camps to do cooking and cleaning. Mexicans and Indians often had been the original settlers of land coveted by whites. Each of these minority groups met with white prejudice, especially when it became evident that the forests and mines would not make everyone rich. California imposed a tax on foreign miners and denied blacks, Indians, and Chinese the right to testify

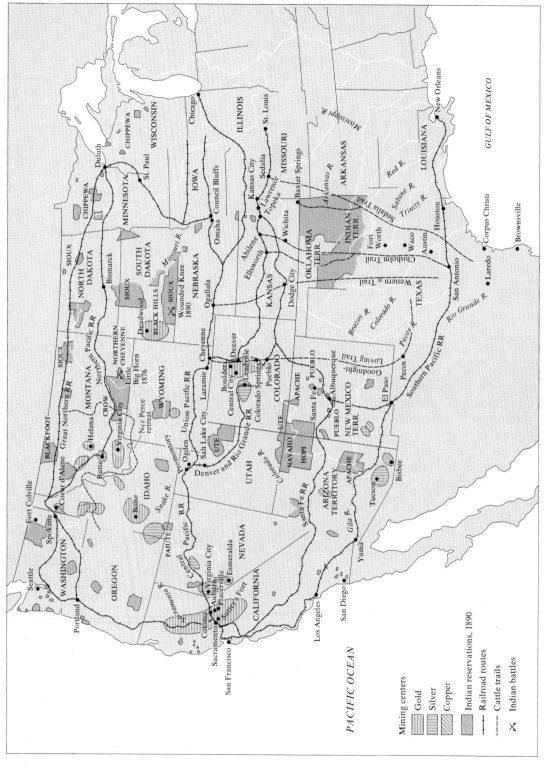

The American West, 1860–1890

Mining centers
Gold
Silver
Copper
Indian reservations, 1890
Railroad routes
Cattle trails
Indian battles

in court. Throughout the West any claims Indians or Mexicans might have had to land sought by white miners were ignored or the land simply was stolen. Blacks and Chinese who worked in mining camps often suffered threats and violence. Nonwhites defended themselves as best they could, but their most common tactic was to pack up and seek jobs and homes in another town or mining camp.

Inevitably, developers of natural resources were more interested in what the land yielded

| Use of public lands |

than in the land itself. They wanted trees and oil, not stripped and scrubby plains. To avoid purchase costs, they used several ploys, some legal and some not. One method was to purchase or rent limited rights to extract resources. Lumbermen would buy permits to fell a certain number of trees on a given forest tract and share the profits with the landowner. Oilmen and iron miners often leased property from private owners or the government and paid royalties on the minerals extracted. Other practices were frankly corrupt or fraudulent. Some lumbermen simply cut trees on public lands without paying a cent. Mining companies bribed and manipulated state and federal legislators for advantages in mineral extraction. Even when Congress and the U.S. Land Office tried to prevent fraud by passing tighter legislation and sending out more investigators, many communities resisted in the fear that such crackdowns would slow local economic growth.

Development of new areas brought western territories to the threshold of statehood. In 1889 Republicans seeking to solidify their control of

| Admission of new states |

Congress pushed through the Omnibus Bill, granting statehood to North Dakota, South Dakota, Washington, and Montana. Wyoming and Idaho were admitted in 1890. Congress denied statehood to Utah until 1896 when the Mormon majority agreed to abandon polygamy.

The mining towns and lumber camps in these states spiced American folk culture and fostered the go-getter optimism that distinguished the American spirit. The lawlessness and hedonism of places like Deadwood, in Dakota Territory, and Tombstone, in Arizona Territory, gave the West notoriety and romance. Moreover, characters like Wild Bill Hickok, Poker Alice, and Bedrock Tom became western folk heroes, and fiction writers like Mark Twain and Bret Harte captured for posterity some of the flavor of mining life. But violence and notoriety were far from common. Most miners and lumbermen worked seventy hours a week and had neither time nor money for drinking and gambling, let alone gunfights. Women worked as long or longer as teachers, cooks, laundresses, storekeepers, and housewives; only a very few were gunslingers or dance-hall queens. For most westerners, life was a matter of adapting and surviving.

The age of railroad expansion

Discovery and development of natural riches provided the base on which the nation's economy expanded. But raw wealth would have been of limited use without means of carrying it to factories, storehouses, marketplaces, and ports. In today's world a railway train, puffing steam and rattling across the countryside, seems almost an anachronism, a relic. But in the half-century following the Civil War, railroads refashioned the American economy. A web of railroad track spread across the country during these years. This expansion helped to boost the nation's steel industry and spawned a number of other related activities, including coal production, passenger and freight-car manufacture, and depot construction. By the turn of the century, the country's railroad network was virtually complete. Henceforth the goods and raw materials of one section would be available in all other sections of the country.

Railroads accomplished much but they did so with some of the largest government subsidies in American history. Railroad executives argued

The Promontory Point Grand Trestle, built in Utah by engineers of the Union Pacific Railroad. This photograph was taken in 1869, the day before workers drove down the golden spike that joined the Union Pacific with the Central Pacific. The Oakland Museum.

Government subsidy of railroads

that their activities were benefiting the public interest and that the government should aid them by giving them land from the public domain. Sympathetic governments at the national, state, and local levels responded by providing railroad companies with massive subsidies. Indeed, the federal government gave the railroads over 180 million acres of land. In an age dominated by the doctrine of laissez faire—the belief that government should not interfere in commerce—capitalists argued against government interference in one breath and accepted government aid in the next. Yet without government help, few railroads could have established themselves sufficiently to attract private investment.

As the nation's rail network expanded, so did competition and duplication. Multiple lines

Competition and discriminatory rate setting

serving individual cities allowed shippers several routes from which to choose. In their quest for new customers, local lines as well as

Chapter 16: Transformation of the West and South, 1877–1892

trunk lines cut rates to attract more traffic and outmaneuver competitors. But rate wars soon cut into profits, and wild vacillations in rates angered shippers and farmers. Some kind of stability was clearly desirable.

Ironically, while railroad rates generally were falling, complaints about excessively high charges were increasing. Railroads often boosted rates as high as possible on noncompetitive routes in order to compensate for unprofitably low rates on competitive routes. Thus pricing was not proportionate to distance: rates on short-distance hauls served by only one line could be far higher than those on long-distance hauls served by competing lines.

Railroads also devised other forms of discrimination, such as special contracts with large shippers and free passenger passes for important shippers and politicians. To reduce competition, several railroads made agreements among themselves called pools, whose participants shared traffic and earnings and set common rates. Such agreements generally discriminated against small shippers.

These discriminatory practices riled several groups of critics, including farmers, small shippers, retailers, bankers, reform politicians, and even some stockholders. During the 1870s, many of these groups demanded that government regulate railroads, especially their pricing

| Government regulation of railroads | practices. By 1880, fourteen states had established commissions or other agencies to limit freight and storage rates |

charged by state-chartered lines. Railroads bitterly fought these laws, but in 1877 the Supreme Court upheld the principle of government regulation of private property in the public interest in *Munn* v. *Illinois*.

Although the principle of regulation had won acceptance, dissatisfaction with state measures grew. Critics charged that state regulatory commissions were either too weak or too subservient to railroad interests. Moreover, state commissioners had little control over interstate lines and thus could not affect the largest, most powerful railroads. The Supreme Court affirmed

this limited authority in 1886 by declaring in the *Wabash* case that only Congress and not the states could regulate rates on interstate commerce. Consequently, reformers called for stronger laws at the federal level.

Congress responded in 1887 by passing the Interstate Commerce Act. The act prohibited pools, rebates, and long-haul–short-haul rate discriminations; and one of its clauses directed that "all charges . . . shall be reasonable and fair." The law also created the Interstate Commerce Commission (ICC) and gave it power to investigate railroads, to issue cease-and-desist orders against illegal practices, and to seek court assistance to enforce compliance with the law. But the provisions for enforcement were blurry and left railroads much room for evasion. Moreover, federal judges chipped away at ICC powers. In the *Maximum Freight Rate* case (1897), the Supreme Court ruled that the act did not grant the ICC power to set rates, and in the *Alabama Midlands* case the same year, the Court shattered prohibitions against long-haul–short-haul discriminations.

In spite of such setbacks, the era of railroad reform opened new paths for future generations. The right of the federal government to regulate railroads as a public enterprise did receive court support. Regulation at the state level continued, especially with regard to safety and intrastate rates. Strong criticism of railroads forced their executives to become more responsive to public opinion. Finally, establishment of the ICC gave further impetus to the movement to eliminate favoritism in all aspects of society and the economy.

The Indians' last stand

Railroad expansion made the vast domain between the Missouri and the Pacific more accessible to settlement. But much of this land was not empty. It was the home of thousands of native American tribespeople, whose ways of life

A Sioux camp in South Dakota, 1891. The Sioux led a nomadic life, living in harmony with the natural environment; when they packed up and moved on, they left the landscape almost undisturbed. This photograph shows the temporary situation characteristic of their camps.   Library of Congress.

differed profoundly from those of most white people and whose presence represented a stubborn barrier to full exploitation of the land.

Beginning in the 1850s, when large numbers of whites first streamed into the West, the Indians faced serious threats to their cultural survival. The newcomers, hungry for land and profits, could not tolerate the humble, nomadic tribes who recognized no individual ownership of lands. Clashes between natives and whites were inevitable and often violent. By 1873 white settlers aided by federal troops had broken most resistance except for periodic raids by young dissidents.

The basic features—and disgraces—of late-nineteenth-century policy toward Indians began with the subjugation of the Great Plains tribes: Sioux and Crows in the north, Pawnee and Cheyenne in the middle Plains, and Comanches and Kiowa in the south. These tribes led a nomadic existence, usually following the buffalo herds. Their economies and cultures revolved around migration. A restless people who took pleasure in the discipline of moving camp, the Plains tribes regarded their relationship with nature as sacred. Though they observed strict sexual divisions of

Culture of the Great Plains tribes

Chapter 16: Transformation of the West and South, 1877–1892

labor, their different roles did not imply a difference in status between the sexes.

Upon their first extensive contacts with whites, the natives accepted the federal government's policy of defining territorial boundaries

| Concentration and reservation policies | for individual tribes and making a separate treaty with each. This tactic, called "concentration," was really a system of divide-and-conquer. It

lasted only until the 1860s, when thousands of whites moved into the Plains and treaties made one week dissolved the next.

A series of bloody battles and massacres prompted a new federal policy in 1867. A commission appointed to establish peace with the Plains Indians decided that all tribes should be concentrated on two reservations, one in Dakota Territory and the other in Oklahoma Territory. Within these reservations, each tribe would occupy a specific piece of land, and white administrators would help them to shed their old ways in favor of a settled agrarian existence. Land agents and government officials cajoled or bribed tribal chiefs into signing treaties to this effect. But whites soon discovered that 125,000 people could not easily be forced to abandon their centuries-old culture. Between 1869 and 1876, many disaffected families left the reservations and vengeful braves fought attempts by the U.S. Army to subdue them.

Moreover, the new agreements made by the government meant little to the whites, as the Sioux discovered in 1875 when federal officials

| Sioux wars | allowed thousands of miners to invade the Dakota reserva-

tion in search of gold. Faced with this latest broken promise—and with the approach of the Northern Pacific Railroad, whose construction threatened their territory—the Sioux rebelled. The revolt, led by Chiefs Rain-in-the-Face, Sitting Bull, and Crazy Horse, peaked June 16, 1876, when 2,500 braves annihilated the troops of the rash General George A. Custer near the Little Big Horn River in southern Montana. But within a few months, shortages of supplies and overwhelming odds led to the collapse of Sioux resistance. By fall 1877, the Sioux war was over and other attempts at resistance had been quelled.

By means of warfare and reservation policy, the government destroyed tribal unity and the power of chiefs. At the same time, white hunters undermined Plains Indian culture even more radically by destroying the huge buffalo herds that provided natives with food, clothing, and tools. The bulky beasts were easy targets for rifle-toting whites, who killed indiscriminately for sport or to collect the $1 to $3 offered by eastern tanneries for hides. Railroads hired sharpshooters like Buffalo Bill Cody to kill buffalo en masse because herds impeded traffic and a stampede could derail a train. By the mid-1880s, only a few hundred remained of the estimated 13 million bison that had existed in the 1850s. Even more decisively than government policy, extermination of the buffalo forced Indians to abandon their nomadic way of life.

One major step remained: breaking down tribal organization and converting the natives into docile citizens. A new era began in 1871, when Congress declared that the government would no longer recognize Indian tribes as independent

| Destruction of tribal sovereignty | nations capable of making treaties with the United States. Between 1883 and 1885, the government en-

couraged natives to establish their own court systems, extended federal jurisdiction over reservations, and prohibited mass religious gatherings.

By 1887 reservation land held in common was the only remaining feature of tribal unity. In that year Congress passed the Dawes Severalty Act, which dissolved community-owned tribal lands and granted individual plots to each native family. To prevent Indians from selling their plots to speculators, the government retained ownership of these lands for twenty-five years. The act also granted citizenship to all who accepted the allotments, and authorized the government to sell unallotted land and to set aside the profits for the education of Indians.

A squadron of farm machines sweeps across a wheat field in Minnesota's Red River valley. Mechanization multiplied production and turned farming into a big business, enabling the United States to become the breadbasket of the world. Photographed in the 1880s.   Montana Historical Society, Helena.

The Dawes Act completed what invasion, force, and buffalo slaughter had begun; it left native Americans bereft of their culture and disadvantaged in a white country. Only in the Southwest, where pueblo-dwelling Indians avoided allotments, did natives succeed in retaining their aboriginal ways of life.

In 1890 the government made one last show of force. Some Sioux Indians had turned to the visionary religion of the Ghost Dance movement as a means of preserving native culture. Inspired by a prophet named Wovoka, the Ghost Dance promised a day when the land and water would swallow up all whites while the Indians danced as ghosts suspended above the calamity. All implements of white civilization, including guns and whiskey,

Ghost Dance movement

would be buried, and all Indians united as brothers would return to reclaim the earth.

Although the Ghost Dance forswore violence, government agents became alarmed about the possibility of renewed Indian uprisings as Wovoka's vision became more popular. Late in 1890, the government sent the Seventh Cavalry, Custer's old regiment, to apprehend some Sioux who were moving north from Pine Ridge, South Dakota, and who were believed to be armed for revolt. During the encounter, at a creek called Wounded Knee, the troops trained their new machine guns on the Indians and massacred two hundred men, women, and children in the snow.

By 1934, 138 million acres of Indian land had dwindled to 48 million acres, half of which was useless for farming or mining. That year federal policy was reversed and tribal land ownership was restored. But this move came too late. Natives had been isolated with only their inner strength and minimal government assistance to enable them to survive. The West was won at their expense.

The ranching frontier

Railroad construction and Indian removal set the stage for one of the West's most colorful and romantic industries, cattle ranching. Early in the nineteenth century, huge herds of cattle, originally introduced by the Spanish, roamed southern Texas and bred with cattle brought by American settlers. The resulting longhorn breed multiplied and became valuable by the 1860s, when the East's growing population increased demand for food, and railroads made transportation of beef more feasible. By 1870 drovers were herding thousands of Texas cattle northward to railroad connections in Kansas, Missouri, and Wyoming. On these long drives, mounted cowboys supervised the herds, which fed on open grassland along the way.

The long drive gave rise to its own romantic lore: rugged cowboys (as many as 25 percent of whom were black) with six-shooters, gaudy clothes, and crude manners; riotous cowtowns with raucous saloons and tough-minded women. But it was not very efficient. In trekking 1,500 miles, cattle lost weight and toughened. Herds traveling through Indian lands and farmers' fields were sometimes shot at and later prohibited from such trespass by state laws. The ranchers' only solution was to eliminate long drives by raising herds near to railroad routes.

Cattle raisers were like timber cutters: they needed vast stretches of land where their herds could graze, and they wanted to incur as little

| Open-range ranching | expense as possible to use such land. Thus they often bought a few acres bordering |

streams and turned their herds loose on adjacent public domain, which no one would want to own because it lacked water access. By this method, called open-range ranching, a cattleman could control thousands of acres by owning only a hundred or so.

By the 1880s the era of the open-range was nearing its end. Ranchers, largely in response to the problem of overgrazing, began to fence in their pastures with barbed wire—even though they had no legal title to the land. Fences destroyed the open range and often provoked disputes between competing ranchers, between cattle raisers and sheep raisers, and between ranchers and farmers who claimed use of the same land. In 1885, President Cleveland ordered removal of illegal fences on public lands and Indian reservations. Although enforcement was slow, the order signaled that free use of public domain was ending.

Open-range ranching made beef a staple of the American diet and created a few fortunes, but its extralegal features could not survive the rush of history. By 1890, well-organized businesses were taking over the cattle industry and applying scientific methods of breeding and feeding. The cowboy became just another corporate wage earner, though the myth of his freedom and individualism grew rather than faded. Most cattle ranchers now owned or leased the land they used, although some illegal fencing of public domain continued.

Meanwhile, two new groups were contending with cattle ranchers for supremacy on the Plains. From California and New Mexico, sheepherders moved into land east of the Rockies. More importantly, the farming frontier advanced into the West.

Farming the Plains

Settlement of the Plains and the West involved the greatest migration in American history. Most migrants were men from either the eastern states or Europe. They were lured by offers of cheap land and credit from states and railroads eager to promote settlement. Between 1870 and 1910 the nation's population rose from 40 million to 92 million, and the total urban population swelled by over 400 percent. As a result, demand for farm products grew rapidly. Meanwhile, scientific advances were enabling farmers to use the soil more efficiently. Agricultural experts developed the technique of dry farming, a system of plowing and harrowing that prevented precious moisture from evaporating. Scientists perfected varieties of "hard" wheat whose seeds could withstand northern winters. Railroad expansion made remote farming regions more accessible, and grain-elevator construction eased problems of shipping and storage.

Still, life on the Plains was hard. Migrants often encountered scarcities of essentials they had

Hardships of life on the Plains

taken for granted back home. Vast stretches of land contained little lumber for housing and fuel. Pioneer families were forced to build houses of sod and to burn manure for heat. Water was as scarce as timber. Few families were lucky or wealthy enough to buy land near a stream that did not dry up in summer and freeze in winter. Most had to haul water long distances or try to collect rainwater.

Even more formidable than the terrain of the Plains was its climate. Weather seldom followed predictable cycles. In summer, weeks of torrid heat and parching winds would suddenly give way to violent storms and flash floods that washed away crops and property. Winter blizzards piled up mountainous snowdrifts that halted all outdoor movement. In March and April, melting snow swelled streams, and flood waters threatened millions of acres. In the fall, a week without rain could turn dry grasslands into tinder, and the slightest spark could ignite a raging prairie fire.

Even when the climate was better behaved, nature could turn vengeful. Weather that was

good for crops was also good for insect breeding. Worms and flying pests ravaged corn and wheat. In the 1870s and 1880s grasshopper plagues literally ate up entire farms. Heralded only by the rising din of buzzing wings, a cloud of insects a mile high and miles long would smother the land and devour everything in sight. As one farmer lamented, the "hoppers left behind nothing but the mortgage."

Settlers of the Plains also had to contend with social isolation, a factor accentuated by the pattern of settlement. Under the Homestead Act of 1862, for example, settlers received rec-

Social isolation

tangular shaped tracts of 160 acres. At most four families could live near each other, but only if they congregated around the same four-corner boundary intersection. In practice, farmers usually lived back from their boundary lines, and at least a half-mile separated farmhouses.

Many observers wrote about the loneliness and monotony of life on the Plains. Men escaped the oppressiveness by working outdoors and taking occasional trips to sell crops or buy supplies. But women were more isolated, confined by domestic chores to the household, where, as one writer remarked, they were "not much better than slaves. It is a weary, monotonous round of cooking and washing and mending and as a result the insane asylum is ⅓d filled with wives of farmers."

Most farm families survived by depending on their inner resolve and by organizing churches and clubs where they could socialize and share experiences a few times a month. By the early 1900s, two external developments had combined to bring rural settlers into closer contact with modern life. Starting in the 1870s and

Mail order companies and Rural Free Delivery

1880s mail-order houses— chiefly Montgomery Ward and Sears Roebuck—expanded and made the products of the industrial society available to almost everyone. And in 1898 the government brought Rural Free Delivery (RFD) to the Plains. Now farmers could receive letters, newspapers, advertisements, and catalogues on a daily basis. Fifteen years later parcel post was inaugurated.

In the years following the Civil War an agricultural revolution was made possible by the expanded use of machinery. When the Civil War

drew many men away from farms in the upper Mississippi River valley, the women and male laborers who remained behind began using reapers and other implements more extensively to meet demand for grain and to take advantage of high prices. After the war, continued demand and high prices encouraged farmers to depend more on machines, and inventors perfected better implements for farm use.

At the same time, Congress and agricultural scientists were making efforts to improve existing crops and develop new ones. The 1862 Morrill Land Grant Act gave

Legislative and scientific aid to farmers

each state public lands to sell in order to finance agricultural and industrial colleges. And the Hatch Act of 1887 provided for agricultural experiment stations in every state, further encouraging the advancement of farming technology.

Farming received a great boost from science in the late nineteenth century. Californian Luther Burbank developed a wide range of new plants by cross-breeding. And George Washington Carver, a black chemist at Tuskegee Institute, created hundreds of new products from peanuts, soybeans, sweet potatoes, and cotton wastes and taught methods of soil improvement and crop diversification. Scientists also developed means of combating corn rot, wheat rust, hog cholera, and hoof-and-mouth disease.

Settlement of the West and the various technological and scientific advances that made it possible altered American agriculture and forced farmers to adjust to a new age. Their adjustments were neither smooth nor painless. The social and economic problems that accompanied agricultural transformation were eventually to

shape a climactic chapter in nineteenth-century American history.

The South after Reconstruction

In 1880 four times as many farmers lived in the South as on the Plains. Ravaged by civil war, southern agriculture recovered slowly. Millions of acres of rich farmland existed, but high prices for seed and implements, falling crop prices, taxes, and indebtedness trapped many families in perpetual poverty. And attempts to industrialize the South were only marginally successful. Whether interested in an industrialized New South or in agriculture, southerners were generally dependent upon northern money.

During and after Reconstruction, a significant shift in the nature of agricultural labor swept the South. Between 1860 and 1880, the total number of farms in southern states more than doubled, from 450,000 to 1.1 million, and the size of the average farm decreased from 347 to 156 acres. Despite the proliferation of farms, the number of land owners did not increase. Instead, southern agriculture became dominated by sharecropping and tenant farming. Over one-third of the farmers counted in 1880 were sharecroppers and tenants, and the proportion increased to two-thirds by 1920.

This system entangled millions of southerners in a web of humiliation. At its center was the crop lien, which worked in the following way.

Crop lien system

Most farmers were too poor ever to have cash on hand. Forced to borrow in order to buy necessities, they could offer as collateral only what they could grow. Thus a farmer in need of supplies would deal with a nearby "furnishing merchant," who would exchange supplies for a certain portion, or lien, of the farmer's forthcoming crop. The prices charged to credit customers averaged 30 to 40 percent higher than those charged to cash customers. Credit customers also had to pay interest of 33 to 200 percent on the advances they received. After the crop was harvested, farmers frequently found that they lacked sufficient funds to pay the full debt owed to the merchant. Their only choice was to commit the next year's crop and sink deeper into debt. The constant need to settle debts forced merchants and farmers to rely almost exclusively on sure-money crops, namely cotton and tobacco. But overproduction of these crops lowered prices, making debts even more difficult to settle.

Black people in the South had to cope not only with the exploitative crop lien system but with new forms of social and political oppression. With slavery dead, white supremacists fashioned new means of keeping blacks in a position of inferiority. Southern leaders, embittered by northern interference in race relations during Reconstruction and anxious to reassert their authority after the withdrawal of federal troops, instituted racist measures in all realms of life. Foremost among these measures were political disfranchisement, segregation laws, and violence.

Fearful that some political faction might manipulate black voters, white leaders decided to circumvent the Fifteenth Amendment and disfranchise blacks. (The amendment prohibited states from denying the vote to people "on the

Disfranchisement of blacks

basis of race, color, or previous condition of servitude.") Beginning with Georgia in 1877, southern states levied taxes of $1 to $2 on all citizens wishing to vote. Though seemingly trivial, these poll taxes were prohibitive to most black voters. Mississippi (1890) required voters to prove that they could read and interpret the Constitution. White registration officials applied stiffer standards to blacks than to whites. Some states utilized the grandfather clause; others held white-only primary elections. These and other devices insured that by the early 1900s blacks in all southern states with the exception of Tennessee had effectively lost their political rights.

Racial discrimination also stiffened in social affairs. A widespread informal system of separation had governed race relations in the antebellum South. After the Civil

Spread of Jim Crow laws

War, this system was codified into law. In a series of cases during the 1870s, the Supreme Court ruled that the Fourteenth Amendment protected citizens' rights only against infringement by state governments. If blacks wanted protection under the law, the Court said, they must seek it from the states. The climax to these rulings came in 1883, when in the *Civil Rights Cases* the Court struck down the 1875 Civil Rights Act, which had prohibited segregation in public facilities such as streetcars, hotels, theaters, and parks. Subsequent lower-court cases in the 1880s established the principle that blacks could be restricted to "separate-but-equal" facilities. The Supreme Court upheld the separate-but-equal doctrine in *Plessy* v. *Ferguson* (1896), and officially applied it to schools in *Cummins* v. *County Board of Education* (1899).

Thereafter, segregation laws–known as Jim Crow laws–spread rapidly. Between 1890 and 1920, discriminatory legislation piled up throughout the South, confronting black people with countless daily reminders of their inferior status. State laws and local ordinances restricted blacks to the rear of streetcars, to separate drinking and toilet facilities, and to separate sections of hospitals, asylums, and cemeteries. Segregation reached such extremes that Atlanta required separate Bibles for black witnesses swearing before court.

Whites reinforced disfranchisement and segregation with violence. Between 1880 and 1918, over 2,400 blacks were lynched in the South, compared to 100 in the North. Race riots–some of them particularly bloody–became more frequent in the South. For black southerners, race relations had improved only nominally since before the Civil War.

In industry, breezes of change were being stimulated by new manufacturing initiatives, but

Industrialization of the South

there too a distinctively southern quality prevailed. Two of the South's leading industries in the late nineteenth century relied on the traditional staple crops, cotton and tobacco. In the 1870s, textile mills began to sprout up in the Cotton Belt states, and by 1920 the South was clearly replacing New England in textile manufacturing supremacy. Proximity to raw materials and cheap labor aided the development of the industry. Mills paid barely half what northern workers received to the women and children from poor white families who tended the machines. Often the company store was as exploitative as the farmer's furnishing merchant.

Northern and European capitalists sponsored other southern industries. In the Gulf states the lumber industry became highly significant, and iron and steel production made Birmingham a boom city. Yet in 1900 the South remained as rural as it had been in 1860. The emergence of a New South would have to wait another era.

Stirrings of agrarian unrest

The inequities of the southern agricultural system gave rise to the first rumblings of a mass democratic movement that was to shake American society in the late nineteenth century. The agrarian revolt was born of the despair brought about by crop liens, furnishing merchants, declining farm prices, rising costs, high interest and railroad rates, weather, insects, and isolation. Once under way, it inspired visions of a truly cooperative, democratic society.

Even before the full impact of their economic problems was felt, farmers had begun to organize to relieve their mounting distress. With aid from government officials, particularly Oliver H. Kelley of the Department of Agriculture, farmers founded a network of local organizations called Granges in almost every state during the late 1860s and early 1870s. | **Grange movement** | By 1875 the Grange had nearly twenty thousand local branches and over 1 million members. Strongest in the Midwest and South, Granges served chiefly as social organizations, sponsoring meetings and educational events to help relieve the loneliness of farm life.

As membership flourished, Granges moved beyond social functions into economic and political action. At its 1874 national convention, the Grange proposed to avoid high retail prices by forming local cooperatives to buy equipment and supplies directly from manufacturers. Granges also encouraged the formation of sales cooperatives, whereby farmers would pool their grain and dairy products and then divide the profits. In politics, Grangers used their numbers to some advantage, electing sympathetic legislators and pressing for laws to regulate transportation and storage rates.

Granges nevertheless declined in the late 1870s because their essentially conservative tactics did not meet members' needs. The requirement that cooperatives run on a cash-only basis excluded large numbers of farmers who never had any cash. Efforts to regulate business and transportation withered when corporations and railroads won court support against "Granger laws." After a brief assertion of influence, the Grange reverted to an organization of farmers' social clubs. Its short-lived agrarian campaign served, however, as a precedent for future action.

Rural activism then shifted to the Farmers' Alliances, two networks of organizations—one in the Plains and one in the South—that by 1890 | **Farmers' Alliances** | constituted a genuine mass movement. The first alliances sprang up in Texas, where hard-pressed farmers rallied against crop liens, furnishing merchants, and railroads in particular, and against money power in general. Alliance leaders extended the movement to other southern states, and by 1889 the Southern Alliance boasted over 3 million members. This number included the powerful Colored Farmers' National Alliance, which claimed over 1 million black members. A similar movement flourished in the Plains, where by the late 1880s 2 million members were organized in Kansas, Nebraska, and the Dakotas.

Important events

1859–60	Gold rushes in Nevada, Colorado, and Idaho
1862–64	Gold rushes in Arizona and Montana
1862	Homestead Act Morrill Land Grant Act
1865–67	War with western Sioux
1873	Major silver discovery of Comstock Lode (Nevada)
1875–76	Indian war in Black Hills
1876	Gold rush in Black Hills
1877	Nez Perce Indian uprising
1878	Timber and Stone Act
1879	Silver discovery at Tombstone, Arizona
1883	*Civil Rights Cases*
1885–86	Disastrous winters in Plains states
1887	Dawes Severalty Act Interstate Commerce Act Farm prices collapse
1889–90	Ghost Dance movement and Battle of Wounded Knee
1890–98	Disfranchisement of blacks in South
1892	Populist convention in Omaha
1896	*Plessy* v. *Ferguson*
1899	*Cummins* v. *County Board of Education*

Motivated by outrage, alliance members not only pushed the Grange concept of cooperation but also proposed a scheme to alleviate the most serious rural problems: lack of cash and credit.

Subtreasury plan

The subtreasury plan called for the federal government to construct warehouses in every major agricultural county. At harvest time, farmers could store their crops in these subtreasuries while awaiting higher prices, and the government would loan farmers treasury notes amounting to 80 percent of the market price the stored crops would bring. Farmers could use these subtreasury notes as legal tender to pay debts and make purchases. Once the stored crops were sold, farmers would pay back the loans plus small interest and storage fees.

Growing membership and rising confidence drew alliances more deeply into politics. By 1890, farmers had elected a number of office-holders sympathetic to their programs—especially in the South. In the Midwest, alliance candidates often ran on independent third-party tickets, and achieved some success in Kansas,

Rise of Populism

Nebraska, and the Dakotas. During the summer of 1890, the Kansas Alliance held a "convention of the people" and nominated candidates who swept the fall elections. The formation of this People's party, whose members were called Populists, gave a name to the movement that grew out of alliance political activism. Two years later, after overcoming regional differences, the People's party held a convention in Omaha, drafted a platform, and nominated a presidential candidate.

The Omaha Platform was one of the most comprehensive reform documents in American history. Most of its planks addressed three central issues: transportation, land, and money. Frustrated with weak state and federal regulation of transportation, the Populists demanded government ownership of railroad and telegraph lines. They called on the federal government to reclaim all land owned for speculative purposes by railroads and aliens. The monetary plank called for a flexible currency system based on free and unlimited coinage of silver that would increase the money supply and enable farmers to pay their debts more easily. Other planks advocated a graduated income tax, postal savings banks, and such reforms as the direct election of U.S. senators and shorter hours for workers. As its presidential candidate, the party nominated James B. Weaver of Iowa, a former Union general.

Although Weaver received only 8 percent of the total popular vote in 1892, Populism had become a national force. Not since 1856 had a third party won so many votes in its first national effort. The party's central dilemma— whether to stand by its ideals at all costs or compromise those ideals in order to gain power—still loomed ahead.

Suggestions for further reading

THE WESTERN FRONTIER Ray A. Billington, *Westward Expansion* (1967); William H. Goetzmann, *Exploration and Empire* (1966); Robert V. Hine, *The American West* (1973); Julie Roy Jeffrey, *Frontier Women* (1979); Frederick Merk, *History of the Westward Movement* (1978); Rodman W. Paul, *The Frontier and the American West* (1971); Henry Nash Smith, *Virgin Land: The American West as Symbol and Myth* (1950); L. Steckmesser, *The Western Hero in History and Legend* (1965).

RAILROADS Robert W. Fogel, *Railroads and Economic Growth* (1964); Edward C. Kirkland, *Men, Cities, and Transportation* (1948); Gabriel Kolko, *Railroads and Regulation* (1965); George R. Taylor and Irene Neu, *The American Railroad Network* (1956); O. O. Winther, *The Transportation Frontier* (1964).

INDIANS AND RANCHING Ralph K. Andrist, *The Long Death: The Last Days of the Plains Indians* (1964); Lewis Atherton, *The Cattle Kings* (1961); Francis Paul Prucha, *American Indian Policy in Crisis* (1976); Wilcomb E. Washburn, *Red Man's Land/White Man's Law* (1971).

SETTLEMENT OF THE PLAINS Gilbert C. Fite, *The Farmer's Frontier* (1966); Fred A. Shannon, *The Farmer's Last Frontier* (1963); Walter Prescott Webb, *The Great Plains* (1931).

THE NEW SOUTH Orville Vernon Burton and Robert C. McMath, Jr., *Toward A New South In Post-Civil War Southern Communities* (1982); Thomas D. Clark and Albert D. Kirwan, *The South Since Appomattox* (1967); Dewey Grantham, Jr., *The Democratic South* (1963); Sheldon Hackney, *Populism to Progressivism in Alabama* (1969); Morgan Kousser, *The Shaping of Southern Politics* (1974); Theodore Saloutos, *Farmer Movements in the South, 1865–1933* (1960); C. Vann Woodward, *Origins of the New South* (1951); C. Vann Woodward, *The Strange Career of Jim Crow* (1966).

FARM PROTEST Gerald Gaither, *Blacks and the Populist Revolt* (1977); Lawrence Goodwyn, *Democratic Promise: The Populist Movement in America* (1976); Earl W. Hayter, *The Troubled Farmer* (1968); John D. Hicks, *The Populist Revolt* (1931); Norman Pollack, *The Populist Response to Industrial America* (1962); Fred A. Shannon, *American Farmers' Movements* (1957).

17

THE MACHINE AGE,

1877–1920

Conrad Carl tried to appear calm, but he was understandably nervous. It was spring 1882, and Carl, who for nearly thirty years had been a tailor in New York City, was appearing before a group of U.S. senators to explain changing work conditions in the tailoring business.

When he first began tailoring, Carl explained, he and his wife and children had pieced together garments by hand. The pace of their work was relaxed, yet he was able to save a few dollars each year. Then, said Carl, "The sewing machine was invented . . . and it stitched very nicely, nicer than the tailor could do; and the bosses said: 'We want you to use the sewing machine. . . .'"

Carl and his fellow tailors used their meager savings to buy machines, hoping they could earn more by producing more. But their employers cut wages instead of raising them. The tailors "found that we could earn no more money than we could without the machine; but the money for the machine was gone now, and we found that the machine was only for the profit of the bosses; that they got their work quicker, and it was done nicer."

Moreover, because the machines were noisy, the Carl family had to confine their work to the daytime hours, so as not to disturb the neighbors. "We work now in excitement—in a hurry. It is hunting; it is not work at all; it is a hunt."

Conrad Carl's testimony to the Senate committee was one worker's view of the industrialization that was relentlessly overtaking Ameri-

can society. The forces prevailing in the new order were both inspiring and ominous. The factory and the machine broke down manufacturing into minute, routinized tasks and organized work according to the dictates of the clock. The city—long the vanguard of commercial growth—now furnished labor, capital, and consumers for industrial transformation. The railroad linked markets and hastened delivery of goods and raw materials. And the large corporation amassed frightening power in the quest for productivity and profits. All these influences profoundly changed the structure of society.

Industrialization is a process whose complexity defies precise definition. It is thus best understood by considering its predominant characteristics, which in America were:

1. production by machine rather than by hand
2. involvement of an increasing proportion of the work force in manufacturing
3. production concentrated in large, intricately organized factories
4. accelerated technological innovation, emphasizing new inventions and applied science
5. expanded markets, no longer merely local and regional in scope
6. growth of a nationwide transportation network based on the railroad, and an accompanying communications network based on the telegraph and telephone
7. increased capital accumulation for investment in expansion of production

8. growth of large enterprises and specialization in all forms of economic activity
9. rapid population increase
10. steady increase in the size and predominance of cities

Technology and the quest for wealth

In 1876, Thomas A. Edison and his associates moved into a long wooden shed in Menlo Park, New Jersey, where Edison intended to turn out "a minor invention every ten days and a big thing every six months or so." He envisioned his Menlo Park laboratory as an invention factory, a place where creative people would pool their ideas and skills to fashion marketable products. Edison, and others like him, helped to make the years between 1865 and 1900 an age of invention. Indeed, the work of inventors was an integral part of American industrialization (see map, page 262).

Perhaps the biggest of Edison's "big-thing" projects began in 1878 when he formed the Edison Electric Light Company and embarked on a search for a cheap, efficient means of indoor lighting. His major contribution was perfection of an incandescent bulb. At the same time he worked out a system of power production and distribution—an improved dynamo (generator) and a parallel circuit of wires. In 1882 he built a power plant that would light eighty-five buildings in New York's Wall Street financial district. When this Pearl Street Station began service with great fanfare, a *New York Times* reporter marveled that working in his office at night "seemed almost like writing in daylight."

Edison's system had a major limitation: it used direct current at low voltage, and could thus send electric power only a mile or two.

Birth of the electrical industry

George Westinghouse, an inventor from Schenectady, New York, solved the problem. Westinghouse used alternating current and transformers to reduce high-voltage power to lower voltage levels, thus making transmission over long distances cheaper.

Once Edison and Westinghouse had made their technological breakthroughs, others helped them distribute their inventions to a wide market. Samuel Insull, Edison's private secretary, deftly attracted investments and organized Edison power plants across the country. In the late 1880s and early 1890s, financiers Henry Villard and J. P. Morgan consolidated patents in electric lighting and merged equipment-manufacturing companies into the General Electric Company. Equally important, General Electric and Westinghouse Electric established research laboratories that paid practical-minded scientists to find new uses for electricity.

But research laboratories did not eliminate individual dreamers. One such optimist was Henry Ford, who in the 1890s worked as an electrical engineer in Detroit's Edison Company and in his spare time experimented with a gasoline-burning internal combustion engine to power a vehicle. Like Edison, Ford had a scheme as well as an invention. His plan was to produce millions of identical cars in exactly the same fashion. The key was mass production, and the watchword was *flow*. On Ford's assembly lines production was broken down so that each worker had responsibility for only one task, constantly repeated, and there was a continuous flow of these tasks from raw materials to finished product. In 1910, the first year the famous Model T was marketed, Ford sold 10,000 cars. By 1914, the year after the first moving assembly line was inaugurated, 248,000 Fords were sold. Many cost only $490 apiece, about a fourth of what they would have cost a decade earlier. In 1914, to put the car within even easier reach of the average worker, who earned only $2 per day, Ford tried to set an example by raising workers' wages to $5 a day. "This is neither charity nor wages," he ex-

Mass production of the automobile

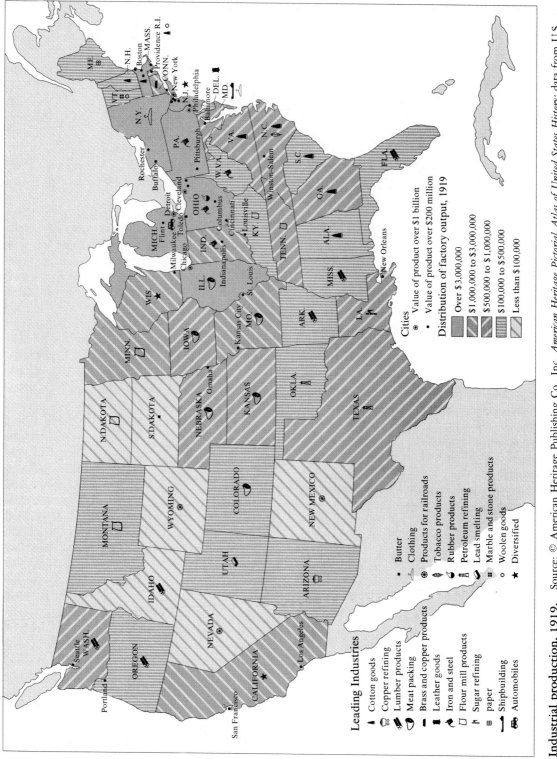

Industrial production, 1919. Source: © American Heritage Publishing Co., Inc. *American Heritage Pictorial Atlas of United States History*; data from U.S. Bureau of the Census, *Fourteenth Census of the United States, 1920.* Vol. IX: *Manufacturing* (Washington: U.S. Government Printing Office, 1921).

A laborer poses by a huge ore breaker at the Utah Copper Company, around 1900. As machines became larger and more efficient, workers' skills became less important.   State Historical Society of Wisconsin.

plained, "but profit sharing and efficiency engineering."

A host of other machines and processes helped to alter the nation's economy and everyday life between 1865 and 1900. The telephone and typewriter revolutionized communications. Sewing machines made mass-produced clothing available to almost everyone. Refrigeration changed American dietary habits by making it easier to preserve food. Streetcars, elevated railroads, and subways extended city limits and enabled people to live farther from their workplaces. Cash registers and adding machines revamped accounting and created new clerical jobs.

All these developments and more thrust the United States into the vanguard of industrial nations. Other effects, however, were less positive. Industrial expansion and mechanization destroyed time-honored crafts and subordinated men and women to rigid schedules and repetitive routines. On another level, manufacturers pooled existing patents and tried to monopolize new discoveries by confining research to their own labs. As in farming and mining, bigness and consolidation were engulfing the individual.

Technology and the quest for wealth

The triumph of industrialism

In the industrial sector, higher production at lower costs resulted in huge profits. As railroads and technological innovations made large-scale production more economical, sizable factories began to replace small ones. Only large factories could afford to buy new machines and operate them at full capacity. And large factories could best take advantage of discount rates for shipping products in bulk and for buying raw materials in quantity. Economists call such advantages *economies of scale.*

Machines and large factories made such efficiencies possible, but profitability was as much a matter of organization as of mechanics. Thus by

| New emphasis on efficiency |

the 1890s, engineers and managers were working intently to increase output economically and efficiently, putting the primary emphasis on time. Of the many people who espoused systems of efficient production, the most influential was Frederick W. Taylor. His experiments involved identifying the "elementary operations of motions" used by specific workers, eliminating "all useless movements," selecting better tools, and devising "a series of motions which can be made quickest and best."

Taylor's writings helped to make time studies and scientific management a national obsession. They heightened the emphasis on large-scale production and economies of scale while minimizing the importance of factory workers relative to clerks and planners. Workers' skills became less valued. Time rather than quality became the measure of acceptable work, and science rather than tradition determined the right ways of doing things. As integral features of the assembly line, employees had become another kind of interchangeable part.

By the late 1880s, large manufacturers were adding new marketing techniques to their technological and organizational innovations. Meat processor Gustavus Swift built branch slaughter-

| New marketing techniques |

houses and refrigerated warehouses and railroad cars in order to enlarge the market for fresh meat. James B. Duke, who organized the American Tobacco Company and made cigarettes a big business, saturated communities with billboards and free samples and offered premium gifts to retailers for selling more cigarettes. Companies like International Harvester and Singer Sewing Machine set up systems for servicing their products and introduced financing schemes to permit customers to buy the machines more easily. Mail-order firms, large department stores, and chain stores eliminated wholesaling costs and in the process invented new methods of retailing.

The corporate consolidation movement

Neither the wonders of industrial production nor the buoyant language of market promotion could mask unsettling factors in the American economy. Competition and the resulting race for higher productivity and new markets had costs as well as benefits. New technology demanded that factories operate at near-capacity in order to produce goods most economically. But the more manufacturers produced, the more they had to sell. And in order to sell more, they had to reduce prices. In order to profit more, they expanded production further and often reduced wages. In order to expand, they had to borrow money. In order to repay the loans, they had to produce and sell even more. This circular process strangled small firms that could not keep pace and thrust workers into conditions of constant uncertainty. The same pressures and consequences affected trade, banking, and transportation as well as manufacturing.

Such conditions encouraged rapid growth—

but optimism could dissolve at the hint that debtors were unable to meet their obligations. In the final third of the nineteenth century, financial panics afflicted the economy at least once a decade, depressing prices and putting workers out of jobs. The depressions that began in 1873, 1884, and 1893 each hovered over the nation for several years. Business leaders failed to agree on what caused the declines. In an effort to combat the uncertainty of the business cycle, many businessmen turned to more centralized and cooperative forms of economic power, notably corporations, pools, trusts, and holding companies.

In the nineteenth century, corporations, with their limited liability for stockholders, were the best instruments for raising the capital needed for industrial expansion. But economic disorder and the urge for profits caused corporation managers to seek stability in new and larger forms of economic concentration. At first consolidation | efforts were tentative and

| *Methods of* | informal, consisting mainly
| *consolidation* | of cooperative agreements

among firms that made the same product or offered the same service. Through these arrangements, called *pools,* competing companies tried to control the market by agreeing how much each should produce and what prices should be charged. Such "gentlemen's agreements" rarely worked for long. The desire for profits often tempted pool members to evade their commitments by secretly reducing prices or selling more than the agreed quota. Because pools were extralegal, pool members could not sue each other for broken promises. The Interstate Commerce Act of 1887 outlawed pools, but by then their usefulness was already fading.

John D. Rockefeller disliked pools, calling them "ropes of sand." In 1879 one of his lawyers adapted an old device called a *trust* whereby companies could turn over control of their stock to a board of trustees, which then supervised all operations. This device allowed Rockefeller to integrate the management of his original Standard Oil Company of Ohio with that of all the other companies he had gobbled up. Then in 1888 New Jersey adopted new incorporation laws allowing corporations chartered there to own property in other states and to own stock in other corporations. This liberalization led to the creation of the *holding company,* which controlled a partial or complete interest in other companies. Holding companies could in turn merge their constituent companies' assets. Thus Rockefeller incorporated Standard Oil of New Jersey and merged the assets of forty companies. Holding companies also encouraged the use of *vertical integration,* which allowed companies to take over several levels of production and distribution, including control of raw materials and transportation as well as manufacturing.

Originally designed as an arrangement whereby responsible individuals would manage the financial affairs of people unwilling or unable to handle them alone, the trust became the answer to industry's search for order. Between 1889 and 1903, some three hundred combinations were formed, most of them trusts and holding companies. By far the most spectacular was the U.S. Steel Corporation, financed by J. P. Morgan. This new enterprise, made up of iron-ore properties, freight carriers, wire mills, plate and tubing companies, and other firms, was capitalized at over $1.4 billion.

The gospel of wealth

Business leaders turned to consolidation under the new forms of corporation both to promote growth and to cut down wasteful competition. But the American public had been raised on an ideology of open competition. It thus became necessary for the defenders of the monopolistic companies to find a means to justify their size and power. They turned to the doctrine of Social Darwinism.

Social Darwinism loosely adapted Charles

Darwin's theory of the origin of species to the traditional principles of laissez faire. Human society had evolved naturally, the Social Dar-

| Social Darwinism |

winists reasoned, and any interference with existing institutions would only hamper progress and aid the weak. In a free society operating according to the principle of survival of the fittest, power would flow naturally to the most capable. Property holding and acquisition were therefore sacred rights, and wealth was a mark of well-deserved power and responsibility.

This philosophy required that people be left free to accumulate and dispose of wealth. In fact, however, the new corporate forms, with their domination of production and finance, prevented most individuals who did not already have wealth from acquiring it. In response to this inconsistency, extensions of Social Darwinist theory gave rise to various forms of paternalism—providing for the needs of those less fortunate or less capable—on the part of the elite. It meant that the wealthy could and should endow churches, hospitals, and schools, since such gifts promoted progress by raising the "moral culture" of all classes. But it also meant that government should not force the rich, through taxation or regulation, to become more humanitarian.

Paradoxically, business executives who exalted individual initiative and independence also pressed for government assistance. They de-

| Government assistance to business |

nounced any measures that might aid unions or regulate factory conditions; such legislation, they said, thwarted natural economic laws. At the same time, though, they lobbied forcefully for subsidies, bounties, loans, and tax relief that would encourage business growth. Tariffs were by far the largest form of government assistance to industry. By putting high import duties on competing goods from abroad, Congress enabled American producers to keep the prices of their goods relatively high. Industrialists argued that tariff protection encouraged the development of

new products and the founding of new enterprises. But tariffs also forced consumers to pay, in the form of artificially high prices, for industrialists' investments.

Dissenting voices

Writers who attacked trusts argued within the same framework of values as did corporate leaders who defended the new economic system. While defenders insisted that trusts were the natural and efficient outcome of economic development, critics charged that trusts were unnatural because they were created by greed, and inefficient because they stifled opportunity. Underlying such charges was a deep-seated fear of monopoly. Those who feared monopoly believed that large corporations could exploit consumers by fixing prices, demean workers by cutting wages, destroy opportunity by eliminating small businesses, and threaten democracy by corrupting politicians.

Characteristically, intellectuals believed there was a better way to achieve progress. By the mid-1880s, a number of young professors began to challenge Social Darwinism and laissez faire. To some, like the pioneering sociologist Lester Ward, a system that guaranteed survival only to the fittest was wasteful and brutal; instead, he reasoned, unified and cooperative activity, fostered by planning and government intervention, was the most progressive means to unity and happiness. Economists Richard Ely, John R. Commons, and Edward Bemis agreed that natural forces should be harnessed for the public good. Instead of the laissez-faire system, they preferred one of positive assistance by the state.

While academics were recommending intervention in and adjustments of the natural eco-

| Utopian economic schemes |

nomic order, others were proposing more utopian schemes for combating monopolies. Reformer Henry

George, the author of *Progress and Poverty*, declared that inequality stemmed from the ability of a few to profit from rising land values. To restore equality, George proposed to tax the "unearned increment"—the rise in land values caused by increased market demand rather than by owners' improvements—and to eliminate all other taxes. By confiscating undue profits, George insisted, this single tax would end monopolistic tendencies and ensure social progress.

Unlike George, who approved of private ownership, novelist Edward Bellamy envisioned a socialist state in which government would own and oversee the means of production and distribution and would unite all people under moral laws. Bellamy outlined his vision in the utopian *Looking Backward, 2000–1887*, published in 1888. He warned that catastrophe would result from the extremes of wealth and poverty that characterized American society. The remedy, said Bellamy, was a fully nationalized state free of the greed of bankers, industrialists, lawyers, and politicians.

Meanwhile, public clamor against monopolies and trusts began to prod legislators into action. By the end of the century, fifteen states had constitutional provisions outlawing trusts, and twenty-seven states had laws forbidding pools. Most of these states were in the South and West. Their laws, along with those regulating railroads, established precedents for government intervention. But state attorneys general lacked the staff and judicial support for a concerted attack on big business, and corporations always found ways to evade restrictions. Consequently, the need for national legislation only became more pressing.

Antitrust legislation

In 1890 Congress passed the Sherman Anti-Trust Act. The act made illegal "every contract, combination in the form of trust or otherwise, or conspiracy in the restraint of trade." People found guilty of violating the law faced fines and jail terms, and those injured by illegal combinations could sue for triple damages. However, the law was vague. It did not define clearly what a restraint of trade was. Moreover, it entrusted interpretation of its provisions to the courts, which at that time were strong allies of business.

The Sherman Anti-Trust Act was intended to encourage free competition by prohibiting unreasonable restraints of trade, but judges—particularly the Supreme Court—made it difficult to distinguish between reasonable and unreasonable. When in 1895 the government prosecuted the so-called Sugar Trust for owning 98 percent of the nation's sugar-refining capacity, eight of the nine Supreme Court judges ruled that control of manufacturing did not necessarily mean control of trade *(U.S. v. E. C. Knight Co.)*.

This interpretation left the antitrust act with only token power to combat industrial bigness. Ironically, the law did serve government officials as a tool for breaking up labor unions. Courts that did not consider monopolistic production a restraint of trade willingly applied antitrust provisions to union strikes that affected trade.

The changing status of labor

By 1880 the status of labor had changed dramatically from what it had been a generation earlier. Most workers could no longer accurately be termed producers—as craftsmen and farmers had traditionally considered themselves. The enlarged working class now consisted mainly of employees—people who worked only when someone else hired them. Whereas producers were paid by consumers according to the quality of what they produced, employees were increasingly paid wages based on time spent on the job.

As mass production subdivided manufacturing into minute tasks, workers spent their time repeating one specialized operation. No longer was it up to the worker to decide when to begin and end the work day, when to rest, and what tools and techniques to use. Especially

Even as work became more routinized, workers held onto traditional customs. In this photograph a cigar maker reads the newspaper to his fellow workers, according to tradition.   International Museum of Photography, George Eastman House.

as assembly-line production spread, employees lost their sense of individualism. Workers reacted to industrialization by struggling to retain old customs such as having a fellow worker read aloud while they labored. Conversely, employers sought to make workers more docile through temperance and moral reform societies.

As machines and assembly-line production reduced the need for skilled workers, employers cut wage costs further by hiring more women and children. In 1870 there were 354,000 women employed in manufacturing (11 percent of all manufacturing laborers); in 1900 there were 1.2 million women (20 percent of all manufacturing laborers), including 45 railroad engineers and stokers, 185

| Employment of women and children |

blacksmiths, and 408 machinists. But most female industrial workers were employed in low-paying, menial jobs in textile mills, laundries, and candy factories, where they earned as little as $1.56 for seventy hours of labor. For similar work, men received $7 to $9.

Although most working children toiled on their parents' farms, the number in nonagricultural occupations tripled between 1870 and 1900. In 1900, 13 percent of all textile workers were below age sixteen. In other industries, too, mechanization created a number of light unskilled tasks (such as running errands and helping machine operators) that children could handle at a fraction of adult wages. Many parents lied about their children's ages to help them get jobs to supplement the family income.

By 1900, child labor laws and further automation had reduced the total number of children working in manufacturing, but many more still held jobs in street trades—shining shoes and peddling newspapers—and as clerks and helpers in stores.

While working conditions loomed as the major issue laborers had to face, the problem of wages was often the immediate catalyst of worker unrest. Many employers believed in the "iron law of wages," which dictated that employees be paid according to the conditions of supply and demand. In practice the principle meant that employers did not have to raise wages—and could even lower them—as long as there were people who would accept low pay. Employers justified the system with references to old-fashioned individual freedom: if a worker did not like the wages being paid, he or she was free to quit and find a job elsewhere. Wage earners saw things differently. They believed the wage system trapped and exploited them.

Moreover, even a steadily employed status was uncertain. Repetitive tasks using high-speed machinery dulled workers' concentration, and the slightest mistake could cause a serious injury. Industrial accidents rose steadily before 1920, killing or maiming hundreds of thousands of people each year. Even as late as 1913, after factory owners had installed some safety devices, some 25,000 people died in industrial mishaps, and close to 1 million were injured.

Families stricken by such accidents suffered acutely, because disability insurance and pensions were almost nonexistent. Nineteenth-century laissez-faire attitudes prevented protective legislation for workers, and employers would not take responsibility for employees' well-being. As one railroad manager told his workers, "If an employee is disabled by sickness or any other cause, the right to claim compensation is not recognized."

Reformers in several states passed laws to ease working conditions, but the Supreme Court

Working conditions

Textile mills and other factories employed thousands of children like Addie Laird, a twelve-year-old spinner in a cotton factory in North Pownal, Vermont. Reformers tried to prevent the exploitation of child labor, but many families could not do without their children's meager wages. Photographed in 1910 by Lewis Hine.   National Archives.

limited their impact by making narrow interpretations of what jobs were dangerous and which workers needed protection. Initially, in *Holden* v. *Hardy* (1896), the Court decided to uphold a law regulating the working hours of miners because their work was so dangerous that long hours would increase the threat of injury. In *Lochner* v. *New York* (1905), however, the Court struck down a law limiting bakery workers to a sixty-hour week and a ten-hour day, because baking was not a dangerous enough occupation for the legislature to restrict the right of workers to sell their labor freely. Then, in *Muller* v. *Oregon* (1908), the Court resorted to a different rationale to uphold a law limiting working hours for women to ten a day. Labor legislation for women was necessary, the Court asserted, because a woman's health "becomes an object of public interest and care in order to preserve the strength and vigor of the race."

Throughout the nineteenth century, tensions rose and fell as different groups of men and women confronted mechanization, government neglect, and wage scales that did not keep pace with the rising cost of living. Some people bent to the demands of the factory, the machine, and the time clock. Others, however, turned to organized resistance.

In many ways, the year 1877 was a historical watershed. In July of that year, a series of strikes broke out among railroad workers who were

| *Worker protest* |

protesting wage cuts. Violence spread across Pennsylvania and Ohio all the way to Chicago and St. Louis. Strikers derailed trains and burned rail yards. Militia companies organized by employers broke up picket lines and fired into threatening crowds. In several areas, factory workers, wives, and even local merchants aided the striking workers, while railroads enlisted strikebreakers to replace union men.

After more than a month of unprecedented carnage that reached from West Virginia and Maryland to Illinois, Texas, and California, President Rutherford B. Hayes sent federal troops to restore order and end the strikes. His action marked the first significant use of troops to quell labor unrest. Thereafter, use of federal and state troops became a normal method of suppressing strikes.

The union movement

Anxiety over their loss of independence drove some workers to unionize to protect their interests. The National Labor Union, which flourished briefly after its founding in 1866, died during the depression of the 1870s. The only broad-based labor organization to survive that depression was the Knights of Labor, founded

| *Knights of Labor* |

in 1860 by Philadelphia garment cutters who opened their doors to other workers during the 1870s. Under the leadership of Terence V. Powderly, the Knights recruited women and blacks as well as immigrants and unskilled and semiskilled workers, who were excluded from craft unions. Membership mushroomed from 10,000 in 1879 to 730,000 in mid-1886.

Strikes presented a dilemma for the Knights. Powderly and other leaders wondered whether the pursuit of immediate goals through this sometimes violent tactic would detract from the union's long-range objective of a Bellamy-type cooperative society. As strikes began to fail in 1886, as Powderly began to denounce radicalism and violence, and as the more militant craft unions broke away, Knights' membership dwindled. The union survived only in a few small towns, where a brief and vain attempt was made to unite with the Populists in the 1890s. The special interests of craft unions overcame the Knights' general appeal, and dreams of the unity of labor faded.

As the depression of the 1870s subsided and better conditions returned in the early 1880s, a number of labor groups, including the Knights of Labor, began to campaign for an eight-hour work day. This effort on the part of workers to regain control of their work gathered most momentum in Chicago, where radical anarchists as

| *Haymarket riot* |

well as various craft unions agitated for the cause. On May 1, 1886, the workers' deadline for achieving their goal, city police were mobilized to prevent possible disorder. Two days later a riot broke out at the McCormick reaper factory where police shot and killed two workers and wounded several others. The next evening, labor groups organized a rally at Haymarket Square, near downtown Chicago, to protest police brutality. As a company of police officers approached the meeting, a bomb exploded near their front ranks, killing seven and injuring sixty-seven. Mass arrests of anarchists and unionists followed. Eventually eight men, all anarchists, were tried and convicted of the bombing, though there was no evidence of their guilt. Four were executed and one committed suicide in prison. The remaining three were pardoned in 1893 by Illinois governor John P. Altgeld, who believed they had been victims of the "malicious ferocity" of the courts.

The Haymarket bombing drew public attention to labor campaigns for better conditions but also revived the long-standing American fear of radicalism. In several cities police forces and armories were strengthened. And employer associations designed to counter labor militancy multiplied.

The newly formed American Federation of Labor was the major workers' organization to emerge after the 1886 upheavals. A combination

| American Federation of Labor |

of national craft unions, the AFL initially had about 140,000 members, most of whom were skilled native workers. Led by Samuel Gompers, the pragmatic and opportunistic head of the Cigar Makers' Union, AFL unions avoided the idealistic rhetoric of worker solidarity to press for specific goals, such as higher wages, shorter hours, and the right to bargain collectively. By 1917 the organization included 111 national unions, 27,000 local unions, and 2.5 million members.

The AFL and the labor movement in general staggered in the early 1890s, when once again labor violence evoked public fears. In July 1892, Henry C. Frick, the stubborn president of the Carnegie Steel Company, closed the company plant in Homestead, Pennsylvania, when the AFL-affiliated Amalgamated Association of Iron and Steelworkers refused to accept pay cuts and went on strike. Shortly thereafter, angry workers attacked and routed three hundred Pinkerton guards hired by Frick to protect the plant. State militia then moved in to protect the factory, and after five months the strikers gave in.

In 1894, workers at the Pullman Palace Car Company walked out in protest over exploitative policies at the company town near Chicago.

| Pullman strike |

The paternalistic company head, George Pullman, owned and controlled the land and all buildings, the school, the bank, and the water and gas systems. The company paid workers' wages, fixed their rents, determined what prices they would pay for the necessities of life, and employed spies to report on disgruntled workers.

One thing Pullman would not do was negotiate with workers. When the depression that began in 1893 threatened his business, Pullman managed to maintain profits and pay dividends to stockholders by cutting wages 25 to 40 percent but holding firm on rents and prices in the town. Workers, squeezed into debt and deprivation, sent a committee to Pullman in May 1894 to protest his policies. Pullman reacted by firing three of the committee. The enraged workers, most of whom had joined the American Railway Union, called a strike. Pullman retaliated by shutting down the plant. When the American Railway Union, led by the charismatic young organizer Eugene V. Debs, voted to aid the strikers by boycotting all Pullman cars, Pullman stood firm and rejected arbitration. The railroad owners' association then enlisted the aid of U.S. Attorney General Richard Olney, who obtained a court injunction to prevent the union from "obstructing the railways and holding up the mails." In response to further worker obstinacy, President Grover Cleveland sent federal troops to Chicago, supposedly to protect the mails but in reality to crush the strike. Within a month the strike was over, and Debs was jailed for six

Important events

1873–78	Depression
1877	Widespread railroad strikes
1879	Henry George, *Progress and Poverty*
	Edison perfects the incandescent light bulb
1882	Formation of Standard Oil trust
1884–85	Depression
1886	Haymarket riot
	American Federation of Labor founded
1888	Edward Bellamy, *Looking Backward*
1890	Sherman Anti-Trust Act
1892	Homestead Steel strike
1893–97	Depression
1894	Pullman strike
1901	United States Steel Corporation founded
1903	Ford Motor Company founded
1910	Ford Model T first marketed
1913	First moving assembly line begins operation at Ford

months for contempt of court in defying the injunction.

After the turn of the century, a number of battles occurred between workers and employers in the mining industry. Out of the western struggles emerged the Industrial Workers of the World (IWW), a radical organization that fused the Knights of Labor vision of worker solidarity with the tactics of strikes and sometimes sabotage. Using the rhetoric of class conflict—

"The final aim is revolution"—the IWW attracted far greater attention than its small membership warranted.

It must be emphasized that during the half-century following the Civil War, only a small fraction of American workers belonged to unions. Labor organizers took no interest in large segments of the industrial labor force and intentionally excluded others. Many unions, such as those of the AFL, were openly hostile toward women. Since the early years of industrialization in America, female workers had organized their own unions; some, such as the Collar Laundry Union of Troy, New York, organized in the 1860s, had been successful in carrying out strikes and achieving higher wages. The first broad-based women's union was the Women's Trade Union League (WTUL), founded in 1903. The WTUL worked for protective legislation for women workers, sponsored educational activities, and joined the cause for women's suffrage. Although the WTUL had some forceful working-class leaders—notably Agnes Nestor, a glove maker, Rose Schneiderman, a cap maker, and Mary Anderson, a shoe worker—it was dominated by middle-class women who had humane but generally nonmilitant purposes in helping working women. Then in the early 1920s, the WTUL fought a constitutional amendment guaranteeing equal rights to women, arguing that women needed protection from exploitation more than they needed equality. Such reasoning fit the assertion of males who argued that women belonged in their own sphere at home, out of the work force and out of unions. Because the WTUL backed away from active union organization, it lost the support of working class women, and by 1930 it had virtually dissolved.

> **Women, immigrants, and blacks in the labor movement**

Organized labor also excluded most immigrant and black workers. Some trade unions welcomed skilled immigrants—in fact, foreign-born craftsmen were prominent leaders of several unions—but only the Knights of Labor and the IWW had firm policies of accepting immigrants and blacks. A few AFL unions included blacks, but exclusion policies kept out the vast majority. Resentments already fueled by long-held prejudices increased when blacks and immigrants worked as strikebreakers. It is likely that few strikebreakers understood the full effects of such employment when they were recruited to fill the jobs of striking workers; but even for those who did, the lure of employment was too great to resist.

For most American workers, then, the machine age had dubious results. Industrial wages rose between 1877 and 1914, boosting purchasing power and enabling the creation of a mass market for standardized goods. Yet in 1900 most employees worked sixty hours a week at wages that averaged 20 cents an hour for skilled work and 10 cents an hour for unskilled work. Factory workers fortunate enough to hold a job all year could expect annual incomes of only $400 to $500. Moreover, as wages rose, living costs increased even faster. The industrial transformation had thrust the United States into international leadership in economic capability. But in factories as well as on farms, some people were beginning to question whether a system based on ever-greater profits was the best way for Americans to create a world of peace and prosperity.

Suggestions for further reading

GENERAL   Daniel J. Boorstin, *The Americans: The Democratic Experience* (1973); Thomas C. Cochran and William Miller, *The Age of Enterprise* (1942); Ray Ginger, *The Age of Excess* (1965); Samuel P. Hayes, *The Response to Industrialism* (1975).

TECHNOLOGY AND INVENTION   George H. Daniels, *Science and Society in America* (1971); Sigfried Giedion, *Mechanization Takes Command* (1948); Frank E. Hill, *Ford: The Times, the Man, the Company* (1954); Mat-

thew Josephson, *Edison* (1959); Leo Marx, *The Machine in the Garden: Technology and the Pastoral Ideal* (1964); Elting E. Morison, *Men, Machines, and Modern Times* (1966); Nathan Rosenberg, *Technology and American Economic Growth* (1972).

INDUSTRIALISM, INDUSTRIALISTS, AND CORPORATE GROWTH   Stuart Bruchey, *Growth of the Modern Economy* (1973); Alfred D. Chandler, *Strategy and Structure: Chapters in the History of American Industrial Enterprise* (1966); David F. Hawkes, *John D.: The Founding Father of the Rockefellers* (1980); Robert Higgs, *The Transformation of the American Economy, 1865–1914* (1971); Matthew Josephson, *The Robber Barons* (1934); Edward C. Kirkland, *Industry Comes of Age* (1961); Glen Porter, *The Rise of Big Business* (1973); Joseph Wall, *Andrew Carnegie* (1970).

ATTITUDES TOWARD INDUSTRIALISM   Sidney Fine, *Laissez Faire and the General Welfare State* (1956); Louis Galambos and Barbara Barron Spence, *The Public Image of Big Business in America* (1975); Richard Hofstadter, *Social Darwinism in American Thought,* rev. ed. (1955).

WORK AND LABOR ORGANIZATION   Alan Dawley, *Class and Community* (1977); Melvyn Dubofsky, *Industrialism and the American Worker* (1975); Philip S. Foner, *The Great Labor Uprising of 1877* (1977); Herbert G. Gutman, *Work, Culture and Society in Industrializing America* (1976); Tamara K. Hareven, *Family Time and Industrial Time: The Relationship Between the Family and Work in a New England Industrial Community* (1982); Susan Estabrook Kennedy, *If All We Did Was To Weep At Home: A History of White Working Class Women in America* (1979); Harold Livesay, *Samuel Gompers and Organized Labor in America* (1978); Milton Meltzer, *Bread and Roses: The Struggle of American Labor, 1865–1915* (1967); David Montgomery, *Workers' Control in America: Studies in the History of Work, Technology, and Labor Struggles* (1979); Daniel J. Walkowitz, *Worker City, Company Town* (1978); Barbara Mayer Wertheimer, *We Were There: The Story of Working Women in America* (1977); Irwin Yellowitz, *Industrialization and the American Labor Movement* (1977).

18

THE CITY AND
EVERYDAY LIFE,
1877-1920

The lure of the city and its appeal over the countryside were expressed by a character in George Fitch's play *The City* when she exclaimed, "Who wants to smell new-mown hay, if he can breathe in gasoline on Fifth Avenue instead! *Think* of being able to go out on the street and *see some one you didn't know by sight!*"

Urbanization brought far more, however, than seeing *"some one you didn't know by sight."* With the growth of the city came the mass migration of Europeans, as well as rural Americans, the myriad of problems associated with rapidly expanding pluralistic cities, and the efforts of political bosses and urban reformers to make their communities function.

The reading, buying, and entertainment habits of Americans were also changed by life in the city. New products were created and advertisers established communities of consumers. Commercial entertainment replaced the church social, and writers developed plots and characters more applicable to the tastes of city dwellers. In short, modern American society—a society largely shaped by the ways people built their cities and adjusted to the new urban environment—was emerging.

These fundamental changes in the national landscape were brought about by both industrialization and urbanization. They occurred in the half-century between the end of Reconstruction and the end of the First World War. From a demographic perspective, the population shifts were dramatic. In the United States of 1880 seven out of every ten people lived on farms or in towns with fewer than 2,500 people. By 1920, a milestone had been reached: a majority of the people—51.4 percent—dwelled in cities.

The birth of the modern city

By the first decade of the twentieth century, the modern American city was reaching maturity. From Boston to San Francisco, developed areas sprawled outward several miles from the original central core. No longer did walking distance determine a city's size, and no longer did different social groups live physically close together—poor near rich, immigrant near native, black near white. Instead, cities were divided into distinct districts: working-class neighborhoods, black ghettos, a ring of suburbs, business districts.

| New shape of the city |

Two forces, mass transportation and economic change, were responsible for this new arrangement. Steam-powered commuter railroads had appeared in a few cities during the 1850s and 1860s, but not until the late 1870s did in-

ventors begin to mechanize municipal mass transit. The first power-driven devices were cable cars—carriages that traveled over tracks by clamping onto a moving underground wire. Cheaper than horse cars, cable cars could also haul passengers up and down steep hills. By the 1890s, however, electric-powered streetcars were replacing the early forms of mass transit. Between 1890 and 1902, total mileage of electrified track in American cities grew from 1,300 to 22,000 miles.

In a few cities, transit companies raised part of their track onto stilts, enabling vehicles to travel through jammed downtown districts without interference from other traffic. And in Boston, New York, and Philadelphia, mass transit companies dug underground passages for their cars, again to avoid tie-ups and delays. These elevated railroads and subways, however, were extremely expensive to construct. They thus appeared only in the few cities where companies could amass enough capital to build them and where there were enough riders to create high profits.

Mass transportation lines launched millions of urban dwellers into outlying neighborhoods and created a commuting public. Now those

Beginnings of urban sprawl

who could afford the fare— usually five cents a ride— could live outside the crowded, dirty central city and still return there for work, shopping, and entertainment. Working-class families, whose incomes rarely topped a dollar a day, found even the nickel fare too high and could not take advantage of the streetcars. But for the growing middle class, a home in a quiet, tree-lined neighborhood became a real possibility. Between 1890 and 1920, for example, developers in the Chicago area opened 800,000 new lots. A home several miles from downtown was inconvenient, but the benefits seemed to outweigh the costs. As one suburbanite wrote in 1902, "It may be a little more

difficult for us to attend the opera, but the robin in my elm tree struck a higher note and a sweeter one yesterday than any *prima donna* ever reached."

Urban sprawl was essentially unplanned. Investors who bought residential land in anticipation of settlement paid little attention to the need for parks, traffic control, and public services. Moreover, construction of mass transit lines was guided by the profit motive and thus served the urban public unevenly. Streetcar lines serviced mainly those neighborhoods that promised the most riders—whose fares, in other words, would provide dividends for stockholders.

Public transportation altered commercial as well as residential patterns. As consumers moved outward along mass transit lines, businesses followed. Branches of downtown department stores and banks joined groceries, theaters, drugstores, taverns, and specialty shops to create neighborhood shopping centers. Meanwhile, the urban core became the work zone, where offices, stores, warehouses, and factories hulked over streets clogged with traffic.

Cities also became the main arenas for industrial growth, generating and attracting concentrations of economic power. As centers of

Urban-industrial development

resources, labor, transportation, and communications, cities provided everything factories needed. Capital accumulated by the early commercial enterprises of cities was used for industrial investment, and urban populations furnished consumers for new products. Thus urban growth and industrialization wound together in a mutually productive spiral. The further industrialization advanced, the more opportunities it created for work and investment in cities. Increased opportunity drew more people to cities; as workers and as consumers, they in turn fueled further industrialization.

Urban growth and industrial development transformed the national economy and freed the United States from dependence on European capital and manufactured goods. Imports and foreign investments still flowed into the country. But by the second decade of the twentieth century, cities and their factories, stores, and banks were converting the United States from a debtor agricultural nation into a major industrial and financial power.

Peopling the cities

The population of any given place can grow in three ways: by the extension of its borders to include nearby land and people; by natural increase—an excess of births over deaths; and by migration—an excess of in-migrants over out-migrants. From the end of the Civil War until the early 1900s, many cities annexed nearby suburbs and other areas, thereby increasing their populations. More important, annexation added land where new city dwellers could live. Cities like Chicago, Minneapolis, and Cincinnati incorporated hundreds of undeveloped square miles into their borders in the 1880s, only to see them fill up in succeeding decades. Although annexation did increase urban populations, its major effect was to enlarge the physical size of cities.

| How cities grew |

Natural increase did not account for more than 20 percent of any city's population increase in any given decade. Instead, migration and immigration made by far the greatest contribution to urban population growth. Each year millions of people were on the move, many of them lured by the cities' promise of opportunity. Although many farm families left rural America for the nation's cities, most of the urban newcomers were immigrants from Europe. A great number of immigrants did not intend to stay. They hoped instead to make enough money to return home and live in greater comfort and security. For every hundred foreigners who entered the country, around thirty left. Still, most of the 26 million European immigrants who ar-

| Major waves of migration and immigration |

rived between 1870 and 1920 stayed, and the great majority settled in cities, where they helped to shape modern American culture (see map).

The influx of immigrants came in two waves. The first began in the 1840s and crested in the 1880s, and the second climaxed between 1900 and 1910. The first wave consisted mainly of Protestants and Catholics from Germany, Scandinavia, Ireland, and England, most of whom entered through eastern ports. At the same time a small number of Chinese and Mexicans arrived in the West and Southwest. The second wave contained mainly Catholics and Jews from eastern and southern Europe, plus smaller contingents from Canada and Mexico. Although immigrants from northern and western Europe continued to arrive after 1890, the shift between the two waves was dramatic. In 1882, for example, 87 percent of the immigrants came from northern or western Europe; a quarter of a century later 81 percent came from southern or eastern Europe. Together, the two waves of immigration helped swell the number of foreign-born people in the United States from 5.7 million in 1870 to 14 million in 1920.

The differences between the two waves of immigrants were in many ways more imagined than real. Many natives feared that the strange customs, non-Protestant religions, illiteracy, and poverty of the "new" immigrants made them less desirable and assimilable than the "old" immigrants, whose languages and beliefs seemed less alien. In reality, however, the old and new immigrants resembled each other in many ways. The majority of both groups were young males who settled in cities. Most lived initially in the old districts of the central city vacated by residents who had moved to newly developed outlying neighborhoods. Perhaps most important, all immigrants brought with them memories of their homelands and adjusted to American life in light of those memories. In their new surroundings immigrants anchored their lives on what they knew best: their culture. Many immigrant neighborhoods were made up

| Immigrant cultures |

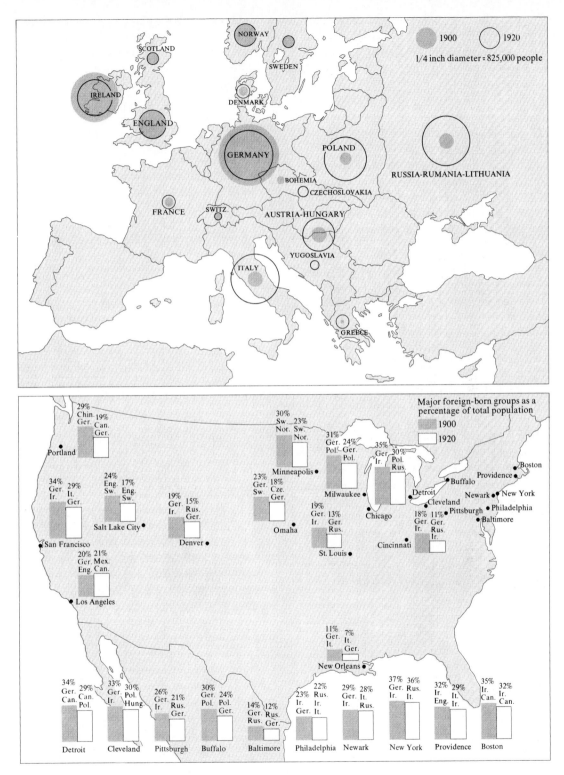

Sources of foreign-born population, 1900 and 1920

277

of enclaves of Irish immigrants from the same county, Italians from the same province, and Russian Jews from the same *shtetl* (village). In these transplanted communities, Old World customs persisted. People practiced their religions as they always had, held traditional feasts and pageants, married within their group, and pursued old feuds with people from rival villages and provinces.

Yet the very diversity of American cities forced most immigrants to modify their attitudes and habits. Few newcomers could avoid contact with people different from themselves, and few could prevent such contacts from altering their traditional ways of life. Although many foreigners identified themselves by their village or region of birth, and organized their mutual benefit and fraternal societies along these lines, some immigrant institutions, like newspapers and churches, had to appeal to an entire nationalist group in order to survive. Immigrants struggled to maintain their native languages and to pass them down to younger generations, but English was taught in the schools and needed on the job; it soon penetrated nearly every community. And because the goods available in America often differed from those of the homeland, immigrants were forced to adjust their lifestyles to resemble those of other Americans. They continued to cook ethnic meals using American foods, but many bought the ready-made clothing and mass-produced furniture that were commonplace in the larger society.

The influx of so many immigrants between 1870 and 1920 transformed the United States from a basically Protestant nation into a society of Protestants, Catholics, and Jews. Newcomers from Italy, Hungary, and what would become Czechoslovakia, Yugoslavia, and Poland joined the Irish and Germans to boost the proportion of Catholics in several large cities. German and eastern European immigrants gave New York one of the largest Jewish populations in the world.

In the 1880s, another group of migrants be-

gan to move into American cities. Thousands of

| Black migration to the cities |

rural blacks moved northward and westward, fleeing crop liens, violence, and political oppression and seeking better employment. Although their numbers would grow much larger after 1915, thirty-two cities contained ten thousand or more blacks by 1900, and 79 percent of all blacks outside the South lived in cities. Black migrants resembled foreign immigrants in their peasant backgrounds and economic motivations, but they differed in several important ways. Because very few factories would employ blacks, most black workers found jobs in the service sector–cleaning, cooking, carting. Also, because the majority of jobs in domestic and personal service were traditionally female jobs, black women outnumbered black men in most cities.

Together the three major migrant groups that peopled American cities–native whites, foreigners, and native blacks–sowed the seeds of modern American culture, to which each group made important contributions. Cities nurtured a rich cultural variety: American folk music and literature, Italian cuisine, Irish comedy, Yiddish theater, Afro-American jazz and dance, and much more. Like their predecessors, newcomers in the late nineteenth century changed their environment as much as they were changed by it.

Straining to meet urban needs

The migration patterns and economic and technological changes of the late nineteenth century segmented urban society into racial, ethnic, and class divisions. Outward residential sprawl separated the most advantaged classes from the jammed inner-city districts housing the least advantaged. Late-nineteenth-century American cities seemed to harbor all the evils that plagued the modern world: crowding, disease,

The Lower East Side of New York City, home of thousands of Russian Jews and other immigrants, was one of the most famous ethnic districts in the nation. Inside the tenements people were jammed to-gether in alarming squalor. But the streets were always alive with peddlers and pedestrians, giving the area a rich cultural fabric. Photographed in the first decade of the twentieth century.   Library of Congress.

crime, poverty, decay, and other unpleasant conditions that result when large numbers of people are packed tightly together. These problems were compounded by rapid growth and by the fact that neither government nor the marketplace was willing or equipped to handle them.

One of the most persistent shortcomings of American cities has been their failure to provide adequate housing to all who need it. This failure has deep roots in nineteenth-century urban development. The low-paying jobs of most working-class household heads forced urban newcomers to rent their living quarters. Few could afford to buy or build a house. Low income families adjusted to high housing costs and short supply by sharing space and expenses. Thus it became common in many big cities for a one-family apartment to be occupied by two or three families or by one family plus a number of paying boarders.

Inside many buildings, living conditions were intolerable. The largest rooms were barely ten feet wide, and interior rooms either had no windows at all or opened onto narrow shafts that

> **Housing problems**

bred vermin and rotten odors. Few buildings had indoor plumbing, coal-burning stoves were the only source of heat, and privacy was nonexistent.

In several places acute housing problems aroused concerned citizens to mount reform campaigns. New York State took the lead in 1867, 1879, and 1901 by legislating light, ventilation, and safety codes for new tenement buildings. A few housing reformers, such as Jacob Riis and Lawrence Veiller, advocated housing low-income families in model tenements, with more spacious, airier rooms and better facilities. Model tenements, however, required landlords and investors to accept lower profits, a sacrifice few were willing to make. And neither humanitarian reformers nor public officials would consider government support of better housing, fearing such a step would undermine private enterprise.

Scientific and technological advances enhanced the quality of urban life. Following the general acceptance of the germ theory of disease, cities established more efficient water purification and sewage disposal systems. Public health regulations helped to reduce the death rate for tuberculosis and to control such diseases as cholera, typhoid fever, and diphtheria. Modernized firefighting equipment and streetlighting made the cities safer places in which to live. None of these improvements, however, lightened the burden of poverty borne by large numbers of city dwellers.

Since colonial days, Americans have never agreed on how much responsibility the general public should assume for poor relief. In the late nineteenth and early twentieth centuries, many people held to the traditional beliefs that anyone could escape poverty through hard work and clean living and that poverty was inevitable only because some people were weaker than others. Yet close observation of the poor caused some social welfare workers to conclude that people's environments, rather than their personal defects, caused poverty.

Even more than crowding and pauperism, crime and disorder alarmed Americans and nur-tured fears that urban growth, especially the growth of slums, was corrupting the nation.

Crime and violence The more cities grew, it seemed, the more they shook with violence. Native whites were quick to blame immigrants and blacks for the so-called crime wave that swept the nation. Yet it is possible that as a greater proportion of the population concentrated in cities, crime merely became more conspicuous and sensational rather than more prevalent. To be sure, urban wealth and the mingling of different kinds of people provided new opportunities for lawless behavior. But how do such activities compare to the lawlessness and brutality of backwoods mining camps and southern plantations? Moreover, in spite of distress over Irish bank-robbery gangs, German pick-pockets, and Italian Black Hand murderers, there is little evidence that more immigrants than natives populated the rogues' gallery.

One thing does seem certain; city life in the late nineteenth and early twentieth centuries supported the thesis that there is a tradition of violence in the United States. Cities served as arenas for many of the era's worst riots. Besides the violence that often erupted during strikes or times of depression, there were race riots: in Wilmington, North Carolina (1898); in Atlanta, Georgia (1906); in Springfield, Illinois (1908). In the Southwest and on the Pacific Coast, Chinese and Mexican immigrants often felt the vicious sting of native intolerance.

Solving the mounting problems of city life seemed to many Americans to demand greater government action. Thus city governments passed more laws and ordinances that regulated housing, provided poverty relief, and expanded police power. Yet public responsibility always ended at the boundaries of private property. Constrained by laissez faire, local governments could do little to provide a better life for many of their citizens. Eventually some advances in housing construction, sanitation, and medical care did reach slum dwellers. But for most people, the only hope was to look to the next generation or to move elsewhere.

Promises of mobility

In the half-century between the Civil War and the First World War, Baptist minister Russell Conwell delivered the same sermon more than six thousand times to untold millions across the United States. Titled "Acres of Diamonds," his immensely popular lecture affirmed the widespread belief that any American could achieve success. People did not have to look very far for riches, Conwell preached; acres of diamonds lay at everyone's feet. Conwell declared to his audiences that it was one's "Christian and Godly" duty to attain riches. But how possible was it for people actually to improve their lot and fulfill that duty?

Basically, there were three ways a person could get ahead: occupational advancement (and the higher income that accompanied it); acquisition of property (and the potential for greater wealth it represented); and migration to an area of better conditions and greater opportunity. In the period between 1877 and 1920, these options were open chiefly to white men. Although many women worked, owned property, and migrated, their social standing was usually defined by the men in their lives—their husbands, fathers, or other kin. Many women did improve their economic status by marrying men with wealth or potential, but other avenues were mostly closed. Men and women who were Afro-American, American Indian, Mexican-American, or members of other racial minorities had even fewer opportunities for success. Pinned to the bottom of society by prejudice, these groups were expected to accept their inherited station.

To a large number of Americans, however, the extensive urban and industrial expansion of the late nineteenth century should have offered broad opportunity for occupational mobility. Thousands of small businesses were needed to | **Occupational mobility** | supply goods and services to burgeoning urban populations. And corporations required a variety of managerial and clerical personnel. Only a very few traveled the rags to riches path, but considerable movement occurred along the path from rags to moderate success.

Rates of occupational mobility in late nineteenth- and early twentieth-century American communities were slow but steady. Some people slipped from a higher to a lower rung of the occupational ladder, but rates of upward movement were almost always double the downward rates. Immigrants generally experienced lower rates of upward mobility and higher rates of downward mobility than natives did. Still, regardless of birthplace, the chances for a white male to rise occupationally over the course of his career or to have a higher-status job than his father had were relatively good.

In addition to or instead of advancing occupationally, a person could achieve social mobility by acquiring property. But property was not | **Acquisition of property** | easy to acquire in turn-of-the-century America. Banks and savings institutions were far stricter in their lending practices than they would become after the 1930s, when the federal government began to bolster real estate financing. Mortgage loans carried high interest rates and short repayment periods. Nevertheless, a general rise in wage rates enabled many families to build savings accounts, which could be used for down payments on property. Indeed, the 1900 federal census noted that the United States had the highest home ownership rate among all Western nations except Denmark, Norway, and Sweden.

Finally, each year millions of families tried to improve their living conditions by packing up and moving elsewhere. In general, Americans | **Residential mobility** | followed the maxim that movement means improvement. The urge to move affected every region, every city. From Boston to San Francisco, from Minneapolis to San Antonio, no more than half the families residing in the city at any point in time could be found there ten years later.

In addition to population movement between cities, extraordinary numbers of people moved from one residence to another within the same city. In contemporary American communities, one in every five families moves in any given year. A hundred years ago, the proportion was closer to one in four, or even one in three. Population turnover affected almost every neighborhood, every ethnic and occupational group.

Rapid residential flux undermined the stability of even the most homogeneous neighborhoods. Rarely did a single nationality comprise a clean-cut majority in any large area, even when

| *Ethnic neighborhoods and ghettos* | that area was known as Little Italy, Jewtown, Over-the-Rhine, or Greektown. Residential change dispersed im- |

migrants from their original areas of settlement into many different neighborhoods. In New York, Boston, and other eastern ports, ethnically homogeneous districts did exist, and people tended to change residences within those districts rather than move away from them. Elsewhere, however, most immigrant families lived dispersed in ethnically mixed neighborhoods rather than in ghettos.

The true meaning of the term *ghetto* as a place of enforced residence from which escape is difficult applied to only one major urban group in this era, black Americans. Prejudice and discrimination not only trapped blacks at the bottom of the occupational ladder but operated in housing markets to limit their residential opportunities. Whites organized protective associations that pledged not to sell homes in white neighborhoods to blacks, and occasionally used violence to scare away black families who did move in. Such efforts seldom worked. Whites who lived on the edges of black neighborhoods often fled, leaving their homes and apartments to be sold and rented to black occupants. By 1920 ten Chicago census tracts were over 75 percent black. In Detroit, Cleveland, Los Angeles, and Washington, D.C., two-thirds or more of the total black population lived in only two or

three wards. Within these districts, blacks nurtured distinct cultural institutions that helped them to adjust to urban life: storefront churches, business and educational organizations, social clubs, and saloons. But the ghettos also bred frustration and escapism, the result of stunted opportunity and racial bigotry. Color, more than any other factor, made the urban experiences of blacks different from those of whites.

All groups, however, including blacks, could and did move—if not from one part of the city to another, then from one city to another. Americans were always seeking greener pastures, and the hope that things might be better somewhere else acted as a kind of safety valve, relieving some of the tensions and frustrations that simmered inside the city. At times these tensions and frustrations erupted into violence; more often, people simply left to seek a better life elsewhere.

The rise of urban boss politics

The sudden growth and mounting rivalry among social and economic interest groups that occurred in the late nineteenth century mired cities in a governmental swamp. From suburbs to slums, burgeoning populations, business expansion, and technological change created urgent needs for water, sewers, police and fire protection, schools, parks, and many other services. Such needs simply strained government institutions beyond their capacities. Furthermore, city governments approached these needs in a disorganized fashion.

Power thrives on confusion and out of this governmental chaos arose the political machine.

| *Political machines and bosses* | Unlike political parties, which ideally exist for higher purposes than merely electing their candidates to of- |

fice, machines were organizations whose main goal was getting and keeping political power. In order to achieve that goal, a machine had to win popular support. Machine politicians routinely used bribery and graft to further their ends. But they could not have succeeded if they had not provided relief, security, and municipal services to large numbers of people. By doing so, machine politicians alleviated many urban problems and accomplished things that other agencies had been unable or unwilling to attempt.

Machines were also beneficiaries of the new urban conditions. As cities grew larger and economically more complex, business leaders either vied to use government to advance their own interests or withdrew from local affairs to pursue their interests in interurban or interregional economic organizations. At the same time, hordes of newcomers, often unskilled and foreign-born, crowded into the cities. Enfranchised by liberal voting qualifications, the men of these groups became a substantial political force. These circumstances bred a new kind of leader: the political boss. Conflicting interest groups needed brokers who could bypass governmental stalemates, and urban newcomers had needs that required government attention. Bosses and machines filled those needs.

The system rested on a popular base and was held together by loyalty and service. City machines were coalitions of smaller machines that derived their power directly from the neighborhoods, particularly inner-city neighborhoods inhabited by the native and immigrant working classes. In return for votes, bosses provided jobs, built parks and bathhouses, distributed food to the needy, and helped when someone ran afoul of the law. Such personalized service cultivated mass attachment to the boss; never before had government or public leaders assumed such responsibility for people in need.

In order to finance their largesse and support their system, bosses exchanged favors for votes or money. Their power over local government enabled machines to control the letting of contracts, the granting of utility or streetcar franchises, and the distribution of city jobs. Recipients of city business and jobs were expected to repay the machine with a portion of their profits or salaries and to cast supporting votes on election day. Bosses called this process gratitude; critics called it graft. Moreover, machines dispensed favors to illegal businesses as well as legitimate ones. Payoffs from gambling, prostitution, and illegal liquor traffic were important sources of machine revenue. In an era when unemployment insurance and welfare were virtually unknown, however, machines were valued despite these shortcomings.

Civic reform

Machine politics between 1877 and 1920 brought some order to city government, met some of the needs of immigrants and other inner-city residents, and lined the pockets of some leaders and their business allies. But the boss system also alarmed the established classes inhabiting the outlying neighborhoods and sensitized many men and women to the problems, real or imagined, of urban growth. At the same time the bosses were consolidating their power, a reform movement was organizing to destroy political machines and improve the quality of urban life. Anxious over the mounting poverty, crowding, and disorder that seemed to accompany population expansion, and convinced that urban services were making taxes too high, civic reformers organized to root out bosses and to install more responsible leaders at the helm of urban administration.

The antiboss, promorality tinge of these good-government groups was accompanied by a distinct antidemocratic bias. To such early reform leaders as E. L. Godkin, editor of *The Nation,* and Moorfield Storey, a Boston lawyer, electing the "best men" to office meant replacing bosses with people like themselves—people of wealth, education, and refinement. They believed they could cleanse politics and topple the machine system by reviving property, literacy, and residency restrictions to ensure that only the most qualified people could vote.

The late nineteenth-century emphasis on eliminating waste and inefficiency in the industrial sector had an impact on reformers' thinking. Business-minded reformers hoped to make government more efficient by running it like a business. In fact, the major accomplishments of reform leaders were to reduce budgets, make government employees work longer, and cut taxes. As another means of introducing sound business principles to government, civic reformers supported a number of structural changes, such as city-manager and commission forms of government and nonpartisan, citywide election of officials. Each of these reforms was aimed at removing politics from government. Experts would control decision making at the local level, and the ward and neighborhood power bases of the bosses would be undermined.

A few reformers did move beyond structural changes to a genuine concern for social problems. Hazen S. Pingree, mayor of Detroit from 1889 to 1896; Samuel "Golden Rule" Jones, mayor of Toledo from 1897 to 1904; and Thomas L. Johnson, mayor of Cleveland from 1901 to 1909, worked to provide jobs for poor people, to reduce charges by transit and utilities companies, and to establish greater governmental responsibility for the welfare of all citizens. Some supported public ownership of gas, electric, and telephone companies—a quasi-socialistic reform that alienated their business allies. But most civic reformers could not match the bosses' political savvy and soon found themselves out of power.

Nevertheless, the seeds of social reform were beginning to sprout outside of politics. Convinced that laissez-faire ideology could no longer work in a complex urban-industrial world, a number of men and women—mostly young and middle-class—embarked on campaigns for social betterment. Driven by an urge to identify and address urban problems, these people thought they could control and solve those problems. Their attempts laid the foundation for the progressive reforms that would become a national movement in the early twentieth century.

Perhaps the most ambitious and inspiring features of the urban reform movement were settlement houses. Patterned after London's Toynbee Hall, settlements were efforts by young, educated, middle-class men and women to live in slum neighborhoods and bridge the gulf between classes, in hopes that people could learn from each other. Early settlement leaders such as Jane Addams, Florence Kelley, and Graham Taylor wanted to improve the lives of working-class people by helping them to obtain an education, an appreciation of the arts, better jobs, and better housing. They provided a wide array of services, from vocational classes to child care for working mothers. But they also attempted to remake the working-class in their own middle-class image.

The National Consumers League provided another reform outlet for educated upper- and middle-class women. Founded by Josephine Shaw, a socially prominent Massachusetts widow, the Consumers League initially worked to improve the wages and working conditions of young women who worked in department stores. After Florence Kelley became the league's general secretary, the organization expanded its activities to include protection of child laborers and licensing of food vendors.

Urban reformers wanted to save cities, not abolish them. They believed that urban life could be improved by restoring feelings of service and cooperation among all citizens. Reformers often failed to realize, however, that cities were diverse places where different people had different views of what reform actually meant. As a result of such attitudes, the accomplishments of urban reform were mixed: the American reform tradition merged idealism with naiveté and insensitivity.

The legacy of urbanism

Urban America seldom functioned smoothly; in fact, there really was no coherent urban community, only a collection of subcommunities. As a result of immigration and urbanization, the United States had become a culturally pluralistic society. Literary critic Randolph Bourne dubbed the United States "a cosmopolitan federation of national colonies." This kind of reasoning produced hyphenated identifications: people considered themselves Irish-American, Italo-American, Polish-American, and the like.

| Cultural pluralism |

Pluralism and its attendant interest-group loyalties made politics an important institution. If America was not a melting pot—a place where various immigrant and racial groups had become assimilated—then different groups were competing with each other for power, wealth, and status. Often they turned to politics to protect their interests. In general, groups that opposed the interference of government in matters of personal liberty identified with the Democratic party, while those that believed government could be an agent of moral reform identified with the Republican party. The former included immigrant Catholics and Jews, who believed that God and faith should guide their behavior through ritual and sacraments. The latter consisted mostly of native and immigrant Protestants, who believed that salvation could best be achieved by purging the world of evil and that legislation might be necessary to protect people from sin.

| Cultural-political alignments |

Adherents of these two cultural traditions battled over how much control government should exercise over people's lives. The most provocative issue was use of leisure time and celebration of Sunday, the Lord's day. In the Puritan tradition, natives supported blue laws designed to prevent the desecration of the Sabbath by prohibiting various commercial and recreational activities. European immigrants, accustomed to feasting and playing after church, fought Sunday closings of saloons and other restrictions on the only day they had free for fun and relaxation. Similar splits developed elsewhere over public versus parochial schools and prohibition versus the free availability of liquor.

Such conflicts illustrate why local and state politics were so heated in the late nineteenth and early twentieth centuries. Some people carried polarization to its extreme and tried to suppress everything new and allegedly un-American. In several communities during the 1890s, the American Protective Association achieved considerable influence by attacking "the diabolical works of the Catholic Church" and demanding an end to immigration. Some of this sentiment influenced national legislation. In 1882, Congress bowed to pressure from West Coast nativists and prohibited Chinese immigration for ten years. In 1902 a new law excluded the Chinese permanently. And periodic attempts were made to prevent foreign-born citizens from voting by imposing literacy tests on them.

Such efforts generally failed, though, because too many people had a stake in the country's cultural diversity. By 1920, immigrants and their offspring outnumbered natives in many cities, and the national economy depended on the new workers and consumers. They had helped to make the United States an urban nation with a rich and varied culture. And modern American political liberalism, with its sensitivity to individual liberty, owes much to them.

Standards of living

If the affluence of a society can be measured by how quickly it converts luxuries into com-

A middle-class girl poses with her newly acquired Christmas gifts. New mass-production and marketing techniques, developed in the late ninteenth century, made such materialism possible. Library of Congress.

monplace articles of everyday life, the United States was indeed becoming affluent in the years between 1880 and 1920. In 1880, for example, almost no one smoked cigarettes, only wealthy women could afford silk stockings, and only residents of Florida, Texas, and California could enjoy the luxury of fresh oranges. In 1921, however, Americans smoked 43 billion cigarettes,

bought 217 million pairs of silk stockings, and ate 248 crates of oranges per 1,000 people. How did Americans afford these goods? How did changes in standards of living come about?

What people can afford depends largely but not entirely on their resources and incomes. Data for the period from 1880 to 1920 are scattered, but there is no doubt that incomes rose.

Chapter 18: The city and everyday life, 1877–1920

As always, the rich got richer. But incomes also rose among the middle classes. For example, be-

Personal income

tween 1890 and 1910 the average pay of clerical workers rose from $848 a year to $1,156 and that of postal clerks and carriers from $878 to $1,049. After the turn of the century, employees of the federal executive branch were averaging $1,072 a year, and college professors $1,100—not handsome sums, but much more than manual workers received. With these incomes, the middle class could afford relatively comfortable housing. A six- to seven-room house cost around $3,000 to buy or build and $15 to $20 per month to rent.

Significantly, average salaries for public school teachers almost doubled between 1890 and 1910. But their extreme meagerness—$256 in 1890, $492 in 1910—reflected continued exploitation of women, who made up the majority of the profession. School teachers were middle class in education and employment, working class in income level.

Wages for industrial workers increased as well, though they varied widely and income figures were deceiving. On the average, the annual wages of industrial workers rose from $486 in 1890 to $558 in 1910. By contrast, farm laborers averaged only $336 in 1910. Regional variations were wide in almost all industries. Wages tended to be much lower in the South than in the Northeast, and generally higher in the Midwest and West.

But wage increases mean little if living costs rise as fast or faster than incomes. In fact, this is

Cost of living

what happened in the United States around the turn of the century. Rarely did the income for a particular occupation rise at the same rate as the cost of living. Thus, particularly for the working class, it was becoming harder, not easier, to pay for life's necessities.

How then could Americans afford the new goods and services that the industrial age offered? Obviously, many could not. A working-class family could raise its income and partake at least partially in consumer society by sending

Expansion of the labor force

children and women into the labor market. Thus in a household where the father made $600 a year, the wages of other family members might lift the total income to $800 or $900. Moreover, many families earned an extra $200 or $300 per year by renting household space to boarders and lodgers. These means of increasing family income allowed people to save more and to spend more.

A new trend in the late nineteenth century was the increased number of southern women who worked for wages. By the 1890s, southern women, most of them white (large numbers of black women were already employed as domestics) were flocking to jobs not only in the rapidly multiplying textile mills but also in binderies, paper factories, and cigarette factories. In addition, thousands of women nationwide were being hired for new white-collar jobs as clerks, stenographers, salespersons, and the like—jobs created by the growth of retail establishments and corporate record keeping.

Most female workers were young, unmarried, and poorly paid. Saleswomen earned only $6 or $7 a week; factory workers often received even less. Some married women worked in factories or offices, but more earned money at home. Censuses and other surveys often missed the large numbers of mothers who took in laundry, strung beads and linked chains for costume jewelry, made artificial flowers, or did mending and tailoring. Such jobs enabled women to tend to their household tasks and earn money as well.

Medical and technological developments eased some of life's struggles. Advances in medicine and better living conditions sharply reduced

Life expectancy

death rates and extended the life span. Between 1900 and 1920, for example, life expectancy rose from 51 to 56.5 years for women, and from 48 to 54 for men. During the same period there were spectacular declines in the death rates from diseases such as typhoid, diphtheria, influenza (except for a harsh epidemic in 1918 and 1919), tuberculosis, and intestinal ailments—diseases that had been the scourge of earlier generations. There were, however, significant increases in deaths from cancer, diabetes, and heart disease. Americans also found new ways to kill themselves: although the suicide rate remained about the same, homicides and automobile deaths soared between 1900 and 1920.

Family life

Though the overwhelming majority of Americans continued to live their lives within a family, this most basic of social institutions underwent considerable strain during the industrial era. As American society became more affluent and complex, it generated new institutions— schools, social clubs, political organizations, and others—that competed with the family to provide nurture, education, companionship, and security. Yet the family retained its fundamental usefulness as a cushion in a hard, uncertain world.

Throughout modern Western history, most people have lived in two overlapping kinds of basic units: the household and the family. A *household* is a residential unit, a group of related and/or unrelated people who live in the same abode. A *family* is a group of people related by kinship, some of whom typically live together. The distinction between household and family is important in describing how Americans lived in the late nineteenth and early twentieth centuries.

At the most elementary level, Americans between 1877 and 1920 grouped themselves in traditional ways. As in the past, the vast majority of American households consisted of *nuclear families*—usually a married couple with or without children and including no other relatives. About 15 to 20 percent of households consisted of *extended families,* which might include grandparents, grandchildren, aunts and uncles, in-laws, cousins, or combinations of such relatives. About 5 percent of the population lived alone.

The relative size of nuclear families did change over time, however. In 1880 the birth rate was 39.9 live births per 1,000 people; by 1920 it had dropped to 27.7. The reasons for this decline remain unclear. The pattern seems to have been that women in the settled eastern areas of the country were ending childbearing at an earlier age than were women in western areas. Possibly the greater availability of arable land in the West encouraged larger families; differences in a child's productivity may also have had an effect. On the farms, where children could work at home or in the fields at an early age, a new child contributed a new set of hands to the family work force. But in the wage-based eastern economy, children could not contribute significantly to the family income for many years.

Though fertility rates among blacks, immigrants, and rural dwellers were consistently higher than those of white native urban dwellers, the birth rates of all groups fell dramatically. As a result, families with six or eight children became less common; three or four children became more common. The size of the nuclear family had declined and had done so over a short time span.

In spite of the predominance of the nuclear family, the household typically expanded and contracted drastically over the lifetime of a given family. First, the size of the family fluctuated as children were born, and later left home. Second, the process of leaving home made for huge numbers of young people—and some older people—who lived as boarders and lodgers, especially in cities. Middle- and working-class families commonly took in boarders to help pay the rent or to occupy unused rooms vacated by grown children.

The practice of boarding stirred middle-class concern about health and morality. Some reformers complained of "the lodger evil." Yet for many immigrants and young people who had left home, boarding was a transitional stage of life. For such people a quasi-family environment was provided.

Within both nuclear and extended families kinship had important functions, especially for immigrants and others in need. At a time when welfare and service agencies were rare, the family continued to be the institution to which people could turn. Immigrants, for example, often took in newly arrived relatives. Nearby family members could help each other out with child care, meals, shopping, advice, consolation, and the like. Relatives also obtained jobs for each other.

The obligations of kinship, however, were not always welcome or even helpful. Immigrant families often put pressure on last-born children to stay at home and care for aging parents, a practice that stifled those children's opportunities for education, marriage, and economic independence. Tensions also developed when one relative felt another was not helping out enough. Nevertheless, kinship, for better or worse, provided people a means of coping with the stresses of urban industrial society.

At the turn of the century, family life and its functions were both changing and holding firm. New institutions were assuming tasks formerly performed by the family. Schools were making education more of a community responsibility. Employment agencies, personnel offices, labor unions, and legislatures were beginning to take responsibility for employee recruitment and job security. In addition, migration and a soaring divorce rate seemed to be splitting families apart: 19,633 divorces were granted in the United States in 1880; by 1920, that number had grown to 167,105. Yet in the face of these changes, the family remained a resilient institution.

The birth of mass culture

Before the end of the nineteenth century, what people consumed, talked about, and did with their spare time were individual matters, often dictated by subsistence needs. Social institutions were local, and contacts with the broader world were limited. But the revolutions in transportation, industrialization, and urbanization upset these traditional patterns. Technological and industrial changes created a variety of new standardized goods and services, as well as a more developed money economy. Urbanization expanded the nation's cultural centers. The most common form of nonwork mass activity was still church attendance, but the industrial age was fostering new recreations that increasingly filled people's spare time. The explosive development of leisure-time pursuits that occurred between 1877 and 1920 eventually gave rise to a genuine mass culture.

For a nation nurtured on a frontier tradition of hard work and distaste for wasted time, the leisure-time revolution of the late nineteenth century marked a dramatic shift. The revolution was made possible by the invention of labor-saving devices. For both factory workers and white collar employees, the work week was reduced.

Increase in leisure time

The vanguard of the trend was sports, of which football and especially baseball were popular among males. In 1845 baseball's rules had been codified, and by 1890 professional games had been played before crowds of more than 51,000 people. And in 1903 the champions of the National League (formed in 1876) played the champions of the American League (formed in 1901) in the first World Series. About the time that baseball was becoming entrenched as the national pastime, the violent sport of football began to attract public attention.

Football had first gained popularity at the intercollegiate level among those who could afford a college education. Soon colleges were employing nonstudents—called "tramp athletes"—to play on their teams. Winning at virtually any cost became important—18 players died and over 150 were seriously injured in 1905. Such violence stirred President Theodore Roosevelt who convened a White House conference to discuss the game. From this meeting came the Inter-

Sports

Opening day at the first World Series, Boston, 1903. This match between Pittsburgh (National League) and Boston (American League) evidenced the growing popularity of professional baseball, as increasing numbers of Americans found the time and money to support spectator sports. Northeastern University, World Series Room.

collegiate Athletic Association (renamed the National College Athletic Association in 1910), an organization designed to police college sports and to make them less violent.

Meanwhile women were also developing an interest in sports. At the college level, basketball became a popular game. The sport's rules were modified by Senda Berenson of Smith College. Her changes limited dribbling and running and encouraged passing. By the turn of the century intercollegiate basketball games among women were common.

There were, of course, sports enjoyed by both sexes. Croquet, which swept the nation after the Civil War, was popular among middle- and upper-class people. And bicycling became so popular that the 1900 census declared, "Few articles . . . have created so great a revolution in social conditions as the bicycle." Both croquet and cycling were important in an era when the removal of work from the home had begun to separate men and women; these two recreational activities created social contact between the sexes.

The "revolution in social conditions" referred to in the 1900 census, however, pertained to clothing styles. The constraints of Victorian fashions gave way to more comfortable and practical styles suitable for cycling, and the freer styles of cycling costumes (divided skirts, and simple undergarments) influenced everyday fashion.

Chapter 18: The city and everyday life, 1877–1920

The rise of American show business paralleled the rise of sports, and similarly became a mode of leisure created by and for the common people. Circuses had existed since the 1820s and 1830s. But after the Civil War, railroads enabled the traveling spectacles to reach more of the country, and the popularity of the big show increased enormously. Circuses offered two main attractions: so-called freaks of nature and the temptation and conquest of death. More important, however, was the sheer astonishment aroused by the trapeze artists, lion tamers, high-wire artists (sometimes on bicycles), acrobats, and clowns.

Circuses

Several branches of American show business matured with the growth of cities. Popular drama, musical comedy, and vaudeville all gave Americans a chance to escape from the ambiguities and harsh realities of urban-industrial life into melodrama, nostalgia, adventure, and comedy. The plots were simple, the heroes and villains instantly recognizable. Virtue, honor, and justice always triumphed in melodramas, reinforcing the popular belief that even in an uncertain and disillusioning world, goodness would nevertheless prevail.

Popular drama and musical comedy

Musical comedies bolstered national optimism with song, humor, and dance. American musical comedy grew out of the lavishly costumed extravaganzas and comic operettas popular in Europe. By introducing American themes (often involving ethnic groups), folksy humor, and catchy tunes and dances, these shows launched the nation's most popular songs and entertainers. George M. Cohan, the master of the American musical comedy after the turn of the century, helped to advance a sense of national superiority with such songs as "Yankee Doodle Dandy" and "You're a Grand Old Flag."

The French term *vaudeville* first referred to light drama with musical interludes, but in the United States vaudeville became a unique form of entertainment with no European roots. Vaudeville was

Vaudeville

probably the most popular entertainment in early twentieth-century America because its variety made it attractive to mass audiences. Shows included magic and animal acts, juggling, stunts, comedy (especially ethnic humor), and song and dance. Unfortunately, vaudeville humor often stereotyped and ridiculed minorities—both ethnic and racial.

But show business also provided new economic opportunities for women, blacks, and immigrants. The opera star Lillian Russell, vaudeville singer and comedienne Fanny Brice, and burlesque queen Eva Tanguay attracted intensely loyal fans, commanded handsome fees, and won respect for their genuine talents. In contrast to the demure Victorian female, they conveyed pluck and creativity.

Before the 1890s, the only form of entertainment open to black performers was the minstrel show. By century's end, however, minstrel shows had given way to more sophisticated Negro musicals, and blacks had begun to break into vaudeville. As stage sets shifted from the plantation to the city, the music shifted from folk tunes to ragtime. Pandering to the prejudice of white audiences, composers and performers of both races ridiculed blacks. Burt Williams, a highly talented black comedian and dancer achieved his tormented success mainly by playing the stereotypical roles of darky and dandy.

Black musicals and ethnic humor

Shortly after 1900, live entertainment began to yield to an even more accessible form of amusement: moving pictures. Perfected by Thomas Edison in the late 1880s, movies began as slot-machine peep shows in penny arcades and billiard parlors. Eventually images were projected onto a screen so large audiences could view them, and a new medium was born. At first, the subject matter of films was unimportant; it was enough merely to awe viewers with moving pictures of speeding trains, galloping horses, roaring surf, and writhing belly dancers.

Movies

Producers soon discovered, however, that a film could tell a story. By 1910 motion pictures had become an art form, thanks especially to the creative (and bigoted) director D. W. Griffith, who pioneered artistic camera angles and editing techniques. Griffith's most famous work, *The Birth of a Nation* (1915) an epic film about the Civil War and Reconstruction, fanned racial prejudice by depicting blacks as threatening white moral values; its exaltation of the Ku Klux Klan also helped to revive the hooded empire. But the film's innovative techniques—close-ups, fade-outs, switchbacks, and battle scenes—gave viewers heightened drama and excitement.

The still camera, modernized by inventor George Eastman, enabled ordinary people to make their own photographic images; and the phonograph, another of Edison's inventions, made possible musical performances at home. The spread of movies, photography, and phonograph records meant that access to live performances no longer limited peoples' exposure to art and entertainment.

The transformation of mass communications

With so many new things to do and buy, how did Americans decide what they wanted? Two new types of communication influenced consumer tastes and mass opinion. Modern advertising molded peoples' needs and consumption patterns; and popular journalism spread mass culture throughout the country.

In the United States, advertising has meant more than just selling. Advertisers aim to *invent* a demand. Indeed, the growth in the late nineteenth century of large companies that mass-produced consumer goods gave advertisers the task of creating "consumption communities"—bodies of consumers loyal to a particular brand name.

The major vehicle for advertising was the newspaper. In 1879 Wanamaker's placed the first full-page ad, and at about the same time newspapers began to allow advertisers to print pictures of products. Such attention-getting techniques transformed advertising into news. More than ever before, people read the newspapers to find out what was for sale as well as what was happening.

Just as advertising became news, news often became a form of advertising, or at least of publicity. Canny publishers made people crave news. Joseph Pulitzer, a Hungarian immigrant who bought the *New York World* in 1883, pioneered

| Popular journalism |

the development of journalism as a branch of mass culture. Believing that newspapers should be "dedicated to the cause of the people rather than to that of the purse potentates," Pulitzer filled the *World* with stories of disasters, crimes, and scandals. Sensational headlines, set in large bold type like that of advertisements, screamed from every page. Pulitzer's journalists not only reported the news but sought it out—and sometimes even created it. Pulitzer also popularized the comics, and the bright yellow garb of a cartoon character ("The Yellow Kid") lent the nickname "yellow journalism" to the new emphasis on the sensational and lurid. The success enjoyed by Pulitzer caused others, most notably William R. Hearst, to adopt his techniques.

By the early twentieth century, the communications media, like the mass consumption of goods, were drawing the country together. Alongside newspapers, mass-circulation magazines offered human-interest stories, muckraking exposés, titillating fiction, and eye-catching advertisements to a growing mass market. And the total number of books published more than quadrupled between 1880 and 1917, reflecting a growing literacy rate (94 percent in 1920).

Other forms of communication were also expanding. By 1920 the telephone was becoming a commonly used instrument, and increasing numbers of people were sending telegrams and letters. Little wonder, then, that the term *community* took on new dimensions. More than ever before, people in different parts of the country knew about and discussed the same staples of mass culture, whether it was a sensational murder, a sex scandal, or the fortunes of a particular entertainer or athlete. America was becoming a mass society.

The public sentiment

American culture has long focused one eye on an increasingly complex technological future while casting the other longingly back at a sentimentalized, simpler past. When modern wonders like telephones, high-speed printing presses, phonographs, cameras, and projectors made information and entertainment more accessible, people demanded diversions that reaffirmed the traditional values of optimism, individualism, and freedom. Thus in 1914, just when they were beginning to fully appreciate automobiles, movies, and electricity, Americans made Edgar Rice Burroughs's *Tarzan of the Apes* a best seller.

Popular fiction writers in tune with the times concentrated on the sensational. After the Civil

| Dime novels |

War low-priced, paperbound adventure stories known as dime novels became the most widely read variety of American literature. Dime novels and similar popular literature offered three types of stories to young readers. The first evoked the Wild West. Intertwining fact and fiction with typically American abandon, writers like Zane Grey wove adventure stories around famous folk heroes like Buffalo Bill Cody and Wild Bill Hickok. During the 1880s, however, many authors began to give their tales urban settings and themes. Detective thrillers became the leading type of popular urban fiction. And just before the end of the century, science fiction and superheroes came to the fore.

One popular witer, Horatio Alger, moved beyond the fantasies of dime novels and offered his readers a formula for contending with new so-

| Moral messages of popular fiction |

cial and economic forces. Each of his 130 books tells the success story of an adolescent boy facing the prob-

lem of finding a place in an urban industrial world. Through ambition, honesty, luck, courage, and thrift, Alger's heroes overcome some obstacle, as well as poverty, and attain success. Alger believed in a cause-and-effect relationship between virtue and wealth.

Just before Alger's death in 1899, one of America's most popular superheroes, Frank Merriwell, was created by Gilbert Patten (whose pen name was Burt Standish). Frank Merriwell's adventures had a common theme that accorded with the way many Americans liked to think of themselves and their nation: he attempted and accomplished the impossible. Merriwell became one of the first character models in popular fiction. A picture of refinement and valor, he taught by example, not by preaching. Even his name symbolized American virtues: according to Patten, "I took the three qualities I most wanted him to represent—frank and merry in nature, well in body and mind—and made the name Frank Merriwell."

Young women found similar escape and inspiration in sentimental tales about growing up and about animals. One of the most widely read was Louisa May Alcott's *Little Women,* published in two parts in 1868 and 1869. This novel recreated the domestic delights and moral trials of four girls based on Alcott and her sisters. A generation later, Gene Stratton-Porter's romantic novels about animals, like *Freckles* (1904) and *Laddie* (1913), became the best sellers of her day. Others in the same vein were Anna Sewell's *Black Beauty* (1890) and Kate Douglas Wiggins's *Rebecca of Sunnybrook Farm* (1903).

Popular literature for adults also oozed with escapism and sentimentality. The best-selling titles of the late nineteenth century included romances about mythical places of chivalry and honor. *Ben Hur* (1880), General Lew Wallace's powerful religious melodrama set in the Roman Empire, was of particular importance because it heralded a rage for historical fiction that has not yet subsided.

While some popular writers focused on escapism, other writers were trying to introduce realism into romance. During the 1870s and

1880s, a number of "local-color" writers began

 producing works that depicted the people and environment of a particular region more realistically. Essentially, they used authentic manners, customs, and speech to depict a romantic, rustic past. The movement was largely centered in the South, whose writers felt compelled to rebuild the region's image. But the realist movement permeated other regions as well. Indeed, it began in the Far West and the Midwest.

One local colorist moved beyond romance and adventure, and in doing so won recognition from intellectuals as well as the masses. Mark

Literary classics Twain (the pen name of Samuel Clemens) was a regional writer by reputation. He was best known for his books about the American West: *Tom Sawyer* (1876), *Life on the Mississippi* (1883), and *Huckleberry Finn* (1884). These antisentimental novels were realistic portrayals of western life and of human weakness. Twain was sensitive to both the comic and the tragic sides of life, and his writing reflected the dynamic energy and materialism of his era.

A number of Twain's contemporaries shunned the falseness of escape writing and focused instead on the moral tests life holds. Realists like William Dean Howells and Henry James wrote chiefly about upper-class Americans, but other realists examined the lives of more ordinary Americans and in so doing opened new literary vistas. These writers, sometimes called naturalists, often viewed life in terms of the survival of the fittest; they portrayed ruthless struggles for life and power in frank detail. Their descriptions of slum life, sexual immorality, and violence portrayed a side of America that local colorists avoided.

The escapism of popular fiction and the realism of serious fiction, though seemingly at odds, offered similar commentaries on the American society of the early twentieth century. It was no coincidence that Frank Merriwell replaced Horatio Alger's heroes in popular fiction around 1900: by then Americans knew that it took more than honesty, energy, and a timely rescue to become rich. Naturalist writers, for example, saw that the new demands the industrial age placed on individuals threatened the traditional American values of family, nature, frugality, and moral restraint.

Suggestions for further reading

URBAN GROWTH   Howard P. Chudacoff, *The Evolution of American Urban Society,* rev. ed. (1981); Arthur M. Schlesinger, *The Rise of the City* (1933); Sam Bass Warner, Jr., *Streetcar Suburbs* (1962); Sam Bass Warner, Jr., *The Urban Wilderness* (1972); Olivier Zunz, *The Changing Face of Inequality: Urbanization, Industrial Development, and Immigrants in Detroit, 1880–1920* (1982).

IMMIGRATION, ETHNICITY, AND RELIGION   Josef J. Barton, *Peasants and Strangers: Italians, Rumanians, and Slovaks in an American City* (1975); John Bodnar, *Immigration and Industrialization* (1977); Robert D. Cross, *The Church and the City* (1967); Leonard Dinnerstein and David Reimers, *Ethnic Americans* (1975); Nathan Glazer and Daniel P. Moynihan, *Beyond the Melting Pot,* rev. ed. (1970); Milton Gordon, *Assimilation in American Life* (1964); Victor Greene, *For God and Country: The Rise of Polish and Lithuanian Ethnic Consciousness in America* (1975); Oscar Handlin, *The Uprooted,* 2nd ed. (1973); Marcus Lee Hansen, *The Immigrant in American History* (1940); John Higham, *Strangers in the Land: Patterns of American Nativism* (1955); Maldwyn A. Jones, *American Immigration* (1960); Matt S. Maier and Feliciano Rivera, *The Chicanos: A History of Mexican Americans* (1972); Henry F. May, *Protestant Churches and Industrial America* (1949); Humbert S. Nelli, *The Italians of Chicago* (1970); Moses Rischin, *The Promised City New York's Jews* (1962).

URBAN NEEDS AND SERVICES   Robert H. Bremner, *From the Depths: The Discovery of Poverty* (1956); James H. Cassedy, *Charles V. Chapin and the Public Health Movement* (1962); Marvin Lazerson, *Origins of the Urban School* (1971); Eric H. Monkkonen, *Police in Urban America, 1860–1920* (1981); James F. Richardson, *The New York Police* (1970); Mel Scott, *American City Planning Since 1890* (1969); David B. Tyack, *The One Best System: A History of American Urban Education* (1974).

MOBILITY AND RACE RELATIONS John Bodnar, Roger Simon, and Michael P. Weber, *Lives of Their Own: Blacks, Italians, and Poles in Pittsburgh, 1900–1960* (1982); Clyde Griffen and Sally Griffen, *Natives and Newcomers* (1977); David M. Katzman, *Before the Ghetto* (1973); Kenneth L. Kusmer, *A Ghetto Takes Shape* (1976); Gilbert Osofsky, *Harlem: The Making of a Ghetto* (1966); Allan H. Spear, *Black Chicago* (1967); Stephan Thernstrom, *The Other Bostonians: Poverty and Progress in the American Metropolis* (1973).

BOSS POLITICS John M. Allswang, *Bosses, Machines and Urban Voters* (1977); Alexander B. Callow, Jr., ed., *The City Boss in America* (1976); Bruce M. Stave, ed., *Urban Bosses, Machines, and Progressive Reformers* (1972).

URBAN REFORM John D. Buenker, *Urban Liberalism and Progressive Reform* (1973); James B. Crooks, *Politics and Progress* (1968); Allen F. Davis, *Spearheads for Reform* (1967); Melvin Holli, *Reform in Detroit* (1969); Roy M. Lubove, *The Progressive and the Slums* (1962); Martin J. Schiesl, *The Politics of Efficiency: Municipal Administration and Reform in America* (1977); John G. Sproat, *The Best Men: Liberal Reformers in the Gilded Age* (1968).

LIVING STANDARDS AND NEW CONVENIENCES Daniel J. Boorstin, *The Americans: The Democratic Experience* (1973); Godfrey M. Lebhar, *Chain Stores in America* (1962); Clarence D. Long, *Wages and Earnings in the United States, 1860–1890* (1960); Lawrence Wright, *Clean and Decent* (1960).

FAMILY AND INDIVIDUAL LIFE CYCLES W. Andrew Achenbaum, *Old Age in the New Land* (1979):

Carl N. Degler, *At Odds: Women and the Family in America* (1980); Michael Gordon, ed., *The American Family in Social-Historical Perspective,* 2nd ed. (1978); Tamara K. Hareven, ed., *Transitions: The Family and Life Course in Historical Perspective* (1978); Joseph Kett, *Rites of Passage: Adolescence in America* (1979); David J. Pivar, *Purity Crusade: Sexual Morality and Social Control, 1868–1900* (1973); Richard Sennett, *Families Against the City* (1970); Virginia Yans-McLaughlin, *Family and Community: Italian Immigrants in Buffalo* (1977).

MASS ENTERTAINMENT AND LEISURE Gunther Barth, *City People* (1980); John E. DiMeglio, *Vaudeville U.S.A.* (1973); Foster R. Dulles, *America Learns to Play* (1966); John F. Kasson, *Amusing the Million: Coney Island at the Turn of the Century* (1978); Arthur Knight, *The Liveliest Art* (1957); Joseph A. Musselman, *Music in the Cultured Generation: A Social History of Music in America,* 1870–1900 (1971); Benjamin G. Rader, *American Sports* (1983); Harold Seymour, *Baseball,* 2 vols. (1960–1971); Robert Sklar, *Movie-Made America* (1976); Robert C. Toll, *On With the Show: The First Century of Show Business in America* (1976); David Q. Voigt, *American Baseball,* 2 vols. (1966–1970).

ADVERTISING AND JOURNALISM George Juergens, *Joseph Pulitzer and the New York World* (1966); Frank L. Mott, *American Journalism,* 3rd ed. (1962); Bernard A. Weisberger, *The American Newspaperman* (1961); James P. Wood, *The Story of Advertising* (1958).

POPULAR LITERATURE John G. Cawelti, *Apostles of Success in America* (1965); Theodore P. Greene, *America's Heroes: The Changing Models of Success in American Magazines* (1970); Frank L. Mott, *Golden Multitudes: The Story of Best Sellers in the United States* (1947); Edmund L. Pearson, *Dime Novels* (1929); Moses Rischin, ed., *The American Gospel of Success* (1965)

19

GILDED AGE POLITICS, 1877–1900

Esther Morris's craggy face must have cracked a satisfied grin as she thought about what was happening on July 23, 1890. On that day, a day celebrating Wyoming's newly won statehood, Mrs. Morris had the honor of presenting a commemorative flag to the governor. She had migrated with her husband and children to Wyoming Territory in 1869. There she had played a chief role in convincing the territorial legislature to legalize full voting rights for women. When Wyoming applied for statehood twenty years later, its constitution retained the women's suffrage provision, the first state constitution to do so.

By a narrow margin Congress approved statehood for Wyoming and its women thus entered the American political process, but they were exceptions. In 1900 the majority of Americans—including women in all other states, black men in many southern states, Indians, and unnaturalized immigrants—still could not vote. Moreover, the political process suffered from more than exclusivity. Corruption and greed were prevalent, and the venality of the era prompted novelists Mark Twain and Charles Dudley Warner to dub it the Gilded Age.

The system faltered in the 1890s when a deep economic depression overspread the nation, exposing the gap between those with political influence and those who were excluded and aggravating conflicts between opposing interest groups: farmers versus businessmen; debtors versus creditors; employees versus employers. In the midst of the depression, a presidential campaign stirred Americans as they had not been stirred for a generation. Two candidates, William Jennings Bryan and William McKinley, and three parties, Democrats, Populists, and Republicans, compressed all the symbols of the era into a single election. The nation emerged from the turmoil of the 1890s with new political alignments, just as it had developed new economic configurations. These new alignments prepared the way for the new century, and for a new era of reform.

Cynical parties and emotional issues

Lord James Bryce, a British historian and diplomat who wrote a classic study called *The American Commonwealth* (1888), penned a disparaging analysis of American political parties in the Gilded Age. Referring to Democrats and Republicans, Bryce observed that "neither party has any principles, any distinctive tenets. . . . Both have certainly war cries, organizations, interests enlisted in their support. But these interests are in the main the interests of getting or keeping the patronage of the government." Henry Adams, grandson and great-grandson of presidents, agreed, noting that the period between 1870 and 1895 "was poor in purpose and barren in results." But were the two major par-

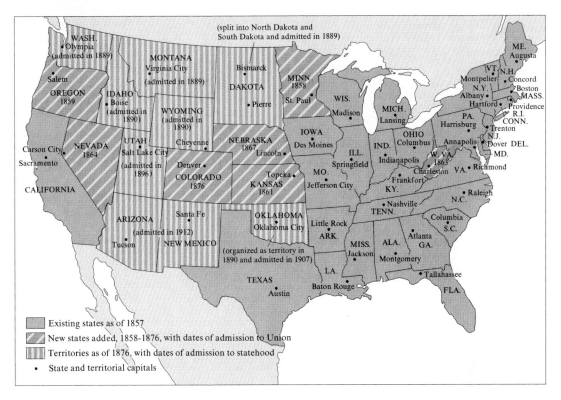

The United States, 1876–1912

ties void of principle and alike in interests? Was the period so barren politically that government could accomplish very little?

From the voters' perspective, politics appeared anything but barren. At no other time in the nation's history was public interest in elec-

Voter participation

tions higher. Except in the South, where blacks endured growing voting restrictions, 80 to 90 percent of eligible voters cast ballots in local and national elections. Politics was the prime form of mass entertainment, outdistancing even baseball, vaudeville, and circuses. For voting was only the last stage in a process that included rallies, parades, picnics, and speeches, all of which were as much public amusement as civic responsibility.

Politics was a personal as well as a community activity. People formed strong loyalties to both individual politicians and parties. These allegiances were usually evenly distributed, so that

no one party predominated for long. Between 1877 and 1897, Republicans held the presidency for twelve years, Democrats for eight. The same party controlled the presidency and both houses of Congress for only three two-year spans: the Republicans twice, the Democrats once. The balance persisted despite the admission of six territories to statehood during this period (see map).

In some ways, the major parties did look the same. Both were led by wealthy men, and both contained large numbers of farmers and wage earners as well as merchants and manufacturers. And internal quarrels split each party. In the Re-

Party factions

publican party, factional feuds and personal rivalries took precedence over national concerns. On one side stood the Stalwarts, led by New York's pompous Senator Roscoe Conkling who sought party influence and government jobs for his supporters over all other political concerns. On the

Cynical parties and emotional issues

other side were the Half-Breeds, led by Senator James G. Blaine of Maine, former Speaker of the House and twice secretary of state. Blaine wanted influence just as much as Conkling, but attempted to disguise his greed and sought the support of independents. On the sidelines were the more idealistic liberals, or Mugwumps, who, like Senator Carl Schurz of Missouri, believed that only righteous, dedicated men like themselves should govern. Meanwhile Democrats tended to subdivide into white-supremacy southerners, immigrant-stock urban machine members, and business interests favoring low tariffs. Like Republicans, Democrats eagerly pursued the spoils of office.

Yet the two parties and the voters differed substantively over long-standing political and economic issues, such as sectional rivalry, tariffs, and the currency. Long after Reconstruction ended, Americans were haunted by the sectional conflict and political disruptions that had followed the Civil War. Whenever they faced a Democratic challenge, Republicans capitalized on the war by "waving the bloody shirt" and claiming that Democrats had been responsible for the war. In the South voters also waved the bloody shirt, calling all Republicans traitors. The use of such emotional appeals persisted well into the 1880s.

| Sectional conflicts |

Politicians were not the only ones who attempted to profit by keeping the memory of the war alive. In the 1880s and 1890s, the Grand Army of the Republic, an organization of Union army veterans numbering over 400,000, allied itself with the Republican party and pressured Congress into legislating generous pensions for former soldiers and their widows. Certainly many pensions were well deserved. Union soldiers had been poorly paid, and the war had widowed thousands of women. But for many other veterans, the emotional wake of the great conflict provided an opportunity to profit at the public's expense.

Few politicians could afford to oppose Civil War pensions, but a number of reformers mustered their energies in an attempt to dismantle the spoils system. The practice of awarding government jobs to party workers, regardless of their qualifications, had blossomed after the Civil War. As federal building construction, the postal service, the diplomatic corps, and other government activities expanded, so did the number of jobs on the public payroll. Elected officials scrambled to control the new appointments as a means of cementing support for themselves and their parties. In return for the relatively short hours and high pay of government jobs, appointees pledged their votes and a portion of their earnings.

| Civil service reform |

A system so susceptible to corruption ruffled a growing number of independents, who began advocating appointments and promotions based on merit rather than connections. The movement gained momentum during the 1870s, when scandals in the Grant administration bared the defects of the spoils system. It reached full flower in 1881 with the formation of the National Civil Service Reform League. That same year the assassination of President James Garfield by Charles Guiteau, a frustrated and demented job-seeker, hastened the drive for civil service reform. Finally, in 1882 Congress passed the Pendleton Civil Service Act, and President Chester Arthur signed it early in 1883.

The law created the Civil Service Commission, which would supervise competitive examinations for government positions. Significantly, however, the act gave the commission jurisdiction over only about 10 percent of federal jobs—although the president could expand the list. Nevertheless the law, and especially one provision outlawing political contributions by officeholders, signaled a change.

Civil service reform has often been considered one of the major accomplishments of the Gilded Age; yet its actual impact can be debated. Certainly the system of hiring government workers needed improvement. But civil service reformers were by no means egalitarians who wanted to give all qualified Americans a chance to participate in government. They were conservatives who wanted to restore an era

Before the Pendleton Act of 1883, many government positions were filled by patronage: hat in hand, job seekers beseeched the president to find a place for them. Here a member of Congress presents constituents for office in return for their past political support.   Library of Congress.

when public servants were chosen from among men whose birth, wealth, and education supposedly fitted them for leadership. Moreover, the spoils system did serve a useful function: it financed the two major political parties in an era when no other form of support existed. And it was an open and accepted system of party support, far less sinister than the system of secret contributions from large corporations that replaced it. Finally, no one has ever proven that the quality of government service improved under civil service.

In the 1880s tariffs and money, not government jobs, attracted the most attention in Congress. Through the mid-nineteenth century Congress had raised most tariff rates to protect **American** manufactured goods and some agricultural products from European competition. By the 1880s there were separate tariffs on over four thousand items, and the resulting revenues were making for an embarrassing surplus in the federal treasury. Though a few economics professors and some farmers argued for free trade,

| Tariff policy |

Cynical parties and emotional issues

most Americans still believed high tariffs were necessary to preserve the prosperity of industrialists and the jobs of wage earners.

The Republican party, claiming responsibility for economic growth, made protective tariffs a core feature of its policies. Democrats and other critics complained that tariffs made prices artificially high, benefiting those interests who products were protected while hurting farmers whose crops were not protected and consumers who had to buy manufactured goods. Although Democrats generally saw a need for some protection of American goods and raw materials, they favored lower tariff rates to encourage foreign trade and to reduce the treasury surplus.

The currency controversy was even more tangled than the tariff issue. In brief, it involved opposing reactions to the fall in prices caused by increased industrial and agricultural production after the Civil War. Farmers, most of whom were debtors, suffered particularly severely because they had to pay fixed mortgage and interest payments even while their incomes declined because prices for their crops were dropping. Correctly perceiving that an insufficient money supply had made their debts more expensive relative to other prices, farmers favored schemes like the coinage of silver to increase the amount of currency in circulation. Creditors, on the other hand, believed that overproduction had caused the price decline. They thus favored a more stable, tightly controlled money supply backed only by gold as a means of maintaining the confidence of native and foreign investors in the American economy.

| Monetary policy |

But the issue involved more than economics. The creditor-versus-debtor conflict translated into haves versus have-nots. It also involved a sectional cleavage: the western silver-mining areas and agricultural regions of the South and West against the industrial Northeast. Finally, the issue had moral, almost religious, overtones. For centuries people had considered gold a God-given symbol of value.

Prior to the 1870s, the government had coined both silver and gold dollars; a silver dollar weighed sixteen times more than a gold dollar, meaning that gold was officially worth sixteen times as much as silver. But gold discoveries since 1849 had increased the supply, lowering gold's market price relative to that of silver. Thus producers of silver, which was now worth more than one-sixteenth the value of gold, preferred to sell their metal on the open market rather than to the government. As a result, silver dollars disappeared from circulation—owners hoarded them rather than spend them—and in 1873 Congress officially stopped coining silver dollars. At about the same time, European nations also stopped buying silver. Thus the United States and many of its trading partners adopted the gold standard, meaning that their currency was backed chiefly by gold.

Within a few years, however, new mines in the American West began to flood the market with silver, and its price dropped. Gold was now worth more than sixteen times what silver was worth. It became profitable to spend silver dollars—and would have been worthwhile to sell silver to the government in return for gold, but the government was no longer buying it. Debtors, who saw silver as a means of expanding the currency supply, now joined with silver producers to denounce the "Crime of '73" and to press for resumption of coinage at the old sixteen-to-one ratio.

Congress, split into silver and gold factions, tried to neutralize the issue with compromise legislation: the Bland-Allison Act of 1878, which required the treasury to buy $2 to $4 million worth of silver each month; and the Sherman Silver Purchase Act of 1890, which fixed the monthly purchase of silver in weight (4.5 million ounces) rather than in dollars. But neither act satisfied the different interest groups. Renewed prosperity in 1879 caused crop prices to rise and gold to flow in from overseas, temporarily calming the silverite fervor. The Sherman Act, passed partially in response to an economic decline in the mid-1880s, failed to expand the money supply: as the price of silver dropped, the government, now required only to buy a certain weight of silver, could spend less to purchase the stipulated number of ounces. Thus the money supply was not increased as substantially as some had hoped.

While debates over tariffs and money raged, Congress and state legislatures began to face the issue of women's suffrage more squarely than ever before. Late in 1869 a Missouri couple, Francis and Virginia Minor, drew up a resolution stating that the Constitution and its amendments had already given women the right to vote. According to the Minors' theory, the Constitution granted citizenship to "all persons born or naturalized in the United States," and no state could abridge the "privileges or immunities" of any citizen, including his—or her—right to vote. Eventually the Minors, with support from the National Woman Suffrage Association (NWSA), sued a St. Louis registrar who had refused to permit Mrs. Minor to vote. In 1874 the Supreme Court ruled that suffrage did not automatically accompany citizenship and that states could legally withhold voting rights from certain classes of citizens, such as criminals, the insane—and women.

Four years later Susan B. Anthony, the indomitable fighter for human rights, convinced her friend Senator A. A. Sargent of California, a strong supporter of women's suffrage, to introduce in Congress a constitutional amendment stating that "the right of citizens of the United States to vote shall not be denied or abridged by the United States or by any state on account of sex." The bill was killed by a Senate committee, but supporters reintroduced it several times over the next eighteen years. On the few occasions when the bill reached the Senate floor, it was voted down by senators who expressed their fears that suffrage would interfere with women's family responsibilities and ruin female virtue.

While the NWSA and others fought for the vote on the national level, the American Woman Suffrage Association worked for constitutional amendments at the state level. Between 1870 and 1910, there were seventeen referenda in eleven states (all but three of which were west of the Mississippi River) to legalize women's suffrage. These attempts almost always failed, but women did attain partial victories. By 1890 nineteen states allowed women to vote on school issues, three granted suffrage on tax and bond issues, and the groundwork was well laid for the next generation's battle for national voting rights.

Thus legislative leaders did address some of the basic issues of the day, but they failed to agree on clear solutions. Congressmen and their constituents were so divided among factions and interest groups that the only passable legislation was the kind, like the Pendleton Act, that was ideal to no one but acceptable to most. And while complex problems like the tariff demanded careful study, most politicians preferred to devote their energies to party and factional concerns.

The decline of the presidency

Woodrow Wilson once said that a good president should be chief administrator, chief of legislation, and chief of the party. In the years between 1877 and 1900, American presidents seldom fulfilled any of these functions. Proper, honorable, and honest, Presidents Hayes, Garfield, Arthur, Cleveland, Harrison, and McKinley won public respect but seldom provoked strong emotions. Not one of them was an inspiring personality, nor could any of them dominate the factional chieftains of their parties.

Rutherford B. Hayes (1877 to 1881) personified the belief that the president was a caretaker elected to execute what Congress initiated. Honest, prudent, and a model of self-control, Hayes avoided such controversial issues as the tariff and sectional rivalry. He did, however, take a conservative position on currency, and ordered out troops to aid local militia during the 1877 railroad strikes. Hayes also pleased civil service advocates by appointing reformer Carl Schurz to the cabinet

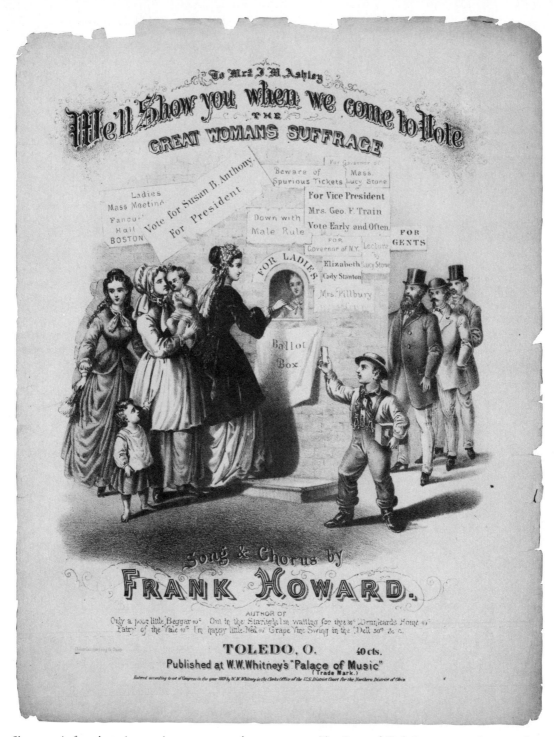

Sheet music for a late-nineteenth-century song about women's suffrage. Women increased their agitation for the vote until in 1878 a constitutional amendment granting them suffrage was introduced in Congress. The Senate killed the measure that year, but women's groups like the National Woman Suffrage Association continued to fight for the cause. American Antiquarian society.

and battling New York's patronage king, Senator Roscoe Conkling. But Hayes also demanded that his own appointees contribute to Republican coffers for the 1878 elections.

When Hayes refused to run for re-election in 1880, Republican factions battled over whom to nominate, then compromised by selecting another Ohio congressman and Civil War hero, James A. Garfield. After defeating the Democrats' Winfield Scott Hancock, also a Civil War hero, by just 40,000 votes out of over 9 million, Garfield spent most of his brief presidency trying to secure an independent position among party potentates like Blaine and Conkling. He did please civil service reformers by refusing to satisfy Conkling's demands, but Garfield's opportunity to make lasting contributions ended with his assassination.

Garfield's vice president and successor was New York politician Chester A. Arthur, a protégé of the notorious Senator Conkling. Arthur had been nominated for vice president only to help the Republicans carry New York state; his elevation to the presidency made reformers shudder. Yet he became a dignified and temperate executive. Like his two predecessors, Arthur had no taste for his office. Suffering from illness, he made little effort to run in 1884.

In the 1884 presidential campaign the Republicans nominated James G. Blaine, and the Democrats named New York's Governor Grover Cleveland. Both parties focused on the opposition's sordid side. On election day Cleveland beat Blaine by only 23,000 popular votes; his tiny margin of 1,149 votes in New York gave him that state's 36 electoral votes, enough to squeeze a 219–182 victory in the electoral college. Cleveland may have won New York solely because in the last week of the campaign a local Protestant minister publicly equated Democrats with "rum, Romanism, and rebellion" (drinking, Catholicism, and the Civil War). The Democrats eagerly publicized the slur among New York's numerous Irish-Catholic population, urging voters to protest by turning out for Cleveland.

Cleveland, the first Democratic president since Buchanan, exercised more vigorous leadership than had his immediate predecessors.

| Cleveland and Harrison |

Cleveland used the veto extensively against outrageous pension bills, and he extended the scope of civil service. But Cleveland's most forceful action was his unsuccessful campaign for tariff reform. When advisers warned him that his stand might weaken his chances for re-election, the president retorted, "What is the use of being elected or re-elected, unless you stand for something?" Cleveland's firmness did not prevail, though. The Mills tariff bill of 1888, passed by the House in response to Cleveland's wishes, would have reduced some rates. But it was killed by the Senate.

The Democrats renominated Cleveland in 1888, and the Republicans selected Benjamin Harrison, the grandson of President William Henry Harrison. The campaign was less savage than the 1884 campaign had been, but it was far from clean. Quite helpful to Harrison was the pervasive bribery and multiple voting that helped him to win Indiana by just 2,300 votes and New York by only 14,000. (Democrats also indulged in bribery and vote fraud, but the Republicans were more successful at it.) These crucial states assured Harrison's victory; though Cleveland outpolled Harrison by 90,000 popular votes, Harrison carried the electoral vote by 233 to 168.

Harrison was the first president since 1875 whose party controlled both houses of Congress, but he did little to take advantage of this circumstance by asserting himself as a party or legislative leader. Several aspects of his administration were contradictory. Harrison was a fiscal conservative, but under his administration Congress passed the first peacetime budget to exceed $1 billion. At Harrison's urging the House passed a bill to protect blacks' civil rights, but senators filibustered and then tabled the bill. And though Harrison supported a boost in protective tariff rates and reciprocity agreements to aid business, he agreed to the Sherman Anti-

Trust Act and the Sherman Silver Purchase Act (1890), both of which were considered damaging to business.

Cleveland and Harrison ran against each other again in 1892. This time Cleveland attracted heavy contributions from business and beat Harrison by 380,000 popular votes and by 277 to 145 electoral votes. The victory was less decisive than it might have been, however, because of James B. Weaver's third-party challenge. The Populist candidate garnered over 1 million votes, winning majorities in four states and 22 electoral votes. The forces of equilibrium were weakening.

In office once more, Cleveland took bolder steps to meet the problems of currency, tariffs, and labor unrest. But his actions reflected a narrow orientation to the interests of business. For example, in the election campaign Cleveland promised sweeping tariff reform, but he made little effort to line up support for such reform in the Senate. And when 120,000 boycotting railroad workers paralyzed western trade in the 1894 Pullman strike, Cleveland bowed to the requests for federal troops from railroad managers and Attorney General Richard Olney. Throughout Cleveland's second term, events—particularly the economic downturn and the Populist ferment—seemed too much for the president.

The depression of the 1890s

Early in 1893, a seemingly minor but ominous economic event occurred: the Philadelphia and Reading Railroad, once a thriving and profitable line, went into bankruptcy. Like other railroads, the Philadelphia and Reading had borrowed heavily to lay more tracks and make costly improvements. But overexpansion cut into revenues; profits dwindled, and the company was unable to pay its debts.

The same problem nagged manufacturers. For example, output at the McCormick farm machinery factories was nine times greater in 1893 than it had been in 1879, but revenues had only tripled. To compensate, the company tried to boost profits by automating its plants (another heavy expense) and squeezing more work out of fewer laborers. But this strategy only enlarged the debt and increased unemployment.

Banks suffered too. As primary lending agents, their problems compounded when customers defaulted. The failure of the National Cordage Company in May 1893 set off a chain reaction of business and bank closings. During the first four months of 1893, 28 banks failed. By May the number had grown to 54, and in June it reached 128. In 1894 one adviser warned President Cleveland, "We are on the eve of a very dark night." He was right; between 1893 and 1897, the nation suffered the worst economic depression it had yet experienced.

Falling prices and mounting unemployment arrived in the wake of business failures. Although records are sketchy, it appears that about 2.5 million people, or nearly 20 percent of the labor force, were out of work for some time during the depression. Many people could not afford basic necessities. New York police estimated that twenty thousand homeless and jobless people roamed the city's streets.

As the depression deepened, currency problems reached a critical stage. The Sherman Silver Purchase Act of 1890 had committed the government to buy 4.5 million ounces of silver each month, but the western mining boom made silver more plentiful, and its value relative to gold fell accordingly. Thus every month the government exchanged gold, whose worth remained fairly constant, for less valuable silver. Fearful that the dollar, which was based on the treasury's holdings in silver and gold, was losing its value, businessmen at home and abroad began to exchange paper money and securities for gold. As a result, the nation's gold reserves dwindled, falling below the psychologically significant level of $100 million in April 1893.

President Cleveland, promising to protect the gold reserves, called a special session of Congress

Currency problems

and secured the repeal of the Sherman Silver Purchase Act. But the run on the treasury continued. By early 1895 gold reserves had fallen to only $41 million. In desperation, Cleveland accepted an offer of 3.5 million ounces of gold in return for $62 million worth of federal bonds from a banking syndicate led by J. P. Morgan. When the bankers resold the bonds to the public, they profited handsomely at the nation's expense. Cleveland claimed that the gold reserves had been saved, but many, especially farmers and silver miners, saw only humiliation in the president's actions.

In the final years of the century, new gold discoveries, good harvests, and saner industrial growth brought better times. But, though few Americans realized it, the depression had hastened the crumbling of an old system and the emergence of a new one. The processes of industrial development and technological change had been under way for some time. But the organizational features of the new business system—consolidation and a trend toward bigness—were just beginning to solidify when the depression hit.

| Interdependent economic structures |

What had happened was that the national economy had reached the point of interdependence, the point at which the fortunes of a business in one part of the country had repercussions elsewhere. By the 1890s railroads were overextended; their reckless investments inevitably crumbled. And when railroads collapsed, they pulled other industries down with them. In the first half of 1893, for example, thirty-two steel companies failed. In all, five hundred banks and sixteen thousand businesses toppled into bankruptcy that same year.

To complicate matters, agriculture too had been languishing for several years. After 1870 commercial farming had expanded to the point that American farmers were competing with foreign producers for world markets. Thus American farmers had to contend not only with fluctuating transportation rates and falling crop prices at home but also with foreign competition. A mounting worldwide supply, and even surplus, of farm products drove down prices further, and American farmers borrowed more in order to produce enough to make ends meet. But the more they produced, the more surplus they created. As a result prices dropped further, forcing them to produce and borrow still more. When farmers fell into debt and lost their purchasing power, their depressed condition in turn affected the economic health of railroads, farm-implements manufacturers, banks, and other businesses. The downward spiral reversed late in 1897, but the depression had left deep scars.

Undercurrents of protest

The depression bared social as well as economic problems in the industrial system. For half a century technological and organizational changes had increasingly widened the gap between employers and employees. By the 1890s workers' protests against exploitation threatened economic and political upheaval. In 1894, when the American economy plunged, there were over thirteen hundred strikes and countless riots. Violence reached an alarming pitch in several places, and radical rhetoric escalated. Contrary to the fears of business leaders, all the protesters were not anarchists or communists. The disaffected included thousands of rural, small-town, and urban men and women who wanted a better chance, regardless of how the government was organized. Far from giving birth to radicalism, the uncertainties of the age merely brought to the surface an activist undercurrent that has flowed throughout American history.

Socialism was part of this undercurrent. Most of the Americans who were socialists were immigrant Marxists. Led by Daniel DeLeon, the fiery West-Indian-born lawyer and lecturer who dominated the Socialist Labor Party, they agreed with Karl Marx, the father of communism, that whoever controlled the means of production held the power to determine how well people lived.

| Socialism |

Marx predicted that workers throughout the world would become so discontented they would revolt and seize factories, farms, banks, and transportation lines. The governments resulting from this revolution would end exploitation and erase class differences, paving the way for a new order of social justice.

The American socialist movement suffered from internal disagreements and a lack of strong leadership, but events in 1894 triggered changes within the movement. That year the government's quashing of the Pullman strike and of the newly formed American Railway Union created a new and inspiring socialist leader. Eugene V. Debs, the railway union's president, had become a socialist while serving a six-month prison term for defying an injunction against the strike. Once released, the bald, forceful Indianan became the leading spokesperson for American socialism, combining visionary Marxism with Jeffersonian and Populist antimonopolism. Though never good at organizing, Debs attracted huge audiences and captivated them with his passion and eloquence.

In 1894, however, it was not the tall, animated Debs but a short, quiet, frustrated businessman from Massillon, Ohio, who captured public attention. His name was Jacob S. Coxey, and like Debs he had a vision. The year before, Coxey had become con-

| Coxey's army |

vinced that, to help debtors, the government should issue paper money unbacked by gold—purposeful inflation, in other words. As the depression spread, Coxey recommended a federal job program financed by an issue of $500 million of this "legal tender" paper money to relieve unemployment and revive consumer spending. He planned to publicize his scheme by leading a march from Massillon to Washington, D.C.

Coxey and his troops, including women and children, entered the capital on April 30. The next day the citizen army of some five hundred people marched to the Capitol, armed with "war clubs of peace." When Coxey and a few others vaulted the wall surrounding the Capitol grounds, a hundred mounted police moved in

and routed the crowd. Coxey tried to speak from the Capitol steps, but the police arrested him for ignoring Keep Off the Grass signs and dragged him away. As the arrests and clubbings continued, Coxey's dreams of a demonstration of 400,000 jobless workers dissolved. Like the strikes, the people's first march on Washington had yielded to police muscle. Strikes and petitions, including the "petition in boots," clearly could not redress the protesters' grievances, but the ballot box remained a possibility. That is where farmers turned in 1896.

The battle of the standards and the election of 1896

William Jennings Bryan arrived at the Democratic national convention in Chicago in July 1896. He was thirty-six years old, avidly religious, and highly distressed by what the depression had done to midwestern farmers. And as a member of the party's resolutions committee, Bryan helped to write a platform calling for free coinage of silver.

When the platform was presented to the full convention, Bryan rose to speak on its behalf. Even in the heat and humidity of the Chicago summer, Bryan's now-famous closing words chilled the delegates:

> Having behind us the producing masses of this nation and the world . . . , we will answer their [the business interests'] demand for a gold standard by saying to them: You shall not press down upon the brow of labor this crown of thorns, you shall not crucify mankind upon a cross of gold.

The speech could not have been more timely; indeed, Bryan planned it to be so. Friends who had been pushing Bryan for the presidential nomination now had no trouble enlisting support. The convention flowed to Bryan, and the "great campaign" had begun in earnest.

Silver was the central issue of the 1890s. Al-

William Jennings Bryan (1860–1925), the spellbinding orator whose speech on behalf of free silver thrilled thousands of western and southern agrarians in 1896.   Library of Congress.

though the currency problem was one of the most complex facing the nation's political leaders, many people, including most Populists, saw silver as a simple solution to America's ills. To Populists, and others, free silver meant the end of special privilege for the rich. Along with government ownership of some businesses and the strict regulation of others, a graduated income tax, direct election of senators, and price stabilization, free silver would help to close the gap between the haves and the have-nots.

In the early 1890s the Populists carried their crusade into local and state elections throughout the West and South. In 1892 their presidential

Growth of the Populist party

candidate drew more than 1 million votes, and Populist candidates in 1894 made good showings. Nevertheless, the party could claim only a few electoral victories. Like all third parties, the Populists were underfinanced and underorganized. They had strong and colorful candidates, but not enough of them to blanket an area and wrest control from the two major parties. Moreover, many sympathetic voters were

Important events

1873	Coinage of silver dollars ends	1888	Mills Tariff passes House, killed in Senate
1873–78	Depression		Benjamin Harrison elected president
1876	Rutherford B. Hayes elected president	1890	Sherman Silver Purchase Act Sherman Anti-Trust Act
1878	Bland-Allison Act	1892	Populist convention in Omaha Cleveland elected president
1880	James A. Garfield elected president	1893	Repeal of Sherman Silver Purchase Act
1881	Garfield assassinated; Chester A. Arthur assumes the presidency National Civil Service Reform League founded	1893–97	Depression
		1894	Pullman strike; Eugene V. Debs arrested and turns to socialism Coxey's march
1883	Pendleton Civil Service Act		
1884–85	Depression	1895	Cleveland deals with bankers to save gold reserve
1884	Grover Cleveland elected president	1896	William McKinley elected president
1887	Collapse of farm prices	1900	McKinley re-elected

reluctant to break old habits and loyalties, and the Populists had trouble luring supporters away from the Republicans and Democrats.

The presidential campaign of 1896 brought the nation's political wanderings to a climax. The Republicans nominated Governor William

Presidential campaign of 1896

McKinley of Ohio. The only real difficulty occurred when the party adopted a moderate platform supporting gold, an action that caused Senator Henry M. Teller of Colorado, one of the party's founders, to walk out of the convention in tears. At the Democratic convention, the nomination of Bryan and the adoption of a silver platform pleased farmers but drove away a dissenting minority of gold Democrats.

Bryan's nomination presented the Populist party with a dilemma. Should Populists join Democrats in support of Bryan, or should they nominate their own candidate and preserve their party's independence? Each faction had its supporters. In the end the party compromised, first naming the Populist Tom Watson of Georgia as its vice-presidential nominee and then nominating Bryan for the presidency.

The election results revealed that the political stand-off had finally ended. McKinley, the symbol of Republican pragmatism and the new economic order, beat Bryan by over 600,000 popular votes and by 271 to 176 in the electoral college. It was the most one-sided presidential election since 1872. As Henry Adams put it, "the majority de-

Election results

clared itself once and for all, in favor of a capitalistic system with all its necessary machinery."

The Populists had done all they could to rally the nation. But the obsession with silver undermined their cause. Silver especially prevented the Populists from building the urban-rural coalition that would have given them political breadth. Urban workers shied away from the silver issue because they feared the high prices that would result. Labor leaders like Samuel Gompers of the AFL, though partly sympathetic, would not join with Populists because they were unconvinced that farmers were employees, like industrial workers. And socialists like Daniel DeLeon denounced the Populists because, unlike socialists, they still believed in free enterprise. Thus the Populist cause fizzled in 1896.

As president, McKinley promptly signed the Gold Standard Act (1900), which required that all paper money be backed by gold, and continued to support high protective tariffs. Good times, brought about by an upswing of the business cycle and an increased money supply from new gold discoveries, enabled McKinley to beat Bryan again in 1900. Freed from the care of the economy, McKinley spent most of his time on foreign affairs.

In future elections, political parties would have to be sensitive to the pluralism of American society. They would have to satisfy a broad spectrum of interests rather than march under the banner of moral perfection. The reform spirit would survive, but its success would depend on cooperation, not on the sermons of righteous evangelists. Ironically, by 1920 many of the Populists' reform goals would be achieved, including regulations of railroads, banks, and utilities; shorter working hours; a variant of the subtreasury system; a graduated income tax; direct election of senators; the secret ballot, and more. These reforms would succeed precisely because a number of groups united behind them. Immigration, urbanization, and industrialization had transformed the United States into a pluralistic society where compromise among interest groups had become a political fact of life. The election of 1896 and

the end of the Gilded Age equilibrium confirmed that transformation.

Suggestions for further reading

GENERAL Ray Ginger, *The Age of Excess* (1965); Richard Hofstadter, *The Age of Reform: From Bryan to FDR* (1955); H. Wayne Morgan, *From Hayes to McKinley* (1969); R. Hal Williams, *Years of Decision: American Politics in the 1890s* (1978).

PARTIES, LEADERS, AND POLITICAL ISSUES John H. Dobson, *Politics in the Gilded Age* (1972); Eleanor Flexner, *Century of Struggle: The Women's Rights Movement in the United States* (1959); J. Rogers Hollingsworth, *The Whirligig of Politics: The Democracy of Cleveland and Bryan* (1963); Ari A. Hoogenboom, *Outlawing the Spoils: The Civil Service Movement* (1961); Matthew Josephson, *The Politicos* (1938); Walter T. K. Nugent, *Money and American Society* (1968); A. M. Paul, *Conservative Crisis and the Rule of Law: Attitudes of Bar and Bench, 1887–1895* (1969); David J. Rothman, *Politics and Power: The United States Senate, 1869–1901* (1966); John G. Sproat, *The Best Men: Liberal Reformers in the Gilded Age* (1968).

UNDERCURRENTS OF PROTEST William M. Dick, *Labor and Socialism in America* (1972); John P. Diggins, *The American Left in the Twentieth Century* (1973); Ray Ginger, *Bending Cross: A Biography of Eugene Victor Debs* (1949); John Laslett, *Labor and the Left* (1970).

POPULISM AND THE ELECTION OF 1896 Paolo Coletta, *William Jennings Bryan: Political Evangelist* (1964); Paul W. Glad, *McKinley, Bryan, and the People* (1964); Paul W. Glad, *The Trumpet Soundeth: William Jennings Bryan and His Democracy* (1964); Lawrence Goodwyn, *Democratic Promise: The Populist Movement in America* (1976); John D. Hicks, *The Populist Revolt* (1931); Stanley L. Jones, *The Election of 1896* (1964); Allan Weinstein, *Prelude to Populism: Origins of the Silver Issue* (1970). See Chapter 16 for other works on farm protest.

20 ✍

THE PROGRESSIVE ERA, 1895–1920

Writing to his friend Henry Ford in 1912, Thomas Edison complained that American society needed overhauling:

> In a lot of respects we Americans are the rawest and crudest of all. Our production, our factory laws, our charities, our relations between capital and labor, our distribution—all wrong, out of gear. We've stumbled along for a while, trying to run a new civilization in old ways, but we've got to start to make this world over.

Americans had always been preoccupied with reforming their society, with "making it over," but between the 1890s and the end of the First World War, an intensified rush of reform swept the country. The efforts made by reformers shaped what came to be called the Progressive era.

By the 1910s the Progressive party had formed to embody the reformers' principles. Since that time historians have used the term *progressivism* to refer to the reform spirit in general, while anguishing over the movement's meaning and its membership. It is probably most accurate to consider the era between 1895 and 1920 as characterized by a series of movements, however, each of them aimed in one way or another at renovating American society.

Who were the progressives?

The new middle class that emerged in the closing years of the nineteenth century formed the vanguard of the progressives. This group consisted mainly of young, educated men and women in the professions who believed they could use their expertise for the betterment of society. Repelled by inefficiency and immorality in business, government, and human relations, they set out to apply scientific and rational techniques to the problems of the larger society. Progressives had strong faith in progress—hence their name—and in the ability of humankind to create a better world. They were confident that if unknowing people were informed about the existence of evil, they would become outraged and demand its eradication. Unlike the period of Populist ferment, the prevailing issues of the Progressive era were urban. The progressive quest for social justice, educational and legal reform, and streamlining of government was actually an extension of the urban reform goals of the previous half-century. Indeed, the formation of the National Municipal League in 1895 signaled the beginning of the new era. The league served as a forum for debate on issues of civic reform, such as bossism versus civil service, revisions of tax laws, nonpartisan elections, and municipal ownership of public utilities.

In the early stages of the Progressive era, reformers were motivated by personal indignation, if not revulsion, at corruption and injustice. This feeling was shared and expressed by journalists

| Muckrakers |

whom Theodore Roosevelt dubbed muckrakers (alluding to a character in *Pilgrim's Progress* who rejected a crown for a muckrake). These writers investigated and attacked social, economic, and political wrongs. Their fact-filled articles and books exposed such offenses as the sale of tainted meat, fraudulent insurance schemes, and prostitution. Lincoln Steffens's articles in *McClure's,* later published as *The Shame of the Cities* (1904), ranked among the highlights of muckraker journalism. Other well-known muckraking efforts included Ida Tarbell's catalogue of abuses by the Standard Oil Company and Upton Sinclair's *The Jungle,* an exposé of the meat-packing industry. Muckrakers hoped their surveys of misrule and unfair privilege would inspire mass indignation and ultimately lead to reform.

Middle-class indignation also revealed itself in opposition to party politics. Reformers had a strong distaste for boss-ridden parties. They felt,

| Political reformers |

as journalist William Allen White did, that machines should "be reduced to mere political scrap iron by the rise of the people." (By "the people" reformers usually meant white middle-class native citizens like themselves.) To improve government and the political process, these progressives advocated such reforms as nominating candidates through direct primaries instead of party caucuses, and nonpartisan elections to prevent corruption and bribery from entering the elective process. To involve more people in the political process and to make legislators more responsible, they advocated three reform devices: the initiative, which would enable voters to propose new laws on their own; the referendum, which would enable voters to accept or reject a law at the ballot box; and the recall, which would allow voters to remove offi-

cials and judges from office before their terms were up. Their goal was to reclaim government by replacing the favoritism of the boss system with rational, accountable management chosen by a responsible electorate.

Progressive reformers, then, had an aversion to party politics, not to government. They turned to government for aid in achieving most of their goals, for they had discovered that only government had the leverage they needed. But political power was only a means toward scientific and bureaucratic ends; to Progressive reformers, especially middle-class professionals, knowledge was the key to progress. Science and the scientific method—system, planning, control, predictability—were central to their values. Just as corporations were applying scientific management to achieve economic efficiency, progressives would use impersonal decision making and planning to achieve social and political efficiency.

Among social reformers, the urge to serve needy people was sometimes translated into paternalism and intolerance of cultural differences. Efforts to teach immigrants and blacks vocational skills and the attempt to control their behavior through prohibition reflected a desire, conscious and unconscious, to keep them in their place. Finally, reformers made only feeble attempts, if any, to ensure high employment and decent wages and to fight racism and sexism.

But not all progressive reformers were middle-class professionals. During this era vital elements of what would become modern American liberalism grew out of the working-class urban experience. By the close of the nineteenth

| Working-class reformers |

century, many urban workers were pressing for government intervention to ensure safety and promote welfare. They wanted improvements in housing and health, safe factories, shorter working hours, workers' compensation, and other reforms. Often these were the very people who supported the political bosses, supposedly the enemies of reform. Workers knew that bosses needed to cultivate support among their constituents and would cater to their needs. And in fact bossism was not necessarily at odds with humanitarianism.

After 1900, voters from inner-city districts populated by migrant and immigrant working-class families elected a number of progressive legislators who had trained in the arena of machine politics. The chief goal of such politicians was to establish government responsibility for alleviating the hardship that had resulted from urban-industrial growth. They opposed such reforms as prohibition, Sunday closing laws, civil service, and nonpartisan elections, all of which conflicted with their constituents' interests.

The progressive spirit also stirred some elite business leaders. Some supported limited government regulation and political reforms as a means of protecting their wealth from more radical elements. Others were genuine humanitarians who worked unselfishly for social justice. Business leaders guided organizations like the Municipal Voters League and the U.S. Chamber of Commerce, which supported limited political and economic reform. And women of the elite classes often led reform organizations like the YWCA and Women's Christian Temperance Union.

Business leaders

But it would be a mistake to imagine that the progressive spirit touched all of American society between 1895 and 1920. There were still large numbers of people, heavily represented in Congress, who opposed reform. They disliked government interference in economic affairs—except when it strengthened the tariff—and saw nothing wrong with existing power structures. Outside government, this outlook was represented by big business leaders like J. P. Morgan, John D. Rockefeller, and E. H. Harriman. Within government this ideology was expressed by old-guard Republicans who had become so accustomed to wielding power that they were contemptuous of democratic reforms. And they had the courts on their side.

With the exception of some minor radical branches of the working-class groups, progressive reformers operated from the center of the ideological spectrum. Moderate, concerned, sometimes contradictory thinkers, they believed on the one hand that the laissez-faire system was obsolete and on the other that radical challenges to the fundamentals of capitalism were dangerous. Like the Jeffersonians, they believed in the conscience and will of the people; like the Hamiltonians, they opted for a strong central government to act in the interest of conscience.

Governmental and legislative reform in the states

By the turn of the century, professionals and intellectuals were accepting the notion that government could and should exert more power to ensure justice and well-being. They were becoming convinced that a simple, inflexible government was ineffective in a complex industrial age, and that public power was needed to counteract corruption and exploitation. But before reformers could use such power in ways they believed to be necessary, they would have to recapture government from the evil politicans whose greed had infected the democratic system. Thus an important thrust of progressive activity was the effort to root out corruption in government.

Reformers first attacked this problem in the cities, trying to redirect government through structural reforms such as civil service, nonpartisan elections, and tighter scrutiny of public expenditures. After 1900 the movement for reform brought into being the city manager and city commission forms of government and stronger regulation of public utilities. But reformers soon found that the city was too small an arena for the kind of political and economic reform they sought. Because of their faith in a strong, fair-minded executive, progressives looked to governors and other elected officials to extend and protect the reforms that had been achieved at the local level.

The reform movement produced a number of

Chapter 20: The Progressive era, 1895–1920

skillful, influential, and often charismatic governors who used executive power to achieve

Progressive governors

change. Their ranks included Braxton Bragg Comer of Alabama and Hoke Smith of Georgia, who introduced business regulations and other reforms in the South; Albert Cummins of Iowa and Hiram Johnson of California, who battled the railroads that dominated their states; Hazen Pingree of Michigan, who carried his fight against private utilities from the city to the state level; and Woodrow Wilson of New Jersey, whose administrative reforms were copied by other governors. Such men were not always saints, however. Smith supported the disfranchisement of blacks, and Johnson discriminated against Japanese-Americans.

Probably the most notable progressive governor was Wisconsin's Robert M. La Follette. A self-made small-town lawyer, La Follette rose through the ranks of the state Republican party to the governorship in 1900. As governor he initiated a multipronged reform program whose highlights were direct primaries, revision of taxes to prevent corporations from benefiting unfairly over other taxpayers, regulation of railroad rates, and the staffing of regulatory commissions with experts. After three terms as governor, "Battling Bob" was elected senator and carried his progressive ideals into national politics. His goal, he once asserted, "was not to 'smash' corporations, but to drive them out of politics, and then to treat them exactly the same as other people are treated."

Not all state leaders were as successful as La Follette. To be sure, the crusade against party politics and corruption did accomplish some permanent changes. By 1916 all but three states had direct primaries, and many states had adopted the initiative, referendum, and recall. And political reformers had achieved a major goal in 1912 when the states ratified the Seventeenth Amendment, which provided for the direct election of U.S. senators (formerly elected by state legislatures). But political reforms did not always bring about the desired results. Party bosses, better organized and more experienced

than reformers, were able to control the new primaries as well as elections. Moreover, political reformers had little durability; professional politicians moved back into power when enthusiasm for reform waned and reform leaders tired of their crusade.

New state laws aimed at bettering social welfare had greater impact than most political reforms, especially in factories. Broadly interpreting their powers to protect the health and safety of their citizens, many states enacted factory inspection laws, and by 1916 nearly two-thirds of the states had insurance for victims of industrial accidents. Under pressure from the National Child Labor Committee, nearly every state established a minimum age for employment (varying from twelve to sixteen), and prohibited employers from working children more than eight or ten hours a day. (Such laws, however, were hard to enforce.) Several groups also joined forces to limit working hours for women. After the Supreme Court upheld Oregon's ten-hour limit in 1908, many more states passed such laws protecting women workers. Finally, the efforts of the American Association for Old Age Security began to succeed in 1914, when Arizona established old-age pensions. Though the law was struck down by the courts, the First World War renewed interest in pensions, and in the 1920s many states drafted laws to provide for needy older people.

Progressive legislation

These and other social reforms were strongly opposed by people who thought them detrimental to their self-interest or a threat to the free enterprise system. The National Association of Manufacturers coordinated the battle against regulation of business and working conditions. And legislators friendly to special interests connived to weaken the new laws by failing to fund their enforcement.

Reformers themselves were not always certain about what was progressive, especially in terms of human behavior. The main problem seemed to be whether or not it was possible to create a desirable moral climate through legislation. Members of

Moral reform

the Social Gospel movement, for example, believed that only church-based inspiration and humanitarian work could transform society. But other people believed state intervention was necessary to achieve purity, especially in drinking habits and sexual behavior.

The formation of the Anti-Saloon League in 1893 marked a new turn in the long campaign against drunkenness and its effects on society. This organized group of reformers joined with the older Women's Christian Temperance Union (founded in 1873) to publicize the connections between alcoholism and health problems, poverty, unemployment, and family break-ups. The result was that a large number of states, counties, towns, and city wards restricted the sale and consumption of liquor. In 1918 prohibitionists induced Congress to pass the Eighteenth Amendment, prohibiting the manufacture, sale, and transportation of intoxicating liquors. After ratification by the states, the amendment was implemented in 1920.

Public outrage boiled over after 1900 when muckraking journalists began to expose interstate and international rings that kidnapped young women and forced them to become prostitutes, a practice called white slavery. Middle-class moralists, already alarmed by a perceived link between immigration and prostitution in the cities, prodded governments to investigate the problem and recommend corrective legislation. By 1915 nearly every state had outlawed brothels and the soliciting of sex. And in 1910 Congress passed the Mann Act, or White Slave Traffic Act, prohibiting interstate and international transportation of women for immoral purposes.

Neither the Prohibition Amendment nor the Mann Act stood squarely in the middle of progressive reform. Even so, they reflected growing sentiment that state and national governments could do something to stamp out social evils. Reformers believed that the source of evil was the social environment. From their perspective, human-made laws could destroy human-made evil.

New ideas in education, law, and the social sciences

Reformers had long envisioned education as a means of bettering society. As early as 1883, psychologist G. Stanley Hall had noted that the experiences of urban children were different from those of their rural-bred parents and grandparents. Thus educational techniques had to change. The progressives, with the educational philosopher John Dewey in the vanguard, took up the cause. According to Dewey, children, not subject matter, should be the focus of school policy, and schools should serve as community centers and instruments of social progress. Above all, said Dewey, education should relate directly to experience. Children should be encouraged to discover things for themselves. Rote memorization and outdated subjects should be replaced by teaching techniques that make knowledge relevant to students' lives and develop skills useful in modern industrial society. To Dewey, it was personal growth, not mastery of a given body of knowledge, that was the goal of human existence.

Progressive education

Personal growth also became the driving principle behind college education. The purpose of American colleges and universities had traditionally been to train a select few for the professions of law, medicine, teaching, and religion. But in the late nineteenth century, places of higher education multiplied, spurred by public aid and increases in the number of people who could afford tuition. Furthermore, educators sought to make learning meaningful to more students. Harvard University, under President Charles W. Eliot, pioneered in substituting electives for required courses and in experimenting with new teaching techniques.

Colleges and universities

As colleges and universities expanded, so did their enrollment of women. Between 1890 and 1910 the number of females enrolled in institutions of higher learning swelled from 56,000 to 140,000. By the latter date, women accounted for 40 percent of all college students, disproving the notion that women were mentally and physically inferior to men. But discrimination lingered; women were discouraged from taking courses in science and mathematics, and most medical schools refused to accept women.

The law, like education, began to exhibit new emphases on experience and scientific principles. Oliver Wendell Holmes, Jr., associate justice of

| *Progressive legal thought* |

the Supreme Court between 1902 and 1932, led the attack on the old view of law as universal and unchanging. Holmes's view that law should reflect society's needs challenged the judicial practice of invoking traditional beliefs to obstruct social legislation. Louis D. Brandeis, a brilliant lawyer who joined Holmes on the Supreme Court in 1916, carried Holmes's views one step further by insisting that judges' opinions be based on factual, scientifically gathered information about social realities. In the landmark case *Muller* v. *Oregon* (1908), Brandeis mustered extensive scientific evidence to convince the Supreme Court to uphold Oregon's law limiting women's working hours. The new legal thought, however, met some tough resistance. Judges brought up on laissez-faire economic theory continued to strike down the kind of law progressive lawyers thought necessary for effective reform.

Meanwhile, a group of young men and women concerned with improving social conditions were setting up residences called settle-

| *Settlement houses* |

ment houses in the inner-city slums. The earliest settlement houses were founded in New York by Stanton Coit, Vida Scudder, and Lillian Wald; in Chicago by Jane Addams and Ellen Gates Starr; and in Boston by Robert A. Woods. After 1900 the idea spread, and by 1910 there were over four thousand settlements scattered across the country. Well-educated and driven by the desire to help others, settlement workers offered classes, sponsored exhibits and

concerts, and undertook surveys of poverty, housing, public health, and other conditions needing reform.

Settlement workers joined with scientists and organizations like the National Consumers League to bring about some of the most far-reaching of progressive reforms: those in the area of public health. After the 1880s, doctors and social reformers began to press local governments for measures to reduce the threat of disease. By 1900 a number of cities were filtering and chlorinating public water supplies, and enlarged staffs of health inspectors were supervising tighter sanitation regulations. Health department expenditures on neighborhood clinics and dispensaries skyrocketed. Progressive women's organizations were particularly successful in sponsoring laws ensuring pure pasteurized milk and regulating the quality of food sold by street vendors.

Thus between the end of the nineteenth century and the First World War, a new breed of men and women pressed for institutional change as well as political reform. Largely middle-class in background, trained by new professional standards, confident that new ways of thinking would bring progress, these people helped to broaden the concept of government's role in meeting the needs of a mature industrial society.

Challenges to racial and sexual discrimination

W. E. B. Du Bois, the forceful black scholar and teacher, ended an essay in his book *The Souls of Black Folk* (1903) with a call that heralded the twentieth-century civil rights movement: "By every civilized and peaceful method," he wrote, "we must strive for the right which the world accords to men."

By "men" Du Bois meant all human beings, not just one sex. But his statement and its con-

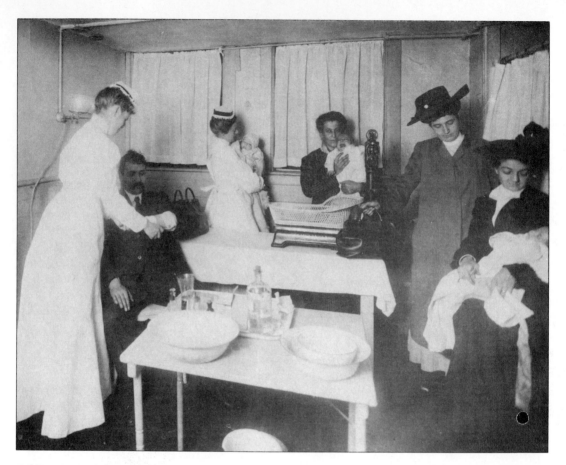

Public health clinics such as this one at Denison House in Dorchester, Boston, were among the most effective projects of progressive reformers. Often sponsored by settlement houses, the clinics ministered to the needs of the inner-city poor, especially mothers caring for infants. Photographed in 1900. The Schlesinger Library, Radcliffe College.

text suggest the dilemma that vexed the two largest groups of underprivileged Americans in the early 1900s: women and nonwhites. Both were trapped in a society dominated by white males. Both suffered from disfranchisement, discrimination, and humiliation. And for both groups the progressive challenge to old ideas and customs gave impetus to their struggles for rights, but it posed thorny questions as well. Should women and blacks strive to become just like white men, with white men's values and power as well as their rights? Or was there

something unique about their racial and sexual identity that should be retained at the risk of sacrificing some gains?

Black leaders differed over the issue of how—and whether—to achieve assimilation. In the wake of emancipation, ex-slave Frederick Douglass had urged "ultimate assimilation through self-assertion, and on no other terms." Other blacks who favored isolation from the cruel white society supported migration back to Africa or the establishment of all-black communities in Oklahoma Territory and Kansas. Still

Black students practicing woodwork at Hampton Institute, Hampton, Virginia. Like Tuskegee Institute, Hampton offered vocational instruction in the belief that by acquiring skills and working hard, blacks could convince whites they were worthy of equal rights.   Library of Congress.

others, like T. Thomas Fortune, editor of the *New York Age* and founder of the Afro-American League, advocated militancy.

Most blacks, however, could neither escape nor conquer white society. They thus had to find other routes to improvement. Self-help, a strategy articulated by educator Booker T. Washington, was one of the most popular alter-

natives. Born a slave in 1856, Washington worked his way through school and in 1881 founded Tuskegee Institute, a vocational school for blacks. There he developed the philosophy that blacks' hopes for assimilation lay in abandoning self-assertion and at least temporarily ac-

commodating themselves to whites. Rather than fighting for political rights, he said, blacks should work hard, acquire property, and prove they were worthy of their rights. Washington voiced his views in a widely acclaimed speech at the Atlanta Exposition in 1895. Whites, including progressives, welcomed Washington's policy of accommodation, and chose to regard him as representative of all blacks.

Although Washington never argued that blacks were inferior to whites, he seemed, to some black leaders, to favor second-class citizenship. In 1905 a group of "anti-Bookerites" met near Niagara Falls and pledged a more militant pursuit of such rights as unrestricted voting, equal access to economic opportunity, integration, and equality before the law. The spokesman for the Niagara movement was W. E. B. Du Bois, a vociferous critic of Washington's policy of accommodation. A New Englander with a Ph.D. from Harvard, Du Bois had the background of a typical progressive. He used scientific methods to compile fact-filled sociological studies of the lives of black ghetto dwellers, and wrote poetically for the cause of civil rights. In his essays and speeches, Du Bois treated Washington politely, but he could not accept Washington's submission to white domination.

Du Bois showed that accommodation was an unrealistic strategy, but his own solution may have been just as fanciful. A blunt elitist, Du Bois believed that an intellectual vanguard of cultivated, highly trained blacks, which he called the Talented Tenth, would save the race by setting an example to whites and other blacks. Inevitably, such elitist sentiments had more attraction for middle-class white liberals than for black sharecroppers. Thus when Du Bois and his allies formed the National Association for the Advancement of Colored People (1909), which aimed to use legal redress in the courts to end racial discrimination, the leadership consisted chiefly of white progressives.

Whatever strategy they pursued—accommodation or agitation—black Americans faced continued oppression. Race riots like the one in Atlanta in 1906 destroyed middle-class as well as working-class black neighborhoods. And the federal government only aggravated conditions. Under the administration of Woodrow Wilson, segregation within the federal government expanded; southern cabinet members supported racial separation in the rest rooms, restaurants, and offices of government buildings and balked at hiring black workers. Once more the nation failed to adhere to its ideals, and once more the dream of black Americans to be treated as human beings was delayed.

During this time too, the progressive challenge to social relations stirred women to seek liberation from the home. But their struggle raised questions of identity. What tactics should women use to achieve equality, and what should be their role in society? Could women achieve equality with men and at the same time change male-dominated society?

By the early 1900s the trend was definitely toward greater freedom for women. In 1900 exactly 20 percent of all adult women were in the labor force. By 1920 the percentage was about the same, but a major shift in the type of employment had occurred. The most significant trend was in the clerical sector. In 1880 there were only 38,000 female clerical workers; forty years later there were 1.9 million. Meanwhile the proportion of women in domestic service declined. Growth also occurred in the number of female factory workers and professionals. Though most women held the lowest-paying jobs, and those offering the least opportunity, wage labor gave them some economic independence as well as social contacts that women confined to the home never enjoyed.

Despite these breezes of change, however, most women failed to break free from traditional restraints. On the job, they had to defer to male bosses who treated them as inferiors and blocked their path upward. Off the job they were typically expected to carry a heavy load of family responsibilities as well. Single women contributed much of their meager wages to help support their parental families, and could only escape domineering parents through marriage and service to another man.

Still, the Progressive era did see a number of efforts by and on behalf of women to extend their influence beyond domestic bounds. Some of these efforts derived from radical impulses. Feminist Charlotte Perkins Gilman sounded a clarion call in her book *Women and Economics* (1898), declaring that domesticity and female innocence were obsolete and attacking the male monopoly on economic opportunity. This and Gilman's other writings moved some women, but even more

W. E. B. Du Bois

Employed women

Charlotte Perkins Gilman

were swept up by the women's club movement, which brought middle-class women together to press politically for the alleviation of social problems.

A number of such women joined the birth control movement led by Margaret Sanger. As a visiting nurse in New York's East Side immigrant neighborhoods, San- | **Margaret Sanger** | grant neighborhoods, Sanger distributed information about contraception in hopes of preventing unwanted pregnancies. Her crusade, however, captured the attention of middle-class women, who wanted to limit their own families and to control the growth of immigrant masses. It also aroused the opposition of men and women who saw birth control as a threat to family and morality. In 1914 the latter group caused Sanger to be indicted for sending obscene literature (actually articles on contraception) through the mail, forcing her to flee the country. Sanger persevered and in 1921 formed the American Birth Control League, which enlisted physicians and social workers to convince judges to allow distribution of birth control information. Most states still prohibited the sale of contraceptives, but the issue had entered the realm of public discussion.

Like birth control, the women's suffrage movement, which dated back to the mid-nine- | **Suffragists** | teenth century, drew much of its support from the middle class. Suffragists achieved their first successes at the local level; by 1912 nine states, all of them in the West, allowed women to vote. After 1900 they pressed increasingly for the vote on the national level. The suffragists' tactics ranged from the moderate but persistent propaganda campaigns of the National American Women Suffrage Association, led by Carrie Chapman Catt, to the active picketing and marching of the National Women's party, led by Alice Paul. More decisive, however, was women's participation on the home front during the First World War as factory laborers, medical volunteers, and municipal workers. Their efforts convinced legislators that women could shoulder public responsibilities and gave

final impetus to passage of the Nineteenth Amendment in June 1919.

While middle-class women organized for suffrage, working women organized unions. The resistance of their male counterparts was immediate and harsh. Of the 8 million female workers | **Women's labor unions** | in 1910, only 125,000 were members of unions, mostly because unions refused to accept women as members. Yet female employees could fight employers as bitterly as men could. The thousands of New York women shirtwaist workers proved as much in 1909, when they struck for three months and laid the foundation for the powerful International Ladies Garment Workers Union.

Some efforts were made to encourage feelings of sisterhood among all classes. Since the early nineteenth century, a number of well-to-do women had recognized that all women had common grievances. Thus Alva Belmont, a wealthy supporter of the shirtwaist workers' strike, said in 1909, "It was my interest in women, in women everywhere and every class that drew my attention and sympathies first to the striking shirtwaist girls." This feeling of sisterhood formed the basis of the feminist movement. For women such as Alva Belmont the Progressive era had helped to clarify the issues that concerned them, but major reforms would await the future.

Theodore Roosevelt and the revival of the presidency

The Progressive era's theme of challenge—to politics, to institutions, to social relations—directed attention to government, especially the federal government, as the ultimate hope of reform. The federal government, however, seemed incapable of assuming such responsibility. Then suddenly, in September 1901, the climate changed. The assassination of President William

President Theodore Roosevelt (1858–1919) giving a typically rousing political speech at a Flag Day rally. Known for his energetic leadership, Roosevelt revitalized the presidency.   Brown Brothers.

McKinley by an anarchist named Leon Czolgosz vaulted Theodore Roosevelt, the young, vigorous vice president, into the White House.

As president, Roosevelt became a progressive hero. At heart, though, he was a conservative and an individualist, not a reformer. His impulsive patriotism, admiration for big business, and compulsive dislike of anything he considered effeminate distinguished him from soft-hearted humanitarians. Yet Roosevelt came to conclusions similar to those reached by progressives. His sense of history convinced him that the kind of small government Jefferson had hoped for would not suffice in the modern industrial era. Instead, economic development necessitated a Hamiltonian system of government powerful enough to guide national affairs.

Roosevelt's presidency inaugurated the government regulation of economic affairs that has characterized twentieth-century American history. Roosevelt first turned his attention to big business, where the combination movement had produced giant trusts that controlled almost every sector of the economy.

Roosevelt's policies toward trusts

Though Roosevelt has a reputation as a trust buster, he actually believed in consolidation as the most efficient means to achieve material and technological progress. Rather than return to uncontrolled competition, he preferred to distinguish between good and bad trusts, and to prevent the bad ones from manipulating markets and fixing prices. Thus he instructed the Justice Department to use antitrust laws to prosecute the railroad, meat-packing, and oil trusts, which he believed had unscrupulously exploited the public. Roosevelt's policy triumphed in 1904 when the Supreme Court ordered the dissolution of the Northern Securities Company, the huge railroad combination created by J. P. Morgan and his powerful business allies. In general, however, Roosevelt preferred coopera-

Chapter 20: The Progressive era, 1895–1920

tion between business and government. And he exerted pressure on business to regulate itself.

Roosevelt also pushed for regulatory legislation, especially after 1904, when he won a resounding electoral victory by garnering the votes of progressives and businessmen alike. After compromising with business representatives in Congress, he succeeded in 1906 in getting passage of the Hepburn Act, which imposed stricter control over railroads and expanded the powers of the Interstate Commerce Commission. The act gave the ICC more authority to fix railroad rates and outlaw free passes, though it did allow the courts to overturn rate decisions.

Roosevelt showed a similar willingness to compromise on legislation to ensure pure food and drugs. For decades reformers had been urging government regulation of patent medicines and processed meat. The outcry against fraud and adulteration heightened in 1906 with the publication of Upton Sinclair's *The Jungle,* an exposé of filthy, rat-infested meat-packing plants in Chicago. On reading Sinclair's novel, Roosevelt ordered an investigation. Finding Sinclair's descriptions accurate, he supported legislation that would become the Pure Food and Drug Act and the Meat Inspection Act, both passed in 1906. Like the Hepburn Act, these laws reinforced the principle of government regulation. But as part of the compromise to obtain their passage, the government had to agree to pay for inspections, and meat packers could appeal government decisions in court.

> **Pure food and drug laws**

On other issues Roosevelt took stands that both thrilled and frustrated progressives. When, for example, the United Mine Workers struck against coal-mine owners in 1902, the president intervened by using the progressive tactics of investigation and arbitration. The mine workers, led by feisty John Mitchell, wanted higher pay and an eight-hour day, but the owners stubbornly refused to recognize the union or arbitrate the grievances. As winter approached and fuel shortages threatened, Roosevelt warned that he would use federal troops to reopen the mines, thereby forcing both sides to accept arbi-

tration of the dispute by a special commission. The commission decided in favor of higher wages and reduced hours, but also declared that the owners did not have to recognize the union. The decision, according to Roosevelt, created a "square deal" for all. The strike settlement established the federal government as an arbiter in labor disputes affecting the public interest. But it also illustrated Roosevelt's belief that the president or his agents should have a say in which labor demands were legitimate and which were not.

On the issue of conservation, Roosevelt displayed the same mix of flamboyant executive action and quiet compromise that he applied to other domestic matters. He built a reputation as a determined conservationist, using presidential power to add almost 150 million acres to the national forests and to preserve vast areas of water and coal from private plunder. True to the progressive spirit, Roosevelt wanted a "well-conceived plan" for resource management. But compromises and factors beyond his control weakened his scheme. Timber and mining companies shunned supervision of their wasteful practices, and Congress never authorized enough funds or personnel to enforce federal regulations.

> **Conservation**

During his last year in office, Roosevelt moved further away from the Republican party's traditional alliance with big business. He lashed out at the irresponsible actions of "malefactors of great wealth" and threw his support behind stronger regulation of business and heavier taxation of the rich. Having promised in 1904 that he would not seek re-election, Roosevelt backed his friend Secretary of War William Howard Taft for the nomination in 1908. The Democrats nominated William Jennings Bryan for the third time, but the Great Commoner lost again.

Early in 1909 Roosevelt went to Africa to shoot game, leaving Taft to face the political problems his predecessor had managed to postpone. Foremost among them were tariff rates. Honoring Taft's pledge to cut rates, the

> **Taft administration**

House passed a bill sponsored by Representative Sereno E. Payne that provided for numerous downward revisions. Senate protectionists prepared to revise the House bill in an upward direction, but progressives, led by La Follette, fought back. In the end the protectionists rewrote the bill, and Taft signed it. To many progressives, Taft had failed the test of filling Roosevelt's shoes.

The progressive and conservative wings of the Republican party were rapidly drifting apart. Soon after the tariff controversy a group of insurgents in the House, led by George Norris of Nebraska, challenged Speaker "Uncle Joe" Cannon of Illinois, whose power over committee assignments and scheduling of debate could make or break a piece of legislation. Taft first supported and then abandoned the insurgents, who nevertheless managed to liberalize procedures by enlarging the important rules committee and removing its appointments from Cannon's control. Meanwhile, Taft also angered conservationists by allowing Secretary of the Interior Richard A. Ballinger to remove 1 million acres of forest and mineral land from the reserved list and to fire Gifford Pinchot, the government's chief forester, when he protested a questionable sale of coal lands in Alaska.

In reality Taft was as sympathetic to reform as Roosevelt was. He prosecuted more trusts than Roosevelt; continued to expand the national forest reserves; signed the Mann-Elkins Act of 1910, which bolstered the regulatory powers of the ICC; and supported such labor reforms as the eight-hour day and mine safety legislation. The Sixteenth Amendment, which enabled the establishment of a federal income tax, and the Seventeenth Amendment, which provided for the direct election of U.S. senators, were initiated during Taft's presidency. Like Roosevelt, Taft was forced to compromise with big business, but he lacked Roosevelt's ability to maneuver and to publicize the issues he supported.

Thus in 1910, when Roosevelt returned from Africa, he found his party fragmented. Anti-Taft reformers formed the National Progressive Republican League and rallied behind Robert La Follette for president in 1912. Another wing of the party stood loyal to Taft. Finally, when La Follette became ill, Roosevelt threw his hat in the ring for the Republican presidential nomination.

Taft's supporters controlled the convention and nominated him for a second term, but the Roosevelt forces formed a third party—the Progressive party—and nominated the fifty-three-year-old former president. Meanwhile, the Democrats selected New Jersey's progressive governor Woodrow Wilson. The Socialists nominated their perennial candidate Eugene V. Debs. The campaign exposed the voters to the most thorough evaluation of the American political and economic system in nearly a generation.

Woodrow Wilson and the extension of reform

Wilson won the election with 42 percent of the popular vote—he was a minority president, though he did capture 435 out of 531 electoral votes. Roosevelt received about 27 percent of the popular vote. Taft finished a poor third, polling 23 percent of the popular vote and only 8 electoral votes. Debs won an impressive 900,000 votes, 6 percent of the total. Thus fully three-quarters of the electorate supported some alternative to the restrained approach to government that Taft represented. The results allowed Wilson to interpret the election as a popular mandate to subdue powerful trusts and broaden the federal government's concern for social reform.

The campaign had featured a sharp debate over the fundamentals of progressive government. On one side stood Roosevelt with a system he called the New Nationalism. Roosevelt foresaw a new era of national unity in which governmental authority would balance and coordinate economic activity. He would not destroy big business, which he saw as an efficient way to organize production. Rather, he would establish regulatory commissions to protect citizens' interests and ensure the wise use of concentrated economic power. Again, Roosevelt was less interested in trust-busting than in supervising corporate enterprise for the general welfare.

Wilson offered a more idealistic scheme in his New Freedom. He believed that the concentration of economic power threatened individual liberty, that monopolies had to be broken so that the marketplace could again become open. But he did not want to restore laissez faire. Like Roosevelt, Wilson would enhance governmental authority to protect and regulate. But Wilson stopped short of the combination of big business and big government inherent in Roosevelt's New Nationalism.

Roosevelt and Wilson stood closer together than their rhetoric implied. Both men strongly supported equality of opportunity, conservation of natural resources, fair wages for workers, and social betterment for all classes. Perhaps more important, both would expand governmental activity through strong personal leadership and bureaucratic reform.

As president, Wilson found that he had to blend his New Freedom ideals with New Nationalism precepts, and in so doing he set the direction of federal economic policy for much of the twentieth century. The corporate merger movement had proceeded so far that restoration of free competition was impossible. Thus Wilson could only acknowledge economic concentration and try to prevent its abuse by expanding the government's regulatory powers. His administration moved toward that end with the passage in 1914 of the Clayton Anti-Trust Act and a measure creating the Federal Trade Commission (FTC). The Clayton Act extended the Sherman Anti-Trust Act of 1890 by outlawing quasi-monopolistic practices such as price wars aimed at destroying

*Expanded
regulation of
business*

competition and interlocking directorates (management of two or more competing companies by the same executives). The FTC, which replaced Roosevelt's Bureau of Corporations, was to investigate corporations and issue cease-and-desist orders against unfair trade practices. Like ICC rulings, accused companies could appeal FTC orders in the courts.

Wilson pushed federal regulation beyond the confines of corporate behavior and into finance with the Federal Reserve Act of 1913. The law established the nation's first centralized banking system since Andrew Jackson destroyed the Second Bank of the United States. Twelve newly created district banks would hold the reserves of member banks throughout the nation. The district banks would loan money to member banks at a low interest rate, called the *discount rate*. By adjusting this rate (and thus the amount of money a bank could afford to borrow), the district banks would be able to increase or decrease the amount of money in circulation. In other words, depending on the nation's needs, the reserve bank could loosen or tighten credit.

Perhaps the only act of Wilson's first administration that re-established free competition was the Underwood Tariff, passed in 1913. For years rising prices had thwarted consumers' desires for the material benefits of the industrial age, partially because tariffs discouraged importation of cheap foreign materials. The Underwood Tariff encouraged imports by drastically reducing or eliminating tariff rates. To recover revenues lost due to the reductions, the act levied a graduated income tax on U.S. residents—an option made possible earlier that year when the Sixteenth Amendment was ratified. The income tax was tame by today's standards. Incomes under $4,000 were exempt; thus almost all factory workers and farmers escaped the tax. People and corporations earning $4,000 to $20,000 had to pay a 1-percent tax, and the rate for higher incomes rose gradually to a maximum of 6 percent on earnings over $500,000. Such rates made no holes in the pockets of the rich.

Important events

1893	Anti-Saloon League founded		1907	Economic panic
1895	Booker T. Washington's accommodation speech at Atlanta Exposition		1908	William Howard Taft elected president *Muller* v. *Oregon*
1898	Charlotte Perkins Gilman, *Women and Economics*		1909	NAACP founded Payne-Aldrich Tariff
1899	John Dewey, *The School and Society*		1910	Mann-Elkins Act White Slave Traffic Act Ballinger-Pinchot controversy
1900	McKinley re-elected		1912	Woodrow Wilson elected president
1901	McKinley assassinated; Roosevelt assumes the presidency		1913	Sixteenth and Seventeenth Amendments ratified Underwood Tariff Federal Reserve Act
1903	Elkins Act Coal strike settled W. E. B. Du Bois, *The Souls of Black Folk*		1914	Federal Trade Commission Act Clayton Anti-Trust Act Margaret Sanger indicted
1904	*Northern Securities* case Theodore Roosevelt elected president Lincoln Steffens, *The Shame of the Cities*		1916	Wilson re-elected Federal Farm Loan Act Adamson Act
1905	Niagara Falls Convention		1919	Eighteenth Amendment ratified (prohibition)
1906	Hepburn Act Pure Food and Drug Act Upton Sinclair, *The Jungle*		1920	Nineteenth Amendment ratified (women's suffrage)

The European war and the approaching presidential campaign prompted Wilson to support stronger reforms in 1916. Concerned that food shortages might result if farmers could not borrow money to sustain production, the president backed the Federal Farm Loan Act of 1916. The measure created twelve federally supported banks that would lend money to farm-

Aid to farmers and workers

ers at moderate interest rates. To stave off railroad strikes that might disrupt transportation at a time of national emergency, Wilson pushed passage of the Adamson Act of 1916, which mandated an eight-hour day and time-and-a-half for overtime for railroad laborers. Finally, Wilson courted the support of social reformers in Roosevelt's camp by backing laws that outlawed child labor and provided workers' compensation for federal employees who suffered from injury or illness.

By emphasizing peace, prosperity, and progressivism, Wilson won a narrow victory in the 1916 presidential election over Republican challenger Charles Evans Hughes, an associate justice of the Supreme Court and former progressive governor of New York. Wilson's second term and the subsequent involvement of the nation in the First World War saw a shift away from competition toward interest-group politics and government regulation.

The Progressive era in perspective

The Progressive era was characterized by a welter of confusing and sometimes contradictory goals. Certainly there was no single progressive movement. On the national level, reform programs ranged from Roosevelt's New Nationalism to Wilson's New Freedom. At the state and local levels, reformers pursued causes as varied as neighborhood improvement, government reorganization, public ownership of utilities, betterment of working conditions, and moral revival.

The failure of many progressive initiatives testifies to the strength of opposition to reform as well as ambiguities within the reform movements themselves. The courts struck down some key progressive legislation. In states and cities, adoption of the initiative, referendum, and recall did not encourage greater participation in government; either those mechanisms were seldom used or they became the tools of special interests. On the federal level, new regulatory agencies rarely had the resources for thorough investigations. Thus government remained under the influence of business and industry, which many people considered quite satisfactory.

Yet in spite of all their weaknesses, the numerous reform movements that characterized the Progressive era did refashion the nation's future. Industrialists became more conscious of public opinion, and politicians became less dictatorial. Progressive legislation gave government tools with which to protect consumers. But perhaps most important, progressives challenged old institutions and old ways of thinking. They raised questions about the quality of American life that, though they remained unresolved, made the nation more aware of its principles and promises.

Suggestions for further reading

PROGRESSIVISM Richard Abrams, *The Burdens of Progress* (1978); John W. Chambers, *The Tyranny of Change: America in the Progressive Era* (1980); Arthur Ekrich, *Progressivism in America* (1974); Samuel P. Hays, *The Response to Industrialism* (1957); Richard Hofstadter, *The Age of Reform* (1955); Henry F. May, *The End of American Innocence* (1959); David W. Noble, *The Progressive Mind,* rev. ed. (1981); William L. O'Neill, *The Progressive Years* (1975); Robert H. Wiebe, *Businessmen and Reform* (1962); Robert H. Wiebe, *The Search for Order* (1968).

STATE AND LOCAL REFORM Richard Abrams, *Conservatism in a Progressive Era: Massachusetts Politics, 1900–1912* (1964); George E. Mowry, *The California Progressives* (1951); David P. Thelen, *The New Citizenship: Origins of Progressivism in Wisconsin* (1972); David P. Thelen, *Robert La Follette and the Insurgent Spirit* (1976); James H. Timberlake, *Prohibition and the Progressive Crusade* (1963).

EDUCATION, LAW, AND THE SOCIAL SCIENCES Loren P. Beth, *The Development of the American Constitution, 1877–1917* (1971); Lawrence Cremin, *The Transformation of the School: Progressivism in American Education* (1961); Allen F. Davis, *Spearheads for Reform* (1967); Samuel J. Konefsky, *The Legacy of Holmes and Brandeis* (1956); Lawrence Veysey, *The Emergence of the American University* (1970).

WOMEN Lois Banner, *Women in Modern America* (1974); Carl N. Degler, *At Odds: Women and the Family in America* (1980); Eleanor Flexner, *Century of Struggle: The Women's Rights Movement in the United*

States (1959); Aileen Kraditor, *The Ideas of the Women's Suffrage Movement* (1965); William L. O'Neill, *Everyone Was Brave: The Rise and Fall of Feminism in America* (1969); Ross Evans Paulson, *Woman's Suffrage and Prohibition* (1973); Rosalind Rosenberg, *Beyond Separate Spheres: Intellectual Roots of Modern Feminism* (1982); Elyce J. Rotella, *From Home to Office: U.S. Women at Work, 1870–1930* (1981); Leslie Woodcock Tentler, *Wage-Earning Women: Industrial Work and Family Life in the United States, 1900–1930* (1979).

BLACKS George Frederickson, *The Black Image in the White Mind* (1971); Louis R. Harlan, *Booker T.* Washington (1972); James M. McPherson, *The Abolitionist Legacy: From Reconstruction to the NAACP* (1975); August Meier, *Negro Thought in America, 1880–1915* (1963); Elliot M. Rudwick, *W. E. B. Du Bois* (1969).

NATIONAL POLITICS John M. Blum, *The Republican Roosevelt,* 2nd ed. (1957); John M. Blum, *Woodrow Wilson and the Politics of Morality* (1956); Paolo E. Coletta, *The Presidency of William Howard Taft* (1973); Arthur S. Link, *Woodrow Wilson and the Progressive Era* (1954); Edmund Morris, *The Rise of Theodore Roosevelt* (1979); George E. Mowry, *The Era of Theodore Roosevelt* (1958).

21 🌊

THE QUEST FOR EMPIRE,
1865–1914

William H. Seward's travels through scenic Alaska in August 1869 revived his enthusiasm for the huge territory he had, as secretary of state, bought from imperial Russia two years earlier. In a speech at Sitka, Seward told white citizens that Alaska was certain to become a "shipyard for the supply of all nations." Seward's oratory reflected the optimism of those nineteenth-century Americans like himself who saw little but grandeur in the nation's future. Indeed, the nation had long been on an expansionist course. According to the Russian minister to the United States, the American "destiny is always to expand."

But the expansionist road, then and later, was not unchallenged, or consistently traveled. Diplomatic crises, wars, and vigorous national debate always accompanied expansionism. Critics slowed expansion with their arguments that it was unnecessary given the undeveloped domain at home. Leaders played politics with foreign policy, complicating the diplomatic process. Still, the quest for land and trade continued and accelerated in the nineteenth century, reaching fever pitch in the tumultuous decade of the 1890s.

Expansionism revived

Foreign policy has always sprung from the domestic setting of a nation—its needs, wants, moods, and ideals. The people who guided

| Domestic roots of foreign policy |

America's expansionist foreign relations were the same people who kindled the spirit of national growth at home. Most Americans paid scant attention to external issues or to the intense international rivalry of the post–Civil War era. But America's leaders were alert to the nation's place in world affairs.

The expansionism so evident at home after the Civil War was deeply intertwined with foreign policy. The national network of railroads, for example, made it possible for Iowa farmers to transport their crops to seaboard cities and then on to foreign markets. Their livelihood was thus tied to international market conditions, to the outcomes of foreign wars, and to the time-honored American principle of freedom of the seas. The tariff too was an issue in both domestic politics and world affairs. Tariff increases designed to protect American industry and agriculture from foreign competition adversely affected those who sold to America, prompting them to enact retaliatory tariffs on American products. And the massive influx of immigrants caused diplomatic problems as well as social upheaval at home. Moreover, notions of racial superiority and Jim Crow practices at home influenced American policies toward Asian and Latin American peoples of color, who were considered inferior. In short, the threads of domestic and foreign policy were densely interwoven.

By 1900 the United States had become a world power. Since the Civil War it had acquired Alaska, the Midway Islands, Samoa, the

| American imperialism | Philippines, Guam, Puerto Rico, Hawaii, and Wake Island. |

It exercised a protectorate over Cuba and was establishing hegemony—that is, dominance—over much of the Caribbean. The United States had also pledged itself to preserve the principle of equal trade opportunities, or the Open Door, in China. The U.S. Navy was taking its place among the world's foremost fleets. And the nation's export trade was second only to that of Great Britain. American missionaries, too, were more active abroad than ever before.

American expansionism led to imperialism: the imposition of control over other peoples, denying them the freedom to make their own decisions, undermining their sovereign independence. Imperialism took a variety of forms, both formal (annexation, colonialism, or military occupation) and informal (the threat of intervention or economic manipulation). Sometimes the United States took territories; sometimes it controlled the economic life of others; sometimes American troops intervened, imposed order, and stayed to govern.

With a characteristic mixture of self-interest and idealism, United States leaders believed that imperialism benefited both Americans and those who came under American control. When they intervened in other lands or lectured weaker states, Americans defended their behavior on the grounds that they were extending the blessings of liberty and prosperity to less fortunate people. To critics at home and abroad, however, American paternalism appeared hypocritical. They charged that the use of coercion to compel resistant foreigners to behave and think like Americans violated cherished American principles.

Visions of greatness

William H. Seward's career spanned pre–Civil War and post–Civil War expansionism. A sena-

tor from New York (1849–1861) and later secretary of state (1861–1869) he envisioned a large

| William H. Seward | coordinated empire encompassing Canada, the Caribbean, Cuba, Central America, |

Mexico, Hawaii, Iceland, Greenland, and certain Pacific islands. This empire would be built not by war but by a natural process of gravitation toward the attractive republican United States. Commerce would hurry the process, he thought.

A host of voices echoed Seward's fervent nationalism and quest for expansion and empire. In the aftermath of the bloody Civil War, American leaders tried to heal sectional wounds with soothing patriotic oratory. Notions of American exceptionalism and Manifest Destiny were revived, and predictions of American supremacy in international affairs became commonplace. To the Reverend Josiah Strong, author of the influential book *Our Country* (1885), Americans were a special, God-favored, superior Anglo-Saxon race destined to lead others. To Social Darwinists, Americans were a superior people who would surely overcome all competition and thrive.

Captain Alfred T. Mahan also believed in American greatness, but assumed that its source was sea power. Since foreign trade was vital to the nation's well-being, the nation required an

| The call for naval power | efficient navy to protect its shipping. And the navy in turn required colonies for |

bases. Mahan's widely read book *The Influence of Seapower Upon History* (1890) sat on every good expansionist's shelf. Senator Henry Cabot Lodge of Massachusetts enthusiastically endorsed Mahan's call for trade, navy, and colonies. An advocate of what he tagged the "large policy," Lodge chided those Americans who shied away from empire.

Articulate spokesmen for a wider field, like Seward and Lodge, belonged to what scholars have variously labeled the foreign-policy elite,

| Foreign policy elite | the foreign-policy public, or the opinion leaders. Better read and better traveled than |

most Americans, more cosmopolitan than provincial in outlook, and politically active, they influenced the making of foreign policy. Unlike domestic policy, foreign policy is seldom shaped by the people. It was this small group whose opinion counted, and increasingly they urged an imperialist course.

Factory, farm, and foreign affairs

Those business people and farmers whose livelihoods depended upon foreign markets also supported expansionism. They sought profits from foreign sales, but fear generated foreign trade as well. The nation's farms and factories produced more than Americans could consume. Foreign commerce, it was believed, could be a safety valve to avert or relieve depression.

The tremendous economic growth of the United States after the Civil War stimulated foreign trade. From the 1860s to 1914, in fact, foreign trade grew faster than the national income. By the 1870s the United States began to enjoy a long-term favorable balance of trade (exporting more than it imported). In 1870 United States exports totaled $451 million; by 1914 they had reached $2.5 billion. Although exports of manufactured items increased, agricultural goods accounted for about three-quarters of the total in 1870 and about two-thirds in 1900. Manufactured goods led export sales for the first time in 1913.

Growth of foreign trade

America's large businesses looked to foreign markets, especially in the 1890s when it became clear that the output of industrial products was outdistancing consumption. In the 1870s and 1880s about two-thirds of all American petroleum was exported, and in succeeding decades the figure was about one-half. Fifteen percent of America's iron and steel, 50 percent of its copper, and 16 percent of its agricultural implements were sold abroad by the turn of the century, making many workers in those industries dependent on exports.

Singer sewing machines were exported throughout the globe in the late nineteenth century. Here the King of Ou (the Caroline Islands, in the Pacific) operates the Great Civilizer. Though the caption for this company-sponsored photograph read "The Herald of Civilization—Missionary Work of the Singer Manufacturing Company," Singer was interested in more than improving the world's standard of living. The profitable business sold 800,000 sewing machines in 1890, about three-quarters of all the sewing machines sold in the world that year. Courtesy, Robert B. Davies, *Peacefully Working to Conquer the World.*

Foreign economic expansion was also measured in other ways. Direct American investments abroad reached $3.5 billion by 1914, placing the United States among the top four investor countries. This high ranking convinced some that the financial center of the world was passing from London to New York.

American economic expansion in Latin America was especially impressive, and aroused the nation's diplomatic interest in its neighbors to the south. United States exports to Latin

America, which exceeded $50 million in the

Economic expansion in Latin America

1870s, topped $300 million in 1914. Investments by United States citizens in Latin America amounted to a towering $1.26 billion in 1914. In Central America, the United Fruit Company, owner of more than 1 million acres of land, became a major political force. By 1910 Americans controlled 43 percent of Mexican property and produced more than half that nation's oil.

Economic expansion abroad meant more than pocketbook profits for farmers and businessmen. For nationalists, a vigorous foreign trade was a sign of greatness, a source of pride. Foreign commerce was also a mechanism for exerting political influence. Indeed, by the early twentieth century American economic interests were influencing policies on taxes and natural resources in countries like Cuba and Mexico. American interests were responsible for drawing Hawaii into the American imperial net and for spreading American cultural values abroad. Religious missionaries and Singer executives, for example, joined hands in promoting the "civilizing medium" of the sewing machine. It is not surprising that many of the recent nationalist revolutions, such as that in Mexico in 1910, were very anti-American.

Transportation, communication, and expansion

Improvements in transportation and communication in the machine age were also significant for American foreign policy: by dramatically reducing the time required to move ships, people, goods, and words, they shrank the globe. Drawn closer to one another by technology, nations found that faraway events became more

Impact of the telegraph

important to their prosperity and security. The world became a huge communica-

tions system. In 1866, through the persevering efforts of Cyrus Field, an underwater transatlantic cable linked European and American telegraph networks. And Americans strung telegraph lines to Latin America, reaching Chile in 1890. Information about markets, diplomatic crises, and war flowed steadily and quickly to the United States.

Commodore George Dewey's flagship, the *Olympia,* belonged to another offshoot of the new technology, the New Navy. Until its modernization, the American navy had been in a

New Navy

sorry state. But in 1883 Congress authorized construction of the first steel steam-powered warships, and a year later the Naval War College was founded at Newport, Rhode Island, to instill professionalism in the officer corps. New Navy ships thrust the United States into naval prominence. In a deliberate effort to kindle patriotism and local support for naval expansionism, many of these vessels were named for states and cities.

The relationship between technology, foreign trade, and ships was also apparent in the campaign for an isthmian canal in Central America.

Panama Canal

Expansionists, including leaders from the political, military, and business communities, wanted an American owned and controlled canal. But three obstacles stood in the way: the enormous expense of construction, approval by the nation through which the canal would be cut, and the Clayton-Bulwer Treaty with England (1850), which provided for joint control of any canal built in the area. Not until Theodore Roosevelt became president did the United States remove the impediments. Roosevelt nudged the British aside in the Hay-Pauncefote Treaty of 1901; urged Panamanian rebels to declare independence from Colombia; sent American warships to the isthmus to ensure the rebels' success; signed a treaty (1903) with the infant nation of Panama awarding the United States a canal zone and long-term rights to its control; and lobbied Congress for the substantial funds to dig and fortify a canal. The Panama Canal opened in 1914.

The Panama Canal under construction, 1910. To build the locks shown here, workers poured 2.4 million cubic yards of concrete from the huge, T-shaped overhead cranes. A monument to American technological genius, the canal cost over $350 million.   Courtesy, Panama Canal Company.

A generation of diplomacy, 1865–1895

The American empire was built gradually, sometimes haltingly, in the years following the Civil War. Though Seward began the process, most of his grandiose plans did not reach fruition during his own tenure as secretary of state. But he did enjoy some successes. When an American naval officer seized the Midway Islands in 1867, Seward laid claim to them for the United States. The same year he paid Russia $7.2 million for the 591,000 square miles of Alaska. The secretary's forceful handling of French in-

terference in Mexico also furthered his reputation. In 1861, Napoleon III had placed Archduke Ferdinand Maximilian of Austria on the throne in Mexico. Preoccupied with the Civil War, Seward could do little to dislodge the intruding Europeans. But in 1866, citing the Monroe Doctrine, he told the French to get out. American troops headed for the Mexican border to buttress the point. Napoleon, troubled at home, abandoned his Mexican venture. But Seward's other schemes for acquiring territory were blocked by a combination of anti-imperialists and political foes.

Seward's successor, Hamilton Fish (1869–1877), inherited the knotty and emotional problem of the *Alabama* claims. The *Alabama* and other vessels built by Great Britain for the Con-

Anglo-American relations

federacy during the Civil War had marauded Union shipping. Fish patiently took to the bargaining table the question of British compensation for the damage. In 1871 Britain and America signed the Washington Treaty, whereby the British apologized and agreed to the creation of a tribunal, which later awarded the United States $15.5 million. Disputes over fishing rights along the North Atlantic coast and the hunting of seals in the Bering Sea near Alaska also dogged Anglo-American relations and would continue to do so for decades. Yet the two powers, however competitive, were slowly coming to the conclusion that rapprochement rather than confrontation or war best served their interests.

The convening of the first Pan-American Conference in Washington, D.C., in 1889 bore witness to the growing ties between the United States and Latin America. The conference was

Pan-American Conference

designed to improve commercial relations. The Latin American conferees toured United States factories and then negotiated several general agreements to promote trade. To improve inter-American cooperation, they founded the Pan American Union. Even so, Pan-Americanism remained more an ideal than a reality.

Hawaii also excited American attention. This key to the Pacific was a major way station for trade with Asia and had long been a site of missionary work. Its undeveloped but strategic port of Pearl Harbor tempted naval expansionists, and the vast sugar plantations of the islands attracted American entrepreneurs. In 1875 the United States signed a treaty granting Hawaiian sugar duty-free entry to the American market; the Hawaiian sugar industry boomed and became dependent on mainland business. When the Congress revised the tariff laws in the early 1890s, however, it eliminated the special protection for Hawaiian sugar and gave American producers a bounty of two cents a pound.

American planters in Hawaii were severely hurt. To gain exemption from American tariffs once and for all, a group of them, called the Annexation Club, plotted a revolution aimed at forcing annexation.

In January 1893 the white minority overthrew the native monarch, Queen Liliuokalani. Their success stemmed in part from the support

Annexation of Hawaii

of the chief American diplomat in Honolulu, John L. Stevens, who saw to it that sailors from the warship *Boston* encircled the royal palace. Stevens informed Washington that the "Hawaiian pear is now fully ripe, and this is the golden hour for the United States to pluck it." Against the protests of Japan, whose nationals outnumbered Americans in Hawaii, President Harrison sent a treaty of annexation to the Senate. But incoming President Cleveland, an expansionist who nevertheless disapproved of forced annexation, withdrew it. Five years later, on July 7, 1898, during the Spanish-American War, President William McKinley successfully maneuvered another treaty through the Senate and added Hawaii to the American empire.

Like the annexation of Hawaii, the Venezuelan crisis of 1895 climaxed a long history of U.S. intervention in that nation's affairs. For decades

Venezuelan crisis

Venezuela and Great Britain had squabbled over the border between Venezuela and British Guiana, for the disputed territory contained rich gold deposits. When Venezuela asked for American help, President Cleveland decided that the "mean and hoggish" British had to be warned away. In July 1895, Secretary of State Richard Olney sent the British a brash 12,000-word message. After reminding them of the Monroe Doctrine, Olney declared, "To-day the United States is practically sovereign on this continent, and its fiat is law upon the subjects to which it confines its interposition."

This statement of United States hegemony did not impress the British, who rejected American interference in what they considered a local issue. But neither London nor Washington wanted war. The British, seeking international

Chapter 21: The quest for empire, 1865–1914

friends to counter an intensifying German competition, quietly retreated from the crisis. In 1896 an Anglo-American arbitration board divided the disputed territory. Throughout the deliberations Venezuela was barely consulted. Thus the United States displayed a trait common to imperialists: a disregard for the rights and sensibilities of small nations.

The Cuban revolution as menace and opportunity

In 1895 another crisis rocked the Caribbean: the Cuban revolution against Spain. From 1868 to 1878 the Cubans had battled their mother country to no avail. Slavery was abolished but independence was denied, and Spanish rule continued to be repressive. The Cuban rebels waited for another chance. José Martí, one of the heroes of Cuban history, collected money, arms, and men in the United States. As in the case of Hawaii, a change in American tariff policy hastened the revolution. The Wilson-Gorman Tariff (1894) imposed a duty on Cuban sugar, which had been entering the United States duty-free. The Cuban economy, highly dependent on exports, was thrown into turmoil.

From American soil, Martí launched a revolution that became gruesome in its human and material costs. Rebels burned cane fields and razed mills. Under the command of Valereano Weyler, soon dubbed the Butcher, Spanish officials instituted a policy of "reconcentration":

hundreds of thousands of Cubans were herded into fortified towns and camps to separate them from the insurgents. Camp conditions were ghastly. As much as one-quarter of the total Cuban population perished in these reconcentration centers.

As tragic stories of atrocity and destruction reached the United States—and were played up by the American yellow press—people grew angry with the Spanish and sympathetic toward the insurrectionists. In late 1897 a new government came to power in Madrid. The Spanish modified reconcentration and promised that Cuba would be given some degree of autonomy. Americans waited to see if the new reforms would subdue the rebellious island and restore peace.

When President McKinley came to office he was already an expansionist. And the 1896 Republican platform on which he ran was a spirited imperialist document that called for Cuban independence. In his annual message of December 1897, however, McKinley surveyed the Cuban crisis and ruled out American intervention while Spain seemed to be walking the path of reform. He was by no means a weak leader, but he wanted to avoid war if at all possible.

Events in the first few months of 1898 sabotaged the Spanish reforms and exhausted American patience. Early in January, anti-reform pro-Spanish loyalists and army personnel rioted in Havana. After the riots, Washington officials ordered the New Navy battleship *Maine* to Havana harbor. On February 16 an explosion ripped through the *Maine,* killing 260 American officers and crew members. Americans were quick to blame Spain for the disaster.

Spain's image in the United States had been undermined a week earlier when William Randolph Hearst's inflammatory *New York Journal* published a stolen private letter from Enrique Dupuy de Lôme, the Spanish minister in Washington. In the letter de Lôme scorned McKinley as "weak and a bidder for the admiration of the crowd" and revealed Spanish determination to fight on in Cuba. The combination of the letter and the sinking of the *Maine* provoked cries for war. In March the president asked for $50 million in defense funds, and Congress complied unanimously. The naval board created to investigate the sinking of the *Maine* then reported that a mine had caused the explosion. (Actually, the explosion was probably accidental.) The panel did not assign responsibility, but restless Americans blamed Spain.

McKinley's diplomatic options were greatly reduced by the impact of these events. The president thought about buying Cuba, but he knew Spain would not sell, the rebels would oppose the deal, and Congress might not fund it. So he settled instead on an ultimatum. In late March the United States insisted that Spain accept an armistice, end reconcentration altogether, and designate McKinley as arbiter if peace had not been achieved by October 1. The American goal became Cuban independence. Yet no Spanish government could have given up Cuba and remained in office.

The Spanish did make concessions. They abolished reconcentration and accepted an armistice on the condition that the insurgents agree first. McKinley had wanted more; he began to write a message to Congress. After completing his speech, however, he received the news that Spain had gone one step further and declared a unilateral armistice. The weary McKinley hesitated but chose to go to Congress with a war message nonetheless. He could no longer tolerate the chronic disorder just ninety miles off the American coast. In his address on April 11, the president did not ask for a declaration of war against Spain but rather for an authorization to use force, as "an impartial neutral," to effect "a rational compromise between the contestants."

War, empire, and public debate

Congress debated for over a week and then on April 19 declared Cuba free and independent, directing the president to use force to remove Spanish authority from the island. The legislators also passed the Teller Amendment, which disclaimed any American intention to annex Cuba. On April 24 Spain declared war on the United States.

The motives of those Americans who favored war were mixed and complex. McKinley's message of April 11 expressed a humanitarian im-

pulse to stop the bloodletting; concern for the

| *Motives for war* |

"very serious injury to the commerce, trade, and business of our people"; and the psychological need to end the nightmarish anxiety once and for all. Republican politicians advised McKinley that they would lose the upcoming congressional elections unless the Cuban question was solved. And many businessmen, who had been hesitant before the crisis of early 1898, joined many farmers in the belief that removing Spain from Cuba would open new markets for surplus production, to which the depression of the 1890s had given urgency.

Inveterate imperialists saw the war as an opportunity to fulfill the "large policy." Naval enthusiasts could prove the worth of the New Navy. Religious leaders too saw merit in war. Social Gospel advocate Washington Gladden remarked that "in saving others we may save ourselves." Some conservatives, alarmed by violent labor strikes and Populism, welcomed war as a national unifier. Sensationalism also figured in the march to war. Assistant Secretary of the Navy Theodore Roosevelt and others too young to remember the inhumanity of the Civil War looked on war as adventure, and the yellow press exaggerated stories of Spanish atrocities. But underlying all explanations of American acceptance of war was the spirit and reality of expansionism, which had been moving the nation ever-outward in the last half of the nineteenth century.

John Hay called it "a splendid little war," but it was hardly splendid. Over 5,400 Americans died, but only 379 of them in combat. The rest fell to malaria and yellow fever. The disease-carrying mosquitos were unrelenting, the food was bad, and medical care was unsophisticated. Soldiers were issued heavy woolen uniforms in a tropical climate, and the stench of body odor was sickening. For black troops there was no relief from racism and Jim Crow.

Before Americans began to fight and die in Cuba, the first news of the war came from far-away Asia where Spain held the Philippine Islands as a colony. It surprised Americans, who knew little about the steady United States push into the Pacific or the dreams of farmers and

| Commodore Dewey in the Philippines |

business people for a huge market in China. On May 1 Commodore George Dewey steamed into Manila Bay, the Philippines, and wrecked the Spanish fleet. Dewey became an instant hero, especially to the informed foreign-policy elite, who had for years cast longing eyes on the islands and the choice Manila harbor.

Facing rebels and Americans in both Cuba and the Philippines, Spanish resistance collapsed rapidly. The Spanish Caribbean fleet, trapped in Santiago Harbor, made a desperate attempt to escape but was destroyed by American warships on July 3. Several days later, Puerto Rico fell to the invading Americans. Manila surrendered in August under pressure from Americans and Filipino insurgents led by Emilio Aguinaldo. Undermanned and ill-equipped, Spain sued for peace. The combatants signed an armistice on August 12.

In Paris in December, American and Spanish negotiators agreed on the peace terms: independence for Cuba; cession of the Philippines, Puerto Rico, and Guam to the United States; and payment of $20 million to Spain for the new territory. Filipino nationalists tried to persuade American officials to set their nation free, but they were rebuffed. The American empire now stretched deep into Asia; and the annexation of Wake Island (1898), Hawaii (1898), and Samoa (1899) gave American traders, missionaries, and naval promoters other stepping stones to China. Puerto Rico provided a long-desired base in the Caribbean that could help protect an American-built isthmian canal. And the United States would soon acquire another naval base at Guantánamo Bay in Cuba.

The Treaty of Paris sparked heated debate in the United States. Anti-imperialists like Mark Twain, Samuel Gompers, William Dean How-

| Debate over the Treaty of Paris |

ells, William Jennings Bryan, William Graham Sumner, Andrew Carnegie, and Senator George Hoar of Massachusetts argued vigor-

ously against annexation of the Philippines. They were disturbed that a war to free Cuba had led to an empire. Some cited the Declaration of Independence and the Constitution: the conquest of people against their will violated self-determination. Other anti-imperialists disliked the increased power of the president in the checks-and-balances system. Anti-imperialist critics emphasized domestic priorities over foreign ventures and argued that the United States could acquire overseas markets without having to subjugate peoples abroad. The imperialists replied with their familiar arguments of patriotism, destiny, and commerce.

But the anti-imperialists entered the debate with many handicaps. Possession of the Philippines was an accomplished fact; the anti-imperialists' role was thus a negative one. Then, too, they were internally divided and never able to launch an effective campaign. Although many of them belonged to the Anti-Imperialist League, they differed on so many domestic issues that it was difficult for them to speak with one voice on a foreign question. They were also inconsistent: Gompers favored the war but not the postwar annexations; Carnegie would accept colonies if they were not acquired by force; Hoar voted for the annexation of Hawaii but against that of the Philippines. The imperialists sneered that some of their critics were hypocrites, showing more concern for Filipinos than for American Indians, blacks, unskilled workers, or destitute immigrants. Indeed, some anti-imperialists feared the absorption of dark-skinned people.

On February 6, 1899, the United States Senate passed the Treaty of Paris by a 57-to-27 vote. Republicans, except for Hoar and Senator Eugene Hale of Maine, voted with their president; twenty-two Democrats voted no, but ten voted for the treaty. The latter group was probably influenced by Bryan, who urged a favorable vote in order to end the war and then push for Philippine independence. An amendment promising independence as soon as the Filipinos formed a stable government was defeated only by the tie-breaking ballot of the vice president.

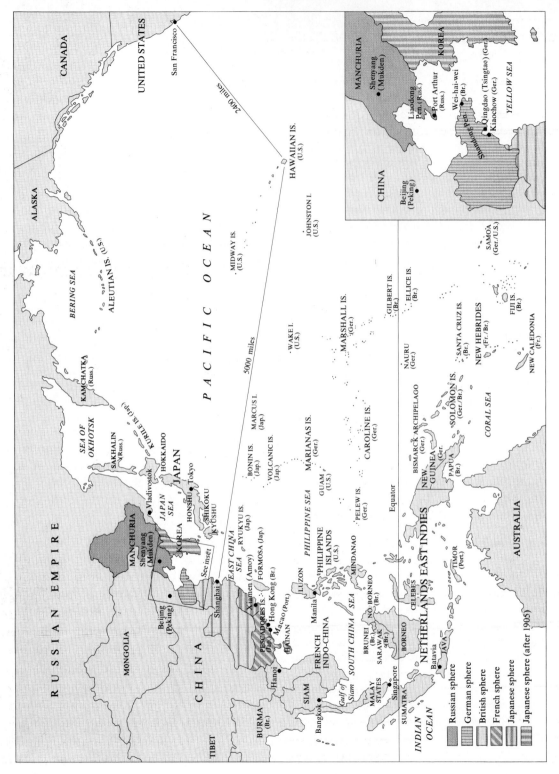

Imperialism in Asia: turn of the century

The fruits and tasks of empire, 1900–1914

Meanwhile the Germans, Japanese, Russians, British, and French were creating spheres of interest (see map) in China—known as the Sick Man of Asia. Within their spheres, the European powers built fortified bases, leased territory, and claimed exclusive economic privileges. American business interests and missionary societies petitioned Washington to halt the dismemberment before they were closed out. What good were the Philippines as stepping-stones to China if there was nothing left to step into? asked some.

Secretary of State John Hay recognized that the United States could not force the imperial powers from China. But he was determined to protect American commerce. In September 1899 Hay sent the imperial nations a note asking them to offer assurances that they would respect an Open Door for all nations in their spheres.

Open Door policy

Germany, France, and the others sent evasive replies. Then in 1900, a secret Chinese society called the Boxers revolted against the foreigners in their midst and laid siege to the foreign legations in Beijing (Peking). The United States joined the imperialists in sending troops to Beijing to lift the siege. And Hay, in a note dated July 3, 1900, again asked for "equal and impartial trade." He also instructed the other nations to preserve China's territorial integrity.

Hay's foray into Asian politics settled little, but the Open Door policy thereafter became a central element in United States diplomacy. Actually, the Open Door had long been an American principle, for as a trading nation the United States opposed barriers to international commerce and demanded equal access to markets. After 1900, when the United States began to emerge as the premier world trader, the Open Door policy became a global instrument first to pry open markets and then to dominate them.

"I'm out for commerce, not conquest," says Uncle Sam in the 1899 magazine cover. Through the Open Door policy, designed to keep the trade door ajar in China, the United States presented itself as a benevolent alternative to European territorial expansionism. Thus a resolute Uncle Sam restrains the threatening militarists as China examines a model locomotive and sewing machine.   The New York Public Library.

For the Open Door was more than a policy; it was an ideology. The tenets of this ideology were that America's domestic well-being required exports, that foreign trade would suffer interruption unless the United States intervened abroad to implant American principles and keep markets open, and that any area closed to American products, citizens, or ideas threatened the survival of the United States itself.

In the Philippines, meanwhile, the United States antagonized its new colonials. Emilio

Aguinaldo, the Philippine rebel leader, had be-

| Filipino Insurrection |

lieved that Dewey promised independence for his country if Aguinaldo and other patriots helped to defeat the Spanish. But after the victory, Aguinaldo was ordered out of Manila and isolated from decisions affecting his nation. Racial slurs like *gugu* and *nigger* infuriated the Filipinos, and the Treaty of Paris angered them. Americans' paternalistic attitude toward their new charges grated on Filipino nationalist feelings.

In January 1899 Aguinaldo proclaimed an independent Philippine Republic, and shooting began shortly thereafter. Before the Philippine Insurrection was suppressed in 1902, over 5,000 Americans and 200,000 Filipinos were dead. The atrocities committed by both sides were abominable. The defeat of the Filipinos was followed by the Americanization of the islands. Later in 1916, the Jones Act promised Filipino independence, but the promise was not fulfilled until after the Second World War.

Possession of the Philippines meant American participation in the turbulent politics of Asia. The major contender for influence in the area was Japan, and the Open Door policy was no deterrent to its advances. After rivalry over Manchuria and Korea led to the Russo-Japanese War (1904–1905), Japan scored quick victories

| Japanese-American relations |

over the stunned Russians. Roosevelt mediated the terms of the peace settlement at the Portsmouth Conference in New Hampshire in an attempt to preserve a balance of power in Asia. In 1905, in the Taft-Katsura Agreement, the United States conceded Japanese hegemony over Korea in return for Japan's pledge not to undermine the American position in the Philippines. To impress the Japanese—and they were duly impressed—Roosevelt sent the Great White Fleet on a world tour, with conspicuous stops in Asia.

Troubles with Japan boiled to the surface in 1906 when the San Francisco School Board, reflecting the anti-Orientalism of the West Coast, segregated all Chinese, Koreans, and Japanese in a special school. Japan protested this discrimination against its citizens. Because there was little President Roosevelt could do to budge the insistent Californians, he struck a gentleman's agreement with Tokyo restricting Japanese immigration to the United States. (In 1913 California denied Japanese residents the right to own property. Tokyo protested again.)

Despite the Root-Takahira Agreement (1908), in which Japan again pledged the security of American possessions in the Pacific and the United States recognized Japan's interests in Manchuria, Japanese-American relations deteriorated. Japan was alarmed by the new President Taft's ineffective attempt at dollar diplomacy, inducing American bankers to join an international consortium to build a Chinese railway. Dollar diplomacy was an effort to use private funds to serve American diplomatic goals and at the same time to garner profits for American financiers. Realizing neither purpose, Taft's venture seemed only to embolden the Japanese to solidify and extend their holdings in China.

In its own backyard of Latin America, the United States was unfettered, and intervention was the order of the day (see map). The Teller Amendment had outlawed American annexa-

| Platt Amendment |

tion but not control of Cuba. American troops remained there until 1902. Marines were there again from 1906 to 1909, in 1912, and from 1917 to 1922. Washington further manifested its hegemony over Cuba by forcing that nation to include the Platt Amendment in its constitution. The Platt Amendment prohibited Cuba from signing a treaty with another nation that might impair Cuba's independence. In short, all treaties had to be approved by the United States. Cuba was also forced to agree that the United States had the right to intervene to preserve the island's independence and to protect "life, property, and individual liberty." Finally, the United States required Cuba to undertake a sanitation program and to lease a naval base (Guantánamo) to the Americans.

As for the rest of the Caribbean, it became an

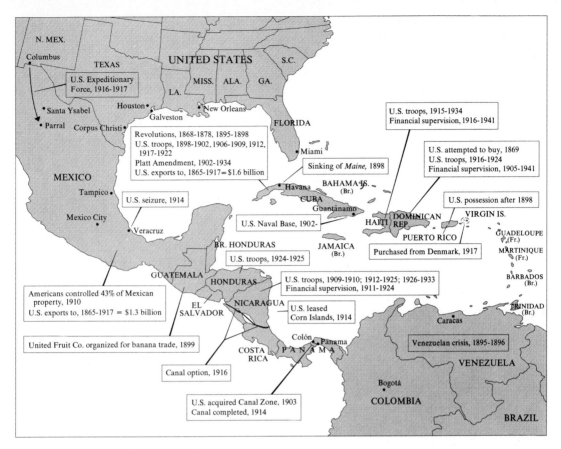

The map contains the following labels:

N. MEX.
Columbus
TEXAS
UNITED STATES
S.C.
MISS. ALA. GA.
U.S. Expeditionary Force, 1916-1917
LA.
Santa Ysabel
Houston
New Orleans
Parral
Corpus Christi
Galveston
FLORIDA
U.S. troops, 1915-1934
Financial supervision, 1916-1941
Miami
Revolutions, 1868-1878, 1895-1898
U.S. troops, 1898-1902, 1906-1909, 1912, 1917-1922
Platt Amendment, 1902-1934
U.S. exports to, 1865-1917=$1.6 billion
Sinking of *Maine*, 1898
U.S. attempted to buy, 1869
U.S. troops, 1916-1924
Financial supervision, 1905-1941
MEXICO
Tampico
Havana
BAHAMA IS. (Br.)
CUBA
Guantánamo
U.S. seizure, 1914
DOMINICAN REP.
VIRGIN IS.
U.S. possession after 1898
Mexico City
HAITI
PUERTO RICO
GUADELOUPE (Fr.)
Veracruz
U.S. Naval Base, 1902-
JAMAICA (Br.)
Purchased from Denmark, 1917
MARTINIQUE (Fr.)
BR. HONDURAS
BARBADOS (Br.)
U.S. troops, 1924-1925
Americans controlled 43% of Mexican property, 1910
U.S. exports to, 1865-1917 = $1.3 billion
GUATEMALA
HONDURAS
U.S. troops, 1909-1910; 1912-1925; 1926-1933
Financial supervision, 1911-1924
TRINIDAD (Br.)
EL SALVADOR
NICARAGUA
U.S. leased Corn Islands, 1914
Caracas
United Fruit Co. organized for banana trade, 1899
Colón
Panama
Venezuelan crisis, 1895-1896
VENEZUELA
Canal option, 1916
COSTA RICA
PANAMA
Bogotá
U.S. acquired Canal Zone, 1903
Canal completed, 1914
COLOMBIA
BRAZIL

The United States and Latin America

American lake. "Speak softly and carry a big stick," said Roosevelt. In 1904 the president released his Roosevelt Corollary to the Monroe Doctrine, warning Latin Americans to stabilize their politics and finances to forestall European meddling in their affairs. "Chronic wrongdoing," he lectured, might require "intervention by some civilized nation, and in the Western Hemisphere the adherence of the United States to the Monroe Doctrine may force the United States, however reluctantly, in flagrant cases of such wrongdoing or impotence, to the exercise of an international police power." Roosevelt and his successors were not bluffing. From 1900 to 1917, when the United States entered the First World War, American

Roosevelt Corollary

troops intervened in Cuba, Panama, Nicaragua, the Dominican Republic, Mexico, and Haiti. American officials took control of customs houses to ensure that tariff revenues were properly spent; they renegotiated foreign debts with American banks; they trained national guards and even ran elections.

The United States set out to police the Caribbean in the name of order. Whether such order was achieved by the landing of marines, the development of a national guard, a managed electoral process, or a manipulated economy, it was deemed necessary to guarantee United States security and prosperity. After Roosevelt helped to slice off Panama from Colombia in 1903 and initiated the construction of the Panama Canal, Washington would not tolerate disturbances

Important events

1861–69	William Seward serves as secretary of state		Part of Samoa annexed First Open Door note Outbreak of Filipino Insurrection
1866	Transatlantic cable completed France withdraws from Mexico	1900	Second Open Door note U.S. exports total $1.5 billion McKinley re-elected, defeating anti-imperialist William Jennings Bryan
1867	Acquisition of Alaska and Midway Islands		
1870	U.S. exports total $451 million (mostly agricultural goods)	1901	Theodore Roosevelt becomes president Hay-Pauncefote Treaty
1871	Anglo-American Washington Treaty settles *Alabama* claims	1902	Advent of U.S. domination in the Philippines
1883	Advent of New Navy	1903	Panama breaks away from Colombia United States granted canal rights in Panama Platt Amendment
1884	Naval War College founded		
1885	Josiah Strong, *Our Country*		
1889	First Pan-American Conference		
1890	Alfred T. Mahan, *The Influence of Sea Power Upon History*	1904	Roosevelt Corollary to the Monroe Doctrine
1891	Diplomatic crisis with Chile	1905	Taft-Katsura Agreement Portsmouth Conference
1893	Hawaiian revolution begins		
1894	Wilson-Gorman Tariff	1906	San Francisco segregates Oriental school children United States invades Cuba
1895	Crisis over Venezuela Cuban revolution begins Japan defeats China		
		1907	Great White Fleet Gentleman's agreement with Japan on immigration
1896	William McKinley elected president as expansionist		
1898	Sinking of the *Maine* Spanish-American War Hawaii and Wake Island annexed Treaty of Paris	1908	Root-Takahira Agreement
		1912	U.S. troops enter Cuba again
		1913	Manufactured goods head U.S. export list for the first time
1899	Senate passes Treaty of Paris, which cedes the Philippines, Guam, and Puerto Rico to the United States	1914	U.S. troops invade Mexico First World War begins Panama Canal opens

that might threaten the vital waterway. Order was believed essential to American commerce and investment too.

Roosevelt, Taft, and Wilson gave varying expression to this quest for order. The Rough Rider saw world affairs as a constant struggle for international power. The United States, in its own interest, had to lay claim to as much power as possible. Taft emphasized dollar diplomacy: dollars, not bullets, he predicted, would effect stability and enhance American interests. Wilson was no less a nationalist or pragmatist in desiring to safeguard and expand American prosperity and security. He justified military force by proclaiming it "our peculiar duty" to teach colonial peoples "order and self-control" and "the drill and habit of law and obedience." Wilson became known for his missionary paternalism, his insistence on liberal capitalism and constitutional government. Whether by means of Roosevelt's big stick, Taft's dollars, or Wilson's sermons—in fact, each president used all three—United States behavior toward its southern neighbors was imperialistic.

From the Civil War to the First World War, expansionism and empire were central to American foreign policy. By 1914 Americans held extensive interests in a world made smaller by modern technology. The outward reach of American policy from Seward to Wilson met opposition from domestic critics, but the trend was never seriously diverted. Ideas of racial supremacy, the belief that the nation needed foreign markets to absorb surplus production so the domestic economy could thrive, a mission to uplift the less fortunate, and emotional appeals to national greatness—all fed the appetite for foreign adventure and commitments.

Expansion, whether at home or abroad, claimed victims. In 1914 Americans braced themselves for the immediate shock of full-scale war in Europe. In the future, though, their foreign policy would be preoccupied with rebellious challenges to United States hegemony from proud and resentful nationalists victimized by American paternalism. And Americans who sincerely believed that they had been helping others to enjoy a better life would feel betrayed and baffled that their foreign clients could be so ungrateful.

Suggestions for further reading

GENERAL Robert L. Beisner, *From the Old Diplomacy to the New, 1865–1900* (1975); Charles S. Campbell, *The Transformation of American Foreign Relations, 1865–1900* (1976); John A.S. Grenville and George B. Young, *Politics, Strategy, and American Diplomacy* (1967); David Healy, *U.S. Expansionism* (1970); Walter LaFeber, *The New Empire* (1963); H. Wayne Morgan, *America's Road to Empire* (1965); Milton Plesur, *America's Outward Thrust* (1971); Emily S. Rosenberg, *Spreading the American Dream* (1982); Rubin F. Weston, *Racism in United States Imperialism* (1972); William Appleman Williams, *The Tragedy of American Diplomacy,* rev. ed. (1962).

DIPLOMATIC LEADERS Howard K. Beale, *Theodore Roosevelt and the Rise of America to World Power* (1956); John M. Blum, *The Republican Roosevelt* (1954); William H. Harbaugh, *The Life and Times of Theodore Roosevelt* (1975); Frederick Marks, III, *Velvet on Iron: The Diplomacy of Theodore Roosevelt* (1979); William C. Widenor, *Henry Cabot Lodge and the Search for an American Foreign Policy* (1980).

ECONOMIC EXPANSION, TECHNOLOGY, AND THE NAVY See the works by Beisner, Campbell, and LaFeber cited above; Benjamin F. Cooling, *Gray Steel and Blue Water Navy* (1979); Robert B. Davies, *Peacefully Working to Conquer the World: Singer Sewing Machines in Foreign Markets, 1854–1920* (1976); Kenneth J. Hagan, *American Gunboat Diplomacy and the Old Navy, 1877–1889* (1973); Walter R. Herrick, *The American Naval Revolution* (1966); David M. Pletcher, *Rails, Mines, and Progress: Seven American Promoters in Mexico, 1867–1911* (1958); Robert Seager, *Alfred Thayer Mahan* (1977); Tom Terrill, *The Tariff, Politics, and American Foreign Policy, 1874–1901* (1973); Mira Wilkins, *The Emergence of the Multinational Enterprise* (1970); William Appleman Williams, *The Roots of the Modern American Empire* (1969).

IMPERIALISM AND THE SPANISH-AMERICAN WAR
Graham A. Cosmas, *An Army for Empire: The United States Army in the Spanish-American War* (1971); Philip S. Foner, *The Spanish-Cuban-American War and the Birth of American Imperialism* (1972); Willard Gatewood, *Black Americans and the White Man's Burden, 1898-1903* (1975); Walter LaFeber, "That 'Splendid Little War' in Historical Perspective," *Texas Quarterly,* 11 (1968), 89–98; Gerald F. Linderman, *The Mirror of War: American Society and the Spanish-American War* (1974); Ernest R. May, *American Imperialism* (1968); Ernest R. May, *Imperial Democracy* (1961); Julius Pratt, *Expansionists of 1898* (1936); David F. Trask, *The War with Spain in 1898* (1981).

ANTI-IMPERIALISM AND THE PEACE MOVEMENT Robert L. Beisner, *Twelve Against Empire* (1968); Charles DeBenedetti, *Peace Reform in American History* (1980); David S. Patterson, *Toward a Warless World* (1976); E. Berkeley Tompkins, *Anti-Imperialism in the United States* (1970); Richard E. Welch, *Response to Imperialism* (1979).

RELATIONS WITH LATIN AMERICA Samuel F. Bemis, *The Latin American Policy of the United States* (1943); David Healy, *Gunboat Diplomacy in the Wilson Era* (1976); David Healy, *The United States in Cuba, 1898-1902* (1963); Walter LaFeber, *The Panama Canal* (1979); Lester D. Langley, *Struggle for the American Mediterranean* (1976); Lester D. Langley, *The United States and the Caribbean, 1900-1976* (1980); David McCullough, *The Path Between the Seas: The Creation of the Panama Canal, 1870-1914* (1977); Dexter Perkins, *The Monroe Doctrine, 1867-1907* (1937); Ramon Ruiz, *Cuba: The Making of a Revolution* (1968); Karl M. Schmitt, *Mexico and the United States, 1821-1973* (1974).

ASIA AND THE PACIFIC Warren I. Cohen, *America's Response to China,* 2nd ed. (1980); Raymond A. Esthus, *Theodore Roosevelt and Japan* (1966); Michael Hunt, *The Making of a Special Relationship* (1983); Akira Iriye, *Across the Pacific* (1967); Akira Iriye, *Pacific Estrangement: Japanese and American Expansion, 1897-1911* (1972); Jerry Israel, *Progressivism and the Open Door* (1971); Thomas J. McCormick, *China Market* (1967); Charles E. Neu, *The Troubled Encounter* (1975) (on Japan); Peter Stanley, *A Nation in the Making: The Philippines and the United States, 1899-1921* (1974); Paul A. Varg, *The Making of a Myth: The United States and China, 1897-1912* (1968); Leon Wolff, *Little Brown Brother* (1961); Marilyn Blatt Young, *The Rhetoric of Empire* (1968).

BRITAIN Alexander E. Campbell, *Great Britain and the United States, 1895-1903* (1960); Charles C. Campbell, *From Revolution to Rapprochement: The United States and Great Britain, 1783-1900* (1974); Bradford Perkins, *The Great Rapprochement* (1968).

22

AMERICA AT WAR,

1914-1920

She was a Southern woman, born into a Presbyterian minister's family, educated at a small Georgia women's college. Ellen Axson Wilson was a mother who made her children's clothing, nursed them through scarlet fever, and planned the family budget. A well-managed and serene household was a matter of self-conscious pride for her. "I wonder how anyone who reaches middle age can bear it," she said "if she cannot feel, on looking back, that whatever mistakes she may have made she has on the whole lived for others and not for herself."

Woodrow Wilson admired her greatly. To him the loving bond that tied them together in twenty-nine years of marriage was central to his own well-being and success. But she had been ill off and on for years. After moving to the White House, fifty-four-year-old Ellen Wilson overworked herself. Wilson was holding her hand when she died on August 5, 1914.

Seldom have such painful personal and official burdens fallen on a president at the same time. The day before, keeping vigil at his wife's bedside, Wilson had drafted a message offering American mediation to end the bloody war the European nations had just begun. At a time of wrenching bereavement, the president was called on to make momentous decisions about America's place in the First World War. He found it difficult to concentrate on the affairs of state.

The state of the nation

The Great War in Europe nevertheless began to consume Wilson's time and energy. Like most Americans, he was shocked by its outbreak. Americans had, of course, witnessed and participated in the years of international competition for colonies, the intense quest for markets, the sporadic military encounters, and the buildup in new weaponry. But full-scale war seemed a thing of the past. "The nineteenth-century view of history as progress," historian Henry F. May has written, "received a shattering blow." Soon after the war began William Allen White remarked "how sad it is that the war is taking the national attention away from justice."

By "justice" White meant reform. But it was not the war alone that seemed to be sapping progressivism of its vitality. After over a decade of reform, the American people were still sorely divided, and social and economic injustices continued to plague the nation. As they entered 1914, Americans suffered an economic downturn. Labor-management struggles commanded headlines. Race relations were strained as well, notably by Wilson's decision to segregate federal buildings in Washington, D.C., and by numerous lynchings of blacks (fifty-one in

| Domestic tensions |

The Wilson family: from left to right, Margaret, Ellen Axson Wilson, Eleanor, Jessie, and President
Woodrow Wilson (1865-1924). After Ellen's death
in 1914, the bereaved president married again, in the
midst of a debate over American preparedness for the
First World War.   Library of Congress.

1914). And nativists angrily protested the fast
pace of immigration. Aware of the emotion the
European war aroused among ethnic groups in
the United States, Wilson appealed for neutrality in thought and action.

While Wilson tried to keep America out of
the war, to protect American interests as a neutral trader, and—just in case—to prepare the nation militarily, his political fortunes grew worri-
some. The Bryan wing of the Democratic party
was in revolt, and many progressives no longer
looked to Wilson for leadership. Thus political
necessity forced him into a turnabout to improve his chances in the election of 1916. Early
that year Wilson appointed Louis D. Brandeis

to the Supreme Court. Brandeis, an antimonop-
olist, defender of small business, "people's advocate," and the first Jewish appointee to the high
court, was a symbol of progressivism. Wilson
also pleased progressives by supporting the
Keating-Owen bill to regulate child labor; the
Farm Loan Act, which provided capital to farmers who found private banks too conservative in
their loan policies; the Adamson Act, which set
an eight-hour day for railroad workers; and
workers'-compensation legislation. With these
political steps, Wilson entered the election of
1916.

The Republicans snubbed Theodore Roosevelt, who wanted the nomination, in favor of

344

Charles Evans Hughes, former reform governor

Election of 1916

of New York and Supreme Court justice. Wilson ran on a platform of peace, progressivism, and preparedness. Many were attracted by the Democratic party's campaign slogan: "He Kept Us Out of War." Hughes led a fractured party, and he could not muzzle Roosevelt, whose bellicose speeches suggested that the Republicans would drag Americans into the world war. Wilson received 9.1 million votes to Hughes's 8.5 million, and the president barely won in the electoral college by a 277-to-254 count. Within several months, the "peace candidate" Woodrow Wilson would lead the United States into the First World War.

The question of neutrality

In 1914, soon after the Allies (Great Britain, France, Russia, and eventually Japan and Italy) and the Central Powers (Germany, Austria, and eventually Turkey) exchanged declarations of war, President Wilson issued a proclamation of neutrality. He also asked Americans to refrain from taking sides. "We definitely have to be neutral," Wilson said privately, "since otherwise our mixed populations would wage war on each other."

Wilson's lofty appeal for American neutrality and unity at home collided with three realities. First, ethnic groups in the United States naturally

Ethnic ties to Europe

took sides. Many German-Americans and vehemently anti-British Irish-Americans (Ireland was then trying to break free from British rule) cheered for the Central Powers, as did Swedish-Americans who shared Sweden's long-standing antagonism toward Russia. Americans of British and French ancestry applauded the Allies. Anglo-American traditions and slogans like "Remember Lafayette," as well as the sheer number of Americans with roots in the Allied nations, drew a majority to the Allied cause.

Second, America's economic links with the Allies rendered neutrality difficult, if not impossible. England had long been one of the nation's best customers. New war-inspired orders

Economic links with the belligerents

flooded American companies and farms, pulling the economy out of its recession. In 1914 American exports to England and France equaled $753 million; in 1916 the figure reached $2.75 billion. In the same period, however, exports to Germany dropped from $345 million to $29 million. Much of the American-Allied trade was financed through private American loans, amounting to $2.3 billion during the period of neutrality; in stark contrast, Germany received only $27 million.

From Germany's perspective, of course, the linkage between the American economy and the Allies signaled an unwelcome and dangerous fact: the United States had become the quite-unneutral Allied arsenal and bank. Under international law the British—who controlled the seas—could buy contraband (war-related goods) and noncontraband from neutrals at their own risk. It was Germany's responsibility, not America's, to stop the trade in ways that international law prescribed: an effective blockade of the enemy's territory or the seizure of all goods from belligerent (British) ships and contraband from neutral (American) ships.

The third reason neutrality did not work derived from the pro-Allied sympathies of Wilson administration officials. For Wilson, a German

Pro-Allied sympathies

victory would destroy government by law and "free industry and enterprise." If Germany won the war, he prophesied, "it would change the course of our civilization and make the United States a military nation." Wilson's chief advisors and diplomats—Colonel Edward House, Secretary of State Robert Lansing, and Ambassador to London Walter Hines Page among them—shared these sentiments.

Wilson and his administration also believed that Wilsonian principles stood a better chance of international acceptance if Britain, rather than the Central Powers, sat astride the postwar

| Wilsonianism |

world. Wilsonianism—the name scholars have given to the body of ideas Wilson espoused—consisted of traditional American diplomatic principles. His ideal world was to be open in every sense of the word: no barriers to commerce, no impediments to democratic politics, no secret diplomatic deals. Empires were to be opened up in keeping with the principle of self-determination. Wilson envisioned free-market, nonexploitative capitalism and political constitutionalism for all nations, to ensure the good society and world peace.

To say that American neutrality was never a real possibility, given ethnic loyalties, economic ties, and Wilsonian preferences, is not to say that Wilson sought to enter the war. He emphatically wanted to keep the United States out of the military conflict, and in fact did so for two and a half years. But by the spring of 1917, whatever remained of the tattered U.S. neutrality was swept away by the intense winds of American national interest, as defined by Woodrow Wilson.

Americans got caught in the Allied-Central Power crossfire. The British, "ruling the waves and waiving the rules," declared a loose, in-

| British naval policy |

effective, and hence illegal blockade; outlawed a broad list of contraband (including foodstuffs) that was not supposed to be shipped to Germany by neutrals; mined the North Sea; and harassed neutral shipping by seizing cargoes. To counter German submarines, the British flouted international law by arming their merchant ships and flying neutral (sometimes American) flags. Wilson frequently protested British violations of neutral rights, but London often deftly defused American criticism by paying for confiscated cargoes.

Germany was determined to lift the injurious blockade and to end American-Allied commerce. These ambitious tasks were assigned to the submarine. In February 1915 Berlin announced that it was creating a war zone around the British Isles. All enemy ships in the area

would be sunk; neutral vessels were warned to stay out so as not to be attacked by mistake; and travelers from neutral nations were warned to stay off enemy ships. President Wilson repeated that the United States was holding Germany to "strict accountability" for any losses of American life and property.

Wilson was interpreting existing international law in the strictest sense. That law held that an attacker had to warn a passenger or merchant ship before attacking, so that passengers and crew could disembark into lifeboats for safety. But the submarine, an extremely vulnerable vessel when surfaced, postdated that rule, and Wilson refused to adjust tradition to this new weapon of war. Berlin frequently complained to Wilson that he was denying the Germans the one weapon they could use to break the British economic stranglehold, disrupt the Allies' substantial connection with American producers and bankers, and win the war. Wilson, of course, did not want the Germans to win.

From the Lusitania to war

Over the next few months the U-boats sank ship after ship. Then the sinking of the *Lusitania* forced the submarine issue for Wilson. The swift, majestic British passenger liner left New York City on May 1, 1915, with over twelve hundred passengers and a cargo of foodstuffs and contraband, including 4.2 million rounds of ammunition for Remington rifles. Before "Lucy's" departure, the newspapers carried an unusual announcement from the German embassy: travelers on British vessels were warned that a war zone existed and that Allied ships in those waters "are liable to destruction." On May 7, off the Irish coast, U-20 unleashed torpedoes at the vessel; the *Lusitania* carried 1,198 people, including 128 Americans, to their deaths.

This brutal assault on innocent people angered and saddened Americans. But Wilson and the American people, however great their hatred

Reaction to the sinking of the Lusitania

for Germany, ruled out a military response. Secretary of State William Jennings Bryan advised the president that the tragedy underscored the urgency of his suggestion that Americans not be permitted to travel on belligerent ships and that passenger vessels not be allowed to carry war goods. Bryan also urged that simultaneous protest notes be sent to London and Berlin.

Wilson moved deliberately. He rejected Bryan's counsel, as well as that of Theodore Roosevelt and others who clamored for war. Instead he sent a note to Berlin insisting on the right of Americans to sail on belligerent ships and demanding that Germany cease its inhumane submarine warfare. The Germans asked Wilson to rethink the relationship between international law and the submarine. Wilson fumed. He dispatched a second letter to Germany reiterating the demand that submarines be kept in port. When the president refused to ban American travelers from belligerent ships, Bryan resigned in protest.

Germany, seeking to avoid war with America, ordered its U-boat commanders to halt attacks on passenger liners. But in mid-August another British vessel, the *Arabic,* was sunk; two American lives were lost. The German ambassador hastened to pledge that never again would an unarmed passenger ship be attacked without warning. And some Americans wondered why their government did not require citizens to travel only on American ships.

In March 1916 an attack on the *Sussex,* a French vessel crossing the English Channel, took the United States a step closer to war. Four Americans on that ship were injured. Stop the marauding submarines, Wilson told Berlin, or he would sever diplomatic relations. Again the Germans backed off, pledging not to attack merchant vessels without warning.

Then in early February 1917, Germany startled the Wilson administration by launching unrestricted submarine warfare. All vessels, bellig-

erent or neutral, warship or merchant, would be attacked if sighted in the declared war zone. This bold decision represented a calculated risk that submarines could impede the valuable munitions shipments from America to England and thus defeat the Allies before Americans could be mobilized and ferried across the Atlantic to enter the fight. Wilson quickly broke diplomatic relations with Berlin. Everybody waited for the inevitable collision.

With this German challenge to American neutral rights and economic interests came a German threat to American security. In late February, the British intercepted, decoded, and

Zimmermann telegram

handed to the American government a telegram addressed to the German minister in Mexico from Foreign Secretary Arthur Zimmermann. The minister was instructed to tell the Mexican government that if it joined a military alliance against the United States, Germany would help Mexico to recover the territories it was forced to give up to its northern neighbor in 1848.

Secretary of State Robert Lansing and Wilson agreed that the Zimmermann telegram constituted "a conspiracy against this country." Shortly thereafter, Wilson asked Congress for "armed neutrality." Specifically, he requested the authority to arm American merchant ships, and more generally the power to "employ any other instrumentalities or methods that may be necessary." In the midst of the debate, Wilson released Zimmermann's telegram to the press; the nation was stunned. Still, antiwar Senators Robert M. La Follette and George Norris, among others, saw the armed-ship bill as a blank check for the president to move the country to war, and filibustered it to death. Wilson, angrily labeling them a "little group of willful men," proceeded to arm America's commercial vessels in spite of them. The decision came too late to prevent the sinking of several American ships. War cries echoed across the nation, and the cabinet unanimously urged war.

On April 2, 1917, the president stepped before a hushed Congress. His solemn address chided the Germans for "warfare against mankind." Wilson enumerated American grievances: Germany's violation of the principle of freedom of the seas, its disruption of American commerce, its attempt to stir up trouble in Mex-

| *Declaration of war* | ico, and its violation of human rights by killing innocent Americans. Wilson's |

most famous words rang out: "The world must be made safe for democracy." Congress quickly declared war against Germany, by a vote of 373 to 50 in the House and 82 to 6 in the Senate. The first woman ever to sit in Congress, Montana's Jeannette Rankin, elected in 1916, cast a ringing "no" vote that won her a high rank in the pantheon of American pacifism.

For principle, for morality, for honor, for commerce, for security—for all these reasons the United States took up arms against Germany. The submarine was certainly the culprit that drew a reluctant president and nation into the maelstrom. In the most general sense, however, America decided for war to reform world politics. By early 1917 Wilson seemed to believe that America could not claim a seat at the peace conference unless it became a combatant. At such a conference, Wilson intended to put into constitutional form the principles he thought essential to a stable world order, to promote democracy and the Open Door, and to outlaw revolution and aggression. Quite simply, Woodrow Wilson decided for war because he wanted a peace fashioned according to American precepts.

Taking up arms

Even before the war decision, the United States had been preparing for combat. Encouraged by such groups as the National Security League and the Navy League, and by mounting public outrage against Germany's submarine warfare, the president in 1915 began to plan a substantial military buildup. Meanwhile, antiwar

| *Antiwar sentiment* | critics vowed to block preparedness. Some pacifist progressives became active in an |

antiwar coalition, the American Union Against Militarism. Jane Addams and Carrie Chapman Catt founded the Women's Peace party, and both Henry Ford and Andrew Carnegie worked for peace. But the peace movement was splintered, some of its followers endorsing peace but not pacifism, and it could not prevent passage of preparedness measures, such as the National Defense Act (1916).

To raise an army after the declaration of war, Congress in 1917 passed the Selective Service Act, requiring the registration of all males be-

| *Raising an army* | tween the ages of twenty and thirty (later changed to eighteen and forty-five). Na- |

tional service, proponents believed, would not only prepare the nation for battle but also promote efficiency, order, democracy, personal sacrifice, and nationalism. Critics, on the other hand, feared that "Prussianism," not democratization, was the likely outcome.

On June 5, 1917, over 9.5 million men signed up for the "great national lottery." By war's end, 24 million men had been registered by local draft boards. Over 4.8 million served in the armed forces, 2 million of whom fought in France. The typical soldier was a draftee between twenty-one and twenty-three years of age, white, single, and poorly educated. About 16 percent of the male labor force was drawn into military service. Although many enlisted men had imbibed Wilson's idealism, others said they did not "care very much about dying for posterity or liberty, or anything else." Many simply wanted action and adventure. American troops' ignorance of the reasons they were fighting so alarmed Wilson administration officials that they put a copy of the president's war message in every knapsack. Over 300,000 men evaded the draft by failing to show up when called, and 4,000 were classified as conscientious objectors.

Jim Crow was in the army too. Fearing a black soldiery, many southern politicians opposed the drafting of blacks. But the army needed men, white and black. The NAACP and W. E. B. Du Bois urged blacks to join the fight for "world liberty," optimistically thinking that a war to make the world safe for democracy would blur the color line at home. They were greatly disappointed. The military segregated facilities, discouraged blacks from becoming officers, and assigned black recruits to menial labor. Ugly racial slurs echoed through the camps. In Houston, Texas, angry black soldiers responded to goading from whites by seizing arms and killing thirteen of them. White retaliation was immediate and excessive. After brief "trials," thirteen blacks were executed; another six were hanged after an unsuccessful appeal of their death sentences; others were court-martialed and given long prison terms.

In France, true to America's unilateralist tradition, General John J. Pershing refused to submerge American troops in Allied units. This independent spirit annoyed Allied leaders, but they welcomed the "doughboys." Firsthand war, the soldiers soon learned, was quite different from the abstractions spoken of at home. They

Americans in combat

came to know the muck and stink of trench warfare and the horrors of poison gas and barbed wire. Fifty-one thousand Americans lost their lives in battle and another 230,000 were wounded; the mortality toll from disease was greater. Many of the 62,000 soldiers and sailors who died from disease were among the 550,000 Americans who were killed by the influenza epidemic of 1918.

It was the influx of American men and materiel that decided the outcome of the First World War. With both sides virtually exhausted, the Americans tipped the balance toward the Allies. Actually the inexperienced Americans did not engage in much combat until after the lull of the severe winter of 1917 and 1918. Then in the spring, after knocking Russia out of the war and closing the eastern front, the Germans launched a major offensive. Kaiser Wilhelm's forces got within fifty miles of Paris; American troops helped to blunt their advance at Château-

Thierry. In June the U.S. 2nd Division recaptured Belleau Wood. In September over 1 million Americans joined British and French troops in the Allied offensive that pushed the Germans back. Its submarine warfare a dismal failure, its ground war a shambles, its troops and cities mutinous, abandoned by Turkey and Austria, Germany sued for peace. The armistice was signed on November 11, 1918.

The armistice was Wilsonian: the president insisted that his Fourteen Points, which he had enunciated in January, be made the general terms for peace negotiations. The Allies balked, but Wilson scared them into acceptance by threatening a separate peace with Germany. The Fourteen Points were a summary of Wilsonianism. The first five called for diplomacy in the "public view," freedom of the seas, lower tariffs, reductions in armaments, and the decolonization of empires. Points 6 through 13 appealed for self-determination for national groups in Europe. For Wilson the last point was the most essential, the vehicle for achieving all the others: "a general association of nations" or League of Nations. Having won the war, the resolute Wilson set out to win the peace.

The home front

"It is not an army that we most shape and train for war," declared the president, "it is a nation." The United States was a belligerent for only nineteen months, but the impact of the war on domestic America was conspicuous. In that comparatively short period the national government quickly geared the economy to war needs and marshaled public opinion. As never before, the state intervened in American life. An unprecedented concentration of bureaucratic power developed in Washington, D.C.

The federal government and private business became partners during the war. Dollar-a-year executives flocked to the nation's capital from major companies; they retained their corporate salaries while serving in administrative and consulting capacities. Early in the war, the government relied on several industrial committees for advice on purchases and prices. But evidence of self-interested businessmen cashing in on the national interest aroused public protest. As a result the committees were disbanded in July 1917 in favor of the War Industries Board (WIB). Business-government cooperation was also stimulated by the suspension of antitrust laws; by cost-plus contracts, which guaranteed companies a healthy profit and a means to pay higher wages to head off labor strikes; by the Webb-Pomerene Act (1918), which granted immunity from antitrust legislation to companies that combined to operate in the export trade; by the virtual abandonment of competitive bidding; and by a floor placed under prices to ensure profits.

Hundreds of new government agencies, staffed largely by businessmen, came into being to wage the war. Some of the superagencies placed unprecedented controls on the economy. The Food Administration, led by Herbert Hoover, undertook programs to improve production and conserve food through voluntary action; it also set prices and regulated distribution. Americans were urged to grow "victory gardens" in their backyards and to tolerate meatless and wheatless meals. The Railroad Administration took over the snarled and financially troubled railway industry. When strikes threatened the telephone and telegraph companies, the federal government seized and ran them.

The largest and potentially most powerful of the wartime agencies was the War Industries Board. Designed as a clearinghouse to coordinate the national economy, and headed after early 1918 by millionaire financier Bernard Baruch, the WIB faced the enormous task of satisfying both Allied and domestic needs. It made purchases, allocated supplies, and fixed prices. Although on paper the WIB was all-powerful, in reality it had to conciliate competing interest groups and compromise with the businessmen whose advice it so valued.

The performance of the mobilized economy was mixed, but it delivered enough men and materiel to France to ensure the defeat of the Central Powers. About a quarter of all American production was diverted to war needs. Farmers enjoyed boom years as they put more acreage into production and watched prices go up. Food exports, which had equaled only about 7 million tons before the war, reached 19 million tons in 1919. Induced to produce more at a faster pace, farmers mechanized as never before. Some industries enjoyed substantial increases because of wartime demand, and the gross national product soared.

Organized labor sought a partnership with government too, but its gains were far less spectacular. Samuel Gompers, president of the AFL,

Wartime labor relations

threw his loyalty to the Wilson administration, promising to calm calls for strikes. He and other moderate labor leaders were rewarded with appointments to high-level wartime government agencies. The War Labor Board, created to mediate labor disputes, ruled out strikes and lockouts but guaranteed workers the right to organize for collective bargaining. As a result unionization moved at a fast pace; from roughly 2.7 million members in 1916 to over 4 million in 1919. But the AFL could not curb strikes by the radical Industrial Workers of the World (IWW) or rebellious AFL locals: in the nineteen war months, over six thousand strikes occurred. During these years, many workers gained a forty-eight-hour week. Increases in real income, however, were held to a minimum by inflation.

As the needs of the military and a decline in immigration affected the traditional sources of laborers, the call went out to women, blacks, and Mexican-Americans. Though the number of

Women in the work force

women in the work force remained steady at about 8 million, many shifted from one job to another, sometimes into formerly male domains. White women left domestic service for factories, moved from clerking in department stores to stenography and typing, and de-

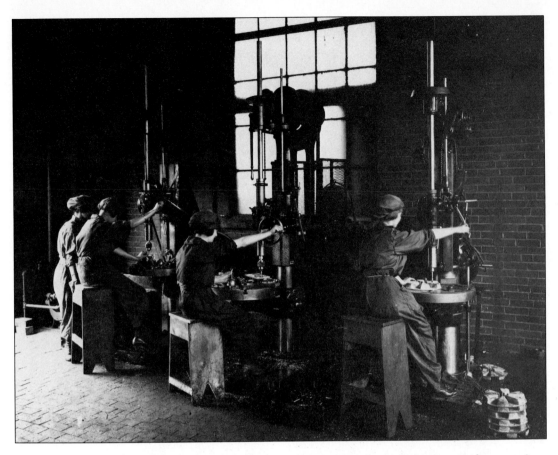

The Bethlehem Steel Corporation, like other defense industries, hired women as never before during the First World War. Here women workers operate drilling machines in Bethlehem's cartridge case shop. Bethlehem Steel Corporation.

parted textile mills for employment in firearms plants. Twenty percent or more of all workers in the wartime manufacture of electrical machinery, airplanes, and food were women. As white women took advantage of the new opportunities, black women took some of their places in domestic service and in textile factories.

The movement of women into jobs that had been the preserve of males generated controversy. Male workers complained that women were destabilizing the work environment with their higher productivity; women answered that they were used to seasonal employment and piecework and hence worked at a faster pace. Men protested that women were undermining the wage system by working for lower pay; women pointed out that male-dominated companies discriminated against them and unions denied them membership. Finally, male employees resented the spirit of independence evident among women whose labor was now greatly valued.

Overall, though, the war years were not a watershed in the history of female labor. The attitude that women's proper sphere was the home changed very little. Married working women found that their husbands and children resented the disruption of home life. Moreover, reformers complained that working mothers were neglecting their children. And when the war was over, many of the gains women had made were reversed.

Wartime mobilization wrought significant changes for the black community. Wartime jobs in the North provided an escape from southern social, political, and economic oppression. During the war years, southern blacks undertook a great migration to northern cities to work

Black migration to the North in railroad yards, packing houses, steel mills, shipyards, and coal mines. In the decade from 1910 to 1920, about a half-million black Americans uprooted themselves to move north. Most were young unmarried males seeking economic opportunity.

New jobs and improved opportunities could not erase the fact that blacks, North and South, continued to be a minority in a white society whose racism sometimes verged on the barbaric. The Ku Klux Klan began to revive and racist films like D. W. Griffith's *The Birth of a Nation* (1915) further fed prejudice. Lynching statistics exposed the wide gap between American declarations of humanity in the war and the American practice of inhumanity at home: between 1914 and 1920, 382 blacks were lynched, some of them in military uniform.

Northern whites who resented the "Negro invasion" vented their anger in riots. In East St. Louis, Illinois, in 1917, whites opposed to black

Race riots employment in a defense plant rampaged through the streets; forty blacks and nine whites lost their lives. In the bloody "Red Summer" of 1919, race riots rocked two dozen cities and towns. The worst race war occurred in Chicago, where thirty-eight people died in a riot sparked by an incident at a segregated beach.

The war also affected Mexican-Americans, whose numbers increased from 385,000 in 1910 to 740,000 in 1920. They lived largely in the southwestern states and California, belonged to the Catholic Church, and worked mostly in agriculture as field laborers. Before the war Mexicans had migrated to the United States largely to seek better incomes and to escape the convulsions of the Mexican Revolution. Many en-

Mexican-American migration tered illegally. But in 1917 the United States passed an immigration act with a head tax and a literacy test that slowed Mexican migration. When the United States entered the First World War, many Mexicans returned home, fearful they would be drafted. Thus, at a time when southwestern growers needed more labor to meet the wartime demand for foodstuffs, their work force was actually shrinking. The growers appealed to Washington for help. Federal officials first assured aliens that they would not be drafted into the armed forces and then exempted agricultural workers from the act of 1917, a waiver that lasted until 1920. As a result, over 100,000 Mexicans migrated to the Southwest. Some filled jobs left vacant by Mexican-Americans who, like blacks, had migrated north to work in industry.

The attack on civil liberties

"Woe be to the man that seeks to stand in our way in this day of high resolution when every principle we hold dearest is to be vindicated and made secure." Woodrow Wilson's passionate words were aimed at dissenters who questioned his war decision, the draft, and his management of wartime affairs. An official and unofficial campaign to silence critics swept the nation. Headed by George Creel, the Committee on Public Information (CPI), in effect a propaganda agency, set out to shape and mobilize public opinion by means of anti-German tracts, speeches, films, and "self-censorship" of the press. The CPI encouraged people to spy on their neighbors and report any suspicious behavior. Exaggeration, fearmongering, distortion, half-truths, and mindless emotionalism were the stuff of the CPI's "mind mobilization."

The Wilson administration also sponsored the Espionage Act (1917) and the Sedition Act (1918). The first statute forbade "false statements" designed to impede the draft or promote military insubordination and banned from the mails materials considered treasonous. The Sedition Act made it unlawful to obstruct the sale of war bonds and to use "disloyal, profane, scurrilous, or abusive" language against the government, the Constitution, the flag, and the military uniform. These loosely worded laws gave the government wide latitude to crack down on those with whom it differed. Over two thousand people were prosecuted under the acts. Among them was Eugene Debs, who received a ten-year sentence for his criticism of the war and defense of free speech.

State and local governments joined the campaign. Officials banned what they considered "pro-German" books from public schools; the governor of Iowa prohibited the use of any language but English in schools and public places; and Pittsburgh banned Beethoven's music. Everywhere teachers who questioned the war faced dismissal by hostile school boards. And at Columbia University, antiwar Professor J. M. Cattell, a distinguished psychologist, was fired. His colleague Charles Beard, a prowar historian, resigned in protest: "If we have to suppress everything we don't like to hear, this country is resting on a pretty wobbly basis."

The point was just that: Wilson tried to crush what he did not like to hear. In particular, the administration concentrated on the IWW and the Socialist party. The war emergency and

Persecution of radicals
the frank opposition of those two radical organizations gave progressives and conservatives alike an opportunity to throttle their political rivals. Soon after the declaration of war, government agents raided union meetings and arrested IWW leaders. The army was sent into western mining and lumbering regions to put down IWW strikes on the pretense that they were pro-German. Under the immigration acts, alien members of the IWW were deported. Town after town evicted the "Wobblies," and by the end of the war most of the union's leaders were in jail. The Socialist party fared little better.

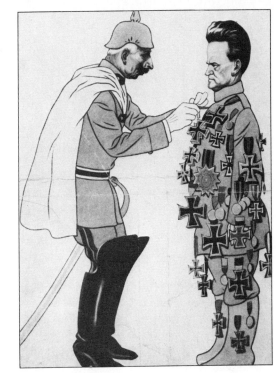

For his opposition to American participation in the First World War, Senator Robert La Follette (1855–1925) was cruelly misrepresented as a traitor. In this cartoon from *Life* magazine he is decorated by the German Kaiser. La Follette believed a majority of Americans, if given the opportunity in a referendum, would vote his way on the war. "The poor . . . who are the ones called upon to rot in the trenches, have no organized power," he once said. State Historical Society of Wisconsin.

The Supreme Court, itself attuned to the pulse of the times, upheld the Espionage Act. Justice Oliver Wendell Holmes, in *Schenck* v. *U.S.* (1919), expressed the Court's unanimous opinion that in time of war the First Amendment could be restricted: "Free speech would not protect a man falsely shouting fire in a theater and causing panic." If words "are of such a nature as to create a clear and present danger that they will bring about the substantial evils that Congress has a right to prevent," Holmes went on, free speech could be limited. In another case, *Abrams* v. *U.S.* (1919), the Court

The attack on civil liberties

voted 7 to 2 that the Sedition Act was constitutional.

The Red Scare

In the last few months of the war, guardians
of Americanism began to label dissenters not
only pro-German, but pro-Bolshevik. After the
Bolshevik Revolution in the fall of 1917, American hatred for Germany was readily transferred
to Communist Russia. And when the new Russian government under V. I. Lenin made peace
with Germany in early 1918, thereby closing the
eastern front, Americans felt betrayed. President
Wilson, who refused to recognize the new regime, actually attempted to subvert the Bolshevik Revolution by ordering troops to Russia and
participating in a blockade of the country. At
home too, the Wilson administration was moving against radicals and others imprecisely defined as Bolsheviks or Communists.

After the war Americans were edgy: the war
had disrupted race relations, the workplace, and
the family; it had increased the cost of living;
postwar unemployment loomed; and in 1919
the Russian Communists established the Com-
intern to promote world revolution. Americans
found it easy to blame their postwar troubles on
new scapegoats. A rash of labor strikes in 1919
sparked the Red Scare. All told, over 3,300
strikes involving 4 million laborers occurred that
year, including a general strike in Seattle in February.

In May, bombs were sent through the mails
to prominent Americans; most of the devices
were intercepted and dismantled, but police
never captured the conspirators. The common
and not unreasonable assumption was that anarchists and others bent on the destruction of
the American way of life were responsible. Next
came the Boston police strike in September,
soon thought to be part of a Bolshevik conspiracy. The governor of Massachusetts, Calvin
Coolidge, gained fame by proclaiming that no-

body had the right to strike against the public
safety. State guardsmen were brought in to replace the striking police force.

Especially ominous was the walkout of
350,000 steel workers. One of the leaders of the
steel strike was William Z. Foster, a radical who
joined the Communist party after the strike. His
presence in a labor move-
ment seeking the satisfaction
of legitimate grievances and bread-and-butter
goals permitted political and business leaders to
dismiss the steel strike as a foreign threat orches-
trated by American radicals. There was actually
no conspiracy. Indeed, the American left was
badly splintered and incapable of mounting a
threat to the established order.

Steel strike

But Attorney General A. Mitchell Palmer insisted on conformity. Palmer believed that the
"blaze of revolution" was "burning up the
foundations of society." To stamp out the radical fire, Palmer created the Bureau of Investigation and appointed J. Edgar Hoover to
run it. Hoover organized a file of thousands of
index cards bearing the names of alleged radical
individuals and organizations. In 1919 agents
jailed IWW members and deported alien radicals like Emma Goldman. Again, state and local
governments took their cue from Washington.
The New York state legislature expelled five
duly elected Socialist members. States passed
peacetime sedition acts under which hundreds of
people were arrested.

The Red Scare reached a climax in January
1920 when the attorney general staged his Palmer Raids. Using information gathered by Hoover, government agents in
thirty-three cities broke into
meeting halls, pool rooms, and homes without
search warrants, seizing materials and people.
Four thousand people were thrown into over-
crowded jails and denied counsel. Of this number, about 550 were deported.

Palmer Raids

Palmer's disregard for elementary civil liberties soon drew criticism. Civil libertarians and
lawyers pointed out that Palmer's blatant tactics
ignored the Constitution, that many of the arrested "Communists" had committed no crimes,

and that some were not even radicals. Palmer's call for a peacetime sedition act alarmed leaders of many political persuasions. His dire prediction that major violence would mar May Day 1920 proved ridiculous. Palmer's exaggerations, his scenarios of Bolshevik conspiracy, simply exceeded the truth so far that he was no longer credible.

The campaign against free speech in the period from 1917 through 1920 left casualties. Critics, radical or otherwise, were afraid to speak their minds. Debate, so essential to democracy, was curbed. Reform suffered as reformers either joined in the antiradicalism or became victims of it. The radical movement was badly weakened, the IWW becoming virtually extinct and the Socialist party paralyzed. Moreover, the actions of the government had threatened the Bill of Rights and reflected the willingness of some progressives to use authoritarian means in their quest to create a homogeneous society.

The peace conference and League fight

As the Red Scare was threatening American democracy, Woodrow Wilson was struggling to make his Fourteen Points a reality. When the president departed for the Paris peace conference in December 1918, he faced obstacles erected by his political enemies, by the Allies, and by himself. Some observers suggested that the ambitious Wilson, confident of his own abilities and religious in his belief that destiny directed his course, underestimated his task.

Wilson's troubles were compounded by the results of the 1918 congressional elections. The Republicans gained control of both houses, signaling trouble for Wilson in two ways. First, any peace treaty would have to be submitted for approval to a potentially hostile Senate; second, Wilson's stature had been diminished in the eyes of foreign leaders. After this setback, Wilson ag-

gravated his political problems by not naming any senator to the American Peace Commission, refusing to take any prominent Republican with him to the conference, and failing to consult with the Senate Foreign Relations Committee before he sailed for Paris.

Another obstacle in Wilson's way was the Allies' determination to impose a harsh, vengeful peace on the Germans who, along with the Russians, were not allowed to participate in the con-

Wilson's clash with the Allies

ference. Georges Clemenceau of France, David Lloyd George of Britain, and Vittorio Orlando of Italy—with Wilson, the Big Four—were formidable adversaries. They had signed secret treaties during the war, and expected to enlarge their empires at Germany's expense. Growing impatient with Wilson's sermons, they scoffed at the headstrong, self-impressed president who wanted to deny them the spoils of war.

The victors demanded that Germany pay a huge reparations bill. Wilson called for a small indemnity, fearing that a resentful and economically hobbled Germany might turn to Bolshevism or disrupt the postwar community in some other way. Unable to moderate the Allied position, the president reluctantly gave way, agreeing to a clause blaming the war on the Germans and accepting the huge reparations figure of $33 billion, an amount he expected Germany could never pay.

As for decolonization and the principle of self-determination, Wilson only partially overcame the land-grabbing mood of the conference. The conferees placed former German and Turkish colonies under the control of other imperial nations in a League-administered "mandate" system. The mandate system was a halfway station between outright imperial domination and independence. In other compromises, Japan was granted influence over China's Shandong Peninsula, and France was permitted occupation rights in Germany's Rhineland. Elsewhere in Europe, however, Wilson's prescriptions fared better. Out of Austria-Hungary and Russia came the new independent states of Austria,

Hungary, Yugoslavia, Czechoslovakia, and Poland. Wilson and his colleagues also built a *cordon sanitaire* of new westward-looking nations (Finland, Estonia, Latvia, and Lithuania) around Russia to quarantine the Bolshevik contagion.

Wilson worked harder on the charter for the League of Nations than on anything else. In the long run, he believed, the League would moder-

League of Nations

ate the harshness of the Allied peace terms and temper imperial ambitions. He devised a League that reflected the power of large nations like the United States: an influential council of five permanent members (great powers) and elected delegates from smaller states; an assembly for discussion; and a World Court. The heart of the League covenant, as well as the centerpiece of Wilson's international reform program, was the collective security provision contained in Article 10, in which members agreed to respect and preserve each other's territorial integrity.

Americans vigorously debated the merits of the treaty. In March 1919, as the conferees in Paris were hammering out the accord, Republi-

Debate over the treaty

can Senator Henry Cabot Lodge of Massachusetts circulated a petition signed by thirty-nine senators (enough to deny the treaty the necessary two-thirds vote) that the League's structure did not adequately protect American interests. Wilson lamented the "pygmy" minds of his antagonists, but persuaded the peace conference to exempt the Monroe Doctrine and domestic matters from League jurisdiction. Having made these concessions to senatorial advice, Wilson would not budge.

Yet criticism mounted. Wilson had bastardized his own principles; he had given Shandong to Japan; he had personally killed a provision affirming the racial equality of all peoples. There was no mention in the treaty of freedom of the seas; there was no reduction in tariffs. Negotiations had been conducted in private, and reparations were impossibly high. And Article 10 raised serious questions: Would the United

States be obligated to use armed force to ensure collective security?

Wilson pleaded for understanding and lectured his opponents. Did they not realize that compromises were necessary given the awesome, stubborn resistance of the Allies, who had threatened to jettison the conference unless Wilson made concessions? Did they not recognize that the league would rectify wrongs? Could they not see that membership in the League would give the United States "leadership in the world"? Senator Lodge was unimpressed. He introduced a number of reservations to the treaty which reflected his belief that the League, as planned, would undermine American freedom of action and intrude on domestic questions. One reservation stated that the nation's immigration acts could not be subject to League decision. Another drew some of the teeth from Article 10 by stating that Congress had to approve any obligation under the article.

Aware that opposition to his masterwork was growing, Wilson took to the road in September for a speaking tour of the United States. Growing more exhausted every day, he dismissed his critics as "absolute, contemptible quitters." In Colorado, while delivering another passionate speech, the president collapsed. A few days later, in Washington, D.C., he suffered a stroke that paralyzed his left side. Although his mind remained alert, he became grumpy and peevish, fearful of displaying weakness and unable to conduct the heavy business of the presidency. Advised by Secretary of State Lansing and Colonel House to placate senatorial critics so the treaty would have a chance of passing, Wilson refused to compromise. From Senate Democrats he demanded loyalty—a vote against all reservations.

The Senate first tested the treaty's strength in November. In two votes, one on the treaty with reservations and one without, the Senate rejected it. A group of sixteen "Irreconcilables,"

Senate rejection of the treaty

determined to defeat any treaty, amended or not, voted nay each time. Again in March 1920, the Senate fell short of the necessary two-thirds vote of approval. Had Wilson permitted Democrats to compromise, to accept the reservations, he could have achieved his fervent goal of American membership in the infant League of Nations.

Who or what was responsible for the defeat of the treaty? The answer lies in the fact that at the core of the debate was a fundamental issue of American foreign policy: whether the United States would endorse collective security or pursue its traditional path of unilateralism, as articulated by George Washington in his Farewell Address and by James Monroe in his famous doctrine. Wilson lost because he could not overcome the tenacity of unilateralism, the desire for freedom of choice in international relations and for nonalignment. He could not persuade Americans to depart from their past.

The experience of war

America emerged from the war years an unsettled mix of the old and the new. Above all else the war exposed the heterogeneity of the American people and the deep divisions among them: white versus black, nativist versus immigrant, capital versus labor, dry versus wet, men versus women, radical versus progressive or conservative, pacifist versus interventionist, nationalist versus internationalist.

The war had brought massive government intervention in the economy. In the period from 1916 to 1919 annual federal expenditures increased 2,500 percent. Wilsonian wartime policies nourished the continued growth of big business and of oligopoly (the control of a whole industry by a few large companies). Moreover, the wartime cooperation of business and government encouraged the growth of trade associations. Standardization of products contributed to the development of a mass society.

The international system born during the war years was fragmented and unstable. The process of decolonization—a major trend of modern history—was set in motion at this time. Nationalist leaders like Ho Chi Minh of Indochina and Mahatma Gandhi of India, taking to heart the Wilsonian principle of self-determination, vowed to achieve independence for their peoples. Communism became a new and disruptive force in world politics, and the Russians bore a grudge against the Allies, who had futilely tried to thwart their revolution. The several new states in Central and Eastern Europe proved weak, dependent on outsiders for security. The new Germany bitterly resented the harsh peace settlement. Nor was the world economy settled. The war debts and reparations problems would dog international order for years. Yet America became the world's leading economic power and shifted from a debtor to a creditor nation.

The war experience also changed the mood of most Americans. The war was grimy and ugly, far less glorious than Wilson's lofty rhetoric had described it. People | *Disillusionment with the war* | recoiled from the photographs of bodies dangling from barbed wire, poison-gas victims, and battleshocked faces. American soldiers were eager to return home. Apparently tired of idealism and cynical about their ability to right wrongs, they craved the latest baseball scores, and stories of the home-run exploits of a new hero, Babe Ruth. Still, for the doughboys the army years were memorable, a turning point in their lives.

Those progressives who had believed entry into the war would deliver the millennium now marveled at their naiveté. Many lost their enthusiasm for crusades, and many others turned away in disgust from the bickering of the victors. Woodrow Wilson himself had remarked soon after taking office in 1913, before the Great War, that "there's no chance of progress and reform in an administration in which war plays the principal part." From the vantage point of 1920, looking back on the array of distempers at home and abroad, Wilson would have to agree with his fellow citizens that progress and reform had been dealt substantial blows.

Important events

1914	First World War begins
	Ellen Axson Wilson dies
1915	Germany declares war zone around British Isles
	German U-boat sinks *Lusitania*
	D. W. Griffith, *The Birth of a Nation*
1916	*Sussex* torpedoed
	Woodrow Wilson re-elected president on peace platform
1917	Germany declares unrestricted submarine warfare
	Zimmermann telegram
	Russian Revolution
	United States declares war against Germany
	Selective Service Act
	Espionage Act
	Race riot in East St. Louis, Illinois
	War Industries Board created
1918	Wilson announces Fourteen Points
	Webb-Pomerene Act

Sedition Act
Eugene Debs imprisoned for violating Espionage Act
American troops fight at Château-Thierry
U.S. troops intervene in Russian civil war
Allied offensive leads to German defeat
Flu epidemic
Republicans win congressional elections
Armistice

1919	Paris Peace Conference at Versailles
	May Day bombings and disturbances
	Red Summer; Chicago race riot
	Widespread labor strikes; steel strike
	U.S. Communist party founded
	President Wilson suffers a stroke
	Treaty of Paris rejected by Senate
	Schenck v. *U.S.*
1920	Red Scare and Palmer Raids

Suggestions for further reading

AMERICA IN THE ERA OF THE GREAT WAR John M. Blum, *Woodrow Wilson and the Politics of Morality* (1956); John W. Chambers, *The Tyranny of Change* (1980); Otis L. Graham, Jr., *The Great Campaigns* (1971); Ellis W. Hawley, *The Great War and the Search for a Modern Order* (1979); Arthur S. Link, *Wilson*, 5 vols. (1947–1965); Henry F. May, *The End of American Innocence* (1964); Ronald Steel, *Walter Lippmann and the American Century* (1980).

WILSONIAN FOREIGN POLICY Thomas A. Bailey and Paul B. Ryan, *The Lusitania Disaster* (1975); Pat-rick Devlin, *Too Proud to Fight* (1975); Ross Gregory, *The Origins of American Intervention in the First World War* (1971); N. Gordon Levin, Jr., *Woodrow Wilson and World Politics* (1968); Arthur S. Link, *Woodrow Wilson: Revolution, War, and Peace* (1979); Ernest R. May, *The World War and American Isolation, 1914–1917* (1959); Robert E. Osgood, *Ideals and Self-Interest in American Foreign Relations* (1953); Daniel M. Smith, *The Great Departure* (1965); Barbara Tuchman, *The Zimmermann Telegram* (1958); Arthur Walworth, *America's Moment* (1977); William C. Widenor, *Henry Cabot Lodge and the Search for an American Foreign Policy* (1980).

PREPAREDNESS AND WAR   Arthur E. Barbeau and Florette Henri, *The Unknown Soldiers: Black American Troops in World War I* (1974); J. Garry Clifford, *The Citizen Soldiers* (1972); Edward M. Coffman, *The War to End All Wars* (1968); Harvey A. DeWeerd, *President Wilson Fights His War* (1968); Thomas C. Leonard, *Above the Battle: War-Making in America from Appomattox to Versailles* (1978); David Trask, *The United States in the Supreme War Council* (1961); Russell F. Weigley, *The American Way of War* (1973).

THE HOME FRONT   Alfred W. Crosby, Jr., *Epidemic and Peace, 1918* (1976); Robert D. Cuff, *The War Industries Board* (1973); Edward R. Ellis, *Echoes of Distant Thunder* (1975); Maurine W. Greenwald, *Women, War, and Work* (1980); Carol S. Gruber, *Mars and Minerva: World War I and the Uses of the Higher Learning in America* (1975); Florette Henri, *Black Migration* (1975); David M. Kennedy, *Over Here* (1980); Seward W. Livermore, *Politics Is Adjourned* (1966); Frederick C. Luebke, *Bonds of Loyalty: German-Americans and World War I* (1974); Mark Reisler, *By the Sweat of Their Brow* (1976) (on Mexican-Americans); Elliott M. Rudwick, *Race Riot at East St. Louis, July 2, 1917* (1964); William M. Tuttle, *Race Riot: Chicago in the Red Summer of 1919* (1970).

WARTIME DISSENT, CIVIL LIBERTIES, AND THE RED SCARE   David Brody, *Labor in Crisis: The Steel Strike of 1919* (1965); Charles Chatfield, *For Peace and Justice: Pacifism in America, 1914–1941* (1971); Stanley Coben, *A. Mitchell Palmer* (1963); Charles DeBenedetti, *Origins of the Modern Peace Movement* (1978); Sondra Herman, *Eleven Against War* (1969); Paul L. Murphy, *World War I and the Origin of Civil Liberties* (1979); Robert K. Murray, *Red Scare* (1955); H. C. Peterson and Gilbert C. Fite, *Opponents of War, 1917–1918* (1968); William Preston, *Aliens and Dissenters: Federal Suppression of Radicals, 1903–1933* (1966): Francis Russell, *A City in Terror, 1919 – The Boston Police Strike* (1975); David P. Thelan, *Robert M. La Follette and the Insurgent Spirit* (1976); James Weinstein, *The Decline of Socialism in America, 1912–1923* (1967).

HOSTILITY TOWARD BOLSHEVIK RUSSIA   Peter G. Filene, *Americans and the Soviet Experiment, 1917–1933* (1967); George F. Kennan, *Russia Leaves the War* (1956); George F. Kennan, *The Decision to Intervene* (1958); Christopher Lasch, *The American Liberals and the Russian Revolution* (1962); John Thompson, *Russia, Bolshevism, and the Versailles Peace* (1966); Betty M. Unterberger, *America's Siberian Expedition, 1918–1920* (1956).

VERSAILLES AND THE LEAGUE FIGHT   Thomas A. Bailey, *Woodrow Wilson and the Great Betrayal* (1945); Thomas A. Bailey, *Woodrow Wilson and the Lost Peace* (1944); Inga Floto, *Colonel House in Paris* (1973); Warren F. Kuehl, *Seeking World Order* (1969); Arno Mayer, *Politics and Diplomacy of Peacemaking* (1967); Ralph A. Stone, *The Irreconcilables* (1970).

AFTERMATH   Stanley Cooperman, *World War I and the American Mind* (1970); Malcolm Cowley, *Exile's Return* (1951); Paul Fussell, *The Great War and Modern Memory* (1975); Stuart I. Rochester, *American Liberal Disillusionment in the Wake of World War I* (1977).

23

THE NEW ERA

OF THE 1920s

At 9:39 P.M. on August 5, 1926, a young American woman trudged out of the rough sea onto the English coast. Nineteen-year-old Gertrude Ederle had left France that morning in an attempt to swim the English Channel, a feat that only five men and no women had ever accomplished. She not only succeeded but swam the treacherous thirty-mile stretch in 14 hours 31 minutes, the fastest time yet recorded.

Ederle's conquest of the Channel, wrote the *Literary Digest,* "would be hailed as a battle won for feminism" and the "unanswerable refutation of the masculine dogma that woman is, in the sense of physical power and efficiency, inferior to man." Yet the name of Ederle was never as renowned as those of the era's most admired males: Dempsey, Ruth, and Lindbergh. And along with adulation, the young woman's feat inspired exploitative swimsuit ads linking physical fitness to sex appeal.

The ads were but another sign of the times. During the 1920s the flower of consumerism reached full bloom. Spurred by advertising and new forms of credit, Americans eagerly bought automobiles, radios, real estate, and stocks. The majority of the population enjoyed an unparalleled standard of living. Perhaps the most fundamental and perplexing trend of the 1920s was the effect of the new mass consumer culture on individuals and communities. Changes in work habits, family responsibilities, and health care fostered new uses of time and new attitudes about proper behavior at home and in society.

In many ways, the Ederle story illustrates the complexities and ironies of the new era of the 1920s. The decade was a time both of great accomplishments—in economic productivity as well as athletics—and of frivolous commercial stunts, contests, and fads. It was a time of swift social change, of frankness and liberation. But the winds of change also stirred up waves of reaction. The new, more liberal values repelled some groups, such as the Ku Klux Klan, immigration restrictionists, and religious fundamentalists. Such groups reacted by trying to restore a society of simpler values, where people knew their place and deviants were not tolerated.

Postwar optimism

Poor Richard's Almanac would have sold poorly in the 1920s. Few Americans of that era had much interest in the virtues of thrift and sobriety that Benjamin Franklin had preached. They saw more attraction in acquisition, speculation, amusement, and salesmanship. Instead of traditional homilies like "waste not, want not," they harkened to the advice of an advertising executive: "Make the public want what you have to sell. Make 'em pant for it." With such an attitude Americans attained the highest standard of living they had yet experienced. Though poverty and social injustice still infected the country, many people shared the belief, as journalist Joseph Wood Krutch put it, that "the future was bright and the present was good fun at least."

The decade did not begin very brightly. Wartime prosperity gave way to a postwar economic slump that hurt farmers the most. Net farm income was $10 billion in 1919; two years later it was $4 billion. Unemployment, which had hovered around 2 percent in 1919, passed 12 percent in 1921. The railroad and mining industries suffered declining profits, and layoffs spread through New England mills as textile companies abandoned outdated factories for the raw materials and cheap labor of the South.

Recovery began in 1922 and continued unevenly until 1929. During this period, industrial output nearly doubled. Elec- tric motors were responsible for much of the rise; by 1929 electricity powered 70 percent of American industry. Powered by electricity and made more efficient by the assembly line, factories turned out an increasing variety of products. The expansion of manufacturing and services led to higher profits and wages. And increased incomes, when combined with installment credit plans, fueled a new consumerism.

Behind the prosperity, an economic revolution was coming to a head. First, the consolidation movement that had given birth to trusts and holding companies in the late nineteenth century reached a new stage. Progressive-era trustbusting had not halted oligopoly. By the 1920s many of these companies dominated not only the production but the marketing, distribution, and even financing of a product. Thus in businesses as varied as automobile manufacturing, steel production, meat processing, and railroads, a few sprawling integrated companies predominated.

The organizational movement that had begun around 1900 also matured in the 1920s. Myriad business and professional associations sprang up to coordinate and protect their members' interests. Retailers and small manufacturers formed trade associations to pool information

and attempt market planning. Farm bureaus and cooperative marketing associations promoted scientific agriculture, lobbied for government protection, and tried to stabilize the market. Lawyers, engineers, and social scientists cooperated with business to promote economic growth.

These developments bespoke not only an economically mature nation but an urbanized one. By the 1920s, the city had become the locus of the national experience, and urban expansion occurred across the nation. Cities in warm climates, such as Miami, Tampa, and San Diego, underwent the most explosive growth.

During the 1920s, an estimated 6 million Americans left their farms for nearby or distant cities. Blacks accounted for a sizable portion of the migrants fleeing farms. Crushed by tenant farming and lured by new industrial jobs, 1.5 million blacks moved cityward during the 1920s. The black populations of New York, Chicago, Philadelphia, Detroit, Cleveland, and Houston doubled during these years. Forced by necessity and discrimination to seek the cheapest and poorest housing, the newcomers squeezed into ghettos—low-rent districts from which escape was difficult at best. When overcrowding burst the boundaries of the black ghetto and blacks spilled over into nearby white neighborhoods, racial violence often resulted.

In response partly to their new urban experiences and partly to race riots and threats, thousands of blacks in northern cities joined movements that glorified black independence. The most influential of these black nationalist groups was the Universal Negro Improvement Association (UNIA), headed by Marcus Garvey, a Jamaican immigrant who believed blacks should separate themselves from a corrupt white society. Proclaiming "I am the equal of any white man," Garvey cultivated race pride and promoted black capitalism. His newspaper, the *Negro World,* refused to publish ads for hair straighteners and skin-lightening cosmetics, and his Black Star shipping line was intended to help blacks emigrate to Africa.

Postwar economic recovery

Climax of urbanization

Marcus Garvey

The UNIA declined in the mid-1920s when the Black Star line went bankrupt (unscrupulous dealers had sold it dilapidated ships) and when the government jailed Garvey for mail fraud and then deported him. Nevertheless, the organization had attracted a huge following (contemporaries estimated it at 500,000; Garvey claimed 6 million) in New York, Chicago, Detroit, and other cities. And Garvey's speeches had served notice that blacks had their own aspirations, which they could and would translate into action.

As urban growth peaked, suburban growth accelerated. Although towns had existed around the edges of urban centers since the nation's earliest years, prosperity and easier transportation—mainly the automobile—made the urban fringe more accessible in the 1920s. Between 1920 and 1930, suburbs of Chicago, Cleveland, and Los Angeles grew five to ten times as fast as the central cities. Most, but not all, of these suburbs were middle- and upper-class bedroom communities.

The bulging cities and suburbs fostered the development of the new mass culture that gave the decade its character. Most of the consumers who jammed retail establishments, movie houses, and sporting arenas were city dwellers. Cities were the places where people flouted law and morality by patronizing speakeasies (illegal saloons), holding petting parties, swearing in public, wearing outlandish clothes, and listening to jazz. And yet Americans could not escape the small-town society of the past. While intellectuals carped that small towns stifled personal growth, other Americans reminisced about the innocence and simplicity of a world gone by. This was the dilemma of a modern nation: how could one anchor oneself in a world of rampant materialism?

Materialism unbound

"One day," Henry Ford recalled, "someone brought to us a slogan which read: 'Buy a Ford and Save the Difference,' I crossed out the 'save' and inserted 'spend'–'Buy a Ford and Spend the Difference.' It is the wiser thing to do. Society lives by circulation and not by congestion." Ford's ardent consumerism was a major theme of the 1920s, to which he contributed materially as well as philosophically.

Indeed, between 1919 and 1929 the gross national product–the total value of all goods and services produced in the United States–swelled by 40 percent. Wages and salaries also increased (though not as much) and consumer price indexes generally fell. The result was that real income–the amount of goods and services money could buy–rose. In other words, people had more purchasing power. And they spent as Americans had never spent. By 1929 two-thirds of all Americans lived in dwellings that had electricity, one-fourth of all families owned electric vacuum cleaners, and one-fifth had electric toasters. Many could afford these and other items only because more than one family member worked or because the breadwinner took a second job. Nevertheless, new products and services were available to more than just the rich.

Of all the era's technological and economic wonders, the automobile was the vanguard. During the 1920s automobile registrations soared from 8 million to 23 million. Mass production and competition had brought down prices, making cars affordable even for some working-class families. By 1926 a Ford Model T cost under $300 and a Chevrolet sold for $700–at a time when workers in manufacturing earned around $1,300 a year and clerical workers about $2,300. The car became a source of pride as well as a means of transportation.

The motor car altered society as much as the railroad had seventy-five years earlier. Public officials were forced to pay more attention to safety regulations and traffic control. The growing choice of models (there were 108 different automobile manufacturers in 1923) and colors allowed automobile owners to express their per-

Growth of the suburbs

Expansion of the consumer society

Effects of the automobile

The age of electrical home appliances dawned in the 1920s. Here a sales force poses with toaster, vacuum cleaners, and washing machine outside an appliance store in Louisville, Kentucky. University of Louisville Photographic Archive; Caufield and Shook Collection 109089.

sonal tastes in a growing mass society. But most important, the car had a leveling effect; it was the ultimate symbol of social equality. As one writer observed in 1924, "It is hard to convince Steve Popovich, or Antonio Branca, or plain John Smith that he is being ground into the dust by Capital when at will he may drive the same highways, view the same scenery, and get as much enjoyment from his trip as the modern Midas."

More than ever, Americans' taste for automobiles and other goods and services was whetted by advertising. By 1929 total advertising expenditures had reached $1.78 billion, nearly as much as was spent on all types of formal education. For many, advertising became the new gospel. In his best-selling *The Man Nobody Knows* (1925), ad-

| Advertising |

vertising executive Bruce Barton called Jesus "the founder of modern business" because he "picked up twelve men from the bottom ranks of business and forged them into an organization that conquered the world."

Although daily newspaper circulation declined during the 1920s, over 10 million families owned radios by the decade's end. A new advertising medium had been discovered. Station KDKA in Pittsburgh pioneered in commercial radio broadcasting beginning in 1920; by 1922 there were 508 such stations. By 1929 the National Broadcasting Company, which had begun to assemble a network of radio stations three years earlier, was charging advertisers $10,000 to sponsor an hour-long show. Commercial intermissions at movie houses and highway billboards also reminded viewers to buy.

Materialism unbound

The business of government, the government of business

In this outburst of materialism, many Americans shed their fear of big business, swayed in part by the testimonials of probusiness propagandists. "Among the nations of the earth today," one writer proclaimed in 1921, "America stands for one idea: *Business. . . .*" All branches of the federal government supported business interests during these years. In 1921 Congress reduced taxes on corporations and wealthy individuals, and in 1922 it raised tariff rates in the Fordney-McCumber Tariff Act. Presidents Harding, Coolidge, and Hoover appointed strong cabinet officers who pursued policies favorable to business. Regulatory agencies cooperated with corporations more than they regulated them. And the Supreme Court upheld big business and struck down reform in cases such as *Bailey* v. *Drexel Furniture Company* (1922), which voided restrictions on child labor; and *Adkins* v. *Children's Hospital* (1923), which overturned a minimum wage law for women because it infringed on liberty of contract.

The pursuit of profits and comfort prompted political analysts to lament the death of progressivism. Yet many of the Progressive era's achievements were sustained and consolidated in these years. Although trustbusting fizzled on the federal level, regulatory commissions and other government agencies still monitored business activities and worked to reduce wasteful practices. And in Congress a sizable corps of reformers, led by George Norris of Nebraska and Robert La Follette of Wisconsin, kept progressive causes alive by supporting labor legislation, federal aid to farmers, and continued government operation of a federally constructed hydroelectric dam at Muscle Shoals, Alabama. Most reform, however, occurred at the state and local levels.

Extension of progressive reforms

Organized labor, which had gained ground during the Progressive era, suffered some setbacks during the 1920s. Public opinion, influenced by prosperity, the new materialism, and probusiness rhetoric, turned against workers who pushed for better wages and disrupted everyday life with strikes. Both the federal government and the Supreme Court frequently stifled union attempts to exercise power during these years. Meanwhile, large corporations worked to counteract the appeal of unions by promising workers pensions, profit sharing, and company-sponsored social and sporting events— a policy that became known as *welfare capitalism*. In such a climate, union membership fell from 5.1 million in 1920 to 3.6 million in 1929.

The epitome of the decade's goodwill toward business was President Warren Gamaliel Harding, a Republican elected in 1920, at a time when the populace wanted to avoid national and international crusades. Harding appointed some capable assistants, notably Secretary of State Charles Evans Hughes, Secretary of Commerce Herbert Hoover, Secretary of the Treasury Andrew Mellon, and Secretary of Agriculture Henry C. Wallace. His problem was that he also appointed some predatory friends to positions from which they infested government with corruption. Charles Forbes of the Veterans Bureau served time in Leavenworth prison after being convicted of fraud and bribery in connection with government contracts. Thomas W. Miller, alien property custodian, was jailed for accepting bribes. Two other officials committed suicide to escape prosecution. Harding's close friend Attorney General Harry Daugherty was implicated in a scheme of accepting bribes and in other fraudulent acts; he escaped prosecution only by refusing to testify against himself. In the most notorious case of all, Secretary of the Interior Albert Fall accepted bribes to lease government property to private oil companies. For his role in the affair, called the Teapot Dome scandal after a Wyoming oil reserve, Fall was fined $100,000 and spent a year in jail. He was the first cabinet officer to be so disgraced.

Harding administration

In June 1923, few Americans knew how corrupt Harding's administration had become. The president, however, had become disillusioned. Amid rumors of mismanagement and crime, he told journalist William Allen White, "My God, this is a hell of a job. I have no trouble with my enemies. . . . But my friends, my God-damned friends . . . they're the ones that keep me walking the floor nights." On a speaking tour of the West that summer, Harding became ill and died in San Francisco on August 2.

Harding's successor, Vice President Calvin Coolidge, was far more solemn and certainly less active. In fact, Coolidge usually slept more than half of each day: at least ten hours a night and another two or three in the afternoon. A dour New Englander, he had first attracted national attention by his firm stand against striking Boston policemen in 1919, a policy that won him the vice-presidential nomination in 1920. Usually, however, he was content to let events take their course.

Coolidge had great respect for private enterprise. Fortunately for him, his administration coincided with extraordinary business prosperity.

 Coolidge prosperity Aided by Andrew Mellon, whom he retained as secretary of the treasury, and other cabinet officers, he balanced the budget, reduced government debt, lowered income-tax rates (especially for the rich), and began construction of a national highway system. The only disruptions arose over farm policy. Responding to farmers' complaints of falling prices, Congress twice passed bills to establish government-backed price supports for staple crops (the McNary-Haugen bills of 1927 and 1928). But Coolidge vetoed the measure both times.

"Coolidge prosperity" was the determining issue in the presidential election of 1924. That year both major parties ran candidates who had no quarrel with business supremacy. The Republicans nominated Coolidge with little dissent. At their national convention, the Democrats endured 103 ballots before settling on John W. Davis, a corporation lawyer from New York. Remnants of the progressive movement, along with various farm, labor, and socialist groups, formed a new Progressive party and nominated Wisconsin's aging reformer, Robert La Follette. Coolidge won 54 percent of the popular vote and 382 of the 531 electoral votes.

In 1928 the Democrats ran New York's Alfred E. Smith; the Republicans, Herbert Hoover. Both were competent men. Hoover had achieved an admirable record as a public administrator, and Smith had supported many social reforms during his governorship. An urbane, gregarious politician of immigrant stock, Smith was the first Roman Catholic to run for president on a major party ticket. As such he had considerable appeal among urban ethnic groups, who were voting in increasing numbers, but he lost the votes of some Protestant southerners and westerners for the same reason. Hoover, who stressed the nation's prosperity, won the popular vote 21 million to 15 million and the electoral vote 444 to 87. But Smith's candidacy had important effects on the Democratic party. Smith carried the nation's twelve largest cities, heretofore Republican, and lured millions of foreign-stock voters to the polls for the first time. From 1928 onward the national Democratic party would solidify this urban labor base, which when combined with its traditional strength in the South made the party a formidable force in national politics.

New trends in the use of time

In contrast to the relative calm of national affairs, change was making constant ripples on the surface of everyday life. Increasingly, people were splitting their lives into three distinct compartments: work, family, and leisure. Work time and family time were both shrinking in the 1920s. Among industrial workers the five-and-one-half-day workweek (half a day on Saturday) was becoming common. Many white-collar employees enjoyed two days off and worked a forty-hour week. Annual vacations were also becoming a standard job benefit for white-collar workers, whose numbers grew by 40 percent during the decade.

Family time is harder to measure, but certain figures suggest important changes. As birth control became more widely accepted, birth rates dropped noticeably between 1920 and 1930, decreasing the proportion of families with five or more children. For women marrying in the 1920s, four or fewer children became the norm. Over the same period the divorce rate rose. In 1920 there was one divorce in every 7.5 marriages; in 1929 the national ratio was 1 in 6. Moreover, between 1920 and 1930 life expectancy at birth increased from fifty-four to sixty years, reflecting better nutrition and medical research in bacteriology and immunology. Nonwhites did not share the results of enhanced medical care equally with whites.

At the same time the availability of ready-to-wear clothes, preserved foods, and mass-produced furniture meant that family members spent less time producing household necessities. *Household management* Wives still spent most of their day cleaning, cooking, mending, and otherwise maintaining the home, but new machines made some of their tasks less rigorous. Instead of being a producer of food and clothing, the wife now became chief consumer, doing the shopping and making sure the family spent its money wisely.

The ready availability of washing machines, hot water, and commercial soap put greater pressure on wives to keep everything clean. Indeed, advertisers tried to coax women into buying products by making them feel guilty for not giving enough attention to cleaning the home, feeding the family, caring for the children, and tending to personal hygiene. Thus, as the industrial and service sectors became more specialized as a result of technological advances, housewives retained a wide variety of responsibilities and added new ones as well.

While family time and work time were decreasing, nonwork, nonfamily activities were expanding. High school enrollment quadrupled between 1910 and 1929; by 1929 over a third of all high school graduates went on to college. And as the use of electricity spread, people stayed up later at night to read or listen to the radio. They filled their expanding leisure time with automobile rides, sports events, motion pictures, shopping, and other forms of amusement.

With more people spending time away from work and family, new values and outlooks were inevitable. Especially among the middle class *Social values* but among the working class too, clothes became a means to personal expression and freedom. The line between inappropriate and acceptable behavior blurred as smoking, swearing, and frankness about sex became more common. Thousands who had never read psychoanalyst Sigmund Freud's theories were certain that he prescribed an uninhibited sex life as the key to mental health. Birth-control advocate Margaret Sanger gained a large following in respectable circles. Newspapers, magazines, motion pictures, and popular songs made certain that Americans did not suffer from "sex starvation."

Still other trends contributed to the breakdown of traditional values. As white-collar and professional occupations proliferated, men seemed to draw more prestige from their work than from their families. And because child-labor laws and compulsory-school-attendance laws kept children in school longer than was common in earlier generations, school now played a greater role in preparing children for adulthood. Parents tended to rely less on family tradition and more on child-care manuals in raising their children. Old-age homes, public health clinics, and workers' compensation reduced the family's responsibilities even further.

Although the home remained the domain of wives and mothers, women continued to stream *Opportunities for women* into the labor force during the 1920s. By 1930 10.8 million women worked, an increase of over 2 million since the war's end. More than a million of these were professionals, mainly teachers and nurses. Some 2.2 million were typists, bookkeepers, and office clerks, a

Chapter 23: The new era of the 1920s

The "new woman," independent and assertive, could tip her hat to a man just as he tipped his to her. Although far from all young women in the 1920s indulged in the frivolity and sexual abandon attributed to the flapper, many did experience some degree of liberation in their behavior and thinking.　Library of Congress.

tenfold increase since 1920; another 736,000 were salespeople in stores. Increasingly large numbers of women took jobs as waitresses and hairdressers. Though almost 2 million women worked in factories, their numbers grew very little over the decade.

As in the past, women struggled to define their place in a male-dominated society. Most employed females were young and single, supervised by males who paid them poorly, bullied them, and blocked their chances to move up the occupational ladder. Few heeded the call for equal pay and equal opportunity voiced by Alice Paul, leader of the National Women's party, who in 1922 supported an equal rights amendment to the Constitution.

Yet women liberated themselves in other ways. Thousands pursued intellectual and artistic careers. By the end of the 1920s, 15 percent of the nation's college and university teachers were women, as were 38 percent of musicians and music teachers, 27 percent of authors, editors, and reporters, and nearly half of artists and art teachers. Alternate lifestyles—or the appearance of them—spread among large numbers of women. Short skirts and bobbed hair, regarded as signs of sexual freedom, became common. And the most popular models of female behavior were not chaste, sentimental heroines but movie vamps like Clara Bow, the "It Girl," and Gloria Swanson, who specialized in torrid love affairs on and off the screen. And though not everyone was a flapper, as the young independent-minded woman was called, many women were clearly asserting their equality with men.

These new social trends represented a final break with the more restrained culture of the nineteenth century. But social change, as always,

New trends in the use of time

did not proceed smoothly. As the decade wore on, various groups prepared to defend against the threat to older, more familiar values.

Lines of defense

In the spring of 1920 the leader of a newly formed organization decided to hire two public-relations experts to help in recruiting members. Using modern advertising techniques, the promoters canvassed communities in the South, Southwest, and Midwest. By 1923 the organization, a revived Ku Klux Klan, claimed 5 million members. Its appeal was based on fear.

The Klan was the most sinister reactionary movement of the 1920s. Re-established in 1915 by William J. Simmons, an Atlanta evangelist

| Ku Klux Klan | and insurance salesman who wanted to purify southern culture, the new Invisible Empire revived the hoods, intimidating tactics, and mystical terms of its forerunner. But the new Klan was broader in membership and in objectives than the old. Its chapters fanned outward from the deep South and for a time wielded frightening power in Ohio, Indiana, Oklahoma, Oregon, and even Pennsylvania, New York, and New England. And unlike the first Klan, which terrorized mostly emancipated blacks, the new Klan directed its venom toward a variety of groups.

One brief phrase expressed the new Klan's objectives: "Native, white, Protestant supremacy." *Native* meant no immigration, no "mongrelization" of white Protestant culture. Klan tactics included the use of threatening assemblies, violence, and political pressure. Assuming the role of moral protector, they meted out vigilante justice to bootleggers, wife beaters, and adulterers; forced schools to adopt Bible readings and stop teaching the theory of evolution; and campaigned against Catholic and Jewish political candidates. By the mid-1920s, however, the Invisible Empire was on the wane, outvoted

by its foreign-stock enemies and rocked by scandal. (In 1925 Indiana Grand Dragon David Stephenson was convicted of kidnapping and raping his secretary, who later committed suicide.)

Nativist sentiment was also reflected in continued fear of radicalism. The most notorious outburst of antiforeign hysteria occurred in 1921, when a court convicted Nicola Sacco and

| Sacco and Vanzetti | Bartolomeo Vanzetti, two immigrant anarchists, of murdering a guard and paymaster during a robbery in South Braintree, Massachusetts. Sacco and Vanzetti's main offenses seem to have been their political beliefs and Italian origins, however, since evidence failed to prove their involvement in the robbery. Judge Webster Thayer nevertheless openly sided with the prosecution, privately calling the defendants "those anarchist bastards." Amid protest, the two men were executed in August 1927.

Congress responded to the mounting nativist pressure in 1921, 1924, and 1927 by passing laws that established yearly immigration quotas for each nationality. These quotas favored northern and western Europeans, reflecting the prejudices of natives against newer immigrant groups from southern and eastern Europe. The Emergency

| Immigration quotas | Quota, or Johnson, Act of 1921 provided that the annual immigration of any given nationality could not exceed 3 percent of the number of immigrants from that nation residing in the United States in 1910. But this law, meant to be temporary, did not satisfy restrictionists' aims, so Congress replaced it with the National Origins Act of 1924. The new law set the quota at 2 percent of each nationality residing in the United States in 1890. The National Origins Act was amended in 1927, at which time Congress set a limit of 150,000 immigrants a year—including 65,721 from Great Britain and 25,957 from Germany, but only 5,802 from Italy and 2,712 from Russia. These laws virtually excluded Orientals, but left the door open to peoples from the Western Hemisphere.

Soon Mexicans and Puerto Ricans became the largest groups of newcomers.

The impulse to protect racial and moral purity also stirred religious fundamentalists. In 1925 fundamentalist Christianity clashed with new scientific theory in a celebrated case in Dayton, Tennessee. Early that year the Tennessee legislature passed a law forbidding

| Scopes trial |

public school instructors to teach the theory that humans had evolved from lower forms of life rather than from Adam and Eve. Shortly thereafter, high school teacher John Thomas Scopes was arrested for violating the law (he had volunteered to serve in a test case). Scope's trial became a headline event, with William Jennings Bryan, former secretary of state and three-time presidential candidate, arguing for the prosecution, and a team of civil-liberties lawyers headed by the famous attorney Clarence Darrow arguing for the defense. Although Scopes was easily convicted—clearly he had broken the law—modernists claimed victory; the testimony, they believed, had shown fundamentalism to be at odds with secular social trends.

The emotional responses Americans made to events during the 1920s were part of a larger attempt to sustain old, local values in a fast-moving, materialistic world. Even as they attempted to hold to the past, however, most Americans adjusted in some way to the new order. They went to movies and sporting events, listened to the radio, and generally tried to find release from societal pressures in a world of leisure.

The age of play

During the 1920s Americans developed an almost insatiable thirst for recreation, to which entrepreneurs responded quickly. The decade marked the flowering of fads, frivolities, and what contemporaries called ballyhoo, a blitz of

| Fads and sports |

publicity that lent exaggerated importance to some person or event. The new games and fancies were particularly attractive to middle-class families with large spendable incomes. In the early 1920s the Chinese tile game of mahjongg was the rage. By the mid-1920s fun seekers were turning to crossword puzzles; a few years later they adopted miniature golf as their new craze. Throughout the decade dance fads like the Charleston riveted public attention, aided by radio music and the growing popularity of jazz.

In addition to their active participation in leisure activities, Americans were avid spectators, particularly of movies and sports. The most popular films were mass spectacles such as Cecil B. DeMille's *The Ten Commandments* and *The King of Kings;* lurid sex tales such as *Sinners in Silk* and *Up in Mabel's Room;* and slapstick comedies. Ironically, the comedies, with their often poignant satire of the human condition, carried the most thought-provoking messages.

Spectator sports also boomed. Each year millions packed stadiums, arenas, gymnasiums, and parks to watch athletic events. Perhaps in an age when technology and mass production had sapped experiences and objects of their uniqueness, sports provided the unpredictability and drama that people craved. Newspapers and radio captured and exaggerated this drama, feeding news to an eager public and often overpromoting events with unrestrained narrative. Baseball seemed to attract the largest following. On discovering that home runs aroused excitement, the leagues redesigned the ball to make it livelier. Thereafter, attendance at major-league games skyrocketed. In 1921 a record 300,000 people attended the six-game World Series between the New York Giants and the New York Yankees.

Sports, movies, and the news gave Americans a panoply of heroes. As society became more collectivized and the individual less significant,

| Sports heroes |

people clung to these heroic personalities as a means of identifying with the unique. Boxing, football, and baseball produced the biggest sports heroes. Heavyweight champion Jack Dempsey, a powerful brawler from Manassa, Colorado, attracted the first of many million-dollar gates in his fight

Patrons of a speakeasy flout Prohibition in this rare photograph of an illegal saloon. Although a constitutional amendment had outlawed the manufacture and sale of alcoholic beverages, many otherwise respectable and law-abiding citizens willfully broke the law. The Bettmann Archive.

with Georges Carpentier in 1921. And Harold "Red" Grange, running back for the University of Illinois football team, thrilled thousands every weekend and became the idol of sportswriters. Baseball's greatest star of the era was New York Yankee outfielder George Herman "Babe" Ruth. Ruth's annual home run totals increased from a record 29 in 1919, to 54 in 1920, 59 in 1924, and 60 in 1927. His exaggerated gestures on the field, defiant lifestyle, and boyish grin endeared him to millions and made him a national legend.

If Americans identified with the physical exploits of sports stars, they fulfilled a yearning for romance and adventure through adulation of movie stars. The films and personal lives of

| Movie stars and public heroes |

Douglas Fairbanks, Gloria Swanson, Charlie Chaplin, and scores of others were discussed in parlors and pool halls across the country. Perhaps the decade's most ballyhooed personality was Rudolph Valentino, whose Latin machismo made women swoon and prompted men to copy his pomaded hairdo and slick sideburns.

News promoters created their own heroes outside the world of athletics and entertainment. Flagpole sitters, marathon dancers, and other record seekers regularly occupied the front pages. The most notable of these news heroes was Charles A. Lindbergh, the pilot whose daring solo flight across the Atlantic in 1927 was cheered by millions. A modest, independent midwesterner whom newspapers dubbed the Lone Eagle, Lindbergh accepted fame but did not try to profit from it. Because his quiet personality contrasted so starkly with the ballyhoo that surrounded him, Americans honored him even more fervently.

In part the adulation of Lindbergh may have reflected guilt. For in their quest for fun and individual expression—liberties that Prohibition

| Prohibition |

seemed to deny—Americans became flagrant lawbreakers and supporters of crime. The constitutional amendment and federal law that prohibited the manufacture, sale, and transportation of alcoholic beverages worked well at first. Per-capita consumption of liquor dropped, arrests for drunkenness diminished, and the price of illegal booze rose higher than the average worker could afford. But after about 1925 the noble experiment broke down in the cities, where the desire for personal freedom overwhelmed the weak means of enforcement.

Criminals were quick to recognize the possibilities of the situation. But though Prohibition encouraged organized crime, it did not create it. Gangs or mobs, the most notorious of which belonged to Chicago's Al Capone, had provided illegal goods and services long before the 1920s.

As Capone explained it, "Prohibition is business. All I do is supply a demand."

Thus during the 1920s Americans were caught between two value systems. On the one hand, the Puritan tradition of hard work, sobriety, and restraint—"waste not, want not"—still prevailed, especially in rural areas where new diversions were unavailable. On the other hand, a liberating age of play beckoned. At no previous time in American history had so many opportunities for recreation presented themselves.

Cultural currents

This tension between value systems pulled artists and intellectuals in new directions and energized an experimental movement in literature, art, and music. Fear that materialism and conformity were being fostered by mass society gave this movement a bitterly critical tinge. Indeed, many of the era's leading literary figures,

| *Literature of alienation* |

finding the vulgar materialism of the time hostile to their art, succumbed to disillusionment and became known as the Lost Generation. Some moved to Europe in protest. Although these writers' main goals were to create new forms of expression and portray emotion realistically, they also produced biting social commentary. The dominant themes of their social criticism were middle- and upper-class materialism and the impersonality of modern society. F. Scott Fitzgerald's novels and Eugene O'Neill's plays exposed America's overemphasis on money and success. The powerful antiwar sentiments of John Dos Passos's *Three Soldiers* (1921) and Hemingway's *A Farewell to Arms* (1929) were skillfully interwoven with passionate critiques of the impersonality of modern relationships.

Perhaps the most trenchant social criticism flowed from the pen of H. L. Mencken. A Baltimore newspaperman and founder of the *American Mercury,* Mencken jabbed at prevailing customs and beliefs with stinging cynicism. No group, no individual was too sacred to escape his satire. He jeered at the inane quest for status of the middle-class "booboisie," labeled Woodrow Wilson a "self-bamboozled presbyterian," and scorned political reformers as "saccharine liberals" and "jitney messiahs."

A spiritual discontent quite different from that of white writers energized the work of a new generation of young black artists. Largely middle-class and well-educated, these writers represented W. E. B. Du Bois's "Talented Tenth" in background, but their outlook seemed closer to Booker T. Washington's racial self-help. They rejected the amalgamation of black and white cultures, exalting the militantly assertive "New Negro," proud of the African

| *Harlem Renaissance* |

heritage. Most of them lived in Harlem, the black neighborhood in upper Manhattan. In this "Negro Mecca" black intellectuals and artists celebrated the development of a modern black culture in what became known as the Harlem Renaissance.

Harlem in the 1920s fostered an extraordinary number of gifted writers, among them Langston Hughes, who wrote forceful and sometimes humorous poems, stories, and essays; Countee Cullen, a poet with moving lyrical skills; and Claude McKay, whose militant verses sounded a clarion call for rebellion against bigotry. Jean Toomer's novels and poems portrayed black life with passionate realism, and Alain Locke's essays gave early direction to the artistic renaissance. Much of this group's writing addressed issues of identity. For though black intellectuals took pride in African culture, they also realized that black Americans had to assert themselves and come to terms with themselves as Americans.

Although black authors did not reach many people, black musicians had considerable influence. The Jazz Age, as the decade is some-

| *Jazz* |

times called, owed its name to the music that grew out of black urban culture. With its emotional rhythms and its emphasis on improvisation, jazz

Important events

1920	Warren G. Harding elected president
	First commercial radio broadcast
1920–21	Postwar deflation and depression
1921	Immigration quotas established
	Sacco and Vanzetti convicted
1922	Fordney-McCumber Tariff
	Economic recovery
1923	Harding dies; Coolidge assumes the presidency
	Peak of Ku Klux Klan activity
1923–24	Exposure of Harding administration scandals
1924	National Origins Act
	Coolidge elected president; La Follette's third-party movement
1925	Scopes trial
1926	Rudolph Valentino dies
1927	First McNary-Haugen bill vetoed
	Sacco and Vanzetti executed
	Charles A. Lindbergh's transatlantic flight
	Babe Ruth hits sixty home runs
1928	Herbert Hoover elected president

blurred the distinction between composer and performer and created a new intimacy between performer and audience.

As blacks moved north, they brought jazz with them. By the 1920s dance halls and bars patronized by whites as well as blacks featured jazz. Gifted black performers like trumpeter Louis Armstrong, trombonist Kid Ory, and singer Bessie Smith enjoyed widespread popu-

larity. The music recorded by these and other black artists gave black Americans a distinctive place in the new consumer culture. More important, jazz endowed America with its most distinctive art form.

In many ways the 1920s were the most creative years the nation had yet experienced. Influenced by jazz and by experimental writing, painters such as Georgia O'Keeffe and John Marin drew on European techniques in an effort to forge a distinctively American style of painting. And although European composers and performers still dominated classical music, Americans such as Henry Cowell, who pioneered electronic music, and Brooklyn-born Aaron Copland, who built exciting orchestral and vocal works around native folk motifs, began careers that later won wide acclaim. In architecture, Frank Lloyd Wright's "prairie style" houses, churches, and schools reflected the magnificence of the American landscape. At the beginning of the decade, essayist Harold Stearns had complained that "the most . . . pathetic fact in the social life of America today is emotional and aesthetic starvation." By 1929 such a contention was hard to support.

Most Americans, especially members of the middle class, seemed to enjoy the 1920s. To be sure, the revived Klan, the Sacco and Vanzetti trial, and the decade's immigration laws reflected traditional American xenophobia. But for most Americans the decade was one of diversion. Speakeasies, Babe Ruth's records, Lindbergh's flight, new dances, miniature golf, movie idols, and a host of other individuals, events, and fads caught the public's attention. In their quest for enjoyment few Americans worried about the health of the economy. The decade was, in their minds, a prosperous one.

Yet there were underlying weaknesses. In 1927 there were about 15,000 more commercial failures than there had been in 1920. Moreover, by 1926 critical industries such as construction, coal mining, and auto manufacturing were manifesting signs of weakness. Stock prices rose to unrealistic levels in 1928 and 1929. A few people including President Hoover and Joseph

Kennedy, father of future president John F. Kennedy, anticipated a market decline and sold their stocks in 1929. But most individuals believed that all was right with the economy.

Suggestions for further reading

OVERVIEWS OF THE 1920s   Frederick Lewis Allen, *Only Yesterday* (1931); Paul A. Carter, *Another Part of the Twenties* (1977); William E. Leuchtenburg, *The Perils of Prosperity* (1958).

ECONOMICS AND LABOR   Irving L. Bernstein, *A History of the American Worker, 1920–1933* (1960); James J. Flink, *The Car Culture* (1975); Jim Potter, *The American Economy Between the Wars* (1974); John Rae, *The Road and the Car in American Life* (1971); Leslie Woodcock Tentler, *Wage-Earning Women: Industrial Work and Family Life in the United States, 1900–1930* (1979).

POLITICS AND LAW   David Burner, *The Politics of Provincialism* (1968); Matthew Josephson and Hannah Josephson, *Al Smith* (1970); Samuel Lubell, *The Future of American Politics* (1952); Donald R. McCoy, *Calvin Coolidge* (1967); Alpheus Mason, *The Supreme Court from Taft to Warren* (1958); R. K. Murray, *The*

Harding Era (1969); George Tindall, *The Emergence of the New South* (1967); Joan Hoff Wilson, *Herbert Hoover: The Forgotten Progressive* (1975).

SOCIAL ISSUES   William H. Chafe, *The American Woman: Her Changing Social, Economic, and Political Roles* (1972); David M. Chalmers, *Hooded Americanism: The History of the Ku Klux Klan* (1965); E. D. Cronon, *Black Moses: The Story of Marcus Garvey* (1955); David H. Fisher, *Growing Old In America* (1977); Norman F. Furniss, *The Fundamentalist Controversy* (1954); Joseph R. Gusfield, *Symbolic Crusade* (1963); John Higham, *Strangers in the Land: Patterns of American Nativism* (1955); Kenneth T. Jackson, *The Ku Klux Klan in the City* (1967); Andrew Sinclair, *Prohibition: The Era of Excess* (1962).

MASS CULTURE   Erik Barbouw, *A Tower of Babel: A History of Broadcasting in the United States to 1933* (1966); Robert Creamer, *Babe* (1974); Kenneth S. Davis, *The Hero, Charles A. Lindbergh* (1959); Randy Roberts, *Jack Dempsey* (1979); Robert Sklar, *Movie-Made America* (1976).

LITERATURE AND THOUGHT   George H. Douglas, *H. L. Mencken* (1978); Robert Elias, *Entangling Alliances with None: An Essay on the Individual in the American Twenties* (1973); Nathan I. Huggins, *Harlem Renaissance* (1971); Roderick Nash, *The Nervous Generation: American Thought, 1917–1930* (1969).

24 🌀

THE GREAT DEPRESSION AND THE NEW DEAL, 1929-1941

"Anything wrong wid my work for company?" asked an autoworker of Slavic descent who had just been fired by the Ford Motor Company after fourteen years of employment. No, his work had been good, but cars were not selling. "I haf' no money now . . . lose my home quick, what I do chil'ren, what I do doctor?" When two of his daughters went to work to support the family and their sick mother, he cried, "I ain't man now."

People like John Boris were among the three thousand men and women who gathered on March 7, 1932, for a hunger march to Ford's huge River Rouge plant in Dearborn, just outside Detroit, Michigan. Most of the marchers were former Ford workers like Boris, now unemployed. Dearborn-Detroit authorities nonetheless blamed the march on the Communist party and met the protesters with a phalanx of police. A battle that erupted took the lives of four marchers.

The fundamental source of this trouble was not the Communist party, not the marchers, not the Dearborn police, not Henry Ford himself, but a nationwide disaster called the Great Depression. It began in 1929 with the stock market crash. Slowly but steadily, cascading tremors moved through the economy, and the nation sank from economic downturn to depression.

Though economic hard times aggravated old tensions, most Americans did not resort to political extremism or violence. Instead, they called on their government to help. When President Hoover refused to take strong measures to relieve their hardship, they turned him out of office and elected a new president, Franklin D. Roosevelt. Promising vigorous action and projecting confidence in the nation's ability to reverse the disaster, Roosevelt brought new hope to despairing Americans.

From the first days of his presidency, Roosevelt displayed a buoyancy and a willingness to experiment that helped to restore public confidence in the government and the economy. Roosevelt's program, which he dubbed the New Deal, inspired opposition from both the left and right. It also expanded both the role of the federal government and the popularity of the Democratic party. But achievement of its ultimate goal—putting people back to work—would await the nation's entry into the Second World War.

The New Day

There was little sense of impending tragedy in 1928, when 62 percent of Wayne County

(Detroit and Dearborn) voters cast their ballots for Republican presidential candidate Herbert Hoover. And in early 1929, when Hoover entered the White House, the byword was optimism. In his inaugural address the president proclaimed a New Day, telling his listeners that the future "is bright with hope."

The new president, popularly known as the Great Engineer, was a proven administrator who had gained a reputation for compassion as well as for brilliance as head of food relief for Europe following the First World War. But not everyone in his administration shared his enlightened attitudes. Sitting in the cabinet, composed

| *Hoover administration* |

largely of businessmen, were six millionaires, including Andrew Mellon, who stayed on as secretary of the treasury. These appointees to high office were smug devotees of the existing order, champions of a capitalist utopia. Innovation was not expected from them. In the lower ranks, on the other hand, Hoover brought in the New Patriots, mostly young professionals who agreed with the president that scientific methods could be applied to government to solve its problems.

Before the Great Depression sapped the national spirit, reverence for what Hoover called "the American system" ran high. The belief that individuals were responsible for their own condition, that unemployment or poverty suggested personal failing, was widespread. Prevailing thought also held that changes in the business cycle were natural and therefore not to be tampered with. As for the government, its job was limited: to ensure equal opportunity and to stimulate the economy through judicious advice and public works projects.

Much of this thinking was, of course, shallow, self-serving, or utopian. Businesspeople had often tinkered with the system out of self-interest. Government had long played favorites or neglected to blow the referee's whistle. Equal opportunity was denied to Americans who were

| *Distribution of wealth* |

nonwhite or female. Finally, income and wealth were maldistributed. In 1929 experts estimated that about 60 percent of America's families lived at or below subsistence level ($2,000 a year); the Federal Trade Commission reported that 1 percent of the American people owned 59 percent of the country's wealth and 87 percent owned only 10 percent. Hoover himself knew that not all was well. "The only trouble with capitalism is capitalists," he complained. "They're too damned greedy." Hoover's ideal capitalist was one who tempered his self-interest to advance the general welfare, who cooperated with others to build a progressive, nonexploitative society. He later admitted that most businesspeople did not approach this ideal.

The great crash and the Great Depression

Toward the end of the 1920s all seemed well to Wall Street brokers. The bull market attracted millions of buyers, many of whom joined the speculative binge of buying their shares on margin (paying only a portion of the cost in cash and borrowing the rest) or investing their savings. One businessman was so enthusiastic about the boom that he proclaimed that "anyone not only can be rich, but ought to be rich" by speculating in the stock market.

The get-rich-quick mentality was jolted in September and early October 1929 when stock prices dropped. Analysts attributed the dip to "shaking out the lunatic fringe." But on Octo-

| *Black Thursday* |

ber 24, Black Thursday, a record number of shares was traded; many stocks sold at low prices, and some could find no takers. At noon, banking leaders met at the headquarters of J. P. Morgan and Company to halt the skid and restore confidence. They put up $20 million, told everybody about it, and ceremoniously began by buying ten thousand shares of United States Steel. The mood changed and some stocks rallied.

Herbert Hoover (1874-1964), the wealthy mining engineer and businessman who gained a reputation for brilliance and compassion as head of a relief program during the First World War—and lost it when as president he faced the Great Depression. Photographed after Hoover's single term as president. Dr. Erich Salomon, Magnum.

But the nation gradually succumbed to panic. News of Black Thursday spread across the country, and trouble ("Sell!") ricocheted back to New York via telephone. Another bolt struck on Black Tuesday (October 29) when stock prices plunged again. Hoover assured Americans that the economy was sound. He shared the popular assumption that the stock market's ills could be quarantined from the general economy, which was considered basically healthy. He was wrong.

The crash ultimately helped to unleash a devastating depression that drained the nation and its people of their vitality and self-assurance. The economic downturn can be explained, first, by noting the increasing weakness of the economy throughout the 1920s. During the decade, the agricultural sector was plagued with overproduction, declining prices for farm products,

mounting debts, bankruptcies, and small bank failures. Some industries, like coal, railroads, and textiles, were in distress long before 1929, and two mainstays of economic growth, autos and construction, also declined early. What all these weaknesses meant by 1929 was that major sectors of the economy were not expanding. Indeed, the opposite was true: unsold inventories were stacking up in warehouses, investments were shrinking, laborers were being sent home, and consumer purchases were dropping off

The depression derived, secondly, from pell-mell, largely unregulated speculation on the stock market. Corporations and banks invested large sums in stocks; some speculated in their own issues. Brokers sold stocks to buyers who put up little cash, borrowed in order to purchase, and then used the stocks they bought as collateral for their loans. When the stocks came tumbling down, so did brokers, bankers, and companies.

Third, both the onset and the severity of the depression can be attributed to under-

| Under-consumption |

consumption. Wages and mass purchasing power had lagged behind the industrial surge of the 1920s; the workers who produced the new consumer products ultimately could not afford to buy them. Why did purchasing decline? Laborers and farmers constituted the great majority of consumers. Overproduction caused farmers economic distress, forcing them to trim their purchases. And as industries like coal, autos, and construction declined, they laid off men and women who then lacked the money to sustain buying. Other laborers lost their jobs because machines displaced them. There was, in short, a sizable nonconsuming group. Moreover, the nation's unequal distribution of wealth compounded the problem. Because income was concentrated at the top of America's economic ladder—with the rich—much of it was put into luxuries, savings, and investments instead of into consumer goods.

Fourth, the American business system was shaky, for a few large corporations in each industry—oligopolies—unbalanced it. Not only did these companies speculate dangerously on the stock market; they built pyramid-like businesses based on shady, if legal, manipulation of assets through holding companies. If one part of the edifice collapsed, the entire structure crumbled. Such was the case with Samuel Insull's mighty electrical empire, wherein one company held the stock of another company, which held the stock of another company, and so on. Even Insull admitted that he was not sure how it all worked; his sixty-five chairmanships, eighty-five directorships, and seven presidencies confused him as much as anybody else. His empire collapsed in 1932.

A fifth explanation for the deepening effects of the economic crisis is international in scope. As the world's leading creditor and trader, the

| International economic troubles |

United States was deeply involved with the world economy. Billions of dollars in loans had flowed into Europe during the First World War and then during postwar reconstruction. Yet in the late 1920s American investors were beginning to keep their money at home, to invest it in the more exciting and lucrative stock market. Europeans, unable to borrow more funds and unable to sell their goods easily in the American market because of high tariffs, began to buy less from America and to default on their debts. Pinched at home, they raised their own tariffs, further crippling international commerce, and withdrew their investments from America.

Finally, government policies and practices contributed to the crash and depression. The federal government failed to regulate the wild speculation. It neither checked corporate power nor raised income taxes to encourage a more equitable distribution of income. Indeed, it lowered taxes, thus promoting the uneven distribution. And the Federal Reserve Board pursued easy-credit policies, even though it knew the easy money was paying for the speculative binge. The "Fed" blundered again in 1931 by tightening the money market at a time when just the opposite was needed: a loosening to spur borrowing and spending.

Despairing Americans

As the economy limped into the 1930s, statistics began to tell the story of a national tragedy. Between 1929 and 1933 a hundred thousand businesses failed; corporate profits fell from $10 billion to $1 billion; and the gross national product was cut in half. But what happened to America's banks—and savings—illustrates especially well the cascading nature of the Great Depression. Banks tied into the stock market or foreign investments were badly weakened; some failed. When nervous Americans made runs on banks to salvage their threatened savings, a powerful momentum—panic—took command. In 1929, 659 banks folded; in 1930 the number of failures climbed to 1,350. The next year proved worse: 2,293 banks shut their doors; another 1,453 ceased to do business in 1932. By 1933, 9 million savings accounts had been lost.

The impact of the depression on individuals was gradual. Most people remained employed, but each day thousands received severance slips. Unemployment increased from 4 million at the beginning of 1930 to 13 million (one-fourth of the work force) in early 1933. And millions more were underemployed. Hoover asked businesspeople not to cut wages. Hourly wages did hold steady for a while, but weekly earnings began to drop off as hours were trimmed back. Then hourly wages were reduced in industry after industry. Overall, labor income dropped by 40 percent during Hoover's presidency.

Blacks, women, and the unskilled lost their jobs first; whites and managerial personnel were let go last. Discriminatory practices based on race and gender were accentuated. Whites displaced many blacks as servants, and Atlanta fired its black sanitation workers to replace them with whites. In the Southwest, signs went up: "No Niggers, Mexicans, or Dogs Allowed." As for working women, one Chicago civic group declared, they "are holding jobs that rightfully belong to the God-intended providers of the household." Some states even passed laws forbidding the hiring of married women for civil service jobs.

People's diets deteriorated, malnutrition became common, and the undernourished fell victim more easily to disease. Some people quietly

Deterioration of public health lined up at Red Cross and Salvation Army soup kitchens or queued in breadlines. Others ate only potatoes, crackers, or dandelions, stole dog biscuits from the local dog pound, or scratched through garbage cans for bits of food. Millions of Americans were not only hungry and ill; they were cold. Unable to afford fuel, some huddled in unheated tenements and shacks. Families doubled up in crowded apartments, but some who were unable to pay the rent were evicted, furniture and all. Under such conditions it is not surprising that the nation's suicide rate increased.

In the countryside economic hardship deepened. Between 1929 and 1933 farm income was cut in half. Though farm prices dropped 60 per-

Plight of the farmers cent, production decreased only 6 percent as individual farmers struggled to make up for lower prices by producing more, thereby creating an excess. And the surplus that so depressed agricultural prices could not be exported, since foreign demand had shrunk. Drought, foreclosure, clouds of hungry grasshoppers, and bank failures further plagued the American farmer.

Some Americans became transients in search of jobs or food. Desperate tenant farmers—husbands, wives, and children—walked the roads of the South. The California Unemployment Commission reported in 1932 that an "army of homeless" had trooped into the state and moved constantly from place to place, forced by one town after another to move on. Hundreds of thousands jumped aboard freight trains—"rode the rods"—or hitchhiked. Some boys and girls wandered on their own, living in hobo jungles usually populated by adults. During these years Mexicans and Mexican-Americans moved south of the border, sometimes willingly, sometimes deported by immigration officials eager to purge them from the relief rolls.

Economic woe and geographical dis-placement strained marriage and family life.

Strains on marriage and the family People postponed marriage, and married couples postponed having children. The self-esteem of jobless husbands and fathers was undermined, especially when women took jobs to support their families.

The tempered protest

Most Americans did not meet the crisis with violence, protest, or political extremes. Instead, shock cut deeply into the American psyche. A psychiatrist describing unemployed miners wrote, "They hung around street corners and in groups. They gave each other solace. They were loath to go home because they were indicted, as if it were their fault for being jobless. A jobless man was a lazy good-for-nothing. . . . They felt despised, they were ashamed of themselves." This was the stuff not of revolution, but of self-hatred and melancholy.

Scattered protests did, however, raise the specter of popular revolt. In Iowa's Cow War of 1931, angry farmers assailed state tuberculin inspectors who condemned diseased cattle but gave farmers little compensation for their losses. In Nebraska, Iowa, and Minnesota, farmers protesting low prices put up barricades, stopped

Farmers' Holiday Association trucks, and dumped milk and vegetables on the road. Some of these demonstrations were organized by the Farmers' Holiday Association whose leader, Milo Reno, urged farmers to take a holiday—keep their products off the market until they commanded better prices. The Sioux City milk strike of 1932 was the association's most dramatic effort, but like others it failed to alter significantly the terrible economic position of farmers.

The most spectacular confrontation shook Washington, D.C., in summer 1932. Congress was considering a bill authorizing immediate issuance of bonuses already allotted to First World War veterans, but not due for payment until 1945. To lobby for the bill, fifteen thousand unemployed veterans and their families

Bonus Expeditionary Force

converged on the tense nation's capital, calling themselves the Bonus Expeditionary Force (BEF). They camped in crude shacks on vacant lots and in empty government buildings. Though President Hoover threw his weight against the bonus bill, the House passed it. The showdown came in the Senate, which voted no after much debate. Many of the bonus marchers then left Washington, but several thousand remained.

In July General Douglas MacArthur, assisted by Majors Dwight D. Eisenhower and George S. Patton, met the veterans and their families with cavalry, tanks, and bayonet-bearing soldiers. The BEF hurled back stones and bricks. What followed shocked the nation. Men and women were chased down by horsemen; children were teargassed; shacks were set afire. When presidential hopeful Franklin D. Roosevelt heard about the government's violent attack on the Bonus Army, he turned to his friend and adviser Felix Frankfurter and said: "Well, Felix, this will elect me."

Hoover holds the line

When daily appeals began being made to the White House for government relief for the jobless, Hoover at first became defensive, if not hostile. He rejected direct relief—derisively called the dole—because he believed it would undermine character and individualism. Hoover thus appeared to a growing number of Americans to be heartless and inflexible. Rather than deal with the quarter of the work force that was jobless, he emphasized the many who were still on the payrolls.

True to his beliefs, the president urged people to help themselves and their neighbors. He ap-

plauded private voluntary relief through charitable agencies. Yet when the

Reliance on private relief

need was greatest, donations declined. State and urban officials found their treasuries drying up, too. Meanwhile, those calling for federal action got no sympathy from Secretary of the Treasury Mellon. The millionaire cabinet member advised the president to "let the slump liquidate itself. Liquidate labor, liquidate stocks, liquidate the farmers, liquidate real estate. . . . It will purge the rottenness out of the system."

But as the depression intensified, Hoover's opposition to federal action diminished. He met with business and labor leaders, winning pledges from them to maintain wages and production and to avoid strikes. He urged state governors to increase their expenditures on public works. And he created the President's Organization on Unemployment Relief (POUR) to generate private contributions for relief of the destitute. Unfortunately, POUR accomplished little.

Hoover's spurring of federal public works projects (including the Boulder, or Hoover, and Grand Coulee dams) did provide some jobs. Help also came from the Federal Farm Board, which supported agricultural prices by lending money to cooperatives to buy products and keep them off the market. To retard the collapse of the international monetary system, Hoover announced a moratorium on the payment of First World War debts and reparations (1931).

The president also reluctantly asked Congress to charter the Reconstruction Finance Corporation (RFC). Created in 1932, the RFC was designed to make loans to banks, insurance companies, and railroads, and later to state and local

Reconstruction Finance Corporation

governments. The theory behind the RFC was that it would lend money to large entities at the top of the economic system, and benefits would trickle down to people at the bottom through a sort of percolation process. It did not work; banks continued to collapse and small companies to go into bankruptcy.

Despite warnings from prominent economists, Hoover also signed the Hawley-Smoot Tariff (1930). Hoover argued that the tariff, which raised rates by about one-third, would help farmers and manufacturers by keeping foreign goods off the market. Actually, the tariff further weakened the economy by making it even more difficult for foreign nations to sell their products and thus earn the money to buy American products.

Like most of his contemporaries, Hoover believed that a balanced budget was sacred, and deficit spending sinful. In 1931 he appealed for a decrease in federal expenditures and an increase in taxes. The following year he supported a sales tax on manufactured goods. The sales tax was defeated, but the Revenue Act of 1932 raised corporate, excise, and personal income taxes. Hoover seemed caught in a contradiction: he urged people to spend to spur recovery, but his tax policies deprived them of spending money.

Although Hoover expanded public works projects and approved loans to some institutions, he vetoed a variety of relief bills presented to him by the Demo-

cratic Congress. He also vetoed a multipurpose development project for the Tennessee River, arguing that its cheap electricity would compete with power from private companies. Clinging to his old viewpoints, Hoover stretched government activities as far as he thought he could without violating his cherished principles.

Tradition in time of crisis: the election of 1932

Herbert Hoover and the Republican party faced dreary prospects in 1932. The tired and sullen president grumbled at reporters, banks continued to close, and memories of the Bonus March persisted. But what soured public opinion most was that Hoover seemed not to lead at a time when innovative generalship was required.

Franklin D. Roosevelt, on the other hand, enjoyed a different reputation. He was born into the upper class of tradition and privilege, the only child of doting parents who heaped on him all sorts of advantages. He graduated from Harvard in 1903, and in fall 1904, he entered the School of Law at Columbia University. A few months later he announced his engagement to his fifth cousin once-removed, Anna Eleanor Roosevelt, the niece of President Theodore Roosevelt. The next spring they were married.

Roosevelt began the practice of law, but had other ambitions—political ones. In 1910, he was elected to the New York State Assembly. In 1912 he accepted Woodrow Wilson's offer of the post of assistant secretary of the navy. For eight years Roosevelt helped expand American naval forces, gaining confidence and shedding much of his smugness. And he learned lessons about the emergence of the United States as a world power and the need for decisive presidential leadership in times of crisis.

In 1920, running as the Democratic vice-presidential candidate, Roosevelt was defeated. He suffered his most devastating loss the next year, however, when he was stricken by polio. Now he was a cripple, totally paralyzed in both legs. What should he do next? Should he retire from public life, a rich invalid? His answer and his wife's was no. Throughout the 1920s Franklin and Eleanor contended with his new handicap. In this personal struggle, he grew more patient and more understanding of those who suffer. People who had known him before commented that polio had made him a "twice born man," that his "fight against that dread disease had evidently given him new moral and physical strength." As Roosevelt explained it: "If you had spent two years in bed trying to wiggle your big toe, after that anything would seem easy."

Re-entering politics, Roosevelt became a spokesperson for progressive Democrats. In 1928 he was elected governor of New York. As governor, he appealed to the American penchant for optimism, undertaking vigorous relief programs and establishing an unemployment commission. He also endorsed and worked for old-age pensions and protective legislation for labor unions. With this record, he became an obvious prospect for the 1932 Democratic presidential nomination. When he accepted that nomination, Roosevelt promised a "new deal for the American people," suggesting his intention of implementing at the national level the types of programs he had started in New York.

The two party platforms differed little, but the Democrats were willing to abandon prohibition and to launch federal relief. Roosevelt,

| Election of 1932 |

playing the political game superbly, would agree with Hoover that the budget had to be balanced, then appeal for costly new programs. When Roosevelt spoke of the forgotten man and declared himself ready to provide direct relief to individuals, Hoover boiled. "This campaign is more than a contest between two men," he said. "It is more than a contest between two parties. It is a contest between two philosophies of government."

To prepare a national political platform, Roosevelt surrounded himself with a "brains

| Roosevelt's "brains trust" |

trust" of lawyers and university professors. Foremost among these advisers were Columbia University professors Rexford G. Tugwell, Raymond Moley, and Adolf A. Berle, Jr. Bigness was unavoidable in the modern American economy, these experts reasoned; thus the cure for the nation's ills was not to go on a rampage of trustbusting, but to place large corporations, monopolies, and oligopolies under effective government control.

Roosevelt and his brains trust agreed that it was essential for the government to take action to restore purchasing power to farmers, blue-collar workers, and the middle classes, and that the way to do so was to cut production. If the demand for a product remained constant and the supply were cut, they reasoned, the price would rise. Producers would make higher profits, and workers would earn more money. This method

In November 1930 Franklin D. Roosevelt (1882–1945) read the good news. Re-elected governor of New York by 735,000 votes, he immediately became a leading contender for the 1932 Democratic presidential nomination. Note Roosevelt's leg braces, rarely shown in photographs because of an unwritten agreement by photographers to shoot him from the waist up.   UPI.

Tradition in time of crisis: the election of 1932

381

of combating a depression has been called the economics of scarcity. Unlike Hoover, Roosevelt also advocated immediate and direct relief to the unemployed. Finally, Roosevelt and his advisers demanded that the federal government engage in centralized economic planning and experimentation to bring about recovery.

More people went to the polls in 1932 than in any election since the First World War. In a crisis-ridden moment Americans quietly, calmly, even routinely followed tradition and peacefully exchanged one government for another. Roosevelt's 22.8 million popular votes far outdistanced Hoover's 15.8 million. The voters also gave the Democrats overwhelming control of the House and the Senate.

From November to March, a lame-duck president, a lame-duck Congress (158 of whose members had been defeated), and a hesitant president-elect took little positive action, and the depression continued to cut its debilitating path. Americans wondered what would happen next. Might not radicals make gains? Some thought Roosevelt would reform the American system enough to forestall radical solutions. Others envisioned demagogues, splinter parties, or violence.

On the afternoon of March 2, 1933, President-elect Roosevelt and his family and friends boarded a train for Washington, D.C., and the inauguration ceremony. Roosevelt was carrying with him rough drafts of two presidential proclamations, one summoning a special session of Congress, the other declaring a national Bank Holiday, suspending banking transactions throughout the nation. Thirty-eight states had closed their banks to prevent a run on funds by nervous depositors. It was time for Roosevelt to produce the New Deal he had promised the American people.

Restoring confidence

"First of all," declared the newly inaugurated president, "let me assert my firm belief that the only thing we have to fear is fear itself—nameless, unreasoning, unjustified terror." In his inaugural address Roosevelt scored his first triumph as president, instilling hope and courage in the rank and file. Roosevelt attacked the nation's bankers, accusing them of having "fled from their high seats in the temple of our civilization." His administration, he said, would take drastic action to "restore that temple to the ancient truths." And if need be, he asserted, "I shall ask the Congress for the one remaining instrument to meet the crisis—broad Executive power to wage a war against the emergency, as great as the power that would be given to me if we were in fact invaded by a foreign foe."

Congress convened in emergency session on March 9 to begin what observers would call the

| Beginning of the Hundred Days |

Hundred Days. The first measure, the Emergency Banking Relief Bill, was introduced just before 1 P.M. on March 9, passed sight unseen by unanimous House vote, approved 73 to 7 in the Senate, and signed by the president that evening. The act provided for the reopening, under treasury department license, of banks that were solvent and the reorganization and management of those that were not. It also gave the president broad powers over credit, currency, and the buying and selling of gold and silver. But it was a conservative law that left the nation's banking system essentially unchanged, with the same people in charge.

On the next day, March 10, the second bill of the New Deal was introduced in Congress. It too was conservative, and ten days later it became law. Called the Economy Act, its purpose was to balance the federal budget by chopping veterans' benefits and allowances by $400 million and reducing by $100 million the pay of federal employees. Under Roosevelt, the budget balancers had won a battle that could not have been won under Hoover. But taking money away from veterans and federal employees was deflationary.

On Sunday evening, March 12, the president

broadcast the first of his fireside chats, and 60

First fireside chat

million people heard his comforting voice on their radios. His message: banks were once again safe places for depositors' savings. On Monday morning the banks opened their doors, but instead of queuing up to withdraw their savings, people were waiting outside to deposit their money. The bank runs were over; people had regained confidence in their political leadership, their banks, and even their economic system. "Capitalism," Raymond Moley later wrote, "was saved in eight days."

Launching the New Deal

On March 16, the president sent to Congress the Agricultural Adjustment Bill, his plan to restore farmers' purchasing power. If over-

Aid to farmers

production was the cause of farmers' problems—falling prices and mounting surpluses—then the government had to encourage farmers to grow less food. Under the domestic allotment plan, as it was called, the government would pay subsidies to farmers to reduce their acreage or plow under crops already in the fields. Farmers would receive payments based on *parity,* a system of regulated prices for corn, cotton, wheat, rice, hogs, and dairy products that would allow them the same purchasing power they had had during the prosperous period of 1909 through 1914. In effect, the government was making up the difference between the actual market value of farm products and the income farmers needed to make a profit. The funds for the subsidies would come from taxes levied on the processors of agricultural commodities. Against vehement opposition, the Agricultural Adjustment Act (AAA) was passed on May 12, implementing a farm policy based upon the economics of scarcity.

Meanwhile, other relief measures became law. On March 21 the president requested massive infusions of relief of three kinds: a job corps called the Civilian Conservation Corps (CCC);

Other relief measures

direct cash grants to the states to provide relief payments for needy citizens; and public works projects. Ten days later Congress approved the CCC, which ultimately put 2.5 million young men between the ages of eighteen and twenty-five to work planting trees, clearing camping areas and beaches, and building bridges, dams, reservoirs, fish ponds, and fire towers. Then on May 12 Congress passed the Federal Emergency Relief Act, which authorized $500 million in aid to state and local governments.

Roosevelt's proposed plan for public works became Title II of the National Industrial Recovery Act (NIRA). Passed on June 16, it established in the Public Works Administration (PWA) a fund of $3.3 billion to build roads, sewage and water systems, public buildings, and a host of other projects, including ships and naval aircraft. The purpose of the PWA was to prime the economic pump—to stimulate consumer buying power, business enterprise, and ultimately employment by pouring billions of dollars into the economy.

A month earlier Congress had enacted an even bolder program for the depressed Tennessee River valley, which ran through Tennessee, North Carolina, Kentucky, Virginia, Mississippi, Georgia, and Alabama. For years progressives led by Senator George Norris of Nebraska had advocated government operation

TVA

of the Muscle Shoals electric power and nitrogen facilities on the Tennessee River. But the Tennessee Valley Authority (TVA), as finally established, was a much broader program than the progressive plan. Its dams would not only serve to control floods; they could also be used to generate hydroelectric power, reclaim and reforest land, and prevent soil erosion. Other provisions of the TVA included the production and sale of nitrate explosives to the government; the digging of a 650-mile navigation channel from Knoxville to Paducah; and the construction of public-power facilities as a yardstick for determining fair rates for privately produced electric power. The goal of the TVA was nothing less than enhancement of the economic well-being of the entire Tennessee River valley.

If the AAA was the agricultural cornerstone of the New Deal, the National Industrial Recovery Act was the industrial cornerstone. The NIRA was a testimony to the New Deal belief in national planning as opposed to an individualistic, intensely competitive laissez-faire economy. Like the War Industries Board, the NIRA granted business exemptions from the antitrust laws, through the agency of the National Recovery Administration (NRA), whose symbol, the Blue Eagle, was meant to encourage cooperation. Under the law, competing businesses met with government mediators and representatives of workers and consumers to draft codes of fair competition, which limited production, assigned markets, and established prices.

With businesses enjoying new concessions, workers wanted a share of the pie too. Congress guaranteed their right to unionize and to bargain collectively in Section 7(a) of the NIRA, which called for industrywide codes establishing minimum wages and maximum hours.

With the passage of the NIRA, Congress adjourned on June 16, its Hundred Days completed. Roosevelt had delivered fifteen messages to Congress, and fifteen significant laws had been enacted. Those not yet mentioned included the Federal Securities Act, to compel brokers to tell the truth about new securities issues; the National Employment System Act, to match funding of state employment agencies; the Banking Act of 1933, to set up the Federal Deposit Insurance Corporation for insuring bank deposits, and divorce investment from commercial banking; and the Emergency Railroad Transportation Act, to encourage financial reorganization of railroads, simplify rate-making, and put railroad holding companies under the supervision of the Interstate Commerce Commission.

Throughout the remainder of 1933 and the spring and summer of 1934, more New Deal bills became law. Indeed, there seemed to be something for everybody in the New Deal. Here was interest-group democracy at work, with government benefits accruing not only to business but to agriculture and labor; to farm and home-owners; to corporations, railroads, and city governments; and to the jobless. In the midst of this coalition of all interests was President Roosevelt, the artful broker who weighed the claims of competing interest groups. And this broker state appeared to be working. In 1933 almost 13 million people had been jobless. Following New Deal legislation the figure fell steadily to 11.4 million in 1934, 10.6 million in 1935, and 9 million in 1936. Net farm income rose from $2.5 billion in 1932 to $5.85 billion in 1935. And manufacturing salaries and wages also increased, jumping from $6.25 billion in 1933 to almost $13 billion in 1937.

There was no doubt about the popularity of either the New Deal or Roosevelt. In the 1934 congressional elections the Democrats added to their majorities in both the House and the Senate. The New Deal, according to Arthur Krock of the *New York Times,* had won "the most overwhelming victory in the history of American politics." As for Roosevelt: "He has been all but crowned by the people," wrote William Allen White.

Reactions against the broker state

Yet there was more than one way to read employment and income statistics and election returns. For example, though unemployment had dropped from a high of 13 million (25 percent) in 1933 to 9 million (16.9 percent) in 1936, it had been only 1.5 million (3.2 percent) in 1929. And though manufacturing wages and salaries had reached almost $13 billion in 1937, that figure was almost $1.5 billion less than the total for 1929. In other words, regardless of the New Deal's successes, it had a long way to go before reaching predepression standards.

With the arrival of partial economic recovery, many businesspeople and conservatives became vocal critics of the New Deal. Some charged

Business critics of the New Deal

there was too much government regulation. Others criticized the deficit financing of relief and public works. According to still others, the New Deal had subverted individual initiative and self-reliance by providing relief and welfare payments.

If businesspeople felt the government was their enemy, others thought the government favored business too much. Farmers, labor unions, individual entrepreneurs, and antitrust critics complained that the NRA set prices too high and favored large-scale producers over small businesses. And the federal courts began to scrutinize the constitutionality of the legislation.

The AAA came under attack as well because of its encouragement of cutbacks in production. In 1933 farmers had plowed under 10.4 million acres of cotton and slaughtered 220,000 sows and 6 million pigs—at a time when people were ill-clothed and ill-fed. Though for landowning farmers the program was successful, the average person found such waste to be shocking. And what about tenant farmers and sharecroppers? They too were supposed to receive government payments for taking crops out of cultivation, but very few of them, especially if they were black, received what they were entitled to. Furthermore, the AAA's hopes that landlords would keep their tenants on the land were not fulfilled. The number of southern sharecropper farms declined by more than 230,000 during the 1930s. The result was a homeless population, some of whom, known in the folklore of the times as "Okies" and "Arkies," took off for California. Others migrated to the cities of the North and West.

As dissatisfaction mounted, so too did the appeal of various demagogues. Father Charles Coughlin, the Roman Catholic priest whose

Plagued by dust storms, evictions, and the unsympathetic policies of the Agricultural Adjustment Administration, thousands of tenant farmers and sharecroppers were forced to leave their land during the Great Depression. Known as "Okies" and Arkies," they took off for California with their few belongings, camping along the side of the road. This famous portrait of an Okie madonna and her children was taken by the photographer Dorothea Lange. Library of Congress.

weekly radio sermons offered a curious combination of anti-Communism, anticapitalism, and anti-Semitism, was one of the more famous. According to Coughlin, the worst abuses of capitalism had been inflicted by Jews. Whatever the reasons for his appeal, Coughlin reportedly received more mail than anyone else in the United States, and he drew larger audiences than the popular radio stars Ed Wynn and Amos 'n' Andy.

Another challenge to the New Deal came from Dr. Francis E. Townsend, who had conceived what he called an Old Age Revolving Pensions plan. Under Townsend's scheme the government would pay monthly pensions of $200 to all citizens over age sixty, on the condition that they spend the money in the same month they received it. Townsend claimed his plan would not only aid the aged but cure the depression by pumping enormous purchasing power into the economy. Though the plan was fiscally impossible, it had a powerful emotional appeal, for it addressed the needs of deprived senior citizens.

Demagogic attacks on the New Deal

And then there was Huey Long, the Kingfish, perhaps the most successful demagogue in American history. In 1928 Long was elected governor of Louisiana with the slogan "Every Man a King, But No One Wears a Crown." As a member of the Senate, Long at first supported the New Deal. Later he found the Economy Act and the NRA too conservative, and began to believe that Roosevelt had fallen captive to big business and big money. Long countered in 1934 with the Share Our Wealth Society, which advocated the seizure by taxation of all incomes over $1 million and all inheritances over $5 million. With those funds, the government would furnish each family a homestead allowance of $5,000 and an annual income of $2,000. By mid-1935 Long's movement claimed 7 million members, and few doubted that Long aspired to the presidency. Though an assassin's bullet extinguished his ambition in September 1935, the Share Our Wealth movement persisted under a new leader, the vitriolic anti-Semite Gerald L. K. Smith.

Some politicians of the 1930s, like Floyd Olson, governor of Minnesota, declared themselves socialists. Olson sought a third party that would

Left-wing critics of the New Deal

"preach the gospel of government and collective ownership of the means of production and distribution." In neighboring Wisconsin the left-wing Progressive party re-elected Robert La Follette, Jr., to the Senate in 1934, sent seven of the state's ten representatives to Washington, and placed La Follette's brother Philip in the governorship. And the old muckraker Upton Sinclair almost won the Democratic gubernatorial nomination in California in 1934 on the platform End Poverty in California (EPIC).

Perhaps the most controversial alternative to the New Deal was the Communist party of the United States of American (CPUSA). In 1932 a number of distinguished writers had endorsed the Communist presidential candidate, William Z. Foster. But membership in the CPUSA remained small until 1935, when the party leadership changed its strategy. Proclaiming "Communism is Twentieth Century Americanism," the CPUSA disclaimed any intention of overthrowing the United States government and began to cooperate with left-wing labor unions, student groups, and intellectual organizations. Still, at its high point for the decade in 1938, the CPUSA had only 55,000 members.

In addition to challenges from the right and the left, the New Deal was threatened by the

Supreme Court decisions against the New Deal

Supreme Court. In January 1935, in *Panama Refining Co.* v. *Ryan,* the Court struck down part of the NIRA. By granting the president power to prohibit interstate and foreign shipment of oil, the Court ruled, Congress had unconstitutionally delegated legislative power to the executive branch. Then on May 27 the Court unanimously struck down the whole NIRA (*Schechter* v. *U.S.*) on the grounds that it gave excessive legislative power to the White House and that the commerce clause of the Constitution did not give the federal government authority to regulate intrastate businesses. Roosevelt's industrial recovery program was dead. In January 1936 his farm program met a similar fate when the Court invalidated the AAA *(U.S.* v. *Butler),* declaring that agriculture was a local problem and thus, under the Tenth Amendment, subject to state action only.

As Roosevelt looked ahead to the presidential election of 1936, he saw that he was in danger of losing his capacity to lead and to govern. His coalition of all interests was breaking up; radicals and demagogues were offering Americans alternative programs; and the Supreme Court was dismantling the New Deal. In the spring and summer of 1935, Roosevelt took the initiative once more, and the New Deal scored some of its biggest victories. So impressive was the new legislation that historians have called it the Second New Deal.

The Second New Deal

The first triumph of the Second New Deal was an innocuous-sounding but momentous law called the Emergency Relief Appropriation Act,

Emergency Relief Appropriation Act

which Congress passed and Roosevelt signed in April 1935. The act authorized the president to issue executive orders establishing massive public works programs for the jobless, including the Works Progress Administration (WPA).

Later renamed the Work Projects Administration, the WPA ultimately employed more than 8.5 million people. By the time it was terminated in 1943, the WPA had built over 650,000 miles of highways, streets, and roads, 125,000 public buildings, and 8,000 parks, as well as numerous bridges, airports, and other structures. But WPA did more than lay bricks. Its Federal Theatre Project brought plays, vaudeville shows, and circuses to cities and towns across the country, and WPA artists painted murals in post offices and other public buildings. The Federal Music Project and the

WPA Dance Theatre sponsored laboratories for young composers and choreographers. And the Federal Writers' Project hired writers like Conrad Aiken, John Cheever, Claude McKay, John Steinbeck, and Richard Wright to write local guidebooks and regional, ethnic, and folk histories.

Besides the WPA, the Emergency Relief Appropriation Act funded other relief and public works measures. The Resettlement Administration (RA) resettled destitute families and organized rural homestead communities and suburban greenbelt towns for low-income workers. The Rural Electrification Administration (REA) generated and distributed electricity to isolated rural areas. And the National Youth Administration (NYA) sponsored work relief programs for people between the ages of sixteen and twenty-five and provided part-time employment for students.

As significant as these achievements were, Roosevelt wanted more legislation, some of it aimed at controlling the activities of big business. The Supreme Court had condemned government-business cooperation, and businesspeople had become increasingly critical of Roosevelt and the New Deal. Now Roosevelt decided that government should "cut the giants down to size" through antitrust suits and heavy corporate taxes. In June he asked Congress to enact five major bills: a labor bill sponsored by Senator Robert Wagner; a Social Security bill; a banking bill; a measure to regulate public-utility holding companies; and a "soak the rich" tax bill.

These were the Second Hundred Days. On July 5 the National Labor Relations (Wagner)

Roosevelt's Second Hundred Days

Act granted workers the right to unionize and to bargain collectively. The act empowered the national Labor Relations Board to supervise the election of bargaining units and agents and to issue cease-and-desist injunctions against harassment of union members by employers.

On August 15 Roosevelt signed the Social

Security Act, which established a cooperative federal-state system of unemployment compensation and old-age and survivors' insurance. Social Security was a conservative measure: the government did not pay for old-age benefits; workers and their bosses did. The tax was also regressive—the more workers earned, the less they were taxed proportionately—and deflationary—it took more money out of people's pockets than it gave back. Finally, many people were ineligible for coverage under the law, including farm workers, domestic servants, and many hospital and restaurant workers. But the act was a milestone. It acknowledged the government's responsibility to establish a system of insurance for the aged, the dependent, the disabled, and the destitute.

In the next two weeks Roosevelt gained the remainder of what he had asked for, including the Revenue (Wealth Tax) Act of 1935. The Wealth Tax Act, which some critics saw as the president's attempt to "steal Huey's thunder," did not result in a redistribution of income, though it did increase the income taxes paid by the wealthy. It also imposed a new tax on excess business profits and increased taxes on inheritances, large gifts, and profits from the sale of property.

The Second Hundred Days indicated not only that the president was once again in charge, but that he was set to run for re-election. The campaign was less heated than might have been expected, however. Naturally the Republican

| Election of 1936 |

nominee, Governor Alf Landon of Kansas, criticized Roosevelt, but he did not advocate a wholesale repeal of the New Deal. When the ballots were counted, Roosevelt had won a landslide victory, polling 27.8 million votes to Landon's 16.7 million. The Democrats carried every state except Maine and Vermont and won huge majorities in the House and Senate.

The Democratic victory of 1936 stemmed from what observers have called the New Deal coalition. The growing strength of the party in the cities, the suffering wrought by the Great Depression, and the New Deal response to social distress had converged to make Roosevelt the champion of the urban masses. Labor, especially the new unions of the Congress of Industrial Organizations (CIO), was an indispensable member of the coalition. And black voters in northern cities, most of whom had been Republicans prior to the 1930s, now cast their lot with the Democratic party. The Democratic party had become the dominant half of the two-party system.

The rise of the CIO

Organized labor benefited as much as farmers and businesspeople did from New Deal legislation. On enactment, Section 7(a) of the NIRA inspired union leaders to organize and recruit new members. "Millions of workers throughout the nation," recalled American Federation of Labor President William Green, "stood up for the first time in their lives to receive their charter of industrial freedom." By October 1933 an additional 1.5 million workers had enlisted in unions, bringing total membership to 4 million.

But these gains did not always come easily. Management put up determined resistance in the early and mid-1930s, hiring armed thugs to intimidate workers and break up strikes. Labor

| Rivalry between craft and industrial unions |

confronted yet another obstacle in the AFL craft unions' traditional skepticism and hostility toward industrial unions. Craft unions typically consisted of skilled workers in a particular trade; industrial unions represented all workers in a given industry, skilled and unskilled. The organizing gains in the 1930s were far more impressive in industrial unions than in craft unions, with hundreds of thousands of workers joining unions in such industries as autos, garments, rubber, and steel. What re-

Strikers in a Fisher Body plant read newspapers as they relax on car seats. The sit-down strike, developed in 1937, proved a powerful weapon in labor-management confrontations. Library of Congress.

sulted was a struggle for control of the labor movement between craft and industrial union leaders.

Attempts were made in the mid-1930s to reconcile the craft and industrial union movements, but in late 1935 John L. Lewis of the United Mine Workers resigned as vice president of the craft union-dominated AFL. He and other industrial unionists within the AFL formed the Committee for Industrial Organization (CIO). In 1938 the AFL expelled the CIO unions, and the CIO reorganized itself as the Congress of Industrial Organizations. By that time CIO membership stood at 3.7 million, more than the AFL's 3.4 million.

The CIO, which in the 1930s evolved into a pragmatic bread-and-butter labor organization, had organized millions of workers who had never before had an opportunity to join unions. Now their dues enabled it to organize even more people. The United Auto Workers (UAW) scored a major victory in late 1936. The

Sit-down strikes

union, 30,000 strong, demanded recognition from General Motors, Chrysler, and Ford. When GM refused, the UAW launched a new kind of strike: the sit-down. Beginning in the Fisher Body plants in Flint, Michigan, workers refused to leave the plants. To discourage the strikers, GM managers turned off the heat; when that tactic failed, they called the police, who were met by a barrage of missiles— iron bolts and door hinges, coffee mugs, and pop bottles. When the police resorted to tear gas, the strikers turned the plant's water hoses on them, and the police retreated.

The strike lasted for weeks. GM obtained a court order to evacuate the plant, but the strikers continued, risking imprisonment and fines. With the support of their families and neighborhoods, the workers stuck to their rigid discipline. Community women wearing red berets organized an "emergency brigade" to picket and deliver food and supplies to the strikers. In the end the UAW prevailed and GM agreed to recognize the union (1937). Chrysler signed a similar agreement, but Ford held out for four more years.

In 1937, too, the Steel Workers Organizing Committee (SWOC) signed a contract with the nation's largest steelmaker, U.S. Steel, that guaranteed an eight-hour day and a forty-hour week. Other steel companies refused to go along, however. Confrontations between these so-called little steel companies and the SWOC led

| Memorial Day Massacre |

to violence. On Memorial Day in Chicago, strikers and their families had joined with sympathizers in a peaceful picket line in front of the Republic Steel plant. Suddenly and without provocation the police opened fire. They continued to shoot into the crowd even as people turned away and began to run. Of the ten fatalities, none had been shot in the front of the body; of the forty gunshot wounds, only four were frontal.

As senseless as the Memorial Day Massacre was, its occurrence was not surprising. During the 1930s industries had hired private police agents and accumulated large stores of arms and ammunition for use in deterring workers from organizing and joining unions. Republic Steel, for example, was the nation's largest single purchaser of tear and sickening gas. Youngstown Sheet and Tube owned 8 machine guns, 369 rifles, 190 shotguns, 450 revolvers, and thousands of rounds of ammunition.

Through it all, the CIO continued to enroll new members. By the end of the decade it had succeeded in organizing most of the nation's mass-production industries.

Mixed progress for nonwhites

For black Americans the early depression years were ones of great trial. Like some earlier Republican presidents, Herbert Hoover tried to push blacks out of the party. This "lily-white"

GOP effort was designed to entice southern whites into the party. Moreover, Hoover appointed few blacks to federal office, disbanded the Negro division of the Republican National Committee, rejected appeals for an antilynching law, and nominated a southern white supremacist to a position on the Supreme Court.

Scottsboro became a celebrated civil liberties case that symbolized the ugliness of race relations in the depression era. One afternoon in

| Scottsboro trials |

March 1931, a freight train pulled into the yard at Paint Rock, near Scottsboro, Alabama. When the train stopped, armed sheriff's deputies arrested nine young blacks, charging them with roughing up some white hobos and throwing them off the train earlier in the day. When two white women who were removed from the same freight claimed that the blacks had raped them, an angry white mob gathered. Within two weeks eight of the "Scottsboro boys" had been convicted of rape by all-white juries and sentenced to death. The ninth, only twelve years old, was favored by a hung jury. But because court-appointed lawyers had offered little defense for the youths, the Supreme Court overturned the convictions (1932) on the grounds that the accused had not been granted adequate legal counsel.

New trials opened in 1933, again with all-white juries. Medical evidence showed that the women had not had intercourse on the train. Nevertheless, the first defendant up for retrial, Haywood Patterson, was once again found guilty. Judge James Horton, who had stated that under American law "we know neither black nor white," was convinced that Patterson was an innocent victim of racial hatred. The courageous Horton overturned the jury's decision.

In 1936 Patterson was retried, found guilty, and given a seventy-five-year sentence. Four of the other youths were sentenced to life imprisonment, and the state dropped charges against the remaining four. Not until 1950 were all five out of jail—four by parole and Patterson by escaping from his work gang.

The nine Scottsboro youths in jail in Decatur, Alabama. Seated with attorney Samuel Leibowitz is Haywood Patterson.   Brown Brothers.

It was against this background of injustice
and insensitivity toward Afro-Americans that
blacks first began to appraise Franklin Roosevelt. They soon found the New York Democrat
to be the most appealing president since Lincoln. Part of Roosevelt's attraction was the
courageous way he bore his physical disability.
And when the president received black visitors
at the White House and created a Black Cabinet, his actions contrasted favorably with Herbert Hoover's.

The Black Cabinet, or black brains trust, was
unique in United States history. Never before
had there been so many
black advisers at the White
House, and never before had they been highly
trained professionals. There were black lawyers,
journalists, and doctors of philosophy; black experts on housing, labor, and social welfare. William H. Hastie and Robert C. Weaver, both of
whom held advanced degrees from Harvard,
served in the Department of the Interior. Mary

| Black Cabinet |

McLeod Bethune, a college president, was director of the Division of Negro Affairs of the National Youth Administration. Eugene Kinckle Jones, executive secretary of the National Urban League, and Lawrence A. Oxley, a professional social worker, served in comparable posts in the Departments of Commerce and Labor. Black social scientists, among them Ralph Bunche, Ira DeA. Reid, Abram L. Harris, and Rayford W. Logan, acted as government consultants.

There were also among the New Dealers some whites who had committed themselves to first-class citizenship for Afro-Americans. Foremost among these people was Eleanor Roosevelt. The president himself, however, remained uncommitted to the black civil rights movement. Fearful of alienating southern whites, he never endorsed two key goals of the civil rights struggle: a federal law against lynching and abolition of the poll tax.

Furthermore, some New Deal programs and agencies functioned in ways that were definitely hostile to black Americans. The AAA, rather than benefiting black tenant farmers and sharecroppers, actually forced many of them off the land. The Federal Housing Administration (FHA) refused to guarantee mortgages on houses purchased by blacks in white neighborhoods, and the U.S. Housing Authority financed segregated housing projects. The CCC was racially segregated, as was much of the TVA. Finally, waiters, cooks, hospital orderlies, janitors, farm workers, and domestics, many of whom were black, were excluded from Social Security coverage and from the minimum-wage provisions of the Fair Labor Standards Act of 1938.

Confronted with the mixed message of the New Deal, many blacks concluded that ultimately they could depend only on themselves and organized self-help and direct-action movements. Nowhere was the trend toward direct action more evident than in the March on Washington movement of 1941. In that year billions of federal dollars flowed into American industry as the nation prepared for the possibility of an-

Antiblack effects of the New Deal

other world war. The government funds generated many thousands of new jobs, but discrimination deprived blacks of their fair share. So in early 1941, A. Philip Randolph, president of the Brotherhood of Sleeping Car Porters, proposed that 50,000 to 100,000 blacks march on the nation's capital to demand equal access to jobs in defense industries. Fearing the possibility of riots and the possibility of Communist infiltration of the movement, Roosevelt announced that if Randolph would cancel the march, he would issue an executive order prohibiting discrimination in war industries and in the government. The result was Executive Order No. 8802, issued on June 25, 1941, which established the Fair Employment Practices Committee (FEPC).

March on Washington movement

Native Americans benefited more directly than blacks from the New Deal. Prior to Roosevelt's inauguration, many Indians had suffered hunger, disease, and even starvation. At the heart of the Indians' suffering was a 1929 ruling by the U.S. comptroller general that landless tribes were ineligible for federal aid. Arguing that these Indians were no longer a national legal responsibility, the Indian Bureau had not requested congressional funds to help them. With the coming of the New Deal, however, federal policy changed. Roosevelt appointed John Collier commissioner of Indian affairs. In the 1920s, as founder of the American Indian Defense Association, Collier had crusaded for Indian land-ownership; now he championed the Indian Reorganization (Wheeler-Howard) Act of 1934, which ended the allotment policy of the Dawes Severalty Act of 1887. Since passage of that bill, Indian landholdings had dropped from 138 million acres to 48 million acres. The Wheeler-Howard Act sought to reverse the process by restoring lands to tribal ownership and forbidding future division of Indian lands into individual parcels. Other provisions of the act enabled tribes to obtain loans for economic development and to establish self-government. Collier also en-

Indian Reorganization Act

couraged the perpetuation of Indian religions and cultures. His reforms would stand until 1953.

Mexican-Americans also suffered extreme hardship during the depression, but no government programs benefited them. During the 1920s, more than 150,000 immigrants from Mexico had entered the United States on permanent visas; by official count the Mexican-born population had increased by 27.8 percent. (Illegal immigration may have equaled or even exceeded the legal figure.) Most of these new immigrants had settled in California, Texas, New Mexico, Arizona, and Colorado, but many others had moved to the Midwest.

When public officials complained that Mexicans were absorbing too large a share of the welfare budget, the Southern Pacific Railroad offered to ship Mexicans to Mexico City at $14.70 per head. Officials of Los Angeles County were eager to accept the offer. It cost the county $77,249 to repatriate 6,024 Mexicans, but it would have cost $424,933 to support them had they remained. According to the federal census, the Mexican-born population of the United States dropped from 617,000 in 1930 to 377,000 in 1940.

| Deportation of Mexican-Americans |

One reason for the large number of deportations was that in the 1930s many employers changed their minds about the desirability of hiring Mexican-American farm workers. They became disenchanted when Mexican-Americans began engaging in prolonged and sometimes bloody strikes. For example, in the San Joaquin valley in October 1933, eighteen thousand cotton pickers walked off their jobs and set up a "strike city" after being evicted from the growers' camps. Shortly after, their union hall was riddled with bullets and two strikers died. The next year labor violence was frequent in the Imperial valley, where police crushed a strike by burning the pickers' camp to the ground. In this dispute and others, Mexican-Americans showed their determination to organize, gain strength from unity, and fight for their rights.

The New Deal offered little help to these Mexican-Americans. Migratory farm workers received no benefits from the AAA, the Social Security Act, the Wagner Act, or the Fair Labor Standards Act (a law establishing a minimum wage and maximum hours for many but by no means all workers). One New Deal agency, the Farm Security Administration (FSA), was established in 1937 to help farm workers, in part by setting up migratory labor camps. But the FSA came too late to help Mexican-Americans, most of whom had by that time been replaced by Okies and Arkies who had fled their drought-stricken farms in Oklahoma, Arkansas, and other "Dust Bowl" states.

Roosevelt's second term: the unrealized promise

Despite the bold and unprecedented steps of his first term, what Roosevelt faced during his second term was a darkening horizon. The economy faltered again between 1937 and 1939, bringing renewed unemployment and suffering. And Europe drew closer to war, threatening U.S. security. In need of support for his foreign and military policies, Roosevelt began to court conservative politicians. The eventual result was the demise of the New Deal.

In several instances Roosevelt created his own defeat. The Supreme Court had invalidated much of the work of the First Hundred Days; now Roosevelt feared it would do the same with the fruits of the Second Hundred Days. So in February 1937 the President sent to Congress

| Roosevelt's Court-packing plan |

his Judiciary Reorganization Bill. What the federal judiciary needed, he claimed, was a more enlightened and progressive world view. Indeed, four of the associate justices of the Supreme Court seemed less attuned to the twentieth century than to a nineteenth-century world of natural selection and survival of the fittest. Three others were liberals, and two were swing votes.

What Roosevelt requested was the authority to appoint a replacement whenever a federal judge failed to retire within six months of reaching age seventy. He wanted the power to name up to fifty additional federal judges, including six to the Supreme Court. Though Roosevelt spoke of understaffed courts and aged and feeble judges, it was obvious that he envisioned using the bill to create a Supreme Court sympathetic to the New Deal.

Opposition to Roosevelt's attempt to pack the Court was widespread and vocal. Naturally, Republicans and some conservative Democrats opposed the bill, but liberals resisted as well. In the end Roosevelt had to concede defeat. The bill he signed made pensions available to retiring judges, but it denied him the power to increase the number of judges.

This episode had an ironic final twist. During the public debate over court packing, the two swing-vote justices began to vote in favor of liberal, pro–New Deal rulings. In spring 1937, for example, the court upheld a Washington state minimum-wage statute, the Wagner Act *(N.L.R.B.* v. *Jones & Laughlin Steel Corp.),* and the Social Security Act, all by 5-to-4 votes. Moreover, encouraged by pensions, judges past the age of seventy did begin to retire, and the president was able to appoint seven new Supreme Court justices between 1937 and 1941. Roosevelt had lost the legislative battle but won the war for a more progressive judicial outlook.

Another New Deal defeat, the renewed economic recession of 1937 through 1939, had no

Recession of 1937–1939

unexpected payoffs. Roosevelt had never abandoned his commitment to the balanced budget. In 1937, confident that most of the problems of the depression had been solved, he began to order drastic cutbacks in government spending. At the same time, the Federal Reserve Board, concerned over a 3.6 percent inflation rate, tightened credit. The two actions sent the economy into a tailspin; unemployment climbed from 7.7 million in 1937 to 10.4 million in 1938. Soon Roosevelt was forced to resume deficit spending.

Roosevelt's campaign against three conservative southern Democrats in the off-year elections of 1938 revealed his increasing desperation. Senators Walter George of Georgia, "Cotton Ed" Smith of South Carolina, and Millard Tydings of Maryland, all critics of the New Deal, won re-election despite Roosevelt's attempts to purge them from the party. As it turned out, Roosevelt would soon need the support of these conservatives for his programs of military rearmament and preparedness.

In spring 1938, with conflict over events in Europe commanding more and more of the nation's attention, the New Deal came to an end. The last significant laws enacted were a new Agricultural Adjustment Act and the Fair Labor Standards Act.

As the presidential election of 1940 approached, many people wondered whether Roosevelt would run for a third term (no presi-

Election of 1940

dent had ever served more than two terms). Roosevelt himself seemed undecided until May 1940, when Hitler's military advances apparently convinced him to stay on. The Republican candidate was Wendell Willkie, a utility executive who had been an anti–New Deal Democrat throughout most of the 1930s.

Willkie campaigned against the New Deal, contending that its meddling in the affairs of business had failed to return the nation to prosperity. He also called the government's military preparedness program inadequate. But Roosevelt pre-empted the defense issue by beefing up military and naval contracts. When Willkie reversed his approach and accused Roosevelt of being a warmonger, the president promised, "Your boys are not going to be sent into any foreign wars."

Willkie never did come up with an effective campaign issue, and when the votes were tallied on election day, Roosevelt had received 27 million votes to Willkie's 22 million. In the elec-

Important events

1928	Herbert Hoover elected president
1929	Federal Farm Board created Stock market crash
1930	Hawley-Smoot Tariff

1931	Scottsboro affair
	Hoover calls for moratorium on
	   World War I debts and
	   reparations
	Iowa's Cow War

1932	Reconstruction Finance
	   Corporation established
	Ford Hunger March in Dearborn,
	   Michigan
	Sioux City milk strike
	Bonus March on Washington,
	   D.C.
	Franklin D. Roosevelt elected
	   president

1933	13 million Americans
	   unemployed
	National Bank Holiday
	Roosevelt's Hundred Days
	Agricultural Adjustment Act
	   (AAA)
	Tennessee Valley Authority
	   (TVA)
	National Industrial Recovery Act
	   (NIRA)

1934	Dr. Francis Townsend's Old Age
	   Revolving Pensions plan
	   established
	Huey Long's Share Our Wealth
	   Society established
	Indian Reorganization (Wheeler-
	   Howard) Act
	Major Democratic victories in
	   congressional elections
	Father Charles Coughlin's

	National Union for Social Justice established

1935	Emergency Relief Appropriation
	   Act
	Works Progress Administration
	Schechter v. *U.S.* invalidates
	   NIRA
	National Labor Relations Act
	Social Security Act
	Huey Long assassinated
	Committee for Industrial
	   Organization (CIO)
	   established

1936	*U.S.* v. *Butler* invalidates AAA Roosevelt re-elected, defeating Landon

1937	United Auto Workers' sit-down
	   strikes
	Roosevelt introduces his "Court-
	   packing" plan
	N.L.R.B. v. *Jones & Laughlin*
	   upholds the Wagner Act
	Memorial Day Massacre
	Farm Security Administration

1937–39	Business recession

1938	AFL expels the CIO unions
	Fair Labor Standards Act
	Roosevelt's unsuccessful "purge"
	   of southern Democratic
	   senators
	10.4 million Americans
	   unemployed

1940	Roosevelt re-elected, defeating Willkie

1941	March on Washington
	   Movement
	Fair Employment Practices
	   Committee (FEPC) established

toral college, Roosevelt buried Willkie 449 to 82. Although the New Deal was over, Roosevelt was still riding its wave of public approval.

The legacy of the New Deal

Any analysis of the New Deal must begin with Franklin Delano Roosevelt. Assessments of his career varied widely during his presidency. Most historians have considered him a truly great president, citing his courage, his buoyant self-confidence, his willingness to experiment, and his capacity to inspire the nation during the most somber days of the depression. But those who have criticized him have charged that he was too pragmatic, that he failed to formulate a bold and coherent strategy of economic recovery and political and economic reform.

Though scholars have debated Roosevelt's performance, they all agree that he transformed the presidency. "Only Washington, who made

Strengthening of the presidency

the office, and Jackson, who remade it," Clinton Rossiter wrote in 1956, "did more than Roosevelt to raise it to its present condition of strength, dignity, and independence." Scholars in a later era would charge that Roosevelt laid the foundations of the "imperial presidency." But whether for good or ill, Roosevelt strengthened not only the presidency but the whole federal government. "For the first time for many Americans," William Leuchtenburg has written, "the federal government became an institution that was directly experienced. More than state and local governments, it came to be *the* government."

The New Deal brought about limited change in the nation's power structure. Beginning in the 1930s, business interests had to share their political clout with others. Finally, the labor movement gained influence in Washington, and farmers got more of what they wanted from Congress and the White House. But there was

no real increase in the power of Afro-Americans and other minorities. And if people wanted their voices to be heard, they had to organize in labor unions, trade associations, or other special-interest lobbies.

The New Deal failed in its fundamental purpose: to put people back to work. As late as

New Deal failure to solve unemployment

1938, over 10 million men and women were still jobless. That year unemployment was 19 percent; over the next two years it fell no lower than 14.6 percent. What plagued the nation throughout the 1930s was underconsumption: people and businesses either could not or would not purchase enough goods to sustain high levels of employment.

Historians have debated whether the New Deal was radical or conservative, revolutionary or evolutionary. Most historians would agree that if the New Deal was a revolution, it was a timid one, with few ideological underpinnings. In the end it was not the New Deal but massive government spending during the Second World War that put people back to work. In 1941, as a result of mobilization for war, unemployment would drop to 9.9 percent, and in 1944, the height of the war, only 1.2 percent of the labor force would be jobless.

Suggestions for further reading

HOOVER AND HIS ADMINISTRATION   David Burner, *Herbert Hoover: A Public Life* (1979); Martin L. Fausold and George T. Mazuzan, eds., *The Hoover Presidency* (1974); Ellis W. Hawley, *The Great War and the Search for a Modern Order* (1979); William E. Leuchtenberg, *The Perils of Prosperity, 1914–1932* (1958); Edgar E. Robinson and Vaughn D. Bornet, *Herbert Hoover* (1975); Albert V. Romasco, *The Poverty of Abundance: Hoover, The Nation, The Depression* (1965); Harris G. Warren, *Herbert Hoover and the Great Depression* (1959); Joan Hoff Wilson, *Herbert Hoover: Forgotten Progressive* (1975).

THE GREAT DEPRESSION AND ITS ORIGINS   Lester
V. Chandler, *America's Greatest Depression 1929–1941*
(1970); John K. Galbraith, *The Great Crash,* rev. ed.
(1972); Charles Kindleberger, *The World in Depression, 1929–1939* (1973); Broadus Mitchell, *Depression Decade* (1947); Jim Potter, *The American Economy Between the Wars* (1974); George Soule, *Prosperity Decade* (1947); Gordon Thomas and Max Morgan-Witts, *The Day the Bubble Burst* (1979).

THE AMERICAN PEOPLE IN HARD TIMES   Andrew
Bergman, *We're in the Money: Depression America and
Its Films* (1971); Irving Bernstein, *The Lean Years: A
History of the American Worker, 1920–1933* (1960);
Caroline Bird, *The Invisible Scar* (1965); Milton Meltzer, *Brother, Can You Spare a Dime?* (1969); Robert
Sklar, *Movie-Made America* (1975); Bernard Sternsher, ed., *Hitting Home: The Great Depression in Town
and Country* (1970).

PROTEST AND ALTERNATIVES   Alan Brinkley,
*Voices of Protest: Huey Long, Father Coughlin and the
Great Depression* (1982); Roger Daniels, *The Bonus
March* (1971); John P. Diggins, *The American Left in
the Twentieth Century* (1973); R. Alan Lawson, *The
Failure of Independent Liberalism, 1930–1941* (1971);
Donald J. Lisio, *The President and Protest: Hoover, Conspiracy, and the Bonus Riot* (1974); Donald R. McCoy,
Angry Voices: Left-of-Center Politics in the New Deal Era
(1958); James T. Patterson, *Congressional Conservatism
and the New Deal* (1967); David Shannon, *The Socialist Party of America* (1955); John L. Shover, *Cornbelt
Rebellion: The Farmers' Holiday Association* (1965);
Frank A. Warren, *Liberals and Communism: The "Red
Decade" Revisited* (1966); Frank A. Warren, *An Alternative Vision: The Socialist Party in the 1930s* (1976); T.
Harry Williams, *Huey Long* (1969); George Wolkskill, *The Revolt of the Conservatives: A History of the
American Liberty League, 1934–1940* (1962).

THE NEW DEAL   Paul K. Conkin, *FDR and the
Origins of the Welfare State* (1967); Otis L. Graham,
Jr., *Encore for Reform: The Old Progressives and the New
Deal* (1967); Ellis W. Hawley, *The New Deal and the
Problem of Monopoly* (1966); William E. Leuchtenburg, *Franklin D. Roosevelt and the New Deal* (1963);
Arthur M. Schlesinger, Jr., *The Age of Roosevelt,* 3
vols. (1957–1960).

FRANKLIN D. ROOSEVELT   James MacGregor
Burns, *Roosevelt: The Lion and the Fox* (1956); Frank
Freidel, *Franklin D. Roosevelt,* 4 vols. (1952–1973); Joseph P. Lash, *Eleanor and Franklin* (1971).

VOICES FROM THE DEPRESSION   James Agee, *Let Us
Now Praise Famous Men* (1941); Ann Banks, ed.,
First-Person America (1980); Federal Writers' Project,
These Are Our Lives (1939); Robert S. McElvaine, ed.,
*Down and Out in the Great Depression: Letters from the
"Forgotten Man"* (1983); Studs Terkel, *Hard Times:
An Oral History of the Great Depression* (1970); Tom
E. Terrill and Jerrold Hirsch, eds., *Such As Us: Southern Voices of the Thirties* (1978).

LABOR   Irving Bernstein, *Turbulent Years: A History of the American Worker, 1933–1941* (1969); Melvin Dubofsky and Warren Van Tine, *John L. Lewis:
A Biography* (1977); Sidney Fine, *Sit-Down: The General Motors Strike of 1936–1937* (1969); David Milton,
*The Politics of U.S. Labor: From the Great Depression to
the New Deal* (1980); H. L. Mitchell, *Mean Things
Happening in This Land* (1979).

AGRICULTURE   Sidney Baldwin, *Poverty and Politics:
The Rise and Decline of the Farm Security Administration*
(1967); David E. Conrad, *The Forgotten Farmers: The
Story of Sharecroppers in the New Deal* (1965); Walter
J. Stein, *California and the Dust Bowl Migration*
(1973); Donald Worster, *Dust Bowl: The Southern
Plains in the 1930's* (1979).

NONWHITES AND RACE RELATIONS   Dan T. Carter,
Scottsboro, rev. ed. (1979); John Hope Franklin, *From
Slavery to Freedom,* 5th ed. (1980); John B. Kirby,
*Black Americans in the Roosevelt Era: Liberalism and
Race* (1980); Carey McWilliams, *North from Mexico*
(1949); August Meier and Elliott Rudwick, *From
Plantation to Ghetto,* 3rd ed. (1976); Donald L. Parman, *The Navajos and the New Deal* (1975); Kenneth
Philip, *John Collier's Crusade for Indian Reform, 1920–
1954* (1977); Mark Reisler, *By the Sweat of Their
Brow: Mexican Immigrant Labor in the United States,
1900–1940* (1976); Harvard Sitkoff, *A New Deal for
Blacks* (1978); Raymond Wolters, *Negroes and the
Great Depression* (1970); Robert L. Zangrando, *The
NAACP Crusade Against Lynching, 1909–1950*
(1980).

Suggestions for further reading

CULTURAL AND INTELLECTUAL HISTORY Daniel
Aaron, *Writers on the Left: Episodes in American Literary Communism* (1961); Richard H. King, *A Southern
Renaissance: The Cultural Awakening of the American
South, 1930–1955* (1980); Jerre Mangione, *The Dream
and the Deal: The Federal Writers' Project, 1935–1943*
(1972); Richard H. Pells, *Radical Visions and American Dreams: Culture and Social Thought in the Depression Years* (1973).

25

DIPLOMACY IN A BROKEN WORLD, 1920-1941

Franklin D. Roosevelt wanted to be like his famous older cousin Theodore. In fact, he set out to ape his cousin's career: both graduated from Harvard, served in the New York State legislature and as governor of that state and assistant secretary of the navy, ran for the vice presidency, and reached the presidency itself. Like his cousin, Franklin Roosevelt believed that the United States should have entered the First World War earlier than it did. He never doubted that the United States should exert leadership in the world community, or that military preparedness and a big navy would ensure American security and prosperity.

During the interwar period, however, F.D.R. talked less about preparedness and more about disarmament and the horrors of war. Alert to public criticism of American military intervention in Latin America, he moved toward a Good Neighbor policy. Convinced that nonrecognition of Soviet Russia was counterproductive, he came to favor diplomatic relations with that power. And bewildered like most Americans by the First World War debts-reparations tangle and the havoc of the Great Depression, Roosevelt tried to protect the nation from global economic troubles while pre-

serving and expanding its share in the international marketplace. When Europe and Asia descended into diplomatic crisis and war in the 1930s, Roosevelt declared that the United States should avoid foreign squabbles, and he signed the "isolationist" Neutrality Acts.

Yet in the late 1930s, like many other Americans, Roosevelt changed his mind. Perceiving Germany and Japan as a terrible menace to the national interest, he first appealed for preparedness and then begged the nation to abandon its neutrality in order to aid Britain and France. German victory in Europe, he reasoned, would imperil Western political principles, destroy traditional American economic links, threaten America's sphere of influence in the Western Hemisphere, and place at the pinnacle of European power a fanatical man—Adolf Hitler.

At the same time Japan seemed determined to dismember America's friend China, to squelch the principle of the Open Door, and to surround and isolate the American colony of the Philippines. To deter Japanese expansion in the Pacific, Roosevelt cut off supplies of vital American products like oil. But economic warfare only confirmed the Japanese suspicion that the

United States was hostile to its empire. Japan's surprise attack on Pearl Harbor finally brought the United States into the Second World War.

Roosevelt and independent internationalism

The man who directed American foreign policy in the vexing depression decade was a believer in personal diplomacy. Roosevelt centralized decision making in the White House, failing on many occasions to inform the Department of State or Secretary Cordell Hull about his thinking. "A good horse trader" by nature, he shunned complex overviews and abstract theories, preferring to work with the issue at hand "by inspiration," as one of his advisers commented. To the consternation of State Department officers, the president's penchant for covering over differences sometimes misled or confused people.

Always the ambitious politician, alert to the temper of the times, Roosevelt both reflected and shaped the public mood in the interwar years. It would be wrong to depict him solely as an opportunistic politician who always did what was expedient; he had his own views. And though he seldom strayed from what he thought was public opinion, he did, when he believed it necessary, influence that opinion in his own direction.

Interwar public attitudes on foreign relations have often been characterized as *isolationist*. Historians agree, however, that the term is misleading in its suggestion that the United States cut itself off from international affairs after the First World War. A more useful and accurate description of interwar foreign policy is *independent internationalism*. That is, in the interwar years the United States was active on a global scale but retained its independence of action, its traditional unilateralism. Even had they wanted to,

Americans could not have escaped the tumult of international relations; their interests were too far-flung and too vast: colonies, client states, overseas naval bases, investments, trade, missionaries.

The desire to avoid war led American leaders to search for nonmilitary means to exercise power. In the aftermath of the First World War, Americans had grown disenchanted with military methods of achieving order and protecting American prosperity and security. American diplomats thus put increasing emphasis on conferences, moral lectures and calls for peace, nonrecognition of disapproved regimes, arms control, and economic and financial ties in accord with the principle of the Open Door.

American leaders deemed this last means to power, economic and financial ties, extremely important. In the early 1920s Secretary of State Charles Evans Hughes, like the nation's business leaders, expected American economic expansion to bring about world stability; out of economic prosperity would spring a world free from political extremes, revolution, aggression, and war.

Interwar economic expansion

United States economic influence became conspicuous after the First World War. By the late 1920s the United States produced about half the world's industrial goods, ranked first among exporters, and acted as the financial capital of the world. To many foreigners, this American economic expansionism was imperialistic. Argentine writer and critic Manuel Ugarte went so far as to assert that the United States was a new Rome: it annexed wealth rather than territory.

Negotiating with the Europeans

Europe lay in shambles at the end of the war. It is estimated that from 1914 to 1921 there were sixty million casualties in Europe from world war, civil war, massacre, epidemic, and famine. Crops, livestock, factories, trains, forests, bridges—little was spared. Currencies lost value and trading patterns were disrupted. The desperate plight of Europeans drew American sympathies and aid in the form of food.

But if Americans won praise from Europeans for their humanitarianism, they earned the nickname Uncle Shylock for their handling of war debts and reparations, an issue that dogged international relations for a decade. Twenty-eight nations were tangled in the web of inter-Allied

| *First World War debts and reparations* | debts, which totaled $26.5 billion, about half of it owed to the United States. Europeans urged Americans to |

forgive the debts as a magnanimous contribution to the war. But American leaders insisted on repayment.

The debts question was linked to Germany's $33 billion reparations bill. Hobbled by inflation and economic disorder, Germany had begun to default on its payments. Americans grew worried that German economic troubles would spawn radicalism. To keep Germany afloat, American bankers poured millions of dollars in loans into the floundering nation. A triangular relationship developed: American investors' money flowed to Germany; German reparations payments went to the Allies; the Allies then paid some of their debts to the United States. The American-crafted Dawes Plan of 1924 greased the financial tracks by reducing Germany's annual payments, extending the repayment period, and providing still more loans. And the United States gradually scaled down Allied obligations, cutting the debt by half during the 1920s.

But the triangular arrangement was dependent on continued German borrowing in the United States, and in 1928 and 1929 American lending abroad declined sharply in the face of more lucrative opportunities in the stock market. The American-negotiated Young Plan of 1929, which reduced the total of Germany's reparations, salvaged little as the international economy sputtered and collapsed. By 1931, when

Hoover declared a moratorium on payments, the Allies had paid back only $2.6 billion. Wracked by depression, they defaulted on the rest.

In the end, American economic power had proved unable to sustain a healthy world economy. But many nations shared responsibility for the failure. The selfish and vengeful Europeans might have trimmed Germany's huge indemnity. The Germans might have borrowed less from abroad and taxed themselves more. The Bolsheviks might have agreed to pay rather than repudiate Russia's $4 billion indebtedness. And Americans might have tried for a comprehensive, multinational settlement and lowered their tariffs, giving Europeans a market in which to earn the money to pay off their debt.

American influence also failed to curb militarism and prevent war. The nation's efforts began at the Washington Conference (1921–1922).

| *Washington Conference* | There the United States discussed limits on naval armaments with eight other na- |

tions. Britain, the United States, and Japan, the three top naval powers, were facing a costly postwar naval arms race, and they welcomed the opportunity to deflect it. In the Five-Power Treaty the delegates set a ten-year moratorium on the construction of large, or capital, ships, and established a total tonnage ratio of 5:5:3:1.75:1.75 among the five top nations (Britain : United States : Japan : France : Italy). The first three nations actually agreed to dismantle some existing vessels to meet the ratio. To assuage the Japanese, who were vexed over their third-place standing, the United States promised not to build new fortifications in the Philippines.

Several other agreements were reached at the conference. The Nine-Power Treaty reaffirmed the Open Door in China. In the Four-Power Treaty, the United States, England, Japan, and France agreed to respect each other's Pacific possessions and to consult in the event of aggression in Asia. In another agreement Japan pledged to pull back from Shandong and Russian Siberia. But although the treaties signed at Washington provided a rare and noble example of mutual disarmament, they did not, critics pointed out, limit submarines, destroyers, or cruisers, and there were no provisions for enforcement of the Open Door declaration.

Peace advocates next placed their hopes in the Kellogg-Briand Pact of 1928, eventually signed by sixty-two nations. The signatories agreed simply to "condemn recourse to war for the solution of international controversies, and renounce it as an instrument of national policy." The treaty's backers billed it as a first step in a long journey toward international co-operation and the outlawry of war. Lacking provisions for enforcement, however, it proved impotent in the 1930s.

The League of Nations, also looked to as a peacemaker, exhibited a conspicuous feebleness, not only because the United States refused to join, but because members themselves usually chose not to use it to settle disputes. Starting in the mid-1920s, however, American officials did participate discreetly in League meetings on public health, prostitution, drug trafficking, and other such questions. And individual jurists like Charles Evans Hughes served on the World Court in Geneva, although the United States also refused to join that institution.

Soviet Russia was a special problem in American foreign relations. Following Wilsonian precedent, the Republican administrations of the 1920s refused to recognize the Soviet government. To Americans, the Communists were godless radicals bent on destroying the American way of life. Nevertheless, communications with Russia gradually increased. By 1930–1931, Russia was the number one foreign buyer of American agricultural and industrial equipment. In the early 1930s, trade began to slump. To stimulate business and help the United States pull out of the depression, some businesspeople began to lobby for diplomatic recognition of Russia. Roosevelt, believing that

Relations with Russia

it was foolish not to recognize such a major country, agreed that a change in policy was necessary. He also recognized that closer Russian-American ties might deter Japanese aggression in Asia. For these reasons the United States recognized the Soviet Union in 1933.

Sphere of influence in Latin America

Before the First World War the United States had thrown an imperial net over much of Latin America. By the 1920s the supposed benefits of American expansionism—hospitals, schools, roads, telephones, and irrigation systems—were evident in much of Latin America. But United States imperialism meant meddling in the internal affairs of Latin American nations. United States financial advisers supervised government budgets in the Caribbean, and in 1920 American soldiers occupied Cuba, the Dominican Republic, Haiti, Panama, and Nicaragua.

Yet these military expeditions to Latin America were becoming unpopular and counterproductive. Congressional critics complained about the denial of self-determination to Latin Americans and the dispatch of troops abroad without congressional approval. Businesspeople feared the destruction of property by angry Latins. And in 1932 Secretary of State Henry L. Stimson, who was concerned about Japanese incursions in China, worried that similar intervention in Latin America by the United States would render his protests meaningless.

Turning away pragmatically from military intervention, then, the United States sought less controversial methods of maintaining its influence in Latin America: Pan-Americanism; support for strong native leaders; the training of national guards; economic penetration; Export-Import Bank loans; and when

Good Neighbor policy

necessary, political subversion. Although the process began before his presidency, Roosevelt gave it a name in 1933: the Good Neighbor policy. Good Neighborism did not mean that Latin America would escape from the United States sphere of influence. It did mean that the United States would be less blatant in its domination.

The training of national guards went hand in hand with support of dictators: many Latin American dictators rose to power through the

Training of national guards

ranks of a U.S.-trained national guard. For example, before the United States withdrew its troops from the Dominican Republic in 1924, American personnel created a constabulary. One of its first officers was Rafael Leonidas Trujillo, who became head of the National Army in 1928. Trujillo became president in 1930 through fraud and intimidation, and ruled the Dominican Republic with an iron fist until his assassination in 1961. "He may be an S.O.B.," as Roosevelt once remarked, "but he is our S.O.B."

In Nicaragua the experience was similar. The United States occupied Nicaragua from 1912 to 1925 and returned in late 1926 during a civil war. The justification for United States involvement was the need to clean up and stabilize Nicaragua's politics. When the marines departed in 1933, they left behind a powerful national guard headed by General Anastasio Somoza. With American backing, the Somoza family would rule Nicaragua from 1936 to 1979 through corruption, political suppression, and torture, while anti-Americanism simmered among the masses.

The Cubans too grew restless under American domination. By 1929 American investments in the Caribbean nation totaled $1.5 billion, up

Domination of Cuba

from $220 million in 1913. The American military uniform was conspicuous at the naval base at Guantánamo Bay. In 1933 Cuban rebels placed Professor Ramon Grau San Martín in the president's seat. Grau declared the Platt Amendment, which accorded the United States

the right to intervene in Cuban affairs, null and void. He seized some American-owned mills, refused to make payments on American bank loans, and talked of land reform.

A startled United States refused to recognize the new government. Instead, Americans encouraged a coup by army sergeant Fulgencio Batista (1934), who ruled Cuba until driven from power in 1959 by Fidel Castro. During the Batista era Cuba protected American investments and granted the United States more military sites. In return it received military aid, loans, abrogation of the Platt Amendment, and a more favorable sugar tariff.

The pattern was different in Mexico. In 1917 the Mexicans adopted a new constitution specifying that all "land and waters" and all subsoil raw

Nationalist fervor in Mexico

materials (like oil) belonged to the Mexican nation—a real threat to American land-holdings and petroleum interests. Here was a unique case: a weak, underdeveloped Latin American nation issuing a direct challenge to the powerful United States.

Washington settled on a policy of nonrecognition of the new government and ardent defense of the interests of American businesses and landowners. In 1923 a compromise led to U.S. recognition, but wrangling continued until 1938, when Mexico expropriated the property of all foreign-owned petroleum companies. In reply the United States cut back on purchases of Mexican silver and encouraged a business boycott of the upstart nation.

The outbreak of the Second World War in 1939 helped to determine the outcome. Fearful that Mexico would sell its oil to the saber-rattling Germans and Japanese, Roosevelt decided to compromise. In 1941 the United States conceded that Mexico owned its raw materials and could treat them as it saw fit; and Mexico compensated American companies for their lost property. American power had been diminished, setting a precedent to which Latin American nationalists would refer in the future.

Roosevelt's movement toward nonmilitary

methods—the Good Neighbor policy—paid off in the Declaration of Panama (1939), wherein the Latin American governments drew a security line around the hemisphere and warned aggressors away. In exchange for more trade and foreign aid, Latin American governments also reduced their sales of raw materials to Germany, Japan, and Italy, and increased shipments to the United States. On the eve of the war, then, the United States' sphere of influence was virtually intact, ready to back American military and diplomatic policies.

The Great Depression and growing isolationism

Secretary of State Cordell Hull liked to say that the character of international relations derived from economic conditions. In the 1930s the effect of economics was particularly apparent. The depression wrecked international finance and trade. In the late 1920s, when First World War debts and reparations proved too much for the shattered European economies to bear, international finance collapsed. Banks failed and world trade faltered.

The United States actually added to the burdens of the world economy with the Hawley-Smoot Tariff (1930), a selfish move that shut off the American market to European nations struggling to earn cash to pay off their war debts. President Hoover's moratorium on debts payments (1931) came too late. By 1932 about twenty-five nations had retaliated against the American tariff by imposing similar restrictions on American imports. And in 1933 President Roosevelt resorted to protectionism at the London Conference (1933), barring American cooperation in international monetary stabilization.

Cordell Hull was beside himself over the world's conspicuous nose-dive into economic nationalism. Calling the protective tariff the "king of evils," Hull successfully pressed Congress to pass the Reciprocal Trade Agreements Act (1934). The act, which would guide American economic foreign policy thereafter, empowered the president to reduce American tariffs by as much as 50 percent through special agreements with foreign countries.

Cordell Hull's economic foreign policy

The central feature of the act was the *most-favored-nation principle*, whereby the United States was entitled to the lowest tariff rate set by a nation with which it had a most-favored-nation agreement. In 1934 Hull also sponsored the creation of the Export-Import Bank, a government agency that provided loans to foreigners for the purchase of American goods. Hull's programs stood as rare examples of internationalism in an era of rampant nationalism.

Meanwhile, as the Great Depression cut a destructive path through the international economy, other nations turned to political extremism. In Germany, Adolf Hitler came to power. Like Benito Mussolini, who gained control of Italy in 1922, Hitler was a fascist. Fascism (called Nazism, or National Socialism, in Germany) was a collection of ideas and prejudices that included supremacy of the state over the individual; of dictatorship over democracy; of authoritarianism over freedom of speech; and of militarism and war over peace. The Nazis vowed not only to revive German economic and military strength, but to "purify" the German "race" of Jewish influence, on which they blamed Germany's problems. In Japan militarists justified aggression in Asia by arguing that their country was so dependent on foreign trade that it could not survive without foreign economic resources.

As for the United States, the depression reinforced isolationist, or independent internationalist, thought. A 1937

Isolationist sentiment

Gallup poll found that nearly two-thirds of the people questioned thought that American participation in the First World War had been a mistake. Conservative isolationists feared higher taxes and increased federal power if the nation went to war again. Liberal isolationists spoke of the need to give domestic problems priority. Other critics feared that by attempting to spread democracy abroad, America would lose it at home.

Isolationism was a truly national phenomenon that cut across socioeconomic, ethnic, party, and sectional lines and attracted a majority of the American people. What united isolationists was the opinion that there were alternatives to American involvement in another futile Old World war. Only when events grew uglier and more menacing toward the end of the depression decade would many, like President Roosevelt, change their minds.

Some liberal isolationists, critical of business practices at home, charged that corporate "mer-

 Business ties with the aggressors

chants of death" were undermining the national interest by assisting the aggressors. From 1934 to 1936 a congressional committee chaired by Senator Gerald P. Nye held hearings on the role of business interests in the American decision to enter the First World War. The hearings did not prove that businesspeople and financiers had dragged reluctant Americans into the war, but they did uncover evidence that corporations had bribed foreign politicians to improve arms sales in the 1920s and 1930s and had lobbied against arms control.

Senator William E. Borah (1865–1940), an influential isolationist and champion of disarmament, the Kellogg-Briand Pact, nonintervention in Latin America, and the neutrality acts. Few spokesmen matched his passionate oratory or fierce independence. Library of Congress.

European upheaval and American neutrality

In 1933, resentful of the punitive terms of the Treaty of Paris (1919), Hitler pulled Germany out of the League of Nations, ended reparations payments, and began to rearm. Secretly laying plans for the conquest of neighboring states, he watched admiringly as Mussolini's troops invaded the African nation of Ethiopia in 1935. The next year Hitler ordered his goose-stepping troopers into the Rhineland, an area the Treaty

of Paris had declared demilitarized. Germany's timid neighbor France did not resist.

Soon the aggressors began to join hands. In fall 1936 Italy and Germany formed an alliance called the Rome-Berlin Axis. Shortly thereafter Germany and Japan united against Russia in the Anti-Comintern Pact. To these events Britain and France responded with a policy of appeasement, hoping to curb Hitler's expansionist appetite by permitting him a few nibbles. But the policy eventually proved disastrous; taking advantage of European caution, the German leader continually raised his demands.

In those hair-trigger times, a civil war in Spain turned into an international struggle: from 1936 to 1939 the Loyalist Republicans battled the fascist-backed insurgents of Francisco Franco. Hitler and Mussolini sent military aid to Franco; Russia assisted the Loyalists. France and Britain held to the fiction of a nonintervention pledge that even Italy and Germany had signed. And a few hundred American volunteers known as the Lincoln Battalion joined the fight on the side of the Republicans. When Franco won in 1939, his victory tightened the grip of fascism on the European continent.

Early in 1938 Hitler once again tested the limits of European patience when he sent his soldiers into Austria to annex that nation. In September of the same year he seized the Sudeten region of Czechoslovakia. Appeasement reached its peak that month at the Munich Conference when France and Britain, without consulting the helpless Czechs, agreed to allow Hitler this one last territorial bite. British Prime Minister Neville Chamberlain returned home to proclaim "peace in our time," confident he had quieted the dictator. But in March 1939 Hitler swallowed the rest of Czechoslovakia. Poland was next on his list. Scuttling appeasement, London and Paris announced they would stand by their ally. Undaunted, Germany neutralized Russia by signing the Nazi-Soviet Pact and struck Poland on September 1. Britain and France, dismissed by Hitler as "worms," declared war on Germany two days later. The Second World War had begun.

However much they were opposed to fascist aggression, Americans tried to stay clear of the conflict. Each new crisis increased isolationist sentiment. In a series of neutrality acts Congress sought to protect the nation by severing the kind of contact that had compromised American neutrality two decades earlier. The Neutrality Act of 1935 prohibited arms shipments to either side in a war once the president had declared the existence of belligerency. The Neutrality Act

Neutrality Acts

of 1936 forbade loans to belligerents. A joint resolution in 1937 declared the United States neutral in the Spanish Civil War; Roosevelt then embargoed arms shipments to both sides. And finally, the Neutrality Act of 1937 introduced the cash-and-carry principle: warring nations wishing to trade with the United States would have to pay cash for their purchases and carry the goods away in their own ships. The act also forbade Americans from traveling on vessels of belligerent nations.

But Roosevelt was deeply troubled by the arrogant behavior of the "three bandit nations," Germany, Italy, and Japan. He was disgusted by Nazi persecution of the Jews and by Japanese slaughter of Chinese civilians. Privately he snarled against the refusal of the British and French to collar Hitler in their own backyards. And he worried that the United States was militarily ill-prepared to confront the aggressors.

The United States had not been neglecting its military. Roosevelt's New Deal public works programs included millions for the construction of new ships. In 1935 the president requested the largest peacetime defense budget in American history; three years later, in the wake of Munich, he urgently asked Congress for funds to build up the air force. The president also began to cast about for ways to encourage the British and French to show more backbone. One result was his agreement in January 1939 to sell bombers to France.

Finally, in his annual message early in 1939, the president lashed out at the international lawbreakers. Soon afterward he urged Congress to

Roosevelt proposes repeal of arms embargo

repeal the arms embargo and permit the sale of munitions to belligerents on a cash-and-carry basis. Roosevelt saw repeal as an aid to Britain, which dominated the seas. And although he did not yet have the votes to win a repeal, he stepped up his public condemnation of the aggressors.

When Europe fell into the abyss of war in

Nazi dictator Adolf Hitler (1889–1945), the maniacal militarist who set out to restore his nation's lost grandeur through annihilation of its enemies. Hitler's seemingly insatiable appetite for conquest convinced many Americans that war was unavoidable. Library of Congress.

September 1939, Roosevelt declared neutrality. But unlike Woodrow Wilson, he did not ask Americans to be neutral in thought, and he pressed again for repeal of the arms embargo.

After much lobbying, debate, and bipartisan consultation, Congress revised the neutrality legislation. In November 1939 it lifted the embargo on contraband and approved cash-and-carry exports of arms. Now Roosevelt was ready to aid the Allies—short of war—and to challenge the isolationists more boldly.

A new order in Asia

If United States power was massive in Latin America and limited in Europe, it was minuscule in Asia. Still, there were American interests in that region that required defense in the interwar period: the Philippines and Pacific islands; religious missions; trade and investments; and the Open Door in China. Americans increasingly saw the Japanese as a threat to these interests, and specifically as strong-willed expansionists bent on subjugating China and unhinging the Open Door doctrine of equal trade and investment opportunity.

The highly nationalistic Chinese Revolution of 1911 still rumbled in the 1920s. In the late 1920s Jiang Jieshi (Chiang Kai-shek) emerged

| *Rise of Jiang Jieshi in China* |

as the pre-eminent leader of this convulsed nation. Jiang ousted Communists from the governing Guomindong party, forcing their leader, Mao Zedong, to flee to the hills with his followers. Americans applauded Jiang's anticommunism and his conversion in 1930 to Christianity. Satisfied with Jiang, the United States signed a treaty in 1928 restoring control of tariffs to the Chinese.

Twentieth-century Japanese-American relations had seldom been cordial. Many causes existed for the stress, the most important of which was the conflict between America's Open Door policy and Japanese drive for Asian raw materials. Relations deteriorated further after the Japanese military seized Manchuria in September 1931 (see map). Only nominally a Chinese region, Manchuria was important to the Japanese

| *Japanese seizure of Manchuria* |

both as a buffer against the hated Russians and as a vital source of coal, iron, timber, and food. More than half of Japan's foreign investments were in Manchuria. Lacking the power to force Japanese withdrawal, the United States responded with a moral lecture called the Stimson Doctrine (1932), which declared that the United States would not recognize any impairment of China's sovereignty or of the Open Door policy.

Hardly cowed by timid protests from Western capitals, Japan continued to harry China. In mid-1937 full-scale Sino-Japanese war erupted. In an effort to help China, Roosevelt refused to declare the existence of war, thus allowing the Chinese to continue to buy weapons in the United States. In a stirring speech denouncing the aggressors in October 1937, he called for a "quarantine" to curb the "epidemic of world lawlessness."

Alarmed by Japan's self-proclaimed "New Order" in Asia, the United States looked for small ways to assist China and thwart Japan in 1938 and 1939. Military equipment flowed to the Chinese, as did a $25 million loan. Secretary of State Hull declared a moral embargo against the shipment of airplanes to Japan. The navy, its eye on the Pacific, continued to grow, helped by a billion-dollar congressional appropriation in 1938. And in mid-1939 the United States abrogated the 1911 Japanese-American trade treaty. Yet America continued to ship oil, cotton, and machinery to Japan. The administration hesitated to initiate economic sanctions for fear they would spark an Asian war at a time when the more serious threat was emanating from Berlin. When war broke out in Europe in 1939, Japanese-American relations were stalemated.

On the brink, 1939 to 1941

Polls showed that Americans strongly favored the Allies, and that most supported aid to Brit-

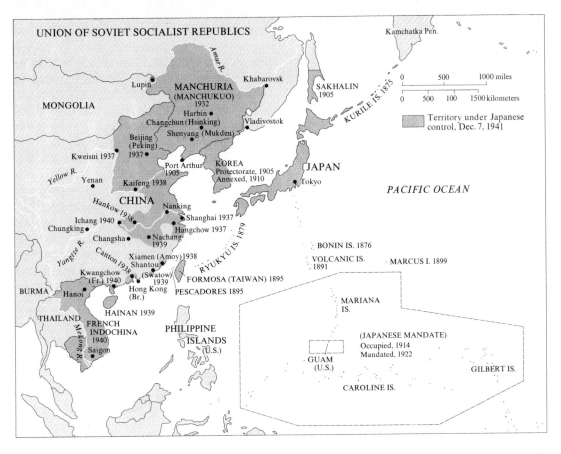

Japanese expansion before Pearl Harbor

ain and France; but the great majority emphatically wanted the United States to remain at peace. Troubled by this conflicting advice—defeat Hitler, aid the Allies, but stay out of war—the president between 1939 and 1941 "moved two steps forward and one back before he took the giant step forward," as historian Robert A. Divine put it. From neutrality the United States moved to undeclared war and then to war itself.

During those tense months of inching toward belligerency, isolationist sentiment declined. Alarmed by the swift

Decline of isolationism clined. Alarmed by the swift defeat of one European nation after another, some liberals left the isolationist fold, which became more and more the province of conservatives. Die-hard isolationists organized the America

First Committee in fall 1940; interventionists, meanwhile, joined the Century Group or the Committee to Defend America by Aiding the Allies (both formed in mid-1940).

In September 1939 Poland succumbed to German stormtroopers in just two weeks (see map, page 410). In November Russia invaded Finland, prompting Roosevelt to denounce "this dreadful rape"; by March 1940 Finland had been defeated. The following month Germany invaded Denmark and Norway, a month later the Netherlands and Belgium. And in June 1940 France collapsed. Would England be next?

In the meantime, Roosevelt began to aid the faltering Allies. In May 1940 he ordered the sale of surplus First World War equipment to Britain and France. In July he cultivated bipartisan

The German advance, 1939–1942

support for the war by naming Republicans Henry L. Stimson and Frank Knox, ardent backers of aid to the Allies, secretaries of war and the navy respectively. In September he announced that by executive agreement he was trading fifty old American destroyers for leases to eight British bases, including Newfoundland, Bermuda, and Jamaica. Two weeks later he signed into law the Selective Training and Service Act, the first peacetime military draft in American history.

Through the fall Roosevelt spoke of the need for a huge foreign aid program to save England from the Nazis. The United States, he implored, must become the "great arsenal of democracy."

| Lend-Lease Act | In January 1941 the controversial Lend-Lease bill was

introduced in Congress. The president argued that America had a moral obligation to provide the British with weapons, just as a neighbor lends a garden hose to fight a fire. The bill cleared Congress in March 1941, and $7 billion was appropriated. By the end of the war $50 billion in Lend-Lease aid had been distributed, mostly to England.

To ensure the safe delivery of Lend-Lease goods, Roosevelt ordered the navy to patrol halfway across the Atlantic and sent American troops to Greenland. Then a stunning turn of events in Europe spurred a new decision. In June 1941 Hitler struck Russia. By November Lend-Lease aid was flowing to appreciative Russians.

In August 1941 Churchill and Roosevelt met

Chapter 25: Diplomacy in a broken world, 1920–1941

for four days off Newfoundland. At this confer-

Atlantic Charter ence the two leaders wrote the Atlantic Charter, a set of war aims reminiscent of Wilsonianism. The Atlantic Charter called for collective security, disarmament, self-determination, economic cooperation, and freedom of the seas. Later, on January 1, 1942, twenty-six nations signed the Declaration of the United Nations, pledging themselves to fulfill the charter.

In September 1941 the United States moved closer to an open confrontation with Germany. After a German U-boat fired at the destroyer *Greer,* Roosevelt denounced the act of "piracy" and declared that the United States would convoy British merchant ships all the way to Iceland. He failed to mention that the *Greer* had been trailing the submarine, giving its position to British airplanes. The next month another American destroyer, the *Reuben James,* was torpedoed, and over one hundred sailors lost their lives. Congress responded by scrapping the cash-and-carry program and authorizing armed American merchant ships to transport munitions to England.

In retrospect it seems ironic that the Second World War came to the United States via Asia, where Roosevelt so wanted to avoid it in order to concentrate American resources on the defeat of Germany. In September 1940 Americans read the stunning news of the Tripartite Pact, an alliance between Germany, Italy, and Japan. After much

Cut-off of trade with Japan debate within the administration, Roosevelt slapped an embargo on shipments of aviation fuel and scrap metal to Japan. The next summer Washington responded to Japanese occupation of French Indochina by freezing Japanese assets in the United States. The action virtually ended Japanese trade with the United States, making it impossible for Japan to secure much needed American oil.

Tokyo recommended a high-level meeting between President Roosevelt and Prime Minister Prince Konoye, but the United States rejected the idea. American officials insisted that the Japanese first agree to respect China's sover-

eignty and territorial integrity and to honor the Open Door policy—in short, to get out of China. Roosevelt also told the Japanese ambassador that his nation would have to withdraw from the Tripartite Pact.

As the president's advisers tried to string out Japanese-American talks in order to buy time to fortify the Philippines and check the fascists in Europe, cryptographers worked on the Japanese code ("Operation Magic"). On breaking the diplomatic code, experts informed Roosevelt that Japan would go to war if the oil embargo

Attack on Pearl Harbor was not lifted. Then on December 1 the president was informed that Japanese task forces were being ordered into battle. Secretary Stimson explained later that the United States let Japan fire the first shot so as "to have the full support of the American people" and "so that there should remain no doubt in anyone's mind as to who were the aggressors." Fearing that they could not win a prolonged war, the Japanese plotted a daring raid on Pearl Harbor in Hawaii. A flotilla of Japanese aircraft carriers crossed three thousand miles of ocean, and on the morning of December 7, planes stamped with the Rising Sun swept down on the unsuspecting American naval base, killing more than 2,400 people, sinking several battleships, and smashing aircraft.

How could Pearl Harbor have happened? Americans asked. Roosevelt did not, as his critics later charged, conspire to leave the fleet vulnerable to attack, so the United States could enter the Second World War through the "back door" of Asia. The base was not ready—not on red alert—because a message of warning from Washington had been sent by Western Union telegraph rather than by navy cable and arrived too late. Base commanders were relaxed, thinking Hawaii, so far from Japan, an unlikely target for all-out attack. They expected the assault to come at British Malaya, Thailand, or the Philippines. Mistakes there were, but not conspiracy.

On December 8, referring to the previous day as a "date which will live in infamy," Roosevelt asked for and received from Congress a declara-

Disaster at Pearl Harbor, December 7, 1941. The surprise attack by the Japanese disabled much of America's Pacific fleet, Investigators later complained of negligence in the Navy and War departments, but no courts-martial were initiated.   National Archives.

tion of war against Japan. Three days later Germany and Italy declared war against the United States. The war was now a global conflict.

Suggestions for further reading

GENERAL   Thomas H. Buckley, *The United States and the Washington Conference, 1921–1922* (1970); James MacGregor Burns, *Roosevelt: The Lion and the Fox* (1956); Wayne Cole, *Roosevelt and the Isolationists, 1933–1945* (1983); Robert Dallek, *Franklin D. Roosevelt and American Foreign Policy, 1932–1945* (1979); Robert A. Divine, *Roosevelt and World War II* (1969);

L. Ethan Ellis, *Republican Foreign Policy, 1921–1933* (1968); Robert H. Ferrell, *American Diplomacy in the Great Depression* (1957); Arnold A. Offner, *The Origins of the Second World War* (1975); Julius W. Pratt, *Cordell Hull*, 2 vols. (1964); Raymond Sontag, *A Broken World, 1919–1939* (1971).

ECONOMIC FOREIGN POLICY   Frederick Adams, *Economic Diplomacy* (1976); Derek H. Aldcroft, *From Versailles to Wall Street, 1919–1929* (1977); Herbert Feis, *The Diplomacy of the Dollar, 1919–1932* (1950); Lloyd C. Gardner, *Economic Aspects of New Deal Diplomacy* (1964); Michael J. Hogan, *Informal Entente: The Private Structure of Cooperation in Anglo-American Economic Diplomacy, 1918–1928* (1977); Charles Kindleberger, *The World in Depression* (1973); Mira Wil-

Important events

1919–20	Senate rejects membership in the League of Nations	1935	Italy invades Ethiopia Neutrality Act
1921–22	Washington Conference on naval arms control	1936	Outbreak of Spanish Civil War Neutrality Act
1922	Mussolini comes to power in Italy	1937	Neutrality Act Roosevelt's quarantine speech
1924	Dawes Plan for German reparations U.S. occupation of the Dominican Republic ends	1938	Mexico nationalizes American-owned oil companies Munich Conference Hitler's persecution of the Jews
1926	American troops occupy Nicaragua (remaining until 1933)	1939	Nazi-Soviet pact Germany invades Poland Second World War begins United States repeals arms embargo
1927	Jiang Jieshi attacks Communists in China		
1928	Kellogg-Briand Pact		
1929	Young Plan for German reparations	1940	Soviets invade Finland Committee to Defend America by Aiding the Allies formed Tripartite Pact Destroyer-bases deal with Great Britain America First Committee formed Selective Training and Service Act
1930	Hawley-Smoot Tariff		
1931	Japan seizes Manchuria		
1932	Stimson Doctrine of nonrecognition		
1933	Hitler comes to power in Germany U.S. recognition of Soviet Russia Good Neighbor policy announced United States subverts Cuban revolution	1941	Lend-Lease Act Germany attacks Russia United States freezes Japanese assets, cutting trade Atlantic Charter meeting of Roosevelt and Churchill *Greer* incident Japan attacks Pearl Harbor
1934	Reciprocal Trade Agreements Act Export-Import Bank founded		

kins, *The Maturing of Multinational Enterprise* (1974); John Hoff Wilson, *American Business and Foreign Policy, 1920–1933* (1971).

LATIN AMERICA   Alton Frye, *Nazi Germany and the American Hemisphere, 1933–1941* (1967); Irwin F. Gellman, *Good Neighbor Diplomacy* (1979); David Green, *The Containment of Latin America* (1971); Lester D. Langley, *The United States and the Caribbean, 1900–1970* (1980); Neil Macaulay, *The Sandino Affair* (1967); Robert I. Rotberg, *Haiti* (1971); Ramon Ruiz, *Cuba: The Making of a Revolution* (1968); Karl M. Schmitt, *Mexico and the United States, 1821–1973* (1974); Bryce Wood, *The Making of the Good Neighbor Policy* (1961).

EUROPE, AMERICAN "ISOLATIONISM," AND WAR
Edward Bennett, *Recognition of Russia* (1970); Charles Chatfield, *For Peace and Justice: Pacifism in America, 1914–1941* (1971); Wayne Cole, *America First* (1953); James V. Compton, *The Swastika and the Eagle* (1967); Charles DeBenedetti, *Peace Reform in American History* (1980); Robert A. Divine, *The Illusion of Neutrality* (1962); Robert A. Divine, *The Reluctant Belligerent* (1979); Manfred Jonas, *Isolationism in America, 1935–1941* (1966); Warren F. Kimball,

The Most Unsordid Act: Lend-Lease, 1939–1941 (1969); William L. Langer and S. Everett Gleason, *The Challenge to Isolation, 1937–1940* (1952); William L. Langer and S. Everett Gleason, *The Undeclared War, 1940–1941* (1953); Joseph P. Lash, *Roosevelt and Churchill, 1939–1941* (1976); Melvyn P. Leffler, *The Elusive Quest* (1979); Arnold A. Offner, *American Appeasement* (1969); David Reynolds, *The Creation of the Anglo-American Alliance, 1937–1941* (1981); Bruce Russett, *No Clear and Present Danger* (1972); John Wiltz, *In Search of Peace: The Senate Munitions Inquiry, 1934–1936* (1963).

CHINA, JAPAN, AND PEARL HARBOR   Dorothy Borg and Shumpei Okomoto, eds., *Pearl Harbor as History* (1973); R. J. C. Butow, *Tojo and the Coming of the War* (1961); Warren I. Cohen, *America's Response to China,* 2nd ed. (1980); Herbert Feis, *The Road to Pearl Harbor* (1950); Waldo H. Heinrichs, Jr., *American Ambassador* (1966); Akira Iriye, *Across the Pacific* (1967); Akira Iriye, *After Imperialism: The Search for a New Order in the Far East, 1921–1931* (1965); Charles Neu, *The Troubled Encounter: The United States and Japan* (1975); Gordon Prange, *At Dawn We Slept* (1981); Michael Schaller, *The United States and China in the Twentieth Century* (1979).

26 ᔒ

THE SECOND

WORLD WAR

AT HOME AND ABROAD,

1941-1945

"We are going on a mission to drop a bomb different from any you have ever seen or heard about," Colonel Paul Tibbets informed his crew on the small Pacific island of Tinian. Silent and incredulous, they listened to "Old Bull" describe the strange new weapon, which packed the destructive power of twenty thousand tons of TNT. Resting in the bay of a converted B-29 named the *Enola Gay,* after Tibbets's mother, was "Little Boy"—a ten-thousand-pound uranium bomb on which the airmen had scribbled anti-Japanese graffitti.

On August 6, 1945 the crew put on welder's goggles and made their run on the unsuspecting city of Hiroshima. When the bomb hit target, a flash of dazzling light shot across the sky; then two violent slaps rocked the plane. "My God!" gasped co-pilot Captain Robert Lewis as he watched a huge purplish mushroom cloud boil 40,000 feet into the atmosphere. Dense smoke, swirling fires, and suffocating dust soon engulfed the ground for miles. Much of the city was leveled almost instantly.

Approximately 130,000 people were killed at Hiroshima; tens of thousands more suffered painful burns and nuclear poisoning. As Hiro-shima suffered its unique nightmare, Washington, D.C., celebrated its military and scientific triumph. "This is the greatest thing in history," exclaimed President Harry S Truman on hearing of the successful mission. The Second World War would soon be over.

Americans had fought for some forty-five months in the Pacific before losing patience with conventional warfare and turning to the atom bomb. In Europe, they had not become significantly involved until June 1944, when they joined the massive crossing of the English Channel that pressed back Nazi forces through France to Germany. Throughout the war the Allies–Britain, Russia, and the United States— were held together by their goal of defeating Hitler. But they squabbled over many issues, from when the second, or western, front would be opened to how Eastern Europe, liberated from the Germans, would be reconstructed.

At home Americans united behind the war effort, collecting scrap iron, rubber, and old newspapers and planting victory gardens. The federal government mobilized all traditional sectors of the economy–industry, finance, agriculture, and labor–as well as new ones: higher education and science. For this was a scientific and technological war, supported by the development of new weapons like the atomic bomb.

For millions of Americans the war was a time to pull up stakes and relocate in other parts of the country. Between 1941 and 1945, over 15 million men and women served in the armed forces. Also on the move during the Second World War were blacks and whites from the South, who migrated to war-production centers in the North and the West. Employers' negative attitudes toward women workers eased during the war, and millions of married middle-class women, many of them over age thirty-five, took jobs for the first time.

In these and other ways the United States and its people underwent profound change during the course of the war. The Second World War was truly a watershed in American history.

Winning the Second World War

"We are now in the midst of a war, not for conquest, not for vengeance, but for a world in which this Nation, and all that this Nation represents, will be safe for our children." President Roosevelt was speaking just two days after the surprise attack on Pearl Harbor. Americans believed with Roosevelt that they were defending their homes and families against aggressive and satanic Nazis and Japanese. Few of them, however, knew much about the principles of the Atlantic Charter or about United States war aims.

In the army's propaganda films and in the popular mind, the Allies were heroic partners in an effort against evil. Actually, wartime relations between the United States, Great Britain, and the Soviet Union ran hot and cold. Although winning the war claimed top priority, Allied leaders knew that military decisions had political consequences. Thus an undercurrent of suspicion ran beneath the surface of Allied cooperation.

Roosevelt, British Prime Minister Winston Churchill, and Soviet Premier Josef Stalin

| Second front controversy |

differed most over the opening of a second front. Stalin pressed for a British-American landing on the northern coast of Europe to draw German troops away from the eastern front, but Churchill would not agree. The Russians therefore did most of the fighting and dying on land, while the British and Americans concentrated on getting Lend-Lease supplies across the Atlantic and harassing the Germans from the air.

Roosevelt was particularly sensitive to the Russian burden. And he feared that Russia might be knocked out of the war, leaving Hitler free to invade England. In 1942 Roosevelt told the Russians they could expect the Allies to open a second front later that year. The move across the English Channel, later tagged Operation OVERLORD, was exactly what Stalin sought to take pressure off his wracked country. But Churchill, fearing heavy British losses in a premature invasion, balked; he favored a series of small jabs at the enemy's Mediterranean forces.

Churchill won the debate. Instead of attacking France, the western Allies invaded North Africa in November 1942. "We are striking back," the cheered president declared. In the same month the Russians began to blunt the German thrust, pushing Hitler's armies back from Stalingrad. But in early 1943 Stalin was told once again that the second front would be delayed. He was not mollified by the Allied invasion of Italy in the summer of 1943. When Italy surrendered in September, it capitulated to American and British officers; Russian officials were not invited to participate. Stalin grumbled that the arrangement smacked of a separate peace.

With the Grand Alliance badly strained, Roosevelt sought reconciliation through personal diplomacy. The three Allied leaders met in Teheran, Iran, in December 1943. Stalin dismissed Churchill's repetitious justifications for further delaying the second front. Roosevelt had had enough too; with Stalin he rejected Churchill's proposal for another peripheral attack, this

D-Day on Omaha Beach, June 6, 1944: army medics administer blood plasma to a survivor of the cross-channel invasion, which opened the second front in Europe. Omaha was strongly defended from high cliffs. Many of the over 25,000 soldiers who jumped into the water from landing craft never made it to shore.   U.S. Army, Department of Defense.

time through the Balkans to Vienna. The three finally agreed to launch OVERLORD in early 1944.

Like a coiled spring bursting free, the second front opened in the dark morning hours of June 6, 1944: D-Day. Two hundred thousand Allied troops

D-Day

under the command of General Eisenhower scrambled ashore in Normandy, France, in the largest amphibious landing in history. After dig-

ging in at now-famous places like Utah and Omaha beaches and gaining reinforcements, Allied forces broke through disorderly German lines and gradually ground inland, reaching Paris in August. That same month another force invaded southern France and threw the stunned Germans back. Allied troops soon spread across the countryside, liberating France and Belgium and entering Germany itself in September. In December German panzer divisions counterattacked in Belgium's Ardennes Forest, hoping to push on to Antwerp to halt the flow of Allied supplies through that major Belgian port. Allied forces were surprised; their defenses buckled. But after weeks of heavy fighting in what has come to be called the Battle of the Bulge—because of the noticeable dent in the Allied line—the Allies pushed the enemy back once again.

Meanwhile battle-hardened Russian troops streamed through Poland and cut a path to the German capital, Berlin. American forces crossed the Rhine in March 1945 and captured the heavily industrial Ruhr valley. Some units peeled off to enter Austria and Czechoslovakia, where they met up with Russian soldiers. In bomb-ravaged Berlin, defended largely by teen-age boys and old men, Adolf Hitler killed himself in his bunker. On May 8 Germany surrendered.

Allied strategists had devised a "Europe first" formula: knock out Germany first and then concentrate on an isolated Japan. Nevertheless the Pacific theater claimed headlines throughout the war, for the American people regarded Japan as the United States' chief enemy. By mid-1942 Japan had seized the Philippines, Guam, Wake, Hong Kong, Singapore, Malaya, and the Dutch East Indies. In the Philippines in 1942 Japanese soldiers forced American prisoners, weak from insufficient rations, to walk sixty-five miles, clubbing, shooting, or starving to death about ten thousand of them. The Bataan Death March hardened even more the American hatred of the Japanese.

In April 1942 Americans began to hit back. They bombed Tokyo, and in May, in the momentous Battle of the Coral Sea, carrier-based U.S. planes halted a Japanese advance toward Australia (see map). The next month American forces defeated the Japanese at Midway, sinking four of the enemy's valuable aircraft carriers. The Battle of Midway broke the Japanese momentum and relieved the threat to Hawaii. Thereafter Japan was never able to match American manpower, sea power, air power, or economic power.

General Douglas MacArthur's strategy was to "island-hop" toward Japan itself, skipping the

| American offensive in the Pacific |

most strongly fortified points whenever possible and taking weaker ones. American forces also set out to sink Japan's merchant marine, without which the enemy could neither supply its armies nor obtain vital raw materials. The first American offensive was at Guadalcanal in the Solomons (1942). Over the next few years U.S. troops attacked the Gilberts (1942), the Marianas (1944), and the Philippines (1944). In 1945 both sides took heavy losses at Iwo Jima and Okinawa. In desperation, Japanese pilots made suicide *(kamikaze)* attacks on American warships, flying their planes directly into the vessels.

Hoping to avoid a humiliating unconditional surrender (and to preserve the emperor's sovereignty), Japanese leaders refused to admit defeat. They hung on while American bombers leveled their cities. In one staggering attack on Tokyo on May 23, 1945, American planes dropped napalm-filled bombs that engulfed the city in a chemically induced firestorm. Eighty-three thousand people died.

Impatient for victory, American leaders began to plan for a fall invasion of the Japanese home islands, an expedition that would bring high casualties. But the successful development of an atomic bomb by American scientists provided another route to victory. Shortly after the atomic bombing of Hiroshima and Nagasaki the Japanese surrendered, on the condition that their emperor would remain, at least theoretically, the nation's ruler. Formal ceremonies were held September 2 aboard the battleship *Missouri.*

The war was over. Everywhere ghostlike people wandered about searching for food and mourning those who would never come home. Russia had lost 15 to 20 million people; Poland 5.8 million; Germany 4.5 million. In all, about 35 million Europeans died as a result of the war. In Asia untold millions of Chinese and 2 million Japanese died. Only one major combatant

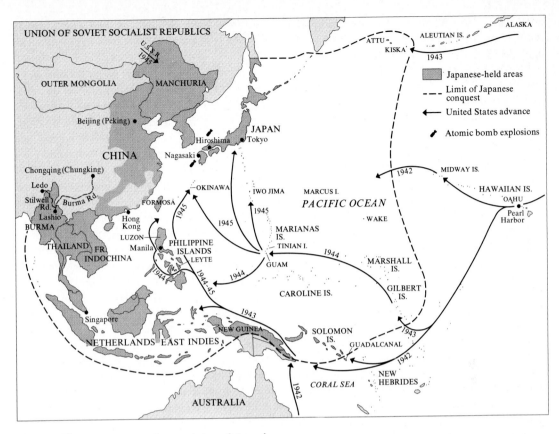

The Pacific war. Source: By permission of the publisher, from *American Foreign Policy: A History* by Paterson *et al.,* p. 474. (Lexington, Mass.: D.C. Heath and Company, 1977).

emerged from the war comparatively unscathed: the United States.

Wartime diplomacy

Throughout the war years the lessons of the 1930s weighed heavily on the minds of American diplomats. Americans vowed to make a peace that would ensure a postwar world free from depression, totalitarianism, and war. Thus American goals included the Open Door and lower tariffs; self-determination for liberated peoples; avoidance of the debts-reparations tangle that had plagued Europe after the First World War; expansion of the United States sphere of influence; and management of world affairs by what Roosevelt once called the Four Policemen: Russia, China, Great Britain, and the United States.

Although the major Allies concentrated on defeating the aggressors, their suspicions of one another undermined cooperation. For the Allies Eastern European questions proved the most difficult. The Russians sought to fix their boundaries where they had stood before Hitler at-

Allied disagreement over Eastern Europe

tacked in 1941. In the case of Poland, this meant that the part of the country the Soviets had invaded and captured in 1939 would become Russian territory. The British and Americans hesitated, preferring to deal with Eastern Europe at the end of the war. Yet in October 1944 Churchill and Stalin, without Roosevelt's participation, struck a bargain: Russia would gain Rumania and Bulgaria as a sphere of influence; Britain would have the upper hand in Greece; and the two would share authority in Yugoslavia and Hungary.

Poland was a special case. In 1943 Moscow had broken off diplomatic relations with the conservative Polish government-in-exile in London. The Poles had asked the International Red Cross to investigate German charges that the Russians had massacred thousands of Polish army officers in the Katyn Forest in 1941. Then an uprising in Warsaw in July 1944 complicated matters still further. To the dismay of the world community, Soviet armies stood aside as German troops slaughtered 166,000 people and devastated the city. Stalin further intensified the Polish question by spawning a pro-Communist government in Lublin. Thus near the end of the war Poland had two competing governments, one in London and another in Lublin.

Early in the war the Allies had begun talking about a new international organization. At Teheran in 1943 Roosevelt called for an institution controlled by the Four Policemen. The next year, in an elegant Washington, D.C., mansion called Dumbarton Oaks, American, British, Russian, and Chinese representatives conferred on the details. The conferees approved a preliminary charter for a United Nations Organization, providing for a supreme Security Council dominated by the great powers and a weak General Assembly. The Security Council would have five permanent members, each with veto power; Britain had insisted that France be one of them. Meanwhile the Russians, hoping to counter pro-British and pro-American blocs in the General Assembly, sought separate membership for its

Creation of the United Nations Organization

sixteen Soviet republics. That issue was not resolved, but the meeting was successful nevertheless.

The diplomatic batting average on another problem, Nazi treatment of the Jews, was considerably lower. Even before the war Nazi officials had targeted Jews throughout Europe for persecution. By war's end, about 6 million Jews had been forced into extermination camps and systematically disposed of by firing squads, unspeakable tortures, and gas chambers. Many others who survived the Holocaust could never forget the terror. During the 1930s the United States and other nations had refused to relax their immigration restrictions to save Jews fleeing persecution. Bureaucrats applied the rules so strictly—requiring legal documents fleeing Jews could not possibly provide—that otherwise qualified refugees were kept out of the country. From 1933 to 1945 less than 40 percent of the German-Austrian quota was filled.

Jewish refugees from the Holocaust

When evidence mounted that Hitler intended to exterminate the Jews, British and American representatives met in Bermuda (1943) but came up with no plans. Secretary Hull made a discouraging report to the president, emphasizing "the unknown cost of moving an undetermined number of persons from an undisclosed place to an unknown destination." Appalled, Secretary of the Treasury Henry Morgenthau, Jr., charged that the State Department's foot-dragging made the United States an accessory to murder. Early in 1944, stirred by Morgenthau's well-documented plea, Roosevelt created the War Refugee Board, which set up refugee camps in Europe and saved thousands from death.

But American officials waited too long to act, and they missed a chance to destroy the gas chambers and ovens at the extermination camp at Auschwitz in occupied Poland. They had aerial photographs and diagrams of the camp, but they argued that bombing it would detract from the war effort or prompt the Germans to step up the anti-Jewish terror. In 1944 American

Chapter 26: The Second World War at home and abroad, 1941–1945

planes bombed synthetic oil and rubber plants in the industrial sector of Auschwitz, only five miles from the gas chambers and crematoria, but left the camp itself untouched.

The Yalta Conference and a flawed peace

With the war in Europe nearing an end, Roosevelt urged another summit meeting. The three Allied leaders met at Yalta, on the Russian Crimea, in early February 1945. Controversy has surrounded the conference ever since. Roosevelt was obviously ill, and critics of the Yalta agreements later charged that Roosevelt was too weak to resist the demands of a guileful Stalin. The evidence suggests, however, that Roosevelt was mentally alert.

Each of the Allies entered into the conference with definite goals. Britain sought a place for France in occupied Germany; a curb on Soviet influence in Poland; and protection for the vulnerable British Empire. Russia wanted reparations from Germany, to assist in the massive task of rebuilding at home; possessions in Asia; continued influence in Poland; and a permanently weakened Germany. The United States lobbied for the United Nations Organization, where it believed it could exercise influence; for a Soviet declaration of war against Japan; for recognition of China as a major power; and for compromise between rival factions in Poland.

Allied goals at Yalta

Military positions at the time of the conference helped to shape the final agreements. Soviet troops had occupied much of Eastern Europe, including Poland, and the Russians were set against the return of the London government. Under Roosevelt's leadership Stalin and Churchill reached a compromise: a boundary favorable to Russia in the east; postponement of the western boundary issue; and the creation of a "more broadly based" coalition government that would include members of the London government-in-exile. Free elections would be held sometime in the future. The agreement was vague, but given Soviet occupation of Poland, Roosevelt considered it "the best I can do."

As for Germany, the Big Three agreed that it would be divided into four zones, the fourth to go to France. Russia and the United States gave in to Britain on that point; they did not believe that France deserved such recognition. On the question of reparations the Russians and Americans agreed that an Allied committee would use a sum of $20 billion as a basis for discussion in the future.

Asian issues were debated, and again tradeoffs were devised. Stalin promised to declare war on Japan two or three months after Hitler's defeat. He also agreed to sign a treaty of alliance with America's Chinese ally Jiang Jieshi (Chiang Kai-shek). In return the United States agreed to give Russia the southern part of Sakhalin Island, Lüshun (Port Arthur), and a hand in the operation of the Manchurian railroads.

Regarding the United Nations Organization, Roosevelt and Churchill gave the Soviets three votes in the General Assembly. The three leaders scheduled the organizing meeting of the United Nations for April 25 in San Francisco (fifty nations launched that body in May). Finally, they restated the Atlantic Charter principles in the Declaration of Liberated Europe, pledging to establish order and to rebuild national economies by democratic methods.

Yalta marked the high point of the Grand Alliance; each of the Allies came away with something, in the tradition of diplomatic give-and-take. But as the great powers jockeyed for influence at the close of the war, neither the spirit nor the letter of Yalta held firm. The crumbling of the alliance became evident at the Potsdam Conference in July and August 1945. Roosevelt had died in April, and Harry S Truman had replaced him. Truman was a novice at international diplomacy, and less patient with the Russians.

Potsdam Conference

The Big Three did agree at Potsdam on some general policies for governing Germany. A Control Council made up of the military commanders of the four zones (French, British, American, and Russian) was empowered to oversee "complete disarmament and demilitarization." But the question of reparations continued to divide the victors. In a compromise they decided that each occupying nation should take reparations from its own zone; but they could not agree on a total figure.

Economic effects of the war at home

The war at home was just as important to victory as the military campaigns abroad. One month after Pearl Harbor, President Roosevelt established the War Production Board (WPB). First on the WPB's list of tasks was the con-

version from civilian production to military production. Factories that had manufactured silk ribbons began to turn out silk parachutes; automobile companies switched to the production of tanks and airplanes; adding-machine companies converted to making automatic pistols. Other factories had to be expanded, and new ones had to be built. Moreover, whole new industries, the best known of which was synthetic rubber, had to be created. The Japanese had captured most of the world's supply of natural rubber. The WPB was so successful that the production of durable goods more than tripled.

To gain the cooperation of business, the WPB and other government agencies met it

more than halfway. Whenever possible, Chairman Donald Nelson said, he wanted "to establish a set of rules under which the game could be played the way industry said it had to play it." So the government offered guaranteed profits in the form of cost-plus-fixed-fee contracts, generous tax

writeoffs, and exemption from antitrust prosecution. And it allowed prime contractors to distribute subcontracts as they saw fit, including those involving scarce war-related materials.

From mid-1940 through September 1944 the government awarded contracts totaling $175 billion, no less than two-thirds of which went to the top one hundred corporations. General Motors received almost $14 billion, or 8 percent of the total; big awards also went to other automobile companies, several aircraft and steel companies, General Electric, AT&T, and Du Pont. Though no one had yet thought to call it the "military-industrial complex," as President Dwight Eisenhower would in 1961, the web of government-business interdependence had begun to be woven.

The big got bigger not only in business but in science and higher education. To develop radar and do other research, the Massachusetts Institute of Technology received seventy-five contracts valued at $117 million. The California Institute of Technology came next with forty-eight contracts totaling $83 million, followed by Harvard, Columbia, the University of California, Johns Hopkins, and the University of Chicago. The most spectacular result of government contract with a university was, of course, the atomic bomb, the testing of which was run by officials at the University of California at Berkeley. Likewise, the first controlled nuclear chain reaction was set off—under contract—at the Metallurgical Laboratory at the University of Chicago.

Big labor also grew bigger during the war. Union membership ballooned from 8.5 million in 1940 to 14.75 million in 1945. In 1942, to minimize labor-management conflict, President Roosevelt created the National War Labor Board (NWLB), sometimes referred to as the Supreme Court for labor disputes. As a result of its Little Steel formula, which limited wage increases to increases in the cost of living, the NWLB was soon confronted with labor disputes. Production time lost through strikes and other labor stoppages tripled in 1943. After three walkouts in two months by United Mine Workers, the government seized the coal mines.

B-17 pilots return from a training flight in their Flying Fortress *Pistol Packin' Mama.* WAF pilots ferried the planes for the Air Corps.   U.S. Air Force Photo.

Agriculture made impressive contributions to the war effort, not only through hard work but through the introduction of labor-saving ma-

> **Increased mechanization of agriculture**

chinery to replace the men and women who had gone to the front or migrated to war-production centers. Farming was in the midst of a transition from the family-owned and operated farm to the large-scale, mechanized agribusiness dominated by banks, insurance companies, and farm co-ops. The Second World War accelerated the trend. Like business and labor, agriculture was becoming more consolidated in the process of contributing to the war effort.

At the head of the burgeoning economy stood the federal government. The WPB and the NWLB were only two of the host of new agencies that sprang up: others included the Office of Price Administration, the War Manpower Commission, the Office of War Mobilization, the Office of War Information, and the Office of Scientific Research and Development. The national debt jumped from $49 billion in 1941 to $259 billion in 1945.

The federal government was, of course, also responsible for mobilizing the military. By 1945 well over 12 million men and women were serving in the armed forces. The army topped the list with 8.3 million, including 100,000 WACS (members of the Women's Army Corps). Though women were prohibited from engaging in combat duty, they worked at a variety of noncombat jobs, not only in the WACS but as WAVES in the navy, as pilots in the WAFS (Women's Auxiliary Ferrying Squadron), and as members of the *Semper Paratus* Always Ready Service (SPARS) and the Women's Reserve of the Marine Corps.

Most troops served overseas for an average of about sixteen months. Some, of course, never returned: total deaths exceeded 405,000; total wounded, 670,000. In terms of human life, the cost of the war was second only to that of the Civil War. Still, compared with losses suffered by other nations, U.S. figures were low. Less than 1 percent of the population was killed or wounded in the war; the Soviet Union lost 8 percent of its population—20 million people.

The war in the popular imagination

Throughout the war, civilians had difficulty relating to a conflict of which they had no first-hand experience. War themes were prominent in popular culture—the movies people saw, the books they read, the songs they listened to—as they struggled to come to grips with the overwhelming event. Their amusements were those of a society marking time until the war's close.

Motion pictures were typically light, fluffy, sentimental escapes from the harsh realities of life. The most popular film of 1944, for example, was Bing Crosby's *Going My Way,* the story of two lovable priests in a New York parish. However, some hard-hitting war films were successful in bringing the realities of war home to the American people. In September 1942, just as the newspapers were filled with stories of Guadalcanal, the film *Wake Island* opened. But even the best of these films tended to be simplistic in their moral outlook. Pitted against unadulterated good was unadulterated evil; the hero always won in the end. Documentaries, such as John Ford's *The Battle for Midway,* and newsreels were more realistic, bringing the war home to civilians.

| The war in the movies |

Like films, most books published during the war lacked substance. Noteworthy exceptions were the nonfiction best sellers *Berlin Diary* by William Shirer, *Mission to Moscow* by Joseph Davies, and *Victory Through Air Power* by Alexander de Seversky. Such books provided insight into the war. Other best sellers discussed the shape of the postwar world. Wendell Willkie's *One World,* written by the Republican presidential candidate of 1940, was probably the most influential book published during the war.

| Literature of the war |

In previous wars Americans had flocked to the colors with flags, wild rallies, and militaristic songs. But as historian Allan Nevins wrote at the conclusion of the conflict, "In this war there was happily no such straw fire of frothy enthusiasm." In 1861, 1898, and 1917, Americans had thought that "the war would be easy." Nevins wrote, "They knew full well in 1941 that it wouldn't." Indeed, this was a war they might even lose. Perhaps for that reason Americans sought escape not only in movies and books, but in music as well. The few popular songs that did relate to the war, such as "Praise the Lord and Pass the Ammunition" and "Coming In on a Wing and a Prayer," tended to emphasize the uncertainties of war, or the longing for lovers in uniform—"I'll Get By" and "I'll Be Seeing You."

Branded members of an enemy race by the government, more than 110,000 Japanese-Americans were rounded up and shipped to internment camps. These people were among the 18,000 Japanese-Americans sent to a race track at Santa Anita, California, where they lived in horses' stalls.   National Archives.

Internment of Japanese-Americans

Civil liberties had been one of the casualties of the First World War. By contrast—and with one enormous exception—the government's record on civil liberties in the Second World War was commendable.

The exception was the internment in "relocation centers" of more than 110,000 Japanese-Americans. Of these people, 70,000 were Nisei, or native-born citizens of the United States.

Charges of criminal behavior were never brought against them; none were ever indicted or tried, though civilian courts were open and accessible. Their imprisonment was based not on suspicion or evidence of treason, but on ethnic origin—the fact that they were of Japanese descent.

"It was really cruel and harsh," recalled Joseph Y. Kurihara, a citizen and a veteran of the First World War. "To pack and evacuate in forty-eight hours was an impossibility. Seeing mothers completely bewildered with children crying from want and peddlers taking advantage and offering prices next to robbery made me feel like murdering those responsible."

The internees were sent to flood-damaged lands at Relocation, Arkansas; to the intermountain terrain of Wyoming and the desert of western Arizona; and to other arid and desolate spots in the West. Although the names were picturesque—Topaz, Utah; Rivers, Arizona; Heart Mountain, Wyoming; Manzanar, California—the camps themselves were bleak and demoralizing. Behind barbed wire stood tarpapered wooden barracks where entire families lived in a single room furnished only with cots, blankets, and a bare light bulb. Toilets and dining and bathing facilities were communal; privacy was almost nonexistent. Besides their freedom, the Japanese-Americans lost property estimated at $500 million, along with their positions in the truck-garden, floral, and fishing industries. Indeed, their economic competitors were among the most vocal proponents of their relocation.

The Supreme Court upheld the government's policy of internment. In wartime, the Court said in the *Hirabayashi* ruling (1943), "residents having ethnic affiliations with an invading enemy may be a greater source of danger than those of different ancestry." And in the *Korematsu* case (1944), the Court, with three justices dissenting, approved the removal of the Nisei from the West Coast. One dissenter, Justice Frank Murphy, denounced the decision as the "legalization of racism." In an even more ominous appraisal, Circuit Court Judge William Denman had written, "the identity of this doctrine with that of the Hitler generals . . . justifying the gas chambers of Dachau is unmistakable."

The decline of liberalism

If civil liberties abuses during the war did not constitute a trend, the decline of liberalism did. Even before Pearl Harbor, liberals had suffered major defeats. Some Democrats hoped to revive the reform movement during the war, but Republicans and conservative Democrats were on guard against such a move. Senator Robert Taft and his fellow conservatives successfully blocked reform.

Part of the Democrats' problem was that, unlike the 1930s, the war years were a time of full employment. Once people had secured jobs and gained some economic security, they began to be more critical of New Deal policies. The New Deal coalition had always had the potential for fragmentation. Southern white farmers had little in common with northern blacks or white factory workers. And in northern cities, blacks and whites who had voted for Roosevelt in 1940 were competing for jobs and housing and would soon collide in the race riots of 1943. It was perhaps too much to expect people not to vote on the basis of their fears and hatreds.

With Republican congressional and gubernatorial victories in 1942, the alliance of conservative southern Democrats and Republicans be- | *Conservative attack on the New Deal* | came a formidable threat to New Deal programs. In 1942 and 1943 the conservative coalition actually abolished several New Deal relief and social-welfare agencies, among them the Civilian Conservation Corps, the Work Projects Administration, and the National Youth Administration.

But though liberalism was enfeebled, it was far from dead. The liberal agenda began with a pledge to secure full employment—meaning, according to Roosevelt, 60 million jobs. Roosevelt emphasized the concept in his Economic Bill of Rights, delivered as part of his 1944 State of the Union address. Every American had a right, the president declared, to a decent job, sufficient food, shelter, and clothing, and financial security in unemployment, illness, and old age. If to accomplish those goals the government had to operate at a deficit, Roosevelt was willing to do so. But first he had to be re-elected.

In 1944 the Republicans were optimistic about their prospects for regaining the presidency, and several governors attempted to se-

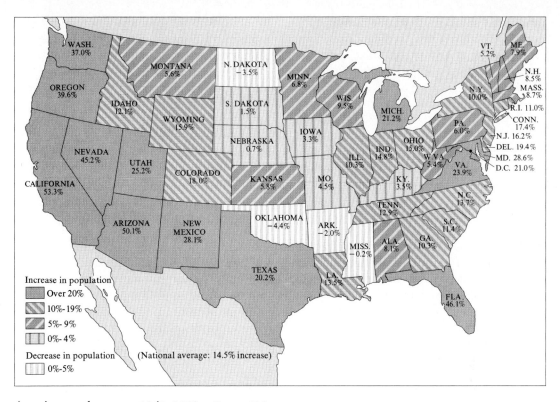

A nation on the move, 1940–1950. Source: U.S. Bureau of the Census, *Portfolio of United States Census Maps, 1950* (Washington: U.S. Government Printing Office, 1953), p. 4.

Increase in population
- Over 20%
- 10%–19%
- 5%–9%
- 0%–4%

Decrease in population   (National average: 14.5% increase)
- 0%–5%

Map labels:
WASH. 37.0% · OREGON 39.6% · MONTANA 5.6% · N. DAKOTA –3.5% · MINN. 6.8% · IDAHO 12.1% · WYOMING 15.9% · S. DAKOTA 1.5% · WIS. 9.5% · MICH. 21.2% · NEVADA 45.2% · UTAH 25.2% · NEBRASKA 0.7% · IOWA 3.3% · ILL. 10.3% · IND. 14.8% · OHIO 15.0% · CALIFORNIA 53.3% · COLORADO 18.0% · KANSAS 5.8% · MO. 4.5% · KY. 3.5% · W. VA. 5.4% · VA. 23.9% · ARIZONA 50.1% · NEW MEXICO 28.1% · OKLAHOMA –4.4% · ARK. –2.0% · TENN. 12.9% · N.C. 13.7% · S.C. 11.4% · MISS. –0.2% · ALA. 8.1% · GA. 10.3% · TEXAS 20.2% · LA. 13.5% · FLA. 46.1% · VT. 5.2% · ME. 7.9% · N.H. 8.5% · N.Y. 10.0% · MASS. 8.7% · R.I. 11.0% · CONN. 17.4% · N.J. 16.2% · DEL. 19.4% · MD. 28.6% · D.C. 21.0%

Election of 1944

cure the party's nomination. New York's Thomas E. Dewey, a moderate with ability and a dull personality, secured the nomination. Despite rumors of ill health, Roosevelt was elected for a fourth term. His margin of victory (53.4 percent), however, was the narrowest since 1916. More than anything else, it was the urban vote that returned Roosevelt to the White House. Wartime population shifts had much to do with the cities' new political clout. New workers—notably southern whites who had been lifelong Democrats and southern blacks who had never before voted—had migrated to the urban industrial centers (see map).

The 1944 Democratic victories, however, did little to change legislative trends in Congress, where the conservative coalition still frustrated liberal initiatives. Even liberals had to admit that wartime economic mobilization had made some reforms unnecessary. With practically all Americans gainfully employed, there was little justification for some New Deal social-welfare programs.

The seeds of the black revolution

For blacks in America, the Second World War would prove to be a watershed, the point at which they determined to make a stand against racial discrimination once and for all. Behind this change were several developments: the presence of 1 million black men and women in the armed services; the mass migration of blacks, particularly from the rural South to the urban North and West, to work in war industries; and the participation of black people in all kinds of wartime activities, from buying war bonds to serving as air-raid wardens.

Though blacks in the service were still segregated, they made some real advances in the direction of racial equality during these years. For the first time the War Department sanctioned the training of blacks as airplane pilots. After instruction at Tuskegee Institute in Alabama, pilots saw heroic service in such all-black units as the Ninety-ninth Pursuit Squadron, winner of eighty Distinguished Flying Crosses. And some blacks reached positions of leadership. In 1940 Colonel Benjamin O. Davis became the first black brigadier general, and blacks were appointed as aides to the secretary of war and the director of Selective Service. Wherever black people were offered opportunities to distinguish themselves, they proved they were just as capable as whites.

| *Blacks in the armed forces* |

Set against these accomplishments, however, were distressing failures in race relations. Serious race riots occurred on a number of military bases, instigated by whites. And white civilians assaulted black soldiers and sailors throughout the South. When the War Department issued an order in mid-1944 forbidding racial segregation in military recreation and transportation, the *Montgomery Advertiser* replied, "Army orders, even armies, even bayonets, cannot force impossible and unnatural social relations upon us."

Of course, experiences such as these caused black soldiers and sailors to wonder what, in fact, they were fighting for. Why, they asked, should they help to defend a nation that treated them like second-class citizens? They noted that the Red Cross separated blood taken from whites and blacks, as if there were some difference. But most telling was the charge that American racism was little different from German racism.

At the same time, there were positive reasons for blacks to participate in the war effort. Per-

haps this was an opportunity, as the NAACP believed, "to persuade, embarrass, compel and shame our government and our nation . . . into a more enlightened attitude toward a tenth of its people." Proclaiming that in the Second World War they were waging a "Double V" campaign (for victory at home and abroad), blacks were more militant than before, and readier than ever to protest. As a result membership in civil rights organizations soared. And in 1942 civil rights activists founded the Congress of Racial Equality (CORE).

Because of the war, blacks found new opportunities in industry. To secure defense jobs, 1.2 million blacks migrated from the South to northern and western industrial centers in the 1940s. More than half a million became members of CIO unions. As their earning power increased, so did their standard of living and political power. Indeed, urban blacks were becoming a swing vote in local, state, and presidential elections.

| *Black war workers* |

But along with the benefits of urban life came liabilities. The migrants had to make enormous emotional and cultural adjustments, and white hostility and ignorance made their task particularly difficult. In 1942 more than half of all northern whites believed that blacks should live in segregated neighborhoods and attend segregated schools. Such attitudes caused many to fear that the summer of 1943 would prove to be another Red Summer. And indeed, almost 250 racial conflicts exploded in forty-seven cities that year. Six people died and over five hundred were injured in race rioting in Harlem. In the Los Angeles Zoot Suit riot, a mob of a thousand whites assaulted blacks and Mexican-Americans in full view of Anglo policemen. Other riots erupted in Beaumont, Texas; Mobile, Alabama; and Newark, New Jersey. But the worst of these episodes bloodied the streets of Detroit in June. At the end of thirty hours of rioting, twenty-five blacks and nine whites lay dead.

| *Race riots of 1943* |

Other than taking unavoidable measures,

such as sending six thousand soldiers to patrol Detroit, a center of war manufacturing, the federal government did practically nothing to prevent further violence. From Roosevelt on down, most federal officials put the war first, domestic reform second. But this time governmental neglect could not discourage Afro-Americans and their century-old civil rights movement. By war's end they were ready to wage the struggle for voting rights and for equal access to public accommodations and institutions.

A milestone for women

If the Second World War was a watershed for Afro-Americans, it was equally or even more so for the women of America. War ended the depression era hostility toward working women. In five years, 6 million women entered the work force and the number of working women increased by 57 percent. Moreover, the typical newcomer was not a young, single woman; she was married and over thirty-five.

But statistics, no matter how impressive, tell only part of the story. There was a change in attitude toward heavy labor for women. Up to the early months of the war employers had insisted that industrial jobs were not suitable for women. "Almost overnight," said Mary Anderson, head of the Women's Bureau of the Department of Labor, "women were reclassified by industrialists from a marginal to a basic labor supply for munitions making." Women became riveters, lumberjacks ("lumberjills"), welders, crane operators, keel benders, tool makers, shell loaders, cowgirls, blast-furnace cleaners, locomotive greasers, police officers, taxi drivers, and football coaches.

Women in war production

The new employment opportunities increased women's geographical and occupational mobility. Over 7 million women moved from their original counties of residence to new locations during the war. Many of them sought jobs in the rapidly expanding aircraft industry, where they availed themselves of the opportunity to move up the occupational ladder from sewing-machine operator to welder to assembler of electronic equipment. Especially noteworthy were the gains made by black women, over 400,000 of whom quit work as domestic servants to enjoy the better working conditions, higher pay, and union benefits of industrial employment.

Public opinion quickly changed from hostility to support of women's war work. The vast majority of people queried in polls said that even more women should take jobs. Newspapers and magazines, radio and movies proclaimed Rosie the Riveter a war hero. But very few people asserted that women's war work should bring about a permanent shift in sex roles. This was merely a patriotic response to a national emergency.

Though women increased their wages when they acquired better jobs, they still received unequal pay for equal work. In 1945 women in manufacturing earned only 65 percent of what men were paid for the same job. And working women, particularly working mothers, suffered in other ways as well. Perhaps the most persistent problem was the near-absence of supportive services such as child-care centers and communal kitchens. Many women who bore the responsibility for childrearing could accept jobs only at the risk of shortchanging their children.

At the same time that millions of women and youths were entering the work force, hundreds of thousands of women were getting married. The marriage rate, which had begun to rise with the economic recovery of the mid-1930s, jumped again in 1939 with the partial return to prosperity and continued to climb during the war. From 1939 to 1942 the marriage rate rose from 73 marriages per 1,000 unmarried women to 93 per 1,000. Some couples scrambled to get married so they could spend time together before the man was sent overseas. Some doubtless married and had children to qualify for military deferments. But

Increase in marriage and divorce rates

Important events

1941 Office of Price Administration
   established
  Office of Scientific Research and
   Development established
  Japan attacks Pearl Harbor
   and United States enters
   Second World War

1942 National War Labor Board
   established
  Bataan Death March
  Allied invasion of North Africa
  Battles of Coral Sea and Midway
   halt Japanese advance
  War Production Board
   established
  Internment of 110,000 Japanese-
   Americans in "relocation
   camps"
  War Manpower Commission
   established
  Office of War Information
   established
  Manhattan Engineering District
   established to develop the
   atomic bomb

1943 Allied invasion of Italy
  Teheran Conference
  Strikes by soft-coal and anthracite
   miners

  Office of War Mobilization
   established
  Race riots in Detroit, Harlem,
   and 250 other locations

1944 War Refugee Board established
  Cross-channel landing at
   Normandy
  Dumbarton Oaks Conference
  United States retakes Philippines
  Roosevelt requests Economic Bill
   of Rights
  Supreme Court upholds Japanese-
   American internment
  Roosevelt re-elected to fourth
   term, defeating Dewey;
   Democrats retain control of
   Congress

1945 Yalta Conference
  Battles of Iwo Jima and Okinawa
  Roosevelt dies: Harry S Truman
   assumes presidency
  United Nations founded at San
   Francisco
  Russians install a Communist
   regime in Poland
  Germany surrenders
  Potsdam Conference
  Atomic bombs devastate
   Hiroshima and Nagasaki
  Japan surrenders

the rush to get married was also fueled by war-related prosperity. Along with the rise in the marriage rate was an increase in the number of divorces. In 1939, 25,000 couples secured divorces; in 1945, 485,000.

Ironically, women's efforts to hold their families together during the war posed problems for returning fathers. Women war workers had brought home the wages; they had taken over the budgeting of expenses and the writing of checks. In countless ways they had proved they could hold the reins in their husbands' absence. Some men had difficulty accepting the idea that their families could survive and even prosper without them.

For many Americans in 1945, life was fundamentally different from what it had been before Pearl Harbor. The Academy Award-winning film for 1946 was *The Best Years of Our Lives,* the painful story of the postwar readjustments of three veterans and their families and friends. Not only veterans' lives had been changed by the experiences of war; with the advent of the Cold War, millions of younger men would be inducted into the armed forces over the next thirty years. Even in peacetime young men over the age of eighteen would have to register with the Selective Service system. War and the expectation of war would become part of American life.

Suggestions for further reading

THE SECOND WORLD WAR AND DIPLOMACY A. Russell Buchanan, *The United States in World War II,* 2 vols. (1964); James MacGregor Burns, *Roosevelt: The Soldier of Freedom* (1970); Peter Calvocoressi and Guy Wint, *Total War* (1972); Diane S. Clemens, *Yalta* (1970); Robert Dallek, *Franklin D. Roosevelt and American Foreign Policy, 1932-1945* (1979); Robert A. Divine, *Roosevelt and World War II* (1969); Herbert Feis, *Churchill, Roosevelt, and Stalin* (1957); George C. Herring, *Aid to Russia, 1941-1946* (1973); Akira Iriye, *Power and Culture: The Japanese-American War, 1941-1945* (1981); Gabriel Kolko, *The Politics of War* (1968); William H. McNeill, *America, Britain, and Russia* (1953); Vojtech Mastny, *Russia's Road to the Cold War* (1979); Samuel Eliot Morison, *The Two-Ocean War* (1963); Arthur D. Morse, *While Six Million Died* (1968); Gaddis Smith, *Diplomacy during the Second World War, 1941-1945* (1965); Mark Stoler, *The Politics of the Second Front* (1977); Gordon Wright, *The Ordeal of Total War, 1939-1945* (1968).

THE HOME FRONT John Morton Blum, *V Was for Victory: Politics and American Culture during World War II* (1976); Jim F. Heath, "Domestic America during World War II: Research Opportunities for Historians," *Journal of American History,* 58 (1971), 384-414; Richard R. Lingeman, *Don't You Know There's a War On? The American Home Front, 1941-*

1945 (1970); Geoffrey Perrett, *Days of Sadness, Years of Triumph: The American People, 1939-1945* (1973); Richard Polenberg, *War and Society: The United States, 1941-1945* (1972).

ECONOMIC MOBILIZATION FOR WAR Bruce Catton, *The War Lords of Washington* (1948); George Q. Flynn, *The Mess in Washington: Manpower Mobilization in World War II* (1979); Eliot Janeway, *The Struggle for Survival* (1951); Paul A. C. Koistinen, *The Hammer and the Sword: Labor, the Military, and Industrial Mobilization, 1920-1945* (1979); Donald Nelson, *Arsenal of Democracy* (1946); Gerald T. White, *Billions for Defense: Government Finance by the Defense Plant Corporation during World War II* (1980).

FARMERS, SOLDIERS, AND WORKERS Melvyn Dubofsky and Warren H. Van Tine, *John L. Lewis: A Biography* (1977); Joel Seidman, *American Labor from Defense to Reconversion* (1953); Samuel A. Stouffer *et al., The American Soldier* (1949); Walter W. Wilcox, *The Farmer in the Second World War* (1947).

STATE AND LOCAL HISTORY Lowell J. Carr and James E. Stermer, *Willow Run: A Study of Industrialization and Cultural Inadequacy* (1952); Alan Clive, *State of War: Michigan in World War II* (1979); Philip J. Funigiello, *The Challenge to Urban Liberalism: Federal-City Relations during World War II* (1978); Robert J. Havighurst and H. Gerthon Morgan, *The Social History of a War-Boom Community* (1951).

JAPANESE-AMERICAN INTERNMENT Roger Daniels, *Concentration Camps U.S.A.: Japanese Americans and World War II* (1971); Bill Hosokawa, *Nisei: The Quiet Americans* (1969); Jacobus ten-Broek *et al., Prejudice, War and the Constitution: Causes and Consequences of the Evacuation of the Japanese Americans in World War II* (1954); Michi Weglyn, *Years of Infamy: The Untold Story of America's Concentration Camps* (1976).

POLITICS James C. Foster, *The Union Politic: The CIO Political Action Committee* (1975); Roland Young, *Congressional Politics in the Second World War* (1956).

AFRO-AMERICANS A. Russell Buchanan, *Black Americans in World War II* (1977); Richard M. Dalfiume, *Desegregation of the U.S. Armed Forces: Fighting on Two Fronts, 1939-1953* (1969); Lee Finkle, *Forum*

for Protest: The Black Press during World War II
(1975); Harvard Sitkoff, "Racial Militancy and Interracial Violence in the Second World War," *Journal of
American History*, 58 (1971), 661–681; Neil A. Wynn,
The Afro-American and the Second World War (1976).

WOMEN Karen Anderson, *Wartime Women: Sex
Roles, Family Relations, and the Status of Women during
World War II* (1981); William H. Chafe, *The American Woman: Her Changing Social, Economic, and Political Roles, 1920–1970* (1972); Leila J. Rupp, *Mobilizing
Women for War: German and American Propaganda,
1939–1945* (1978).

27

COLD WAR POLITICS
AND FOREIGN POLICY,
1945–1961

The insult stung deeply and was not soon forgotten. In August 1955, the ambassador from India, G. L. Mehta, walked into a restaurant at the Houston International Airport, sat down, and waited to order. But Texas law required that whites and blacks be served in separate dining facilities. The dark-skinned diplomat, who had seated himself in a white-only area, was told to move.

From Washington, D.C., Secretary of State John Foster Dulles telegraphed his apologies, fearful that the incident would injure relations with a nation whose allegiance the United States was seeking in the fight against communism. Such embarrassments were common in the postwar era. Segregationist practices, Dulles complained, were becoming a "major international hazard," a threat to United States efforts to gain the friendship of new nations in Asia, the Middle East, and Africa. Thus when the attorney general appealed to the Supreme Court to strike down segregation in public schools, his introductory remarks took note of the international implications. The humiliation of dark-skinned diplomats, he said, "furnished grist for the Communist propaganda mills." When the Court finally did order school desegregation in the 1954 *Brown* decision, the Voice of America, a United States propaganda agency, quickly broadcast the good news overseas in thirty-five different languages.

American concern over the repercussions of segregation abroad reflected a change in the international distribution of power. In the years following the Second World War, the United States, which had emerged from the war the most powerful nation on earth, moved to center stage in international relations. "We are now concerned with the peace of the entire world," General and later Secretary of State George C. Marshall said in 1945. This new attitude, called globalism, reflected lessons learned during the depression and the war: that events in faraway places seriously affect American prosperity and security; and that the United States must possess the power to thwart threats to its overseas interests. Unfortunately, the new perspective also helped to spawn a new kind of crisis, the postwar Soviet-American diplomatic confrontation called the Cold War. In this new conflict, competitive propaganda, reconstruction programs, alliances, atomic arms development, and spheres of influence condemned the world once again to instability and fear. Just five years after the Second World War, armed conflict erupted again on the peninsula of Korea.

At home, the nation reconverted from war to peace under the new president, Harry S Truman.

433

The economic transition was not smooth. And in the Cold War atmosphere, politics proved volatile; black civil rights and an anticommunist witch-hunt called McCarthyism were the most highly charged issues. The outbreak of the Korean War in 1950 enhanced domestic discontent. In 1952 Americans rejected the Democratic candidate and cast their votes for the popular General Dwight D. Eisenhower.

Like his predecessor, Eisenhower had to deal with Korea, McCarthyism, civil rights struggles, and corruption. The Korean question was settled early in his first term, and in 1954 Senator McCarthy was condemned by his colleagues in the Senate. During the rest of Eisenhower's eight-year presidency the nation seemed quiescent both politically and intellectually. But Soviet-American relations remained tense as the Cold War moved through thaws and freezes, the nuclear arms race accelerated, and the United States intervened in the affairs of developing nations.

Origins of the Cold War

At the close of the Second World War, diplomats gazed out over a vastly altered international landscape. In country after country political affairs were in disarray, as right and left struggled to re-establish a semblance of authority. With the European countries in political tumult and economic crisis, their Asian colonies began to break away. For the great powers, there were friends to be won and strategic and economic interests at stake in the outcomes of these contests. And the economic reconstruction of the rubble-strewn nations of Europe and Asia also stimulated competition between the great powers.

But more important, with Japan and Germany eliminated as centers of power, with Britain and France hobbled, Russia and America now began acting as if in a vacuum. The two nations clashed constantly, "like two big dogs chewing on a bone," as Senator J. William Fulbright remarked. This bipolar structure of power would be one of the Second World War's lasting legacies.

The existence of the newly developed atomic bomb heightened U.S.–Soviet tension. Indeed, diplomatic considerations had sped the decision to drop the bomb on Hiroshima and Nagasaki. Truman and his advisers had envisioned the real and psychological power the bomb would bestow on the United States. It might serve as a deterrent against aggression; it might intimidate Russia into making concessions in Eastern Europe; it might end the war in the Pacific before Russia could claim a role in the management of Asia.

Atomic diplomacy

The Russians were alert to such thinking. It was hardly a secret that Secretary of State James F. Byrnes liked to use the implied threat of the bomb during Soviet-American negotiations. Retiring Secretary of War Henry L. Stimson was among the few who opposed the use of the bomb in this way. He told the president in September 1945, if Americans continued to have "this weapon rather ostentatiously on our hip, their [the Russians'] suspicions and their distrust of our purposes and motives will increase."

Suspicions and distrust were the stuff of the emerging Cold War. In an economically devastated world, Russians and Americans glared at one another, shouted at one another, and supplied client states with the weaponry to fight one another. Each sought leadership in reassembling world order; each sought to build up its own sphere of influence; each was driven by an ideology and a sense of righteousness.

Why did American leaders become active participants in this fierce contest? For one thing, they were determined never to repeat the experiences of the 1930s. No more Munichs, no more appeasement, they vowed. It seemed to many that Nazi Germany had merely been replaced by Soviet Russia, that communism was simply the other side of the totalitarian coin. The popular term "Red fascism" captured this sentiment. In short, the United States intended to challenge countries it perceived to be expansionist, like the Soviet Union.

American decision makers also knew that the nation's economic well-being depended on an activist foreign policy. In the postwar years the United States was the largest supplier of goods to world markets. Indeed, exports constituted about 10 percent of the gross national product; tied to this export trade were the jobs of workers who produced the export items. And without the profits from exports, the United States could not afford to import strategic raw materials. Economic expansion thus remained a central feature of postwar foreign relations.

New strategic theory also propelled the United States toward an activist, expansionist, globalist diplomacy. To be ready for a military challenge in the postwar air age, the nation's defense had to begin far beyond its own borders. Thus the United States had to acquire overseas air bases. And where would its navy float? "Wherever there is a sea," Navy Secretary James Forrestal declared.

President Truman shared these assumptions. And his personality tended to increase the tension that characterized post-

| Truman as Cold Warrior |

war international relations. Critics said Truman's curt style hampered negotiations. He seldom displayed the appreciation of subtleties so essential to successful diplomacy; for him issues were sketched in black and white, not shades of gray. After his first meeting with the Soviet V. M. Molotov, Truman commented: "I gave it to him straight 'one-two to the jaw.' I let him have it straight." This simplistic display of toughness became a trademark of American Cold War diplomacy.

As for the Soviets, they were not easy to get along with either. Dean Acheson, a high-ranking diplomat from 1945 to 1947 and secretary of

| Provocative Soviet actions |

state from 1949 to 1953, found them rude and abusive. Indeed, Premier Stalin's blunt *nyets* stung American ears. The Soviets also annoyed Americans by walking out of meetings, arguing the same point over and over

again, and sometimes changing positions abruptly. But more than Soviet style bothered Americans. In occupied Eastern Europe Russian officials did not hesitate to suppress non-Communists in conspicuous shows of military might and political manipulation. Americans were outraged.

For their part, the Russians remembered how the West had ostracized them before. Driven by memories of the past, by fear of a revived Germany, by the huge task of reconstruction, and by Marxist-Leninist doctrine, the Soviets suspected capitalist nations of plotting once again to extinguish the Communist flame. If Americans feared "Communist aggression," Russians feared "capitalist encirclement." In mirror image, each side saw the other as the aggressor, the obstacle to peace.

"After World War II," Senator Fulbright remembered, "we were sold on the idea that Stalin was out to dominate the world." This globalist point of view, common among historians in the 1950s, pitted a generous United States against a selfish Soviet Union. But Fulbright came to believe, as have many so-called revisionist histo-

| Revisionist interpretation of the Cold War |

rians, that Americans exaggerated the Soviet menace. Russia had neither the resources nor, apparently, the intention of dominating the world; it was a regional power in Eastern Europe. Americans perceived the Soviet threat as global largely because they fixed their attention on the utopian Communist aim of world revolution rather than on actual Soviet behavior.

The Cold War and containment in Europe and the Mideast, 1945–1950

The United States and Russia moved from one crisis to another in the aftermath of the war.

The first clash came in Poland in 1945, when the Russians refused to admit conservative Poles from London to the Lublin government, as agreed at Yalta. The Russians also snuffed out civil liberties in the former Nazi satellite of Rumania. And after allowing free elections in Hungary and Czechoslovakia, they supported Communist coups in both nations. First Hungary (1947) and then Czechoslovakia (1948) succumbed to Communist subversion.

The two adversaries also collided in Iran. By wartime agreement, British, American, and Russian troops occupied Iran.

| Crisis in Iran |

When American petroleum companies asked the Iranian government for an oil concession, Moscow sniffed a capitalist plot on its border. In March 1946, the date agreed on for troop withdrawal, the Russians stayed on in violation of the wartime treaty. Americans angrily accused the U.S.S.R. of intending to take over Iran. Iranian and Soviet diplomats managed to negotiate a settlement in April: Soviet soldiers would depart from Iran in exchange for an oil concession. Americans claimed a Cold War victory, believing their tough words had forced the Soviets to withdraw their troops. In 1947 they turned the tables by persuading the Iranians to go back on their promise of a Russian oil concession. Moscow cried that it had been double-crossed.

Soviets and Americans clashed on every front in 1946. They could not agree on the unification of Germany, so they built up their zones independently. Efforts to establish international control of atomic energy failed. (The American Baruch Plan would have denied Russia the right to develop its own bomb while the United States kept its own.) Even the new World Bank and International Monetary Fund, created at the 1944 Bretton Woods Conference to stabilize trade and finance, became tangled in the Cold War struggle. The Soviets refused to join because the United States so dominated both institutions. In early 1946 Washington unilaterally extended a $3.5 billion loan to Great Britain but turned down a similar Soviet request.

When in early February 1946 Stalin gave a pre-election speech depicting a world threatened by capitalist acquisitiveness, the American chargé d'affaires in Moscow, George F. Kennan, concluded that Russian fanaticism made even a temporary understanding impossible. Kennan's pessimistic telegram to Washington, which was widely read, fed the growing belief that only toughness would work with the Russians. A few weeks later Winston Churchill made his stirring Iron Curtain speech, warning that Eastern European countries were being cut off from the West by Russia.

The Cold War expanded further on March 12, 1947. In response to a request from the British, who could no longer afford to fund their Greek client government against Communist-

| Truman Doctrine |

led rebels, the president went to Congress and in alarmist language asked for $400 million in aid to Greece and Turkey. The United States must help "free peoples who are resisting attempted subjugation by armed minorities or by outside pressure," Truman declared; it was time to contain communism. The president's statement became known as the Truman Doctrine. There was no evidence that the Soviets were involved in the Greek civil war. Nevertheless the money was appropriated and the insurgents defeated.

In July 1947 George F. Kennan offered another statement of what became known as the containment doctrine. Writing under the name "Mr. X" in the magazine *Foreign Affairs,* this expert on Soviet affairs advocated a "policy of firm containment, designed to confront the Russians with unalterable counterforce at every point where they show signs of encroaching upon the interests of a peaceful and stable world." Together with the Truman Doctrine, Kennan's article became the chief manifesto of Cold War foreign policy. Critic Walter Lippmann complained that the policy did not distinguish between areas vital and peripheral to American security.

Lippmann was happier with the Marshall Plan. On June 5, 1947, Secretary of State

George C. Marshall announced that the United States would finance a massive European Recovery Program. Though Marshall did not exclude Eastern Europe or the Soviet Union, few American leaders believed that Russia would want to

| Marshall Plan | join an American project. Congress voted overwhelmingly for the necessary funds. Launched in 1948, the Marshall Plan poured $13 billion into Western Europe before it ended in 1952 (see map, page 438). To stimulate business at home, the plan provided that the foreign aid dollars had to be spent in the United States. The recovery program helped revive Western Europe and gave way to military assistance in 1951. By 1952, in fact, 80 percent of American aid to Western Europe was military in nature.

To strengthen the nation's defenses, Truman worked with Congress to streamline the government's administrative structure under the National Security Act (July 1947). The act created the Department of Defense (replacing the War Department), the National Security Council (NSC) to advise the president, and the Central Intelligence Agency (CIA) to conduct spying and information gathering. By the early 1950s the CIA had expanded its functions to include covert (secret) operations aimed at overthrowing unfriendly foreign leaders.

One of the most electric moments in the Cold War came in June 1948, when the Russians cut off Western access to the jointly occupied city of Berlin, located well inside the Soviet zone of Germany. Before the Soviets' bold move, the Americans, French, and British had agreed to fuse their zones. The three allies planned to integrate the new West Germany, including the three Western sectors of Berlin, into the Western European economy, complete with a reformed German currency. The Soviets, fearing a resurgent Germany tied to the American Cold War camp, may have sparked the Berlin crisis to stimulate negotiations. But if they thought Truman would compromise, they guessed wrong. Instead the president ordered a massive airlift of food, fuel, and other supplies to the isolated city—a plane almost every min-

ute. Finally, in May 1949, their image badly damaged, the Soviets lifted the blockade. They had stimulated the very thing they feared, the creation of the Federal Republic of Germany (West Germany) that month. In retaliation they founded the German Democratic Republic (East Germany). As for the United States, it claimed another victory for toughness.

On April 4, 1949, believing that a military shield should be added to the economic shield of the Marshall Plan, the United States, Canada, and much of Western Europe founded the North Atlantic Treaty Organization (NATO). The treaty aroused considerable debate at home,

| Creation of NATO | for not since 1778 had the United States joined a formal European military alliance. Critics feared that the treaty would provoke Russia, cause American troops to be stationed in Europe, and allow the president to commit forces to combat without a declaration of war. Truman responded that NATO would give Europeans the will to resist communism. And it would function as a "tripwire," bringing the full military and atomic force of the United States to bear on the Soviet Union if it dared to cross the East-West line. The Senate ratified the treaty, as it did all Truman's major foreign policy requests.

The American nuclear monopoly ended in 1949 when the Soviets exploded an atomic bomb. Early in 1950 President Truman ordered the production of the hydrogen bomb. And in May Congress finally endorsed funds for technical assistance to developing nations, to draw them into the American sphere of influence (a plan called the Point Four Program, after point 4 of Truman's 1949 inaugural address).

A month before, the National Security Council had delivered to the president a top-secret document numbered NSC-68. Predicting con-

| NSC-68 | tinued tension with the Communists and describing a "shrinking world of polarized power," the report appealed for an enlarged military budget to counter the Soviet global design American strategists mistakenly believed existed. Adminis-

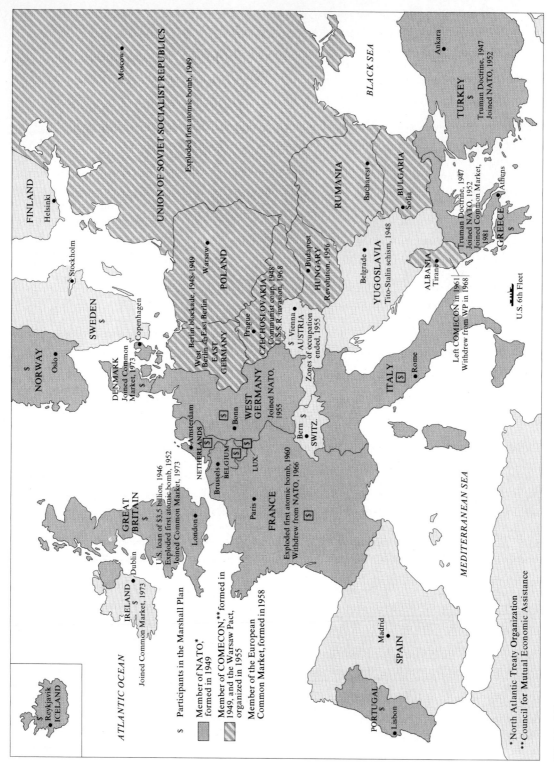

Divided Europe

ATLANTIC OCEAN

ICELAND
$
Reykjavik
Joined Common Market, 1973

IRELAND
$
Dublin

GREAT
BRITAIN
London
U.S. loan of $3.5 billion, 1946
Exploded first atomic bomb, 1952
Joined Common Market, 1973

NORWAY
$
Oslo

SWEDEN
$
Stockholm

FINLAND
Helsinki

DENMARK
Joined Common
Market, 1973
Copenhagen

UNION OF SOVIET SOCIALIST REPUBLICS
Moscow
Exploded first atomic bomb, 1949

NETHERLANDS
Amsterdam
$

BELGIUM
Brussels
$

LUX
$

WEST
GERMANY
Bonn
$
Joined NATO,
1955

EAST
GERMANY
Berlin blockade, 1948-1949
West
Berlin East Berlin

POLAND
Warsaw

Prague
CZECHOSLOVAKIA
Communist coup, 1948
U.S.S.R. invasion, 1968

FRANCE
Paris
$
Exploded first atomic bomb, 1960
Withdrew from NATO, 1966

SWITZ.
Bern $

AUSTRIA
Vienna $
Zones of occupation
ended, 1955

HUNGARY
Budapest
Revolution, 1956

RUMANIA
Bucharest

YUGOSLAVIA
Belgrade
Tito-Stalin schism, 1948

BULGARIA
Sofia

ALBANIA
Tirane
Left COMECON in 1961
Withdrew from WP in 1968

BLACK SEA

TURKEY
Ankara
Truman Doctrine, 1947
Joined NATO, 1952

GREECE
Athens
Truman Doctrine, 1947
Joined NATO, 1952
Joined Common Market,
1981

ITALY
Rome
$

SPAIN
Madrid

PORTUGAL
$
Lisbon

MEDITERRANEAN SEA

U.S. 6th Fleet

Participants in the Marshall Plan

$

Member of NATO,*
formed in 1949

Member of COMECON,** formed in**
1949, and the Warsaw Pact,
organized in 1955

Member of the European
Common Market, formed in 1958

*North Atlantic Treaty Organization
**Council for Mutual Economic Assistance

438

tration officials worried about how to sell this strong prescription to the voters and budget-conscious congressional representatives. "We were sweating over it, and then—with regard to NSC-68—thank God Korea came along," recalled one of Acheson's aides.

The Cold War in Asia, 1945–1951

When the Korean War erupted in mid-1950, it came in the wake of vast changes in Asia. The Second World War accelerated the process of decolonization begun during the First World War. Occupied with defending themselves and then with rebuilding after the war, mother countries were no longer able to resist their colonies' demands for independence. Britain gave up India and what is now Pakistan in 1947, Burma and Ceylon in 1948. And the Dutch reluctantly let go of Indonesia in 1949. The French fought on in Indochina, finally retiring from that outpost in 1954.

The defeat of Japan brought about the division of its empire among the victors. Korea was divided between the United States and the Soviet Union. The Pacific islands (the Marshalls, Marianas, and Carolines) came under American control. Half of Sakhalin went to Russia as agreed at Yalta, and Formosa (Taiwan) was returned to the Chinese. As for Japan itself, the United States monopolized its reconstruction. General Douglas MacArthur, the director of the

| Reconstruction of Japan | American occupation, wrote a democratic constitution for Japan, revitalized its economy, and destroyed the weapons and warships of the Japanese military.

Though United States supremacy in Japan was an established fact, the Russians would not recognize it. Thus, after squabbling with Russia for years over a peace treaty with Japan, the United States finally signed a separate peace in 1951. The treaty restored Japan's sovereignty, ended the occupation, granted the United States a military base at Okinawa, and permitted American troops to be stationed in Japan. Tokyo and Washington also initialed a defense pact. The people who had been called beasts after their surprise attack on Pearl Harbor were now American allies.

Meanwhile, America's Chinese allies were faltering. The United States was feeding and fueling Jiang Jieshi's (Chiang Kai-shek's) Nationalist armies in their battle against Mao Zedong (Mao Tse-tung) and Zhou Enlai's (Chou Enlai's) Communists. Despite $3 billion in American aid from 1945 to 1949, however, Jiang proved a weak and unreliable friend. His government was both corrupt and out of touch with the peasants, who were attracted by Communist promises of land reform.

Still, American leaders saw Jiang as the only viable alternative to Mao. In the *White Paper* of 1949—a long government report on America's efforts to contain communism through aid to Jiang—Secretary Acheson asserted that the "Communist leaders have . . . publicly announced their subservience to a foreign power." Thus the United States rejected overtures for talks from the Chinese Communists. But Americans overestimated Mao's dependence on Russia. The Soviets had given Mao little support; indeed they preferred a weak China under Jiang to a strong one under Mao. Truman's refusal to allow talks with the Communists, however, left Mao little choice; he leaned toward the Soviets.

Following his defeat in the fall of 1949, Jiang fled to the island of Formosa, and Mao proclaimed the People's Republic of China. For several reasons the United States

| Nonrecognition of the People's Republic of China | decided not to recognize the new government. First, American officials were alarmed by a new Sino-Soviet treaty of friendship (1950). Second, Mao's followers had seized American-owned property in China. Third, Mao was now openly hostile toward the United States. Finally, a noisy group of

Republican critics, called the China lobby, were attacking the Truman administration for having "lost" China. The United States would not recognize the People's Republic of China until 1979.

Reaching for some way to offset Jiang's collapse, the National Security Council urged the president to fortify "friendly and independent" states in Asia as a bulwark against Communist expansion. In February 1950 the United States recognized the French puppet regime of Bao Dai in Vietnam, and a few months later decided to extend aid to the beleaguered French there. In April the National Security Council sent the president its alarming report NSC-68. And in May more funds went to Jiang Jieshi in Formosa.

Postwar adjustments at home, 1945–1946

As the Truman administration struggled with the Cold War abroad, it also faced the huge task of economic conversion from war to peace.

| Postwar job layoffs | Even before the war ended, cutbacks in production had caused layoffs. Ten days after

the victory over Japan, 1.8 million people received pink slips and 640,000 filed for unemployment compensation. The peak of postwar unemployment came in March 1946, when 2.7 million people were seeking work.

Despite these figures, the United States was not teetering on the brink of depression in 1945; in fact, it had blasted off into a quarter-century of unprecedented boom. People had plenty of savings to spend in 1945, and suddenly there were new houses and cars for them to buy. Easy credit and new war-inspired industries like synthetic rubber and electronics promoted the buying spree. As a result, though war production began to wind down in 1944, the gross national product continued to rise in 1945. Thus the na-

tion's postwar problem was not depression; it was inflation. Throughout 1945 and 1946 prices skyrocketed; the inflation rate for 1946 was 18.2 percent.

Truman declared his determination to combat both unemployment and inflation. On September 6, 1945, he delivered to Congress a

| Truman's reconversion plan | 21-point message urging extension of unemployment compensation; an increase in the minimum wage; adop-

tion of permanent farm-price supports; and new public works projects. Truman revived Roosevelt's Economic Bill of Rights: every able-bodied American, he declared, had a right to a job. Should the economy fail to provide one, the government should create one. At the same time, Truman warned of the danger of inflation.

Congress responded to Truman's message with the Employment Act of 1946, which announced that the government would use all its resources, including deficit spending if necessary, to achieve "maximum employment, production, and purchasing power." The act established the three-person Council of Economic Advisers to assist the president. Though Congress had deleted a commitment to full employment, Truman nevertheless touted the legislation as the beginning of the Fair Deal, the name he gave his domestic program.

Meanwhile, though prices were rising, many people were earning less than they had during the war. The wartime Little Steel formula had limited workers to cost-of-living pay increases, and the end of war production had eliminated much of their overtime work. But while wages and salaries had declined slightly in 1946, net

| Upsurge in labor strikes | profits had reached all-time highs. Indignant that they were not sharing in the in-

creased prosperity, over 4.5 million men and women left their jobs to strike in 1946. Workers forced nationwide shutdowns in the coal, automobile, steel, and electric industries and halted railroad and maritime transportation.

John L. Lewis's United Mine Workers was among the most powerful unions to walk off the job. Coal was the nation's primary source of energy in 1946; when soft-coal production stopped on April 1, steel and automobile output plummeted, railroad service was canceled, and thousands of people were laid off. Though the miners' demands were legitimate—higher wages, a federal safety code, and a royalty of ten cents per ton to finance health services and welfare and pension funds—a two-week truce in May failed to produce a solution. On May 21 Truman ordered the seizure of the mines. Lewis and the government reached an accord a week later and the miners returned to work. But within six months the agreement had collapsed, and once again the government seized the mines.

There was no doubt about the growing unpopularity of labor unions and their leadership. In 1946 Truman seized the railroads, over a hundred meat-packing plants, a couple of dozen oil-refining companies, and even the tugboats in New York harbor. Public opinion backed him up. A 1946 Gallup poll, for example, indicated that 66 percent of those interviewed favored more laws to control labor.

Truman's attack on the unions

Truman had hopped aboard the antiunion bandwagon in May. In a dramatic appearance before Congress, he asked for authority to draft into the military strikers who refused to honor a presidential order to return to work. Truman's speech alienated union members in general. Many dedicated themselves to defeating him in the 1948 elections.

Truman fared little better in his direction of the Office of Price Administration. Now that the war was over, powerful interests wanted OPA controls lifted. Consumers were impatient with shortages and black-market prices, and manufacturers and farmers wanted to jack up prices legally. Yet when most controls expired in mid-1946 and inflation spiraled higher, people became angry.

Consumer discontent

Republicans made the most of public discontent. "Got enough meat?" asked Republican Congressman John M. Vorys of Ohio. "Got enough houses? Got enough OPA? . . . Got enough inflation? . . . Got enough debt? . . . Got enough strikes?" When the votes were tabulated, the Republicans had won a majority in both houses of the Eightieth Congress. The White House in 1948 seemed within their grasp.

The Eightieth Congress and the election of 1948

The politicians who ruled the Eightieth Congress, both Republicans and southern Democrats, were committed conservatives. Although they supported Truman's foreign policy, they perceived the Republican landslide as a mandate to reverse the New Deal. For Truman, working with the Eightieth Congress would be an unsuccessful and a frustrating experience. Ironically, congressional actions would help to elect Truman in 1948.

For if the president had angered union members, farmers, and liberals, the new Congress made them livid. One extremely unpopular measure was the Taft-Hartley Act, which Congress adopted over Truman's veto in 1947. A revision of the Wagner Act of 1935, the bill prohibited union use of the closed shops, in which only union members could be hired. Moreover, the Taft-Hartley Act forbade union contributions to political funds in federal elections; required union leaders to sign non-Communist affidavits; and mandated an eighty-day cooling-off period in strikes that imperiled the national security. Because the act became a touchstone distinguishing supporters of labor from opponents, Truman's veto of the bill vindicated him in the eyes of organized labor.

Taft-Hartley Act

Throughout 1947 and into 1948 the Eightieth Congress offended numerous interest groups, which in turn swung back to Truman. For example, the president asked Congress for continued price supports for farmers; the

So few pollsters predicted that President Harry S Truman (1884–1972) would win in 1948 that the *Chicago Tribune* announced his defeat before all the returns were in. Here a victorious Truman pokes fun at the newspaper for its premature headline.   UPI.

Eightieth Congress responded with weakened price supports. The president requested nationwide health insurance; the Eightieth Congress refused. It was the same with federal funding of public housing and aid to public education; with broadened and increased unemployment compensation, old-age and survivors' benefits, and the minimum wage; and with antilynching, anti–poll tax, and fair-employment legislation. Truman proposed; Congress rejected or ignored his requests.

But Republicans seemed oblivious to public opinion. Not since 1928 had they been so confident of capturing the presidency, and most political experts agreed. "Only a political miracle," stated *Time,* "or extraordinary stupidity on the part of the Republicans can save the Democratic party." At their national convention, Republicans strengthened their position by nominating for president and vice president the governors of the nation's two most populous states: Thomas E. Dewey of New York and Earl Warren of California.

Election of 1948

Truman, who received the Democratic nomination, found himself fighting more than just Republicans. Leftist elements of the party, especially those critical of the Truman Doctrine, started a new Progressive party under the leadership of former vice president Henry Wallace. Segregationists, angered over the Democratic party's adoption of a civil rights plank, formed the States Rights Democratic party (Dixiecrats) and nominated Governor Strom Thurmond of South Carolina. If Wallace's candidacy did not destroy Truman's chances, experts said, the Dixiecrats certainly would.

But Truman had ideas of his own. He called

the Eightieth Congress into special session and demanded that it enact all the planks in the Republican platform. If Republicans really wanted to transform their ideals into law, said Truman, this was the time to do it. After Congress had met for two weeks and accomplished nothing of significance, Truman took to the road. Traveling more than 30,000 miles by train, he delivered scores of whistle-stop speeches denouncing the "do-nothing" Eightieth Congress. Still, no amount of furious campaigning on Truman's part seemed likely to change the predicted outcome. Hours before the returns were in, the *Chicago Tribune* announced, "DEWEY DEFEATS TRUMAN."

Yet as the votes were counted early into the morning, it became clear that Truman had confounded the experts. The final tally was 24.1 million popular and 304 electoral votes for Truman; 21.9 million popular and 189 electoral votes for Dewey. Not only had Truman won four more years in the White House, but the Democrats had regained control of Congress—in the House by a majority of ninety-three, in the Senate by twelve.

Truman on civil rights

The postwar years were a period of gathering strength for Afro-Americans. Truman and other politicians knew they would have to compete for the growing black vote in urban-industrial states like California, Illinois, Michigan, Ohio, Pennsylvania, and New York. Many Republicans now cultivated the black vote. Thomas Dewey, who as governor of New York had pushed successfully for the establishment of a fair employment practices commission, was particularly popular with blacks. In Harlem, which had gone Democratic by a 4 to 1 margin in 1938, Dewey won by large margins in 1942 and 1946.

Political reality may have made Truman aware of the black vote, but what also caused

him to act was a report that police in Aiken, South Carolina, had gouged out the eyes of a black sergeant just three hours after he had been discharged from the army. Several weeks later Truman signed an executive order establishing the President's Committee on Civil Rights.

A year later the committee delivered its report, *To Secure These Rights,* to the president.

| President's Committee on Civil Rights |

Among the committee's recommendations, which would become the agenda for the civil rights movement for the next twenty years, were the enactment of federal antilynching, antisegregation, antibrutality, and anti–poll-tax laws. *To Secure These Rights* also called for law guaranteeing voting rights and equal employment opportunity, and for the establishment of a permanent commission on civil rights and a civil rights division within the Department of Justice. Congress failed to act, but for the first time since Reconstruction, a president acknowledged the federal government's responsibility to protect Afro-Americans.

Truman also used the power of the executive to proclaim a policy of "fair employment throughout the federal establishment." And his Committee on Equality of Treatment and Opportunity in the Armed Services issued a report, *Freedom to Serve,* in 1950 stating that racial desegregation would "make for a better Army, Navy, and Air Force." Though strong opposition to desegregation existed within the military, by the outbreak of the Korean War segregated units were becoming a thing of the past.

Blacks also benefited from a series of Supreme Court decisions. The trend toward judicial support of civil rights had begun in the late 1930s,

| Supreme Court decisions on civil rights |

when the NAACP established its Legal Defense Fund. At the time the NAACP was trying to destroy the separate-but-equal doctrine by insisting on its literal interpretation. The NAACP calculated that in higher education the cost of racially separate schools was prohibitive. "You can't build a cyclotron for one [black] student," the president of the University of Oklahoma acknowledged. Through legal action the NAACP was able to secure the admission of black students into a number of professional and graduate schools in the 1940s. And in *Smith* v. *Allwright* (1944) the NAACP's attorneys convinced the Supreme Court to abolish the whites-only primaries held in several southern states. Two years later in *Morgan* v. *Virginia* the Supreme Court outlawed segregation in interstate bus transportation. Of comparable significance was the 1947 decision of the Justice Department to submit friend-of-the-court briefs on behalf of the civil rights movement.

A change in social attitudes accompanied these gains in black political and legal power. Books such as Gunnar Myrdal's *An American Dilemma* (1944) and Richard Wright's *Native Son* (1940) and *Black Boy* (1945) had increased white awareness of the social injustice that plagued blacks. A new black middle class had emerged, composed of college-educated activists, veterans, and union workers. Blacks and whites were working together in CIO unions and with service organizations such as the National Council of Churches. And in 1947 a black baseball player, Jackie Robinson, cracked the major-league color barrier and electrified crowds with his spectacular plays at second base.

McCarthyism

A common misperception of the postwar era is that anti-Communist hysteria began in 1950 with the furious speeches of Senator Joseph R. McCarthy. Actually, anticommunism had been part of the American political temper every since the First World War and the Red Scare of 1919 and 1920. McCarthy did not create it; he manipulated it to his own advantage. Undeniably, though, he was the most successful and frightening redbaiter the country had ever seen.

To a great extent President Truman initiated the postwar crusade against communism. Truman was concerned over the wartime increase in the nation's Communist party membership (80,000 in 1943–1944) and by the revelation in 1945 that classified government documents had been found in the offices of *Amerasia,* a little-known magazine whose editors sympathized with the Chinese Communists. He was also bothered by a report that Soviet spies were operating in Canada.

Spurred by these revelations, Truman in March 1947 ordered investigations into the loyalty of the more than 3 million employees of the U.S. government. In 1950 the government began discharging people deemed "security risks." Some were purged for homosexuality or alcoholism; others became victims of guilt by association. None were allowed to confront their accusers.

Truman's loyalty probe

The wellspring of this fear of communism was the Cold War, and Truman was not alone in peddling fear. Conservatives and liberal Democrats joined him. Republicans used the same technique to attack the Democratic candidates for president in 1948 and 1952; liberal Democrats used it to discredit the far-left, pro-Wallace wing of their party. In other words, rather than being a bottom-up grassroots movement, the anti-Communist hysteria of the late 1940s was largely a top-down phenomenon created by professional politicians.

Despite the false accusations, there was some real cause for concern—especially in 1949. In that year, the Russians exploded their first atomic bomb, and the Chinese Communists, finally victorious in the civil war, proclaimed the People's Republic of China. Furthermore, in 1949, a former State Department official, Alger Hiss, was on trial for denying that he had passed to the Russians "numerous secret, confidential and restricted documents." When Truman and Secretary of State Dean Acheson came to his defense,

Hiss trial

some people began to suspect that the Democrats had something to hide. In 1950 Hiss was convicted of perjury. That same year the British arrested Klaus Fuchs, a nuclear scientist, for providing Soviet agents with secrets from the atomic-bomb project at Los Alamos, New Mexico.

It was in this atmosphere that Senator Joseph McCarthy mounted a rostrum in Wheeling, West Virginia, and gave the existing state of mind a name: McCarthyism. The State Department, he asserted, was "thoroughly infested with Communists," and the most dangerous person in the State Department was Dean Acheson. Reporters wrote that the senator claimed to have a list of 205 Communists working in the State Department; later McCarthy lowered the figure to "57 card-carrying members," then raised it to 81. No matter the number; what McCarthy needed was a winning campaign issue, and he had found it. Republicans, distraught over losing what had appeared to be a sure victory in 1948, were eager to support his attack.

McCarthy's attack on the State Department

The widespread support for anti-Communist measures was apparent in the adoption, over Truman's veto, of the Internal Security, or McCarran, Act of 1950. The act made it unlawful for anyone to "contribute to the establishment . . . of a totalitarian dictatorship," required members of "Communist-front" organizations to register with the government, and prohibited such people from holding defense jobs or traveling abroad. And in a telling decision in 1951 *(Dennis et al.* v. *U.S.),* the Supreme Court upheld the Smith Act, a law passed in 1940 making it illegal to support or belong to an organization advocating the overthrow of the government by force, and ordered the imprisonment of eleven American Communist leaders.

McCarthy and McCarthyism gained momentum throughout 1950. Nothing seemed to slow the senator down, not even attacks by other

As a member of the House Committee on Un-American Activities, Congressman Richard M. Nixon (1913–   ) of California had led the investigation into the Alger Hiss case. In December 1948 Nixon (right) and the committee's chief investigator, Robert L. Stripling, viewed microfilm copies of government papers that Hiss had allegedly given to Wittaker Chambers, a confessed ex-Communist. Wide World Photos.

Republicans. Seven Republican senators broke with their colleagues and publicly condemned McCarthy for his "selfish political exploitation of fear, bigotry, ignorance, and intolerance." A Senate committee reported that his charges against the State Department were "a fraud and a hoax." But McCarthy had much to sustain him, including the arrest for espionage of Julius and Ethel Rosenberg in July and August. In 1951 the Rosenbergs were found guilty of recruiting and supervising a spy at the Los Alamos atomic laboratory and were sentenced to death. In spite of protests that the Rosenbergs were victims of anti-Communist hysteria, they were executed in 1953. Perhaps even more helpful to

McCarthy, however, was the outbreak of the Korean War in June 1950.

The Korean War

In the early morning hours of June 25, 1950, thousands of troops under the banner of the Democratic People's Republic of Korea (North Korea) moved across the 38th parallel into the Republic of Korea (South Korea). For years the two Koreas had skirmished along the border the great powers had drawn for them in 1945. Both regimes sought reunification of the divided country, but each on its own terms. Now it appeared that the North Koreans, armed by the Russians, would realize their goal by force.

After huddling with his advisers, President Truman decided to intervene; he ordered MacArthur to send arms to South Korea and to attack North Korean forces from the air. Thinking beyond Korea, he directed the Seventh Fleet to patrol the waters between the Chinese mainland and Jiang's sanctuary, Formosa. Finally, on June 30, Truman ordered American troops into battle. After the Security Council, in the Soviet delegate's absence, voted to assist South Korea, MacArthur became United Nations Commander.

Truman acted decisively for war because he believed, in the Cold War mentality of the time, that the Soviets had masterminded the North

Origins of the Korean War

Korean attack. Unanswered questions, however, dog the thesis that Russia started the Korean War. The Soviet delegate was absent when the Security Council voted to aid South Korea, because he was protesting the United Nations' refusal to seat the People's Republic of China. If the Soviets had fomented the war in Korea, it is puzzling that their delegate was not present to veto aid to South Korea. Then too, why did the Soviets give so little aid to North Korea once the war broke out? Did the war, as

some historians have suggested, begin as a Korean civil conflict rather than as part of the Soviet-American confrontation?

At first the war went badly for American troops, who accounted for about 90 percent of United Nations forces. Pushed into the tiny Pusan perimeter at the base of South Korea, the Eighth Army weathered numerous North Korean assaults. Then on September 15, 1950, MacArthur launched an amphibious landing at Inchon, several hundred miles behind North Korean lines. The operation was so successful it enabled American leaders to redefine their goals from the containment of North Korea to the reunification of Korea by force.

Within several weeks American troops had driven deeply into North Korea; the Chinese watched warily. Mao issued public warnings that China could not permit the continued bombing of its transportation links with Korea or the annihilation of North Korea itself. But MacArthur and officials in Washington shrugged off the statements. In late October Americans tangled with some Chinese soldiers, who pulled back quickly after the encounter—another signal, historians have concluded, that the United States should stop its advances. A month later an unmoved MacArthur sent his Eighth Army northward in a new offensive. On November 26, tens of thousands of Chinese troops counterattacked, surprising the general's forces and driving them pellmell southward. Embarrassed, MacArthur demanded that Washington order a massive air attack on China. Truman, after reflecting upon the costs of a wider war, rejected MacArthur's advice.

MacArthur moves against North Korea

By March 1951 the military lines had stabilized around the 38th parallel. Truman contemplated negotiations, and the Soviets stated publicly that they favored a political settlement. But MacArthur had other ideas. The general was making reckless public statements, calling for an attack on China or for Jiang's return to the mainland. He also hinted that the president was practicing appeasement, and he denounced

Truman fires MacArthur

the concept of limited war. On April 10 Truman fired the general for insubordination. MacArthur returned home to a hero's welcome, and Truman's popularity sagged. Truman was backed, however, by the chairman of the Joint Chiefs of Staff, General Omar Bradley. Escalation could bring Russia into battle, Bradley pointed out, and it was unwise to exhaust American resources in Asia when there were allies in Europe to be protected.

Armistice talks began in July 1951, but the fighting continued for two more years, into a new administration. Though Truman's successor, Dwight D. Eisenhower, went to Korea personally in December 1952 to fulfill a campaign pledge, his postelection visit brought no settlement. The sticking point in the negotiations was the fate of the prisoners of war (POWs); thousands of North Korean and Chinese captives did not want to return home. On July 23, 1953, an armistice was finally signed. The combatants agreed to hand the POW question over to a special panel of neutral nations (which later gave prisoners their choice of staying or leaving). The North Korean–South Korean line was set close to the 38th parallel, the prewar boundary. Thus ended a frustrating war—a limited war that Americans, accustomed to victory, found difficult to accept. The experience was indeed sobering, as was the casualty list of 34,000 Americans dead and 103,000 wounded.

The Korean War had major consequences. Bipartisanship in foreign policy eroded further, and the powers of the presidency grew as Congress deferred to Truman time and again. Truman had never gone to Congress for a declaration of war, for he believed that as commander-in-chief he had the authority to send troops to Korea. The war also set off a great national debate.

Debate over globalist policy

Conservative critics of globalism suggested that America should reduce its overseas commitments and draw its defense line in the Western Hemisphere. But Republican John Foster Dulles countered that "a defense that accepts encirclement quickly decomposes."

The advocates of global defense won the debate. Increased aid flowed to allies around the world, and military budgets remained high.

I like Ike

As the 1952 presidential election approached, the Democrats foundered. Added to frustration with the war and hysteria over communism was the revelation of influence-peddling by some of Truman's cronies. Known as "five-percenters," these presidential appointees had offered government contracts in return for 5-percent kickbacks. In exchange for help in expediting the importation of perfume ingredients, Truman's military aide and friend Major General Harry Vaughn had accepted a freezer. An employee of the executive branch admitted under oath, "I have only one thing to sell and that is influence." Once again the Democratic party seemed doomed.

What sealed the fate of the Democratic party was the Republican candidate, General Dwight D. Eisenhower. "Ike" was a bona fide war hero with a winning smile and a catchy campaign slogan: "I Like Ike." His opponent was Adlai Stevenson, the thoughtful, literate, and witty governor of Illinois. During the campaign, Eisenhower remained silent on the subject of McCarthyism, while his running mate, Senator Richard M. Nixon of California, scored points by referring to Stevenson as "Adlai the appeaser . . . who got a Ph.D. from Dean Acheson's College of Cowardly Communist Containment." The election was never much of a contest; Eisenhower won almost 34 million popular votes and 442 electoral votes to Stevenson's 27 million popular and 89 electoral votes.

Election of 1952

The new president approached his duties with a philosophy of "dynamic conservatism," explaining that he would be "conservative when it

| Dynamic conservatism | comes to money and liberal when it comes to human beings." But his was a business-oriented administration. |

One journalist referred to Eisenhower's cabinet as "eight millionaires and a plumber"—a literally accurate description. In keeping with the philosophy of his appointees, Eisenhower gave top priority to slicing the federal budget and minimizing government regulation of the economy. And he sought, but generally failed, to repeal or chisel away at two New Deal achievements: farm price supports and federally subsidized hydroelectric power.

But Eisenhower did not envision a complete rollback of New Deal and Fair Deal legislation. In fact, during his eight years in the White House, social security coverage was expanded, minimum-wage levels were raised, and federal funding for education, housing, and health increased. And like his Democratic predecessors, Eisenhower resorted to deficit financing to buffer the impact of the three recessions that occurred during his presidency.

The Eisenhower administration was also innovative at times. Officials lobbied successfully in Congress for the St. Lawrence Seaway, established the Department of Health, Education, and Welfare, and initiated a huge federal-state highway system. Occasionally, however, they exhibited a desire to withdraw the government entirely from the business of helping people. When the Salk polio vaccine was distributed free in the mid-1950s, the secretary of health, education, and welfare denounced the policy as a scheme to promote socialized medicine "through the back door."

Aside from the Korean War, the most pressing challenge confronting the new administration was the wave of anti-Communist hysteria generated by Senator McCarthy's speeches. Eisenhower was hesitant to denounce McCarthy.

| Downfall of McCarthy | Indeed, in 1953 he cooperated in the hysteria by suspending the security clearance |

of J. Robert Oppenheimer, the brilliant atomic physicist who had directed the top-secret Los Alamos project. Oppenheimer's crime was not Communist sympathies but his opposition to the crash project to build a hydrogen bomb. Eisenhower did condemn "book burners" after two of McCarthy's aides, Roy Cohn and G. David Schine, demanded the removal of "subversive" and "un-American" books from the libraries of the U.S. Information Agency.

McCarthy finally brought about his own downfall by taking on the U.S. Army in front of millions of television viewers. At issue was the senator's accusation that the army was shielding and even promoting Communists. The Army-McCarthy hearings, held by a Senate subcommittee in 1954, served as a showcase for his abusive treatment of witnesses. McCarthy alternately ranted and, appearing drunk, slurred his words. Finally, after he had attacked a young lawyer who was not even involved in the hearings, Joseph Welch, counsel for the army, asked: "Have you no sense of decency, sir?" The gallery applauded, and McCarthy's career as an anti-Communist witch-hunter was over. In October the Senate condemned McCarthy for sullying the dignity of the Senate.

The same year McCarthy was finally condemned, black Americans scored a historic victory against segregation. The

| Brown v. Board of Education of Topeka | 1954 Supreme Court decision in Brown v. Board of Education of Topeka concluded that "in the field of public educa- |

tion the doctrine of 'separate but equal' has no place. Separate educational facilities are inherently unequal." A year later the Court ordered compliance with the Brown decision "with all deliberate speed."

Though some border states quietly implemented the order, the majority of southern communities defied the Court, at times violently. Business and professional people formed White Citizens' Councils for the express purpose of resisting the order. Known familiarly as "uptown Ku Klux Klans," the councils used their economic power against black civil rights activists, foreclosing on their mortgages and seeing to it that they were fired from their jobs

On September 4, 1957, angry whites taunted this black student in Little Rock, Arkansas, as she attempted to enroll in the all-white Central High School. Governor Orval E. Faubus called out the Arkansas National Guard to prevent the court-ordered desegregation of the school.   Wide World Photos.

or denied credit at local stores. The Klan itself experienced a resurgence. But the most effective resistance tactic was the enactment of state laws that paid tuition for white children attending private schools and ordered the closing of desegregated schools.

Eisenhower, who sympathized with white southerners on the school desegregation issue, hoped to avoid a confrontation over it. He did not get his wish. In 1957 the governor of Arkansas, Orval Faubus, not only defied a federal court order but mobilized the Arkansas National Guard to prevent the desegregation of Little Rock's Central High School. When violence erupted, Eisenhower reluctantly federalized the guard and dispatched paratroopers to Little Rock. Two years passed before Central High School was finally desegregated.

Meanwhile, the civil rights movement was gaining momentum. With the passage of the Civil Rights Act of 1957, which established the U.S. Commission on Civil Rights, Congress joined the executive branch in acknowledging its responsibility to protect the rights of black

| Black protests for civil rights |

citizens. But what is more significant, blacks had resolved to stand up for their own rights. In 1955, Rosa Parks refused to give up her seat to a white passenger on a bus in Montgomery, Alabama. Her arrest sparked a year-long black boycott of the city's bus system. Inspired by twenty-seven-year-old Baptist minister Martin Luther King, Jr., blacks voiced their determination to carpool or walk to work rather than take a seat at the back of the bus. With the aid of a Supreme Court verdict, they won. Jim Crow received another jolt in 1960 when four black students from North Carolina Agricultural and Technical College sat down at a segregated lunch counter in Greensboro and ordered coffee. Their action started a sit-in movement that would sweep the South in the 1960s, ending the segregation of public accommodations.

Eisenhower, Dulles, and the global watch in the 1950s

In foreign affairs Eisenhower confronted continued Cold War tension as well as increasing rebellion against American influence throughout the world. As in domestic affairs, the president's style was low-key; in fact, his appearance of passivity exasperated Democrats who charged him with a failure of leadership.

For the most part, Eisenhower and Secretary of State John Foster Dulles continued Truman's containment policy, but they introduced some

| Eisenhower- Dulles policies |

memorable phrases to distinguish their administration from Truman's. Thinking containment too defensive a concept, Dulles invented the concept of *liberation* (but did not explain precisely how the nations of Eastern Europe could be freed from Soviet control). *Massive retaliation* was the administration's

phrase for the consequences of Soviet aggression: the nuclear obliteration of the Soviet state or its assumed client, the People's Republic of China. The United States' ability to make such a threat was thought to provide *deterrence,* or the prevention of hostile Soviet actions.

Related to both massive retaliation and deterrence was the so-called New Look of the American military. Eisenhower and Dulles emphasized air power and nuclear weaponry and de-emphasized conventional forces. The president's preference for heavy weapons stemmed in part from his desire to trim the federal budget and reduce taxes while maintaining a strong defense posture. With this huge military arsenal, Eisenhower and Dulles practiced a kind of diplomatic brinkmanship: not backing down in a crisis, even if it meant taking the nation to the brink of war. Adopting a globalist perspective on wrenching changes throughout the Third World, they conducted a diplomacy best described as holding the line—against Soviet Russia, Communist China, neutralism, communism, socialism, nationalism, and anti-imperial revolution everywhere. Still, Eisenhower seemed an uneasy Cold Warrior. He noted sadly that "every gun that is made, every rocket fired signifies . . . a theft from those who hunger. . . . The cost of one modern heavy bomber is this: a modern brick school in more than 30 cities."

After the death of Stalin in 1953, Eisenhower attempted with mixed results to achieve better relations with the Kremlin. A temporary thaw in the Cold War occurred in 1955 when Russia and the United States agreed to end their ten-year joint occupation of Austria, making it an independent neutral state. The same year Eisenhower and Soviet Premier Nikita Khrushchev journeyed to Geneva for a summit conference, where they disagreed over how to unite Germany.

The two sides also raced to accumulate arms and allies. The United States had superior strength in intercontinental bombers and nuclear weapons, including hydrogen bombs (first tested in 1952). The Soviet Union exploded its own thermonuclear bomb in 1954. In 1955 the

United States and its European allies welcomed West Germany into NATO. That year, too, the Southeast Asia Treaty Organization (SEATO) went into effect, bringing Britain, France, Australia, New Zealand, Pakistan, Thailand, and the Philippines into alliance with the United States against China, considered a Soviet ally. Finally, the United States signed defense treaties with the Nationalist Chinese government on Taiwan and with Turkey, Iraq, Britain, Iran, and Pakistan (the Baghdad Treaty). The goal of these alliances was to surround Communist nations with allies and thus contain them. The Soviets responded in 1955 with the Warsaw Pact in Eastern Europe.

Khrushchev unwittingly caused new troubles in 1956, when he called for "peaceful coexistence" between capitalists and Communists, denounced Stalin for his crimes against the Russian people, and suggested that Moscow would tolerate different brands of communism. Soon revolts against Soviet power erupted in Poland and Hungary. Moscow quickly crushed the rebellions. The Eisenhower administration, which had gone on record as favoring the liberation of Eastern Europe, found itself unable to aid the rebels without igniting a third world war.

In 1957 the Soviets shocked Americans by launching the first man-made satellite *(Sputnik)* into outer space and firing the first inter-

| Missile race |

continental ballistic missile (ICBM). Americans now felt vulnerable to attack by air and inferior to the Soviets in rocket technology. Though the United States already had the nuclear capability to destroy the Soviet Union, critics charged that Eisenhower had allowed the United States to fall behind in the missile race. On the defensive, Eisenhower ordered a speed-up of the missile program. By the end of 1960 the United States had deployed intermediate-range Thor and Jupiter missiles in Europe; developed long-range (intercontinental) Atlas and Titan missiles; and produced a fleet of Polaris-missile-bearing submarines. As the nation entered the 1960s, it enjoyed overwhelming strategic dominance over the Soviet Union.

Secretary of State John Foster Dulles (1888–1959) traveled extensively because he preferred face-to-face negotiations, in which he could use his formidable debating skills. Foreigners often complained that Dulles was too rigid, passing up chances for compromise. The secretary dismissed Soviet peace initiatives as "Trojan doves," for instance. *The Reporter*, 1956. Copyright 1956 by The Reporter Magazine Company, Inc.

In an effort to ease tensions, Khrushchev and Eisenhower planned a summit meeting for Paris in May 1960. But two weeks before the confer-

Important events

1945	President Roosevelt dies; Harry S Truman assumes presidency	1950	Scotland Yard arrests Klaus Fuchs as atomic spy

1945   President Roosevelt dies; Harry S
        Truman assumes presidency
        Russians install a Communist
           regime in Poland
        Truman's 21-point economic
           message to Congress
        Strikes

1946   American-Russian crisis over Iran
        George F. Kennan's telegram
        Winston Churchill's Iron Curtain
           speech
        Employment Act of 1946
        Strikes by coal miners
        Inflation reaches 18.2 percent
        Republican majorities elected to
           both houses of Congress

1947   Truman Doctrine
        Truman orders loyalty probe of
           government workers
        Taft-Hartley Act
        President's Committee on Civil
           Rights releases *To Secure These
           Rights*
        Communist takeover in Hungary
        Kennan appeals for containment
           doctrine in "Mr. X" article
        Marshall Plan announced

1948   Communist coup in
           Czechoslovakia
        Berlin blockade and airlift
        State of Israel founded
        Truman elected president

1949   Russia explodes an atomic bomb
        Chinese Communists proclaim
           People's Republic of China
        NATO founded

1950   Scotland Yard arrests Klaus
           Fuchs as atomic spy
        Alger Hiss convicted of perjury
        Sino-Soviet treaty
        NSC-68
        Point Four Program launched
        United States supports French in
           Indochina
        Korean War begins
        U.S. troops cross the 38th parallel
        Chinese troops enter the Korean
           War

1951   Armistice talks begin in Korea
        Supreme Court upholds Smith
           Act *(Dennis et al v. U.S.)*;
        Communist leaders imprisoned

1952   Eisenhower elected president,
           defeating Stevenson
        Republican majorities elected to
           both houses of Congress

1953   Department of Health,
           Education, and Welfare
           established
        Execution of Rosenbergs
        Korean War ends

1954   United States intervenes in
           Guatemala
        Brown v. *Board of Education of
           Topeka*
        Army-McCarthy hearings
        Senator McCarthy condemned by
           the Senate
        SEATO formed (into effect
           1955)

1955	Baghdad Pact formed	1957	Little Rock, Arkansas, school
	Formosa Resolution		desegregation crisis
			Civil Rights Act of 1957
1956	Montgomery bus boycott		Soviet Union launches Sputnik
	Federal Highway Act		
	Suez Crisis	1959	Fidel Castro to power in Cuba
	Eisenhower re-elected, defeating	1960	Greensboro, North Carolina,
	Stevenson		sit-in
	Eisenhower Doctrine		U-2 incident

ence an American U-2 spy plane crashed 1,200 miles inside the Soviet Union. Moscow announced that it had been shot down. At first Washington denied that its planes flew over Soviet territory, but Russian officials blasted that story by displaying the captured pilot, Francis Gary Powers, his aircraft, and the pictures he had been snapping of Soviet military installations. Moscow demanded an apology, Washington refused, and the Russians walked out of the Paris summit.

American relations with Communist China were also strained. To the Chinese, America had a demonstrated record of hostility: aid to Jiang Jieshi on Formosa; warfare in Korea; positioning of the Seventh Fleet in the Formosa Straits; nonrecognition of the People's Republic; and blockage of their membership in the United Nations. To Washington, China was a Soviet ally, an enemy in Korea, a vocal advocate of colonial rebellion, and an international outlaw for the seizure of American property in China (1949). Moreover, Mao Zedong's demand that Formosa become part of the People's Republic threatened an American ally.

In 1954 and 1955 a crisis brought the two nations to the brink of war. Just a few miles off the Chinese coast sat the tiny islands of Quemoy

| Quemoy and Matsu |

and Matsu. Occupied by sixty thousand of Jiang's troops, they served as bases for commando raids against the People's Repub-

lic. In fall 1954 Chinese officials ordered the bombardment of the islands in an attempt to liberate them from Jiang's control. Although China had the better legal case, and the small islands were hardly essential to either American or Formosan security, Congress passed the Formosa Resolution (1955), which authorized the president to send American troops to Formosa and its adjoining islands. Secret Sino-American talks failed to produce a settlement. Two years later the United States installed missiles capable of carrying nuclear warheads on Formosa. And again in 1958 Chinese guns boomed over Quemoy and Matsu.

If Eisenhower and Dulles believed they had contained the Sino-Soviet threat, they were less sure about challenges elsewhere in the world. In Latin America, anti-American feeling grew. For example, in Guatemala in 1951, the leftist President Jacobo Arbenz Guzman tried to fulfill a promise of land reform by expropriating uncultivated land from the American-owned United Fruit Company. Though compensation was offered, the company dismissed it as inadequate. Instead, United Fruit set out to rally Washington by falsely claiming that a Communist threat existed in Guatemala.

Officials cut aid to Guatemala, and the CIA began Operation el Diablo, a secret attempt to

| CIA in Guatemala |

subvert the Guatemalan government. When Arbenz learned the CIA was working against him, he turned to Russia, thus confirming American suspicions. The CIA airlifted arms into Guatemala, dropping them at United Fruit facilities, and in June 1954 CIA-supported forces struck from Honduras. American planes bombed Guatemala City, the invaders drove Arbenz from power, and the new pro-American regime returned United Fruit's land. Latin Americans wondered what had happened to Roosevelt's Good Neighbor Policy.

In the Middle East the Eisenhower administration faced several challenges to United States influence. American stakes there included the survival of the Jewish state of Israel and extensive oil holdings. Oil-rich Iran was a special friend, for the ruling shah had granted American oil companies a 40 percent interest in a new petroleum consortium in return for CIA help in the overthrow of his rival Mohammed Mossadegh (1953).

The major threat to American interests in the Middle East came from Egypt, where the fervent Arab nationalist Gamal Abdel Nasser rose to power determined to push the British out of the Suez Canal Zone and the Israelis out of Palestine. The United States was

> **Suez crisis**

caught in a double bind. It did not wish to anger the Arabs, for fear of losing its oil holdings, nor did it wish to lose its ally Israel. But when Nasser declared neutrality in the Cold War, Dulles lost patience with him. Officials decided to withdraw their offer to help finance the Aswan Dam, a project Nasser had dreamed would provide inexpensive electricity and water for thirsty Egyptian farmlands. Nasser responded by nationalizing the British-owned Suez Canal (1956) and using its $25 million annual profit to finance the dam.

Fearing interruption of the Middle Eastern oil trade, from which Western Europe received 75 percent of its oil, the British and French now conspired with Israel "to knock Nasser off his perch." On October 29, 1956, the Israelis invaded the Suez, joined two days later by Britain and France. Eisenhower, who had not been consulted, fumed. He bluntly told London, Paris, and Tel Aviv to pull out. The foreign troops

withdrew, Egypt paid $81 million for the canal, and Russia built the Aswan Dam.

In 1957, in an effort to improve the Western position in the Middle East and protect American interests there, the president proclaimed what became known as the Eisenhower Doctrine. The United States would intervene in the Middle East, he said, if any government threatened by a Communist takeover asked for help. Fourteen thousand American troops scrambled ashore in Lebanon the next year to quell an internal political dispute, while American critics protested that the United States was wrongfully acting as the world's policeman.

The age of consensus

Eisenhower's presidency appeared to be what people desired in the 1950s. Americans seemed to feel little need for the kind of domestic leadership that would challenge and inspire. Instead, they clung fiercely to the status quo, believing that postwar economic growth would eliminate the need for economic and social reform. There was also a consensus on foreign policy. Americans agreed that they were locked in a life-or-death struggle with the Russians and other Communists around the world.

In this age of consensus there was virtually no left wing. A noisy minority on the right vilified the government for its wishy-washy approach to communism, but both liberal Democrats and moderate Republicans shunned

> **Vital center**

extremism and struggled to occupy "the vital center." In the mortal struggle with communism, people believed one should support, not criticize, the government.

Along with this intensely nationalistic feeling went trust in and respect for established leadership and authority. Americans preferred to let those at the top—particularly the financial elite—bargain on their behalf. And they preferred to address only economic goals, not moral issues, for which they believed there were no workable solutions anyway. Like their leaders, Americans saw mass movements as threats to stability. In this era of conformity even college students shunned political activism.

Thus the scholars of the 1950s proclaimed the "end of ideology" in America. No longer did historians tell the American story in terms of conflict—rich against poor, North against South, farmer against banker. Instead, they wrote about stability, continuity, and cultural wholeness. Quite clearly, their interpretation did not prepare the nation for the 1960s—a period of considerable conflict. But it served the interests of most Americans in the 1950s.

"End of ideology"

Suggestions for further reading

GENERAL DIPLOMACY Stephen Ambrose, *Rise to Globalism,* 2nd ed. (1980); Richard Barnet, *Roots of War* (1973); Robert A. Divine, *Foreign Policy and U.S. Presidential Elections, 1940–1960,* 2 vols. (1974); John L. Gaddis, *Russia, the Soviet Union, and the United States* (1978); Alexander L. George and Richard Smoke, *Deterrence in American Foreign Policy* (1974); Walter LaFeber, *America, Russia, and the Cold War, 1945–1980,* 4th ed. (1980); Ronald Steel, *Walter Lippmann and the American Century* (1980); Adam B. Ulam, *Expansion and Coexistence,* 2nd ed. (1974); William Appleman Williams, *Empire as a Way of Life* (1981); Lawrence Wittner, *Rebels Against War* (1974).

ORIGINS OF THE COLD WAR Barton J. Bernstein, ed., *The Atomic Bomb* (1976); Committee for the Compilation of Materials on Damage Caused by the Atomic Bombs in Hiroshima and Nagasaki, *Hiroshima and Nagasaki* (1981); Herbert Feis, *The Atomic Bomb and the End of World War II* (1966); John L. Gaddis, *The United States and the Origins of the Cold War, 1941–1947* (1972); Louis Halle, *The Cold War as History* (1967); Gregg Herken, *The Winning Weapon* (1981); Gabriel Kolko and Joyce Kolko, *The Limits of Power* (1972); Thomas G. Paterson, *On*

Every Front: The Making of the Cold War (1979); Thomas G. Paterson, *Soviet-American Confrontation* (1973); Chalmers M. Roberts, *The Nuclear Years* (1970); Martin J. Sherwin, *A World Destroyed* (1975); Gaddis Smith, *Dean Acheson* (1972); William Taubman, *Stalin's American Policy* (1980); Adam Ulam, *The Rivals* (1971); Daniel Yergin, *Shattered Peace* (1977).

THE TRUMAN DOCTRINE AND CONTAINMENT Thomas H. Etzold and John L. Gaddis, eds., *Containment* (1978); Richard M. Freeland, *The Truman Doctrine and the Origins of McCarthyism* (1972); Bruce R. Kuniholm, *The Origins of the Cold War in the Near East* (1980); Walter Lippmann, *The Cold War* (1947); Thomas G. Paterson, ed., *Containment and the Cold War* (1973); Samuel F. Wells, Jr., "Sounding the Tocsin: NSC-68 and the Soviet Threat," *International Security,* 4 (1979) 116–158.

COLD WAR ORIGINS IN ASIA Dorothy Borg and Waldo Heinrichs, eds. *Uncertain Years* (1980); Warren I. Cohen, *America's Response to China,* 2nd ed. (1980); Herbert Feis, *Contest Over Japan* (1967); Akira Iriye, *The Cold War in Asia* (1974); E. J. Kahn, Jr., *The China Hands* (1975); Gary May, *China Scapegoat: The Diplomatic Ordeal of John Carter Vincent* (1979); Charles E. Neu, *The Troubled Encounter: The United States and Japan* (1975); Michael Schaller, *The United States and China in the Twentieth Century* (1979); William W. Stueck, Jr., *The Road to Confrontation: American Policy toward China and Korea, 1947–1950* (1981); Christopher Thorne, *Allies of a Kind* (1978); Tang Tsou, *America's Failure in China, 1941–1950* (1963).

THE TRUMAN ADMINISTRATION Barton J. Bernstein, ed., *Politics and Policies of the Truman Administration* (1970); Barton J. Bernstein and Allen J. Matusow, eds., *The Truman Administration: A Documentary History* (1966); Bert Cochran, *Harry Truman and the Crisis Presidency* (1973); Robert J. Donovan, *Conflict and Crisis: The Presidency of Harry S Truman, 1945–1948* (1977); Robert J. Donovan, *Tumultuous Years: The Presidency of Harry S Truman, 1949–1953* (1982); Robert H. Ferrell, ed., *Off the Record: The Private Papers of Harry S Truman* (1980); Alonzo L. Hamby, *Beyond the New Deal: Harry S Truman and American Liberalism* (1973); V. O. Key, *Southern Poli-*

Suggestions for further reading

tics in State and Nation (1949); Norman D. Markowitz, *The Rise and Fall of the People's Century: Henry A. Wallace and American Liberalism, 1941–1948* (1973); Harry S Truman, *Memoirs* (1955–1956); Allen Yarnell, *Democrats and Progressives: The 1948 Presidential Election as a Test of Postwar Liberalism* (1974).

MCCARTHYISM Daniel Bell, ed., *The Radical Right* (1955); David Caute, *The Great Fear: The Anti-Communist Purge under Truman and Eisenhower* (1978); Robert Griffith, *The Politics of Fear: Joseph R. McCarthy and the Senate* (1970); Victor Navasky, *Naming Names* (1980); Richard H. Rovere, *Senator Joe McCarthy* (1959); Athan Theoharis, *Seeds of Repression: Harry S Truman and the Origins of McCarthyism* (1971); Allen Weinstein, *Perjury: The Hiss-Chambers Case* (1978).

THE KOREAN WAR Ronald J. Caridi, *The Korean War and American Politics* (1969); Bruce Cummings, ed., *Child of Conflict* (1983); Glenn D. Paige, *The Korean Decision* (1968); David Rees, *Korea: The Limited War* (1964); Robert R. Simmons, *The Strained Alliance* (1975); John W. Spanier, *The Truman-MacArthur Controversy and the Korean War* (1959); I. F. Stone, *The Hidden History of the Korean War* (1952); Allen Whiting, *China Crosses the Yalu* (1960).

THE EISENHOWER ADMINISTRATION Charles C. Alexander, *Holding the Line: The Eisenhower Era, 1952–1961* (1975); Robert L. Branyan and Lawrence H. Larson, eds., *The Eisenhower Administration, 1953–1961:A Documentary History,* 2 vols. (1971); Dwight D. Eisenhower, *Mandate for Change, 1953–1956* (1963) and *Waging Peace, 1956–1961* (1965); William Bragg Ewald, Jr., *Eisenhower the President: Crucial Days* (1981); Robert H. Ferrel, ed., *The Eisenhower Diaries* (1981); Emmet John Hughes, *The Ordeal of Power: A*

Political Memoir of the Eisenhower Years (1963); Peter Lyon, *Eisenhower: Portrait of the Hero* (1974); Herbert Parmet, *Eisenhower and the American Crusades* (1972).

CIVIL RIGHTS Numan V. Bartley, *The Rise of Massive Resistance: Race and Politics in the South during the 1950's* (1969); Richard M. Dalfiume, *Desegregation of the U.S. Armed Forces: Fighting on Two Fronts, 1939– (1969)*; Elizabeth Huckaby, *Crisis at Central High, Little Rock, 1957–1958* (1980); Martin Luther King, Jr., *Stride Toward Freedom: The Montgomery Boycott* (1958); Richard Kluger, *Simple Justice: The History of Brown v. Board of Education and Black America's Struggle for Equality* (1975); Donald R. McCoy and Richard T. Ruetten, *Quest and Response: Minority Rights and the Truman Administration* (1973); Harvard Sitkoff, *The Struggle for Black Equality, 1954–1980* (1981).

EISENHOWER-DULLES DIPLOMACY Charles Alexander, *Holding the Line* (1975); Blanche W. Cook, *The Declassified Eisenhower* (1981); Robert A. Divine, *Eisenhower and the Cold War* (1981); Louis Gerson, *John Foster Dulles* (1967); Michael Guhin, *John Foster Dulles* (1972); Townsend Hoopes, *The Devil and John Foster Dulles* (1973); Richard Immerman, *The CIA in Guatemala* (1982).

THE AGE OF CONSENSUS Daniel Bell, *The End of Ideology: On the Exhaustion of Political Ideas in the Fifties* (1960); Ronald Lora, *Conservative Minds in America* (1971); George H. Nash, *The Conservative Intellectual Movement in America: Since 1945* (1976); David M. Potter, *People of Plenty: Economic Abundance and the American Character* (1954); David Riesman with Nathan Glazer and Reuel Denney, *The Lonely Crowd* (1950); William H. Whyte, *The Organization Man* (1956).

28 ॐ

LIFE IN THE

MIDDLE CLASS,

1945–1960

"The remarkable thing," recalled Chuck Faust, "was that I had never expected to do anything other than follow in my father's footsteps as a farmer in central Kansas." But when he was seventeen years old, a historic event changed Chuck's life: the attack on Pearl Harbor. Just days after graduating from high school, Chuck enlisted in the army.

When he returned home in 1945, Chuck's mind was fixed not on farming but on college. The service had broadened his horizons and the Servicemen's Readjustment Act, or GI Bill, enabled him to attend college. Chuck married his high school sweetheart, Annie Kempton, and the two moved to Lawrence, Kansas. For the next four years the Fausts lived in a leftover quonset hut near the University of Kansas campus. By graduation time, their first child, an early member of the postwar baby boom, had been born.

In the 1950s Chuck and Annie added three more children to their family. Chuck became a sales representative for a farm-machinery company, and his healthy income enabled them to buy a comfortable home in a suburb of Kansas City. Two decades later, when Chuck declined to take over the family farm, his parents sold their home and land to an agribusiness. "We're no longer farm people," mused Annie. "We and

our children, who are now pretty much grown up, are all suburbanites." The Fausts had joined the middle class.

For many people like the Fausts, the American dream seemed to have come true. Whatever the nation's faults, it was the world's foremost land of opportunity. Americans boasted that they enjoyed political self-determination through the vote and social mobility through the melting pot. The postwar economic boom had raised their standard of living, and public education, "the engine of democracy," guaranteed a better life to all who studied and worked hard. The obvious exceptions to the dream—the social and educational segregation, political disfranchisement, and economic victimization of nonwhite Americans—went unnoticed by most Americans. And the lack of equal opportunities for women was concealed by an emphasis on femininity, piety, and family togetherness.

The postwar economic boom

As Americans entered the postwar era, some wondered whether it would resemble another postwar epoch, the get-rich-quick Roaring

457

Twenties. Most Americans expected a replay not of the 1920s, however, but of the 1930s. After all, it was the war that had created jobs and prosperity; surely the end of war would bring a slump. So fearful were people of a return to the hardships of the 1930s that observers coined the term *depression psychosis* to describe their state of mind.

As it turned out, neither prediction was correct. The United States in 1945 was on the verge of one of its longest, steadiest periods of growth and prosperity. The key to this success was increasing output: in the twenty-five years after 1945 the American economy grew at an average rate of 3.5 percent per year. Even with occasional recessions the gross national product seldom faltered, rising from just over $200 billion in 1946 to close to $1 trillion in 1970.

What were the causes of this unparalleled economic growth? One was the increase in the birth rate that followed the Second World War.

| Baby boom | It was of course natural for the birth rate to soar immediately following the war. What was confounding was that it continued to do so throughout the late 1940s and the 1950s, reversing the downward trend in birth rates that had prevailed for two hundred years.

The baby boom spelled business for builders, manufacturers, and school systems. "Take the 3,548,000 babies born in 1950," wrote Sylvia F. Porter in her syndicated newspaper column. "Bundle them into a batch, bounce them all over the bountiful land that is America. What do you get?" Porter's answer: "Boom. The biggest, boomiest boom ever known in history. Just imagine how much these extra people, these new markets, will absorb—in food, in clothing, in gadgets, in housing, in services. Our factories must expand just to keep pace."

Another cornerstone of the postwar economic boom was military spending. When the Defense Department was established in 1949, the nation was spending just over $13 billion on

| Military spending | defense. By 1951, the two-year-old Defense Department's budget was over $22

billion. Two years later it was over $50 billion. Except for a short dip from 1954 to 1958, when the Eisenhower administration stressed "more bang for the buck," it has been on an upward spiral ever since.

The invention of the transistor in 1948 inaugurated the computer revolution and staggering advances in electronics. In a split second a computer could perform a task that had formerly taken hours or even days to accomplish. Businesses and governments were so eager to buy electronic data-processing machines that sales zoomed from $25 million in 1953 to $1 billion in 1960. By the early 1960s thousands of computers had been produced and sold.

The evolution of electronics was a tradeoff for the American people. Computers brought about a rapid rise in productivity through the automation of numerous industries. But in doing so they stimulated technological unemployment: fewer workers were required to accomplish the same amount of work. The spread of electronic technology also promoted the ever-increasing concentration of ownership in industry. Often only large corporations could afford the new technology; small corporations were shut out of the market. Indeed, large corporations with capital and experience in high technology became so powerful they began to expand into related industries.

But not all expansion was a matter of diversification into related fields. Beginning in the early 1950s a third great merger wave swept

| Conglomerate mergers | American business. But unlike the first two waves in the 1890s and 1920s, this new wave was distinguished by conglomerate mergers. A *conglomerate* merged companies in totally unrelated fields as a hedge against instability in a particular market or industry. The new wave of mergers resulted in unprecedented concentration of industrial assets.

Even the labor movement experienced a merger. In 1955 the American Federation of Labor and the Congress of Industrial Organizations put aside their differences and established the AFL-CIO. Most new jobs, however, were

Babies meant big business for companies that produced baby foods, clothing, toys, and diapers. "In its first year as a consumer," read the caption for this 1958 *Life* photo, "baby is a potential market for $800 worth of products." Yale Joel, *Life Magazine* © 1958 Time Inc.

opening up not in the heavy industries but in the union-resistant white-collar service trades. Thus union membership remained fairly constant.

The postwar years were good times for unionized blue-collar workers, many of whom, especially if their wives were working, were able to obtain mortgages for suburban homes. Workers with union cards were also more secure against inflation. In 1948 General Motors and the United Auto Workers Union agreed on automatic cost-of-living adjustments (COLAS) in workers' wages. Thirty years later almost 10 percent of the nation's jobholders were protected against inflation by COLA clauses.

The trend toward economic consolidation brought changes in agriculture as well as business and labor. New machines like mechanical cotton, tobacco, and grape-pickers and crop-

Rise of agribusiness dusting planes revolutionized farming methods, and increased use of fertilizers and pesticides raised the cash value of farm output by 120 percent (in constant dollars) between 1945 and 1970. Meanwhile labor productivity tripled and the farm labor force shrank by 56 percent. The resulting improvement in profitability drew large investors into agriculture. By the 1960s it took money—big money— to become a farmer. In many cases only banks, insurance companies, and other large businesses could afford the necessary land, machinery, and fertilizer.

The significant changes that economic growth produced in industry and agriculture during the postwar years were matched by equally significant changes in Americans' buying habits and lifestyles. For many Americans, especially the middle class, the postwar economic boom brought what the economist John Kenneth Galbraith called the affluent society.

The affluent society

If America's productivity grew by leaps and bounds in the postwar years, so did its appetite for goods and services. In the affluent postwar years middle-class Americans could afford to satisfy desires for a home or a car that they had had to defer during the depression and the war. If they lacked the cash to buy what they wanted, they borrowed the money. Credit to support the nation's shopping spree grew from over $8 billion worth of short- and intermediate-term loans in 1946 to a whopping $127 billion in 1970. Here indeed was the economic basis of the consumer culture.

As Americans consumed goods and services, they were using up the world's resources. Consumption of crude petroleum soared 118 percent from 1946 to 1970, but domestic production increased only 97 percent. The extra oil had to be imported. Electricity use jumped too, from 270 billion kilowatt-hours to 1.6 trillion. By the mid-1960s the United States, with only 5 percent of the world's population, produced and consumed over one-third of the world's goods and services.

A particularly happy effect of postwar prosperity was advances in public health. The aver-

age life span increased from 65.9 years in 1945 to 70.9 in 1970. Regular prenatal and pediatric care led to a major reduction in the infant mortality rate. New wonder drugs, streptomycin, for example, cut the number of deaths caused by influenza and postsurgical infection. And the dreaded disease polio was virtually eliminated in 1955 when the Salk vaccine was approved for public use.

By no means were all the effects of economic growth beneficial to the average American. In agriculture the movement toward consolidation threatened the survival of the family farm. From 1945 to 1969 the nation's farm population declined from 24.4 million to just over 10 million. The South lost almost a quarter of its farm population in just six years, from 1970 to 1976. As one Iowa farmer lamented, "We lost country life when we moved to tractors."

Many of the people forced off farms in the postwar years ended up in the industrial areas of

Growth of the southern rim

the South and West, along with young families from the industrial North and East. This mass migration to the Sunbelt had begun during the Second World War, when GIs and their families were ordered to new duty stations and war workers moved to the shipyards and aircraft factories of San Diego and other cities. Soon it encompassed the entire southern rim, the area running from southern California across the Southwest and South all the way to the Carolinas, Georgia, and Florida.

The millions of people who departed the chilly, drab industrial cities of the North and East for sunnier climes strengthened the political clout of the Sunbelt. In a book published in 1969, Kevin Phillips, a conservative Republican, predicted an emerging Republican majority based on the votes of the South and West. Richard Nixon's triumph in the presidential election of 1968 seemed to support Phillips's thesis. So did the tendency of political parties to nominate Sunbelt candidates for national office. (The nation's four most recently elected presidents have hailed from the Sunbelt. And in 1980 the Census Bureau made it official: for the first time in the nation's history, voters in the South and West accounted for a majority of those eligible to cast ballots.)

Millions, especially the elderly, nonwhites, and divorced, widowed, and deserted women, did not share in the new affluence. They were overlooked in part because they were literally not seen: most lived in the inner cities and in ru-

Levittown, Long Island, as it appeared in 1958. The first of the postwar suburbs, Levittown offered low-cost mass-produced housing to accommodate veterans and their new families.   The Bettmann Archive.

ral areas, out of sight of the prosperous middle class. For up-and-coming Americans had moved to suburbia, where poverty was rare.

The growth of suburbs

A combination of motives drew the middle class to the suburbs. Many families wanted to leave behind the sounds and smells of the cities and to be closer to nature. They wanted homes with yards where their children could play, safe from traffic. Or they wanted the privacy and quiet that detached homes provided, as well as family rooms, extra closets, and utility rooms.

Many were also looking for a community of like-minded people, a place where they could have a measure of political influence. Big-city government was dense and impenetrable. In the suburbs citizens could become involved in government and have an impact, particularly on the education their children received. Indeed, the general welfare of their children seemed to be the major concern of suburbanites.

Government funding and policies helped these new families to settle in the suburbs. Low-interest GI mortgages and Federal Housing Administration mortgage insurance made the difference for people who would otherwise have been unable to afford a home. Such easy credit combined with postwar prosperity to produce a con-

| Housing boom |

struction boom. From 1945 to 1946 housing starts climbed from 326,000 to over 1 million, and in 1950 they approached 2 million. Never before had new starts exceeded 1 million; not until the 1980s would they dip below that level.

Another factor contributing to the growth of suburbs was the rise in automobile production. Between 1945 and 1960 the number of registered automobiles in the nation increased from 25.8 million to 61.7 million. At the same time highway construction opened up rural lands for the development of suburban communities. In

| Highway construction |

1947 Congress authorized the construction of a 37,000-mile chain of highways, and in 1956 President Eisenhower signed the Interstate Highway Act, which launched a 42,500-mile nationwide network.

The spurt in highway construction combined with the mushrooming of suburbia to produce the *megalopolis*, a term first used by urban experts in the early 1960s to refer to the almost uninterrupted metropolitan complex stretching along the northeastern seaboard of the United States. Beginning in Boston and extending 600 miles south through New York, Philadelphia, Baltimore, and Washington, "Boswash" encompassed parts of eleven states and a population of 49 million people, all tied together by interstate highways. Although the suburbs within the megalopolis were politically independent, they were economically dependent on the cities and connecting highways. Other megalopolises that took shape following the Second World War encompassed the areas from Chicago to Pittsburgh and from San Francisco to San Diego.

The white middle class benefited far more than other Americans from the government-supported housing and highway boom. For example, the FHA refused to guarantee suburban home loans to the poor, nonwhites, Jews, and other "inharmonious racial and ethnic groups." And some federal programs actually worsened conditions for the poor. The National Housing Act of 1949 was passed to provide for urban re-

development (slum clearance) and the construction of 810,000 units of low-income public housing in four years. But twenty years passed before the housing units were built. Meanwhile, existing housing for the poor was removed and replaced by parking lots, highways, public buildings, and shopping centers.

Ideals of motherhood and the family

Change also occurred within the American family, and some of it was due to the publication in 1946 of Dr. Benjamin Spock's *Baby and Child Care*. The book, which quickly became the bible for new parents, answered many

| Dr. Spock on childrearing |

common questions about childrearing. But unlike earlier manuals, *Baby and Child Care* urged mothers to think of their children first and foremost, even at the expense of their own mental and physical health. Dr. Spock's predecessors had advised mothers to consider their own needs as well as their children's. But women who embraced Spock's philosophy tried to be mother, teacher, psychologist, and buddy to their children all at once. If they failed in any of these prescribed roles, guilt often resulted.

At the same time Philip Wylie, author of the book *Generation of Vipers*, denounced such selfless behavior as Momism. In the guise of sacrificing for her children, Wylie wrote, Mom was pursuing "love of herself." She smothered her children with affection so they would become emotionally dependent on her and would not want to leave home. Other experts agreed. Even the army blamed mom for recruits' nervous disorders.

But women were caught in a double bind. If they pursued a life outside the home they were accused of being "imitation men" or "neurotic" feminists. Echoing the psychoanalyst Sigmund Freud, critics of working mothers contended that a woman could be happy and fulfilled only through domesticity. Reflecting on the contradictory expectations of women, anthropologist Margaret Mead wrote in 1946, "Choose any set of criteria you like, and the answer is the same: women—and men—are confused, uncertain, and discontented with the present definition of women's place in America."

Despite the controversy, women continued the wartime trend toward work outside the home. The female labor force rose from 16.8 million in 1946 to 31.6 million in 1970. These women entered the labor force without the support of an organized women's movement and without challenging sex-role stereotypes. Many of them, of course, were their families' sole source of income; they had to work. Still others took jobs not to challenge notions of male dominance but to earn additional family income, enjoy adult company, or bolster their self-esteem. Despite the cult of motherhood, most of the new entrants to the job market were married and had children.

Middle-class American families were preoccupied with education, the key to their children's future financial success. But the Soviet

Education of the baby boom generation

launching of *Sputnik* (1957) made education a matter of national security as well. Congress responded in 1958 with the National Defense Education Act (NDEA), which funded public school programs in mathematics, foreign languages, and science and college loans and fellowships. Parents were quick to endorse the new programs. After all, public education was the engine of democracy, a guarantee of both upward social mobility and military superiority.

Just as education became intertwined with national security, religion became synonymous with patriotism. As President Eisenhower put it, "recognition of the Supreme Being is the first, the most basic expression of Americanism." In

America's Cold War with the godless Soviet Union, ministers, priests, and rabbis became foot soldiers in the battle for souls. Religious leaders emphasized family togetherness in their appeals for new converts. "The family that prays together stays together," was a famous slogan used during the 1950s. The Bible topped the best-seller lists, and books with religious themes, such as the Reverend Norman Vincent Peale's *The Power of Positive Thinking* (1952), sold in the millions. Meanwhile evangelist Billy Graham exhorted television viewers and stadium audiences throughout the country. From 1945 to 1970 church membership nearly doubled, and money spent on church and charities quintupled.

If Americans were eager to improve their minds and souls, they were not ready to liberate themselves sexually. When Dr. Alfred Kinsey, director of the Institute for Sex Research at Indiana University, published his pioneering book *Sexual Behavior in the Human Male* (1948), the American public was shocked. On the basis of interviews with numerous men, Kinsey estimated that 95 percent of American men had engaged in masturbation, premarital or extramarital intercourse, or homosexual behavior. Five years later Kinsey caused even more of a disturbance with *Sexual Behavior in the Human Female,* which revealed that 62 percent of women masturbated and 50 percent had intercourse before marriage. Sex was nothing new, of course, but its existence was seldom spoken of in polite conversation.

Socially, the tremendous emphasis on family togetherness tended to isolate the suburban family. Writing in 1957, sociologist David Riesman

Critics of suburban life

criticized "the decentralization of leisure in the suburbs . . . as the home itself, rather than the neighborhood, becomes the chief gathering place for the family—either in the 'family room' with its games, its TV, its informality, or outdoors around the barbecue.' " Even the floor plan of the ranch-style home, at whose center

Cowboy star William Boyd ("Hopalong Cassidy") adorned this late-1940s advertisement for a bigger, brighter, clearer TV. Note the elaborate cowboy outfit worn by his young fan.   Howard Frank.

Middle-class America at play

The affluence that marked the postwar era was reflected in the materialistic values and pleasures of the period. Having satisfied their basic needs for food, clothing, and shelter, growing numbers of Americans turned their attention to luxury items. Indeed, the quest of middle-class families for the latest conveniences made shopping a form of recreation.

Of the new luxuries, television was the most revolutionary in its effects. One man who grew up in the postwar era recalled the purchase of the first family TV set in 1950. "And so the monumental change began in our lives and those of millions of other Americans. More than a year passed before we again visited a movie theater. Money which previously would have been spent for books was saved for the TV payments. Social evenings with friends became fewer and fewer still because we discovered we did not share the same TV program interests."

> **Effects of television**

As television brought the world into their living rooms, Americans began to read newspapers and news magazines a little less carefully, and to listen to radio a lot less frequently. But despite the lure of the tube, book readership went up. One reason for the increased consumption of literature was the mass marketing of the inexpensive paperbound book. Pocket books hit the market in 1939; soon westerns, detective stories, and science fiction filled the newstands, supermarkets, and drug stores. The comic book, which had become popular in 1939 with the introduction of Superman, became another drugstore standard. Reprints of hardcover books and condensed books also did well. Finally, book clubs experienced phenomenal growth. All in all, funds spent for books doubled between 1946 and 1960.

One obvious casualty of the stay-at-home suburban culture was the motion picture. While Americans continued to buy paperbacks and comic books in large numbers, many of them stopped visiting movie theaters. From 1946 to

was the TV set enthroned on a swivel, was ideally suited to the stay-at-home lifestyle.

Riesman was only one of many critics of suburban living and family togetherness. The word *suburbia,* Scott Donaldson wrote in *The Suburban Myth* (1969), had "unpleasant overtones, suggesting nothing so much as some kind of scruffy disease." And C. Wright Mills, a sociologist, castigated white-collar suburbanites, who "sell not only their time and energy but their personalities as well. They sell . . . their smiles and their kindly gestures."

When all the pluses and minuses were added up, however, most residents of suburbia—male and female, children and adults—seemed to prefer family togetherness to any other lifestyle of which they were aware. Of the college students interviewed by Riesman in the 1950s, the vast majority looked forward to living in the suburbs.

1948 Americans had attended movies at the rate of nearly 90 million a week. By 1950 the figure had dropped to 60 million a week; by 1960, 40 million. Thus the postwar years saw the steady closing of movie theaters—with the notable exception of the drive-in, which appealed to car-bound suburban families.

There was one crucial exception to the downturn in moviegoing. By the late 1950s the first children of the postwar baby boom had become adolescents, and though their parents preferred

| *Rise of the youth subculture* |

to stay home and watch television, they themselves flocked to the theaters. No less than 72 percent of moviegoers during the 1950s were under age thirty. Hollywood responded to this youthful new audience with films portraying young people as sensitive and intelligent, adults as boorish and hostile: *The Wild One, Rebel Without a Cause, Blackboard Jungle.* The cult of youth had been born.

Soon the music industry was catering to teens with cheap 45 rpm records. Bill Haley, the Everly Brothers, and Buddy Holly thrilled teenagers with a primitive but joyful music called rock-and-roll. Elvis Presley horrified their parents with his suggestive gyrations. Although the roots of the new music lay in black rhythm-and-blues, most white stars did not acknowledge the debt. Presley's hit tune "Hound Dog," for example, had originally been performed by the black singer Big Mama Thornton, but Thornton received little credit for her contribution. The lone black rock-and-roll superstar of the 1950s was Chuck Berry.

While white performers copied black rhythm-and-blues, black jazz artists like Charlie Parker and Dizzy Gillespie were experimenting with "bebop." In the 1950s jazz became increasingly fused with classical themes, compositions, and instrumentation. Intellectuals began to study this art form, which had once been looked down on as vulgar.

In the arts Martha Graham was lauded in international dance circles, and Jackson Pollock became the pivotal figure of the abstract expres-

sionist movement, which in the 1950s established New York City as a center of the art world. Rather than work with the traditional painter's easel, Pollock spread his canvas on the floor, where he was free to walk around it, "work from the four sides and literally be *in* the painting." He and other "action painters" worked with sticks, trowels, and knives, and they played with new materials like heavy impasto with "sand, broken glass and other foreign matter added." In the 1960s artists of the Pop Art movement satirized the consumer society, using commercial techniques to depict everyday objects. Andy Warhol painted Campbell soup cans; other artists did blowups of ice-cream sundaes, hamburgers, and comic-strip panels.

Every era has its fads; the 1950s had 3-D movies (audiences wore special glasses that enhanced the three-dimensional effect of a film)

| *Fads* |

and hula hoops (children spun large hoops around their waists by imitating a hula dancer). Although such crazes were short-lived, they created multimillion-dollar industries and effectively promoted dozens of movies and TV shows. Other postwar crazes are still with us—Scrabble, Monopoly, canasta, paint-by-number sets, and Barbie dolls, to name just a few. Frisbee-throwing has not only survived but prevailed over similar outdoor games. Many of these toys and games succeeded because they brought the whole family together.

Needless to say, the consensus society of the 1950s was not conducive to social criticism. The filmgoing public preferred noncontroversial movies. Readers bought novels and retreated into the criminal underworld, the Wild West, or the science-fiction fantasy worlds of Ray Bradbury and Arthur C. Clarke. Even serious artists tended to ignore the country's social problems. Respected novelists such as Saul Bellow and Bernard Malamud stressed the inner life, and J. D. Salinger's *Catcher in the Rye* (1951) offered only the innocence of childhood and the Zen Buddhist retreat as alternatives to adult hypocrisy.

There were exceptions. Ralph Ellison's *Invis-*

Important events

1945	Demobilization of 12 million GIs
1946	Beginning of the baby boom Dr. Benjamin Spock, *Baby and Child Care*
1947	Gross national product ($231.3 billion) begins postwar rise
1948	Postwar rise in women's employment Alfred C. Kinsey, *Sexual Behavior in the Human Male*
1949	National Housing Act
1950	Women's employment reaches 18.4 million
1951	J. D. Salinger, *Catcher in the Rye*
1952	Norman Vincent Peale, *The Power of Positive Thinking* Ralph Ellison, *The Invisible Man*
1953	Alfred C. Kinsey, *Sexual Behavior in the Human Female*
1955	Government approves use of Salk polio vaccine AFL-CIO merger *Rebel Without a Cause,* starring James Dean
1956	Interstate Highway Act Allen Ginsburg, *Howl*
1957	Peak of baby boom (4.3 million births) Soviet Union launches *Sputnik* Jack Kerouac, *On the Road*
1958	National Defense Education Act
1960	Gross national product reaches $503.7 billion Women's employment reaches 22.5 million

ible Man (1952) gave white Americans a glimpse of the psychic costs to black Americans of exclusion from the white American dream. Two films—*Gentleman's Agreement* (1947) and *Home of the Brave* (1949) examined anti-Semitism and white racism. And in the 1950s, one group of writers repudiated the conventional world of the middle class and the suburbs. The writers of the Beat (for "beatific") Generation flaunted their freewheeling sexuality and consumption of drugs. The Beats produced some memorable prose and poetry, including Allen Ginsberg's long poem *Howl* (1956) and Jack Kerouac's *On the Road* (1957), and they offered American youth an alternative to their parents' materialism and righteous self-congratulation. Though the Beats were mostly ignored during the fifties, millions of young Americans would discover their writings and lifestyle in the late 1960s.

> **Beat Generation**

One of the most influential books of postwar years was the best-selling *The Affluent Society* (1958), by economist John Kenneth Galbraith. Galbraith's thesis dovetailed with the middle-class belief that economic growth would bring prosperity to everyone. Some would have more than others, of course, but in time everybody would have enough. "Production has eliminated the more acute tensions associated with [economic] inequality," Galbraith wrote. Not until Chapter 23 did the author mention poverty; when he did, he dismissed it as not "a universal or massive affliction," but "more nearly an afterthought."

Only in the 1960s would middle-class Americans discover that there were millions of poor people living in America: Indians; blacks in urban ghettos and rural shacks; whites in the Appalachian Mountains; tenant farmers and migrant workers; aged men and women; nonunion workers in restaurants, hospitals, laundries, and on garbage crews; and working women, many of whom headed households. Politically and culturally, the 1960s would be vastly different from the consensus years. Ironically, it was to be the products of suburbia—the middle-class children of the baby boom—who would form the vanguard of the assault not only on poverty, but on the whole value system of the American middle class.

Suggestions for further reading

THE AFFLUENT SOCIETY John Kenneth Galbraith, *American Capitalism: The Concept of Countervailing Power* (1952); John Kenneth Galbraith, *The Affluent Society* (1958); Robert Heilbroner, *The Limits of American Capitalism* (1966); John L. Shover, *First Majority—Last Minority: The Transforming of Rural Life in America* (1976); Robert Sobel, *The Age of Giant Corporations: A Microeconomic History of American Business, 1914–1970* (1972); Harold G. Vatter, *The U.S. Economy in the 1950's* (1963).

THE BABY BOOM Richard A. Easterlin, *Birth and Fortune: The Impact of Numbers on Personal Welfare* (1980); Landon Y. Jones, *Great Expectations: America & the Baby Boom Generation* (1980).

SUBURBIA William B. Dobriner, *Class in Suburbia* (1963); Philip C. Dolce, ed., *Suburbia: The American Dream and Dilemma* (1976); Scott Donaldson, *The Suburban Myth* (1969); Herbert J. Gans, *The Levittowners* (1967); Robert C. Wood, *Suburbia: Its People and Their Politics* (1959).

MOTHERHOOD AND FAMILY William H. Chafe, *The American Woman: Her Changing Social, Economic, and Political Role, 1920–1970* (1972); Carl Degler, *At Odds: Woman and the Family in America from the Revolution to the Present* (1980); Betty Friedan, *The Feminine Mystique* (1963); Mirra Komarovsky, *Blue-Collar Marriage* (1962); Mirra Komarovsky, *Women in the Modern World: Their Education and Their Dilemmas* (1953); F. Ivan Nye and Lois Wladis Hoffman, eds., *The Employed Mother in America* (1963); Benjamin Spock, *Baby and Child Care* (1946).

POPULAR CULTURE John W. Aldridge, *In Search of Heresy: American Literature in an Age of Conformity* (1956); Ann Charters, *Kerouac* (1973); Andrew Dowdy, *The Films of the Fifties* (1973); Albert Goldman, *Ladies and Gentlemen Lenny Bruce!!* (1971); Maxwell Geismar, *American Moderns: From Rebellion to Conformity* (1958); Richard Kostelanetz, ed., *The New American Arts* (1965); Douglas T. Miller and Marion Novak, *The Fifties: The Way We Really Were* (1977); Robert Sklar, *Movie-Made America* (1975); John Tytell, *Naked Angels: The Lives and Literature of the Beat Generation* (1976).

TELEVISION Leo Bogart, *Age of Television* (1958); George Comstock *et al., Television and Human Behavior* (1978); Marshall McLuhan, *Understanding Media* (1964); Marshall McLuhan, *The Medium Is the Massage* (1967); Jerry Mander, *Four Arguments for the Elimination of Television* (1978).

29

AMERICA IN A REVOLUTIONARY WORLD: FOREIGN POLICY SINCE 1961

CIA officials assured the new president that they could deliver "another Guatemala," toppling the unfriendly government just as they had that of Jacobo Arbenz Guzman in 1954. So John F. Kennedy approved the invasion of Cuba. In mid-April 1961, 1,400 American-trained and supplied Cuban exiles landed at the Bay of Pigs.

On the beach the commandos met early disaster. Fidel Castro's militia was waiting for them; after a short skirmish, they were captured. Castro boasted of his victory over the mighty United States, and Soviet Premier Nikita Khrushchev warned Washington not to threaten Cuba again. Too late Kennedy realized that the ill-advised venture had provided his critics "a stick with which they would forever beat him."

The Cuban invasion was just one of many attempts by recent presidents to influence affairs in the powerful bloc of nations referred to as the Third World. Third World nations are so named because they belong neither to the first world of capitalism—the West—nor to the second world of communism—the East. Often called develorin nations, they are pre-

dominantly nonwhite, nonindustrialized, and located in the southern half of the globe. Many became independent states in the process of decolonization that followed the Second World War (see map, page 470). By the 1970s, Third World nations dominated the United Nations, controlled vital raw materials such as oil, and threatened world peace by warring among themselves.

In American eyes, the Third World challenge only complicated the Cold War. American leaders could have interpreted the anti-imperialism, the attacks on foreign-owned properties, the racial, religious, and ethnic tensions, and the political instability and civil war in the Third World as expressions of nationalism, as the natural restlessness of new nations, or as regional disputes. Instead, most American leaders took the globalist perspective, blaming Soviet Russia for most crises in the Third World and worrying that revolutionary movements there endangered American economic interests. Thus a combination of Cold War and economic motives led the United States to intervene in Third World affairs, discrediting itself in the eyes of its hoped-for allies.

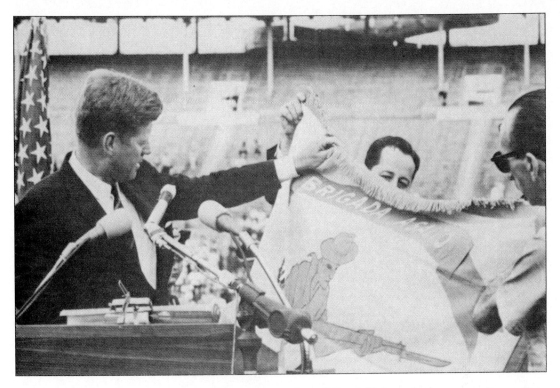

In December 1962, in Miami's Orange Bowl, President John F. Kennedy (1917–1963) welcomed home the newly released members of the CIA-sponsored landing force captured by the Cuban militia at the Bay of Pigs. Still determined to unseat Castro, Kennedy received the troops' combat banner, promising, "This flag will be returned to this Brigade in a free Havana." Wide World Photos.

The long American intervention in Vietnam revealed how difficult it was to resist Third World revolutionary nationalism.

The rise of the Third World

With Cold War lines drawn fairly tightly in Europe by the late 1940s, Soviet-American rivalry shifted increasingly to this part of the

| *Soviet-American rivalry in the Third World* |

world. Here were raw materials and markets, investment opportunities, military and intelligence bases, and votes in the United Nations. But Third World states, such as India, Ghana, Egypt, and Indonesia, did not wish to take sides in the contest between the great powers. To the dismay of both Washington and Moscow, they declared themselves neutral, or nonaligned, in the Cold War.

Most Americans considered the new nations' refusal to become involved in the life-and-death struggle of the Cold War immoral, perhaps even an indication of pro-Communist leanings. If a negative view of neutralism inhibited United States efforts to strengthen relations with emerging states, so did American hostility to-

| *American intolerance of revolution* |

ward revolution. Despite its own history, the United States was intolerant of revolutionary disorder. Third World revolutions were directed against America's Cold War allies. Or, as in the case of Cuba,

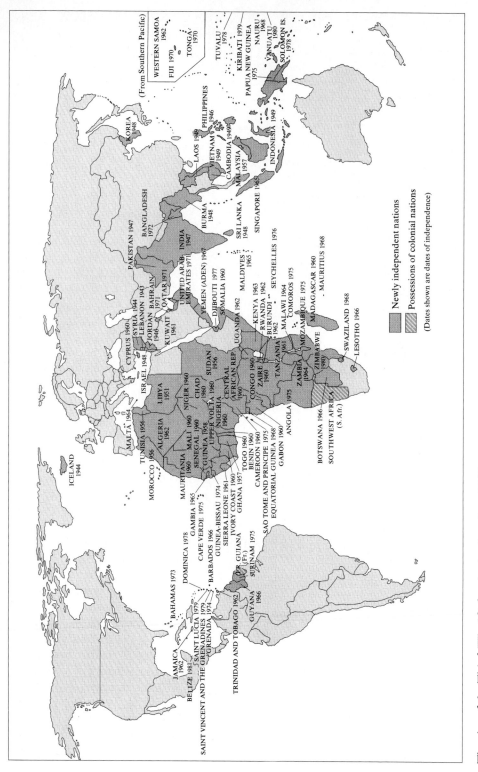

The rise of the Third World: decolonization since 1943

they threatened American investments, markets, and military bases.

Still another obstacle in America's relations with the rising Third World was the United States' great wealth. Foreigners both envied and resented the "people of plenty." American movies offered enticing glimpses of middle-class materialism; American products drew attention at international trade fairs and were coveted items at native marketplaces. And Americans stationed overseas often flaunted their superior standard of living. Also, many foreign peoples resented the ample profits that giant American corporations extracted from them. Finally, American segregationist practices at home deprived blacks of economic opportunity and civil rights, and Third World peoples thus criticized Americans for celebrating democracy but debasing it too. For all these reasons, the United States found itself not the model of revolution but the target.

The Soviet Union enjoyed only a slight edge, if any, in the race to win friends in the Third World. It was true that communist ideology encouraged anticolonialism. But Moscow could not easily explain away its brutal, sometimes military subjugation of neighboring countries. The Soviet takeover of Czechoslovakia in 1968 and invasion of Afghanistan in 1979 earned Russia international condemnation. And though Premier Nikita Khrushchev had toured India and Burma in the mid-1950s and offered aid to nonaligned Egypt and Indonesia, those nations had refused to become Soviet clients. They were not about to replace one imperial master with another. Ultimately the Soviets, like the Americans, concluded that Third World nations were playing the two superpowers against each other in order to garner larger amounts of aid and armaments.

Taking the globalist perspective, American officials assumed that troubles in the Third World were caused by Communist agents. But Third World troubles frequently sprouted from native soil, not from Communist plots. Nonetheless, to stem the perceived Communist threat, to curb revolution and civil war, the United States poured money and arms into the Third World. Beginning in the 1950s, CIA agents attempted to overturn uncooperative foreign governments. They succeeded in some cases—Iran in 1953, Guatemala in 1954, Chile in 1973—but failed in others—Indonesia in 1958 and Cuba in 1961. The Voice of America and the United States Information Agency advertised American achievements abroad. And the American military sometimes took action, as in the invasion of the Dominican Republic in 1965 and the long war in Vietnam.

These many interventions convinced the Soviets and numerous Third World leaders that the United States was a major menace in world affairs. Some Third World leaders blamed an exploitative United States for persistent hunger and poverty in their countries, although their own decisions sometimes hindered their nations' progress. Nonetheless, American interventionism was extensive enough to arouse continued criticism of the United States and to undermine American efforts to win the Third World to its side in the Cold War.

Kennedy, Cuba, and the quest for Cold War victory

In 1960 John F. Kennedy was elected president and a new chapter in the Cold War opened. Although Kennedy and his opponent in the election, Richard M. Nixon, differed little on foreign policy, Kennedy promised Cold War victory instead of stalemate. His attitude owed much to the past. Remembering the tragedy of

| Kennedy as Cold War activist |

appeasement in the 1930s, he concluded that that decade had "taught us a clear lesson: aggressive conduct, if allowed to go unchecked and unchallenged, ultimately leads to war." That there would be no halfway measures was apparent in Kennedy's Inaugural Address: "Let every nation know that we shall pay any price, bear any burden, meet any hardship, support any friend, oppose any foe to assure the survival and the success of liberty."

Khrushchev responded to Kennedy's rhetoric with an endorsement of "wars of national liberation" in the Third World. The Soviet leader also bragged about Russian ICBMs. Although American intelligence data showed that the Soviets were militarily inferior, Kennedy used Khrushchev's actions to justify a military build-up based on the principle of *flexible response*. Junking Eisenhower's concept of massive retaliation, Kennedy sought ways to meet any kind of warfare, from guerilla combat in the jungles to a nuclear showdown. In this way, he reasoned, he could contain both the Soviet Union and Third World revolutionary movements. Kennedy's actions only helped to goad Russia into an accelerated arms race.

During this time Berlin continued to claim headlines. The Russians again demanded nego-

| **Berlin Wall** | tiations to end the Western occupation of Berlin. But Kennedy saw the city as "the great testing place of Western courage and will." Instead of negotiating, Kennedy asked Congress in 1961 for an additional $3.2 billion for defense and the authority to call up reservists. The Soviets responded by erecting the Berlin Wall to halt the exodus of East Germans into West Berlin. In 1963 Kennedy visited the wall and stirred a mass rally of West Berliners with the words "Ich bin ein Berliner" ("I am a Berliner").

But it was over Cuba, a nation whose allegiance the United States had taken for granted since 1898, that Kennedy had his most serious confrontation with the Soviets (see map). Cuba became an obsession of American policy makers in 1959, when Fidel Castro emerged from his mountain-based guerrilla camp to oust America's long-time ally Fulgencio Batista. (Under the friendly Batista, American investments in Cuba had totaled about $1 billion.) President Eisenhower had made a last-minute attempt to install a friendly military regime there and to deny Castro his hard-fought revolutionary triumph. Incensed, Castro determined to break the influence of American business by confiscating some American-owned property, suspending promised elections, indulging in anti-American rhetoric, and signing a trade treaty with Russia (February 1960).

In mid-1960 Eisenhower reduced American purchases of Cuban sugar, and Castro responded by seizing American-owned companies. The Cuban premier also began to appeal to Russia for support and to mouth communist slogans. Russia came to his assistance with loans and trade.

Alarmed, Eisenhower ordered the CIA to train Cuban exiles for an invasion of the island. Just before he left office he broke diplomatic relations with Castro and advised Kennedy to ad-

| **Bay of Pigs** | vance plans for the invasion. But when the Bay of Pigs attack began in April 1961, the Cuban people did not rise up in sympathy with the invaders as had been anticipated, and within two days the invasion collapsed.

Kennedy did not suffer defeat easily. Soon he and his advisers set about finding other means to unseat Castro. As part of a plan called Operation Mongoose, government agents moved to disrupt the Cuban economy and to oust the nation from the Organization of American States. They continued to aid anti-Castro groups in Miami and plotted with organized crime leaders to assassinate Castro.

Kennedy's preoccupation with Cuba eventually led to one of the scariest crises of the Cold War, the Cuban missile crisis (1962). Had there been no Bay of Pigs, and no Operation Mongoose, there very likely would have been no missile crisis. To Castro, American hostility threatened Cuban independence. To Moscow, American actions were a challenge to the only pro-Communist regime in Latin America. In an attempt to counter American intervention, Castro and Khrushchev devised a daring plan: installation of Soviet missiles and nuclear bombers in Cuba.

Although the Kennedy administration was aware of a Soviet military buildup on the island, it was not until October 14, 1962, that a U-2 plane photographed nuclear-missile launching

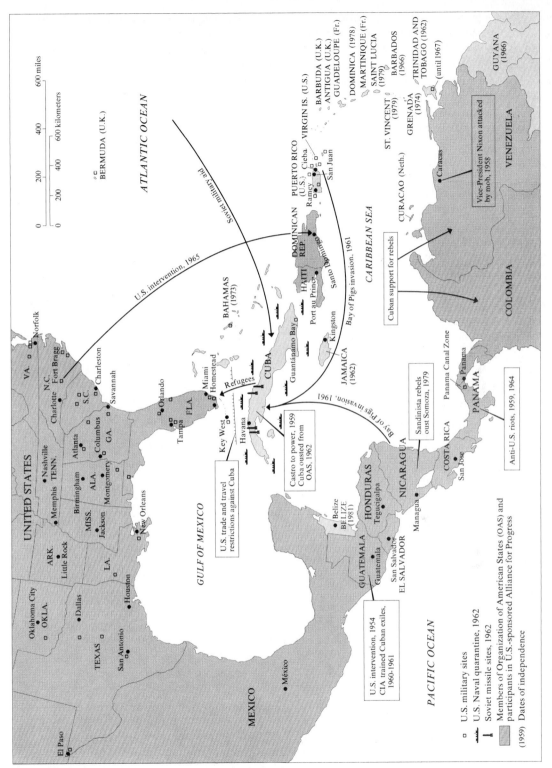

The United States, the Caribbean, and Cuba

UNITED STATES

Norfolk
VA.
N.C.
Fort Bragg
Charlotte
Charleston
S.C.
Savannah
Nashville
TENN.
Atlanta
Memphis
Columbus
Birmingham
GA.
ALA.
Orlando
Montgomery
FLA.
Tampa
MISS.
Jackson
Key West
ARK.
New Orleans
Little Rock
LA.
Oklahoma City
OKLA.
Dallas
TEXAS
Houston
San Antonio
El Paso

Miami
Homestead
Refugees
Havana
Santiago

GULF OF MEXICO

MEXICO
México

PACIFIC OCEAN

GUATEMALA
Guatemala
EL SALVADOR
San Salvador
HONDURAS
Tegucigalpa
NICARAGUA
Managua
COSTA RICA
San José
PANAMA
Panama
Panama Canal Zone
BELIZE
Belize
(1981)

CUBA
Guantánamo Bay
JAMAICA
(1962)
Kingston

BAHAMAS
(1973)
Port au Prince
HAITI
DOMINICAN REP.
Santo Domingo

PUERTO RICO
(U.S.)
Ramey
Ceiba
VIRGIN IS. (U.S.)
San Juan

BERMUDA (U.K.)

ATLANTIC OCEAN

BARBUDA (U.K.)
ANTIGUA (U.K.)
GUADELOUPE (Fr.)
DOMINICA (1978)
MARTINIQUE (Fr.)
SAINT LUCIA (1979)
ST. VINCENT (1979)
BARBADOS (1966)
GRENADA (1974)
TRINIDAD AND TOBAGO (1962)
(until 1967)

CARIBBEAN SEA

CURAÇAO (Neth.)

VENEZUELA
Caracas

COLOMBIA

GUYANA (1966)

U.S. intervention, 1965

Soviet military aid

Bay of Pigs invasion, 1961

Bay of Pigs invasion, 1961

Cuban support for rebels

Vice-President Nixon attacked by mob, 1958

Castro to power, 1959
Cuba ousted from OAS, 1962

U.S. trade and travel restrictions against Cuba

U.S. intervention, 1954
CIA trained Cuban exiles, 1960-1961

Sandinista rebels oust Somoza, 1979

Anti-U.S. riots, 1959, 1964

600 miles
600 kilometers
0   200   400   600

□ U.S. military sites
↑ U.S. Naval quarantine, 1962
⚓ Soviet missile sites, 1962
▓ Members of Organization of American States (OAS) and participants in U.S.-sponsored Alliance for Progress
(1959) Dates of independence

473

sites under construction there. The president ordered his special advisory executive committee to find a way to remove the missiles from Cuba. One committee member advised an air strike, but Attorney General Robert Kennedy, not wanting a Pearl Harbor on his brother's record, scotched the idea. The Joint Chiefs of Staff favored a full-scale invasion, but that might have provoked a prolonged war in Cuba, a Soviet move against Berlin, or even nuclear war. Direct negotiations with the Soviets, private overtures to Castro, and an appeal to the United Nations were also rejected. Secretary of Defense Robert S. McNamara proposed the most acceptable solution: a naval blockade of Cuba. This halfway response gave the administration the flexibility to escalate or negotiate, depending on the Russian response.

Cuban missile crisis

Over national television on October 22, Kennedy informed the Soviets of American policy and demanded their retreat. Throughout the world, the American military went on a full alert. Khrushchev first replied that the missiles would be withdrawn if Washington pledged never to attack Cuba again. Then he demanded the removal of American missiles from Turkey. Kennedy accepted the first condition but rejected the second. (Privately the administration made a loose promise to the Russians to withdraw the missiles from Turkey sometime in the future.) On October 28 Khrushchev accepted the American pledge to respect Cuban sovereignty and promised to dismantle the missiles and return them to the Soviet Union. Americans breathed a collective sigh of relief; this was, said many, Kennedy's finest hour.

But critics have asked whether the crisis was necessary. Why did Kennedy resort to public brinkmanship rather than private talks? Was he motivated by the forthcoming congressional elections? Did he need to prove his toughness? After all, the strategic balance of power was not seriously altered by the placement of missiles in Cuba.

The Cuban missile crisis humiliated the Soviets. Exposed as nuclear inferiors, the Soviets vowed to catch up—and they managed to do so by the late 1960s. The crisis did produce some relaxation in Soviet-American relations. The superpower leaders installed a telephone hot line between the White House and the Kremlin, signed a test-ban treaty, and refrained from further confrontation in Berlin.

Elsewhere in the Third World, Kennedy called for "peaceful revolution" based on the concept of *nation building*. The plan was to bring Third World countries into the American orbit by helping them through the infant stages of nationhood. Programs like the Peace Corps and, in Latin America, the Alliance for Progress focused on improving agriculture, transportation, health care, and communications.

Nation building

Besides such special development programs, Kennedy relied on *counterinsurgency:* the training of native police forces by American military and technical advisers. The assumption was that American soldiers—especially the Special Forces units, or Green Berets—would provide a protective shield against insurgents while American civilian personnel worked on economic projects. But as presidential adviser Arthur M. Schlesinger, Jr., later wrote, counterinsurgency proved "a ghastly illusion. Its primary consequence was to keep alive the American belief in their capacity and right to intervene in foreign lands."

Descent into the longest war: Vietnam

The belief in the right to influence the internal affairs of other countries led to disaster in Southeast Asia. How Vietnam became the site of America's longest war (1950-1975), how the world's most powerful nation spent itself in a futile attempt to subdue a peasant people, how those people suffered enormous losses of life and property and yet persisted, is one of the tragic stories of modern history.

The story begins with the French takeover of Vietnam during the late nineteenth century. For decades the French exploited the colony for its

History of imperialism in Vietnam

rice, rubber, tin, and tungsten, beating back peasant rebellions against their rule. Not until the Second World War, when the Japanese moved into Indochina, did French authority collapse.

Seizing their chance, the Viet Minh, an anti-imperialist coalition led by Communists, began guerilla warfare against the Japanese. Under the leadership of the nationalist Ho Chi Minh, they collaborated with American Office of Strategic Services (OSS) agents to harass the Japanese. OSS officers who worked with Ho in Vietnam were impressed by his frequent references to the United States as a revolutionary model. When Ho declared Vietnam's independence from France in September 1945, he wrote to the Truman administration requesting political support and economic assistance for his new government. His letters were never answered. The United States did not recognize Vietnamese independence, preferring to support its Cold War ally, France, against a Communist who had lived for a time in Russia.

Because of France's attempt to restore colonial rule, Vietnam was initially seen as a French problem. But when Jiang Jieshi (Chiang Kaishek) went down to defeat in China, the United States was roused to action. The Truman administration made two crucial decisions in early 1950. First, it recognized the French puppet government of Bao Dai. Second, the administration agreed to send ammunition, guns, aircraft, and ultimately military advisers to the French. By 1954 the United States had invested over $2 billion in the war and was bearing 78 percent of its cost.

Despite American aid, the French lost steadily to the Viet Minh. Finally, in 1954 Ho's forces surrounded the French fortress at Dienbienphu. What would the United States do? Eisenhower was cautious. If American forces became directly involved in the war—as distinct from merely advising the French—he might not be able to limit the nation's involvement. And as General Matthew Ridgway pointed out, air power alone could not guarantee victory.

Nevertheless, Eisenhower worried aloud at the prospect of a Communist victory, comparing the weak nations of the world to a row of dominoes, all of which would topple if just one fell. He asked the British to help, but they would make no commitment. At home, members of Congress refused to support military action unless the British went along.

To add to the administration's problems, the French wanted out. They agreed to peace talks

Geneva Conference

at Geneva, where France, the United States, Russia, Britain, China, Laos, and Cambodia joined the two competing Vietnamese regimes. When the Geneva Accords of 1954 were agreed on, American delegates grumbled about French weakness. Vietnam was temporarily divided at the 17th parallel, with Ho's Democratic Republic confined to the North. National elections would be held in 1956, and the country would thereupon be unified. Neither North nor South was to join a military alliance or permit foreign military bases on its soil.

Certain that the Geneva agreements would ultimately mean Communist victory, the United States refused to sign and set about to sabotage them. Thus American CIA personnel began secret operations against the North, and in the South support flowed to the anti-French leader Ngo Dinh Diem. A Catholic in a Buddhist nation, Diem lacked popular support. But with American aid and a rigged election, he beat back his opponents.

Diem soon became a dictator. He abolished village elections, jailed thousands of dissenters,

Civil war in South Vietnam

and shut down newspapers critical of his government. Communists and non-Communists alike struck back. The Viet Minh assassinated hundreds of Diem's village officials. With the support of peasants who had been victimized by Diem's regime, in late 1960 they organized the National Liberation Front, or Viet Cong. Civil war had erupted in South Vietnam.

In the United States, the newly elected President Kennedy decided to stand firm against the Viet Cong. Kennedy had suffered the humiliations of the Bay of Pigs and the Berlin Wall; he feared further criticism should the United States back down in Asia. But more important, he sought a Cold War victory. By late 1963, 16,700 American "advisers" were stationed in Vietnam, 489 of whom died that year. The same year an American project called the strategic hamlet program, which aimed to separate peasants from the Viet Cong by uprooting them, backfired. Meanwhile, when Diem's troops attacked Buddhist protesters, monks poured gasoline over their robes and ignited themselves in the streets of Saigon.

Diem, American officials decided, had to go. Through the CIA, the United States quietly encouraged South Vietnamese generals to stage a coup. With the ill-concealed backing of Ambassador Henry Cabot Lodge, the generals struck in early November 1963. Diem was captured and murdered—only a few weeks before Kennedy himself met death by an assassin's bullet and Vice President Lyndon B. Johnson became president.

With new governments in Saigon and Washington, some analysts thought it an appropriate time for reassessment. The Viet Cong, United Nations General Secretary U Thant, France, and others called for a coalition government in South Vietnam. But Johnson, would have none of it; he would settle only for victory.

Johnson and the war without victory

Johnson saw the world in simple terms— them against us—and privately disparaged both his allies and his enemies. Vietnam was a "raggedy-ass fourth-rate country," his critics "rattlebrains." Johnson sometimes lied or exaggerated, creating what reporters referred to as a credi-

bility gap. His greatest liability, however, was that he held firmly to fixed ideas about American superiority, the menace of communism, and the necessity of global intervention.

By early 1964 the Viet Cong controlled nearly half of South Vietnam. Because the new Saigon government was shaky and seemed to be leaning toward neutralism, United States officials cooperated in a second coup. In neighboring Laos, American bombers hit supply routes connecting the Viet Cong with the North Vietnamese, thus widening the scope of the war. Then in August an alleged incident in the Gulf of Tonkin, off the coast of North Vietnam, drew the United States even deeper into the Vietnamese quagmire. While assisting South Vietnamese raiders, the U.S.S. *Maddox* and *C. Turner Joy* reported that they were attacked in international waters by North Vietnamese gunboats (see map). Weather conditions that night were adverse, making suspect the sonar and radar reports on which the initial assumption of attack was based. Indeed, the historian George C. Herring states that "no evidence has ever been produced to demonstrate that they [the gunboats] committed hostile acts."

Johnson, however, seized the chance to go on national television and announce retaliatory air strikes above the 17th parallel. He also secured

| *Tonkin Gulf resolution* |

from Congress the Tonkin Gulf resolution, which authorized the president to "take all necessary measures to repel any armed attack against the forces of the United States and to prevent further aggression." The vote was 466 to 0 in the House and 88 to 2 in the Senate. Over time the Tonkin Gulf resolution would come to serve as the declaration of war Congress never voted on. Only in 1970 would senators repeal it.

Johnson won the presidency in his own right in the fall of 1964, his popularity buoyed by his forceful response to the Tonkin Gulf incident. At his direction the military planned stepped-up bombing of North Vietnam and Laos. Following an enemy attack at Pleiku in February 1965, Johnson initiated Operation Rolling Thunder, a

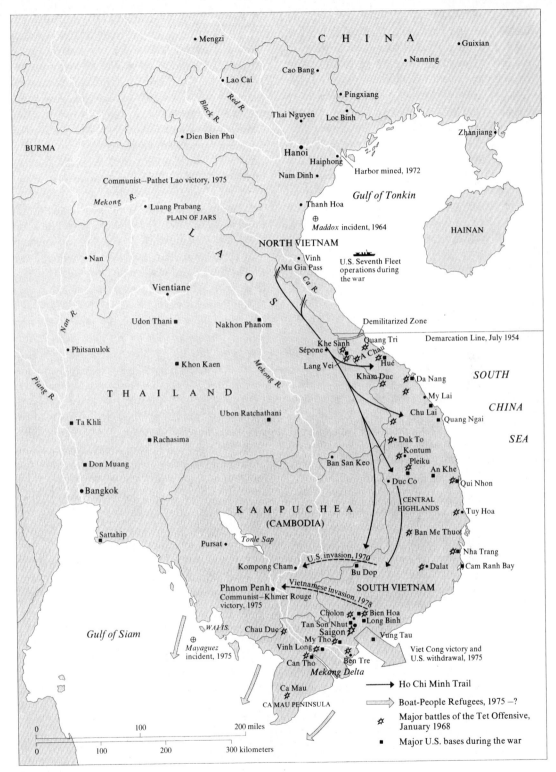

Southeast Asia and the Vietnam War

sustained bombing program above the 17th parallel. Before the war's end, the United States would drop more bomb tonnage on Vietnam than it had in all of the Second World War. The president also sent more troops to the South; by 1969, 542,000 American troops were stationed there.

The "Americanization" of the war in Vietnam under Johnson bothered growing numbers of Americans, especially as increased television coverage brought the ugliness of combat into their homes. The pictures and the stories were not pretty: innocent civilians caught in the line of fire; refugee-flooded "pacification" camps; countryside denuded by chemical defoliants; villages burned to the ground. Stories of atrocities made their way home too. Most gruesome was the My Lai massacre in March 1968. An American unit, frustrated by its inability to pin down an elusive enemy, shot to death scores of unarmed women and children.

By 1968 Johnson faced criticism both inside and outside the government. Secretary of Defense McNamara and Undersecretary of State George Ball resigned in protest. Senator William Fulbright began to conduct hearings on whether the national interest was being served by pursuing the war. And Senator Eugene McCarthy decided to challenge Johnson for the Democratic presidential nomination.

Johnson dug in, snapping at his critics and vowing to continue the battle against communism. At times he halted the bombing to encourage Ho Chi Minh to negotiate. Such pauses, however, were often accompanied by increases in American troop strength. Unpersuaded, the North demanded a complete stop to the destruction before they would sit down at the conference table. Indeed, American terms were unacceptable to the Communists: nonrecognition of the Viet Cong; withdrawal of northern soldiers from the South; and an end to North Vietnamese aid to the Viet Cong.

Then in January 1968, a shocking event forced Johnson to reappraise his position. During Tet, the Vietnamese lunar new year, Viet

Tet offensive Cong and North Vietnamese forces struck all across South Vietnam, hitting and capturing the provincial capitals. In Saigon raiders actually occupied the grounds of the American embassy for several hours. American and South Vietnamese units eventually regained much lost ground, inflicting heavy casualties on the enemy. But the Tet offensive jolted Americans. If all of America's firepower and dollars and half a million troops could not defeat the Viet Cong, could anything?

The impact of the Tet offensive on public opinion hit the White House like a thunderclap. The new secretary of defense, Clark Clifford, told Johnson the war could not be won, even if the 206,000 more soldiers requested by the army were sent to Vietnam. Strained by exhausting sessions with advisers, realizing that further escalation would not bring victory, and faced with serious opposition within his own party, Johnson changed course. In an appearance on national television (March 31) he announced that he had stopped the bombing of most of North Vietnam, asked Hanoi to begin negotiations, and stunned the nation by dropping out of the presidential race. The United States, knowing it could not win, would at least try not to lose.

Richard M. Nixon, Johnson's successor, decided to pursue "peace with honor" through "Vietnamization" of the war–building up South Vietnamese forces to replace American troops. And he announced the Nixon Doctrine: that the United States would help those Asian nations that helped themselves. Slowly he began to withdraw American troops from Vietnam, decreasing their number to 139,000 by the end of 1971. But he also increased the bombing in the North, hoping to pound Hanoi into making concessions. Nixon's national security adviser, Henry A. Kissinger, called it jugular diplomacy.

In April 1970 American and South Vietnamese troops invaded Cambodia in search of enemy forces and arms depots. The escalation sparked renewed protest at home. Demonstrations swept college campuses; the Senate forbade the ex-

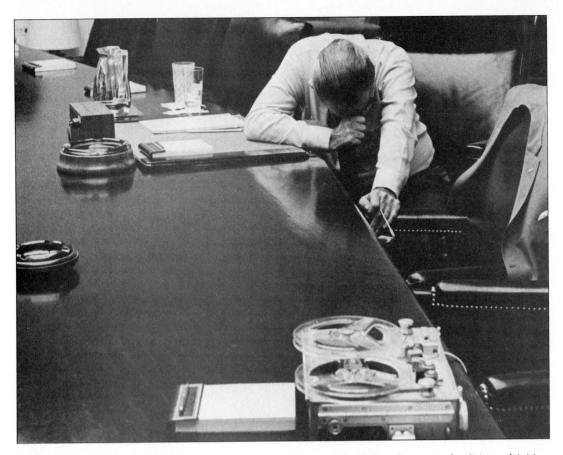

In July 1968 a war-weary President Lyndon B. Johnson (1908–1973) pondered what to do next. Just months before, stunned by the Tet offensive, Johnson had decided to drop out of politics and initiate peace talks.   Lyndon Baines Johnson Library.

penditure of funds on the new war. But Nixon and Kissinger were unmoved. They continued to escalate the war, ordering "protective reaction strikes" against the North; the secret bombing of Cambodia; the mining of Haiphong Harbor, near the northern capital, Hanoi; and in December 1972, a massive air strike that demolished every kind of northern structure.

Meanwhile the peace talks seemed to be going nowhere. But Kissinger was meeting privately with Le Duc Tho, the chief delegate from North Vietnam. Finally, on January 27, 1973, Kissinger and Le signed a cease-fire agreement. The United States promised to withdraw its remaining troops within sixty days. Other troops would stay in place, and a coalition government that included the Viet Cong would eventually be formed in the South. Pleased that a peace had been made, critics nonetheless noted that the terms of the agreement could have been accepted in 1969 and over twenty thousand American lives spared.

American withdrawal from Vietnam

Leaving behind some advisers, the United States pulled its troops out of Vietnam and reduced its aid program. Both North and South soon violated the cease-fire, and full-scale war

The architects of détente, Soviet Communist party boss Leonid Brezhnev (1906–1982) and President Richard M. Nixon (1913–), enjoy a light moment after signing the Strategic Arms Limitation Treaty. UPI.

erupted once more. As many had predicted, the feeble South Vietnamese government could not hold out. On April 29, 1975, South Vietnam collapsed, and shortly after Saigon was renamed Ho Chi Minh City.

The overall costs of the war were immense. Over 57,000 Americans and hundreds of thousands of Asians died. In monetary terms the war cost the United States more than $150 billion; another $200 billion would be paid in future veterans' benefits. At home the war brought inflation, political schism, attacks on civil liberties, and retrenchment from reform programs. The war also had negative consequences internationally: delay in moving toward better relations with the Soviet Union and the People's Republic of China; friction with allies; contin-

ued turmoil in Southeast Asia; and the alienation of Third World nations.

Nixon, Kissinger, and détente

With the war over, Nixon and Kissinger pursued a foreign policy designed to promote a global balance of power, or "balance of restraint," and to curb revolution and radicalism in the Third World. The popular word for the new posture toward the Soviets was *détente,* meaning limited cooperation through negotiations, within a general environment of rivalry. But détente was essentially the old policy of containment refurbished. Its purpose was to check Soviet expansion and limit the Soviet arms buildup.

Nixon and Kissinger pursued détente with extraordinary energy. To slow the costly arms race, they initiated Strategic Arms Limitations Talks (SALT) with the Soviets. In 1972 the talks produced a SALT treaty that limited anti-

| Strategic Arms Limitations Talks (SALT) |

ballistic missile systems (defensive systems that made offensive missiles less vulnerable to attack). A second agreement placed a five-year freeze on the number of offensive nuclear missiles each side could have. At the time of the agreement the Soviets had an advantage in total missiles, but the United States had more warheads per missile. American MIRVs (multiple independently targeted reentry vehicles) could fire several warheads at different targets in midflight. In short, the United States had a 2-to-1 advantage in deliverable warheads. Since SALT did not restrict MIRVs, the arms race continued.

Nixon and Kissinger also tried to restrain the Soviets indirectly, by making overtures to a Russian enemy. In February 1972 Nixon made a his-

| Accommodation with the Chinese Communists |

toric trip to the People's Republic of China. The United States shared one goal with China: to limit Soviet influence in Asia. Nixon also hoped to open the Chinese market to American products, and he wanted China to sign the Nuclear Non-Proliferation Treaty negotiated in 1968 by the Johnson administration. So he and Kissinger journeyed to a country that the United States had refused to recognize since 1949. At the end of the trip they issued a communique that said in essence that the United States and China agreed to disagree on a number of issues, but agreed on one: Russia should not be permitted to make gains in Asia. Official diplomatic recognition and exchange of ambassadors was effected in 1979.

Tortuous events in the Middle East, however, revealed how fragile the Nixon-Kissinger grand strategy was. When Nixon took office in 1969

| Arab-Israeli hostilities |

the Middle East was, in the president's words, a "powder keg." In the Six-Day War (1967), Israel had seized the West Bank and the ancient city of Jerusalem from Jordan, the Golan Heights from Syria, and the Sinai Peninsula from Egypt (see map, page 482). To complicate matters, Palestinian Arabs, many of them expelled from their homeland in 1948 when the nation of Israel was created, had organized the Palestine Liberation Organization (PLO) and pledged to destroy Israel.

On October 6, 1973, Egypt and Syria attacked Israel. In spite of détente, Moscow and Washington were soon locked in confrontation; both superpowers put their armed forces on alert. At the same time, in an attempt to pressure Americans into taking a pro-Arab stance, the powerful Organization of Petroleum Exporting Countries (OPEC) imposed an embargo on shipments of oil to the United States. OPEC also raised prices dramatically.

Faced with an energy crisis at home, the Nixon administration had to find a way to end Middle-Eastern hostilities. In October Kissinger arranged for a cease-fire; beginning in December he undertook "shuttle diplomacy," flying back and forth between Middle Eastern capitals in an exhausting search for a settlement. OPEC ended its embargo early in 1974. In 1975 Kissinger persuaded Egypt and Israel to allow a United Nations peace-keeping force in the Sinai and pledged them to resolve their differences peacefully. But other problems remained: the homeless Palestinian Arabs; Israeli occupation of Jerusalem and the West Bank; Israel's insistence on building settlements in occupied lands; and Arab threats to destroy the Jewish state.

In Latin America, Nixon continued Cold War interventionist policies. In 1970, when the

| Intervention in Latin America |

people of Chile elected the Marxist Salvadore Allende president, Nixon suspended foreign aid to Chile. The CIA moved to disrupt the Chilean economy, fuel anti-Allende criticism and encourage a military coup. In 1974 a military junta ousted and killed Allende.

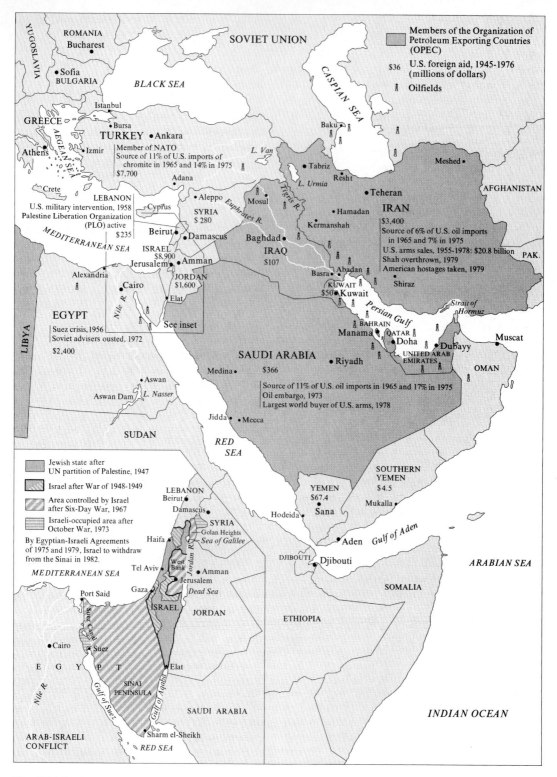

Members of the Organization of Petroleum Exporting Countries (OPEC)

$36 **U.S. foreign aid, 1945–1976 (millions of dollars)**

Oilfields

YUGOSLAVIA

ROMANIA
Bucharest

SOVIET UNION

BLACK SEA

• Sofia
BULGARIA

CASPIAN SEA

Istanbul

GREECE
AEGEAN SEA
Athens •

• Bursa
TURKEY • Ankara

Baku •

Meshed •

• Izmir

Member of NATO
Source of 11% of U.S. imports of
chromite in 1965 and 14% in 1975
$7,700

L. Van

• Tabriz

Resht •

AFGHANISTAN

Crete

Adana

L. Urmia

• Teheran

PAK.

LEBANON
U.S. military intervention, 1958
Palestine Liberation Organization
(PLO) active
$235

Cyprus

• Aleppo

SYRIA
$ 280

Mosul •

Euphrates R.

Tigris R.

• Hamadan

IRAN

• Kermanshah

$3,400
Source of 6% of U.S. oil imports
in 1965 and 7% in 1975
U.S. arms sales, 1955–1978: $20.8 billion
Shah overthrown, 1979
American hostages taken, 1979

MEDITERRANEAN SEA

Beirut •
• Damascus

Baghdad •

ISRAEL
$8,900
Jerusalem •• Amman

IRAQ
$107

Basra •

Abadan •

JORDAN
$1,600

Alexandria

• Cairo

KUWAIT
$50• Kuwait

• Shiraz

Strait of
Hormuz

• Elat

See inset

Persian Gulf

• Muscat

EGYPT

Suez crisis, 1956
Soviet advisers ousted, 1972
$2,400

BAHRAIN
Manama • QATAR
• Doha
• Dubayy

SAUDI ARABIA

Medina •

$366

• Riyadh

UNITED ARAB
EMIRATES

OMAN

LIBYA

• Aswan

Nile R.

Aswan Dam

L. Nasser

SUDAN

Jidda •

Source of 11% of U.S. oil imports in 1965 and 17% in 1975
Oil embargo, 1973
Largest world buyer of U.S. arms, 1978

• Mecca

RED
SEA

SOUTHERN
YEMEN

$4.5

YEMEN
$67.4

Mukalla •

Hodeida •
Sana •

Aden •
Gulf of Aden

ARABIAN SEA

DJIBOUTI
Djibouti •

SOMALIA

ETHIOPIA

INDIAN OCEAN

Jewish state after
UN partition of Palestine, 1947

Israel after War of 1948–1949

Area controlled by Israel
after Six-Day War, 1967

Israeli-occupied area after
October War, 1973

By Egyptian-Israeli Agreements
of 1975 and 1979, Israel to withdraw
from the Sinai in 1982.

LEBANON
Beirut •
Damascus •

SYRIA
Golan Heights
Sea of Galilee

Haifa •

MEDITERRANEAN SEA

Jordan R.

Tel Aviv •

West
Bank
• Amman

Port Said •

Gaza •
• Jerusalem
Dead Sea

JORDAN

Suez Canal

• Cairo
• Suez

ISRAEL

E G Y P T

Nile R.

• Elat

SINAI
PENINSULA

Gulf of Suez

Gulf of Aqaba

SAUDI ARABIA

ARAB-ISRAELI
CONFLICT

Sharm el-Sheikh •
RED SEA

The Middle East

In the wake of the crisis, critics asked why the United States continued to meddle in the affairs of other nations. Part of the explanation was that the United States continued to have an economic interest in them. By the mid-1970s American investments abroad totaled over $133 billion, and the nation's economy was heavily dependent upon imported raw materials. National needs, as well as Kissinger's belief that economic instability creates political instability, still encouraged American intervention abroad.

Carter, Reagan, and continued global tension

When he took office in 1977, President Jimmy Carter vowed to reduce the American military presence overseas (about 700,000 military personnel were stationed abroad); cut back arms sales (they totaled about $10 billion); and slow the nuclear arms race. He said he would continue détente and speed up the peace process in the Middle East. And he promised to be more understanding of Third World aspirations. Finally, "the soul of our foreign policy," Carter said, would be the championing of individual human rights abroad. In practice, however, the president used a double standard, applying the human-rights test to some nations but not to American allies like Iran, the Philippines, and South Korea.

Carter's human-rights policy

Despite Carter's goals, détente deteriorated and the Cold War revived during his administration. The president first angered the Soviets by calling on them to respect their citizens' human rights and tolerate dissent. Moscow told him to mind his own business. Then American officials denounced Russia for backing Cuban troops in Africa. And as Sino-American relations improved following the Nixon visit, Soviet leaders worried that the United States was playing its "China card"—building up their rival in order to threaten them.

A thaw came in 1979 when negotiations produced a new treaty, SALT II, that acknowledged Soviet-American nuclear parity. The agreement placed a ceiling of 2,250 delivery vehicles (long-range bombers, ICBMs, and submarine-based missiles) on each side and imposed limits on the number of warheads and the development of new kinds of nuclear weapons. Critics from the right charged that the treaty favored the Soviets; critics from the left protested that it did not go far enough toward quelling the arms race. As if to prove both sides correct, Carter soon announced that the United States would construct an expensive new MX missile system that would shuttle ICBMs back and forth along a vast maze of underground tunnels designed to confuse attackers.

Meanwhile, events in Afghanistan led to a Soviet-American confrontation. In December 1979 the Red Army bludgeoned its way into the Soviets' southern neighbor to shore up the faltering Communist government, under siege by Moslem rebels. But the rebels persisted, with some aid from the CIA, and analysts predicted that the Soviet Union had sunk into its own Vietnam. Determined to make the U.S.S.R. "pay a concrete price for their aggression," an embittered Carter shelved SALT II, suspended shipments of grain and high-technology equipment to Russia, and launched an international boycott of the 1980 Summer Olympics in Moscow. The president also announced what was quickly dubbed the Carter Doctrine: the United States would intervene, unilaterally and militarily if necessary, against any Soviet aggression in the petroleum-rich Persian Gulf. But all his efforts failed to cause the Soviets to withdraw.

Carter met his toughest test in Iran, where in early 1979 the shah was toppled from his throne by revolutionaries under the leadership of Ayatollah Ruhollah Khomeini, a wrathfully anti-American Moslem cleric. In November, after the exiled shah was admitted to the United States for medical treatment, mobs stormed the American embassy in Teheran and took American personnel as hostages, demanding the return

Hostage crisis in Iran

of the shah for trial, along with his wealth. Although the Iranians eventually released a few of the prisoners, 52 others languished over a year under Iranian guard.

Carter would not return the shah to Iran or apologize for past American involvement there. Unable to gain the hostages' freedom through public appeals, foreign emissaries, or United Nations delegations, the president took steps to isolate Iran economically. He froze Iranian assets in the United States and appealed to American allies, largely unsuccessfully, to reduce trade with the Moslem state. In April 1980 Carter broke diplomatic relations with Iran and ordered a daring rescue mission that miscarried after an equipment failure in the sandy Iranian desert. The hostages were not freed until January 1981, 444 days after their capture. In the agreement that led to their release, the United States unfroze Iranian assets and promised not to intervene again in Iran's internal affairs.

Carter brought to fruition Henry Kissinger's efforts to defuse the feud between Egypt and Israel. Through his personal diplomacy, Egyptian President Anwar Sadat and Israeli Prime Minister Menachem Begin met at Camp David in 1979. With the president's help they agreed to a treaty providing for Israel's phased withdrawal from the Sinai Peninsula, which it had occupied since 1967. Other Arab states denounced the agreement for not requiring Israel to relinquish other occupied territories. But the treaty at least ended warfare along one boundary in this troubled area of the world.

Carter also had some success elsewhere in the Third World. His appointment of Andrew Young, a black civil rights activist and congressman, as ambassador to the United Nations earned goodwill among developing nations. Young believed that the United States should stay out of local disputes, even if Communists were involved. Third World leaders were shocked, however, when Young was forced to resign in 1979 after meeting privately with representatives of the Palestine Liberation Organization, which the United States did not recognize.

In Latin America, Carter concluded two treaties with Panama that provided for gradual return of the Canal Zone to that Central American nation. He also compromised with nationalist forces in Nicaragua, which had been ruled for decades by the dictatorial Somoza family. When leftist rebels overthrew Somoza in 1979, Carter at first tried to tame their radicalism, but failing, then recognized the revolutionary government. To have resisted it, the president argued, would have been to push Nicaragua into the Cuban or even the Soviet camp.

Carter's achievements in Latin America

Carter's diplomatic record did not satisfy Americans who wanted superiority in foreign affairs—a reinstatement of the considerable military edge the United States had had in the early years of the Cold War. Critics chided the administration for a post-Vietnam "loss of will." An Oklahoma couple urged Carter to take up once again Teddy Roosevelt's big stick. "And club the hell out of them if you need to," grumbled the husband.

This nostalgia for old-fashioned American militancy found a ringing voice in President Ronald Reagan, elected in 1980 after a campaign charging that the United States was falling behind the Soviets in the arms race and retreating under fire from the Third World. Reagan promised to abandon détente and SALT II, dramatically increase the military budget, and support authoritarian right-wing governments that stood by American foreign policy. His first secretary of state, former Nixon aide and NATO commander, Alexander M. Haig, believed that "there are more important things than peace . . . there are things which we Americans must be willing to fight for."

Reagan and Cold War revival

Not only Reagan's vehemently anti-Communist rhetoric but his actions were reminiscent of the past. By 1983 the United States had stationed thirty-seven military advisers in El Salvador, a war-torn country where leftist insurgents were attempting to topple a repressive government. American covert aid went to Nicaraguan

Important events

1961	Peace Corps founded
	Alliance for Progress
	Bay of Pigs disaster
	Berlin crisis
	American military build-up in Vietnam
1962	Cuban missile crisis
1963	Test ban treaty
	Diem assassinated in Vietnam
	Kennedy assassinated; Lyndon B. Johnson assumes the presidency
1964	Tonkin Gulf resolution
1965	U.S. intervenes in the Dominican Republic
1967	Six-Day War in the Middle East
1968	Tet offensive in Vietnam
	My Lai massacre
	Nuclear Non-Proliferation Treaty
	Soviet invasion of Czechoslovakia
	Vietnam peace talks open in Paris
	Richard M. Nixon elected president
1969	Détente policy toward the Soviet Union announced
1970	Invasion of Cambodia
1972	Nixon visits China
	SALT I treaty
1973	Vietnam cease-fire agreement
	U.S. helps overthrow government of Chile

	Arab-Israel War
	Arab oil embargo
1975	Egyptian-Israeli peace agreement signed
	South Vietnam falls to Communists
1976	Jimmy Carter elected president
1977	Human-rights policy launched
1978	Panama Canal Treaties
1979	Egyptian-Israeli peace accord struck at Camp David
	American embassy officials seized by mob in Teheran, Iran
	SALT II nuclear-arms-control treaty signed
	Soviets invade Afghanistan
	Carter imposes grain embargo on Soviets and organizes boycott of Moscow Olympic Games
1980	Ronald Reagan elected president
1981	American hostages in Iran released after 444 days of captivity
	U.S. becomes more deeply involved in El Salvador
	Defense budget sharply increased
1982	Israel invades Lebanon
	American marines in Lebanon
1983	Schultz mission to the Middle East
	Funding for MX
	Soviets shoot down Korean commercial airliner

exiles who were attempting to overthrow the leftist Sandinista government. The president also proposed a five-year defense package costing an unprecedented $1.5 trillion. Like Carter, Reagan wanted an MX system, but instead of a mobile one, he proposed a "dense pack"—a tight configuration of missiles within a confined geographic area. His expensive plan encountered criticism from congressional representatives who believed that domestic problems were more pressing. By the summer of 1983 "dense pack" was dead, but Congress appropriated funds for the development of the MX.

The Soviets reinforced Reagan's hard line and spurred his quest for increased defense spending. On September 1, 1983, a Soviet fighter plane shot down a Korean commercial airliner that had violated Russian air space. This inhumane act took the lives of 269 people. The Reagan administration used the incident to focus world condemnation on the Soviets. The American people reacted with outrage, and a renewed anti-Communist emotionalism swept the country.

Continued violence in the Middle East also worried the Reagan administration. In 1982 Israel invaded Lebanon, which was partially occupied by Syrian troops and had become a staging area for PLO attacks on Israel. After defeating the PLO and forcing their withdrawal, Israel agreed to the entry of an international peace-keeping force. American marines participated in that effort. In 1983 Secretary of State George Schultz worked to secure the removal of all foreign troops from Lebanon. Israel agreed to remove its troops if Syrian forces also withdrew; but the Syrians remained reluctant to pull back their forces. By the fall of 1983, hostile fire from one of the Lebanese factions had taken the lives of several marines.

The global watch continued under Reagan. Still, America in the 1980s was not the power it had been in the 1940s and 1950s. Nations devastated by the Second World War had recovered to challenge American business and technology. Third World nations had thrown off their colonial status. Growing consumption produced an energy shortage, making the United States dependent on imports from other nations. And Russia's nuclear arsenal matched America's. "His is a kind of 1952 world," one of Reagan's former advisers said. Yet the world had markedly changed.

Suggestions for further reading

KENNEDY AND JOHNSON DIPLOMACY Graham Allison, *Essence of Decision: Explaining the Cuban Missile Crisis* (1971); Warren I. Cohen, *Dean Rusk* (1980); Herbert Dinerstein, *The Making of a Missile Crisis* (1976); Robert A. Divine, ed., *The Cuban Missile Crisis* (1971); Philip Geyelin, *Lyndon B. Johnson and the World* (1966); David Halberstam, *The Best and the Brightest* (1972); Jim Heath, *Decade of Disillusionment* (1975); Doris Kearns, *Lyndon Johnson and the American Dream* (1976); Herbert S. Parmet, *JFK* (1983); Walt W. Rostow, *Diffusion of Power* (1972); Arthur M. Schlesinger, Jr., *A Thousand Days* (1965); Arthur M. Schlesinger, Jr., *Robert Kennedy and His Times* (1978); Richard Walton, *Cold War and Counterrevolution* (1972).

THE UNITED STATES AND THE THIRD WORLD Rudolf von Albertini, *Decolonization* (1981); Richard J. Barnet, *Intervention and Revolution*, rev. ed. (1972); John L. S. Girling, *America and the Third World* (1980); Melvin Gurtov, *The United States Against the Third World* (1974); Robert C. Johansen, *The National Interest and the Human Interest* (1980); Gabriel Kolko, *The Roots of American Foreign Policy* (1969); Richard B. Morris, *The Emerging Nations and the American Revolution* (1970); Robert A. Packenham, *Liberal America and the Third World* (1973); Ronald Steel, *Pax Americana* (1967); Jennifer S. Whitaker, ed., *Africa and the United States* (1978).

LATIN AMERICA Samuel Baily, *The United States and the Development of South America, 1945–1975* (1977); Cole Blasier, *Hovering Giant* (1974); Richard R. Fagen, ed., *Capitalism and the State in U.S.-Latin American Relations* (1979); Marvin E. Gettleman *et al.*, eds., *El Salvador: Central America in the New Cold War* (1981): Walter LaFeber, *The Panama Canal*

(1979); Walter LaFeber, *Inevitable Revolutions: The United States in Central America* (1983); Robert H. McBride, ed., *Mexico and the United States* (1981); Ramon Ruiz, *Cuba: The Making of a Revolution* (1968); Peter Wyden, *Bay of Pigs* (1979).

MIDDLE EAST Chester L. Cooper, *The Lion's Last Roar: Suez, 1956* (1978); George Lenczowski, *The Middle East in World Affairs,* 4th ed. (1980); William B. Quandt, *Decade of Decision: American Policy toward the Arab-Israeli Conflict, 1967–1976* (1977); Barry Rubin, *Paved with Good Intentions: The American Experience and Iran* (1980); Amin Saikel, *The Rise and Fall of the Shah* (1980); Robert W. Stookey, *America and the Arab States* (1975).

SOUTHEAST ASIA AND THE VIETNAM WAR Chester Cooper, *The Lost Crusade* (1970); Frances Fitzgerald, *Fire in the Lake* (1972); Leslie H. Gelb and Richard K. Betts, *The Irony of Vietnam: The System Worked* (1979); George C. Herring, *America's Longest War* (1979); George M. Kahin and John W. Lewis, *The United States in Vietnam,* rev. ed. (1969); Earl C. Ravenal, *Never Again* (1978); Guenter Lewy, *America in Vietnam* (1978); Herbert Y. Schandler, *The Unmaking of a President: Lyndon Johnson and Vietnam* (1977); William Shawcross, *Sideshow: Kissinger, Nixon, and the Destruction of Cambodia* (1979); James C. Thompson, *Rolling Thunder* (1980).

NIXON, KISSINGER, AND DÉTENTE Richard J. Barnet, *The Giants: Russia and America* (1977); Thomas M. Franck and Edward Weisband, *Foreign Policy by Congress* (1979); Charles Gati and Toby T. Gati, *Debate Over Détente* (1977); Lloyd C. Gardner, ed., *The Great Nixon Turnaround* (1973); Seymour M. Hersh, *The Price of Power: Kissinger in the Nixon White House* (1983); Stanley Hoffmann, *Primacy or World Order* (1978); Stanley Hoffmann, "The Case of Dr. Kissinger," *New York Review of Books,* 16 (6 December 1979), 14ff; Bernard Kalb and Marvin Kalb, *Kissinger* (1974); Roger Morris, *Uncertain Greatness: Henry Kissinger and American Foreign Policy* (1977); Fred Warner Neal, ed., *Détente or Debacle* (1979); Edward R. F. Sheehan, *The Arabs, Israelis, and Kissinger* (1976); John G. Stoessinger, *Henry Kissinger* (1976); Adam Ulam, *Dangerous Relations* (1983); Tad Szulc, *The Illusion of Peace* (1978); Garry Wills, *Nixon Agonistes* (1970).

NUCLEAR ARMS COMPETITION Robert A. Divine, *Blowing on the Wind* (1978); Jerome H. Kahan, *Security in the Nuclear Age* (1975); Michael Mandelbaum, *The Nuclear Question* (1979); John Newhouse, *Cold Dawn: The Story of SALT* (1973); George Quester, *Nuclear Diplomacy: The First 25 Years* (1970); Chalmers M. Roberts, *The Nuclear Years* (1970); Strobe Talbott, *Endgame: The Inside Story of SALT II* (1979); Thomas W. Wolfe, *The SALT Experience* (1979).

THE WORLD ECONOMY Richard J. Barnet, *The Lean Years* (1980); Richard J. Barnet and Ronald Müller, *The Global Reach: The Power of the Multinational Corporations* (1974); Lloyd N. Cutler, *Global Interdependence and the Multinational Firm* (1978); Alfred E. Eckes, *A Search for Solvency: Bretton Woods and the International Monetary System, 1941–1971* (1975); Alfred E. Eckes, *The U.S. and the Global Struggle for Minerals* (1979); Burton I. Kaufman, *The Oil Cartel Case* (1978); Stephen D. Krasner, *Defending the National Interest* (1978); William Paddock and Paul Paddock, *Time of Famines* (1976); Joan E. Spero, *The Politics of International Economic Relations,* 2nd ed. (1981); Mira Wilkins, *The Maturing of Multinational Enterprise* (1974).

30

REFORM,

RADICALISM, AND DISAPPOINTED

EXPECTATIONS,

1961–1973

In 1963 the Millers moved with their eight children from Alabama to Boston. The black family had heard from friends and relatives in the North who would "write and tell us it was different . . . because you were in the city, and there wasn't the sheriff to beat you up if you waited a second before obeying a white man. And you could get more relief money, and the big city hospitals took you in . . . whether you had a dollar or not."

But as Mr. Miller explained, "it never worked out." With little formal education, he could not secure work; because he was living at home, his family was ineligible for welfare. "So that's how I'm doing," he admitted, "real bad. I sit around and go look for a job and hide when the welfare lady comes."

The Miller children grew up differently in Boston than they would have in the South. "They're not afraid, like I was," Mrs. Miller explained. When race riots broke out in Boston in the summer of 1967, the Miller children joined in "like everyone else."

While Boston was erupting in racial violence, other northern cities were boiling over. During a three-week period that summer, dozens of

people were killed and thousands injured. A year later the National Advisory Commission on Civil Disorders (Kerner Commission) released its report on the causes of the race riots. "The nation is rapidly moving toward two increasingly separate Americas . . . a white society principally located in suburbs, in smaller central cities, and in peripheral parts of large central cities; and a Negro society largely concentrated within large central cities."

In the early 1960s, hope had run high among "the other Americans," the nation's poor. President John F. Kennedy's call for a New Frontier had galvanized liberal Democrats and young idealists in a campaign to eliminate poverty, segregation, and voting rights abuses. But the events of that decade—assassinations, race riots, the war in Vietnam—shattered the Kennedy optimism. The social turbulence resulting from these disastrous events brought down the presidency of Kennedy's successor, Lyndon Johnson, and gave rise to Black Power, the radical politics of the New Left, and a revived women's movement. By 1973 many Americans of all races and classes had ceased to believe in the American Dream.

The other America

What had happened? In the postwar years, while millions of middle-class whites were settling in the suburbs, the unskilled and illiterate had been congregating in the inner cities. Start-

| Inner-city poor |

ing with the wartime industrial boom of the early 1940s, almost 4.5 million poor blacks had made the trek to the cities from the rural South. By 1970 the black population had become 81.4 percent urban. Joining Afro-Americans in the exodus to the cities were poor whites from the southern Appalachians, who moved to Cincinnati, Baltimore, St. Louis, Columbus, Detroit, and Chicago. Latin Americans were arriving in growing numbers from Puerto Rico, Mexico, the Dominican Republic, Colombia, Ecuador, and Cuba.

Next to Afro-Americans, the largest group of urban newcomers were the Mexican-Americans, or Chicanos. Like blacks, their migration had begun during the Second World War, when the United States had negotiated the *bracero* program with Mexico to encourage the immigration of farm workers. Pressured by growers after the war, the government had continued to encourage workers to cross the border to harvest seasonal crops. Millions came, and increasingly they remained to make their lives in the United States.

American Indians also moved to the cities in the 1950s and 1960s, particularly after Congress acted in 1953 and 1954 to end their status as wards of the United States. The new policy, called *termination,* was an unabashed attempt to liquidate the reservations and grab the Indians' lands. During the 1950s more than sixty thousand Indians (about one in every eight) had abandoned their reservations under the program, which provided them a small relocation allowance and a menial job in the city. Accustomed to the rural, semicommunal life of the reservation, many Indians had difficulty adjusting to the city.

In the postwar age of abundance, middle-

Walking to their limousine on the way to the inauguration, president-elect John F. Kennedy (1917–1963) and his wife Jacqueline seemed to symbolize youthful energy and idealism. Kennedy's inaugural promise of a New Frontier gave hope to nonwhites and the poor.   San Francisco Public Library.

class suburbanites found it particularly hard to acknowledge the presence of poverty in their midst. Indeed, they were generally unaware that the poor were still ill-housed and ill-fed. But according to the Bureau of Labor Statistics, in 1962 about 42.5 million Americans—nearly one out of every four people—were poor. Age, race, education, and marital status were all factors in their poverty. One-fourth of the poor were over age sixty-five. More than a third of the poor were under eighteen. One-fifth were nonwhite.

Two-thirds lived in households headed by a person with an eighth-grade education or less, and one-fourth lived in households headed by a single woman.

In 1962, with the publication of Michael Harrington's *The Other America,* more and more people began to ask whether anyone in the United States should have to suffer so. America's poor, wrote Harrington, were "the strangest poor in the history of mankind": they "exist within the most powerful and rich society the world has ever known. Their misery has continued while the majority of the nation talked of itself as being 'affluent.'" Crowded into the cities or living in rural isolation, the poor had "dropped out of sight and out of mind; they were without their own political voice." With the election of John F. Kennedy, however, these forgotten Americans caught a glimmer of hope.

Kennedy and the New Frontier

As a senator, John F. Kennedy had generally avoided controversial issues like civil rights, and

| Election of 1960 |

except on matters of direct concern to his district, he tended to vote conservatively. In 1960 he won the Democratic party's nomination for president after defeating better-known rivals, including Lyndon Baines Johnson of Texas, the powerful majority leader of the Senate. Because the Democrats feared losing the South to the Republicans, Kennedy offered Johnson the vice-presidential nomination. Together, the two campaigned for federal aid to education, medical care for the elderly, an end to racial discrimination, and government action to end the recession the country was suffering.

Kennedy's major liability was his Roman Catholicism. But he addressed the issue head-on, boldly traveling to the Bible belt to do so. Speaking to a group of ministers in Houston, Kennedy expressed his commitment to "an America where the separation of church and state is absolute." Kennedy scored points with

black voters when he responded to an appeal to help the black Baptist minister and civil rights activist Martin Luther King, Jr., gain release from a Georgia county jail. He also promised to sign an executive order forbidding segregation in federally subsidized housing.

Partly in response to these actions, blacks in inner cities turned out in large numbers for Kennedy, providing him with crucial electoral margins in Illinois, Texas, and elsewhere. Kennedy defeated the Republican nominee, Vice President Richard M. Nixon, by a razor-slim margin: 49.7 to 49.6 percent of the popular vote. The electoral college margin, 303 to 219, was actually much closer than the numbers suggest. Nixon would have been the victor with only 9,000 more votes in Illinois and 56,000 more in Texas. But Kennedy's civil rights stand, combined with the economic recession, the U-2 incident, and Kennedy's alarmist charge that the United States was trailing behind the Soviet Union in the missile race, spelled Nixon's downfall. Nixon also suffered from an unsavory TV image (he came across as surly and heavy-jowled in televised debates with Kennedy).

In a departure from the Eisenhower administration's staid, conservative image, Kennedy surrounded himself with "the best and the brightest," young men of intellectual verve and

| "Best and the brightest" |

impeccable credentials. (He appointed no women to significant posts.) Secretary of Defense Robert McNamara, forty-four, had been the whiz-kid president of the Ford Motor Company. Kennedy's special assistant for national security affairs, McGeorge Bundy, forty-one, had become a dean at Harvard at age thirty-four with only a bachelor's degree

Kennedy's program, the New Frontier, was immensely ambitious, promising no less than civil rights for blacks; federal aid to farmers and to education; medical care for all; and the abolition of poverty. But Kennedy promised far more than he could deliver. By August 1961, eight months into his first term, it was evident that Kennedy lacked the ability to move Congress.

At the Washington Monument in 1963, the Reverend Martin Luther King, Jr. (1929–1968) moved a crowd of 250,000 with his most famous speech. "I have a dream," King declared fervently, "that my four little children will one day live in a nation where they will not be judged by the color of their skin but by the content of their character." Bob Adelman/ Magnum Photos.

The new president pursued civil rights with a notable lack of vigor. Blacks struggled on without him, using the tactic of nonviolent civil disobedience. Volunteers organized by Martin Luther King's Southern Christian Leadership Conference (SCLC) deliberately violated segregation laws by sitting-in at whites-only lunch counters, libraries, and bus stations throughout the South. When arrested they went to jail as an act of conscience. Freedom Riders with the racially integrated Congress of Racial Equality (CORE) braved attacks by white mobs for daring to desegregate interstate transportation. Meanwhile black students in the South were joining the Student Non-Violent Coordinating Committee (SNCC). More than any other volunteers, it was the SNCC field

Civil Rights movement

workers who walked the dusty back roads of Mississippi and Georgia, encouraging blacks to resist segregation and register to vote.

As the civil rights movement gained momentum in the early 1960s, President Kennedy gradually made a commitment to first-class citizenship for blacks. In September 1962 he ordered U.S. marshals to protect and assist James Meredith, the first black student to attend the University of Mississippi. Finally in June 1963 Kennedy requested legislation to outlaw segregation in places of public accommodation. When more than 250,000 people gathered at the Lincoln Memorial during the March on Washington that August, they did so with the knowledge that President Kennedy was at last on their side.

Meanwhile, television news shows brought civil rights struggles into Americans' homes.

The story was sometimes grisly. In 1963 Medgar Evers, director of the NAACP in Mississippi, was murdered in his own driveway. That same year police under the command of Commissioner of Public Safety "Bull" Connor of Birmingham, Alabama, attacked civil rights demonstrators with snarling dogs, firehoses, and cattle prods.

Then, while Kennedy's public accommodations bill was being held up by a Senate filibuster, two horrifying events helped to convince reluctant politicians to act. In September white terrorists exploded a bomb during Sunday services at Birmingham's Sixteenth Street Baptist Church; four black girls were killed. A little more than two months later, on November 22, 1963, John Kennedy was assassinated.

Historians have wondered what John Kennedy would have accomplished had he lived. Although his legislative achievements were meager, he inspired idealism in Americans. Kennedy had created a sense of national purpose through his support of the space program. And thousands of Americans joined the Peace Corps, volunteering to spend two years of their lives in this Kennedy-created program. Moreover, in his last few months in office, Kennedy had begun to grow as president, making a moving appeal for racial equality and softening his views on the Cold War. Then there was the Kennedy aura. He was, as James Reston of the *New York Times* wrote, "a story-book President," handsome, graceful, "with poetry on his tongue and a radiant young woman at his side."

Johnson and the Great Society

The new president, Lyndon Johnson, made civil rights his top legislative priority. "No memorial oration or eulogy," he told a joint session of Congress five days after the assassination, "could more eloquently honor President Kennedy's memory than the earliest passage of the civil rights bill." Within months Johnson had signed into law the Civil Rights Act of 1964,

Civil Rights Act of 1964

which outlawed not only segregation in public accommodations, but job discrimination against blacks and women. The act authorized the government to withhold funds from public agencies that discriminated on the basis of race, and it gave the attorney general powers to guarantee voting rights and end school segregation.

Johnson also steered through Congress the Economic Opportunity Act of 1964, which allocated almost $1 billion to fight poverty. Forty percent of the money was earmarked for youth training, 30 percent for community action programs, and the remainder for family farms, small businesses, and adult training programs. The act was the opening salvo in Johnson's War on Poverty. Finally, Johnson secured the $12 billion tax cut for which Kennedy had labored unsuccessfully.

In the year following Kennedy's death, Johnson sought to govern by consensus, by appealing to the shared values and aspirations of the majority of the nation. Judging by his lopsided victory over his Republican opponent in 1964,

Election of 1964

Senator Barry Goldwater of Arizona, he succeeded. Johnson garnered 61 percent of the popular vote and the electoral votes of all but six states.

Riding on Johnson's coattails, the Democrats won staggering majorities in both the House (295 to 140) and the Senate (68 to 32). Johnson knew that the moment for reform had arrived. "Hurry, boys, hurry," Johnson told his staff just after the election. "Get that legislation up to the Hill and out. Eighteen months from now ol' Landslide Lyndon will be Lame-Duck Lyndon." Congress responded in 1965 and 1966 with the most sweeping reform legislation since 1935.

Three of the bills enacted in 1965 were legislative milestones. The Medicare program insured the elderly against medical and hospital bills. The Elementary and Secondary Education Act became the first general program of federal aid to education. And the Voting Rights Act of 1965 empowered the attorney general to supervise voter registration in areas where fewer than half the minoriry residents of voting age were registered. When Johnson became president, only one-fourth of the South's black population was registered to vote; when he left office in 1969 the percentage was approaching two-thirds.

Perhaps even more ambitious was Johnson's War on Poverty. Because the gross national product had increased, Johnson and his advisers reasoned that the government could expect a "fiscal dividend" of several billion dollars in additional tax revenues. They decided to spend the extra money to wipe out poverty through education and job training programs. As the War on Poverty evolved in 1965 and 1966, it included the Job Corps and Neighborhood Youth Corps, to provide marketable skills, work experience, remedial education, and counseling for young people; the Work-Experience Program for unemployed fathers and mothers; Project Head Start, to prepare low-income pre-schoolers for grade school; and Upward Bound, for impoverished high school students who aspired to a college education. Other antipoverty programs were Legal Services for the Poor; Volunteers in Service to America (VISTA); and the Model Cities program, which directed federal funds toward the upgrading of employment, housing, education, and health in targeted neighborhoods. Through Johnson's programs and an expanding economy, the number of people living in poverty dropped from an estimated 42.5 million in 1962 to 22 million in 1967.

Johnson had the good fortune to preside at the same time as a liberal Supreme Court. In 1962, led by Chief Justice Earl Warren, the Court began handing down a series of liberal decisions. In *Baker* v. *Carr* (1962) and subsequent rulings, the Court declared that the principle of "one person, one vote" must prevail at both state and national levels, thus forcing reapportionment of state legislatures. And it outlawed required Bible readings and prayers in public schools, explaining that such practices placed an "indirect coercive pressure upon religious minorities" (1962).

Later in the 1960s the Court upheld both the Civil Rights Act of 1964 and the Voting Rights Act of 1965. In *Loving* v. *Virginia* (1967) it invalidated state prohibitions against interracial marriages. The Court also broadened the interpretation of the Fourteenth Amendment by outlawing segregation in private businesses. And in several rulings that particularly upset conservatives, it decreed that books, magazines, and films could not be banned as obscene unless they were "found to be utterly without redeeming social value."

Perhaps most controversial was the Court's transformation of the criminal justice system. Beginning with *Gideon* v. *Wainwright* (1963), the Court ruled that a poor person charged with a felony had the right to a state-appointed lawyer. In *Escobedo* v. *Illinois* (1964), it decreed that the accused had the right to counsel during interrogation, and could remain silent if he or she chose. And in *Miranda* v. *Arizona* (1966), it added that criminal suspects had to be informed by the police not only that they could see a lawyer and remain silent, but that any statements they made could be used against them.

The period of liberal ascendancy was short-lived. Disillusioned with America's deepening involvement in Vietnam, many of Johnson's allies rejected both him and his liberal consensus. At the same time, black civil rights activists questioned the benefits of a racially integrated society and proclaimed the rise of Black Power. Johnson, who had won an overwhelming victory in the election of 1964, less than four years later recognized the depths of his unpopularity

War on Poverty

Liberal rulings of the Warren Court

and announced that he would not be a candidate for re-election.

Black Power and black separatism

Even as the civil rights movement was registering moral and legislative victories, some activists were beginning to grumble that the federal government was not to be trusted. During the Mississippi Summer Project of 1964, hundreds of college-age volunteers from the North had joined SNCC and CORE field workers to establish "freedom schools" for black children. Many of these volunteers believed that the Federal Bureau of Investigation was hostile to the civil rights movement. They alleged that FBI Director J. Edgar Hoover was a racist. And they were disturbed by rumors, later proved true, that Hoover had wiretapped and bugged Martin Luther King, Jr.'s home. Why, activists asked themselves, had President Johnson allowed Hoover and his agents to remain in office?

Indeed, some FBI informants had not only joined the Ku Klux Klan, they had become leaders of the terrorist group. One of them had reportedly organized the bombing of Birmingham's Sixteenth Street Baptist Church in 1963. Small wonder that during summer 1964 there was an upsurge in racist violence in the South, particularly in Mississippi. White vigilantes bombed and burned two dozen black churches between June and October, and three civil rights workers were murdered in Philadelphia, Mississippi, by a mob that included sheriff's deputies. Instead of protecting the civil rights workers, southern police, county sheriffs, and state troopers had assaulted and arrested them.

Meanwhile, northern blacks began to consider their situation. They knew their circumstances were deteriorating. Their neighborhoods were more segregated than ever, for whites had responded to the black migration from the South by fleeing to the suburbs. Their median income was little more than half that of whites, and black unemployment in the mid-1960s was twice that of whites. For black males between eighteen and twenty-five it was five times as high. Many black families, particularly those headed solely by women, lived in perpetual poverty. Such were the conditions in 1964 that caused the first of the "long hot summers" of race riots in northern cities. In Harlem and Rochester, New York, and in several cities in New Jersey black anger boiled over.

If 1964 was a fiery and violent year, 1965 was even more so. In August blacks gutted the Los Angeles neighborhood of Watts; thirty-four people died (see map). Other cities exploded in rioting between 1966 and 1968. Unlike the race riots of 1919 and 1943, white mobs did not provoke the violence; instead, blacks exploded in fury over their joblessness and lack of opportunity, looting white-owned stores, setting fires, and throwing rocks. Still, as indicated several years later by the Kerner Commission, "white society is deeply implicated in the ghetto. White institutions created it, white institutions maintain it, and white society condones it."

| Watts race riot |

It was obvious that many blacks, especially in the North, had begun to question whether the nonviolent civil rights movement had ever been relevant to their needs. In 1963 Martin Luther King, Jr., had appealed to whites' humanitarian instincts in his famous "I have a dream" speech, delivered before the Washington Monument. But another voice was beginning to be heard, one that urged blacks to seize their freedom "by any means necessary." It was the voice of Malcolm X, a one-time pimp and street hustler who had converted to the Black Muslim religion in prison.

| Malcolm X |

The Black Muslims, a small sect that espoused separatism from white society, condemned the "white devil" as the chief source of evil in the world. They attempted to dissociate themselves from white society, exhorting blacks to help themselves by leading sober lives and

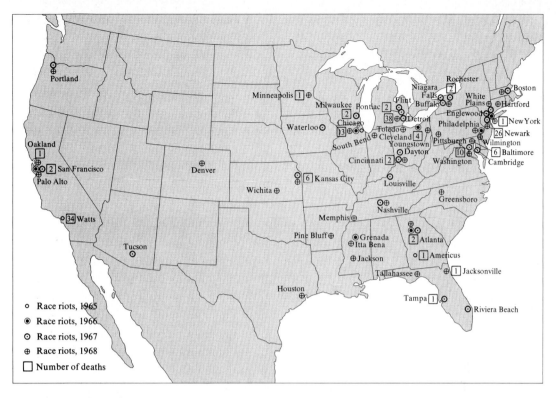

Race riots, 1965–1968

practicing thrift and industriousness. Unlike Martin Luther King, Jr., they advocated violence in self-defense. By the early 1960s Malcolm X had become their chief spokesperson, and his advice was straightforward. "If someone puts a hand on you, send him to the cemetery."

Malcolm X was murdered in a hail of bullets in February 1965; his assassins were Black Muslims who believed he had become a traitor to their cause. It was true that he had modified some of his ideas just before his death. He had met whites who were not devils, he said, and he had expressed cautious support for the nonviolent civil rights movement. Still, for both blacks and whites Malcolm X symbolized black defiance and self-respect.

Within a year of Malcolm X's death, Stokely Carmichael, chairman of SNCC, called on blacks to assert Black Power. According to Carmichael,

<table>
<tr><td>**Black Power**</td></tr>
</table>

in order to be truly free from white oppression, blacks had to control their own institutions–businesses, politics, schools. Soon organizations that had once been committed to integration and nonviolence began to embrace Black Power. Both SNCC and CORE purged their white members, arguing that blacks needed power, not white friendship.

The wellspring of this new militance was black nationalism, the concept that black peoples everywhere in the world shared a unique history and cultural heritage, one that set them apart from whites. Students in colleges and universities pressed for the establishment of black studies programs, and blacks began to call themselves black or Afro-American rather than Negro. At the same time a sense of urgency developed among reform-minded whites, especially college students. On college campuses across the nation, a vocal minority of the baby boom generation set out to "change the system."

The New Left and the counterculture

In the fall of 1964 Mario Savio returned to Berkeley from Mississippi where he had been working in a SNCC summer project. There Savio had become convinced that the same power structure that dominated black lives in the South also controlled students' lives in the university. "Last summer I went to Mississippi to join the struggle there for civil rights. This fall, I am engaged in another part of the same struggle, this time in Berkeley. . . . The same rights are at stake in both places," Savio wrote.

What was wrong with Berkeley? In 1964 the University of California was in many ways a model university, with a worldwide reputation for excellence. Its chancellor, the economist Clark Kerr, had written a book entitled *The Uses of the University,* in which he likened the university to a big business. But it was just that that bothered some students. Berkeley, a "multiversity" with tens of thousands of students, had become hopelessly impersonal. The students of the baby boom had begun to feel like computer cards lost in a vast bureaucracy. "I am a student," rang one lament of Berkeley's Free Speech Movement (FSM). "Do not fold, spindle, or mutilate."

The struggle between students and administration began shortly after the chancellor placed a ban on political recruitment in Sproul Plaza, the students' traditional gathering place. When Savio and others defied the ban, they were suspended, and some were arrested. On October 1 several thousand students surrounded a police car in which one of the militants was being held, immobilizing it for thirty-two hours. Then

in December the FSM seized and occuped Sproul Hall, the main administration building. Governor Pat Brown dispatched state police to Berkeley, and over eight hundred people were arrested. Angry students shut down classes in protest. By the end of the decade, the activism born at Berkeley would spread to hundreds of other campuses.

Over two years before the confrontation in Berkeley, another group of students had met in *Students for a Democratic Society (SDS)* Port Huron, Michigan, to form Students for a Democratic Society (SDS). Like their leaders, Tom Hayden and Al Haber, most SDS members were white college students, the children of middle-class Americans. In their platform, the Port Huron Statement, they condemned racism, the Cold War, poverty amidst plenty, and the anti-democratic tendencies of wealthy, powerful corporations. As the SDS saw it, Americans needed to practice their democratic ideals, not just pay them lip service. The SDS sought nothing less than the revitalization of democracy through the return of power to the people.

Inspired by the Free Speech Movement and SDS, a small minority of students joined the *New Left* New Left. Some were Marxists, others black nationalists, anarchists, or pacifists. Some believed in pursuing social change through negotiation; others were revolutionaries who thought compromise impossible. All were united in their hatred of racism and the war in Vietnam.

In the wake of the New Left appeared a phenomenon observers called the counterculture. *Counter-cultural revolution* Revolutionary figures like Mao Zedong became campus idols. Millions of students experimented with marijuana, amphetamines ("speed"), and hallucinogenic drugs. But it was music more than anything else that reflected the new attitudes. Long before the Beatles sang "There's gonna be a revolution," it was evident that their music had inspired one. Soon music was the chief vehicle for the countercultural assault on the status quo.

Barry McGuire warned of nuclear holocaust in "Eve of Destruction," and Bob Dylan sang of revolutionary answers "blowin' in the wind." Young people cheered Jimi Hendrix, who sang of life in a drug-induced "purple haze"; Janis Joplin, who brought black blues to white Americans; and the Buffalo Springfield, who urged youth to stop and "look what's goin' down."

Rock festivals became cultural happenings, the most famous of which was Woodstock (1969), an upstate New York festival that attracted 400,000 people. The huge crowd endured several days of rain and mud together, without shelter and without violence. Some among them began to dream of a peaceful "Woodstock nation" based on love, drugs, and rock music. Beatle John Lennon expressed it best: "All we are saying is give peace a chance."

While some youths sought alternative experiences through drugs and music, others tried to construct alternative ways of life. Among the most conspicuous were the hippies who were drawn to the San Francisco Bay Area. In the Haight-Ashbury section of the city, "flower children" created an urban subculture as distinctive as that of any Chinatown or Little Italy. "Hashbury" inspired numerous other communal living experiments.

Just as the New Left attracted a minority of students, so the counterculture represented only a small proportion of American youth. But to disconcerted middle-class parents, hippies seemed to be everywhere. Parents carped about long hair, love beads, and patched jeans. They complained that "acid rock" was deafeningly loud, discordant, and even savage. And they feared their children would suffer lifelong damage from drugs. Perhaps most disturbing to parents were the casual sexual mores their children adopted, partly as a result of the availability of birth-control pills. For many young people, living together was no longer equivalent to living in sin. And as attitudes toward premarital sex changed, so did notions about pornography, nudity, homosexuality, sex roles, and familial relationships.

For both cultural and political reasons, the slogan "Make Love, Not War" became popular at mid-decade. With the escalation of the war in Vietnam, the New Left and the counterculture discovered a common cause. Students held teach-ins on the war—open forums for discussion among students, professors, and guest speakers. The first teach-in was held at the University of Michigan in March 1965, shortly after the beginning of Operation Rolling Thunder. In May a Berkeley teach-in lasted thirty-six hours and drew some twelve thousand people. State Department officials dispatched to the teach-ins to defend U.S. policy in Southeast Asia were met by hecklers and demonstrators.

Antiwar movement	

Thousands of young men expressed their opposition to the war by fleeing the draft. By the end of 1972 more than 30,000 draft resisters were living in Canada, an additional 10,000 had fled to Sweden, Mexico, and other countries, and 10,000 more were living under false identities in the United States. During the war half a million men committed draft violations, including an estimated quarter-million who never registered for the draft and another 110,000 who burned their draft cards in protest.

The rebirth of feminism

The New Left and the counterculture were not the only by-products of the civil rights movement. After a long period of quiescence, feminism was reborn in the 1960s. As they had in the nineteenth century when fighting slavery, women discovered that even in movements dedicated to equal rights, they were second-class citizens. Instead of making policy, they were expected to make the coffee, take the minutes, and sometimes even provide sexual favors. As Stokely Carmichael put it, "the position of women in our movement should be prone."

When women examined their place in society as a whole, they were no more encouraged. In *The Feminine Mystique* (1963), Betty Friedan

The Feminine Mystique wrote that the American home had become a "comfortable concentration camp." TV advertisers, magazine writers, beauticians, and psychiatrists had conspired to create the image of a woman "gaily content in a world of bedroom, kitchen, sex, babies and home." Any woman who was dissatisfied with such a role was considered neurotic. But as Friedan pointed out, the wife-mother who spent her life in a world of children sacrificed her adult frame of reference and sometimes her very identity.

For the working woman, the outlook was just as bleak. Her problems were sex discrimination in employment, lack of professional opportunities, unequal pay for equal work, the lack of adequate day care for children, and prohibitions against abortion. In 1963 the average woman earned 63 cents for every dollar a man earned. Ten years later the figure had fallen to 57 cents.

Friedan's book inspired the founding in 1966 of the National Organization for Women (NOW), which battled for "equal rights in partnership with men" in courts and in Congress. Not long after its formation a new generation of radical feminists emerged—once again,

Radical feminism the baby boom was making an impact on American life. Most of these new feminists were white, economically secure, and well educated; many were the daughters of working mothers. Most had been raised in the era of sexual liberation, in which birth-control pills and other contraceptives were taken for granted. The intellectual ferment of their movement produced a new literature in which feminists challenged everything from women's economic, political, and legal inequality to sexual double standards and sex-role stereotypes.

Despite significant opposition, women made impressive gains in the early 1970s. They entered

Educational and legal advances for women professional schools in record numbers: from 1969 to 1973, the numbers of women law students almost quadrupled and of women medical students more than doubled. Under Title IX of the Educational Amendments Act of 1972, female college athletes gained the right to the same financial support as male athletes. In the same year Congress approved the Equal Rights Amendment and sent it to the states for ratification. (The Equal Right Amendment states, "Equality of rights under the law shall not be denied or abridged by the United States or by any State on account of sex.") Two years later the Supreme Court ruled that a woman desiring an abortion had the right to control her own body (*Doe* v. *Bolton* and *Roe* v. *Wade*).

As a result of these victories the women's movement gained new confidence. "If the 1960s belonged to the blacks, the next ten years are ours," remarked one feminist.

1968: a year of protest, violence, and loss

As stormy and violent as the years from 1963 through 1967 had been, many Americans still hoped that the nation's distress would simply go away. But in 1968 a series of quakes hit them even harder. The first shock came in January when the *U.S.S. Pueblo,* a navy intelligence ship, was captured by the North Koreans near the port of Wonsan. A week later came the Tet offensive. For the first time many Americans believed they might lose the war. Meanwhile, American casualties had been climbing. In a two-week period in May more than eleven hundred U.S. soldiers died.

Controversy over the war deepened. Within the Democratic party, two men rose to challenge Johnson for the 1968 presidential nomination. One of them, the war hawk Governor George C. Wallace of Alabama, exhorted Americans to "stand up for America." The other, Senator Eugene McCarthy of Minnesota, entered the New Hampshire primary solely to contest Johnson's war policies. On March 12 McCarthy won 42 percent of the popular vote and 20 of 24 convention delegates. Yet another Democrat, Senator Robert F. Kennedy of New York, would soon enter the fray.

On March 31, President Johnson went on national television and announced a scaling-down of the bombing in North Vietnam. Then he hurled a political thunderbolt. "I have concluded that I should not permit the Presidency to become involved in the partisan divisions that are developing in this political year," with "America's sons in the field far away . . . with our hopes . . . for peace in the balance every day." Johnson would not be a candidate for re-election.

Less than a week later a white assassin named James Earl Ray shot and killed Martin Luther

King, Jr., in Memphis. Ray's crime aroused instant rage in the nation's ghettos. Blacks rioted in 168 cities and towns, looting and burning white businesses and property. Thirty-four blacks and five whites died in the violence. In Chicago, Mayor Richard Daley ordered police to shoot to kill arsonists. Across the nation hatred mounted on both sides.

Student protests multiplied that spring not only in the United States but in Paris, Mexico City, and elsewhere in the world. Between January and June 1968 over two hundred demonstrations rocked colleges and universities across the country. Students protested the involvement of universities in the military-industrial complex. They denounced the spread of urban universities into surrounding poor neighborhoods, the elimination of low-income housing to build gymnasiums, parking garages, and dormitories. In New York students at Columbia University occupied the president's office and other buildings for ten days. On April 30, at the request of Columbia's president, one thousand club-swinging city policemen stormed the occupied buildings, injuring 150 protesters and onlookers.

In April and May Gallup polls reported Robert Kennedy the front-running presidential candidate among Democrats. Kennedy had lost to

McCarthy in the Oregon primary but won in California that June. While he was celebrating his victory in Los Angeles, a young man named Sirhan Sirhan stepped forward with a .22-caliber revolver and fired repeatedly at Kennedy. The assassin, it turned out, was an Arab nationalist who despised Kennedy for his unwavering support of Israel.

The poor were especially grief-stricken by the assassination. Kennedy had been a friend to blacks and Mexican-Americans. When Cesar Chavez had led the United Farm Workers in their strike against growers in 1965, Kennedy had traveled to California to stand with them. Antiwar liberals also felt they had lost a friend in Kennedy.

Violence erupted again in August at the Democratic national convention in Chicago. The Democrats were divided among Vice President Hubert Humphrey, Lyndon Johnson's candidate; peace candidate Eugene McCarthy; and Senator George McGovern of South Dakota, who had inherited some of Kennedy's support. Adding to the dissension were several mule-drawn wagons driven by blacks from the Poor People's Campaign; thousands of antiwar protesters; and the Youth International Party, or Yippies, who had traveled to Chicago for a Festival of Life, which they contrasted pointedly to "Lyndon and Hubert's celebration of death."

The Chicago police force was still in the psychological grip of Daley's shoot-to-kill directive. Twelve thousand police were assigned to twelve-hour shifts and another twelve thousand army troops and National Guardsmen were on call with rifles, bazookas, and flamethrowers. On Michigan Avenue, in front of the Conrad Hilton Hotel, they attacked, wading into ranks of demonstrators, reporters, and TV camera operators. Throughout the nation viewers watched as club-swinging police beat protesters to the ground. When onlookers rushed to shield the injured, they too were clubbed.

The Democratic convention nominated Humphrey for president and Senator Edmund Muskie of Maine for vice president. Like Johnson, Humphrey was a political descendant of the New Deal and an unstinting supporter of the war. Opposing Humphrey were Richard M. Nixon, the Republican nominee, and Governor George Wallace of Alabama, who ran as the nominee of the American Independent party.

When the votes were tabulated, Nixon emerged the winner. Just four years after the Goldwater debacle, the Republicans had captured the White House, though by the slimmest of margins. Wallace garnered almost 10 million votes, or 13.5 percent of the total, the best performance by a third party since 1924. His strong showing made Nixon a minority president, elected with only 43 percent of the popular vote.

Nixon and the persistence of chaos

Richard Nixon's presidency was born in chaos. In 1969 a hundred black students armed with rifles and shotguns seized the student union at Cornell University and occupied the building for thirty-six hours. Harvard students took over the president's office before being evicted by police. Bloody confrontations occurred at Berkeley, San Francisco State, Wisconsin, and scores of other colleges and universities. And in October 1969, three hundred Weathermen, members of an SDS splinter group, raced through Chicago's Loop, smashing windows and attacking police officers in an attempt to inspire armed class struggle. A month later half a million people assembled peacefully at the Washington Monument to protest the war. While they appealed to the nation's leaders, President Nixon watched football on TV.

The next year was worse. On April 30, 1970, the president appeared on television to announce that the United States had launched an "incursion" into Cambodia. Four days later

Killings at Kent State University

Ohio National Guardsmen fired into a group of protesting students at Kent State University, killing four and wounding eleven. Throughout the country outraged students went on strike, shutting down 250 campuses and pouring into the nation's capital to lobby against the war. Nixon referred contemptuously to the protesters as "these bums, you know, blowing up the campuses."

If soldiers waged official violence in 1970, revolutionaries conducted an unofficial campaign of terror. That year they bombed the New York offices of Mobil Oil, IBM, General Telephone and Electronics, and various banks. And there were scores of politically motivated skyjackings.

Worst of all, as far as many Americans were concerned, was street crime. Sales of pistols, burglar alarms, and bullet-proof vests soared. Conservatives accused liberals of causing the crime wave by coddling criminals.

Fear of crime

In the wake of this new wave of riots and violent crime, Nixon became convinced that the nation was descending into anarchy. And he worried, as had Lyndon Johnson before him, that the antiwar movement was Communist-inspired. In June 1970 he ordered the directors of the FBI, the CIA, the National Security Agency, and the Defense Intelligence Agency to formulate a coordinated attack on "internal threats." "Everything is valid," a Nixon aide told the group, "everything is possible." FBI Director J. Edgar Hoover refused to cooperate.

The administration also worked to put the Democratic party on the defensive. Vice President Spiro Agnew took to the road in September to warn the country of

Politics of divisiveness

the threats to its internal security and exhort people to vote Republican in the upcoming congressional elections. The campaign strategy was to portray

A distraught bystander mourns a slain student at Kent State University, May 1970. Ohio National Guardsmen had fired into a crowd of antiwar protesters, killing four. Kent State University News Service.

Democrats as a radical fringe. But Republican attempts to discredit the Democrats failed. In the election the Democrats gained twelve seats in the Senate and dropped only two in the House. The Republicans lost eleven state governorships.

Nixon's fortunes declined further in 1971. On June 13 the *New York Times* began to publish the Pentagon Papers, a top-secret study of

Pentagon Papers

the Vietnam War ordered in 1967 by former Secretary of Defense Robert McNamara. The *Times* had obtained the papers from Daniel Ellsberg, a disillusioned defense analyst with the Rand Corporation, a "think tank" for analyzing national defense policies. Publication of the study revealed that the government had consistently lied to the American people about the war.

In 1971 Nixon also had to contend with inflation, a problem not entirely of his own mak-

Skyrocketing inflation

ing. Rather, it was Lyndon Johnson's policy of guns and butter—massive deficit financing to support both the Vietnam War and the Great Society—that had fueled inflation. By January 1971 the United States was suffering from a 5.3 percent inflation rate and a 6 percent unemployment rate. Soon the word *stagflation*

Important events

1960	John F. Kennedy elected president	1966	Stokely Carmichael calls for "Black Power" National Organization for Women (NOW) established
1961	Congress of Racial Equality's Freedom Ride	1967	Race riots in Newark, Detroit, and other cities Antiwar March on the Pentagon
1962	Students for a Democratic Society founded		
1963	Betty Friedan, *The Feminine Mystique* March on Washington for Afro-American civil rights Birmingham, Alabama, Baptist church bombed Kennedy assassinated; Lyndon B. Johnson assumes the presidency	1968	U.S.S. *Pueblo* captured by North Korea Tet offensive Martin Luther King, Jr., assassinated Race riots in 168 cities and towns Student antiwar protests escalate Robert F. Kennedy assassinated Violence at Democratic convention in Chicago Richard Nixon elected president
1964	Economic Opportunity Act launches War on Poverty Civil Rights Act of 1964 First of the "long hot summers" Free Speech Movement founded Lyndon Johnson elected president	1969	Woodstock festival
		1970	U.S. invades Cambodia Four students killed at Kent State University
1965	Malcolm X assassinated Antiwar demonstrations Voting Rights Act of 1965 Watts race riot	1971	Daniel Ellsberg releases Pentagon Papers
		1972	Equal Rights Amendment (ERA) approved by Congress Nixon re-elected

would be coined to describe this coexistence of economic recession (stagnation) and inflation.

The southern strategy and the election of 1972

Political observers believed that Nixon would have a hard time running for re-election on his first-term record. Having urged Americans to use "cool" words and "lower our voices," he had ordered Vice President Agnew to denounce the press and student protesters. Having espoused unity, he had practiced the politics of polarization. Having campaigned as a fiscal conservative, he had authorized near-record budget deficits. And having promised peace, he had widened the war in Southeast Asia.

Congressional legislative accomplishments had been made more in spite of Nixon than because of him. Eighteen-year-olds gained the

vote, social security payments and food-stamp funding were increased, and the Environmental Protection Agency and Occupational Safety and Health Administration were established. Congress responded to the growing environmental movement by passing the Clean Air Act, the Water Quality Improvement Act, and the Resource Recovery Act. (Nixon opposed most of these social welfare, environmental, and voting rights bills.)

In his campaign for re-election, Nixon was less interested in running on his record than in employing a "southern strategy." A product of

the Sunbelt himself, Nixon was attuned to the growing political power of that conservative area. Thus he appealed to "the silent majority," the white suburbanites, blue-collar workers, Catholics, and ethnic groups of "middle America." As in the 1970 congressional elections, Nixon equated the Republican party with law and order and the Democratic party with permissiveness, crime, drugs, pornography, the hippie lifestyle, student radicalism, black militancy, feminism, homosexuality, and the dissolution of the family. And he spoke out strongly against busing.

To a great extent the campaign waged by Nixon's Democratic opponent, Senator George McGovern of South Dakota, handed victory to the president. In the California primary McGovern suggested that the federal government bestow $1,000 on all Americans "from the poorest migrant workers to the Rockefellers." A fiscally irresponsible idea—and a frightening one to the middle classes, who surmised they would have to pay for it—McGovern's pledge provided deadly ammunition to the Republicans in the general election. When McGovern committed himself to a $30-billion cut in the defense budget, people began to fear he was a neo-isolationist who would reduce the United States to a second-rate power. McGovern's proposals split

the Democrats between his supporters—blacks, feminists, antiwar activists, young militants—and old-guard urban bosses, labor and ethnic leaders, and southerners.

Nixon's victory in November was overwhelming. He polled 47 million votes, or 60.7 percent of the votes cast. McGovern garnered only 29 million and won in just one state, Massachusetts. Nixon's southern strategy was supremely successful: he carried all of the Deep South, which had once been solidly Democratic. He also gained a majority of the urban vote, winning over such long-time Democrats as blue-collar workers, Catholics, and ethnics. Only blacks, Jews, and low-income voters stuck with the Democrats. But Nixon's great victory would soon be tarnished by a scandal of his own making.

Suggestions for further reading

GENERAL Ronald Berman, *America in the Sixties* (1968); Godfrey Hodgson, *America in Our Time* (1976); Peter Joseph, *Good Times: An Oral History of America in the Nineteen Sixties* (1973); William O'Neill, *Coming Apart: An Informal History of America in the 1960s* (1971); Milton Viorst, *Fire in the Streets: America in the 1960s* (1979).

THE OTHER AMERICANS Joseph H. Cash and Herbert T. Hoover, eds., *To Be an Indian: An Oral History* (1971); J. Wayne Flynt, *Dixie's Forgotten People: The South's Poor Whites* (1979); Leo Grebler *et al.*, *The Mexican-American People* (1970); Michael Harrington, *The Other America: Poverty in the United States* (1962); Susan Estabrook Kennedy, *If All We Did Was to Weep at Home: A History of White Working-Class Women in America* (1979); Herman P. Miller, *Rich Man, Poor Man* (1971).

THE KENNEDY ADMINISTRATION David Halberstam, *The Best and the Brightest* (1972); Jim F. Heath, *Decade of Disillusionment: The Kennedy-Johnson Years* (1975); Arthur M. Schlesinger, Jr., *A Thousand Days: John F. Kennedy in the White House* (1965); Theodore

C. Sorenson, *Kennedy* (1965); Theodore H. White, *The Making of the President 1960* (1961).

THE JOHNSON ADMINISTRATION Lyndon B. Johnson, *The Vantage Point: Perspectives of the Presidency, 1963-1969* (1971); Doris Kearns, *Lyndon Johnson and the American Dream* (1976); Sar A. Levitan, *The Great Society's Poor Law: A New Approach to Poverty* (1969); Theodore H. White, *The Making of the President 1964* (1965).

CIVIL RIGHTS AND BLACK POWER Carl M. Brauer, *John F. Kennedy and the Second Reconstruction* (1977); Stokely Carmichael and Charles Hamilton, *Black Power* (1967); Clayborne Carson, *In Struggle: SNCC and the Black Awakening of the 1960s* (1981); William H. Chafe, *Civilities and Civil Rights: Greensboro, North Carolina, and the Black Struggle for Freedom* (1980); August Meier and Elliott Rudwick, *CORE: A Study in the Civil Rights Movement, 1942-1968* (1973); David L. Lewis, *King: A Critical Biography* (1970); Malcolm X and Alex Haley, *The Autobiography of Malcolm X* (1965); Stephen B. Oates, *Let the Trumpet Sound: The Life of Martin Luther King, Jr.* (1982).

THE NEW LEFT AND THE COUNTERCULTURE Morris Dickstein, *Gates of Eden: American Culture in the Sixties* (1977); Todd Gitlin, *The Whole World Is Watching: Mass Media in the Making and Unmaking of the New Left* (1980); Kenneth Keniston, *Young Radicals* (1968); Seymour Lipset and Sheldon Wolin, eds.,

The Berkeley Student Revolt (1965); Michael Medved and David Wallechinsky, *What Really Happened to the Class of '65* (1976); Philip Norman, *Shout! The Beatles in Their Generation* (1981); Theodore Roszak, *The Making of a Counter Culture* (1968); Kirkpatrick Sale, *SDS* (1973); Philip Slater, *The Pursuit of Loneliness,* rev. ed. (1976).

THE NIXON ADMINISTRATION Rowland Evans and Robert Novak, *Nixon in the White House: The Frustration of Power* (1971); Richard M. Nixon, *RN: The Memoirs of Richard Nixon* (1978); Leon E. Panetta and Peter Gall, *Bring Us Together: The Nixon Team and the Civil Rights Retreat* (1971); Kevin Phillips, *The Emerging Republican Majority* (1969); Jonathan Schell, *The Time of Illusion* (1975); Theodore H. White, *The Making of the President 1968* (1969); Theodore H. White, *The Making of the President 1972* (1973); Garry Wills, *Nixon Agonistes* (1970).

THE REBIRTH OF FEMINISM William H. Chafe, *The American Woman: Her Changing Social, Economic, and Political Role, 1920-1970* (1972); Sara Evans, *Personal Politics: The Roots of Women's Liberation in the Civil Rights Movement and the New Left* (1978); Shulamith Firestone, *The Dialectic of Sex: The Case for Feminist Revolution* (1970); Betty Friedan, *The Feminine Mystique* (1963); Kate Millett, *Sexual Politics* (1970); Robin Morgan, ed., *Sisterhood is Powerful* (1970); Gayle Graham Yates, *What Women Want: The Ideas of the Movement* (1975).

31

A DISILLUSIONED PEOPLE: AMERICA SINCE 1973

Night watchman Frank Wills was making his rounds at the Watergate apartment-office complex in Washington, D.C., on June 17, 1972, when he noticed that two doors connecting the building to an underground garage had been taped to keep them from locking. Wills removed the tape, but when he returned thirty minutes later he found it had been replaced. He promptly telephoned the police to report the illegal entry. At 2:30 A.M., police arrested five men who were attaching listening devices to telephones in the sixth-floor offices of the Democratic National Committee.

One of the men arrested was James W. McCord, a former CIA employee who had become security coordinator of the Committee to Re-elect the President (CREEP). The other four were anti-Castro Cubans from Miami. Unknown to the police, two other men had been in the Watergate building illegally at the time of the break-in. One was E. Howard Hunt, a one-time CIA agent who had become CREEP's security chief. The other was G. Gordon Liddy, a former FBI agent serving on the staff of the White House Domestic Council. What did these men hope to overhear on the telephones? Who had ordered the break-in?

In the next twenty-two months Americans watched as the story of Watergate unfolded.

And while they worried about morality in government, the nation's economic troubles deepened. The Arab oil embargo of 1973 led to the realization that the United States was not a fortress that could stand alone; it was dependent for its survival on imported oil. Long gasoline lines, the declining value of the dollar, and persistent stagflation dogged Americans; the postwar economic boom was over.

Politicians seemed unable to cope with the floundering economy. President Gerald Ford's weak WIN program did not impress voters, who turned him out of office in 1976. Jimmy Carter, who defeated Ford, fared just as badly. Under Carter inflation reached new heights and unemployment remained high.

Women and nonwhites were particularly hard hit by inflation and unemployment, for they were usually the last hired and the first to be laid off. Minorities did achieve some victories in the 1970s, though. Women made educational gains and scored legislative victories in Washington and in various statehouses. Many Afro-Americans attended college and joined the middle class or were elected to political office. But opposition to their aspirations mounted steadily. The feminist movement was confronted by an increasingly vocal and effective antifeminist, or "profamily," movement. And blacks had to contend with antibusing agitation and a resurgent Ku Klux Klan.

Some Americans decided that if they could not reform society, they could at least develop their own individual potential. Millions of people took to the streets as joggers; others meditated, ate health food, or developed their assertiveness skills. Such seemingly carefree enthusiasms reflected an undercurrent of desperation. By 1980 public opinion polls disclosed that most Americans found the present worse than the past, and believed the future would be worse yet.

It was in this context that Ronald Reagan rode a wave of conservatism into office, promising a return to old-fashioned morality and a balanced budget. But Reagan soon found those goals were easier to talk of than to achieve.

The Watergate scandal

Watergate actually began in 1971, with the establishment by the White House not only of CREEP but of the overlapping Special Investigations Unit, known familiarly as the Plumbers. Created to stop the leaking of confidential information to the press following publication of the Pentagon Papers, the Plumbers burglarized the office of Daniel Ellsberg's psychiatrist in an attempt to find information that would discredit him. It was the Plumbers who broke into the Democratic National Committee's headquarters to photograph documents and install wiretaps. And it was CREEP that raised the money to pay the Plumbers' expenses.

The arrest of the Watergate burglars generated furious activity in the White House. Incriminating documents were shredded, E.

White House cover-up

Howard Hunt's name was expunged from the White House telephone directory, and tens of thousands of dollars in $100 bills were removed from safes and paid as hush money to the burglars. In addition, Nixon ordered his chief of staff, H. R. Haldeman, to discourage the FBI's investigation into the burglary on the pretext that it might compromise national security.

Had it not been for the diligent efforts of reporters, government special prosecutors, federal judges, senators and congressional representatives, and an aroused public, Nixon might have succeeded in disguising his involvement in Watergate. Slowly, however, the ball of fabrications and distortions began to unravel. In spring of 1973, U.S. District Court Judge John Sirica tried the burglars, one of whom, James McCord, implicated his superiors in CREEP and at the White House. Meanwhile, the Senate Select Committee on Campaign Practices, chaired by Senator Sam Ervin, heard testimony from White House aides. White House counsel John Dean acknowledged not only that there had been a cover-up, but that the president had directed it. Another aide, Alexander Butterfield, shocked the committee and the nation by disclosing that Nixon had had a taping system installed in the White House, and that conversations about Watergate had been recorded.

Watergate hearings and investigations

Nixon feigned innocence, but on April 30 he announced the resignations of his two chief White House aides, John Ehrlichman and H. R. Haldeman. And he appointed Archibald Cox, a Harvard law professor, as special Watergate prosecutor. But when Cox sought nine White House tapes by means of a court order, Nixon decided to fire him. Both Attorney General Elliot Richardson and his deputy, William Ruckelshaus, resigned rather than carry out the president's order to dismiss Cox. Finally the special prosecutor was fired by the next-ranking official in the Department of Justice. The public outcry provoked by the so-called Saturday Night Massacre compelled the president to ap-

Saturday Night Massacre

AUTH

During testimony before a Senate committee investigating Watergate, a White House aide revealed that President Nixon had had tape recorders installed in the White House. This cartoon, which needs no caption, suggests the public's reaction to the electronic surveillance. Reprinted by permission of the Chicago Tribune–New York News Syndicate, Inc.

point a new special prosecutor, Leon Jaworski. When Nixon still refused to surrender the tapes, Jaworski took him to court.

From mid-1972 through mid-1974, enterprising reporters uncovered details of the break-in, the hush money, a dirty-tricks campaign against Democratic candidates, and a cover-up involving even the president. White House aides and CREEP subordinates began to go on trial, with Nixon cited as their "unindicted co-conspirator." As Nixon's story became less credible, his hold on the tapes became more and more tenuous. In late April 1974 the president finally released an edited ("expletive deleted") version of the tapes.

The tapes, however, were replete with gaps. They swayed neither the public nor the House Judiciary Committee, which had begun to draft articles of impeachment against the president. Nixon was still trying to hang onto the tapes when on July 24 the Supreme Court unanimously ordered him to surrender the recordings to Judge Sirica. At about the same time, the Judiciary Committee began to conduct nationally televised hearings. After several days of testimony the committee voted for impeachment on three of five counts: obstruction of justice; defiance of a congressional subpoena of the tapes; and the use of the CIA, the FBI, and the

Impeachment hearings

The Watergate scandal

507

IRS to deprive Americans of their constitutional rights.

On August 5 the president finally handed over the complete tapes, which he knew would condemn him. Four days later he resigned, the first president to do so.

Nixon's successor was the new vice president, Gerald R. Ford. Vice President Spiro Agnew had resigned in October 1973 after pleading no contest to charges of income-tax evasion and acceptance of bribes. Under the provisions of the Twenty-fifth Amendment, Nixon had nominated Ford, minority leader of the House, to replace Agnew. Ford's colleagues hailed the new president as a "decent" and "good" man, but Ford's first substantive act provoked a cry of public indignation: he pardoned Nixon.

The Watergate scandal prompted the reform of abuses of presidental power, some of which

| *Post-Watergate restrictions on executive power* | dated from the Roosevelt administration. In 1973 Congress passed the War Powers Act, which mandated that

"in every possible instance" the president must consult with Congress before sending American troops into foreign wars. And in 1974 Congress produced the Congressional Budget and Impoundment Control Act, which prohibited the impoundment of federal money—a tactic Nixon had used to thwart congressional legislation. In actions directly related to Watergate, Congress attacked campaign fund-raising abuses and the misuse of government agencies. The Federal Election Campaign Act of 1972 had restricted campaign spending to no more than ten cents per constituent, and required candidates to report individual contributions of more than $100. In 1974 Congress enacted additional legislation that set ceilings on campaign contributions and expenditures for House, Senate, and presidential elections. Finally, to aid citizens who were victims of dirty-tricks campaigns, Congress strengthened the Freedom of Information Act. The new legislation permitted access to "reasonably" described government documents and provided penalties if the government "arbitrarily or capriciously" withheld such information.

The energy crisis and the end of the postwar economic boom

The fallout from Watergate was not the only problem confronting the nation in the early 1970s. More disruptive in the long run was the Arab oil embargo of 1973. The American people had grown up on cheap, abundant energy and made no effort to conserve it. By fall 1973 the country was consuming so much energy that it had to import one-third of its oil supplies.

Price increases ordered by the Organization of Petroleum Exporting Countries (OPEC) struck the United States another blow. From January

| *OPEC price increases and rising inflation* | 1973 to January 1974 oil prices rose 350 percent. Angry Americans yearned for a confrontation with the

Arabs. But the Saudi Arabian oil minister reminded them, "We could blow up the oil fields and then everyone would have to get along without Saudi Arabian oil."

Inevitably the boost in the price of imported oil reverberated through the entire economy. Inflation jumped from 3.3 percent in 1972 to 6.2 percent in 1973 and a frightening 11 percent in 1974. At the same time recession hit the auto industry. In Detroit General Motors laid off thirty-eight thousand workers—6 percent of its domestic work force—indefinitely, and furloughed another forty-eight thousand for periods of up to ten days. The reason was obvious: sales of gas-guzzling American autos had plummeted as consumers hurried to purchase energy-efficient foreign subcompacts.

The auto companies that were not selling cars were not buying steel, glass, rubber, or tool-and-die products either. Soon the recession in the auto industry spread to other manufacturers. But unlike earlier postwar recessions, this one did not fade away in a year or two. Part of the reason was the coexistence of inflation. In earlier recessions, increased government spending had stimulated the economy and revived industry. But in 1974 inflation was running out of control, and government officials hesitated to fuel it further through massive spending.

There were other problems too. One was a slowing of increases in productivity, or the average output of goods per hour of labor. Between 1949 and 1959 American productivity had increased at an average rate of 3.2 percent a year. But from 1969 to 1979 productivity increased only 1.3 percent a year. Meanwhile, Japan's productivity had been growing at about four times that rate due to heavy automation. The resulting cost savings to Japanese manufacturers made their products more competitive in the American market, and cut into American manufacturers' sales.

Lagging productivity

The lag in productivity was not matched by a decrease in workers' expectations. Wage increases regularly exceeded production increases, and some economists blamed the raises for inflation. Indeed, wages and prices that went up seldom came down again, regardless of market conditions. Managers of the nation's basic industries—steel, autos, rubber—complained that the automatic cost-of-living adjustments in their labor contracts left them little margin to restrain price hikes.

Some businesspeople and economists blamed government regulation for inflation. The cost of obeying federal health and safety laws and pollution controls inevitably added to the price of goods, they said. Critics estimated that the regulations imposed a cost of tens of billions of dollars annually on industry. They urged officials to abolish the Environmental Protection Agency and the Occupational Safety and Health Administration, and pressed for deregulation of the oil, airline, and trucking industries on the theory that competition would bring prices down.

Criticism of government economic policy

Above all, critics attacked the federal government's massive spending programs. Since the New Deal, both Republican and Democratic administrations had resorted to pump priming to cure recessions. But the Johnson administration's attempt to finance both the War on Poverty and the Vietnam War had evidently backfired. Critics of Keynesian pump priming pointed to the resulting stagflation as evidence of the failure of New Deal economics.

Whatever its causes, inflation was getting out of hand. It had begun to climb in 1966 and 1967; when it reached 5.9 percent in 1970, President Nixon had reacted by trying to restrain federal spending, and the Federal Reserve Board had tightened credit. By the time Gerald Ford became president in 1974, OPEC price increases had pushed the rate to 11 percent. Appalled, Ford created WIN (Whip Inflation Now), a voluntary program that encouraged businesses, consumers, and workers to save energy and form grassroots anti-inflation organizations.

Government response to the economic crisis

WIN was much too weak to be effective. Ford's ultimate response to inflation, like Nixon's, was to curb federal spending and encourage the Federal Reserve Board to tighten credit. As before, these actions prompted a recession—only this time it was the worst recession in forty years. While the economy stagnated, tax revenues plummeted. As a result the federal deficit for the fiscal year 1976 to 1977 hit $60 billion, and unemployment jumped to 8.5 percent in 1975.

Neither Nixon nor Ford devised lasting solutions to the energy crisis. Nixon did outline a six-point energy program. But when OPEC ended the embargo (March 1974), the crisis seemed to pass, and with it the incentive to prevent future shortages.

The energy crisis intensified public debate over nuclear power. For the sake of energy independence, advocates asserted, the United States had to rely more on nuclear energy. Environmental activists countered that the risk of nuclear accident was too great, that there was no proven safe way to store nuclear waste. Some activists launched protests in an effort to impede the construction of nuclear plants. Accidents in the nuclear plants at Brown's Ferry, Alabama (1975), and Three Mile

Brown's Ferry and Three Mile Island

Island, Pennsylvania (1979), gave credence to the activists' claims. By 1979, however, ninety-six reactors were under construction, and thirty more were on order.

The failed promise of the Carter presidency

While Ford struggled with the nation's problems, the Democrats prepared for the presidential election of 1976. Against the background of

Election of 1976

Watergate secrecy and corruption, one candidate in particular promised honesty and openness. "I will never lie to you." pledged Jimmy Carter, an obscure former one-term governor of Georgia. When this born-again Christian promised voters efficiency and decency in government, they believed him. Carter secured the Democratic nomination and chose Senator Walter Mondale, a liberal from Minnesota, as his running mate.

Neither Carter nor President Ford, the Republican candidate, inspired much interest. On election day only 54 percent of the electorate voted. Nevertheless, an analysis of the turnout was instructive. One political commentator concluded that the vote was "fractured to a marked degree along the fault line separating the haves and the have-nots." Carter gained almost 90 percent of the black and Mexican-American vote and squeaked to victory by a slim 1.7 million votes out of 80 million. Ford's appeal was strongest among middle- and upper-middle-class voters.

In office, Carter's major accomplishments were in energy, transportation, and conservation policy. To encourage domestic production of oil

Carter administration

he instituted phased decontrol of oil prices. To spur development of alternative fuels he created the Synthetic Fuels Corporation. And to moderate the social effects of the energy

crisis he called for a windfall-profits tax on excessive profits resulting from decontrol, and grants to the poor and elderly for the purchase of heating fuel. He deregulated the airline, trucking, and railroad industries and persuaded Congress to ease federal control of banks, which were running short of funds due to the low ceiling on interest rates. His administration established a $1.6 billion "superfund" to clean up abandoned chemical-waste sites. And finally, in what Carter called "the most important decision on conservation matters that the Congress will face in this century," the president placed over 100 million acres of Alaskan land under the federal government's protection as national parks, national forests, and wildlife refuges.

Despite his accomplishments, Carter soon alienated party members. Elected as an outsider, he remained one, failing to develop working relationships with congressional leaders. Moreover, his support of deregulation and his opposition to wage and price controls and gasoline rationing ran counter to the liberal Democratic position. Seeing inflation as more of a threat to the nation's economic health than either recession or unemployment, Carter announced that his top priority would be to cut federal spending, even though doing so would add to the jobless rolls.

By 1980 the economy was a shambles. Inflation had jumped to 12.4 percent, and buyers around the world had lost confidence in the dollar, causing unprecedented increases in the price of gold. To steady the dollar and curb inflation, the Federal Reserve Board had taken drastic measures in late 1979: it had raised the rates at which it loaned money to banks. As a result auto loans became progressively more difficult to obtain, mortgage interest rates leaped beyond 15 percent, and the prime lending rate (the rate charged to businesses) hit 20 percent. Worse still, by 1980 the nation was in a full-fledged recession, with an unemployment rate of 7.5 percent. And the combined high inflation and high unemployment rates had produced a staggeringly high discomfort index of just under 20 percent (see figure).

Chapter 31: A disillusioned people: America since 1973

The divided women's movement

In the 1970s, while Nixon, Ford, and Carter wrestled with the economy, increasing numbers of women were committing themselves to the struggle for equality with men. Feminists had scored some impressive legislative victories. In 1974 Congress passed the Equal Credit Opportunity Act, which enabled women to get bank loans and obtain credit cards on the same terms as men. Even more significant were the gains women made along with blacks and other minorities as a result of affirmative action in hiring. As mandated by the Civil Rights Act of 1964 and the establishment of the Equal Employment Opportunity Commission, women and minorities had to receive the same consideration as white males when applying for a job. In the field of criminal law, many states revised their statutes on rape, prohibiting lawyers from stressing the previous sexual experience of rape victims.

Still, women continued to encounter barriers in their quest for equality. One of the most formidable was the antifeminist, or "profamily,"

> **Antifeminist movement**

movement, which contended that men should lead and women should follow, particularly within the traditional family. Antifeminism became an increasingly powerful political force in the 1970s. In defense of the family, antifeminists campaigned against the Equal Right Amendment (ERA), the gay rights movement, and abortion on demand. A number of them, such as Anita Bryant and Phyllis Schlafly, gained fame by arguing that all these issues were interrelated, and that they endangered traditional American values.

Antifeminists successfully blocked ratification of the Equal Rights Amendment, which whizzed through thirty-five state legislatures in the late 1970s and then faltered three votes short of the required three-fourths. Schlafly's STOP ERA campaign had falsely claimed that the ERA would abolish alimony, force women to fight in combat, and prohibit separate-sex rest-

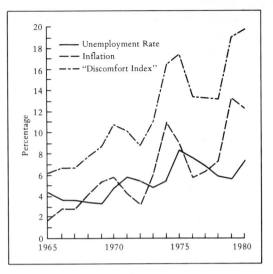

Discomfort index (unemployment plus inflation), 1965–1980. Source: *Economic Report of the President: 1980* (Washington: U.S. Government Printing Office, 1981), pp. 238, 263.

rooms. Shortly after the deadline for ratification (June 1982) the ERA was reintroduced in Congress, and the long process of amendment began again.

Along with Catholics and other religious opponents of abortion, antifeminists supported the efforts of Representative Henry Hyde of Illinois to cut off most Medicaid funds for abortion (1976). In 1980 the Supreme Court upheld the Hyde Amendment, deciding that the government had no obligation to make even medically necessary abortions available to the poor *(Harris v. McRae)*.

As activists in the women's struggle looked to the future, they had to acknowledge certain harsh realities. One was the impact of the eco-

> **Effects of a shrinking job market**

nomic recessions of the 1970s and early 1980s. In a contracted job market, many women found affirmative action meaningless. Before they could receive promotions or even jobs, economic conditions would have to improve. But in the early 1980s, experts were predicting a protracted period of high unemployment.

Another harsh reality women encountered

was "occupational segregation," which became even more pronounced as women flooded into low-paying entry-level jobs in female-dominated fields like secretarial and clerical work. Women complained of "occupational ghettos": half of all working women in 1980 were in jobs that were at least 70 percent female. Some women with college educations earned less than men with eighth-grade educations. As a consequence, feminists began to argue for "equal pay for work of equal value." Why should a secretary earn considerably less than a carpenter, they reasoned, if the two jobs required comparable skills and involved comparable responsibilities?

Perhaps the most disturbing trend was what *Newsweek* called "the Superwoman Squeeze."

| Increased burdens on women |

According to a report by the Worldwatch Institute in 1980, most working wives and mothers, even those with full-time jobs, "retained an unwilling monopoly on unpaid labor at home." Husbands were generally less than eager to do household tasks.

By the early 1980s it appeared that the feminist ferment of the 1970s had waned. Some women seemed to take for granted the gains of that decade, believing that equality of opportunity had been secured for all time. Others were concentrating on planning their lives so they could have both a career and a family without shortchanging either—or themselves—in the process.

Nonwhites in a shrinking economy

Nonwhites too made social gains in the 1970s that were offset by the effects of a contracting job market. As a result of the sluggish economy, poverty was still a national problem in 1980, and blacks made up a disproportionate share of the poor. By 1978, though the overall poverty rate had decreased to 11.4 percent, the rates for black families and families of Hispanic origin were 27.5 and 20.4 compared with 6.9 percent for white families. Unemployment figures were equally discouraging. In 1980 the unemployment rate for black teen-agers in the inner city hovered at 50 percent.

Tied to the high unemployment rate was the increase in the number of young black families headed by single women. Between 1960 and 1975 the number of fatherless black families rose 130 percent. Many of these families were headed by unmarried teenagers who were forced to rely on welfare to support their children. Other mothers earned meager incomes as domestic servants, laundresses, or kitchen helpers. Like young black males, welfare mothers suffered from a sense of futility. Most of them were children of the welfare system; it was the only life they knew.

Some whites and even other blacks grumbled that poor blacks were responsible for their own poverty. Their own forebears had seized the opportunities at hand and raised themselves up by their bootstraps, whites insisted; why couldn't

| Declining job opportunities for blacks |

today's blacks do the same? But the job market was far different in the 1980s from what it had been twenty-five, fifty, or seventy-five years before. Most jobs required skills the poor and undereducated did not have.

But even as the plight of the black poor worsened, the black middle class expanded.

| Black middle class |

Black college students increased from 282,000 in 1966 to over 1 million in 1976. During this period an estimated 30 percent of the urban black population joined the middle class, and many moved to the suburbs or to better housing in the cities. By 1980 about one-third of all black high school graduates were going on to college, the same proportion as among white youths. At least at the upper levels of black society, the dream of equality was being realized.

In his provocative book *The Declining Signifi-*

In Boston in 1976, antibusing protesters tried to impale a black man with a flagstaff. This photograph of the ugly incident won a Pulizer Prize. Stanley Forman/Boston Herald American.

cance of Race (1978), William Julius Wilson spoke of the emergence of two black Americas, one very poor, the other affluent. Wilson concluded that "the life chances of blacks" were "based far more on their present economic class position than on their status as black Americans." In other words, many middle-class blacks had begun to have more in common with middle-class whites than with the poor black society they had left behind in the inner cities.

As middle-class blacks were making gains, resentful whites complained that they were being victimized by "reverse discrimination." To meet federal affirmative-action requirements, some schools and companies had established quotas for minorities and women. In some cases the requirements for quota groups were lower than those for whites. In a five-to-four ruling in 1978 the Supreme Court outlawed quotas but upheld the principle of affirmative action (*Bakke* v. *University of California*).

Anger over a special standard for blacks combined with the effects of stagflation and opposition to busing to produce an upsurge in racism in the 1970s. (As part of the effort to create racially balanced schools, courts ordered students to be transported from one section of a city to

| *White backlash* |

another.) In Boston, where busing caused numerous riots, a group of white students protesting busing attacked a black passer-by outside City Hall, running at him with the sharp end of a flagstaff flying an American flag. Tension rose not only in Boston, but across the nation. Membership in the Ku Klux Klan grew from about five thousand in 1978 to ten thousand just two years later. The organization was active in California, Connecticut, Michigan, and other northern states as well as in the South.

Blacks were tense, too, and they showed it more openly than in the past. "After 350 years of fearing whites," Charles Silberman wrote in *Criminal Violence, Criminal Justice* (1978), "black Americans have discovered that fear runs the other way, that whites are intimidated by their very presence. . . . The taboo against expression of anti-white anger is breaking down, and 350 years of festering hatred has come spilling out." That hatred erupted several times in summer 1980, most notably in Miami and Chattanooga, after all-white juries acquitted whites of the murder of blacks. (In Miami the defendants were white policemen; in Chattanooga, Ku Klux Klansmen.) Miami's three days of rioting left eighteen dead, four hundred injured, and $100 million worth of property damage.

Every bit as angry as blacks were American Indians. Their new militancy had burst into the headlines in November 1969, when a small group of Indians seized Alcatraz Island in San Francisco Bay. Arguing that an 1868 Sioux treaty entitled them to possession of unused federal lands, the Indians occupied the island until summer 1971. Two years later, members of the American Indian Movement (AIM) seized eleven hostages and a trading post on the Pine Ridge Reservation at Wounded Knee, South Dakota, the place where in 1890 troops of the 7th Cavalry had massacred the Sioux. Their seventy-one-day confrontation with federal marshals ended with a government agreement to examine the treaty rights of the Oglala Sioux.

Like blacks, Indians seemed trapped in poverty. In the late 1970s the unemployment rate among Indians was 40 percent. Nine out of ten Indians lived in substandard housing, and the high school drop-out rate averaged 53 percent. Being an Indian was also unhealthy: Native Americans suffered the highest incidence of alcoholism, tuberculosis, and suicide of any ethnic group in the United States. Though their population had risen since the Second World War to about 1 million (650,000 on or near reservations and 350,000 in the "red ghettos" of the cities), that was only a fifth of their number when the first Europeans arrived in North America.

Since 1924 Indians have had dual legal status as United States citizens and as members of tribal nations subject to special treaty agreements with the United States. But their dual status has proved a curse, in large part because the government has not honored its treaty commitments—especially when Indian lands contained valuable *Indian suits for lost lands* minerals. In 1946 Congress established the Indian Claims Commission to compensate Indians for lands stolen from them. Under the legislation lawyers for the Native American Rights Fund and other groups scored notable victories in the 1970s. The Chippewa in the upper Midwest, Indians in the Puget Sound area of Washington, and the Cheyenne-Arapaho tribes in Oklahoma won protection of their hunting and fishing rights and restitution of their land and water. In 1971 President Nixon signed a bill returning to the Taos Pueblo their sacred forest of Blue Lake in New Mexico. And in 1980 the Supreme Court ordered the government to pay $117 million plus interest to the Sioux Indian Nation for the Black Hills of South Dakota, stolen from them when gold was discovered there in the 1870s.

As Indians fought to regain old rights, Hispanics struggled to make a place for themselves in the United States. An influx of immigrants *Hispanic-Americans* unequaled since the turn of the century coupled with a high birth rate had made Hispanic peoples the United States' fastest-growing minority by 1978. Projections were that they

Chapter 31: A disillusioned people: America since 1973

would overtake blacks as the nation's largest minority by the mid-1980s. Of the more than 20 million Hispanics living in the United States in the 1970s, 8 million were Mexican-Americans concentrated in California, Arizona, New Mexico, Colorado, and Texas. Several million Puerto Ricans and perhaps 1 million Cubans clustered mostly on the East Coast.

Besides these officially acknowledged Hispanics, between 8 million and 12 million more undocumented workers, or illegal aliens, lived in the United States. Beginning in the mid-1960s, large numbers of poverty-stricken Mexicans began to cross the poorly guarded 2,000-mile border between Mexico and the United States. The movement north continued in the 1970s; in the last eight years of that decade the Chicano population increased 60 percent. By the end of the 1970s one out of every four Texans and one out of every five Californians was Mexican-American. And in the early 1980s, worsening economic conditions in Mexico encouraged continued flight across the border.

But poverty awaited these new immigrants, as it had previous groups of newcomers. The median family income for Mexican-Americans in 1979 was $11,421, as compared with $16,284 for non-Hispanic families. Nineteen percent of Mexican-Americans lived below the poverty line. Puerto Ricans were worse off, with a median family income of about $8,300, and 30 percent of their number living in poverty. Though the problems with which Hispanics contended were similar to those confronting other non-whites, they also faced a language barrier.

Most Hispanics preferred their family-centered culture to Anglo culture, and for that reason they resisted assimilation. "What we are

| **Hispanic cultural pride** |

saying," explained Daniel Villanueva, a TV executive, "is that we want to be here, but without losing our language and our culture. They are a richness, a treasure that we don't care to lose."

Instead, like other minorities, Hispanics wanted power—"brown power." Cesar Chavez's United Farm Workers had been the first His-

panic interest group to attract national attention. Another group, the militant Brown Berets, attracted notice for their efforts to provide meals to preschoolers and courses in Chicano studies and consciousness-raising to older students. And throughout the 1970s the Mexican-American political party La Raza Unida was a potent force in the Southwest and East Los Angeles. Still, for a group soon to become the nation's largest minority, Hispanics exercised a disproportionately small share of political power.

The Me Decade

At the beginning of 1980, the editors of *Time* magazine observed that the 1970s had been "erected upon the smoldering wreckage of the '60s." In the 1970s the nation had turned apathetic, and perhaps nowhere was this new attitude more evident than among youth. In the 1960s American youths had worked for change in the nation's social, political, and cultural life. But in the 1970s their younger brothers and sisters rejected revolutionary idealism. Older Americans took refuge, too, from a lost war, political scandal, and economic distress. As a theologian put it, Americans "have a beleaguered sense in their bones that the old order is dying. Very few want a radical alternative, but few also are working to develop a rationale for the system we've got."

Instead, in the 1970s, a period the social commentator Tom Wolfe called the Me Decade, Americans turned inward. Transactional Analysis (TA), a form of psychotherapy emphasizing

| **Human potential movement** |

interpersonal relationships, was popularized in Eric Berne's *Games People Play* (1969) and Thomas Harris's *I'm Ok–You're OK* (1969). Transcendental Meditation (TM), a yogic discipline, drew 350,000 adherents and spawned over two hundred teaching centers. In addition to these fads, Zen, yoga, the Sufi, Hare Krishna, and other new therapies and exotic religions flourished.

As millions of Americans sought to fill spiritual and emotional voids through esoteric movements, millions more were drawn to more traditional beliefs. According to a 1977 survey, about 70 million Americans defined themselves as born-again Christians, and 10 million claimed to have had the experience since 1975. Religious revivals and evangelical sects were not new, of course, but by the mid-1970s they were a growth industry. In the latter years of the decade evangelicals were grossing $200 million annually in sales of religious books, and the Virginia-based Christian Broadcast Network was earning nearly $60 million from its four stations and 130 affiliates.

| Spiritual revival |

Besides the relatively harmless human potential movements and the traditional religious enthusiasms, a dark undercurrent of cult-like adherence to charismatic leaders ran through the 1970s. In 1973 and 1974, the Reverend Sun Myung Moon, founder of the Unification Church, toured the United States and converted young Americans to his religion, a curious blend of Christianity, anti-Communism, and worship of Moon as a messiah. "Moonies" disposed of their possessions, moved into communes, and raised funds for the church by selling ginseng tea, candles, flowers, and peanuts. Critics charged that Moon and his disciples had brainwashed their converts, and soon worried parents were attempting to rescue their children from the influence of the church by kidnapping them.

| Messianic cults |

Yet another facet of "me-ness" was the phenomenon called "Roots." The 1977 television series, based on a best-selling book by Alex Haley, dramatized the author's family history beginning with his ancestor, Kunta Kinte, a Gambian boy sold into slavery. "Roots" spawned an interest in family trees that touched all races and ethnic groups. More important, the sheer numbers of Americans exposed to the book and television series (130 million watched the eight-part series) helped to sensitize the public to the agonies of slavery and racism.

If Americans went running to libraries to research their family trees during the 1970s, they probably did so in an expensive pair of Nikes, Pumas, or Adidas, for this was the decade of the jogger. James Fixx's *Complete Book of Running* (1977) enjoyed tremendous popularity, and literature on running, physical fitness, diet, and health jammed book shelves and magazine racks. Perhaps America was no longer the best nation it could be, but Americans were determined to make themselves the best, or at least the healthiest, individuals they could be.

| Physical fitness craze |

As the decade drew to a close, Christopher Lasch, a history professor at the University of Rochester, condemned the nation's behavior as self-indulgent and apolitical. In *The Culture of Narcissism* (1979), Lasch branded Americans an emotionally shallow, anxiety-ridden people desperately trying to ignore the waning of their nation's power. He cited advertising and the human potential movement as causes of the nation's malaise. But there was little evidence that the trend was changing. In a decade of exhausted public passions, private passions reigned supreme.

A turn to the right

By 1980 the nation's mood had turned conservative. In 1978 California voters had approved a tax-cutting referendum called Proposition 13, which had reduced property taxes and put stringent limits on state spending for social programs. On the national level conservatives lobbied for a constitutional amendment to prohibit federal budget deficits and organized for the 1980 elections. One conservative campaign group, the National Conservative Political Action Committee (NCPAC), targeted a number of liberal senators for defeat. And a number of evangelical Christians joined with the conservatives, hoping to use the body politic in their fight against abortion, gay rights, sex in movies, and the ERA.

| Resurgence of conservatism |

In 1981 President-elect Ronald Reagan (1911–   )
and his wife Nancy smiled for photographers. Reagan had swept the nation, beating both Jimmy Carter and John Anderson in 43 states.   Liaison.

From the beginning, the front-runner for the
Republican presidential nomination was conservative Ronald Reagan, a former movie star
and two-term governor of California. Reagan
appealed to both traditional political conservatives and the new breed of
social-issue conservative. In
the Democratic party, Presi-
dent Carter easily beat back Senator Edward
Kennedy's challenge for the nomination. As the
incumbent, Carter had to accept political responsibility not only for high inflation and
unemployment but for the Americans being
held hostage in Iran. When the votes were
counted, Reagan had won 51 percent of the
popular vote and all but forty-nine electoral
votes. Carter carried only six states, Reagan all
the rest. John Anderson, a Republican who ran
as an independent, garnered 8 percent of the
popular vote.

Election of 1980

Reagan took office at a time when polls indicated that the ailing economy was uppermost
in the minds of Americans. Reasoning that old
economic theories had failed, the president
turned to conservative "supply-side" economics for the
solution to the nation's ills. A revived version of
the Republicans' 1920s trickle-down theory,
supply-side theory was based on the idea that
tax reductions would stimulate the economy by
encouraging capital investment. With the help
of conservative southern Democrats, nicknamed
the Boll Weevils, Republicans in Congress
passed Reagan's tax bill in August 1981. The
law lowered the capital gains tax paid by corporations and handed individuals an across-the-
board, three-step tax reduction totaling 25 percent. Wealthy people saved the most under the
bill.

Reagan also encouraged the Federal Reserve

Reaganomics

Important events

1973	Trials of Watergate burglars	1977	Resurgence of evangelical

1973   Trials of Watergate burglars
        Hearings by the Senate Select
            (Ervin) Committee on
            Campaign Practices
        White House aides John
            Ehrlichman and H. R.
            Haldeman resign
        Confrontation between the
            American Indian Movement
            and the federal government at
            Wounded Knee, South
            Dakota
        War Powers Act
        Arab oil embargo
        Vice President Spiro Agnew
            resigns
        Congressman Gerald R. Ford
            appointed as vice president

1974   Oil price increases by the
            Organization of Petroleum
            Exporting Countries (OPEC)
        Equal Credit Opportunity Act
        Supreme Court orders President
            Nixon to release the White
            House tapes
        House Judiciary Committee votes
            to impeach Nixon
        Nixon resigns the presidency;
            Ford becomes president
        President Ford pardons Nixon
        Ford's WIN (Whip Inflation
            Now) program

1975   Nuclear accident at Brown's
            Ferry, Alabama

1976   Hyde amendment cuts off
            Medicaid funds for abortions
        Jimmy Carter elected president

1977   Resurgence of evangelical
            Christianity

1978   Supreme Court upholds
            affirmative action (*Bakke* v.
            University of California)
        California voters approve
            Proposition 13

1979   Nuclear accident at Three Mile
            Island, Pennsylvania
        Federal Reserve Board tightens
            the money supply

1980   Economic recession
        Phased decontrol of oil prices and
            deregulation of transportation
            industries
        One hundred million acres of
            Alaskan land placed in reserve
            for national parks, forests,
            and wildlife refuges
        Supreme Court rules that the
            federal government must
            compensate the Sioux Indian
            Nation for the Black Hills
        Ronald Reagan elected president
        Republicans gain control of U.S.
            Senate

1981   Fifty-two hostages in Iran
            released after 444 days

1982   Unemployment rises to 10.8
            percent
        Congressional elections weaken
            Reagan's position

1983   Inflation wanes

Board to lower the prime lending rate, which stood at a record high 21.5 percent in December 1980. By February 1983 the rate had fallen to 10.5 percent, the depressed housing industry had begun to revive, and the stock market had become bullish again. At the same time inflation slowed, from 11.2 percent in the first quarter of 1981 to less than 5 percent by the last quarter of 1982. Reagan could not claim all the credit for these improvements, however. The weakening of the OPEC oil cartel, increased energy conservation, and reduced factory output due to recession produced an oil glut that lowered prices significantly.

Moreover, Reagan's successes had some negative consequences. To balance his tax cuts, the president had slashed social programs for the poor. Women were especially hard hit by these reductions. Even fundamental programs like Social Security were threatened. In 1983 administration officials began to worry that without some cutbacks, the program, a mainstay of retired Americans, would go bankrupt. And perhaps most disturbing, the lowered inflation rate had been achieved at the cost of high unemployment. In December 1982, 10.8 percent of the nation was out of work; in some states the rate hit 17 percent.

As unemployment levels reached postdepression highs, Republicans worried about the political consequences of hard times, and about the growing "gender gap." Women, hard hit by cutbacks in social programs and the defeat of the ERA, were beginning to desert the GOP. In the 1982 elections the Democrats gained 26 seats in the House. Republicans maintained their 54 to 46 majority in the Senate but lost 7 governorships.

The new Congress was not friendly toward Reagan. Democrats as well as Republicans were alarmed at the rising deficit: in 1982 the national debt increased by $110.7 billion, and estimates for fiscal year 1983 hovered around $200 billion. Liberal Democrats were bent on preventing additional cuts in social programs, and the president was determined to spend even more on defense. A major fight was brewing, one that

might not be resolved until the next presidential election.

Suggestions for further reading

WATERGATE   John W. Dean, *Blind Ambition: The White House Years* (1976); Leon Jaworski, *The Right and the Power: The Prosecution of Watergate* (1976); J. Anthony Lukas, *Nightmare: The Underside of the Nixon Years* (1976); John J. Sirica, *To Set the Record Straight: The Break-in, the Tapes, the Conspirators, the Pardon* (1979); Bob Woodward and Carl Bernstein, *All the President's Men* (1974).

ENERGY SHORTAGES, ECONOMIC WOES   Richard J. Barnet, *The Lean Years: Politics in the Age of Scarcity* (1980); Daniel Bell, *The Coming of the Post-Industrial Society: A Venture in Social Forecasting* (1973); Barry Commoner, *The Politics of Energy* (1979); Robert L. Heilbroner, *An Inquiry into the Human Prospect* (1974); Frances Moore Lappé and Joseph Collins, *Food First: Beyond the Myth of Scarcity* (1977); Harry Mauer, *Not Working: An Oral History of the Unemployed* (1979); James Ridgeway, *Who Owns the Earth* (1980); Emma Rothschild, *Paradise Lost: The Decline of the Auto-Industrial Age* (1973); Lester C. Thurow, *The Zero-Sum Society: Distribution and the Possibilities for Economic Change* (1980).

THE FORD ADMINISTRATION   Gerald R. Ford, *A Time to Heal: The Autobiography of Gerald R. Ford* (1979); Jerry Hartmann, *Palace Politics: An Inside Account of the Ford Years* (1980); Richard Reeves, *A Ford, Not a Lincoln* (1975).

THE CARTER ADMINISTRATION   Betty Glad, *Jimmy Carter: From Plains to the White House* (1980); Haynes Johnson, *In the Absence of Power: Governing America* (1980); Laurence H. Shoup, *The Carter Presidency & Beyond* (1980); Jules Witcover, *Marathon: The Pursuit of the Presidency, 1972–1976* (1977).

WOMEN'S STRUGGLES   Susan Brownmiller, *Against Our Will: Men, Women and Rape* (1975); Barbara Ehrenreich, *The Hearts of Men: American Dreams and the Flight from Commitment* (1983); Jo Freeman, *The*

Politics of Women's Liberation (1975); Kenneth Keniston, *All Our Children: The American Family Under Pressure* (1977); Christopher Lasch, *Haven in a Heartless World: The Family Besieged* (1977); Maggie Scarf, *Unfinished Business: Pressure Points in the Lives of Women* (1980).

NONWHITES IN CONTEMPORARY AMERICA Vine Deloria, *Custer Died for Your Sins: An Indian Manifesto* (1969); Dorothy K. Newman *et al.*, *Protest, Politics, and Prosperity: Black Americans and White Institutions, 1940–1974* (1978); Julian A. Samora and Patricia Vandel Simon, *A History of the Mexican-American People* (1977); Carol B. Stack, *All Our Kin: Strategies for Survival in a Black Community* (1975); J. Harris Wilkinson III, *From Brown to Bakke: The Supreme Court and School Integration, 1954–1978* (1979); William Julius Wilson, *The Declining Significance of Race: Blacks and Changing American Institutions* (1978).

THE ME DECADE Christopher Lasch, *The Culture of Narcissism: American Life in an Age of Diminishing Expectations* (1978); Gail Sheehy, *Passages: Predictable Crises in Adult Life* (1976); Tom Wolfe, "The 'Me' Decade and the Third Great Awakening," *New York*, 9 (1976), 26–40.

THE NEW CONSERVATISM AND THE ELECTION OF RONALD REAGAN Lou Cannon, *Reagan* (1982); Alan Crawford, *Thunder on the Right: The "New Right" and the Politics of Resentment* (1980); Kirkpatrick Sale, *Power Shift: The Rise of the Southern Rim and Its Challenge to the Eastern Establishment* (1975); Peter Steinfels, *The Neoconservatives: The Men Who Are Changing America's Politics* (1979).

Appendix

Historical reference books by subject

Encyclopedias, dictionaries, atlases, chronologies, and statistics

GENERAL AND BIOGRAPHICAL *Concise Dictionary of American Biography* (1977); *Dictionary of American Biography* (1928–   ); *Dictionary of American History* (1976); *Encyclopedia of American History* (1981); *Family Encyclopedia of American History* (1975); George H. Gallup, *The Gallup Poll: Public Opinion, 1935–1971* (1972); George H. Gallup, *The Gallup Poll: Public Opinion, 1972–1977* (1978); John A. Garraty, ed., *Encyclopedia of American Biography* (1974); Bernard Grun, *The Timetables of History: A Horizontal Linkage of People and Events* (1975); Stanley Hochman, *Yesterday and Today: A Dictionary of Recent American History* (1979); *International Encyclopedia of the Social Sciences* (1968–   ); Thomas H. Johnson, *The Oxford Companion to American History* (1966); R. Alton Lee and Archie P. McDonald, eds., *Encyclopedia USA* (1983–   ); Richard B. Morris, *Encyclopedia of American History* (1976); *National Cyclopedia of American Biography* (1898–   ); U.S. Bureau of the Census, *Historical Statistics of the United States: Colonial Times to 1970* (1975); Charles Van Doren, ed., *Webster's American Biographies* (1974).

THE AMERICAN REVOLUTION Mark M. Boatner, III, *Encyclopedia of the American Revolution* (1974).

ARCHITECTURE William D. Hunt, Jr., ed., *Encyclopedia of American Architecture* (1980).

ATLASES John L. Andriot, ed., *Township Atlas of the United States* (1979); Lester J. Cappon, ed., *Atlas of Early American History: The Revolutionary Era, 1760–1790* (1976); Edward W. Fox, *Atlas of American History* (1964); Edwin S. Gaustad, *Historical Atlas of Religion in America* (1976); *International Geographic Encyclopedia and Atlas* (1979); Kenneth T. Jackson and James T. Adams, *Atlas of American History* (1978); Douglas W. Marshall and Howard H. Peckham, *Campaigns of the American Revolution* (1976); *Rand-McNally Atlas of the American Revolution* (1974); Craig L. Symonds, *A Battlefield Atlas of the Civil War* (1983); U.S. Department of the Interior, Geological Survey, *National Atlas of the United States of America* (1970); U.S. War Department, *The Official Atlas of the Civil War* (1958); U.S. Military Academy, *The West Point Atlas of American Wars, 1689–1953* (1959).

BLACKS Peter M. Bergman, *The Chronological History of the Negro in America* (1969); John Hope Franklin and August Meier, eds., *Black Leaders of the Twentieth Century* (1982); Rayford W. Logan and Michael R. Winston, eds., *The Dictionary of American Negro Biography* (1983); W. A Low and Virgil A. Clift, eds., *Encyclopedia of Black America* (1981); Harry A. Ploski and William Marr, eds., *The Negro Almanac* (1976); Erwin A. Salk, ed., *A Layman's Guide to Negro History* (1967); Mabel M. Smythe, ed., *The Black American Reference Book* (1976); Edgar A. Toppin, *A Biographical History of Blacks in America* (1971).

THE CIVIL WAR Mark M. Boatner, III, *The Civil War Dictionary* (1959); E. B. Long, *The Civil War Day by Day: An Almanac, 1861–1865* (1971); Jon L. Wakelyn, ed., *Biographical Dictionary of the Confederacy* (1977); Ezra J. Warner and W. Buck Yearns, *Biographical Register of the Confederate Congress* (1975).

CONSTITUTIONAL HISTORY Congressional Quarterly, *Guide to the Supreme Court* (1979); Leon Friedman and Fred I. Israel, eds., *The Justices of the United States Supreme Court, 1789–1978: Their Lives and Major Opinions* (1980); *Judges of the United States* (1980).

ECONOMIC HISTORY Glenn Porter, *Encyclopedia of American Economic History* (1980).

EDUCATION Lee C. Deighton, ed., *The Encyclopedia of Education* (1971); Joseph C. Kiger, ed., *Research In-*

stitutions and Learned Societies (1982); John F. Ohles, ed., *Biographical Dictionary of American Educators* (1978).

ENTERTAINMENT Tim Brooks and Earle Marsh, *The Complete Directory to Prime Time Network TV Shows, 1946–present* (1979); John Chilton, *Who's Who of Jazz* (1972); John Dunning, *Tune in Yesterday* [radio] (1976); Stanley Green, *Encyclopedia of the Musical Film* (1981); *Notable Names in the American Theater* (1976); *New York Times Encyclopedia of Television* (1977); Andrew Sarris, *The American Cinema: Directors and Directions, 1929–1968* (1968); Evelyn M. Truitt, *Who Was Who on Screen* (1977).

FOREIGN POLICY Alexander DeConde, ed., *Encyclopedia of American Foreign Policy* (1978); John E. Findling, *Dictionary of American Diplomatic History* (1980); Richard B. Morris and Graham W. Irwin, eds., *Harper Encyclopedia of the Modern World* (1970); Jack E. Vincent, *A Handbook of International Relations* (1969).

IMMIGRATION AND ETHNIC GROUPS Matt S. Meier and Feliciano Rivera, *Dictionary of Mexican American History* (1981); Stephen Thernstrom, ed., *Harvard Encyclopedia of American Ethnic Groups* (1980).

INDIANS Frederick J. Dockstader, *Great North American Indians: Profiles in Life and Leadership* (1977); *Handbook of North American Indians* (1978–); Barry Klein, ed., *Reference Encyclopedia of the American Indian* (1978).

LABOR Gary M. Fink, ed., *Biographical Dictionary of American Labor Leaders* (1974); Gary M. Fink, ed., *Labor Unions* (1977).

POLITICS AND GOVERNMENT Congressional Quarterly, *Congress and the Nation, 1945–1976* (1965–1977); Congressional Quarterly, *Guide to U.S. Elections* (1975); Roy R. Glashan, comp., *American Governors and Gubernatorial Elections, 1775–1978* (1979); Melvin G. Holli and Peter d' A. Jones, eds., *Biographical Dictionary of American Mayors, 1820–1980: Big City Mayors* (1981); Joseph E. Kallenbach and Jessamine S. Kallenbach, *American State Governors, 1776–1976* (1977); Mark E. Neely, Jr., *The Abraham Lincoln Encyclopedia* (1982); Svend Peterson, *A Statistical History of the American Presidential Elections* (1963); *Political Profiles, Truman Years to . . .* (1978); John

W. Raimo, *Biographical Directory of American Colonial and Revolutionary Governors, 1607–1789* (1980); William Safire, *Safire's Political Dictionary* (1978); Richard M. Scammon, ed., *America at the Polls: Handbook of Presidential Election Statistics* (1965); Edward L. and Frederick H. Schapsmeier, eds., *Political Parties and Civic Action Groups* (1981); Arthur M. Schlesinger, Jr., and Fred I. Israel, eds., *History of American Presidential Elections, 1789–1968* (1971); Robert Sobel, ed., *Biographical Directory of the United States Executive Branch, 1774–1977* (1977); U.S. Congress, Senate, *Biographical Directory of the American Congress, 1774–1971* (1971); Robert Vexler, *The Vice-Presidents and Cabinet Members: Biographies Arranged Chronologically by Administration* (1975).

REGIONS AND STATES Robert Bain, *et al.,* eds., *Southern Writers: A Biographical Dictionary* (1979); John Clayton, ed., *The Illinois Fact Book and Historical Almanac, 1673–1968* (1970); Howard R. Lamar, ed., *The Reader's Encyclopedia of the American West* (1977); David C. Roller and Robert W. Twyman, eds., *The Encyclopedia of Southern History* (1979); Walter Prescott Webb, H. Bailey Carroll, and Eldon S. Banda, eds. *The Handbook of Texas* (1952, 1976).

RELIGION Henry Bowden, *Dictionary of American Religious Biography* (1977); John Tracy Ellis and Robert Trisco, *Guide to American Catholic History* (1981); J. Gordon Melton, *The Encyclopedia of American Religions* (1978); Arthur C. Piepkorn, *Profiles in Belief: The Religious Bodies of the United States and Canada* (1977–1979).

SCIENCE Charles C. Gillispie, ed., *Dictionary of Scientific Biography* (1970–); National Academy of Sciences, *Biographical Memoirs* (1877–).

SPORTS Ralph Hickok, *New Encyclopedia of Sports* (1977); Ralph Hickok, *Who Was Who in American Sports* (1971); Frank G. Menke and Suzanne Treat, *The Encyclopedia of Sports* (1977); Paul Soderberg, *et al., The Big Book of Halls of Fame in the United States and Canada* (1977).

WARS AND THE MILITARY R. Ernest Dupuy and Trevor N. Dupuy, *The Encyclopedia of Military History* (1977); Robert Goralski, *World War II Almanac, 1931–1945* (1981); Holger H. Herwig and Neil M.

Heyman, *Biographical Dictionary of World War I* (1982); *Louis L. Snyder's Historical Guide to World War II* (1982); Thomas Parrish, ed., *The Simon and Schuster Encyclopedia of World War II* (1978); *Webster's American Military Biographies* (1978); Peter Young, ed., *The World Almanac Book of World War II* (1981).

WOMEN   Edward T. James, Janet W. James, and Paul S. Boyer, eds., *Notable American Women, 1607–1950* (1971); Barbara Sicherman and Carol Hurd Green, eds., *Notable American Women, The Modern Period* (1980).

Declaration of Independence in Congress, July 4, 1776

The unanimous declaration of the thirteen United States of America

When, in the course of human events, it becomes necessary for one people to dissolve the political bonds which have connected them with another, and to assume, among the powers of the earth, the separate and equal station to which the laws of nature and of nature's God entitle them, a decent respect to the opinions of mankind requires that they should declare the causes which impel them to the separation.

We hold these truths to be self-evident: That all men are created equal; that they are endowed by their Creator with certain unalienable rights; that among these are life, liberty, and the pursuit of happiness; that, to secure these rights, governments are instituted among men, deriving their just powers from the consent of the governed; that whenever any form of government becomes destructive of these ends, it is the right of the people to alter or to abolish it, and to institute new government, laying its foundation on such principles, and organizing its powers in such form, as to them shall seem most likely to effect their safety and happiness. Prudence, indeed, will dictate that governments long established should not be changed for light and transient causes; and accordingly all experience hath shown that mankind are more disposed to suffer, while evils are sufferable, than to right themselves by abolishing the forms to which they are accustomed. But when a long train of abuses and usurpations, pursuing invariably the same object, evinces a design to reduce them under absolute despotism, it is their right, it is their duty, to throw off such government, and to provide new guards for their future security. Such has been the patient sufferance of these colonies; and such is now the necessity which constrains them to alter their former systems of government. The history of the present King of Great Britain is a history of repeated injuries and usurpations, all having in direct object the establishment of an absolute tyranny over these states. To prove this, let facts be submitted to a candid world.

He has refused his assent to laws, the most wholesome and necessary for the public good.

He has forbidden his governors to pass laws of immediate and pressing importance, unless suspended in their operation till his assent should be obtained; and, when so suspended, he has utterly neglected to attend to them.

He has refused to pass other laws for the accommodation of large districts of people, unless those people would relinquish the right of representation in the legislature, a right inestimable to them, and formidable to tyrants only.

He has called together legislative bodies at places unusual, uncomfortable, and distant from the depository of their public records, for the sole purpose of fatiguing them into compliance with his measures.

He has dissolved representative houses repeatedly, for opposing, with manly firmness, his invasions on the rights of the people.

He has refused for a long time, after such dissolutions, to cause others to be elected; whereby the legislative powers, incapable of annihilation, have returned to the people at large for their exercise; the state remaining, in the mean time, exposed to all the dangers of invasions from without and convulsions within.

He has endeavored to prevent the population of these states; for that purpose obstructing the laws for naturalization of foreigners; refusing to pass others to encourage their migration hither, and raising the conditions of new appropriations of lands.

He has obstructed the administration of justice, by refusing his assent to laws for establishing judiciary powers.

He has made judges dependent on his will alone, for the tenure of their offices, and the amount and payment of their salaries.

He has erected a multitude of new offices, and sent hither swarms of officers to harass our people and eat out their substance.

He has kept among us, in times of peace, standing armies, without the consent of our legislatures.

He has affected to render the military independent of, and superior to, the civil power.

He has combined with others to subject us to a

jurisdiction foreign to our constitution, and unacknowledged by our laws, giving his assent to their acts of pretended legislation:

For quartering large bodies of armed troops among us;

For protecting them, by a mock trial, from punishment for any murder which they should commit on the inhabitants of these states;

For cutting off our trade with all parts of the world;

For imposing taxes on us without our consent;

For depriving us, in many cases, of the benefits of trial by jury;

For transporting us beyond seas, to be tried for pretended offenses;

For abolishing the free system of English laws in a neighboring province, establishing therein an arbitrary government, and enlarging its boundaries, so as to render it at once an example and fit instrument for introducing the same absolute rule into these colonies;

For taking away our charters, abolishing our most valuable laws, and altering fundamentally the forms of our governments;

For suspending our own legislatures, and declaring themselves invested with power to legislate for us in all cases whatsoever.

He has abdicated government here, by declaring us out of his protection and waging war against us.

He has plundered our seas, ravaged our coasts, burned our towns, and destroyed the lives of our people.

He is at this time transporting large armies of foreign mercenaries to complete the works of death, desolation, and tyranny already begun with circumstances of cruelty and perfidy scarcely paralleled in the most barbarous ages, and totally unworthy the head of a civilized nation.

He has constrained our fellow-citizens, taken captive on the high seas, to bear arms against their country, to become the executioners of their friends and brethren, or to fall themselves by their hands.

He has excited domestic insurrection among us, and has endeavored to bring on the inhabitants of our frontiers the merciless Indian savages, whose known rule of warfare is an undistinguished destruction of all ages, sexes, and conditions.

In every stage of these oppressions we have petitioned for redress in the most humble terms; our repeated petitions have been answered only by repeated injury. A prince, whose character is thus marked by every act which may define a tyrant, is unfit to be the ruler of a free people.

Nor have we been wanting in our attentions to our British brethren. We have warned them, from time to time, of attempts by their legislature to extend an unwarrantable jurisdiction over us. We have reminded them of the circumstances of our emigration and settlement here. We have appealed to their native justice and magnanimity; and we have conjured them, by the ties of our common kindred, to disavow these usurpations, which would inevitably interrupt our connections and correspondence. They, too, have been deaf to the voice of justice and of consanguinity. We must, therefore, acquiesce in the necessity which denounces our separation, and hold them, as we hold the rest of mankind, enemies in war, in peace friends.

We, therefore, the representatives of the United States of America, in General Congress assembled, appealing to the Supreme Judge of the world for the rectitude of our intentions, do, in the name and by the authority of the good people of these colonies, solemnly publish and declare, that these United Colonies are, and of right ought to be, FREE AND INDEPENDENT STATES; that they are absolved from all allegiance to the British crown, and that all political connection between them and the state of Great Britain is, and ought to be, totally dissolved; and that, as free and independent states, they have full power to levy war, conclude peace, contract alliances, establish commerce, and do all other acts and things which independent states may of right do. And for the support of this declaration, with a firm reliance on the protection of Divine Providence, we mutually pledge to each other our lives, our fortunes, and our sacred honor.

JOHN HANCOCK
and fifty-five others

Constitution of the United States of America and Amendments

PREAMBLE

We the people of the United States, in order to form a more perfect union, establish justice, insure domestic tranquillity, provide for the common defense, promote the general welfare, and secure the blessings of liberty to ourselves and our posterity, do ordain and establish this Constitution for the United States of America.

ARTICLE I

Section 1 All legislative powers herein granted shall be vested in a Congress of the United States, which shall consist of a Senate and a House of Representatives.

Section 2 The House of Representatives shall be composed of members chosen every second year by the people of the several States, and the electors in each State shall have the qualifications requisite for electors of the most numerous branch of the State Legislature.

No person shall be a Representative who shall not have attained to the age of twenty-five years, and been seven years a citizen of the United States, and who shall not, when elected, be an inhabitant of that State in which he shall be chosen.

Representatives and direct taxes shall be apportioned among the several States which may be included within this Union, according to their respective numbers, *which shall be determined by adding to the whole number of free persons including those bound to service for a term of years and excluding Indians not taxed, three-fifths of all other persons.* The actual enumeration shall be made within three years after the first meeting of the Congress of the United States, and within every subsequent term of ten years, in such manner as they shall by law direct. The number of Representatives shall not exceed one for every thirty thousand, but each State shall have at least one Representative; *and until such enumeration shall be made, the*

Passages no longer in effect are printed in italic type.

State of New Hampshire shall be entitled to choose three, Massachusetts eight, Rhode Island and Providence Plantations one, Connecticut five, New York six, New Jersey four, Pennsylvania eight, Delaware one, Maryland six, Virginia ten, North Carolina five, South Carolina five, and Georgia three.

When vacancies happen in the representation from any State, the Executive authority thereof shall issue writs of election to fill such vacancies.

The House of Representatives shall choose their Speaker and other officers; and shall have the sole power of impeachment.

Section 3 The Senate of the United States shall be composed of two Senators from each State, *chosen by the legislature thereof,* for six years; and each Senator shall have one vote.

Immediately after they shall be assembled in consequence of the first election, they shall be divided as equally as may be into three classes. The seats of the Senators of the first class shall be vacated at the expiration of the second year, of the second class at the expiration of the fourth year, and of the third class at the expiration of the sixth year, so that one-third may be chosen every second year; *and if vacancies happen by resignation or otherwise, during the recess of the legislature of any State, the Executive thereof may make temporary appointments until the next meeting of the legislature, which shall then fill such vacancies.*

No person shall be a Senator who shall not have attained to the age of thirty years, and been nine years a citizen of the United States, and who shall not, when elected, be an inhabitant of that State for which he shall be chosen.

The Vice-President of the United States shall be President of the Senate, but shall have no vote, unless they be equally divided.

The Senate shall choose their other officers, and also a President *pro tempore,* in the absence of the Vice-President, or when he shall exercise the office of President of the United States.

The Senate shall have the sole power to try all impeachments. When sitting for that purpose, they shall be on oath or affirmation. When the President of the United States is tried, the Chief Justice shall preside: and no person shall be convicted without the concurrence of two-thirds of the members present.

Judgment in cases of impeachment shall not extend further than to removal from the office, and disqualification to hold and enjoy any office of honor, trust or profit under the United States: but the party convicted shall nevertheless be liable and subject to indictment, trial, judgment and punishment, according to law.

Section 4   The times, places and manner of holding elections for Senators and Representatives shall be prescribed in each State by the legislature thereof; but the Congress may at any time by law make or alter such regulations, except as to the places of choosing Senators.

The Congress shall assemble at least once in every year, and such meeting *shall be on the first Monday in December, unless they shall by law appoint a different day.*

Section 5   Each house shall be the judge of the elections, returns and qualifications of its own members, and a majority of each shall constitute a quorum to do business; but a smaller number may adjourn from day to day, and may be authorized to compel the attendance of absent members, in such manner, and under such penalties, as each house may provide.

Each house may determine the rules of its proceedings, punish its members for disorderly behavior, and with the concurrence of two-thirds, expel a member.

Each house shall keep a journal of its proceedings, and from time to time publish the same, excepting such parts as may in their judgment require secrecy; and the yeas and nays of the members of either house on any question shall, at the desire of one-fifth of those present, be entered on the journal.

Neither house, during the session of Congress, shall, without the consent of the other, adjourn for more than three days, nor to any other place than that in which the two houses shall be sitting.

Section 6   The Senators and Representatives shall receive a compensation for their services, to be ascertained by law and paid out of the treasury of the United States. They shall in all cases except treason, felony and breach of the peace, be privileged from arrest during their attendance at the session of their respective houses, and in going to and returning from the same; and for any speech or debate in either house, they shall not be questioned in any other place.

No Senator or Representative shall, during the time for which he was elected, be appointed to any civil office under the authority of the United States, which shall have been created, or the emoluments whereof shall have been increased, during such time; and no person holding any office under the United States shall be a member of either house during his continuance in office.

Section 7   All bills for raising revenue shall originate in the House of Representatives; but the Senate may propose or concur with amendments as on other bills.

Every bill which shall have passed the House of Representatives and the Senate, shall, before it become a law, be presented to the President of the United States; if he approve he shall sign it, but if not he shall return it with objections to that house in which it originated, who shall enter the objections at large on their journal, and proceed to reconsider it. If after such reconsideration two-thirds of that house shall agree to pass the bill, it shall be sent, together with the objections, to the other house, by which it shall likewise be reconsidered, and, if approved by two-thirds of that house, it shall become a law. But in all such cases the votes of both houses shall be determined by yeas and nays, and the names of the persons voting for and against the bill shall be entered on the journal of each house respectively. If any bill shall not be returned by the President within ten days (Sundays excepted) after it shall have been presented to him the same shall be a law, in like manner as if he had signed it, unless the Congress by their adjournment prevent its return, in which case it shall not be a law.

Every order, resolution, or vote to which the concurrence of the Senate and House of Representatives may be necessary (except on a question of adjournment) shall be presented to the President of the United States; and before the same shall take effect, shall be approved by him, or being disapproved by him, shall be repassed by two-thirds of the Senate and House of Representatives, according to the rules and limitations prescribed in the case of a bill.

Section 8   The Congress shall have power

To lay and collect taxes, duties, imposts, and excises, to pay the debts and provide for the common defense and general welfare of the United States; but all duties, imposts and excises shall be uniform throughout the United States;

To borrow money on the credit of the United States;

To regulate commerce with foreign nations, and among the several States, and with the Indian tribes;

To establish an uniform rule of naturalization, and uniform laws on the subject of bankruptcies throughout the United States;

To coin money, regulate the value thereof, and of foreign coin, and fix the standard of weights and measures;

To provide for the punishment of counterfeiting the securities and current coin of the United States;

To establish post offices and post roads;

To promote the progress of science and useful arts by securing for limited times to authors and inventors the exclusive right to their respective writings and discoveries;

To constitute tribunals inferior to the Supreme Court;

To define and punish piracies and felonies committed on the high seas and offenses against the law of nations;

To declare war, grant letters of marque and reprisal, and make rules concerning captures on land and water;

To raise and support armies, but no appropriation of money to that use shall be for a longer term than two years;

To provide and maintain a navy;

To make rules for the government and regulation of the land and naval forces;

To provide for calling forth the militia to execute the laws of the Union, suppress insurrections, and repel invasions;

To provide for organizing, arming, and disciplining the militia, and for governing such part of them as may be employed in the service of the United States, reserving to the States respectively the appointment of the officers, and the authority of training the militia according to the discipline prescribed by Congress;

To exercise exclusive legislation in all cases whatsoever, over such district (not exceeding ten miles square) as may, by cession of particular States, and the acceptance of Congress, become the seat of government of the United States, and to exercise like authority over all places purchased by the consent of the legislature of the State, in which the same shall be, for erection of forts, magazines, arsenals, dockyards, and other needful buildings;—and

To make all laws which shall be necessary and proper for carrying into execution the foregoing powers, and all other powers vested by this Constitution in the government of the United States, or in any department or officer thereof.

Section 9   The migration or importation of such persons as any of the States now existing shall think proper to admit shall not be prohibited by the Congress prior to the year 1808; but a tax or duty may be imposed on such importation, not exceeding $10 for each person.

The privilege of the writ of habeas corpus shall not be suspended, unless when in cases of rebellion or invasion the public safety may require it.

No bill of attainder or ex post facto law shall be passed.

No capitation, or other direct, tax shall be laid, unless in proportion to the census or enumeration herein before directed to be taken.

No tax or duty shall be laid on articles exported from any State.

No preference shall be given by any regulation of commerce or revenue to the ports of one State over those of another; nor shall vessels bound to, or from, one State, be obliged to enter, clear, or pay duties in another.

No money shall be drawn from the treasury, but in consequence of appropriations made by law; and a regular statement and account of the receipts and expenditures of all public money shall be published from time to time.

No title of nobility shall be granted by the United States; and no person holding any office of profit or trust under them, shall, without the consent of the Congress, accept of any present, emolument, office, or title, of any kind whatever, from any king, prince, or foreign state.

Section 10   No State shall enter into any treaty, alliance, or confederation; grant letters of marque and reprisal; coin money; emit bills of credit; make anything but gold and silver coin a tender in payment of debts; pass any bill of attainder, ex post facto law, or law impairing the obligation of contracts, or grant any title of nobility.

No State shall, without the consent of Congress, lay any imposts or duties on imports or exports, except what may be absolutely necessary for executing its inspection laws: and the net produce of all duties and imposts laid by any State on imports or exports, shall be for the use of the treasury of the United States; and all such laws shall be subject to the revision and control of the Congress.

No State shall, without the consent of Congress, lay any duty of tonnage, keep troops or ships of war in time of peace, enter into any agreement or compact with another State, or with a foreign power, or engage in war, unless actually invaded, or in such imminent danger as will not admit of delay.

ARTICLE II

Section 1 The executive power shall be vested in a President of the United States of America. He shall hold his office during the term of four years, and, together with the Vice-President, chosen for the same term, be elected as follows:

Each State shall appoint, in such manner as the legislature thereof may direct, a number of electors, equal to the whole number of Senators and Representatives to which the State may be entitled in the Congress; but no Senator or Representative, or person holding an office of trust or profit under the United States, shall be appointed an elector.

The electors shall meet in their respective States, and vote by ballot for two persons, of whom one at least shall not be an inhabitant of the same State with themselves. And they shall make a list of all the persons voted for, and of the number of votes for each; which list they shall sign and certify, and transmit sealed to the seat of government of the United States, directed to the President of the Senate. The President of the Senate shall, in the presence of the Senate and House of Representatives, open all the certificates, and the votes shall then be counted. The person having the greatest number of votes shall be the President, if such number be a majority of the whole number of electors appointed; and if there be more than one who have such majority, and have an equal number of votes, then the House of Representatives shall immediately choose by ballot one of them for President; and if no person have a majority, then from the five highest on the list said house shall in like manner choose the President. But in choosing the President the votes shall be taken by States, the representation from each State having one vote; a quorum for this purpose shall consist of a member or members from two-thirds of the States, and a majority of all the States shall be necessary to a choice. In every case, after the choice of the President, the person having the greatest number of votes of the electors shall be the Vice-President. But if there should remain two or more who have equal votes, the Senate shall choose from them by ballot the Vice-President.

The Congress may determine the time of choosing the electors and the day on which they shall give their votes; which day shall be the same throughout the United States.

No person except a natural-born citizen, *or a citizen of the United States at the time of the adoption of this Constitution,* shall be eligible to the office of President; neither shall any person be eligible to that office who shall not have attained to the age of thirty-five years, and been fourteen years a resident within the United States.

In case of the removal of the President from office or of his death, resignation, or inability to discharge the powers and duties of the said office, the same shall devolve on the Vice-President, and the Congress may by law provide for the case of removal, death, resignation, or inability, both of the President and Vice-President, declaring what officer shall then act as President, and such officer shall act accordingly, until the disability be removed, or a President shall be elected.

The President shall, at stated times, receive for his services a compensation, which shall neither be increased nor diminished during the period for which he shall have been elected, and he shall not receive within that period any other emolument from the United States, or any of them.

Before he enter on the execution of his office, he shall take the following oath or affirmation:—"I do solemnly swear (or affirm) that I will faithfully execute the office of the President of the United States, and will to the best of my ability preserve, protect and defend the Constitution of the United States."

Section 2 The President shall be commander in chief

of the army and navy of the United States, and of the militia of the several States, when called into the actual service of the United States; he may require the opinion, in writing, of the principal officer in each of the executive departments, upon any subject relating to the duties of their respective offices, and he shall have power to grant reprieves and pardons for offenses against the United States, except in cases of impeachment.

He shall have power, by and with the advice and consent of the Senate, to make treaties, provided two-thirds of the Senators present concur; and he shall nominate, and by and with the advice and consent of the Senate, shall appoint ambassadors, other public ministers and consuls, judges of the Supreme Court, and all other officers of the United States, whose appointments are not herein otherwise provided for, and which shall be established by law: but Congress may by law vest the appointment of such inferior officers, as they think proper, in the President alone, in the courts of law, or in the heads of departments.

The President shall have power to fill up all vacancies that may happen during the recess of the Senate, by granting commissions which shall expire at the end of their next session.

Section 3   He shall from time to time give to the Congress information of the state of the Union, and recommend to their consideration such measures as he shall judge necessary and expedient; he may, on extraordinary occasions, convene both houses, or either of them, and in case of disagreement between them, with respect to the time of adjournment, he may adjourn them to such time as he shall think proper; he shall receive ambassadors and other public ministers; he shall take care that the laws be faithfully executed, and shall commission all the officers of the United States.

Section 4   The President, Vice-President and all civil officers of the United States shall be removed from office on impeachment for, and on conviction of, treason, bribery, or other high crimes and misdemeanors.

Article III
Section 1   The judicial power of the United States shall be vested in one Supreme Court, and in such inferior courts as the Congress may from time to time ordain and establish. The judges, both of the Supreme and inferior courts, shall hold their offices during good behavior, and shall, at stated times, receive for their services a compensation which shall not be diminished during their continuance in office.

Section 2   The judicial power shall extend to all cases, in law and equity, arising under this Constitution, the laws of the United States, and treaties made, or which shall be made, under their authority;—to all cases affecting ambassadors, other public ministers and consuls;—to all cases of admiralty and maritime jurisdiction;—to controversies to which the United States shall be a party;—to controversies between two or more States;—*between a State and citizens of another State;*—between citizens of different States;—between citizens of the same State claiming lands under grants of different States, and between a State, or the citizens thereof, and foreign states, citizens or subjects.

In all cases affecting ambassadors, other public ministers and consuls, and those in which a state shall be party, the Supreme Court shall have original jurisdiction. In all the other cases before mentioned, the Supreme Court shall have appellate jurisdiction, both as to law and fact, with such exceptions, and under such regulations, as the Congress shall make.

The trial of all crimes, except in cases of impeachment, shall be by jury; and such trial shall be held in the State where said crimes shall have been committed; but when not committed within any State, the trial shall be at such place or places as the Congress may by law have directed.

Section 3   Treason against the United States shall consist only in levying war against them, or in adhering to their enemies, giving them aid and comfort. No person shall be convicted of treason unless on the testimony of two witnesses to the same overt act, or on confession in open court.

The Congress shall have power to declare the punishment of treason, but no attainder of treason shall work corruption of blood, or forfeiture except during the life of the person attainted.

Article IV
Section 1   Full faith and credit shall be given in each State to the public acts, records, and judicial pro-

ceedings of every other State. And the Congress may by general laws prescribe the manner in which such acts, records, and proceedings shall be proved, and the effect thereof.

Section 2 The citizens of each State shall be entitled to all privileges and immunities of citizens in the several States.

A person charged in any State with treason, felony, or other crime, who shall flee from justice, and be found in another State, shall on demand of the executive authority of the State from which he fled, be delivered up, to be removed to the State having jurisdiction of the crime.

No person held to service or labor in one State, under the laws thereof, escaping into another, shall, in consequence of any law or regulation therein, be discharged from such service or labor, but shall be delivered up on claim of the party to whom such service or labor may be due.

Section 3 New States may be admitted by the Congress into this Union; but no new State shall be formed or erected within the jurisdiction of any other State; nor any State be formed by the junction of two or more States, or parts of States, without the consent of the legislatures of the States concerned as well as of the Congress.

The Congress shall have power to dispose of and make all needful rules and regulations respecting the territory or other property belonging to the United States; and nothing in this Constitution shall be so construed as to prejudice any claims of the United States, or of any particular State.

Section 4 The United States shall guarantee to every State in this Union a republican form of government, and shall protect each of them against invasion; and on application of the legislature, or of the executive (when the legislature cannot be convened), against domestic violence.

ARTICLE V

The Congress, whenever two-thirds of both houses shall deem it necessary, shall propose amendments to this Constitution, or, on the application of the legislatures of two-thirds of the several States, shall call a convention for proposing amendments, which, in either case, shall be valid to all intents and purposes, as part of this Constitution, when ratified by the legislatures of three-fourths of the several States, or by conventions in three-fourths thereof, as the one or the other mode of ratification may be proposed by the Congress; provided *that no amendments which may be made prior to the year one thousand eight hundred and eight shall in any manner affect the first and fourth clauses in the ninth section of the first article;* and that no State, without its consent, shall be deprived of its equal suffrage in the Senate.

ARTICLE VI

All debts contracted and engagements entered into, before the adoption of this Constitution, shall be as valid against the United States under this Constitution, as under the Confederation.

This Constitution, and the laws of the United States which shall be made in pursuance thereof; and all treaties made, or which shall be made, under the authority of the United States, shall be the supreme law of the land; and the judges in every State shall be bound thereby, anything in the Constitution or laws of any State to the contrary notwithstanding.

The Senators and Representatives before mentioned, and the members of the several State legislatures, and all executive and judicial officers, both of the United States and of the several States, shall be bound by oath or affirmation to support this Constitution; but no religious test shall ever be required as a qualification to any office or public trust under the United States.

ARTICLE VII

The ratification of the conventions of nine States shall be sufficient for the establishment of this Constitution between the States so ratifying the same.

Done in Convention by the unanimous consent of the States present, the seventeenth day of September in the year of our Lord one thousand seven hundred and eighty-seven and of the Independence of the United States of America the twelfth. In witness whereof we have hereunto subscribed our names.

GEORGE WASHINGTON
and thirty-seven others

Amendments to the Constitution*

AMENDMENT I

Congress shall make no law respecting an establishment of religion, or prohibiting the free exercise thereof; or abridging the freedom of speech, or of the press; or the right of the people peaceably to assemble, and to petition the government for a redress of grievances.

AMENDMENT II

A well-regulated militia being necessary to the security of a free State, the right of the people to keep and bear arms shall not be infringed.

AMENDMENT III

No soldier shall, in time of peace, be quartered in any house without the consent of the owner, nor in time of war, but in a manner to be prescribed by law.

AMENDMENT IV

The right of the people to be secure in their persons, houses, papers, and effects, against unreasonable searches and seizures, shall not be violated, and no warrants shall issue but upon probable cause, supported by oath or affirmation, and particularly describing the place to be searched, and the persons or things to be seized.

AMENDMENT V

No person shall be held to answer for a capital, or otherwise infamous crime, unless on a presentment or indictment of a grand jury, except in cases arising in the land or naval forces, or in the militia, when in actual service in time of war or public danger; nor shall any person be subject for the same offense to be twice put in jeopardy of life or limb; nor shall be compelled in any criminal case to be a witness against himself, nor be deprived of life, liberty, or property, without due process of law; nor shall private property be taken for public use without just compensation.

AMENDMENT VI

In all criminal prosecutions, the accused shall enjoy the right to a speedy and public trial, by an impartial

* The first ten Amendments (the Bill of Rights) were adopted in 1791.

jury of the State and district wherein the crime shall have been committed, which district shall have been previously ascertained by law, and to be informed of the nature and cause of the accusation; to be confronted with the witnesses against him; to have compulsory process for obtaining witnesses in his favor, and to have the assistance of counsel for his defense.

AMENDMENT VII

In suits at common law, where the value in controversy shall exceed twenty dollars, the right of trial by jury shall be preserved, and no fact tried by a jury shall be otherwise reexamined in any court of the United States, than according to the rules of the common law.

AMENDMENT VIII

Excessive bail shall not be required, nor excessive fines imposed, nor cruel and unusual punishments inflicted.

AMENDMENT IX

The enumeration in the Constitution, of certain rights, shall not be construed to deny or disparage others retained by the people.

AMENDMENT X

The powers not delegated to the United States by the Constitution, nor prohibited by it to the States, are reserved to the States respectively, or to the people.

AMENDMENT XI
[Adopted 1798]

The judicial power of the United States shall not be construed to extend to any suit in law or equity, commenced or prosecuted against one of the United States by citizens of another State, or by citizens or subjects of any foreign state.

AMENDMENT XII
[Adopted 1804]

The electors shall meet in their respective States, and vote by ballot for President and Vice-President, one of whom, at least, shall not be an inhabitant of the same State with themselves; they shall name in their ballots the person voted for as President, and in distinct ballots the person voted for as Vice-President, and they shall make distinct lists of all persons voted for as President, and of all persons voted for as Vice-President, and of the number of votes for each, which lists they shall sign and certify, and transmit sealed to the seat of government of the United States, directed to the President of the Senate;—the President of the Senate shall, in the presence of the Senate and House of Representatives, open all the certificates and the votes shall then be counted;—the person having the greatest number of votes for President shall be the President, if such number be a majority of the whole number of electors appointed; and if no person have such majority, then from the persons having the highest numbers not exceeding three on the list of those voted for as President, the House of Representatives shall choose immediately, by ballot, the President. But in choosing the President, the votes shall be taken by States, the representation from each State having one vote; a quorum for this purpose shall consist of a member or members from two-thirds of the States, and a majority of all the States shall be necessary to a choice. And if the House of Representatives shall not choose a President whenever the right of choice shall devolve upon them, before *the fourth day of March* next following, then the Vice-President shall act as President, as in the case of the death or other constitutional disability of the President.

The person having the greatest number of votes as Vice-President shall be the Vice-President, if such number be a majority of the whole number of electors appointed; and if no person have a majority, then from the two highest numbers on the list the Senate shall choose the Vice-President; a quorum for the purpose shall consist of two-thirds of the whole number of Senators, and a majority of the whole number shall be necessary to a choice. But no person constitutionally ineligible to the office of President shall be eligible to that of Vice-President of the United States.

AMENDMENT XIII
[Adopted 1865]

Section 1 Neither slavery nor involuntary servitude, except as a punishment for crime whereof the party shall have been duly convicted, shall exist within the United States, or any place subject to their jurisdiction.

Section 2 Congress shall have power to enforce this article by appropriate legislation.

AMENDMENT XIV
[Adopted 1868]

Section 1 All persons born or naturalized in the United States, and subject to the jurisdiction thereof, are citizens of the United States and of the State wherein they reside. No State shall make or enforce any law which shall abridge the privileges or immunities of citizens of the United States; nor shall any State deprive any person of life, liberty, or property, without due process of law; nor deny to any person within its jurisdiction the equal protection of the laws.

Section 2 Representatives shall be apportioned among the several States according to their respective numbers, counting the whole number of persons in each State, excluding Indians not taxed. But when the right to vote at any election for the choice of Electors for President and Vice-President of the United States, Representatives in Congress, the executive and judicial officers of a State, or the members of the legislature thereof, is denied to any of the male inhabitants of such State, being twenty-one years of age and citizens of the United States, or in any way abridged, except for participation in rebellion, or other crime, the basis of representation therein shall be reduced in the proportion which the number of such male citizens shall bear to the whole number of male citizens twenty-one years of age in such State.

Section 3 No person shall be a Senator or Representative in Congress, or Elector of President and Vice-President, or hold any office, civil or military, under the United States, or under any State, who, having previously taken an oath, as a member of Congress, or as an officer of the United States, or as a member of any State legislature, or as an executive or judicial officer of any State, to support the Constitution of the United States, shall have engaged in insurrection or rebellion against the same, or given aid or comfort to the enemies thereof. Congress may, by a vote of two-thirds of each house, remove such disability.

Section 4 The validity of the public debt of the United States, authorized by law, including debts incurred for payment of pensions and bounties for services in suppressing insurrection or rebellion, shall not be questioned. But neither the United States nor any State shall assume or pay any debt or obligation incurred in aid of insurrection or rebellion against the United States, or any claim for the loss of emancipation of any slave; but all such debts, obligations, and claims shall be held illegal and void.

Section 5 The Congress shall have power to enforce, by appropriate legislation, the provisions of this article.

AMENDMENT XV
[Adopted 1870]

Section 1 The right of citizens of the United States to vote shall not be denied or abridged by the United States or by any State on account of race, color, or previous condition of servitude.

Section 2 The Congress shall have power to enforce this article by appropriate legislation.

AMENDMENT XVI
[Adopted 1913]

The Congress shall have power to lay and collect taxes on incomes, from whatever source derived, without apportionment among the several States, and without regard to any census or enumeration.

AMENDMENT XVII
[Adopted 1913]

Section 1 The Senate of the United States shall be composed of two Senators from each State, elected by the people thereof, for six years; and each Senator shall have one vote. The electors in each State shall have the qualifications requisite for electors of [voters for] the most numerous branch of the State legislatures.

Section 2 When vacancies happen in the representation of any State in the Senate, the executive authority of such State shall issue writs of election to fill such vacancies: Provided, that the Legislature of any State may empower the executive thereof to make temporary appointments until the people fill the vacancies by election as the Legislature may direct.

Section 3 This amendment shall not be so construed as to affect the election or term of any Senator chosen before it becomes valid as part of the Constitution.

AMENDMENT XVIII
[Adopted 1919; Repealed 1933]

Section 1 After one year from the ratification of this article the manufacture, sale, or transportation of intoxicating liquors within, the importation thereof into, or the exportation thereof from the United States and all territory subject to the jurisdiction thereof, for beverage purposes, is hereby prohibited.

Section 2 The Congress and the several States shall have concurrent power to enforce this article by appropriate legislation.

Section 3 This article shall be inoperative unless it shall have been ratified as an amendment to the Constitution by the legislatures of the several States, as provided by the Constitution, within seven years from the date of the submission thereof to the States by the Congress.

AMENDMENT XIX
[Adopted 1920]

Section 1 The right of citizens of the United States to vote shall not be denied or abridged by the United States or by any State on account of sex.

Section 2 The Congress shall have power to enforce this article by appropriate legislation.

AMENDMENT XX
[Adopted 1933]

Section 1 The terms of the President and Vice-President shall end at noon on the 20th day of January, and the terms of Senators and Representatives at noon on the 3d day of January, of the years in which such terms would have ended if this article had not been ratified; and the terms of their successors shall then begin.

Section 2 The Congress shall assemble at least once in every year, and such meeting shall begin at noon on the 3d of January, unless they shall by law appoint a different day.

Section 3 If, at the time fixed for the beginning of the term of the President, the President-elect shall have died, the Vice-President-elect shall become President. If a President shall not have been chosen before the time fixed for the beginning of his term, or if the President-elect shall have failed to qualify, then the Vice-President-elect shall act as President until a President shall have qualified; and the Congress may by law provide for the case wherein neither a President-elect nor a Vice-President-elect shall have qualified, declaring who shall then act as President, or the manner in which one who is to act shall be selected, and such persons shall act accordingly until a President or Vice-President shall have qualified.

Section 4 The Congress may by law provide for the case of the death of any of the persons from whom the House of Representatives may choose a President whenever the right of choice shall have devolved upon them, and for the case of the death of any of the persons from whom the Senate may choose a Vice-President whenever the right of choice shall have devolved upon them.

Section 5 Sections 1 and 2 shall take effect on the 15th day of October following the ratification of this article.

Section 6 This article shall be inoperative unless it shall have been ratified as an amendment to the Constitution by the Legislatures of three-fourths of the several States within seven years from the date of its submission.

AMENDMENT XXI
[Adopted 1933]

Section 1 The eighteenth article of amendment to the Constitution of the United States is hereby repealed.

Section 2 The transportation or importation into any State, Territory, or Possession of the United States for delivery or use therein of intoxicating liquors, in violation of the laws thereof, is hereby prohibited.

Section 3 This article shall be inoperative unless it shall have been ratified as an amendment to the Constitution by conventions in the several States, as provided in the Constitution, within seven years from the date of submission thereof to the States by the Congress.

AMENDMENT XXII
[Adopted 1951]

Section 1 No person shall be elected to the office of President more than twice, and no person who has held the office of President, or acted as President, for more than two years of a term to which some other person was elected President shall be elected to the office of President more than once. But this article shall not apply to any person holding the office of President when this article was proposed by the Congress, and shall not prevent any person who may be holding the office of President, or acting as President, during the term within which this article becomes operative from holding the office of President or acting as President during the remainder of such term.

Section 2 This article shall be inoperative unless it shall have been ratified as an amendment to the Constitution by the legislatures of three-fourths of the several States within seven years from the date of its submission to the States by the Congress.

AMENDMENT XXIII
[Adopted 1961]

Section 1 The District constituting the seat of Government of the United States shall appoint in such manner as the Congress may direct:

A number of electors of President and Vice-President equal to the whole number of Senators and Representatives in Congress to which the District would be entitled if it were a State, but in no event more than the least populous State; they shall be in addition to those appointed by the States, but they shall be considered for the purposes of the election of President and Vice-President, to be electors appointed by a State; and they shall meet in the District and perform such duties as provided by the twelfth article of amendment.

Section 2 The Congress shall have the power to enforce this article by appropriate legislation.

Amendment XXIV

[Adopted 1964]

Section 1　The right of citizens of the United States to vote in any primary or other election for President or Vice-President, for electors for President or Vice-President, or for Senator or Representative in Congress, shall not be denied or abridged by the United States or any State by reason of failure to pay any poll tax or other tax.

Section 2　The Congress shall have the power to enforce this article by appropriate legislation.

Amendment XXV

[Adopted 1967]

Section 1　In case of the removal of the President from office or of his death or resignation, the Vice President shall become President.

Section 2　Whenever there is a vacancy in the office of the Vice President, the President shall nominate a Vice President who shall take office upon confirmation by a majority vote of both Houses of Congress.

Section 3　Whenever the President transmits to the President pro tempore of the Senate and the Speaker of the House of Representatives his written declaration that he is unable to discharge the powers and duties of his office, and until he transmits to them a written declaration to the contrary, such powers and duties shall be discharged by the Vice President as Acting President.

Section 4　Whenever the Vice President and a majority of either the principal officers of the executive departments or of such other body as Congress may by law provide, transmit to the President pro tempore of the Senate and the Speaker of the House of Representatives their written declaration that the President is unable to discharge the powers and duties of his office, the Vice President shall immediately assume the powers and duties of the office as Acting President.

Thereafter, when the President transmits to the President pro tempore of the Senate and the Speaker of the House of Representatives his written declaration that no inability exists, he shall resume the powers and duties of his office unless the Vice President and a majority of either the principal officers of the executive department[s] or of such other body as Congress may by law provide, transmit within four days to the President pro tempore of the Senate and the Speaker of the House of Representatives their written declaration that the President is unable to discharge the powers and duties of his office. Thereupon Congress shall decide the issue, assembling within forty-eight hours for that purpose if not in session. If the Congress, within twenty-one days after receipt of the latter written declaration, or, if Congress is not in session, within twenty-one days after Congress is required to assemble, determines by two-thirds vote of both Houses that the President is unable to discharge the powers and duties of his office, the Vice President shall continue to discharge the same as Acting President; otherwise, the President shall resume the powers and duties of his office.

Amendment XXVI

[Adopted 1971]

Section 1　The right of citizens of the United States, who are eighteen years of age or older, to vote shall not be denied or abridged by the United States or by any State on account of age.

Section 2　The Congress shall have power to enforce this article by appropriate legislation.

The American people: A statistical profile

Population of the United States

YEAR	NUMBER OF STATES	POPULATION	PERCENT INCREASE	POPULATION PER SQUARE MILE	PERCENT URBAN/ RURAL	PERCENT MALE/ FEMALE	PERCENT WHITE/ NONWHITE
1790	13	3,929,214		4.5	5.1/94.9	NA/NA	80.7/19.3
1800	16	5,308,483	35.1	6.1	6.1/93.9	NA/NA	81.1/18.9
1810	17	7,239,881	36.4	4.3	7.3/92.7	NA/NA	81.0/19.0
1820	23	9,638,453	33.1	5.5	7.2/92.8	50.8/49.2	81.6/18.4
1830	24	12,866,020	33.5	7.4	8.8/91.2	50.8/49.2	81.9/18.1
1840	26	17,069,453	32.7	9.8	10.8/89.2	50.9/49.1	83.2/16.8
1850	31	23,191,876	35.9	7.9	15.3/84.7	51.0/49.0	84.3/15.7
1860	33	31,443,321	35.6	10.6	19.8/80.2	51.2/48.8	85.6/14.4
1870	37	39,818,449	26.6	13.4	25.7/74.3	50.6/49.4	86.2/13.8
1880	38	50,155,783	26.0	16.9	28.2/71.8	50.9/49.1	86.5/13.5
1890	44	62,947,714	25.5	21.2	35.1/64.9	51.2/48.8	87.5/12.5
1900	45	75,994,575	20.7	25.6	39.6/60.4	51.1/48.9	87.9/12.1
1910	46	91,972,266	21.0	31.0	45.6/54.4	51.5/48.5	88.9/11.1
1920	48	105,710,620	14.9	35.6	51.2/48.8	51.0/49.0	89.7/10.3
1930	48	122,775,046	16.1	41.2	56.1/43.9	50.6/49.4	89.8/10.2
1940	48	131,669,275	7.2	44.2	56.5/43.5	50.2/49.8	89.8/10.2
1950	48	150,697,361	14.5	50.7	64.0/36.0	49.7/50.3	89.5/10.5
1960	50	179,323,175	19.0	50.6	69.9/30.1	49.3/50.7	88.6/11.4
1970	50	203,235,298	13.3	57.5	73.5/26.5	48.7/51.3	87.6/12.4
1980	50	226,504,825	11.4	64.0	73.7/26.3	48.6/51.4	83.2/16.8

NA = Not available.
*1979 figures

Immigrants to the United States

IMMIGRATION TOTALS BY DECADE

YEARS	NUMBER	YEARS	NUMBER
1820	8,385	1901–1910	8,795,386
1821–1830	143,439	1911–1920	5,735,811
1831–1840	599,125	1921–1930	4,107,209
1841–1850	1,713,251	1931–1940	528,431
1851–1860	2,598,214	1941–1950	1,035,039
1861–1870	2,314,824	1951–1960	2,515,479
1871–1880	2,812,191	1961–1970	3,321,677
1881–1890	5,246,613	1971–1980	3,962,000
1891–1900	3,687,546	Total	49,124,638

REGIONAL ORIGINS OF IMMIGRANTS (in percentages)

PERIOD	TOTAL EUROPE	EUROPE			WESTERN HEMISPHERE	ASIA	ALL OTHER
		NORTH AND WEST[a]	EAST AND CENTRAL[b]	SOUTH AND OTHER[c]			
1821–1830	69.2	67.1	—	2.1	8.4	—	22.4
1831–1840	82.8	81.8	—	1.0	5.5	—	11.7
1841–1850	93.3	92.9	0.1	0.3	3.6	—	3.1
1851–1860	94.4	93.6	0.1	0.8	2.9	1.6	1.1
1861–1870	89.2	87.8	0.5	0.9	7.2	2.8	0.8
1871–1880	80.8	73.6	4.5	2.7	14.4	4.4	0.4
1881–1890	90.3	72.0	11.9	6.3	8.1	1.3	0.3
1891–1900	96.5	44.5	32.8	19.1	1.1	1.9	0.5
1901–1910	92.5	21.7	44.5	26.3	4.1	2.8	0.6
1911–1920	76.3	17.4	33.4	25.5	19.9	3.4	0.4
1921–1930	60.3	31.7	14.4	14.3	36.9	2.4	0.4
1931–1940	65.9	38.8	11.0	16.1	30.3	2.8	0.9
1941–1950	60.1	47.5	4.6	7.9	34.3	3.1	2.5
1951–1960	52.8	17.7	24.3	10.8	39.6	6.0	1.6
1961–1970	33.8	11.7	9.4	12.9	51.7	12.9	1.7
1971–1979	18.4	4.8	4.4	9.2	44.9	34.1	2.5

[a] Great Britain, Ireland, Norway, Sweden, Denmark, Iceland, Netherlands, Belgium, Luxembourg, Switzerland, France.

[b] Germany (Austria included, 1938–1945), Poland, Czechoslovakia (since 1920), Yugoslavia (since 1920), Hungary (since 1861), Austria (since 1861, except 1938–1945), U.S.S.R. (excludes Asian U.S.S.R. between 1931 and 1963), Latvia, Estonia, Lithuania, Finland, Romania, Bulgaria, Turkey (in Europe).

[c] Italy, Spain, Portugal, Greece, and other European countries not classified elsewhere.

Source: Stephan Thernstrom, ed., *Harvard Encyclopedia of American Ethnic Groups* (1980), p. 480; and U.S. Bureau of the Census, *Statistical Abstract of the United States, 1982–1983* (1982), p. 89. Reprinted by permission of Harvard University Press.

MAJOR SOURCES OF IMMIGRANTS BY COUNTRY (in thousands)

PERIOD	GERMANY	ITALY	GREAT BRITAIN	IRELAND	AUSTRIA-HUNGARY	RUSSIA	CANADA	DENMARK, NORWAY, SWEDEN	MEXICO	WEST INDIES
1821–1830	7	–	25	51	–	–	–	–	–	–
1831–1840	152	2	76	207	–	–	–	2	–	–
1841–1850	435	2	267	781	–	–	–	14	–	–
1851–1860	952	9	424	914	–	–	–	25	–	–
1861–1870	787	12	607	436	8	3	–	126	–	–
1871–1880	718	56	548	437	73	39	–	243	–	–
1881–1890	1,453	307	807	655	354	213	–	656	–	–
1891–1900	505	652	272	388	593	505	–	372	–	–
1901–1910	341	2,046	526	339	2,145	1,597	179	505	50	108
1911–1920	144	1,110	341	146	896	921	742	203	219	123
1921–1930	412	455	330	221	64	62	925	198	459	75
1931–1940	114	68	29	13	11	1	109	11	22	16
1941–1950	226	57	132	27	28	1	172	26	61	50
1951–1960	478	185	192	57	104	6	378	57	300	123
1961–1970	191	214	206	40	26	8	413	43	454	470
1971–1979	68	124	122	11	15	28	156	13	584	668
Total	6,983	5,299	5,036	4,723	4,317	3,384	3,074	2,494	2,149	1,633

Source: Stephan Thernstrom, ed., *Harvard Encyclopedia of American Ethnic Groups* (1980), p. 480; and U.S. Bureau of the Census, *Statistical Abstract of the United States, 1982–1983* (1982), p. 89. Reprinted by permission of Harvard University Press.

The American Farm

YEAR	FARM POPULATION (IN THOUSANDS)	PERCENT OF TOTAL POPULATION	NUMBER OF FARMS (IN THOUSANDS)	TOTAL ACRES (IN THOUSANDS)	AVERAGE ACREAGE PER FARM
1850	NA	NA	1,449	293,561	203
1860	NA	NA	2,044	407,213	199
1870	NA	NA	2,660	407,735	153
1880	21,973	43.8	4,009	536,082	134
1890	24,771	42.3	4,565	623,219	137
1900	29,875	41.9	5,740	841,202	147
1910	32,077	34.9	6,366	881,431	139
1920	31,974	30.1	6,454	958,677	149
1930	30,529	24.9	6,295	990,112	157
1940	30,547	23.2	6,102	1,065,114	175
1950	23,048	15.3	5,388	1,161,420	216
1960	15,635	8.7	3,962	1,176,946	297
1970	9,712	4.8	2,949	1,102,769	374
1980	6,051	2.7	2,428	1,042,000	429

NA = Not available.

YEAR	TOTAL NUMBER OF WORKERS*	MALE WORKERS		FEMALE WORKERS		PERCENT OF CIVILIAN LABOR FORCE UNEMPLOYED	PERCENT OF WORKERS IN LABOR UNIONS*
		NUMBER*	PERCENT OF TOTAL WORKERS*	NUMBER*	PERCENT OF TOTAL WORKERS*		
1870	12,506,000	10,670,000	85	1,836,000	15	NA	NA
1880	17,392,000	14,745,000	85	2,647,000	15	NA	NA
1890	23,318,000	19,313,000	83	4,006,000	17	4 (1894 = 18%)	NA
1900	29,073,000	23,754,000	82	5,319,000	18	5	3
1910	38,167,000	30,092,000	79	8,076,000	21	6	6
1920	41,614,000	33,065,000	79	8,550,000	21	5 (1921 = 12%)	12
1930	48,830,000	38,078,000	78	10,752,000	22	9 (1933 = 25%)	7
1940	52,705,000	39,818,000	76	12,887,000	24	15 (1944 = 1%)	17
1950	58,646,000	42,126,000	72	16,520,000	28	5	22
1960	68,144,000	45,763,000	67	22,381,000	33	6	24
1970	82,715,000	51,195,000	62	31,520,000	38	5	23
1980	104,400,000	60,100,000	58	44,300,000	42	7	20†

*Figures for 1870–1930 are for all workers, civilian and military; figures for 1940–1980 are for civilian workers only.
†1978 figure.
NA = Not available.

Territorial Expansion of the United States

TERRITORY	DATE ACQUIRED	SQUARE MILES	HOW ACQUIRED
Original states and territories	1783	888,685	Treaty with Great Britain
Louisiana Purchase	1803	827,192	Purchase from France
Florida	1819	72,003	Treaty with Spain
Texas	1845	390,143	Annexation of independent nation
Oregon	1846	285,580	Treaty with Great Britain
Mexican Cession	1848	529,017	Conquest from Mexico
Gadsden Purchase	1853	29,640	Purchase from Mexico
Alaska	1867	589,757	Purchase from Russia
Hawaii	1898	6,450	Annexation of independent nation
The Philippines	1899	115,600	Conquest from Spain (granted independence in 1946)
Puerto Rico	1899	3,435	Conquest from Spain
Guam	1899	212	Conquest from Spain
American Samoa	1900	76	Treaty with Germany and Great Britain
Panama Canal Zone	1904	553	Treaty with Panama (returned to Panama by treaty in 1978)
Corn Islands	1914	4	Treaty with Nicaragua (returned to Nicaragua by treaty in 1971)
Virgin Islands	1917	133	Purchase from Denmark
Pacific Islands Trust (Micronesia)	1947	8,489	Trusteeship under United Nations (some granted independence)
All others (Midway, Wake, and other islands)		42	

Admission of States into the Union

STATE	DATE OF ADMISSION	STATE	DATE OF ADMISSION
1. Delaware	December 7, 1787	26. Michigan	January 26, 1837
2. Pennsylvania	December 12, 1787	27. Florida	March 3, 1845
3. New Jersey	December 18, 1787	28. Texas	December 29, 1845
4. Georgia	January 2, 1788	29. Iowa	December 28, 1846
5. Connecticut	January 9, 1788	30. Wisconsin	May 29, 1848
6. Massachusetts	February 6, 1788	31. California	September 9, 1850
7. Maryland	April 28, 1788	32. Minnesota	May 11, 1858
8. South Carolina	May 23, 1788	33. Oregon	February 14, 1859
9. New Hampshire	June 21, 1788	34. Kansas	January 29, 1861
10. Virginia	June 25, 1788	35. West Virginia	June 20, 1863
11. New York	July 26, 1788	36. Nevada	October 31, 1864
12. North Carolina	November 21, 1789	37. Nebraska	March 1, 1867
13. Rhode Island	May 29, 1790	38. Colorado	August 1, 1876
14. Vermont	March 4, 1791	39. North Dakota	November 2, 1889
15. Kentucky	June 1, 1792	40. South Dakota	November 2, 1889
16. Tennessee	June 1, 1796	41. Montana	November 8, 1889
17. Ohio	March 1, 1803	42. Washington	November 11, 1889
18. Louisiana	April 30, 1812	43. Idaho	July 3, 1890
19. Indiana	December 11, 1816	44. Wyoming	July 10, 1890
20. Mississippi	December 10, 1817	45. Utah	January 4, 1896
21. Illinois	December 3, 1818	46. Oklahoma	November 16, 1907
22. Alabama	December 14, 1819	47. New Mexico	January 6, 1912
23. Maine	March 15, 1820	48. Arizona	February 14, 1912
24. Missouri	August 10, 1821	49. Alaska	January 3, 1959
25. Arkansas	June 15, 1836	50. Hawaii	August 21, 1959

Presidential Elections

YEAR	NUMBER OF STATES	CANDIDATES	PARTIES	POPULAR VOTE	% OF POPULAR VOTE	ELEC-TORAL VOTE	% VOTER PARTICI-PATION
1789	11	**GEORGE WASHINGTON**	No party			69	
		John Adams	designations			34	
		Other candidates				35	
1792	15	**GEORGE WASHINGTON**	No party			132	
		John Adams	designations			77	
		George Clinton				50	
		Other candidates				5	
1796	16	**JOHN ADAMS**	Federalist			71	
		Thomas Jefferson	Democratic-Republican			68	
		Thomas Pinckney	Federalist			59	
		Aaron Burr	Democratic-Republican			30	
		Other candidates				48	
1800	16	**THOMAS JEFFERSON**	Democratic-Republican			73	
		Aaron Burr	Democratic-Republican			73	
		John Adams	Federalist			65	
		Charles C. Pinckney	Federalist			64	
		John Jay	Federalist			1	
1804	17	**THOMAS JEFFERSON**	Democratic-Republican			162	
		Charles C. Pinckney	Federalist			14	
1808	17	**JAMES MADISON**	Democratic-Republican			122	
		Charles C. Pinckney	Federalist			47	
		George Clinton	Democratic-Republican			6	
1812	18	**JAMES MADISON**	Democratic-Republican			128	
		DeWitt Clinton	Federalist			89	
1816	19	**JAMES MONROE**	Democratic-Republican			183	
		Rufus King	Federalist			34	
1820	24	**JAMES MONROE**	Democratic-Republican			231	
		John Quincy Adams	Independent Republican			1	
1824	24	**JOHN QUINCY ADAMS**	Democratic-Republican	108,740	30.5	84	26.9
		Andrew Jackson	Democratic-Republican	153,544	43.1	99	
		Henry Clay	Democratic-Republican	47,136	13.2	37	
		William H. Crawford	Democratic-Republican	46,618	13.1	41	

YEAR	NUMBER OF STATES	CANDIDATES	PARTIES	POPULAR VOTE	% OF POPULAR VOTE	ELEC-TORAL VOTE	% VOTER PARTICI-PATION
1828	24	**ANDREW JACKSON**	Democratic	647,286	56.0	178	57.6
		John Quincy Adams	National Republican	508,064	44.0	83	
1832	24	**ANDREW JACKSON**	Democratic	688,242	54.5	219	55.4
		Henry Clay	National Republican	473,462	37.5	49	
		William Wirt	Anti-Masonic	101,051	8.0	7	
		John Floyd	Democratic			11	
1836	26	**MARTIN VAN BUREN**	Democratic	765,483	50.9	170	57.8
		William H. Harrison	Whig			73	
		Hugh L. White	Whig	739,795	49.1	26	
		Daniel Webster	Whig			14	
		W. P. Mangum	Whig			11	
1840	26	**WILLIAM H. HARRISON**	Whig	1,274,624	53.1	234	80.2
		Martin Van Buren	Democratic	1,127,781	46.9	60	
1844	26	**JAMES K. POLK**	Democratic	1,338,464	49.6	170	78.9
		Henry Clay	Whig	1,300,097	48.1	105	
		James G. Birney	Liberty	62,300	2.3		
1848	30	**ZACHARY TAYLOR**	Whig	1,360,967	47.4	163	72.7
		Lewis Cass	Democratic	1,222,342	42.5	127	
		Martin Van Buren	Free Soil	291,263	10.1		
1852	31	**FRANKLIN PIERCE**	Democratic	1,601,117	50.9	254	69.6
		Winfield Scott	Whig	1,385,453	44.1	42	
		John P. Hale	Free Soil	155,825	5.0		
1856	31	**JAMES BUCHANAN**	Democratic	1,832,955	45.3	174	78.9
		John C. Frémont	Republican	1,339,932	33.1	114	
		Millard Fillmore	American	871,731	21.6	8	
1860	33	**ABRAHAM LINCOLN**	Republican	1,865,593	39.8	180	81.2
		Stephen A. Douglas	Democratic	1,382,713	29.5	12	
		John C. Breckinridge	Democratic	848,356	18.1	72	
		John Bell	Constitutional Union	592,906	12.6	39	
1864	36	**ABRAHAM LINCOLN**	Republican	2,206,938	55.0	212	73.8
		George B. McClellan	Democratic	1,803,787	45.0	21	
1868	37	**ULYSSES S. GRANT**	Republican	3,013,421	52.7	214	78.1
		Horatio Seymour	Democratic	2,706,829	47.3	80	
1872	37	**ULYSSES S. GRANT**	Republican	3,596,745	55.6	286	71.3
		Horace Greeley	Democratic	2,843,446	43.9	*	
1876	38	**RUTHERFORD B. HAYES**	Republican	4,036,572	48.0	185	81.8
		Samuel J. Tilden	Democratic	4,284,020	51.0	184	
1880	38	**JAMES A. GARFIELD**	Republican	4,453,295	48.5	214	79.4
		Winfield S. Hancock	Democratic	4,414,082	48.1	155	
		James B. Weaver	Greenback-Labor	308,578	3.4		

YEAR	NUMBER OF STATES	CANDIDATES	PARTIES	POPULAR VOTE	% OF POPULAR VOTE	ELEC- TORAL VOTE	% VOTER PARTICI- PATION
1884	38	**GROVER CLEVELAND**	Democratic	4,879,507	48.5	219	77.5
		James G. Blaine	Republican	4,850,293	48.2	182	
		Benjamin F. Butler	Greenback- Labor	175,370	1.8		
		John P. St. John	Prohibition	150,369	1.5		
1888	38	**BENJAMIN HARRISON**	Republican	5,477,129	47.9	233	79.3
		Grover Cleveland	Democratic	5,537,857	48.6	168	
		Clinton B. Fisk	Prohibition	249,506	2.2		
		Anson J. Streeter	Union Labor	146,935	1.3		
1892	44	**GROVER CLEVELAND**	Democratic	5,555,426	46.1	277	74.7
		Benjamin Harrison	Republican	5,182,690	43.0	145	
		James B. Weaver	People's	1,029,846	8.5	22	
		John Bidwell	Prohibition	264,133	2.2		
1896	45	**WILLIAM McKINLEY**	Republican	7,102,246	51.1	271	79.3
		William J. Bryan	Democratic	6,492,559	47.7	176	
1900	45	**WILLIAM McKINLEY**	Republican	7,218,491	51.7	292	73.2
		William J. Bryan	Democratic; Populist	6,356,734	45.5	155	
		John C. Wooley	Prohibition	208,914	1.5		
1904	45	**THEODORE ROOSEVELT**	Republican	7,628,461	57.4	336	65.2
		Alton B. Parker	Democratic	5,084,223	37.6	140	
		Eugene V. Debs	Socialist	402,283	3.0		
		Silas C. Swallow	Prohibition	258,536	1.9		
1908	46	**WILLIAM H. TAFT**	Republican	7,675,320	51.6	321	65.4
		William J. Bryan	Democratic	6,412,294	43.1	162	
		Eugene V. Debs	Socialist	420,793	2.8		
		Eugene W. Chafin	Prohibition	253,840	1.7		
1912	48	**WOODROW WILSON**	Democratic	6,296,547	41.9	435	58.8
		Theodore Roosevelt	Progressive	4,118,571	27.4	88	
		William H. Taft	Republican	3,486,720	23.2	8	
		Eugene V. Debs	Socialist	900,672	6.0		
		Eugene W. Chafin	Prohibition	206,275	1.4		
1916	48	**WOODROW WILSON**	Democratic	9,127,695	49.4	277	61.6
		Charles E. Hughes	Republican	8,533,507	46.2	254	
		A. L. Benson	Socialist	585,113	3.2		
		J. Frank Hanly	Prohibition	220,506	1.2		
1920	48	**WARREN G. HARDING**	Republican	16,143,407	60.4	404	49.2
		James M. Cox	Democratic	9,130,328	34.2	127	
		Eugene V. Debs	Socialist	919,799	3.4		
		P. P. Christensen	Farmer- Labor	265,411	1.0		
1924	48	**CALVIN COOLIDGE**	Republican	15,718,211	54.0	382	48.9
		John W. Davis	Democratic	8,385,283	28.8	136	
		Robert M. La Follette	Progressive	4,831,289	16.6	13	
1928	48	**HERBERT C. HOOVER**	Republican	21,391,993	58.2	444	56.9
		Alfred E. Smith	Democratic	15,016,169	40.9	87	

YEAR	NUMBER OF STATES	CANDIDATES	PARTIES	POPULAR VOTE	% OF POPULAR VOTE	ELEC-TORAL VOTE	% VOTER PARTICI-PATION
1932	48	**FRANKLIN D. ROOSEVELT**	Democratic	22,809,638	57.4	472	56.9
		Herbert C. Hoover	Republican	15,758,901	39.7	59	
		Norman Thomas	Socialist	881,951	2.2		
1936	48	**FRANKLIN D. ROOSEVELT**	Democratic	27,752,869	60.8	523	61.0
		Alfred M. Landon	Republican	16,674,665	36.5	8	
		William Lemke	Union	882,479	1.9		
1940	48	**FRANKLIN D. ROOSEVELT**	Democratic	27,307,819	54.8	449	62.5
		Wendell L. Wilkie	Republican	22,321,018	44.8	82	
1944	48	**FRANKLIN D. ROOSEVELT**	Democratic	25,606,585	53.5	432	55.9
		Thomas E. Dewey	Republican	22,014,745	46.0	99	
1948	48	**HARRY S TRUMAN**	Democratic	24,179,345	49.6	303	53.0
		Thomas E. Dewey	Republican	21,991,291	45.1	189	
		J. Strom Thurmond	States' Rights	1,176,125	2.4	39	
		Henry A. Wallace	Progressive	1,157,326	2.4		
1952	48	**DWIGHT D. EISENHOWER**	Republican	33,936,234	55.1	442	63.3
		Adlai E. Stevenson	Democratic	27,314,992	44.4	89	
1956	48	**DWIGHT D. EISENHOWER**	Republican	35,590,472	57.6	457	60.6
		Adlai E. Stevenson	Democratic	26,022,752	42.1	73	
1960	50	**JOHN F. KENNEDY**	Democratic	34,226,731	49.7	303	64.0
		Richard M. Nixon	Republican	34,108,157	49.5	219	
1964	50	**LYNDON B. JOHNSON**	Democratic	43,129,566	61.1	486	61.7
		Barry M. Goldwater	Republican	27,178,188	38.5	52	
1968	50	**RICHARD M. NIXON**	Republican	31,785,480	43.4	301	60.6
		Hubert H. Humphrey	Democratic	31,275,166	42.7	191	
		George C. Wallace	American Independent	9,906,473	13.5	46	
1972	50	**RICHARD M. NIXON**	Republican	47,169,911	60.7	520	55.5
		George S. McGovern	Democratic	29,170,383	37.5	17	
		John G. Schmitz	American	1,099,482	1.4		
1976	50	**JIMMY CARTER**	Democratic	40,830,763	50.1	297	54.3
		Gerald R. Ford	Republican	39,147,793	48.0	240	
1980	50	**RONALD REAGAN**	Republican	43,901,812	50.7	489	53.0
		Jimmy Carter	Democratic	35,483,820	41.0	49	
		John B. Anderson	Independent	5,719,722	6.6	0	
		Ed Clark	Libertarian	921,188	1.1	0	

Candidates receiving less than 1 percent of the popular vote have been omitted. Thus the percentage of popular vote given for any election year may not total 100 percent.

Before the passage of the Twelfth Amendment in 1804, the Electoral College voted for two presidential candidates; the runnerup became vice president.

Before 1824, most presidential electors were chosen by state legislatures, not by popular vote.

*Greeley died shortly after the election; the electors supporting him then divided their votes among minor candidates.

Presidents and Vice Presidents

1.	President	GEORGE WASHINGTON	1789–1797
	Vice President	John Adams	1789–1797
2.	President	JOHN ADAMS	1797–1801
	Vice President	Thomas Jefferson	1797–1801
3.	President	THOMAS JEFFERSON	1801–1809
	Vice President	Aaron Burr	1801–1805
	Vice President	George Clinton	1805–1809
4.	President	JAMES MADISON	1809–1817
	Vice President	George Clinton	1809–1813
	Vice President	Elbridge Gerry	1813–1817
5.	President	JAMES MONROE	1817–1825
	Vice President	Daniel Tompkins	1817–1825
6.	President	JOHN QUINCY ADAMS	1825–1829
	Vice President	John C. Calhoun	1825–1829
7.	President	ANDREW JACKSON	1829–1837
	Vice President	John C. Calhoun	1829–1833
	Vice President	Martin Van Buren	1833–1837
8.	President	MARTIN VAN BUREN	1837–1841
	Vice President	Richard M. Johnson	1837–1841
9.	President	WILLIAM H. HARRISON	1841
	Vice President	John Tyler	1841
10.	President	JOHN TYLER	1841–1845
	Vice President	none	
11.	President	JAMES K. POLK	1845–1849
	Vice President	George M. Dallas	1845–1849
12.	President	ZACHARY TAYLOR	1849–1850
	Vice President	Millard Fillmore	1849–1850
13.	President	MILLARD FILLMORE	1850–1853
	Vice President	none	
14.	President	FRANKLIN PIERCE	1853–1857
	Vice President	William R. King	1853–1857
15.	President	JAMES BUCHANAN	1857–1861
	Vice President	John C. Breckinridge	1857–1861
16.	President	ABRAHAM LINCOLN	1861–1865
	Vice President	Hannibal Hamlin	1861–1865
	Vice President	Andrew Johnson	1865
17.	President	ANDREW JOHNSON	1865–1869
	Vice President	none	
18.	President	ULYSSES S. GRANT	1869–1877
	Vice President	Schuyler Colfax	1869–1873
	Vice President	Henry Wilson	1873–1877
19.	President	RUTHERFORD B. HAYES	1877–1881
	Vice President	William A. Wheeler	1877–1881
20.	President	JAMES A. GARFIELD	1881
	Vice President	Chester A. Arthur	1881

21.	President	CHESTER A. ARTHUR	1881–1885
	Vice President	none	
22.	President	GROVER CLEVELAND	1885–1889
	Vice President	Thomas A. Hendricks	1885–1889
23.	President	BENJAMIN HARRISON	1889–1893
	Vice President	Levi P. Morton	1889–1893
24.	President	GROVER CLEVELAND	1893–1897
	Vice President	Adlai E. Stevenson	1893–1897
25.	President	WILLIAM McKINLEY	1897–1901
	Vice President	Garret A. Hobart	1897–1901
		Theodore Roosevelt	1901
26.	President	THEODORE ROOSEVELT	1901–1909
	Vice President	Charles Fairbanks	1905–1909
27.	President	WILLIAM H. TAFT	1909–1913
	Vice President	James S. Sherman	1909–1913
28.	President	WOODROW WILSON	1913–1921
	Vice President	Thomas R. Marshall	1913–1921
29.	President	WARREN G. HARDING	1921–1923
	Vice President	Calvin Coolidge	1921–1923
30.	President	CALVIN COOLIDGE	1923–1929
	Vice President	Charles G. Dawes	1925–1929
31.	President	HERBERT C. HOOVER	1929–1933
	Vice President	Charles Curtis	1929–1933
32.	President	FRANKLIN D. ROOSEVELT	1933–1945
	Vice President	John N. Garner	1933–1941
		Henry A. Wallace	1941–1945
		Harry S Truman	1945
33.	President	HARRY S TRUMAN	1945–1953
	Vice President	Alben W. Barkley	1949–1953
34.	President	DWIGHT D. EISENHOWER	1953–1961
	Vice President	Richard M. Nixon	1953–1961
35.	President	JOHN F. KENNEDY	1961–1963
	Vice President	Lyndon B. Johnson	1961–1963
36.	President	LYNDON B. JOHNSON	1963–1969
	Vice President	Hubert H. Humphrey	1965–1969
37.	President	RICHARD M. NIXON	1969–1974
	Vice President	Spiro T. Agnew	1969–1973
		Gerald R. Ford	1973–1974
38.	President	GERALD R. FORD	1974–1977
	Vice President	Nelson A. Rockefeller	1974–1977
39.	President	JIMMY CARTER	1977–1981
	Vice President	Walter F. Mondale	1977–1981
40.	President	RONALD REAGAN	1981–
	Vice President	George Bush	1981–

Justices of the Supreme Court

	TERM OF SERVICE	YEARS OF SERVICE	LIFE SPAN		TERM OF SERVICE	YEARS OF SERVICE	LIFE SPAN
John Jay	1789–1795	5	1745–1829	Horace Gray	1882–1902	20	1828–1902
John Rutledge	1789–1791	1	1739–1800	Samuel Blatchford	1882–1893	11	1820–1893
William Cushing	1789–1810	20	1732–1810	Lucius Q. C. Lamar	1888–1893	5	1825–1893
James Wilson	1789–1798	8	1742–1798	*Melville W. Fuller*	1888–1910	21	1833–1910
John Blair	1789–1796	6	1732–1800	David J. Brewer	1890–1910	20	1837–1910
Robert H. Harrison	1789–1790	–	1745–1790	Henry B. Brown	1890–1906	16	1836–1913
James Iredell	1790–1799	9	1751–1799	George Shiras, Jr.	1892–1903	10	1832–1924
Thomas Johnson	1791–1793	1	1732–1819	Howell E. Jackson	1893–1895	2	1832–1895
William Paterson	1793–1806	13	1745–1806	Edward D. White	1894–1910	16	1845–1921
*John Rutledge**	1795	–	1739–1800	Rufus W. Peckham	1895–1909	14	1838–1909
Samuel Chase	1796–1811	15	1741–1811	Joseph McKenna	1898–1925	26	1843–1926
Oliver Ellsworth	1796–1800	4	1745–1807	Oliver W. Holmes	1902–1932	30	1841–1935
Bushrod Washington	1798–1829	31	1762–1829	William R. Day	1903–1922	19	1849–1923
Alfred Moore	1799–1804	4	1755–1810	William H. Moody	1906–1910	3	1853–1917
John Marshall	1801–1835	34	1755–1835	Horace H. Lurton	1910–1914	4	1844–1914
William Johnson	1804–1834	30	1771–1834	Charles E. Hughes	1910–1916	5	1862–1948
H. Brockholst Livingston	1806–1823	16	1757–1823	Willis Van Devanter	1911–1937	26	1859–1941
Thomas Todd	1807–1826	18	1765–1826	Joseph R. Lamar	1911–1916	5	1857–1916
Joseph Story	1811–1845	33	1779–1845	*Edward D. White*	1910–1921	11	1845–1921
Gabriel Duval	1811–1835	24	1752–1844	Mahlon Pitney	1912–1922	10	1858–1924
Smith Thompson	1823–1843	20	1768–1843	James C. McReynolds	1914–1941	26	1862–1946
Robert Trimble	1826–1828	2	1777–1828	Louis D. Brandeis	1916–1939	22	1856–1941
John McLean	1829–1861	32	1785–1861	John H. Clarke	1916–1922	6	1857–1945
Henry Baldwin	1830–1844	14	1780–1844	William H. Taft	1921–1930	8	1857–1930
James M. Wayne	1835–1867	32	1790–1867	George Sutherland	1922–1938	15	1862–1942
Roger B. Taney	1836–1864	28	1777–1864	Pierce Butler	1922–1939	16	1866–1939
Philip P. Barbour	1836–1841	4	1783–1841	Edward T. Sanford	1923–1930	7	1865–1930
John Catron	1837–1865	28	1786–1865	Harlan F. Stone	1925–1941	16	1872–1946
John McKinley	1837–1852	15	1780–1852	*Charles E. Hughes*	1930–1941	11	1862–1948
Peter V. Daniel	1841–1860	19	1784–1860	Owen J. Roberts	1930–1945	15	1875–1955
Samuel Nelson	1845–1872	27	1792–1873	Benjamin N. Cardozo	1932–1938	6	1870–1938
Levi Woodbury	1845–1851	5	1789–1851	Hugo L. Black	1937–1971	34	1886–1971
Robert C. Grier	1846–1870	23	1794–1870	Stanley F. Reed	1938–1957	19	1884–1980
Benjamin R. Curtis	1851–1857	6	1809–1874	Felix Frankfurter	1939–1962	23	1882–1965
John A. Campbell	1853–1861	8	1811–1889	William O. Douglas	1939–1975	36	1898–1980
Nathan Clifford	1858–1881	23	1803–1881	Frank Murphy	1940–1949	9	1890–1949
Noah H. Swayne	1862–1881	18	1804–1884	*Harlan F. Stone*	1941–1946	5	1872–1946
Samuel F. Miller	1862–1890	28	1816–1890	James F. Byrnes	1941–1942	1	1879–1972
David Davis	1862–1877	14	1815–1886	Robert H. Jackson	1941–1954	13	1892–1954
Stephen J. Field	1863–1897	34	1816–1899	Wiley B. Rutledge	1943–1949	6	1894–1949
Salmon P. Chase	1864–1873	8	1808–1873	Harold H. Burton	1945–1958	13	1888–1964
William Strong	1870–1880	10	1808–1895	*Fred M. Vinson*	1946–1953	7	1890–1953
Joseph P. Bradley	1870–1892	22	1813–1892	Tom C. Clark	1949–1967	18	1899–1977
Ward Hunt	1873–1882	9	1810–1886	Sherman Minton	1949–1956	7	1890–1965
Morrison R. Waite	1874–1888	14	1816–1888	*Earl Warren*	1953–1969	16	1891–1974
John M. Harlan	1877–1911	34	1833–1911	John Marshall Harlan	1955–1971	16	1899–1971
William B. Woods	1880–1887	7	1824–1887	William J. Brennan, Jr.	1956–	–	1906–
Stanley Matthews	1881–1889	7	1824–1889	Charles E. Whittaker	1957–1962	5	1901–1973
				Potter Stewart	1958–1981	23	1915–

	TERM OF SERVICE	YEARS OF SERVICE	LIFE SPAN		TERM OF SERVICE	YEARS OF SERVICE	LIFE SPAN
Byron R. White	1962–	–	1917–	William H. Rehnquist	1972–	–	1924–
Arthur J. Goldberg	1962–1965	3	1908–	John P. Stevens, III	1975–	–	1920–
Abe Fortas	1965–1969	4	1910–	Sandra Day O'Connor	1981–	–	1930–
Thurgood Marshall	1967–	–	1908–				
Warren C. Burger	1969–	–	1907–				
Harry A. Blackmun	1970–	–	1908–				
Lewis F. Powell, Jr.	1972–	–	1907–				

*Appointed and served one term, but not confirmed by the Senate.   NOTE: Chief justices are in italics.

INDEX